P9-BZT-960

"*Joy* was just always there; my mother has one, I have one, every woman I know has one (and so do most of the men). Reading Mendelson's lively book has the same effect on the imagination as seeing pictures of your grandmother when she was young: you'd taken for granted that she had always been your grandmother, and suddenly you realize that she has a past, and you look at her in a whole new way. *Stand Facing the Stove,* which could so easily have turned out to be merely a curiosity, is, in addition to being an entertaining double biography of a mother and daughter, a detailed social history that opens up to offer a broad view of twentieth-century America. Mendelson is excellent on the social mores of the Midwest and . . . witty, too."

—*The New Yorker*

"A wonderful story . . . Food historian Anne Mendelson tells it splendidly."

—*Newsweek*

"It would doubtless have been a source of gratification to both Irma Rombauer and her daughter to think that the story of their record-breaking and much-beloved book could be used so effectively to trace a larger piece of history."

—*Oxford Companion to Food*

"A delightful social history of Americans' changing cooking and eating habits."

—*Publishers Weekly*

"A winning account of the life of one of America's standard cookbooks, with portraits of the mother and daughter who brought it into millions of homes."

—*Kirkus Reviews*

"An astonishing work of homage and research."

—*New York Newsday*

"Excellent . . . Anne Mendelson writes with a keen and delightful flair for language."

—*San Jose Mercury News*

"A cogent, insightful history of American cookery . . . A lively and meticulously detailed account of one of the few bits of Americana to be regarded with almost biblical reverence."

—*San Francisco Chronicle*

Stand Facing the Stove

Irma in her thirties, probably between 1912 and 1915.

Marion at age eighteen, in 1921.

Stand Facing the Stove

The Story of the Women Who Gave America the *Joy of Cooking*®

Anne Mendelson

SCRIBNER ◆ NEW YORK LONDON TORONTO SYDNEY SINGAPORE

SCRIBNER
1230 Avenue of the Americas
New York, NY 10020

Copyright © 1996, 2003 by Anne Mendelson

All rights reserved, including the right of reproduction in whole
or in part in any form.

First Scribner trade paperback edition 2003

Scribner and design are trademarks
of Macmillan Library Reference USA, Inc., used under
license by Simon & Schuster, the publisher of this work.

For information about special discounts for bulk purchases,
please contact Simon & Schuster Special Sales: 1-800-456-6798 or
business@simonandschuster.com

Photographs courtesy of Ethan Becker
Designed by Paula R. Szafranski

Manufactured in the United States of America

1   3   5   7   9   10   8   6   4   2

Library of Congress Cataloging-in-Publication Data is available.

ISBN 0-7432-2939-8

An extension of this copyright appears on page 475.

This book is dedicated to
Colleen Mohyde, Beth Crossman,
and the memory of Patty Eiser

CONTENTS

PREFACE

The oddities of this book reflect the fact that it took more than ten years to complete, not the year or so I naively expected when the Becker family gave me access to a vast hoard of documents and memorabilia stretching from the late nineteenth century to the time of Marion Becker's death in 1976. As I saw it, these papers would almost automatically group themselves into a complete story. Certainly they form the backbone of the book I did finally write, but there was nothing automatic about the process.

It was not long before I saw that the Becker-Rombauer papers added up to an extremely fragmentary, confused story. At times their very voluminousness obscured rather than revealed certain exceedingly bitter, tangled histories whose existence I had barely suspected. The most important of these was the long and acrimonious relationship of the Rombauers with their publisher, the Bobbs-Merrill Company.

From what remained of this once great firm I received no cooperation whatever. As a result, reconstructing lengthy wars in a manner that would be fair to both sides turned into a slow, uncertain, groping effort. Almost the only Bobbs-Merrill records I have seen pertaining to *The Joy of Cooking* are copies of letters actually sent to Irma Rombauer and Marion Becker (or their lawyers) and preserved in the family papers, and a fascinating trove of documents from a very few early years in the vexed author-publisher relationship, now owned by the Lilly Library of Indiana University at Bloomington. After that I was mostly confronted either with complete blanks or with obviously partial pictures of things as the Rombauer side saw them.

Rapidly running out of the wherewithal to continue a project that clearly had to be done with some regard for justice or not at all, I had to set it aside for long periods and get back to it at broken intervals. But the very difficulty of getting on with the story as an accurate chronological account eventually made me think about certain aspects of *The Joy of Cooking* more probingly than I might have if my path had been smoother. I realized that no study of any cookbook author or phase of modern food writing had ever dealt with a cookbook as a commercial publication—a property that must be acquired by a publisher, read in manuscript, edited, set in type, proofread, indexed, bound, and (when all of that has been done) marketed according to a more or less definite strategy. What is equally curious, no one has looked at successive editions of any cookbook with the detailed attention to changes in content that students of literary history commonly apply to other sorts of texts, and only a few investigators have tried to study the shifting culinary-cultural contexts out of which a particular cookbook springs.

My book, as it eventually shaped itself after many struggles with both documentation and overall concept, thus ended up as a peculiar composite some distance from the pair of straightforward life stories I had originally expected to write. The main narrative chronicles both the authors' (and their families') lives and the efforts that brought each major edition of the cookbook into being. Two long pauses in the narrative proper are filled by the chapters "Chronicles of Cookery," which discuss the place in culinary history occupied by the *Joy of Cooking* editions that are not now in print and are rarely or never seen by contemporary cooks.

Probably I have laid less emphasis than some readers might expect on a few aspects of the cookbook's history. I have carefully avoided calling it "the best-selling American cookbook" or anything of the kind, and have alluded to its sales record only as forming a general outline of success at different stages. The truth is that people who know something about books tend to be very leery of sales figures. There is no subject on which authors more bitterly distrust the word of publishers under the best of circumstances. As will be seen, the Bobbs-Merrill selling strategies were a terrible bone of contention with the authors from the moment of the book's arrival at best-sellerdom in

1943. And no matter what sort of calculation is used, *The Joy of Cooking* surely has no claim to be the best-selling cookbook in American publishing history. As of 1996, the original *terminus ad guem* of my research, it was probably the best-selling *trade* cookbook—i.e., a work issued through an ordinary publisher whose wares are primarily distributed to retail bookstores. But as regards copies sold, it then lagged well behind *The Better Homes and Gardens Cook Book*, which always drew on the distribution resources of the parent magazine, and *The Betty Crocker Cookbook*, which (until it was reissued in 2000 by a trade publisher as *Betty Crocker's Cookbook*) primarily depended on the research and marketing muscle of General Mills. Both, of course, were the work of committees. What was remarkable about *Joy* is that it was brought into being and continued, until 1997, by individuals.

Bibliographically minded readers may wonder why my account of *Joy*'s publishing history seldom mentions the "fourth edition," the "twelfth edition," and so on. The reason is that the information on the copyright pages is of very little help in identifying the major stages of the book's history. There is even a supposed edition that is a pure phantom—1942, which somehow got onto the copyright page more than fifty years ago with no real 1942 copyright being in existence, and has remained there ever since. The editions that mark genuine stages of the book's development are eight in number: the original privately published *Joy of Cooking* (1931), the first Bobbs-Merrill edition (1936), the best-selling wartime edition (1943), the first postwar edition (1946, actually printed from the 1943 plates with a very few changes), the first Rombauer-Becker edition (1951), the unauthorized edition (1962), the first authorized edition prepared by Marion Becker (1963), and Marion's last revision (1975).

I must mention an important fact about the two women who are the subject of this book. Though I detest what has been called "psychobiography" or "pathography," it will be obvious to any reader that much of my story rests on my own reading of people's characters and relationships. (Another advantage of the ten years I spent poring over the evidence of Irma and Marion's lives when my original writing schedule had collapsed was that I found many of my judgments being altered or refined in the way one might expect in thinking about living acquaintances over such a span of time.) Certain sensitive aspects of the mother-daughter relationship as I describe it are no invention of mine. They were alluded to with stunning consistency by most people who knew both of them well in either private or professional connections.

A note on some names belonging to the major dramatis personae: Various members of Irma's own family styled themselves "von Starkloff" or "Starkloff" without great consistency. I have (mostly) opted for "von Starkloff" for her parents and herself, partly to make it easier to distinguish between her father (Dr. Hugo Maximilian von Starkloff) and her half-brother (Dr. Maximilian Carl Starkloff), who both show up as "Dr. Max Starkloff" in accounts of the time. Irma herself used the "von" more often in youth than in later years, but I have retained it for consistency's sake. The nicknames of Edgar R. Rombauer Jr. and Mary Whyte Hartrich are given in the spellings they themselves used, "Put" and "Mazie" (other people often rendered the names as "Putt" and "Maizie" or "Maisie").

The cookbook itself began life as *The Joy of Cooking* and was so registered in all copyright applications until 1962/1963, when the definite article was dropped—but even in those editions Marion Becker's dedication keeps the "The." I have used the title *The Joy of Cooking* for all editions because I like it better, bibliographically right or wrong.

ACKNOWLEDGMENTS

Dozens of people helped bring this project into being. I can only apologize to anyone whom I have inadvertently forgotten to thank.

My first debt is to Pat Brown and Arline Inge, who encouraged me to write the 1981 article for *Cuisine* magazine that sparked my later curiosity about *The Joy of Cooking*. Alex Ward helped keep my interest going by commissioning a brief article on the family for the *New York Times* Living Section in 1984.

The Becker family and other surviving relatives provided generous help. To Ethan Becker, who gave me the free run of his mother's and grandmother's uncatalogued papers at Cockaigne and offered unfailing hospitality and cooperation without asking to "authorize" a word I wrote, I owe a simply unrepayable debt. Edgar R. Rombauer Jr., Irma's only living child, placed his knowledge and insight at my disposal and with his wife, Marjorie, entertained me most graciously in Seattle. Mark and Jennifer Becker shared their memories in many stimulating conversations. My profound thanks also to Joan W. Becker, Jeffrey Rombauer, Elsa Muench Hunstein, and Abby Dittmann Wise.

Over the years Ethan Becker's staff at Cockaigne pitched in with endless photocopying and searches for needles I knew I'd seen in some haystack around the place. I am grateful to Judy Bossio, the late Dana

Leonard, Mary Gilbert, and The Usual Suspects—Debbie Gibson and the late Patty Eiser.

Several editors lent timely help at different stages, beginning with Ann Bramson at the very start of the project. My great thanks to Genevieve Young, who acquired the book for Little, Brown, and Roger Donald, who took it over. Colleen Mohyde was there at the right moments, first as my editor at Little, Brown and then as my agent when the project was moved to Henry Holt and Company. I am boundlessly grateful to her and to the intrepid Beth Crossman, who tackled a mess of a manuscript with unflagging good sense and moral reinforcement. My general thanks to Henry Holt and Company, and specifically to production editor Lisa Goldberg and copy editor Annette Corkey for their perceptive reading and attention to historical detail. At the Doe Coover Agency, thanks as well to Colleen's partner, Doe Coover, and the ever helpful Frances Kennedy.

Like any serious researcher, I can't imagine what I would have done without several important libraries, newspaper morgues, and other special collections. My sincere thanks to Alison Ryley and her colleagues at the New York Public Library. I was also helped by the following collections and persons: the Lilly Library of Indiana University at Bloomington (Saundra Taylor, Curator of Manuscripts, and Kate S. Medicus); the Indiana State Library in Indianapolis; the Indianapolis/Marion County Public Library; the Indiana Historical Society (Carolyn Autry, Joan E. Hostetler); the St. Louis Public Library; the Mercantile Library of St. Louis (Charles E. Brown, Head of Reference); the Missouri Historical Society (Martha Clevenger, Kathy Corbett, Peter Michel, Dennis Northcott, Barbara Stole, Jean Streeter, Carol Verble); the library of the Missouri Botanical Garden (Martha Riley, Connie Wolf); the Cincinnati Public Library; the Philadelphia Free Library; Princeton University Library (Jean F. Preston, Curator of Manuscripts); the New York Academy of Medicine Library (Anne Pascarelli); the Schlesinger Library at Radcliffe College (Barbara Haber, Curator of Printed Books); and the libraries of the *St. Louis Post-Dispatch* (Mike Marler, Nan Stoddard), *Indianapolis News/Indianapolis Star* (Charlesetta Means, Nadine Moore), and *Cincinnati Enquirer* (Mona Branson, Ray Zwick).

The St. Louis Regional Medical Center and the Christian R. Holmes Hospital provided me with (respectively) Irma Rombauer's and Marion Becker's medical records. Useful information also came from the Vassar College Alumnae/i Association (Mary Gesek in Poughkeepsie, Betty Ann Glas Wolf in Cincinnati).

I was fortunate to be able to interview (by phone or in person) a number of former Bobbs-Merrill employees, who among them helped amplify my picture of author-publisher dealings. My best thanks to Angus Cameron, Judith Cross-Henley, William J. Finneran, Leo Gobin, Marian Israel, Patricia Jones, the late Harrison Platt, the late Eugene Rachlis, Grace Shaw, and Guernsey Van Riper.

I have also been variously helped by Dorothy Merkel Alexander, A. William J. Becker III, Joe Bettenmann, Joan Bricetti, Lydia Rombauer Brown, Cecily Brownstone (who could herself write a splendid book about the Rombauers), the late Jane Brueggeman, Rebecca Busselle, the late Molly Byrne, Wallace H. Cheney, Julia Child, Robert Clark, Peggy Frank Crawford, Evvie Denny, David W. Detjen, Dr. Rudolf Donath, Janet Cameron Duffy, Patricia Egan, Marilyn Einhorn, Emma K. Fischer, Janice Rebert Forberg (who gave me two of the beautiful original drawings for *Wild Wealth*), Helen-Marie Fruth (who put me in touch with many other Rombauer friends), Alice Gerdine, Daniel J. Giannini, Cynthia Gibbons, Elizabeth Goltermann (who lent me valuable materials and offered hospitality at Irma's old cabin in Jefferson County), Marion Gore, Fred Greenman, James Gregory, Eugene A. Hartrich, Karen Hess (who took time to read parts of the book in manuscript and saved me from several terrible blunders), Polly and the late Julian Hill, Margaret Hilliker, Ginnie Hofmann, Robert Isaacson, Marian Judell Israel, Judith and the late Evan Jones, Martin Knorr, George Lang, Merna Lazier, Dr. Silbert Lipton, Jeanne Lesem, Ikki Matsumoto, Ruth Mead, Sidney Mintz, Dr. Muller of the Staatsarchiv Bremen, Terry Nicholson, Edwin L. Noel (who had the Armstrong, Teasdale, Schlafly & Davis file on *Hartrich* v. *Becker* copied for me), Sharon I. B. Paradowski, the late Harriet Pilpel, Bob Pilpel, Frances Jones Poetker and the late Joseph Poetker, Max Putzel, Joan Reardon, Koerner Rombauer, Steven Rowan, Jim Schluter, George and Placide Schriever, Charlotte Selver, Laura Shapiro, Ruth Stalley, Dr. Gene Starkloff, the late Dr. Max and Ardath Starkloff, Anne Stern, Kate Terry, Joyce Toomre, the late Laurent Torno, Laurent Torno Jr., Marian Tracy, Hans Trefousse, Sarah Van Ausdal, the late Charles Van Ravenswaay, Geoffrey Vincent, Kurt Vonnegut, Barbara Vonnegut, Richard C. Vonnegut (who provided much information on Irma's mother's family), Dorothy Wartenberg, Nach and Maron Waxman (who not only filled book requests en masse but commented usefully on a part of the book in manuscript), Barbara Wheaton, Louis A. Williams, Franz Wippold, James Woodress, Helen Worth, and Gary and Pam Yohler.

My last but not least thanks go to my father and stepmother, Emanuel S. Mendelson and Ruth Miner, and my husband, Martin Iger.

Joy and woe are woven fine,
A clothing for the soul divine.

—WILLIAM BLAKE

INTRODUCTION

We are told that a hard-boiled professional cook, when asked what she regarded as primary briefing for a beginner, tersely replied: "Stand facing the stove."
—**1975 *Joy of Cooking***

Most people who have heard of *The Joy of Cooking* have a vague idea that it was written by a mother and daughter. More remember the name of the former than the latter, which is as both would have wanted it; Irma Rombauer, who began the work, loved stardom as much as Marion Rombauer Becker, her eventual collaborator and successor, loved privacy. When I began investigating the story of authors and cookbook, I discovered a strange phenomenon among many cooks who had first used *Joy* in older, pre-Becker editions: an active partisanship in some mother-daughter contest that they perceived in the pages of the book. Their loyalty was invariably to the mother, and they believed that Marion Becker had either performed a kind of sabotage on the Rombauer *Joy of Cooking* or at least imposed her own inferior taste on it.

This view of *The Joy of Cooking* didn't make much sense to me for some years, and still strikes me as fairly misguided. Yet the sheer frequency of the claim at last told me something. So many lay and professional observers from drastically varied backgrounds seem to have discerned an emotional and culinary tug-of-war in the book itself as to give any would-be historian pause. After a time it dawned on me that the very impulse to choose sides—or even think that there are sides to be chosen—is a clue to an important quality of the work: its authors inhabit it more genuinely, more personally, than most cookbook authors inhabit their creations. To the end of their lives, both of the Rombauers put themselves into *The Joy of Cooking* in a way rare among commercially published manuals of any sort but very common among what are called "vanity books."

The Joy of Cooking did in fact start life as a vanity book: a brainchild for which the author pays the publisher, not vice versa. Thousands of such books appear each year, parading their begetters' assaults on the sonnet form, agendas for saving the world, or favorite recipes. In 1931 this one cost Irma Rombauer some $3,000 of the modest legacy her husband had left her on blowing his brains out—an amount equivalent to a year's low-level white-collar wages in the second year of the Great Depression. She was fifty-four years old when the volume appeared, an utter amateur with no known qualifications for publishing a cookbook.

Her forlorn gamble paid off. Eventually it would inspire among a sizable coterie of users a love and loyalty surpassing the common attachment of cooks to cookbooks. A major reason for the affection in which its particular public held it is that somehow it never entirely lost the inner being of a vanity book. Its authors persisted in the amateurs' belief that those who might cook from their manual were as good as personal friends. What is more, they were right. It is true that there are plenty of cooks who don't much like *Joy* or find themselves more annoyed than enthralled by its assumption of a confidential friendship. But people on a certain wavelength tend to be habitués, cheerleaders, partisans. It was in fact Irma and Marion's well-placed faith in a sure author-reader bond that enabled them to put across such an unlikely slogan as "the joy of cooking."

What on earth is joyous about cooking? People who do not know its capacity to bore, weary, and frustrate are people who have never cooked. When Marion Becker came to publish a brief memoir of the book's first thirty-odd years, one of the mementos of its success that she chose to reprint was a 1944 *New York Times Book Review* cartoon in which a well-upholstered dowager lies propped on a sofa gracefully perusing *The Joy of Cooking* while her harassed maid glares from a steaming kitchen. Marion and her mother knew very well that people do not find joy where they do not perceive freedom, control, leisure, or esteem. To put the matter in bald historical perspective, such things were not socially appropriate to cooking in the days when it was done by servants or those too poor to hire them. Ministering to the cook's morale became the task of cookbooks only when the cook was also the mistress of the household—or sometimes, as life got more complicated, the master.

The Depression did not initiate the departure of hired cooks from American households, a demographic readjustment that had begun at least a century earlier. But it speeded up the process for middle-class families, leaving many people occasionally or permanently responsible for producing meals that they would previously have paid someone else to get on the table. Irma was born into and remained in a somewhat privileged sisterhood who did more of their own cooking than their counterparts of a few generations back but could rely on "domestics" (as some tactfully called them) to see to a good part of the week's meals. She knew, however, that millions of women who might once have told the cook what to make for dinner now were their own cooks. It was to assure such people that their new responsibility really wasn't menial that the social implications of cookery could now be enlarged to include "joy," a discreet rearrangement of necessity so as to make it not only a virtue but a delight.

Irma Rombauer was not the only cookery writer who sought to infuse a note of genteel optimism into the subject when changing times expanded the ranks of those who had to cook. But she did it better than anyone else. Where other culinary morale-builders habitually coated a bitter pill with large doses of cuteness and synthetic cheer, she was neither trivial nor affected. Readers light-years removed from her dignified existence responded instinctively to the unique help she held out: her own companionship. She did not, like dozens of professional food writers, contrive a silly illusion of sociability from bits of mechanical claptrap. She had an inborn command of the real thing. Throughout her belated writing career she always managed to give the impression of taking her public with her on a private lark—an impression she could not have conveyed if she had not completely believed in it herself. She never lost the stance of an amateur addressing amateurs, calling not so much on an infallible knowledge of cooking (which in any case she did not possess) as on the perfectly correct belief that she was fun to be with. There was something in her presence to tell the most discouraged beginner why cooking and joy deserved to be mentioned in the same breath.

Irma's gifts as a writer are discussed elsewhere in this book; suffice it to say here that Marion did not share them. When she took over *The Joy of Cooking* from her mother, she worked very hard (with a great deal of help from her husband) to simulate the original tone and style, and probably did better at it than anyone else could have. But "simulate" is the operative word. Something had gone out of the book. The Irma loyalists who picked up new editions and felt that the beloved presence—fey, shrewd, saucy, practical, airily homespun—had been infringed on were not mistaken. Their resentment is the measure not of Marion's failure to be Irma but of her success in being Marion—in other words, maintaining the extraordinarily personal, vanity-book quality of *The Joy of Cooking.* Had she not thoroughly infused it with her own sensibility, that quality would have been falsified. Earnest and careful where her mother had been insouciant and waggish, she was nonetheless equally dedicated to a notion of real, concrete friendship with one's readers that would not have occurred to most professional food writers. This bond had much to do with the fact that both women had come to the business of cookbook writing rather late in life, never having thought of cooking as a particularly momentous priority during their careers as wives and mothers. The years they had spent cooking for only ordinary domestic motives set their work apart from even very good cookbooks cranked out by trained recipe developers with planned agendas to set before the reader.

The joy that the daughter sought to encourage in cooking did not exactly match the blithe example that was the mother's striking contribution. The generation for which Marion wrote was both more bone-ignorant of culinary basics and more occupied with high-flown talk of cooking as an "art," one of the signal delusions of our time. What she tried to point to was the joy of *learning*—exploring the splendid richness of cookery as a body of knowledge to be absorbed by the brain en route to the fingertips. She could not, like Irma, effortlessly conjure up her own personality in her writing, but here and there she wove in small talismans of her own private being, offered quite sincerely to readers as tokens of friendship.

These two highly individual presences do not coexist in *The Joy of Cooking* in an ideally seamless manner. But part of their book's energy and long-term drawing power lies in incongruities that more practiced professional hands might have smoothed out. The collision between the two authors' personalities is just one of these. The work is rife with not only personal but culinary contradictions—a weakness, but also a strength. Its approaches to cooking are provincial and cosmopolitan, muddled and lucid, scrupulous and free-spirited. It messily crams in tokens of many eras past (harking back to Irma's mother and grandmother) and present (just emerging at the end of Marion's life). At no time in *Joy*'s career has it been one polished summary of all the kitchen virtues. Rather it exudes an imperfect hybrid vigor easier to feel than to describe.

Irma and Marion were both unabashedly amateur cooks—and haste-driven ones at that. Of course neither had any kind of career schooling in cookery. What is more, neither was known in private life for concocting arduous, elaborate dinners from scratch. Both were very fond of various canned shortcuts and loved more than anything to assemble a quick, simple luncheon or supper that could be fitted in among more important claims on their time. Arbiters of taste who go to *The Joy of Cooking* looking for one masterly dish after another will find that the recipes in any edition from 1931 on present a picture of American cooking filled with wild inconsistencies—the inconsistencies of real people's real preferences, from canned-soup sauces to homemade noodles.

Nor has *Joy* ever stood as an imparter of infallible culinary expertise. It has always had small (or not so small) lapses and lacunae. The scope of what the Rombauers tried to do grew with every edition, and so did what they succeeded in doing. But there is much that they might more wisely not have attempted. Irma herself sometimes ventured onto shaky ground, and in the last two revisions Marion often bit off more information than she could chew. One can find the mother telling people to ferment cabbage for sauerkraut at 85°F (a sure recipe for a putrid mess) and the daughter spilling much ink on the foundations of French cooking without conveying the sense of something honestly and naturally mastered. Yet in an unaccountable way, *The Joy of Cooking* always has lighted up the subject of cooking far better than some more rigorously correct books. There is nothing to compare with it for cutting through the perplexities to reveal what makes sense.

The famous old cookbook as I have come to know it is patchy, accidental, inconsistent. That is just what is best about it. It records the sheer improbability of twentieth-century American cooking from the Great Depression to the Ford administration, a lawless mélange of blueprints for progress, nostalgic hankerings, gourmet cults, timesaving expedients, media-inspired fads, and unexpected rebellions. The accomplishment would have been possible only for inspired amateurs following their own instincts, buoyed by a strange but completely justified sense of solidarity with their audience.

Irma thanked her "friends, known and unknown," for letting her feel "far more useful than I ever expected to be." Marion, who considered *Joy* a touchstone of disinterestedness in a terribly mercenary field, believed that its authors should "owe no obligation to anyone but themselves and you," the reader. Both felt honestly privileged to meet millions of people through their book. I hope that meeting them through the story of their lives will be a reciprocal privilege for admirers of *The Joy of Cooking*, as it was for me.

PART I

1

The Golden Age of St. Louis

Throughout his life T. S. Eliot recalled the city of St. Louis as having "affected me more deeply than any other environment has ever done" and counted himself "fortunate to have been born here, rather than in Boston, or New York, or London."[1] St. Louis did indeed—at least in a brief and glorious interval after the Civil War—seem one of the finest spots on earth to dwell on special blessings: the happy accident that had put the Mississippi and Missouri Rivers where they were, the divine wisdom of the Louisiana Purchase, the continent-spanning genius of railroad builders past and present, the thrilling sense of the Wild West still (as the small Tom Eliot felt) just beyond Forest Park. It was also, more enduringly, a splendid city in which to be a high-minded civic reformer like Eliot's grandfather and mother, or a thoroughgoing political graft artist like any one of a succession of mayors, or a *Lebenskünstler* like Dr. Hugo Maximilian von Starkloff.

Lebenskünstler is as untranslatable as any word in the German language, which is saying a good deal. It implies a civilized command of living as an art form like singing or painting. German-English dictionaries lamely offer explanations like "one who appreciates the finer things of life." "Life artist" is the baldly literal rendering, and perhaps as good as any. "Life artist," replied the old and very ill Marion Rombauer Becker in 1974, when an attorney taking a deposition asked her occupation.[2] She was undoubtedly thinking of a family story about her mother, Irma von Starkloff Rombauer, as an uncommonly imposing five-year-old making the acquaintance of an aunt newly arrived from Germany. "Ach, du bist eine treue Lebenskünstlerin!" ("Oh, you are a staunch life artist!") exclaimed the visitor.[3] For Irma Rombauer herself, the word was essentially the property of her father, a genially self-important man who had arrived in the environs of St. Louis around 1860 to set up a medical practice in a community that seemed well suited to the life art.

At the time of his arrival from northern Illinois, St. Louis and Carondelet, the large adjacent southern suburb where he settled, were a crazy quilt of elements still bearing some trace of the first French and Spanish presence in the Louisiana territories. Settlers from Virginia and Kentucky were the most visible American-born group, cautiously coexisting with a large contingent of Northerners, particularly transplanted liberal New Englanders like William Greenleaf Eliot, the poet's grandfather. Thousands of poor Irish had also come to the region, especially after the potato famine of 1845–46. They competed for work as laborers, artisans, and servants with large numbers of Germans fleeing comparable poverty. Dr. von Starkloff belonged to a very different community brought by the abortive stirrings of liberal German nationalism after 1830 and more markedly 1848. They were articulate professionals, or sometimes minor nobility, who rejoiced in a peculiarly German marriage of cultural ideals, consciously enlightened convictions, and creature comforts. The young Swabian-born physician almost summed up the type.

He was the second son of a military family that is first heard of in sixteenth-century Courland, a small Baltic state now incorporated into Latvia and Lithuania. By the time of the Napoleonic Wars the soldiering Starkloffs had added a "von" to their name, wandered through various allegiances, and settled down in the employ of the electors (later kings) of Württemberg. Max, born in Ulm in 1832, was nine at the death of his father, Baron Karl von Starkloff, who had married Sophie von Rapp-Frauenfeldt, the daughter of a lieutenant colonel in the imperial Austrian army. He must have had a considerable streak of independence, for in his mid-teens he insisted on leaving the infantry regiment to which he had been attached as a cadet and completing the classical course at a nearby *Gymnasium* in preparation for medical school; he attended first the University of Tübingen, later Heidelberg and Prague.

He was only twenty when he embarked for New York. He had survived the troubles of 1848 with, it appears, no ruinous political attachments—though some were later invented for him in admiring histories of the "Forty-eighters," the crew of energetic political refugees with which he soon linked himself. Irma wrote that she was sure her father's only real motive in leaving "his beloved Schwabenland" (Swabia, the site of the Black Forest and the rise of the Danube) was "his yen for adventure."[4] Max set out a few months after receiving his degree in 1852; apparently he planned to work his way from New York to the Wild West. He almost didn't make it. At Buffalo he signed on as a deckhand on the steamer *Griffith*, which caught fire halfway across Lake Erie and burned to the water, happily not before Max had been rescued by a passing ship. The survivors were set down in Cleveland, from which the greenhorn doctor eventually managed to make his way to California as surgeon to the American Fur Company, the sprawling empire founded by John Jacob Astor.

His family never learned much of his next few years except for stories of dashing adventure. Just why and when he wandered back to the Mississippi Valley is a mystery. He is first heard of in northern Missouri and Illinois, trying to set up practice in Hannibal and nearby Palmyra, as well as Quincy and Galesburg on the other side of the river. It was in Hannibal that his first child, Johann Alexander von Starkloff, was born in November of 1855. Irma knew nothing of the little boy's mother, Hermine Auguste Reinhardt, except that she was "a beautiful widow" whom Max had married on coming east.[5] No date is given for the marriage in the genealogy that Max had drawn up in later years. Johann died in the spring of 1857, a month before the birth of another son, Emil Arthur. Hermine and Max's last child, Maximilian Carl, was born at the end of 1858.

Max's frequent moves during this period (Emil was born in Palmyra, the little Max Carl in Quincy) suggest that he was not having an easy time establishing a practice. The St. Louis–Carondelet area was the largest urban center of the then Far West. Altogether the neighborhood offered a more encouraging start for a young professional than the smaller towns to the north. There is no record of exactly when Max arrived in Carondelet, but he was in the thick of important German doings there by 1861. He had found the ideal venue for his talents.

The chief fact about greater St. Louis was, of course, the Mississippi River, still unbridged and usually unpredictable in this silt-laden stretch just below the entry of the Missouri. It made St. Louis the great conduit of goods reaching the West and the central river valley from the East and the Gulf of Mexico, as well as eastward-bound furs from the Pacific Coast and ore from the new mines of southeast Missouri and New Mexico. Arriving and departing river traffic was the backbone of the city's routine. The traveler reaching St. Louis by steamer saw first the broad man-made plateau of the city levees, swarming with teamsters' wagons and lined with warehouses. The land rose to a modified grid of streets, orderly enough on paper but at most seasons of the year fed by an inexhaustible supply of mud reputed not to differ greatly from the St. Louis drinking water. The region was visited with harsh Midwestern winters, while in summer the incredibly suffocating air of the Gulf Coast surged up the river valley, often with an introductory fanfare of spring tornadoes. But the hardy trading post considered itself a city of some substance by 1860. It had a population of nearly 161,000, and supported a small handful of theaters and a large handful of music societies (well populated with Germans), a library, the new St. Louis Academy of Sciences, Washington University, several foundries, the Pacific Railroad (stretching a magnificent 176 miles westward), a noisy range of political opinions, and sundry German- and English-language newspapers. The Sunday supplement of the *Westliche Post*, surveying the ungainly metropolis in 1859, decided that the descriptive talents of "someone like old Homer" would be required to capture the riches of Broadway a few blocks west of the levee—"a colorful mixture of everything for sale that human imagination or mood is capable of conceiving" and only one instance of why St. Louis "is the most interesting city there is for one who is wont to watch people living and striving."[6]

The observer did not, however, mention another sort of activity that added its own flavor to the civic bustle and that greatly troubled the liberal German refugees: the thousands of black slaves funneled each year through the thriving St. Louis auction. The city was in the strange position of being both a major slave-trading post (another result of its location as the "Gateway to the West") and a hotbed of antislavery sentiment chiefly (though not exclusively) fueled by the German Forty-eighters.

Even in the decades before this influx of zealots, the newly arrived Germans had not much liked the spectacle of people being bought and sold on the St. Louis courthouse steps. One of those who could not reconcile such things with America was Gustave Koerner, a young radical who had been wounded in the Frankfurt student uprisings of 1833 and had fled to the New World. Finding a free black from another state about to be sold under Missouri law, he himself purchased the man's freedom and—along with many like-minded immigrants—put the Mississippi River between himself and the institution of slavery by settling in nearby St. Clair County, Illinois.[7]

Here, in the rolling country near the county seat of Belleville, a large number of German intellectuals popularly known as the "Latin Farmers" (presumably for knowing more about books than turnips) formed a sort of free-state auxiliary of St. Louis, lending moral support to their antislavery neighbors in the increasingly embattled city. Koerner promptly applied himself to learn enough English to pass the bar examination, and exchanged German reformist causes for the travails of the Democratic Party and the Free Soil issue. By 1860 he had held a number of offices in Illinois and was a political confidant of Abraham Lincoln. The influence of such men was a considerable drawing card for later German arrivals like Dr. Starkloff (at this period he rarely used the "von"). So was the intellectual élan of the city's German community, as evidenced in a large range of cultural activities and a press that considered itself at the forefront of enlightenment.

Forty-eighter-led editorial writers and vigilante organizers, many of whom had followed Gustave Koerner's defection to the new Republican Party in 1856, spearheaded a struggle to detach Missouri from the Confederacy as it became clear that the threat of Southern secession would erupt into reality. Dr. Starkloff was in Carondelet in time to see the Missouri Unionists' great adventure of the war, the Camp Jackson affair.[8]

This episode would subsequently be related to St. Louis schoolchildren as a major turning point of the Civil War, though a certain comic-opera-gone-wrong quality also catches the eye. It occurred shortly after the attack on Fort Sumter in April of 1861. The secessionist governor of Missouri, Claiborne Jackson, had dispatched several state militia companies to the vicinity of a Federal arsenal. While they were covertly bringing up guns and cannons to an encampment christened for the governor, Missouri's first contribution to the other side was also hastening to the spot. This was a group that had been drilling for some time in the headquarters of the Tenth Street *Turnverein* (German physical culture society) as the "St. Louis Home Guard" before having itself sworn into the new Union Army as several regiments of "Missouri Volunteers." Among Max Starkloff's fellow recruits in this grand force—in fact, among the fomenters of the whole idea—were the fighting Rombauer brothers from Hungary: Robert, Roderick, Roland, and Raphael. (A fifth, Richard, had died in the service of Kossuth's army.) Like him, they would ever after relate the ensuing deed with immense pride.

On May 10 the Missouri Volunteers marched out and surrounded the Missouri militia, which surrendered without firing a shot. The victorious troops were marching their prisoners to the arsenal when a large crowd of St. Louisans appeared, mostly armed with picnic lunches and ready to watch history being made. Some, however, carried brickbats and guns. It was never clear how the shooting started, but as the crowd grew uglier the new Union soldiers fired into it, wounding many and killing fifteen people on the spot. There was a storm of outrage throughout the city for the next few weeks, but by the time the war was over Camp Jackson was firmly fixed in the pantheon of Union triumphs, particularly German triumphs. (Of course the Home Guard had not been exclusively German, but German-speakers had formed a highly energetic core.) The St. Louis Forty-eighters always spoke of it as a decisive engagement, and in truth it must have helped to blunt early secessionist impetus in a state that could have contributed significantly to the Confederacy.

Most of Max Starkloff's subsequent Civil War service was as an army surgeon rather than a combatant. Like many Missourians in the administrative chaos of the state, he eventually signed on with the Forty-third Illinois Volunteer Regiment, which had been organized by Gustave Koerner in the wake of the first Southern secessions. As a child, Irma listened to horror stories of the Union doctors running out of medical supplies at the battle of Shiloh in April of 1862. But on the whole, Max seems to have thrived, enjoying his involvement in a branch of the family métier that he had so obstinately left in his teens. He emerged from the war as medical director of the First Division of the Seventh Army Corps, with the rank of major.

The end of the war signaled the beginning of a happy era for the likes of Dr. Starkloff. It was the grand age of the St. Louis *Deutschtum*—another untranslatable term that means something like "German community" but contains other nuances, like "German character," "German mores," or "patriotic German identity." It may be slangily but aptly rendered as "the whole German thing." The educated, ambitious Forty-eighters who had fought in the war were not the whole of this world within the city, but they were its most prestigious symbol.

In the postwar prosperity of a burgeoning metropolis that liked to call itself "the Future Great City of the World"—popularly just "Future Great"—men of Max Starkloff's stripe devoted themselves to a civilized German-American existence surrounded by bibelots, music, and congenial conversation made more congenial by good food and wine—the very image of the *Lebenskunst*.

Max was a joiner by nature, and a man with a taste for public eminence that stopped short of any hunger for substantial elective office. He became active in St. Louis Republican politics and eventually in various German-American groups with some political cast, from the local freethinkers' organization and the "Schiller Union"—dedicated to the memory of the liberty-loving poet—to the German-American National Alliance and the *Turnerbund*, the national federation of clubs dedicated to a curious German version of *mens sana in corpore sano*, whose local branch had provided drilling quarters for the Home Guard. But for many years his chief public concern was the St. Louis School Board.

Carondelet was incorporated into St. Louis in 1870, and Max—who had helped found the smaller town's school board four years before—became a member of the central St. Louis board just as the city school system was beginning to be regarded as one of the most extraordinarily innovative in the country. Of course, this renown was of little use to the rapidly multiplying black children of St. Louis, who were entitled to attend only segregated schools—and not even those beyond the elementary grades until 1875, when Roderick Rombauer as attorney to the School Board pointed out that the state constitution required the system to provide a high school education for all pupils.[9] For the whites, all sorts of lofty goals were proposed by high-powered educational talent. One of the most celebrated experiments approved by the School Board ushered in the first public school kindergarten in the United States, to be modeled on much-admired German originals. In one way or another, it was apparently the St. Louis kindergarten program that brought to America a young woman named Emma Kuhlmann.

Later family accounts had Miss Kuhlmann coming to St. Louis as one of the founders of the pioneering city kindergarten, a claim that no student of the school system's history has been able to document. What is certain is that a young St. Louis educational philanthropist, Susan Blow, was sent by the School Board on a study-and-recruiting mission to Germany in 1872 and returned a year later with the makings of a kindergarten faculty and curriculum.[10] Probably Emma Kuhlmann came with her. It is not known whether Emma was a kindergarten teacher—something that then implied strict and very specific training in the theories of the kindergarten movement's founder, Friedrich Froebel—or simply a German-recruited governess in the Blow family who helped in some informal prototype of the eventual St. Louis public kindergarten. But the sequel is beyond doubt: not long after arriving from Germany Emma Kuhlmann met the newly widowed School Board member Max Starkloff, and married him on January 23, 1876.

Hermine Starkloff had died the year before, of a sudden illness described in the *St. Louis Daily Globe* obituary only as "inflammation of the brain."[11] She left two grown sons. It appears that School Board or no School Board, Dr. Starkloff had given them both expensive private educations after the elementary grades. Max Carl, the younger, was an industrious, earnest, rather stubborn young man who had attended Chester Military Academy in Pennsylvania before deciding, like his father, that he wanted to study medicine. Emil had still other ideas. He had been sent to school in Lausanne, Switzerland, where Max had a sister. Later events suggest that this grand gesture may have been meant to put some distance between Emil and an early misdeed. In the year of his father's remarriage he entered the U.S. Naval Academy at Annapolis, departing very prematurely amid rumors of a cheating ring. Emil returned to St. Louis and took a job as a postal clerk—the prelude to his life's work, mail fraud.[12]

Max Carl and Emil's stepmother was only a few years older than they. Emma Clara Christiana Kuhlmann came from a well-to-do north German family. Her mother, Wilhelmine Minlos, belonged to a long line of Lübeck merchants who had rubbed elbows with Thomas Mann's forebears in the city senate. Her father, Carl Bernhard Kuhlmann, was a lawyer and *Oberamtmann* (something like "First Selectman") in the pretty lakeside town of Eutin in Holstein.[13] There were no noble titles to match that of Max's mother, the Austrian-born Countess Sophie von Rapp-Frauenfeldt, but the north German merchant and professional families considered themselves more than the equals of anyone. Why (and exactly how) Emma came to America is not certain; Irma wrote of "an unhappy love affair."[14] She was twenty-six at the time of her marriage, eighteen years Max's junior. Photographs show a tall, fair, mild-featured woman with a look of dignified reticence, a pretty foil to the dark, bearded Max with his important stare at the camera. In his house she was majordomo and nurse-receptionist. She ran his accounts (he had a grand imprecision in matters of money), ordered his dinner from the housemaid-cook, supervised the office boy and Dave, the hired man, and coped with a stream of patients during office hours and emergencies at other hours. The house-cum-office on Main Street in Carondelet was a six-mile trip from downtown St. Louis by buggy or the Iron Mountain Railroad, and her husband's absences in the course of myriad activities—school matters, Republican strategy, *Turner* meetings, the music societies that thrived in St. Louis like tomatoes in August—were many and long. He was at a School Board meeting on the night of October 11, 1876, when Emma gave birth to her first child, Elsa Sophie Wilhelmine.

Her first year of motherhood coincided with uneasy times in the Future Great. St. Louis was now a center of heavy industry and a major (if not *the* major) rail nexus of the Midwest, linked to the East by a massive bridge. Some branches of local opinion held that the national capital should be moved there from Washington, D.C. Growth had come, however, at the price of increasing grime and crime. The Carondelet skyline near the Starkloff home was lit up at night with the unearthly glow of the Vulcan Iron Works and a cluster of other metal smelters, even as other areas were being transformed into leisured, amiable reaches of greenery and fine sandstone houses. In an act of shortsighted hubris, the city seceded from St. Louis County in 1876 to become the only major free city in the United States, touching off a rancorous election-fraud dispute over the ratification of the home-rule charter and cutting itself off from sources of revenue soon to be needed to shore up shaky infrastructures for a burgeoning population that did not see itself sharing in Future Greatness. There had been a huge influx of poor Southern blacks—the reason for the debate over a right to postelementary schooling—following the shambles of Reconstruction. A large white labor population began to take a line terrifying to the staider St. Louis citizenry. Many festering discontents came to a head in July of 1877, when a general strike paralyzed St. Louis for four days. Carondelet metal workers seized several plants—though without violence; the threat of citywide insurrection did not materialize. The strikers disbanded without accomplishing any of their goals, and the city had been calm for several months when Emma gave birth to her second and last child, Irma Louise, on October 30, 1877. It was another School Board night.

St. Louis would be Irma's universe all her life. She never lived elsewhere except for a few years in her teens, and always readily defined herself within circles not far removed from her upbringing in the

Deutschtum. The world she knew as a child was one of soundly insulating comfort and predictability, light-years from strikes or controversies. But Irma herself, as she emerges from her own words and the memories of those close to her, was neither comfortable nor predictable. It is fitting that the very earliest thing she could remember being conscious of—a "first hurtling into reality" that mysteriously seemed to trigger a bewildering awareness of everything around her—was being suddenly awakened one late winter night by the violent crash of the ice breaking up on the river a few city blocks from her bed: "A sense of security and comfort shattered by a terrific detonation—that was my first impression in life." She thought she must have been two or three.[15]

Her early surroundings ministered well to Irma's sense of self-importance. She was quicker than Elsa to seize opportunities for adventure. It was she who almost from babyhood got to accompany their father on his horse-and-buggy rounds in the fine rolling countryside around Carondelet. She was agreeably fussed over by the staff of the army post at Jefferson Barracks, the nuns at a local Catholic convent, and the wealthy old French families in their river-bluff mansions. Dr. Starkloff delighted in her startling likeness to him: stocky, round-faced, with a short, turned-up nose, a well-marked brow above deep-set brown eyes, and a forceful set of mouth. It was one of those almost comic resemblances that most men find irresistible. She was just as obviously his daughter in temperament, fearless and forward, apt, rather boastful, a glutton for attention. Elsa, ladylike and fastidious even as a toddler, worshiped him with silent tenacity but left the long jolting rides over dusty roads to her sister.

Emma taught them both at home in the first years. The little girls soon showed themselves to be creatures of very different orders. Irma rushed upon everything with a passion to be seen excelling, though without great ceremony. She quarried for mudpie ore, tended to smell of the stables, and hung around the kitchen hoping to find a diamond in a chicken gizzard. She mastered simple tasks and lessons with the pride of a born show-off, and would be bursting with answers while Elsa set her back to the wall with a determined "Aber, Mama, ich kann es nicht." ("But, Mama, I *can't.*") The elder sister had little stomach for contests and loathed anything that involved mussing one's clothes. A photograph of the two at about six and seven shows the dreamy-faced Elsa cuddling a doll with an air of gentle maternal competence while Irma, her own doll braced uncomfortably upright in a toy washtub, stares at her sister with the self-possessed, noticing gaze that marks nearly every picture of her from infancy to old age.

In her quietness and inwardness, Elsa was very much the child of Emma Kuhlmann. All of Max's vanity and bustle were lavishly expressed in Irma. But while Elsa developed a jealous devotion to their father, Irma curiously enough responded to a sense of something remarkable in their mother as one of those cool, unsung, practical, but unexpectedly radiant people without whom life could not go on for the more flamboyant. Emma had a streak of mildly debunking irony that must have been well exercised in her marriage. The fragmentary autobiography left by Irma indicates that without much fanfare, Emma remained an alert and well-informed mind who "flirted with the *Zeitgeist*"—i.e., suffragette opinion—while keeping aloof from the "Mary Wollstonecraft or Susan B. Anthony" category of active feminists.[16]

Max's medical practice flourished in Carondelet to a point that called for a partnership. After a brief rift with his son Max Carl—who had been so foolish as to marry a penniless Irish girl in 1879—he had patched things up sufficiently to establish a joint practice at the address on Main Street (the name was later changed to Broadway). By 1882 Irma and Elsa, at respectively four and five, had become the aunts of Max Carl and Molly's daughter, Adele. The elder Max was already meditating on grander things. In 1883 he moved on to larger quarters, leaving his son to occupy their shared office at the old address. His new hilltop house above the river at the corner of Loughborough and Michigan Avenues in Carondelet occasioned not only a notice of the move in the *Post-Dispatch* but, three days later, a further item stating, "Dr. Starkloff will have his office on Broadway connected by telephone with his residence on Michigan avenue."[17]

During the general upset of the move, Emma was advised to escape temporarily from the dreadful St. Louis summer—part of the reason the British Foreign Service classified the city as hardship duty—to the merciful air of the Great Lakes states, which were already a standard seasonal refuge for affluent Mississippi Valley residents. She had been so ill following a miscarriage that the Kuhlmanns in Germany had dispatched extra nursing care in the form of her younger sister "Dada" (Louise), the aunt who at once recognized Irma as a "life artist." She was an elegant young woman with a bracing air of knowing what she thought and a French wardrobe that fascinated her small nieces. Accompanying Emma and the little girls to the reviving coolness of Oconomowoc in eastern Wisconsin, Dada met a vacationing matron from Indiana who quickly bethought herself of a newly bereaved brother with small children. Dada's rapid engagement and marriage to the young widower, Louis Hollweg, presented Emma's girls with three instant cousins.

Perhaps the greatest pleasure of Irma's young life was the frequent family visits to Indianapolis (another city with a solid German stratum), where the Hollwegs' rambling curio-filled house on North Meridian Street always appeared to her a magical place of holidays and joyous companionship. She made a lifelong friend in the youngest of Dada's stepchildren, the clever and troublesome Julia. Irma and Elsa never would be confidantes—to the end of her sister's life, Irma found her a mystery, "a person barricaded against all others" and imbued with "a streak of melancholy frustration and defeat"[18]—but Julia was a ready ally and soul mate at a time when Irma did not have much companionship of her own age.

From the new house on Michigan Avenue the Starkloff girls were now sent to a nearby public school, where a frustration already half sensed became plainer to Irma: she was not an "American." That term, in quotation marks, was the best she could do to identify the transplanted Eastern, irreproachably Anglo-Saxon stock representing a norm toward which everyone else aspired, notwithstanding that second-generation German children now made up more than 46 percent of the St. Louis public school enrollment. Though Irma had somehow learned English by the time she was five, she stood outside a charmed circle observing with envy:

> Our "American" neighbors were a constant source of interest and curiosity to me. They did not sew on Sundays, nor sing nor play. [The German idea of a good Sunday—listening to music at one of the city's glorious beer gardens—horrified Sabbath-observing "Americans."] They made and consumed quantities of Catsup, lounged on beds, had hot cakes with sirup for breakfast, popped corn, made candy and sang sentimental songs. . . . The older girls sat on the porch and had callers. These gay blades drove buckboards with frisky horses and were incredibly romantic as was the whole plan of "American" living to me.[19]

Emma filled the newly perceived lack by hiring an indubitably "American" governess, the Massachusetts-born Mattie Parker, who introduced Elsa and Irma to English-language children's magazines and her own enthusiasm for natural history. But the sense of a baffling gap between cultures was not something that could have faded easily from Irma's young memory. Other elements of St. Louis had come to resent or mock the arrogance and (as they thought) privilege of the *Deutschtum*, while Max Starkloff was always traveling to meetings of German-oriented pressure groups opposing movements that were seen as anti-German—prohibition, for example. It was a matter of increasingly defensive pride to the old guard to have the finest German taught to their children in the city schools and to keep commemorating their own binational patriotism as something that had helped save the Union. On Camp Jackson Day and other public occasions, Irma's father or some other worthy in resplendent Civil War uniform was sure to wind up a noble convolution of German syntax with the lines from Goethe's *Faust* known to every schoolchild:

> *Was du ererbt von deinen Vätern hast,*
> *Erwirb es, um es zu besitzen!*
> —Part I, 682–683

[Or in the rendering Irma would later quote in *The Joy of Cooking*, "That which thy fathers have bequeathed to thee, earn it anew if thou wouldst possess it."]

After a couple of years on Michigan Avenue, Max began dreaming of new professional vistas—in central St. Louis, if possible. Carondelet was now something of a backwater, while a splendid burst of residential construction was taking place in the area just to its north (the new "South St. Louis") and in various downtown fringes. Taking his cue from the dawning vogue of medical clinics and research facilities inspired by Pasteur and Robert Koch, he talked of starting an orthopedic institute in a fairly central location, preferably in a building large enough to provide living quarters as well. Emma was opposed to this further uprooting. But in 1887, while she was firmly holding her ground, an epidemic of diphtheria began in the city. Both children were stricken, Irma the more seriously. It was uncertain at first that she would live, and later that she would recover. She remained disoriented, cross-eyed, and partly paralyzed for weeks, while the exhausted Emma spelled round-the-clock nursing with a younger medical colleague and Republican ally of Max's, Dr. Carl Barck.

At the end of this ordeal Emma decided that the cause of medical research deserved to carry the day. She told Max that she was prepared to go along with the plan. Accordingly, he and a partner leased a mansion on Chouteau Avenue on the southern fringe of center city, in a somewhat declining pocket of erstwhile grandeur now subject to the din and dirt of the Mill Creek Valley railroad.

Irma was nearly ten now, and had seen downtown St. Louis only on occasional train trips from Carondelet. Her most vivid memories had been of the two prosperous downtown coffeehouses, Speck's and Leonhard's, where the children would be taken to marvel at the glories of the German pastrycook's art: *Bienenstich* (a flat coffee cake topped with a honey or syrup glaze and nuts), *Mohrenköpfe* ("Moors' heads," balls of sponge cake filled with whipped cream and covered with a dark chocolate coating), "sausages" of quince paste filled into casings, chocolate mice. The two years she spent at the Chouteau Avenue house were her first experience of a city neighborhood with a street life she could follow for herself—the noisy playground the local children had made for themselves on an isolated block of La Salle Street behind the Starkloffs', grown-up comings and goings at the nearby Germania Club, the traffic of the "free lunch" saloons that were starting to replace the grand houses. The Starkloff girls promptly became acquainted with a pair of slightly older sisters, Fanny and Nellie Hoblitzelle, the orphaned granddaughters of George Knapp, the publisher of the *St. Louis Republic*, the major Democratic paper in the city. (The *Globe-Democrat*, naturally, was Republican.) This friendship echoed Irma's still unquenched yearning to belong to something higher than the *Deutschtum*. "To me they and their family personified all I then admired most in Americans—a high standard of social life and an inborn grace of manner," she wrote. To her admiring envy, it was the elusive Elsa who seemed to have the right qualities for belonging: an air of having been "born a worldling," a social gift consisting in intuitive "correctness, good manners, a poised bearing, and above all an awareness of the reactions of others."[20] These endowments were not Irma's by nature, though she would eventually master them.

The girls, who had duly progressed in the three Rs at the Blow School in Carondelet, continued through the middle grades at the Clinton School near their new home. For all her obvious cleverness, none of it made much of a dent on Irma. It does not appear that Max and Emma ever envisioned any sort of rigorous intellectual attainments for their daughters, much less any need to make a living. "I was brought up to be a 'young lady,' heaven save the mark!" Irma told an interviewer many years later.[21] Much of what she knew came not from school—no serious branch of study ever became a real part of her mental equipment—but from the Starkloff version of the *Lebenskunst*. Emma had inculcated good doses of "Bible stories, myths, legends, fairy tales, poems, fables, and songs,"[22] later supplemented by Mattie Parker and *St. Nicholas Magazine*; there was always some musical project going on in Max's life; national politics were discussed with gusto and often with raised voices. Irma drank in these things with energetic intelligence if no special application. She shone at what would now be termed "creative" activities, then minor feminine graces. She had a talent for drawing, quite likely a gift that might have gone beyond desultory graces with some serious encouragement. She was an apt musician, though again it does not appear that she was encouraged to work at it with real fervor. She read greedily, with a special fondness for the American humorists of the age, and could quote swatches of Mark Twain and Josh Billings by heart.

She was emerging as an impetuous and ever-impatient, gregarious, rather stormy spirit with a strong appetite for admiration, especially male admiration. At six she had been able to boast of having a "beau," to the intense envy of her cousin Norma Hollweg; by eleven or twelve "my life was never lacking in masculine companionship."[23]

In 1889, the year after Benjamin Harrison's election, Max decided to seek some of the rewards of nearly twenty-five years' service to Republican tickets. Newspaper accounts suggest that he had been very strongly angling for a consulship as a piece of patronage owed to the German interests in the party and had a special eye on Hamburg. But that summer he was informed that he had been selected for the less well paid post in Bremen. (The *St. Louis Republic* was still moved to complain about preferential treatment as "a sop to the German element.")[24] The news of his appointment was anything but welcome to Emma and the girls, who were vacationing in Wisconsin with Dada and the Hollweg cousins. The prospect of a sudden uprooting was all the more dismaying as Max promptly disappeared from all the moving preparations with the explanation that he had to talk to the President at once in Washington. "Das hat der Präsident so nötig wie der Elephant Ohrringe," remarked Emma ("The President needs that as much as an elephant needs earrings"), and got everything ready to leave St. Louis in about ten days, soon enough to cram in a last few days with the Hollwegs in western Maryland.[25] The family sailed from Hoboken on August 10, on the North German Lloyd's steamer *Elbe.* They expected to return in about a year, but one thing seems to have led to another until well into the next Presidential administration.

Irma was not quite twelve when her father took up his post and not quite seventeen when the von Starkloffs came back to St. Louis in the summer of 1894. (They seem to have adopted the "von" among the Bremers and to have used it regularly, though not invariably, after their return.) Five years spent close to her German roots, among trappings of some official importance, must have been a decisive epoch for the adolescent would-be "American." In adult life she would cling mightily to family pride and a deep sense of German identity.

Bremen, the oldest of the German Hanseatic ports, was in its own right only about a third the size of St. Louis, which was getting on for 452,000 souls in 1890. But hordes of emigrants on their way from eastern Europe to the great ship terminals now crowded its staid confines. An immensely dignified merchant aristocracy, corresponding precisely to Emma's antecedents in Lübeck only a day's journey away, dominated the circles in which the von Starkloffs moved. "Years later I saw in the Boston of *The Late George Apley* a miniature Bremen," Irma recalled.[26] The family did not find the town so fascinating, or the consular duties so pressing, as to claim their constant presence. They seem to have traveled more or less at will about Europe, even returning to the United States for one visit of several months early in 1891.

The children were introduced to flocks of relatives on both sides, but it was their mother's connections whom they saw oftenest and who seem to have made the strongest impression on Irma. There is no sign of her having kept up close ties with the German Starkloffs, though quite possibly some evidence has disappeared. By contrast, it is clear that she and later Marion went to some lengths to stay loyally in touch with the surviving Kuhlmanns for years after World War II, and made a point of keeping their letters. She developed a firm belief in a distinction between the northern and southern temperaments, as applicable to Germany, she insisted, as to "Maine and Louisiana."[27] In American terms, one might say that she came to admire an equivalent of the New England character—upright, domestic, capable, the very model of the Kuhlmanns.

The von Starkloff children were taken to visit Emma's older brother Willi Kuhlmann, a musician at the grand ducal court of Oldenburg some thirty miles from Bremen, and her older sister "Mally" (Amalie) Schroeder, a Lutheran pastor's wife in the village of Spieka on the coastal headland of Wursten. These regions were a far cry from the fine and rolling but landlocked terrain of eastern Missouri. The flat ditch-crossed Wursten landscape with its quasi-Dutch tidiness and austere vistas of sky and sea made a tremendous impression on Irma, as did the unpretentious but civilized *Gemütlichkeit* of the Spieka parsonage. She always remembered family evenings in the rural isolation of the Schroeder home listening to her uncle Georg read aloud "in his splen-did ringing voice" from Fritz Reuter (Mark Twain's great north German contemporary), while lamplight "fell upon a red plush table-covering, a large bowl of apples and one of walnuts, and on a circle of family faces frequently convulsed with laughter."[28] She would retain a great fond-ness for the "dour peasants" of Wursten and Oldenburg: "It always pleased me that they [the Oldenburgers] held out for years against Hitler and gave him lots of trouble."[29]

South Germans were another matter to Irma: "less rigid," "warmer," "more emotionally unstable"—in a word, more like her father, the Schwabenlander. She loved Max devotedly but with reser-vations. She eventually developed a skepticism about his sublime accounts of his own deeds and always associated him with the braggart Tartarin in Daudet's *Tartarin de Tarascon*. The moments she most cherished in their relationship were those in which he played the genial *Lebenskünstler* by his own fireside, something he had far more time to do in Europe than in St. Louis. When at home, he took to fill-ing his abundant leisure evenings with hours of reading aloud to the family. "That was the best part of the day and the best part of our years abroad," Irma wrote.[30] It was also probably the best-absorbed part of her education—hours of anything from Goethe, Schiller, and Shake-speare to the much-loved nineteenth-century German verse humorist Wilhelm Busch. Mark Twain, another of the evening favorites, crossed the von Starkloffs' path in person during one of his later European vis-its. (Marion records a family story that he "made a particular friend of 'Irm'" and "presented her with an autographed edition of his work.")[31]

Irma's formal education was fairly desultory. She and Elsa were placed (sometimes together, sometimes separately) with various girls' schools and governesses, and both spent some time in Lausanne, prob-ably at a school run there by Max's sister Emma Rambert. But the European years were generally filled with the "young lady's" upbring-ing that Irma later found so preposterous. The entertainment at the formal afternoon teas to which she and Elsa would be asked by Bremen contemporaries usually consisted of the girls' playing the piano or reading plays aloud in parts (probably the classic French and German dramatists and Shakespeare, a national German passion). It was a life well suited to confer what she later called "an intellectual patina" but no great capacity for intellectual exertion.[32] "Ill taught, vaguely informed, moderately gifted," the scrawled notes accompanying her fragmentary autobiography coolly sum up her Bremen self.[33] In an age to come she would keenly feel the paucity of her academic training, for degrees from the Eastern women's colleges would be widely recognized new badges of social standing by the time Irma was a competitive young matron. But the leisurely, higgledy-piggledy education she did receive was the sort that an agile mind can make much of in later years.

The uneventful official life of the consul's family was interrupted in August of 1892, when a great panic broke out following reports of cholera in several parts of Russia and then in the nearby port city of Hamburg (linked with Bremen by frequent trains). Actual cases were soon diagnosed on steamers carrying passengers from Cherbourg and Hamburg to England and the United States. An intense panic swept over New York, the main emigrant destination; meanwhile, several cases turned up in Bremen itself. For the first time in his consulship, Dr. von Starkloff was called upon to deal with a medical emergency.[34]

While the city hastily drew up sanitary measures, Dr. von Starkloff and the management of the North German Lloyd's shipping line, which largely controlled the emigrant traffic from Bremen, undertook the screening of the American-bound passengers. The great Robert Koch, who had been called in from Berlin to consult with the Bremen authorities, met with Max at the instigation of North German Lloyd's and lent his approval to the suggested measures of the American doctor. These, according to Max's report to the U.S. State Department, included daily monitoring of the emigrant hotels and boardinghouses, detention of all arriving emigrants for at least two days' observation, and strict examination and disinfection of all steerage passengers and their luggage before they were allowed to embark. The threatened outbreak was completely contained in the city within a matter of weeks, with not a single emigrant carrying the disease from Bremen. Max was widely credited with having done a good deal to prevent a multinational epidemic. Many decades later, one of the Hollweg cousins mentioned another family memory of the episode in a letter to Marion: that he had also "made a lot of money at that time" vaccinating would-be emigrants.[35]

Dr. von Starkloff's efforts during the cholera emergency were probably the reason he was asked to stay on in Bremen, in an unusual
gesture of bipartisan goodwill, when the Democrats and Grover Cleveland returned to the White House in 1892. But that winter he was in
poor health himself, requiring an operation on his larynx and some
respite from the dank, English-style Bremen climate. At some point
during the next year he asked to be relieved of his duties, citing his
affected health. On July 31, 1894, he was replaced as consul by George
Keenan, and the von Starkloffs were back in St. Louis less than a
month later.

Max was now prepared to live in the grand style in St. Louis. His
next venue would be the newly fashionable enclave of Compton
Heights, a particularly magnificent corner of "South St. Louis" (the
affluent German-dominated realm between center city and the old
Carondelet), where the cream of German society was now settling.
Here, at Compton Avenue and Longfellow Boulevard, Max built one of
the most striking and luxurious mansions in a neighborhood of palatial houses. He had installed his family and his practice in the new
home by the summer of 1895, and settled down to a comfortable elder
statesmanship—he was now sixty-four—in the German community
and the Republican Party.

It was an agreeable time in the family fortunes, though the doings
of Emil (no longer living regularly in St. Louis) sometimes would come
to embarrassing notice. There are family stories of stints as a riverboat
gambler and a pimp; eventually he would be working several Eastern
and Midwestern cities with phony get-rich schemes involving gold
bricks and fictitious mines. In the meanwhile, Max Carl Starkloff—
who always eschewed the "von"—was well on his way to an eminence
that would eventually eclipse his father's. He was by now in his late
thirties, a staunchly industrious man with a strong medical-crusader
streak and the family devotion to Republican causes. He had spent several years as president of the St. Louis area board of Federal pension
examiners—another token of the Harrison administration's local debts
to the elder Max—when Mayor Cyrus Walbridge appointed him City
Health Commissioner. It was an office that would be his own nearly
for life.[36]

Aside from his work, his twin passions were yachting—he loved
treating his young half-sisters to river outings—and hunting. In the fall
season he kept the tables of various family members well supplied
with game, and he had a knowledge of fine guns. He was a man of deep,

not to say stubborn, loyalties, unable to be talked out of a "boundless admiration" for the disgraced Emil, whom, according to Irma, "he assisted repeatedly, always deploring that such gifts, so much intelligence and power should have been misapplied."[37]

Max C. Starkloff had not been long installed in the Health Commissioner's office, or the elder Max's family in the Longfellow Boulevard mansion, when the greatest natural disaster in the history of St. Louis reduced large stretches of the city to rubble. The young lawyer Edgar Rombauer, who was working at the time in downtown chambers, later described the event as having followed a spring of unusual winds and storms. On the hot, sunny afternoon of May 27, 1896, he looked out the office window to see "incessant flashes of lightning in the southwest," shortly followed by answering flickers in the northwest, while the sky in between remained perfectly clear. He was about to start for home and had in fact reached the street when a friend with experience of similar things in Kansas pointed to the sky:

> Moving to meet the clouds coming from the northwest and southwest was a tremendous white cloud coming from the east. It did not move steadily westward, but seemed to move forward with a bound, and then make a stop before bounding forward again, much as a swan swims; and the front of the cloud was curled up and over like the rollers on certain kinds of ice skates, and as it bounded forward it emitted a hissing sound, much as a boat being propelled through waves against a strong headwind. Pretty soon it began to grow dark and the wind blew at a tremendous speed in all directions. I waited near the front entrance of the building until I saw a horse and buggy being blown up the street like a piece of newspaper and then I retreated into the rotunda of the building.[38]

It was an hour before the terrible wind and rain subsided enough for him to venture home through tangles of live wires, finding his parents' house on Geyer Avenue (a few blocks from the von Starkloffs') still standing despite the hundreds of uprooted trees and wall-less buildings that marked the storm's path.

At Longfellow Boulevard, the tornado had swallowed up massive chunks of Max's new mansion within a few minutes. There is a family story that Irma had gone to sketch in Forest Park behind the present St. Louis Art Museum, some three miles away, and could not be found until four days after the storm, when she turned up in a state of amnesia. Edgar Rombauer's account, however, mentions no such episode. He wrote simply that Irma and the von Starkloffs "escaped only because they took refuge in the cellar."[39] The younger Max Starkloff emerged from the disaster a hero. He was at the Health Commissioner's office at City Hall when the storm broke, and bravely or rashly set out on foot in the direction of his chief responsibility, City Hospital, more than a mile and a half to the south. His right arm was at once broken by a falling flagstaff. He promptly improvised a sling, hailed a horse-drawn ambulance, and arrived at the hospital to find it in ruins. He worked through the night and the next day to bring patients out of the wrecked building into hastily commandeered quarters, and personally escorted seventeen prisoners from the hospital prison ward to the safety of the jail. It was an accurate indication of the qualities he would bring to the Health Commissioner's duties for some thirty years.

When the dust had settled, it was gradually estimated that about 140 people had died in the May 27 tornado, with 1,000 injured and some 8,000 buildings completely destroyed.[40] Max von Starkloff, like many thousands more, had to rebuild a great deal of his house. Present descendants relate that some months after the storm Emma was sitting in a friend's drawing room when her eye fell on an oddly familiar chair. "Where did you get that?" she inquired. It turned out to have appeared, undamaged, from the belly of the whirlwind moments after having flown out of the Longfellow Boulevard premises.[41]

Irma and Elsa had now reached the age at which, as little as ten years later, a family like the von Starkloffs would surely have been sending their daughters to college. Irma had been much among clever people, and her later accounts make it evident that she wanted to do clever things herself. But just what she had the power to do cannot have seemed very clear, beyond the power to excite admiration. She was small and neatly made, with a great flair for wearing clothes and in general making herself interesting to others, especially men. Her looks and bearing might in another age have evoked terms like "cute little brunette," and would have been called "dainty" in her own. (Elsa was tall and blond, with finely drawn features and a dignified air bordering on melancholy.) Irma had—there is no getting around the phrase—a sparkling gaze. She met people with a lovely, rather capricious sprightliness of manner that masked some sort of dimly felt ambition or discontent.

On coming back from Bremen she had enrolled in art classes at Washington University, though apparently without any thought of matriculating for a degree. For the next few years she seems to have worked at painting and sketching with some consistency, while performing an unadventurous round of maidenly activities like playing the piano at afternoon musicales and acting in amateur theatricals. Her chief confidante was her cousin Julia, just Irma's age and now an Indianapolis debutante. Norma, the oldest of the Hollwegs, had married and moved from home, and her brother Ferdinand was also grown. Ina, Louis Hollweg's only surviving child by his marriage to Dada, was nine years younger than Julia, and her eagerness for Irma's company is understandable. The two girls paid frequent visits back and forth during the Longfellow Boulevard era, and Irma spent several summers in Indianapolis. On one of her stays with Julia, in the last weeks of 1897, she was introduced to the unemployed and determinedly bohemian twenty-eight-year-old son of an otherwise respectable family living two blocks from the Hollwegs.

Newton Booth Tarkington, who since graduating from Princeton had done nothing to earn a living except bombard publishers with manuscripts (mostly rejected by return post), did not stand high in the then opinion of Indianapolis society. He in turn nourished much disdain for the common rout of Indianapolis. Not surprisingly, their sudden mutual attraction aroused prompt suppressive measures from Irma's relatives. The affair apparently had been buried for many decades when in 1953 the scholar James Woodress, a St. Louisan with a good memory for names, spotted some letters from "Irma von Starkloff" among the Tarkington papers at Princeton and sent an inquiry to the esteemed author of *The Joy of Cooking.*

Today the only records of the ill-starred romance are the few details that Irma provided, by letter and by interview, for Woodress's biography of Tarkington; the three brief letters of hers that the researcher had already found at Princeton; and an impassioned sixteen-page letter from Tarkington written just after he had seen her for the last time. She did not mention this last—the only one of Tarkington's letters that she kept, and the only surviving love-letter that she received from anyone—to Woodress, and it is not clear whether even Marion knew of its existence.

"We met at a spelling bee," Mrs. Rombauer wrote in answer to the biographer's inquiries. "I misspelled a word—I still do—and found him by my side, ready to defend my 'logical' interpretation as against the conventional one." The relationship was "brief, turbulent, and intense."[42] Tarkington was at once taken with, as he thought, her rarefied perceptions. He also found her inordinately charming in a tricky, half-perverse way. He took every occasion to monopolize her at their few meetings, talking and talking like a frustrated lecturer unleashed and deluging her with lofty counsel fit for a chosen spirit. Irma had been used to attracting male admirers almost since she was out of apron strings, but this high-minded ardor struck her with a new sort of confused fascination.

There were according to Tarkington only "four times we were together a little," which may mean when they met at all or (more probably) when they were able to talk intimately.[43] This was enough to bring up heavy artillery in the form of the "rigid and disapproving relatives" by whom "we were torn asunder," as Irma told James Woodress.[44] She was packed off to St. Louis by a Monday morning train on December 20, after impulsively asking him to come by one last time the previous evening. They sat through an embarrassing visit at the watchful Hollwegs', with Tarkington at his most urgently prolix and the dainty Miss von Starkloff at her most capricious.

By the end of this awkward farewell she had nonetheless managed to ask him to write her in St. Louis, a familiarity not then taken for granted by well-bred young people. In response to her "pretty challenge," Tarkington at once went home and poured out a torrent of impassioned admiration and reproach:

> My mind is entirely full of you,—to indulge the flat, outright truth,—and also I follow my will to write before you have forgotten me, Lady-Who-Forgets-No-One! . . . Why did you ask me to write? Won't you try the experiment I am trying—of being utterly and completely frank? You see, it puzzles me. You declared me a great bore, you know. You must have known I shouldn't have dared to ask permission, of course. It was splendidly generous and kind to give me the privelege [sic]—*and to promise to answer*; and you cannot realize how thoroughly grateful I am. It was so tantalizing to catch these few glimpses of you and then to lose you completely by that brute of a train tomorrow. . . . But what made you ask me? I *want* to think it was because you wished, a little, to keep in touch with me, but I find large doubts in my heart.[45]

Irma replied with hesitant encouragement. She had, she assured him, been sincere in asking him to write. She had been struck by the difference between the wayward figure of Indianapolis gossip and the reality of "what I admire above all things, a broad mind. . . . Living as I do, among many narrow people (for nowhere do they seem as narrow as in a large city), hearing from you would be a delight and I did not feel the indifference I feigned before you answered my question."

Clearly unsure of what tack to take, she protested that she did not have the brains or depth to have held his interest more than momentarily had they had more time together, but also hinted that he had touched some vital nerve:

> I *want* to be truthful and will. If I were to fib you would find me out. To be honest I am a little afraid of you. To most people I am a riddle not worth solving. No one has ever understood me as you seem to. I can't write you exactly what I think and how I feel—and have a horror of being misunderstood. The thought that you may be criticising my "style," even my spelling—that unfortunate word of Buffon's, "Le style c'est l'homme"—all help to make me feel stupid and awkward when addressing you.[46]

How long they continued to write is not clear, since the surviving letters are obviously an incomplete record. But distance soon had exactly the effect desired by Irma's family—whose disapproval, though she did not mention it in her letters to Tarkington, remained a vivid memory in her account to James Woodress. Within a few months she had taken a very different tack, telling him with brusque flippancy that their December encounter had been "*so* long ago, and you are right, I *have* lost interest." She coolly turned aside any question of revisiting Indianapolis for several years. But she could not forbear some sort of ambiguous encouragement, hinting that she would like to see him—"Do you ever visit this smoky place?" She thanked him for his interest in her mind and asked him to suggest good books, while neatly contriving to put him in the wrong for having got under her skin:

> I resent your knowledge of my character. You saw me so little and know me so well—at least you know my faults, and kindly attribute a number of good qualities I do not possess—

it makes me feel uneasy, unnatural, when I write you, and that makes writing unpleasant.[47]

In truth, their initial flash of mutual attraction was not the stuff of an attachment durable enough to bridge the difference in background. St. Louis Germans of the von Starkloff girls' backgrounds were still generally marrying within the *Deutschtum*; any "American" suitors had better be of irreproachable solidity, not misunderstood genius. There is no evidence that Irma seriously tried to overcome her family's objections to the Indianapolis ne'er-do-well. Within a short while she was receiving attentions from a far more eligible admirer. In all probability she never saw Booth Tarkington again.

But their brief acquaintance must have made a considerable mark on the unquiet mixture of elements that was the mature Irma, if for no other reason than that Booth Tarkington shortly confounded every Indianapolis naysayer by publishing a highly successful novel. His great breakthrough came in 1899 with *The Gentleman from Indiana*. If his heroine, Helen Fisbee, had such un-Irmalike qualities as gray eyes and the ability to take over a small-town newspaper from an ailing editor, he also made her—like the young lady who became Mrs. Edgar Rombauer a few months after the book's publication—"a dainty little figure about five feet high," with "light brown hair" and "a short upper lip like a curled rose-leaf."[48] Within a decade he would be a household name throughout the United States. That in itself would have been sufficient to keep green in Irma's memory a glimpse of an existence and a potential self quite unlike any future that her own circles had held out to her as she emerged into young womanhood. It was a challenge that in the end she had not pursued. She would remain in her own proper St. Louis world, tugging and worrying at its borders with a competitive discontent plain to all who knew her closely.

2

Beginnings and Endings

Marrying a man like Edgar Rombauer was exactly what might have been expected of a girl like Irma von Starkloff. On the face of it, he was eligible merchandise from the same drawer as Julius Muench, the worthy young scion of a prominent Forty-eighter family whom Elsa had married a year before. But the Rombauers were, even by the standards of the Forty-eighters, an uncommonly contentious and ideological lot. There was a certain troublemaking streak in most of them, though Edgar was one of the less fractious Rombauers.

They were a large tribe of exiled Hungarians—more accurately, ethnic Germans whose forebears had lived for centuries west of the Carpathian Mountains in the city of Löcse (now Levoča in the republic of Slovakia). The Saxon-descended communities of the region were important enough to have a name of their own, the "Zipsers." Edgar's grandfather, Theodore Rombauer, was an ironworks director who supported the Kossuth revolt of 1848 and held a major post in the national munitions program under the ill-fated revolutionary government. When the new regime was crushed by the united forces of Austria and Russia in 1849, Theodore and his wife, Bertha, fled to America with their seven surviving children.[1]

Roderick, born in 1833, was the most ambitious and complex of the refugee family, a would-be poet who had early seen that he had no great genius in that direction and turned to the law. Before the Civil War he had worked his way through law school at Harvard by wrenching effort and sheer privation (he once declined a chance to dine with Longfellow because he thought his clothes too disgraceful). He and his brothers had been among the early drillers in the St. Louis Home Guard, and Roderick had been able to boast himself captain of the first company of the first Union regiment formed from the Home Guard. When his army service was cut short by illness, he turned to politics, quickly finding a suitable bride in Augusta Koerner, a daughter of the Illinois Republican elder statesman Gustave Koerner. By the time of their marriage in 1865, Roderick had already won himself a seat on the St. Louis Law Commissioners Court, later reorganized as the Circuit Court of St. Louis County. The second of their seven children, Edgar Roderick Rombauer, was born on July 3, 1868, near the Koerners' home in Belleville, the seat of the old "Latin Farmers" across the river from St. Louis.

After the Civil War Irma's and Edgar's fathers took equally to the roles of community pillars and Republican stalwarts. Their paths regularly crossed through their School Board connections (Roderick was for many years attorney to the Board). They also were often speakers at the same civic occasions, Dr. von Starkloff usually reading his orotund remarks from a prepared German text and Judge Rombauer speaking in his sharply pointed (though accented) English. But they were not particular friends, or even particular allies. Roderick had a restless and skeptical turn of mind and a powerful streak of ambition that turned first to notions of the U.S. Senate, later of the Supreme Court. But as he grandly declared of himself, he "was always far too independent in his political views, to entitle him to count on the sincere support of professional politicians."[2] He loudly supported woman suffrage when it was the most ridiculed of fringe causes.[3] He thought it his duty to bolt his party when a principle warranted it, and his privilege to complain of the consequences. By 1884, when he was running for a seat on the St. Louis Court of Appeals, he had gravitated toward the "Mugwump" wing of Republicanism, whose alliances with liberal Democrats produced Grover Cleveland's victory over James Blaine that November. (The next day Max von Starkloff picked up the paper and hurled it down on the breakfast table roaring, of the Mugwumps, "Die gottverdammten Schweinhunde haben die Wahl gestohlen!" ["The dirty goddamned rats stole the election!"])[4] Roderick won his race, but he would advance no further in the local, much less Federal, judiciary.

His autobiography, a curious document written in the third person and surveying his accomplishments with mingled self-approbation and restlessness, conveys something of his upright, harsh, yet eager nature. It cannot have been easy to belong to his domestic orbit. A generation later, his young granddaughter Marion Rombauer would shrink from the chilling atmosphere of his household. Little can be gathered of Augusta Koerner Rombauer except that she must have been unflinchingly loyal and patient under difficult circumstances, financial and other. Edgar always remembered his mother's grace throughout several years when, he wrote, "she never had any other than a calico dress" as a result of strapped finances after Roderick, who always offered himself and others up to unpleasant duties with obstinate relish, undertook to pay the bad debts of a brother-in-law. She also bore the provocation not just of her husband's acrimonious nature but of his belief—apparently put into practice on more than one extramarital occasion—in what he called "the freedom of the affections."

From Edgar's account, the happiest times in his early childhood were summer vacations among the good-natured tribe of Koerners and Engelmanns (Augusta's mother's family) around Belleville. Later there was Colorado. Roderick was advised in the late 1870s to seek mountain air for his health and lost no time in gratifying a passion, nourished by boyhood readings of Fenimore Cooper, for the idea of the great and lofty wilderness. The whole family, small children and all, set out for an extended camping trip in a northerly mining district about sixty miles west of Denver, in Clear Creek County close to the Continental Divide. Judge Rombauer, who had never lost a youthful yen to find gold, shortly acquired several properties, including a shaft mine and a "placer" (hydraulic) mine near North Empire. These were not dramatically productive, but they provided an excuse for many summers spent seeking the challenge of the outdoor existence—something that brought a more amiable tinge to Roderick's curdled romanticism and instilled his son with a lifelong fondness for the healing power of nature.

It was virtually a foregone conclusion that whether he wanted to or not, Edgar would be groomed for the law and the Koerner-Rombauer political mantle. By paternal fiat, he was frog-marched into the class of 1888 at the law school of Washington University. As Edgar later explained to his own children:

> The study of the law was not my natural inclination but I had no voice in the matter. Your grandfather, who was a very pos-

itive man, simply said to me, "Either you do as you are told and go to law school or I will apprentice you to a shoemaker," and as I did not wish to become a cobbler I had no other choice than to become a lawyer.[5]

Since after two years of the law course the boy was still too young to qualify for the Missouri bar, Roderick packed him off at twenty to an unsalaried post as assistant in the Chicago law firm of Smith and Pence, where the Koerners had some connection. For his first six months' expenses Roderick agreed to lend him twenty-five dollars a month, which poor Edgar thought would be plenty. His mistake was soon horribly clear. But starving seemed better than asking for more from the man who had once turned down Longfellow's dinner invitation rather than reveal his poverty. Edgar, too young and confused to find another stratagem, took a closet-sized room for eleven dollars a month and prepared to live on the remaining fourteen dollars. With the aid of "an alcohol lamp, a coffee pot, a knife, a spoon and some ground coffee," he devised a diet consisting of a cup of coffee and half a loaf of bread for breakfast and supper, with "a bowl of milk and crackers, or soup, or a small steak, at some very cheap restaurant," for lunch.[6]

This regimen continued unchanged for about a year and with only slight mitigation—he was now earning a tiny salary but had asked Roderick to discontinue anything more from home—for most of another. But Edgar's fortunes soon took a more hopeful turn. In the summer of 1889 a lawyer named John Maynard Harlan joined the firm of Smith and Pence. Several months after his arrival he sounded out the young clerk on the idea of becoming private secretary to his father, Supreme Court Justice John Marshall Harlan.

Judge Rombauer was loudly opposed. The comfortable salary ($1,600 a year) and the attractions of Washington appeared to him just the thing to seduce a young man into a life of ignoble pencil-pushing. But Edgar stood his ground. It may have occurred to him that his father begrudged him a ringside seat at events that the older man had long hungrily followed from afar. He thought that if he had been "strong enough to live on dry bread and coffee for two meals a day for two years," he would be strong enough to use this offer wisely. He moved to Washington at the end of 1889, having promised that he would stay no more than two or three years before getting back to his own legal career.

He kept his word. The job was an excellent one; Edgar not only handled Harlan's correspondence but got to review and summarize critical material in all of the cases before the Court. Justice Harlan himself would tip off the young secretary to particularly exciting debates scheduled for the House or Senate floor. But though Harlan, the great enunciator of civil rights principles that would not become the law of the land until 1954, took an encouraging interest in Edgar and surely would have helped him to other positions, the young man came back to Chicago (having been admitted to the Illinois bar) in the spring of 1892.

At first all seemed to go smoothly with his new practice. But something was amiss. "Towards fall I began to feel that I was not well," he tersely recorded in his autobiography. Edgar tried to fight the unknown malaise until about a year after his return, when he suddenly collapsed on the street in excruciating pain. After a couple of months of blundering medical attentions in Chicago and St. Louis, he set out for six months' convalescence in the Rockies. On the day of his departure he received a telegram offering him the position of associate counsel to the American interest at an international tribunal recently convened in Paris to settle U.S. and Canadian claims over Bering Sea sealing rights. It had been sent at the instigation of Justice Harlan, who had been named to the tribunal and clearly wanted to extend a timely coattail to his able ex-secretary.[7] Too sick even to think of accepting, Edgar continued on to Colorado. He would never again entertain any career option beyond St. Louis.

The illness that had baffled the doctors was the first of Edgar Rombauer's many "nervous breakdowns," an elastic term that then covered all sorts of collapse. What modern psychiatry would have made of it is at best a hazy question. For all the fondness with which his family remembered Edgar and the scrupulous detail of the autobiography he wrote for his small children, it is not easy to form an idea of his inner life that might confidently support much psychiatric sleuthing. That he was the product of a coldly autocratic upbringing (at least on Roderick's side) seems plain, but this does not necessarily explain the intervals of misery that would overtake him all his adult life. The contemporary label that probably is most consistent with his history—periods of energy that would see him through amazing bouts of overwork alternating with paralyzing episodes of anxiety and withdrawal—is manic depression.

In the gratefully familiar mountain air of Clear Creek County, Edgar quickly came back to normal health and spirits over the summer of 1893. Chicago and the practice seemed about to bring on a relapse that fall, but just at that moment he received a welcome proposition from his older brother Theodore, who had spent a time as a civil engineer before turning to the law and who now suggested setting up an office with Edgar in St. Louis. The arrangement did not last long because of Theodore's own failing health (in his engineering travels he had contracted some chronic disease, perhaps malaria). But after their father was defeated for a further term on the Court of Appeals in 1896, he decided to return to private practice with Edgar. It was probably Roderick's presence that brought in a number of excellent commissions, many of them connected with the grandiose hopes of contemporary railroad-builders.

The beginning of Edgar's serious interest in Irma von Starkloff, according to the characteristically careful reckoning in his autobiography, dated from about the time of an unsuccessful campaign he headed to nominate a Republican mayoral candidate in 1897. Together with his unmarried suffragette sisters Bertha and Sophie, he was then living at his parents' home on Geyer Avenue, on the fringes of fashionable South St. Louis. He had first noticed Irma at a dance several years before but had been in no financial position to pay addresses to wealthy young ladies. Now he and she were cast as man and wife in an amateur dramatic production. He took to escorting her to and from rehearsals several times a week, and was shortly asking himself how on earth he could ever afford to seek the hand of this lovely creature.[8]

As he later described it to their son and daughter, the qualities that drew Edgar to Irma were "her beauty, her vivaciousness, and her frankness," along with what he was rash enough to call an "essentially sunny" disposition. Irma left no corresponding comment, though she did much later in life tell a young engaged couple that "young people have ice water in their veins" by comparison with her and her fiancé's passion. She must have found his fine blue eyes and forceful, dignified features an immense contrast to the lantern-jawed and homely Booth Tarkington. As for the rest, the single epithet that she can be found to have written about him—after his death she discussed Edgar with very few people—is "exuberant."[9] That would have counted for a great deal with Irma.

He seems to have spent more than a year calling on her and taking her to the theater before he asked her to be his wife. It was not a proposal he was sure he could afford to make, but he writes that he was "terribly in love." They became engaged in February 1899, with little hope of marrying in the foreseeable future. While Edgar was gloomily reminding himself how uncertain his financial prospects were, a deus ex machina appeared in the person of a railroad manager who chose the young St. Louis lawyer to represent his local interest in a couple of complex, sprawling suits. It was the $1,000 that he received for one of these cases—"my first large fee"—that enabled Edgar to marry Irma von Starkloff on October 14, 1899.

Emma and Max gave the young couple a lavish civil wedding from the Longfellow Boulevard mansion, which was done up to the nines in pink and white roses, trailing vines, and color-coordinated draperies. (Elsa had had a church wedding, but on this occasion the freethinking von Starkloffs and more or less atheistic Rombauers followed their natural inclinations.) The new pair moved into a rented apartment on Botanical Avenue, a few blocks from Irma's parents in South St. Louis. They meant to live on an economical plan befitting Edgar's still-chancy income. Much later, Irma would relate to her great-niece Elsa Muench Hunstein that she had set up housekeeping with no servants, not even a cook.[10] This would have been outlandish indeed for a bride of her social position; the story may well be one of the exaggerations (if not inventions) that Irma liked to spin when she had become famous. That she had to start married life with meager and undependable help is quite likely. But she cannot have spent much time playing at brave young self-reliance. In a matter of weeks she was pregnant, and on July 27, 1900, she gave birth to her first child, Roland.

There are only a few photographs of Roland, cursory glimpses of anonymous infant features surrounded by the lavish muslin baby clothes of the period. Edgar's account is as touchingly scant:

> He was a source of great joy to us while he lived. But from the beginning he was not strong and in the following March [1901] he died very suddenly after an illness of but a few hours.[11]

Irma was, he says, "inconsolable." It seems that she was a great deal more. She must, in fact, have gone into a prolonged state of collapse beyond anything Edgar could cope with, because they had to break up the apartment on Botanical Avenue and move in for the time being with the unstintingly generous von Starkloffs.

After a few months Edgar tried the solace that had done so much for him, the bright alpine terrain of Colorado. Irma, however, developed an alarming fever in the high altitude. She seemed little better when he brought her back to new quarters in an old house on Kennett Place near Lafayette Park, somewhat east of the main enclave of South St. Louis. By the time she began to respond to (or recover in spite of) the rest cure prescribed by the doctor, Edgar knew that he was about to suffer his first nervous breakdown of their marriage.[12]

Again he fought against the coming collapse for many months. It was March of 1902 when, unable to continue any pretense of a normal life, he accepted the advice of his doctors and went with Irma to the hill country resort of Eureka Springs, in northwestern Arkansas near the Missouri border. (His cherished spots in Colorado were unreachable until far later in the year.)

Irma never wrote of what she felt during this appalling crisis—the first extended period of the marriage that had not been colored by the prospect or presence of a baby. It cannot have been anything other than a nightmare, even without the foreknowledge that Edgar's illnesses would continue for the whole of their married life. By the time they reached Eureka Springs, Edgar was in a state of constant weakness and exhaustion, abjectly depressed and full of irrational fears: "If my gums bled when I washed my teeth I was sure I had tuberculosis." Irma rose to the occasion, as she always would. "Your mother had the patience of a saint, and but for her lively, uncomplaining, cheerful disposition I am sure I would have grown steadily worse."

Either Irma's efforts, the beauty and tranquillity of the surroundings, or some self-limitation of the disease gradually prevailed. Within a few weeks Edgar was able to ride with her through the unspoiled hilly countryside. It was the height of spring; later he remembered violets underfoot and dogwood and wild peach trees blooming throughout the woods. They made many excursions to nearby scenic spots and shared a seriocomic introduction to the barbarian ways of "the hill natives of Arkansas." It was perhaps the most idyllic moment of their life together. They returned to Kennett Place around the middle of April, in a state of joyous restoration. Their only daughter, Marion Julia Rombauer, was born not quite eight months later, on January 2, 1903.

Marion was a small baby beset with neonatal digestive problems. Edgar and Irma must have been in constant fear of another loss. They weighed her every Sunday, elated by any tiny gain in weight. She did not exactly thrive, but she survived to grow into a somewhat ailing child, generally "sunny," in the eyes of her father, but given on occasion to "very violent fits of temper."

Kennett Place, in Marion's first memories, was a rather lonely home. There were few children of her own age, and Irma soon took to dashing out of the house in pursuit of nondomestic interests. Marion peopled her days with imaginary playmates to supply the lack of real ones. In later life she would remember two of them: "Arnie," whose origin she never did figure out, and "Bernard Shaw," whom she guessed to have sprung from Irma's growing involvement with improving activities like literary discussion groups.[13]

In Marion's early solitude, the von Starkloff grandparents provided much of what tenderness and domesticity she knew. She loved their pleasant household as much as she instinctively recoiled from the forbidding chill of the senior Rombauers' home. With both daughters married, Max and Emma had moved from Longfellow Boulevard to a slightly more modest corner of South St. Louis, on Cleveland Avenue close to the Missouri Botanical Gardens—"Shaw's Garden," as the great collection was and is universally known in St. Louis. With them Marion felt a sense of reassuring routine not always to be found in her mother's turbulent wake. Like Irma twenty-five years earlier, she would ride with Dr. von Starkloff on his rounds and listen to him tell stories, or watch him get dressed up to celebrate the receding memory of Camp Jackson Day. Emma, meanwhile, quietly supplied things that might otherwise have been scanted while the young Mrs. Rombauer was—as Marion later tactfully put it—"busy developing our environment and ourselves" anywhere except at home. It was she who "had time to teach me to sew, knit, crochet, tat, and cook cookies and the kinds of things children love to make."

At the von Starkloffs', too, Marion could meet one of the few children she knew who were close to her own age: her "always protective," slightly older cousin Max Muench, Elsa and Julius's only child. She loved the aftermath of long, talkative German Sunday dinners at Cleveland Avenue, when she and Max would creep from their own little *Katzentisch* (literally, "cats' table") and disappear under the big dinner table to play in the shadow of the long damask tablecloth. All too soon, "Back to Kennett Place in the late afternoon and once more dependent on my imaginary companions."

In 1906 the domestic circle underwent a sudden convulsion when Edgar's widowed brother Theodore died, leaving a will that named Edgar as the guardian of his nearly fourteen-year-old son, Rod. At once a bitter family struggle broke out. Roderick senior wanted to bring up the boy in his own home. It is possible that his opinion of Irma figured in this intention, for there was no love lost between those two restless souls. Nor was Irma a great favorite with his strong-minded spinster daughters Bertha and Sophie, whom she apparently considered chips off the old block.[14]

Edgar insisted on carrying out Theodore's wishes. If the cold authoritarianism of his own upbringing had not been enough to decide him, the unsuitability of turning a lively boy over to two elderly grandparents and two maiden aunts would have been. Probably he also thought unsuitable his father's defiantly proclaimed penchant for "the freedom of the affections," notably one particular affection for a lady who had been secretary to the School Board.

Edgar prevailed, at the cost of much ill feeling. Irma found herself—amid voluble criticisms from her father-in-law's household—obliged to play mother to a well-grown, rebellious adolescent with the energy of a live hand grenade. The happiest person involved was Marion, who adored Rod as a gloriously dashing daredevil older brother. She was even more overjoyed when they moved from Kennett Place to Rod's own home, the house on Flad Avenue where he had lived with Theodore.

This was a large though not palatial house in the neighborhood of the splendid park complex formed by Tower Grove Park and Shaw's Garden. The two sets of grandparents were only a few blocks away. It was not the poshest area of South St. Louis (which was starting to lose its old cachet), but it was infinitely more companionable for children than Kennett Place. Marion was happily supplied with real rather than imaginary playmates.

Rod, however, began to become wilder and wilder. Because of his parents' long illnesses, he had known little of orthodox adult supervision. He was affectionate enough to his idolizing small cousin, but he did not care to have his extremely decided wishes thwarted by his equally strong-willed uncle. After Rod and a friend had tried to run away and gotten some thirty miles toward the promised land of Montana, Edgar decided to send his unruly charge away to school. He may have been prompted to this measure by the fact that Irma, already at the end of her tether with the boy, was again pregnant. With a few skirmishes Rod was successfully installed at Culver Military Academy in Indiana, and ended by taking very happily to the discipline.

On August 15, 1907, Irma gave birth to her third and last child, Edgar Roderick Rombauer Jr. For a few years, as Edgar noted, "our happiness seemed complete." Two photographs sum up the contentment of which he speaks. In one—probably taken in 1908—he is lying propped on one elbow in the backyard, laughing up at the joyously crowing Edgar Junior. The other, from about 1911, is an exquisitely posed outdoor grouping from a vacation in Michigan. Irma, radiant in summer white, sits sweetly pensive with a child on either side.

That image of serene motherhood had little in common with the real impression projected by Irma as a young matron. Even when Marion was small it was clear that her mother's hungry spirit scorned the tedium of *Kinder und Küche.* Her home was a place teeming with life and energy and treasured belongings, but it was not a homebody's home, or a terribly orderly person's. Marion's later recollection of the "highly contrasting" von Starkloff sisters and their surroundings captures Irma's heedless impact:

> Elsa, tall, distinguished, somewhat melancholy, with elegant taste and a possessive nature. Irma, my mother, lively, outgoing, and vigorously interested in people. She too loved "things," but they always managed to have a somewhat battered quality compared with the carefully placed, well-dusted and polished objects in Aunt Elsa's well-waxed ménage.[15]

Irma's home tended to be a launching pad. In another era, she would undoubtedly have sought a career outside it. In her own time, such a choice would not have seemed right or natural to a professional man's wife—though the Rombauers were just enough more progressive than the von Starkloffs to believe in careers for women, or at least for their own unmarried daughters. Irma's sisters-in-law Bertha and Sophie had cheerfully gone out to learn stenography and find jobs. She disdained such a lowering option for herself, a married woman of position. Yet she unceasingly sought to be involved in a world larger than her own four walls. The nearest approach to serious activity that her St. Louis could give lay in the new arena of women's clubs and organized female philanthropy. The two or three decades before World War I were the golden age of these endeavors in America.

For women like Irma Rombauer, the new women's associations offered bridges to desired social circles while making possible a sort of substitute career and even a voice in civic policy. She flung herself into an array of groups, a born mover and shaker who had found a sphere of action. Almost from the children's earliest memories she was rushing out the door to plan and campaign, leaving them to the care of nursemaids or "generals"—maids of all work, who also did most of the cooking. (Irma's table was considered more memorable for interesting conversation than magnificent food.)[16] What people who knew her during this period chiefly remembered was the blazing, irresistible energy with which she launched herself into everything.

"Immediacy determined my tempo," she wrote in her half-begun autobiography, and, making another stab at the same idea, "I was born with a sense of immediacy, so life has always pulsated around me tumultuously."[17] She was that peculiarly modern phenomenon, a born shopper; she sailed through antique stores (one of her passions) or hat shops like a small tornado, considering and rejecting whole parades of merchandise at a glance before pouncing on what she wanted and sailing out. Her approach to people was not very different. Her likes and dislikes were instant and nearly unchangeable. Anyone she had taken against at first sight rarely got a second chance. Those who got along well with her either learned to like her caprices or were lucky enough to be shielded from them.

By middle age she was already a woman of exceedingly impressive bearing. No one could be long in her diminutive presence without sensing an air of concentrated intelligence, strength, self-possession, charm, and dignity that seemed to sweep all before it—except that she knew how to soften it with disarming feminine self-deprecation and sheer fun. She was a wonderful talker, attentive and literate. But it was also hard to deal with her for long without finding that she had developed a vigorous talent for manipulative intrigue. People either adored or detested her, or sometimes both. In her clubs, she was usually embroiled in some faction.

Some of the groups in which she was active throughout most of her marriage brought her as close to the fringes of politics as a conventional South Side matron could get. At some point when the children were small, she took the momentous step of bringing the family into a church—a nearby Unitarian congregation with a female auxiliary, the "Women's Alliance." No Rombauer ever developed the faintest pretense of belief. (It was left to Marion, more than half a century later, to redeem the tribal legacy by filling in the optional "Religious Affiliation" space on a college alumnae questionnaire with a resolute "Atheist.") But this gesture of assimilation with the city's prestigious liberal New England heritage put Irma to work on Women's Alliance–sponsored causes like programs to provide penny lunches for underprivileged schoolchildren or attractive playgrounds to lend a little pleasure and physical stimulation to their existence. She rapidly became involved with other fund-raising and lobbying groups.

Her civic-improvement concerns often echoed some of Max C. Starkloff's goals—for instance, safe milk and other measures to reduce infant mortality. But on at least one memorable occasion they collided. His chief idée fixe as custodian of the public health was venereal disease, on which the young cousins remembered him annually holding forth for hours over the Thanksgiving table. When he decided to combat syphilis and gonorrhea by instituting compulsory detention, examination, and treatment of all prostitutes at a newly organized clinic in the Good Shepherd Convent, Irma and her intrepid ally Edna Fischel Gellhorn were outraged. With a handful of other women they got up a petition to the mayor protesting these high-handed dealings with unfortunates. They also announced that they wanted to inspect the venereal disease clinic. Commissioner Starkloff, not at all fazed by seeing his sister at the head of a hostile delegation, invited them to go ahead. His version of the event (as related by his son Gene) was that once face to face with the scabby and foul-mouthed whores, Mrs. Gellhorn fainted, Irma gasped, "Brother Max, this is horrible," and the ladies hastily agreed to abandon the mission.[18] It is a reasonable bet that had Mrs. Gellhorn or Mrs. Rombauer left any account, it would have been quite different.

Later Irma—like her father before her—would be closely involved with the musical life of St. Louis (she became a fixture of St. Louis Symphony affairs). She also spent much time in literary discussion groups; this interest must have developed early, if Marion's "Bernard Shaw" is any clue. But the object that dwarfed all others was the Wednesday Club.

This organization, founded in 1885, represented a social ambition not within every vulgar grasp. To join it would be a decisive step beyond the confines of the old *Deutschtum* (though it did already have a scattering of German and Jewish members). Its cachet owed much to its links with "American" luminaries, chiefly the Eliot family. For many years its leading light had been Charlotte Champe Eliot, the daughter-in-law of the late Reverend William Greenleaf Eliot, whose many visible legacies in St. Louis included the Unitarian Church of the Messiah, Washington University (originally Eliot Seminary), City General Hospital, and much about the public schools (he had been an early president of the School Board). Charlotte Eliot appears to have been an equally gifted leader.[19] She lent moral fervor and the prestige of a New England–derived social elite to a great variety of progressive causes such as adequate nutrition and housing for the poor and the establishment of a juvenile court system. She was also a woman of strong literary interests, who wrote poetry herself and encouraged talent in others. Indeed, she virtually embodied the energies that fueled the early women's clubs.

The Rombauers are more likely than Irma's own family to have inspired her foray into the club that Mrs. Eliot had so strongly shaped. Their interests had brought them further into "American" society than the von Starkloffs. Roderick, who enjoyed a reputation as a marvelous raconteur and after-dinner speaker, had ties with a handful of salon leaders and the circle associated with the brilliant William Marion Reedy of *Reedy's Mirror*, at that time one of the foremost literary magazines in the country. Indeed, St. Louis around the turn of the century could still be perceived by a newcomer—the civil libertarian Roger Baldwin, who was teaching in the infant School of Social Economy at about the time the sixtyish Augusta Rombauer attended classes there—as having the aura "of an intellectual elite, a cosmopolitan elite as well."[20] The Wednesday Club in its first decades contained many who hobnobbed with just such elements. Irma's parents did not particularly care about the cutting edge of culture and civic awareness in "American" St. Louis, but the Rombauers were genuinely keen on such things. So was she. Augusta, who joined the Wednesday Club in 1901, probably paved the way for her. Irma became a member in 1911, when her youngest child was four years old.[21]

It is easy to forget today that organizations like the Wednesday Club and Irma's many do-gooder groups made a conspicuous and far from trivial contribution to the emancipation of women. In the decades when woman suffrage appeared a very distant goal indeed, these associations represented a tremendous impulse to channel otherwise unused female abilities. When the clubs and church auxiliaries dabbled in "causes," they legitimized the role of women as lobbyists, occasionally acting in recognized cooperation with elected officials, consistently moving beyond old-style charity to the search for adequate community response to problems now seen as affecting society as a whole. When they turned to cultural enrichment, they helped semischooled middle-class or upper-class women like Irma Rombauer make shift to compensate for the gaps in their education, exposing them to notable currents in art, literature, and contemporary thought. In her early Wednesday Club years Irma might have heard the anarchist Emma Goldman (on a 1911 visit to St. Louis) lecture on Tolstoy and Galsworthy, or participated in discussions of the younger British poets. In the course of her own committee assignments she spoke on the theater of Gerhart Hauptmann and presented programs on subjects like "The Present and Future of Vocational Work in St. Louis" and "The Possibilities of Moving Pictures in Education."

Her civic and cultural associations were not just a hobby, but something close to the center of Irma's life until the unexpected success of her book several decades later. Yet they did not in the least appease her restlessly competitive instincts. She sensed and resented limitations that she could do nothing about. She could not, after all, be a political figure or a cultural eminence in her own right. Moreover, her abilities were impulsive and scattershot. She could not, like some women of good education and concentrated purpose, become the galvanic center of a difficult long-term crusade.

In later life she told a friend that her life would have been entirely different if she had gone to college.[22] She was surely right. She had a wonderful ability to pick up bits of ideas and fashions, but she could not transform herself into a trained intellect or climb some path to really august social standing. Her "favorite reading" by Marion's account, "biographies, memoirs, and studies of seventeenth and eighteenth century historical figures," hints at an existence she would have loved—sparkling among Restoration notables in the circle of Pepys or intriguing among Saint-Simon's compeers at the court of Louis XIV.[23]

As she grew toward middle age, Irma became fiercer in her need not only to shine but to outshine. She did make a satisfying peace with the fact of being a German-American in a society now perfectly amenable to daily interchange and even intermarriage. She developed a great pride in the legacy of the Kuhlmann and von Starkloff forebears. But she recoiled with a shudder from associations unbefitting a great power of the Wednesday Club. It was a horror to her to be the sister of a known criminal—by this time, one very well known indeed to the Federal authorities.

Emil Starkloff had become part of a large crime ring specializing in various sorts of "bunko" (swindles). In 1910 he and a frequent partner in crime named George W. Post were arrested in Philadelphia (where they were passing themselves off as retired bankers) on mail-fraud charges involving a "gold brick" scheme—a gold ingot shown to a victim as a supposed sample of a phony mine in which he was invited to invest. It was only one of numerous swindles on which the Federal authorities and many police departments had been trying to nail them for years.

Accounts of the trial were embarrassingly noticeable in the St. Louis papers for a while, until the two jumped bail. Five years later Emil finally began serving a two-year sentence at the Federal Penitentiary in Atlanta, where he coolly improved his leisure hours with the Eureka Violin Method and a textbook of Spanish until he was released in 1917 to continue his career.[24] Max C. Starkloff always took Emil's criminal pursuits in stride and welcomed him gladly when he happened to pass through St. Louis with no minions of the law behind him. He did not feel in the least threatened by having a resourceful crook for a brother. Irma, however, treated his existence as a family secret too dark to be hinted to the world at large. In her seventies she still felt defiled by "his shadow, menacing and noxious, on our otherwise happy family life."[25] The Health Commissioner needed no one to tell him that he was an important person in his own right. Irma as a woman always had to define herself by those around her.

Irma the eternal seeker for unassailable standing might have done very well as a successful politician's wife, and she probably came within inches of being one. The early years on Flad Avenue saw the beginning of Edgar's political career—and also its rapid end. It is likely that he had thought of politics for some time. He had readily acquired the libertarian convictions that came so naturally to the Rombauers. St. Louis had need of such men. By the time Edgar was in practice with his father in 1896, it was generally agreed to be one of the nation's most corrupt cities. Roderick, unwillingly out of office, would angrily speechify about brazen voting fraud and lootings of the public treasury, and he was dead on the mark.

The equally venal Democratic and Republican party machines, which took turns muscling their way into City Hall, would periodically shrug off attempts to push through slates of reform candidates. Edgar had been trying to field one of these at the time of his first attentions to Irma, but the victory had gone to the machine Republican. The reformers always sounded a few well-worn themes that always were equally timely: filthy streets, filthier water of a murky typhoid-carrying cast, miasmic and soot-laden air that defied the belief of visitors, crime-ridden slums, public coffers where money performed all sorts of wingèd flights, nimble-footed hirelings who could vote at half a dozen polls in the twinkling of an eye.

Around the turn of the century, a burst of cleanup efforts occurred when the city managed to have itself chosen as the site of the "Louisiana Purchase Exposition" honoring the centennial of that event. A few progressive activists of Roger Baldwin's stripe were making themselves heard in St. Louis. An administration willing to do more than talk about housecleaning began wielding a vigorous broom. Actual indictments were obtained against notorious boodlers. A wide range of projects from smoke abatement to trolley-line construction sought to make St. Louis more presentable to the world. The water supply was transformed from what Mayor Rolla Wells described as "a liquefied pall"[26] into the dazzling cynosure of a gorgeous waterworks display illuminated by the novel radiance of electric light. It is true that the fair was a year behind schedule when it opened in the spring of 1904, but it was probably the most successful major exposition ever mounted in America. For a few years thereafter some observers claimed to detect a solid civic renaissance.

Edgar Rombauer as the bright young son of an incorruptible Republican jurist was a natural magnet for those seeking to push through further reforms while the éclat of the World's Fair was still fresh in memory. Clearly he was promising material: clever, practical, strong-minded, conscientious, and deeply concerned with public issues. In the year or two after Edgar Junior's birth his moment seemed to have come. Following a brief involvement with the local logistics of William Howard Taft's Presidential campaign in 1908, Edgar led the next year's effort of the Young Men's Republican Auxiliary to do something about the smelly and discountenanced House of Delegates, at that time the lower house of a bicameral city legislature. He canvassed indefatigably for weeks—Edgar was capable of incredible strength and endurance when he was committed to something. The resulting Republican reform slate was elected almost to a man (the Democrats carried only four wards), and Edgar was chosen Speaker of the House of Delegates. At the close of his two-year term Mayor Frederick Kreismann (who had also entered office on reform pledges in 1909) appointed him to revise the city code of ordinances. He completed the work in 1912, and never undertook any public charge again.

Why he so abruptly left politics is a mystery. One possibility is that he could not stomach the necessary bilge. It does not appear that Edgar was known for suffering fools gladly. Years later a *Post-Dispatch* obituary writer would quote a sharp remark of Speaker Rombauer's made at a time when every grandstander of the city was nobly denouncing a schedule of much-hated railroad bridge charges that in truth were completely outside the jurisdiction of any St. Louis authority. Edgar did not care how popular the "Free Bridge" stance might be with the electorate. "The people are right sometimes, and perhaps they are always right in the long run, but how do we know when they are right?" he remarked. "Such utterances do not make for a long career in politics," the reporter dryly observed.[27] It is distinctly possible that Edgar foresaw and rejected a future of frustration in a civic climate becoming alarmingly friendlier to bigots and demagogues, especially on issues of race.

An alternative explanation is the state of his health. If he had one of his periodic breakdowns while in office, he may well have chosen not to risk exposing his infirmity to public conjecture in future. However, there is no knowing whether such a thing did happen. The factor that is likely to have made the greatest difference is his desire to be with his children. Marion never commented on her father's decision to abandon barely explored political hopes. But remembering him years later, she was convinced that in general he had striven hard to put his family ahead of his career. He had been much absent during his brief stint in the House of Delegates. Apparently he felt the danger of becoming a cipher in the children's lives, and he hints that this was the reason he sat down to write a private autobiography for their benefit—probably at around the time he finished the revision of the city ordinances, since this is the last event mentioned in the manuscript. Marion was then nine and Edgar Junior five.

By her account, he made it his business to set aside large amounts of time for them throughout the years the Rombauers thereafter spent together as a family. "In the evenings Father read aloud from Shakespeare and Scott and Dickens"; he listened seriously to their ideas of things; he made it a nearly unbreakable rule to arrange an annual hiatus in his law schedule during their school vacations in order to share long, leisurely summers with them and Irma on Lake Michigan. Later Marion would believe that the time he spent with them involved a certain amount of professional and financial sacrifice.[28]

Irma, a parent of quite different priorities, made no secret of wishing that he would achieve some grand pinnacle. Their marriage seems to have been fairly stormy. By most reasonable standards Edgar was a successful and highly regarded man. He was attorney to some well-known firms, and privately he was admired for his dedication to the cause of race relations, an ever-worsening miasma in St. Louis. But he would not fight his way to summits of rank and wealth, nor would he let himself be bossed around to suit his wife's notions. According to their son, he once insisted on returning a bonus of $5,000 to a corporate client for some reason of conscience, though Irma told him he was crazy.[29] On all their accounts, she was as jealously ambitious as the fisherman's wife in the fairy tale.

She did, however, treat his recurrent breakdowns with unselfish compassion. Every few years Edgar would sink into an impenetrable withdrawal, unable to work or carry on ordinary social activity. For weeks or months he would sit all day in his room doing crossword puzzles or putting together obsessive private scrapbooks of dreadful world events. At these times Irma left him to his own devices, looking after his wants with little fuss and waiting sympathetically but matter-of-factly for the episode to run its course. If she ever confided her thoughts about these ordeals to anyone, no record remains. As for the children, their father's periodic collapses were part of their early memories, something accepted with as little anxiety as Irma's calm management of the episodes could accomplish.

Eventually he would come back to himself. When in good health he was a sane and steadying influence on them all. But he carried within him a deep sense of defeat. He had failed to continue the public heritage of his father and his grandfather Koerner; he never contrived to live in the grand von Starkloff style. His brother-in-law, the Health Commissioner, knew that Edgar believed he was a failure and also that he had thought of killing himself. Whether Commissioner Starkloff mentioned this to Irma is not known.

The children understood early that their mother pinned great hopes on them. Marion—"Mary" was the name she always insisted on using with her closest family—was the more promising raw material for maternal ambition. She was a bright, rather serious little girl, plagued with frequent unexplained bouts of illness but rapidly manifesting the hunger for activity and eagerness to give pleasure to others that would strike even casual acquaintances throughout her life. Toward those she loved she possessed a passionate loyalty that brooked almost no acknowledgment of faults. At seventy she was not much different from the very small girl who was observed by a Rombauer family friend flashing up in wrath at another child's comment, "Your father has bowlegs." "That's the way legs *ought* to be!" his outraged daughter informed the critic. She belonged to that tribe of enthusiasts who virtually make a religion out of their loyalties and interests. Her isolation in the first years may have intensified this trait. In later life she scribbled down a mention of one early passion that speaks worlds. On cold mornings when their parents were asleep Mary and her brother (then only a toddler) would sit for a long time poring over the tiny volumes of her favorite author, "comforted by the companionship emanating from the world Beatrix Potter had created from her acute loneliness."[30]

She had a vast talent for making friends, either in spite of the fact that she was not pretty or because of it. Almost from the first she was large, ungraceful, and plain-featured. The chic little Irma visited immense cruelty on her for this sin. Marion never ceased to be aware of having been the lumpish, homely daughter of a woman who might have been born to embody the epithets "petite" and "feminine."[31] Irma did not belong to the "Beauty is only skin deep" school. In her mind there were right and wrong ways to look, the wrong way being a betrayal of breeding and ambition. She was no Greek goddess herself, but she had a brand of useful looks that animation, will power, and sheer consciousness of effect can make dazzling. She could not tolerate a child's failure in this department, and she did not trouble to conceal her anger. Marion loved to please, but in this matter there was no pleasing the person with the most power to hurt her.

Marion could not learn to be pretty. But she could, and early did, learn to be liked. In any group, she always managed to find herself among friends. She developed the knack of arranging herself and her surroundings to best effect.

She was quick to acquire a sense of design and a feeling for values of color and texture. She set herself to master some kinds of grace. Dance probably was one of the first things she dreamed of as a career— for unlike her mother, she was brought up with the knowledge that a girl could expect a career. At about ten or eleven Marion was taken to see Pavlova dance *Swan Lake* in St. Louis, "when the Russian Ballet with its Bakst costumes struck us like lightning."[32] She was soon stirred by what she could read of the experimenters Isadora Duncan and Ruth St. Denis. She became obsessed with images of dance, collecting photographs of ballerinas and "interpretative" dancers as avidly as she and her friends had earlier collected baseball cards. By the time she was sophisticated enough to understand that still photographs of dancers intrinsically kill all that matters about motion, she had amassed a mammoth scrapbook that she kept for decades in memory of her early ambition (eventually turning it over to the ballet-struck young daughter of her friend Buckminster Fuller). This effort in itself was prophetic for one who would be a lifelong article clipper and compulsive hoarder of all sorts of personal memorabilia—a complete contrast to Irma, who discarded the lumber of existence with unceremonious impatience. Loyal even to objects, Marion liked to keep things and think about them.

Irma was determined that her daughter would not be shortchanged with the inadequate flourishes that had been her own education. To see her children at well-known schools meant much to her. Luckily Marion, an obedient learner who actually enjoyed doing what was expected of her, took to reading and writing as to breathing air. She was a natural left-hander who was successfully "corrected" after the practice of the epoch but always retained the odd (though, as will be seen, useful) ability to write backward with her left hand as easily as most people write from left to right.

In 1916 Marion, hitherto educated at public schools, was sent to Mary Institute, a first-rate girls' school. It was yet another local legacy of William Greenleaf Eliot, who had founded it in 1859, naming it after a child he had lost very young. Having one's daughters educated there was one of the respectable "American" customs the more assimilated Germans had been acquiring when Irma was a young girl. Her friend Edna Gellhorn, another adventurous-minded product of the *Deutschtum*, had gone to Mary before being sent to Bryn Mawr College. Irma, who had just missed such advantages for herself, was bent on securing them for the next generation. The new school involved a long, complicated streetcar ride and did much to cement Marion's early sense of the world as a place of weighty Monday-morning responsibilities. But she was, as always, surrounded by chums and successful at any expected task.

Irma had a very different creature to deal with in Edgar Junior, who had been christened "Putty" or "Put" (rhymes with "but") by Marion after a reading of *Jemima Puddleduck* and was never known by any other name in St. Louis. From the age of three until long after he had left home, he was giving as good as he got in a state of ongoing war with his mother. Their battles were the talk of the South Side. Put was always stealing a ride on the back of a delivery truck or swinging by one knee from some dangerous height; her attempts at discipline usually degenerated into mutual tantrums. He was clearly as bright as anyone in the family, but he resisted most kinds of official polish with furious obstinacy—oddly enough, resembling old Roderick Rombauer in his school-hating Hungarian childhood. Irma was burning to set him on the same auspicious route as Marion: elite private schools, Harvard or Yale, a life in professional or public circles befitting a descendant of von Starkloffs and Koerners. Put preferred being what Mark Twain's good women would have called "low." Once she caught him selling newspapers on a street corner in an early fit of private enterprise, and exploded in wrath at the idea that a child of hers should be seen doing anything so vulgar. As an added insult, he was doing nothing more than Marion to carry on the good looks of his parents. He had not at all the sort of nose his mother would have chosen for him, and she resented it.

The subject of looks was a sore point she could not leave alone. Marion, in most regards a model daughter, was never to be spared her mother's criticisms over "what she considered, quite rightly, my peasant build and poor features." Of course eyeglasses, which Marion badly needed, were mightily resisted by the dissatisfied parent. The little girl's vision had been seriously affected by a bout of scarlet fever at about ten. Irma decreed a course of sight-improvement exercises with the same Dr. Carl Barck who had nursed her back from diphtheria a quarter of a century before. These helped introduce Marion to Dr. Barck's interest in Southwest American Indian religious rites but did nothing for her eyes.

At last she had to be fitted for glasses, a defeat that proved to have a silver lining. The oculist who examined her thought some of her symptoms might be due to allergies. His lucky guess was the clue to a pattern of strange systemic upsets that had been baffling Marion's parents and the doctors since she was a baby. At odd intervals she would suffer bouts of conjunctivitis, hives, and an indescribable intestinal distress that she referred to as "internal hives" (the doctors' term was "bilious attack"). She was nearly grown by the time the allergy hypothesis was suggested. There followed years of often unpleasant tests, which established that Marion was allergic to lemons and other citrus fruits, strawberries, raspberries, walnuts, and a goodly list of other things—fortunately not including her greatest craving, chocolate. The reason for her inevitable illness on February 23 of every year was the hazelnuts in the cake for her grandmother Rombauer's birthday on February 22. Other unpredictable upsets were eventually traced to the tomatoes that Irma urged on both children for the sake of those newly discovered miracles, "vitamines." For the rest of her life Marion was obliged to take pains to avoid the long list of culprits. It was the beginning of her attraction to the subject of nutrition.[33]

For part of Marion and Put's childhood theirs was a five-member household, at least when their cousin Rod came home from school. In their minds he was as good as an older brother, the beloved idol of their small fan club. But at the age of twenty Rod fell in love with a girl of eighteen and decided to take over his parents' house for himself and his bride. Edgar and Irma moved to a smaller house a few doors away on Flad Avenue. Here they remained from 1912 until the children were grown, on friendly terms with Rod Rombauer's new household.

The five and later four Rombauers always projected an infectious camaraderie no matter what their internal battles. They were a pleasant crew to hang around, and Irma for all her anger and ambition could be a delightful parent. Marion remembered both their Flad Avenue homes as magnets for friends and activities. Her mother was a marvelously welcoming hostess—not known, it is true, as the world's most sedulous cook, but gifted with the knack of making guests of all ages glad they had come. It was a companionable neighborhood, a rich source of playmates. There was a large Irish family nearby who had solved all menu problems by sitting down to steak and potatoes three times a day and enjoyed having Marion come by for breakfast. A crew of the children's friends would congregate at the Rombauers' when the much-loved Edgar was around, and Irma might help them get up an amateur theatrical to raise a dollar or two for one of her causes like the Babies' Free Milk Fund. The elders were part of a jovial South Side group given to robust parties with robust German food.

One of the principal ornaments of these last occasions was a wealthy, very beautiful young South St. Louis matron named Adele Dittmann Becker, who played the piano with great flair and would accompany when the Rombauers got up a *Schnitzelbank* (a sort of musical charade, with comic verses by Edgar and impromptu drawings by Irma). Mrs. Becker was the daughter of William Dittmann, one of the many boot manufacturers who had contributed to St. Louis's reputation as "first in booze, first in shoes, and last in the American League"—this last by courtesy of the beloved but erratic St. Louis Browns. Her husband, Philip August Becker, son of a merchant who had had several stores across the river in East St. Louis, had settled comfortably into his father-in-law's business and big Longfellow Boulevard house. They belonged to a staider and grander stratum of the German community than Edgar and Irma, circles more moneyed indeed than the von Starkloffs at the height of Max's eminence. But Phil and Adele got along capitally with the whole Rombauer family.

Marion had always known their older son, John William Becker, a year her senior, bookish and agreeable. When she was sent to Mary Institute, she found a slightly younger ally in their sharp-tongued, irreverent daughter, Virginia. Jinny and John took to spending a good deal of time in the hospitable busy-ness of the Rombauer household and after a while Marion and John developed a strong common interest in art. He did not exactly become one of her recognized boyfriends (of whom there was always an ample supply), but he seemed to be around rather regularly. He had taken quite a shine to Irma.

Marion, who loved to see the family together and did not like all the separate claims on everyone's time in St. Louis, was never so happy as when they set off together for the North every summer. (Edgar's beloved Colorado was impracticably distant.) From the time the children were small, their regular vacation home was the Michigan settlement of Bay View close to the northern tip of the Lower Peninsula, a few miles east of Petoskey near Little Traverse Bay. Bay View had developed from a Methodist camp meeting site into a large summer colony revolving around one of the biggest and most ambitious Chautauqua institutes in the country. The Beckers usually summered a short distance away, at Alden.

For many years the Rombauers leased a cottage on the edge of the woods in the Bay View settlement. Here all of them acquired some of Edgar's love for the unspoiled outdoors. From him Irma learned the pleasures of fishing and simply rusticating. (She would later credit him with also having taught her to cook, from his own camping skills.)[34] But it was the Chautauqua classes—comprising a huge curriculum at all levels of child and adult education—that were the irresistible attraction of Bay View in her mind. "For Mother cultural indoctrination knew no season," Marion wrote. She remembered having been put into a class of the Swedish carpentry-for-everyone known as "sloyd," and sawing away unavailingly at a planned dollhouse wardrobe until the teacher told her mother that "I was the most patient and least gifted child she'd ever handled." During the mid-nineteen-teens Irma herself sampled various courses, including cooking lessons. According to Marion, she discovered a great flair for cake decoration. Irma had no unusual renown as a cook, but with this newfound skill she took to producing charmingly festooned and garlanded chefs d'oeuvre for family birthdays.[35]

For Marion, a principal legacy of the Bay View vacations was an interest in ecology that would eventually be a great part of what she considered her true life's work. Most of the Rombauers had a sort of hankering to get back to nature, but with her it was also a real curiosity about living habitats. At home she loved getting things to grow— an interest she had inherited from Irma, who was always nursing along some plant. Marion developed an early feeling for the different things that belonged to different places. Bay View, some five hundred miles northeast of St. Louis and quite remote from it in geology and climate, offered pine forests, beech and maple stands, rocky littoral, swampland, creeks lined with wildflowers and birch trees, and a general sense of another environment. Here she prowled under the tutelage of an amateur forester who was another of the Bay View regulars: "as he held forth on the balance of nature the whole concept of succession and ecological relationships became as natural as breathing." Closer to home, her imagination was similarly stirred when her father or grandfather would take her on expeditions to a property of Roderick's sixty miles south of St. Louis on the Mississippi, at a shifting sometime-island called Brickey's. It was a landscape deeply and dramatically carved by the river, with wild ravinelike valleys and high river bluffs contrasting with the Illinois farmland on the other side. Marion remembered it all her life as one of the triggers to her enduring fascination with what distinguishes particular ecosystems.

Like Irma, Marion would always be a true child of the old St. Louis *Deutschtum* and its leisurely, civilized stability. But throughout her girlhood that stability was vanishing fast—so fast that Put, only four years younger, would remember far less of the German world than she. Not only were the original Forty-eighters a dwindling breed, but the remaining few and the second generation found themselves punching bags for forces that were roughly rearranging St. Louis in general.

There was little talk now of the "Future Great." St. Louis had been decisively outdistanced in population and importance by Chicago. The city's manufacturing base was in incipient decline and some of the all-crucial national railroad traffic had gone elsewhere. Even as the euphoria of the World's Fair lingered in memory, an ugly spirit was abroad. Its chief victims would be St. Louis Germans and—on a much more terrifying scale—the poor Southern blacks who continued to swarm into the metropolis and its grimy Illinois appendage of East St. Louis, competing with resentful white laborers and reawakening the race consciousness of a region always more Southern than Northern. It was an embittering time for both Germans and "Americans" of the old liberal convictions. In 1914 a new city charter was pushed through with much populist fanfare, part of a continuing fallout from the reform efforts that Edgar had helped lead. One of its vaunted merits was a provision for direct legislative initiative to get around the hacks and boodlers. As if to prove that the people may not be right, within two years this clause had been used to enact America's first direct-petition Jim Crow housing law. The Supreme Court quickly struck down segregated-housing ordinances of this stripe.[36] But the reality that the measure stood for has not vanished from St. Louis to this day.

Some heirs of the Forty-eighter abolitionists cheerfully countenanced the segregated-housing initiative. The Rombauers, however, were among many Germans who thought they had better earn anew what their fathers had bequeathed to them—and who surely helped to avert bloodshed in St. Louis when East St. Louis erupted in murderous race riots in 1917. Edgar began working with the local Urban League and was its president for many years. He regularly represented black clients, some of them indigent. After his death Irma staunchly supported integration, eventually becoming involved with a biracial community arts center.[37] But in the early days no well-meaning St. Louis white liberal could imagine such a thing as integration. Marion would later realize that as a child she had had virtually no contact with black people as anything but menials.

Closer to home for most of the Germans was a developing hostility that at first seemed not to make sense, in view of how greatly the old German-versus-"American" boundaries had softened. The post–World's Fair civic-cleanup impetus became embroiled in arguments over the enforcement of Sunday liquor sales laws, which the German community considered an unreasonable provocation specifically aimed at them and their Sunday beer-garden excursions. During the next ten or fifteen years, the Deutsch-Amerikaner National Bund, or National German-American Alliance—one of Max von Starkloff's perennial causes, later to be familiarly known as the *Bund*—increasingly assumed the role of defensive and angry apologist for the German-American community as the local extension of the Fatherland.[38]

The accumulating tension had another aspect. The Sunday-sales issue attracted the big guns of the Anti-Saloon League and eventually the Women's Christian Temperance Union (WCTU), among the most powerful advocates of woman suffrage. The oft-repeated suffragist argument that giving women the vote would enable decent Americans to run the filthy liquor industry out of business once and for all put the liberal Germans, some of whom had been supporting suffrage for decades, in a terrible position. (In the event, Prohibition and woman suffrage became law within eighteen months of each other in 1919 and 1920, while the nation was still reeling from recent domestic wounds incurred in these strangely intertwined causes.) It is notable that Irma, for all her own activist warmth in many causes, never referred to suffragism or feminism in any but brusquely noncommittal terms. Probably suffragists had played too large a part in the dangerous polarization that overshadowed her father's last years.

The National Alliance could not have been fighting the beer-garden battle at a worse time. The massive arming of Germany under Kaiser Wilhelm II fueled a great growth of anti-German sentiment in the American press. No less a figure than Theodore Roosevelt spearheaded an ugly nationwide crusade to wipe out "hyphenism"—i.e., the disloyal practice of calling oneself "German-American" or "Irish-American" rather than 100 percent plain *American*. In a city like St. Louis, the young men who should have been the heirs of the Forty-eighters found themselves in the intolerable position of either acquiescing in policies designed to affront their ethnic cohorts or having their American patriotism called in question. Ironically, it was easier and safer for Irma to dabble on at least the fringes of civic affairs in amity with "American" fellow clubwomen than it would have been for a young male politician of Edgar's background to forge similar coalitions.

Max von Starkloff and the National Alliance marched straight on declaring solidarity with Germany as the level of anger rose. The dangers of this course are sadly illustrated by the "Naked Truth" affair, which began in 1913 when the South St. Louis German leadership got up a fund for a memorial to honor three late pioneers of German-language journalism in the city and appointed a jury to select a commemorative statue.[39] Passing over the sketches of six American-born contestants, the jury chose the submission of the lone German national, Wilhelm Wandschneider of Berlin. The uproar over the choice was soon matched by howls over the design, which depicted Truth as an unclad female form bearing up a pair of mighty torches before the names of the three heroes. The image gave the prudish an occasion to point out that Germans were sex fiends as well as sots and to complain about the intimation that one people had a special claim on undoctored facts. Trying to honor the artist's wishes without adding more fuel to the fire, Max on behalf of the *Denkmalverein*

(Memorial Association) at length persuaded Wandschneider to cast the statue in bronze so that it would not *look* quite so naked as the originally intended white marble. Nobody could come up with a better solution. Dr. von Starkloff gave a suitably nonpartisan address at the dedication ceremony in June of 1914. Within weeks, Archduke Ferdinand had been assassinated in Sarajevo; World War I rapidly broke out in Europe.

The local chapter of the WCTU took the occasion to suggest that Naked Truth be melted down and her bronze donated for Allied munitions. Max, already in frail health when the first *Denkmalverein* fracas began, failed swiftly over the summer and died on October 31 at the age of eighty-two. He had quitted the scene just in time to be spared the devastating humiliation of all he held dear.

The onset of the European war did not give the St. Louis Germans a moment's pause in their local war. They went on defiantly parading their German loyalties—indeed, at the *Denkmalverein* dinner in memory of Dr. von Starkloff the entire company broke into "Die Wacht am Rhein," and Kaiser Wilhelm's consul in St. Louis dwelt lengthily on the significance of Naked Truth combating anti-German lies.[40] For more than two years the National Alliance continued raising money for the Kaiser's troops and getting up committees to argue against local prohibitionist initiatives everywhere in America. As a result, the *Deutschtum* was sitting far out on a half-sawed limb when the United States declared war on Germany in April of 1917.

Both Put and Marion were old enough to have keen memories of the anti-German frenzy that broke loose in St. Louis (and all other cities with German populations). While the adults confronted mob violence, defacing of German-owned stores, and sequestration of business assets, German schoolchildren were being taunted as the junior branch of a bestial, baby-killing horde. Put Rombauer remembers the jeers of "Horrible Hun" to this day.

The war and the awful years leading up to it coincided with wrenching personal disasters for Irma and Edgar. When the fighting was over, much in their lives was also over. In 1916 Roderick had suffered a stroke that left him partly paralyzed and almost helpless. The family was obliged to arrange for permanent nursing care in Barnes Hospital. Augusta was markedly affected by the shock. Though she seemed to recover some strength for a time, she succumbed on March 31, 1918, to what Edgar described as "grippe" followed by pneumonia. By then Elsa Muench, Irma's sister, was terribly ill with stomach cancer. She died on May 31, remembered by many of her St. Louis acquaintances as "the most beautiful woman I ever saw" and by Irma as a tantalizing, not-quite-understood image of some marvelous aspiration. She was only forty-two.

Several months later came the real season of death for the community at large: the "Spanish influenza" that arrived not long before the Armistice, prefaced by scattered reports of strange fatal outbreaks during the late spring and summer. The first major wave hit the Midwest in the fall. Rod Rombauer, Put and Marion's childhood idol, was typical of the victims: vigorous young adults in their twenties, apparently stronger and healthier than many who were spared. Rod caught the disease at the army camp where he was stationed in Texas and died at twenty-six without ever seeing battle. He left a young widow and three small children.

Max C. Starkloff was the hero of the St. Louis epidemic of 1918. An inveterate autocrat where issues of public sanitation were concerned, he rushed into action much faster than the health authorities of some other large cities. Despite furious protests from all quarters, he forced Mayor Henry Kiel to order a six-week shutdown of schools, churches, both stage and movie theaters, and most retail businesses. As Kiel later observed, "Doc" Starkloff "was the sort of fellow who would write out an order, say, 'Henry, you've got to sign this'—and you had to sign it to get rid of him."[41] It was generally believed that his dictatorial approach saved many lives, holding the death rate in St. Louis to a lower level than in comparable cities.

The rest of the family emerged from this epoch of horrors into a mere shell of the former *Deutschtum*. The community had been obliged to half dismantle itself. At the declaration of war the German-Americans, at once realizing their complete vulnerability, had done the only thing that could have prevented a major bloodbath: pledged undeviating loyalty to America and pitched in to the war effort. Many of them did so with a sense of ignominious capitulation to something they knew for witch-hunting but had no power to resist. Others were able to retool their allegiance with good grace. Jinny Becker remembered that her more or less apolitical family, at first "pro-German in a kind of automatic way," promptly "became pro-Ally without turning a hair" when America entered the war.[42] Irma and Edgar, though among those who never forgave the perpetrators of mass hysteria, did all that was expected of loyal Americans. Not surprisingly, Edgar suffered one of his breakdowns during the war.

According to Put, he was also physically ill at about this time, having been diagnosed with a cancer of the bladder that required a course of excruciatingly painful treatments with electric needles inserted through the urethra. He retreated from his practice and sat in his room obsessively poring over accounts of the European fighting. (This was at least safer than discussing the two sides' chances in public, a rash act that landed one of Max von Starkloff's old National Alliance colleagues in jail for sedition.) Irma and her chief Unitarian Women's Alliance confederates, a redoubtable trio of sisters named Bella, Grace, and Charlotte Taussig, set up a Red Cross unit, where Marion dutifully stopped by three days a week after school to roll bandages and knit socks for the troops.

The South Side citizens would never again enjoy what Marion and her parents always had known: a confidence that their German heritage was simply a natural extension of their ancestral homeland on American soil. Many people stopped speaking German during the war, even in their own homes. Proposals had been heard that it be made a crime to speak German. Children ceased to be bilingual; Put Rombauer grew up with no knowledge of what Max von Starkloff would have called "the tongue of Schiller and Goethe." (Marion was luckier, and always retained the ability at least to understand German, the language she had known in the nursery.) Most of the German-language press did not long survive the war. Even some of the old music societies fell away. Public and private surgery was performed on many local names. Berlin Avenue became Pershing Avenue, and John Becker's uncle William Dietrich Becker, a rising lawyer with an eye to political office, discreetly changed his name to William Dee Becker.

Edgar occupied himself during part of this bitter time with writing a set of brief biographical sketches he had undertaken on behalf of Augusta's mother's family, the Engelmanns, an original nucleus of the "Latin Farmers" in Belleville. On one of the Engelmann farms a few miles east of Belleville, many of the earlier immigrant members lay buried in a tiny tree-surrounded cemetery on a fine, rolling wooded hilltop. Edgar's memorial sketches apparently were meant to account for all of the deceased up to about 1918. The tree-crowned site and what it stood for meant much to all of them, for Irma and Edgar had always brought the children and a good lunch to this beautiful sanctuary every May for the annual cemetery picnic of the still cohesive Engelmann-Koerner clan.

Roderick Rombauer, ever the frustrated poet—he had continued to compose German and English verse through all his years in America—had contributed the lines that are still inscribed by the entrance, beginning:

Einst war es, vor vielen, vielen Jahren,
Von des Rheines Reb-bekränztem Strand,
Kamen Pilger übers Meer gefahren,
Gründeten ein Heim im freien Land.

[Once it was, upon a time now lost,
From the Rhineland's vine-enwreathèd strand,
Voyagers who late the sea had crossed
Founded their new home in the free land.]

The verses were written in 1903, the year of Marion's birth. By the time the war was over and she was finishing her school years at Mary Institute, they were a signpost to something that was no more, except in a few tenacious memories. Edgar had tried to acknowledge it through writing the sketches. Irma, by now as proud of her German heritage as her father had ever been, would later try in her own way. So would Marion, the Rombauers' last link of memory with the vanished world of the freedom-seeking German exiles and their life art.

3

The Rombauers After the War

As the war receded in memory, Irma made inroads on some of her ambitions. In 1921 Marion entered Vassar. Despite a spotty academic record, Put was shortly trundled off to Country Day School, then the most prestigious private boys' school in the St. Louis area. Meanwhile Irma, having risen through the committee ranks at the Wednesday Club, began a two-year term (1921–23) as first vice president, the overture to the presidency.[1]

The Beckers were less fortunate. Around the beginning of the twenties the family business, the Dittmann Shoe Company, failed. John and Virginia's father tried other ventures without being able to make a great success of anything. John had gone to Harvard a couple of years before Marion started at Vassar, but now he came back to St. Louis to finish up at Washington University. Jinny, who otherwise would have joined Marion and a contingent of other Mary Institute alumnae at Vassar, also had to make do with Washington—a fine school that carried little glamour for young people dreaming of loftier venues. Both of the young Beckers longed for other horizons. It was harder now to discern in St. Louis the aura of a cosmopolitan elite that Roger Baldwin had noted twenty years before. The gracious old circles of the affluent South Side German community were sadly shrunken since the war (though one of the younger Becker cousins remembers that liveried

footmen at Christmas parties were still a familiar sight into the 1930s).
To an outsider, "St. Louis German" was not likely to convey associations of liberality or enlightenment.

Educated young people in all areas of the country were now quicker
than they had been to measure the cultural worth of their own communities against Eastern models and to think of seeking their fortunes
in places like New York. Certainly the idea had occurred to John.
Though no terribly industrious student, he was an apt one stimulated
by contact with alert minds. He rapidly gravitated toward thoughts of
an intellectual life and a huge disdain for anything smacking of Philis-
tinism. He was not a young man to think of making shoes as his father
had done. Most of those who knew John from youth to old age recall
two salient facts about him: he was almost shockingly handsome
(always contriving to look charming and distinguished in anything
from a tuxedo to old shorts), and he enjoyed being an arbiter of elegancies. A fellow student at Washington University later remembered
him as "already something of an exquisite in dress and manners,"[2] a
tendency that would grow more pronounced with age. He fancied himself as a writer and thought of trying his hand at short stories or a
novel. He began to cultivate a taste for the niceties of English usage
and the cutting edge of modern art. After a time another idea occurred
to him: to study architecture. This ambition may well have been stimulated by his friendship with "Rom," as everyone called his sister's old
schoolfellow.

Marion, a diligent rather than brilliant student, had nonetheless
been marked by her Eastern years. In later life she would sometimes
shrug off Vassar as having taught her little more lasting than how to
set up a card file. This is not likely to have been the case. The school
almost surely set her on a lifelong path of attacking any new challenge
by getting a large book on the subject or seeking out certifiable experts
and asking questions. More particularly, Vassar made her a connoisseur of the visual arts.

The catalyst for her new interest was Agnes Rindge, a young
instructor whom Marion met in her sophomore year and a dashing
exponent of the relatively new discipline of art history (as opposed to
the older approach in which one simply soaked oneself in an aura of
masterworks). For Marion it was like being converted to a new religion. Henceforth she would be a *Lebenskünstlerin*, a life artist, not in
the instinctive mode of her mother and grandfather but through a sort
of conscious doctrinal effort. This popular, robust, rather thickset

young woman with a cheerful greeting always on her lips and a fondness for a good game of golf actually dreamed of a life founded on the best modern aesthetic and scientific principles. Some of the guiding stars in her heaven were primitive art of many sorts, modern painting of various schools, and the art of Japan (she developed an enduring fascination with the civilization of the Heian period, roughly A.D. 800–1200). Through Miss Rindge's involvement with the current art scene, Marion also acquired the habit of keeping up with the latest gallery doings in New York.

Even at this stage, John's and Marion's interests were probably rubbing off on each other. At the instigation of her grandmother von Starkloff—"a woman of extraordinary charm and good sense,"[3] as Marion later wrote—she returned to St. Louis to spend her junior year at Washington University in order to cement her local ties. Marion did not repine. She liked the atmosphere of the big, busy city campus and the chance to catch up with old friends, including Jin and John. "Rom" (her invariable nickname) had a mutual bond with John in their experience of distinguished Eastern schools closer than Washington to some ripples of the Zeitgeist.

Some of the trends that they zealously took up were latter-day offshoots of the old arts and crafts movement; others bespoke a new curiosity about mass production and industrial engineering. Together they drank in advanced ideas of the "applied arts," from textile and clothing design to ceramics and book graphics. It was an age in which bright young minds could easily conceive that there was a scientific, enlightened twentieth-century "design for living," preferably to be realized within some socialist framework and encompassing anything from the way airplanes were constructed to the way kitchens were planned. The concept of the object honestly shaped to life's everyday purposes would be a cornerstone of the creed Marion and John jointly adopted. It was also the major intellectual conviction that they would later bring to *The Joy of Cooking*.

Irma, though as fervent as ever about keeping up with the new books and ideas of the twenties, was not equal to all of the young friends' dogmas. She had a sense that Marion tended to set herself up as a superior mind—a mind, nonetheless, that her mother was proud of. She wanted Marion to have not just the advantage of a prestigious college degree but some opportunity even further beyond the common way.

Ever one to act first and plan later, Irma produced her masterstroke late in Marion's senior year at Vassar. At that moment—March of

1925—the household at Flad Avenue was a disaster zone. Put had broken a foot on the soccer field. Irma, who had been having menopausal problems for some time, had been in the hospital receiving the latest treatment, radium implants in the uterus to stop persistent bleeding. Edgar was in the middle of one of his breakdowns, possibly a result of recent crises, including his father's death a year earlier and (according to Put) another bout of successful but very painful treatments for bladder cancer. On this occasion he had been home for weeks unable to work. On Irma's first day back from the hospital Put arrived home on crutches to find the house turned upside down. "Son, we're going to Europe," she greeted him. It was Monday afternoon. Somehow Irma got the contents of three floors and an attic—the accumulated possessions of her twenty-five-year marriage—packed up and put in storage in time to convey herself, Edgar, and the crutch-bound Put to the noon sailing of the SS *New Amsterdam* from New York on Saturday, March 14.[4]

It was something that she had been urging on Edgar for years, only to hear that he was too busy or couldn't spare the money. But that week she had burst forth from her hospital bed with a scheme that addressed all family contingencies and brooked no nay-saying. The moment could not have been better. Irma's Wednesday Club presidency had ended a few months before, leaving her like Alexander in need of other worlds to conquer. Put, whose chances of getting through Country Day School fluctuated dramatically, could perhaps be salvaged for college through a few terms at a foreign boarding school. (It did not hurt that the U.S. dollar stood at a euphorically favorable rate of exchange in postwar Europe.) For Marion, an extended spell abroad would be a much more magnificent—and educational—reward than the summer versions of the Grand Tour that were now standard graduation presents for well-heeled young people. Besides, the sudden stimulus of it all was just what Edgar (who had never seen Europe) needed to bring him back to himself.

She was right about the effect of this unexpected *coup de foudre* on Edgar. He seems to have regained his usual energy and spirits almost as soon as they set out for Europe. At every stage of travel he sent delighted reports back to his office in St. Louis. There his letters were faithfully typed and circulated among family and friends by his secretary, Mary Josephine Whyte.[5]

Mary Whyte—always called "Mazie" or "Maizie"—was a pleasant young Irishwoman, the niece of one of Edgar's closest friends, Charlie Maguire. The Rombauers were fond of Mazie, and when her father died suddenly, leaving his finances in ruin, Edgar had her trained for legal secretarial work and brought her into his office. She was devoted to him and endlessly willing to go an extra mile for any of the Rombauers. Her typescript of Edgar's letters records a family jaunt necessarily less imposing than the five-year sojourn of Irma's adolescence but still meant to provide the children with a leisurely enrichment beyond that of their peers.

The idea was that Irma, Edgar, and Put would travel through England and the Low Countries until Marion could join them after commencement; the whole party would then continue south through Germany, Switzerland, and Italy. Edgar would have to return to St. Louis in the fall, but the others were to remain until next summer—Put at boarding school in Switzerland, Marion and Irma investigating the dance schools at which Marion hoped to study in Italy and Germany.

It was all a glorious success. Irma, as always, was hideously seasick during the Atlantic and Channel crossings (at one point Put saw a blanket-covered bench skating violently back and forth across the deck with the ship's pitching, while the mound that was his mother lay as insensible as a sack of meal). But once on terra firma she was unstoppable, buoyed by this return to scenes of the von Starkloffs' happiest years. Edgar was deeply moved by the sight of Germany, now defeated but in his mind the ever-splendid home of the liberty-loving Koerners and Engelmanns. Marion, who joined them in August after a leisurely tour of English cathedral towns, was looking forward to profound intellectual and artistic experiences. She was not disappointed. Having deposited Put at the Institution Sillig in Vevey and said goodbye to her father in Naples, she and Irma took in parts of Sicily and Spain, then prepared to explore the modern dance schools for which Marion yearned.

In 1925 Marion may well still have been thinking of an actual career in dance, a hope she had cherished as a schoolgirl. Large and lumpish though she always felt herself next to her mother, she had learned to move with grace and to love the language of the body. All aspects of dance would always fascinate her, but what she especially wanted to investigate in Europe was the modern posterity of the eurythmic school, originally an attempt to translate the experience of hearing music into a system of concrete gestures.

After a time Marion became immersed in an approach less concerned with concert performance than with physical and spiritual self-discovery. The teacher who brought about her conversion to this way of thinking was Elsa Gindler of the Bode School for Expressive Movement in Munich.[6] As a young woman Miss Gindler had cured herself of tuberculosis after the doctors had given up on her. From her own road back to health she had developed a system of techniques and exercises—though words like "system" and "techniques" obscure what was an empirical rather than a theoretical style of instruction—meant to make the student experience the act of breathing. All else followed from this elemental rhythm, the wellspring of bodily motion and the key to an awareness of what goes on in the slightest alteration of position. Like yoga, Miss Gindler's teaching sought to resolve unconscious tensions and constraints on both a physiological and spiritual level. The epithet "well-adjusted," later to be trivially popularized as a supposed clue to mental health, may suggest the mutually reinforcing harmony of physical and psychological attitude for which the Gindler teaching strove.

Munich, the home of the Bode School, was only one of Marion and Irma's destinations. Throughout the winter and spring of 1925–26 they wandered through Vienna, Salzburg, Berlin, and the old haunts of Irma's mother's family in the north of Germany. Marion, like her mother, was particularly taken with the idea of the sturdy merchant princes who had built the Minlos mansion (by 1925 it had become a cigar warehouse, but the lovely proportions of the ex-ballroom remained) on the river Trave in Lübeck. She was fascinated by the long-ago world she seemed to enter on being introduced to Emma and Dada's only surviving sibling, "Onkel Willi" Kuhlmann, a retired court musician at the Grand Duchy of Oldenburg. But Munich would be the most important of their stops, and not only for the weeks or months that Marion spent dancing with Elsa Gindler.

At this stage of the Weimar era the city was second only to Berlin (if indeed second) in the brilliance of its cultural life. It was the home of many artists and thinkers, and Marion would have known it as the old headquarters of the now-disbanded "Blue Rider," the Expressionist group that had included Kandinsky and Klee. It was here that they gratified Irma's long-standing passion for Bernard Shaw by attending a performance of *Back to Methuselah,* a marathon affair spread over the five nights that Shaw wanted but was rarely able to get producers to agree to. At a small shop dealing in art books and prints, Marion "stood transfixed before the first Mondrians I had ever seen"—a kind of revelation, and a stunning embodiment of the prospects that Agnes Rindge had opened up to her at Vassar. In Munich, too, she had a love affair.

Ernst Kropp, Marion later wrote, was "a man twice my age,"[7] which means that he must have been nearly as old as Irma. He was probably Jewish. He had an odd, expressive face that Irma later saw unexpectedly mirrored in the French comedian Fernandel.[8] Irma and Marion most likely met Kropp through his work for the Deutscher Werkbund, perhaps the most serious European legacy of the turn-of-the-century English arts and crafts movement. The Werkbund, founded in 1907, had set some of the best German talents to considering how to make the everyday objects in people's lives more beautiful, useful, and rationally planned.[9] At the time the Rombauers met him in Munich, Kropp was designing furniture and textiles for the Werkbund and completing a book about his ideas of the true spiritual and societal mission of twentieth-century art.

Irma was present at the early stages of the unlikely romance between the middle-aged idea-spinner and the young American girl with her bent for radiant enthusiasms. Marion would always be attracted to people with a sense of mission, something Kropp possessed in abundance. He was scraping along like a church mouse while dreaming of a future order in which the old representational art with its daubs and effigies of scenic vistas or famous faces would be blotted out and replaced by a *Kunstgewerbe*, or fusion of the applied arts, as simple and harmonious as the natural world itself. Men and women would then forget arty pursuits, living without fuss among exquisitely right and beautiful household furniture, textiles, tableware, and other necessities as instinctively formed as living leaves, insect wings, and all the inspiring models of the creation.

Irma and Marion were both charmed, though Irma doughtily stuck up for the dignity of the old-style arts. (To show him that she was no dinosaur, she presented him with a German translation of *Back to Methuselah* with its vistas of expanded future human scope.) Marion listened to him read aloud from the manuscript of his book, and he shortly let her know that he had never met one with so great a gift for appreciating his ideas.

At this interesting juncture Irma cut short her trip to return to St. Louis, leaving Marion to make her own way back with Put in a few months. (Irma was a creature of impulse, and the reason for the change of plans is not clear, but she later wrote that it had been prompted by the sight of a lemon meringue pie in an American magazine advertisement.)[10] Marion certainly got the better end of this decision, which would have been unthinkable in her mother's youth. Irma arrived in

New York to be greeted by customs authorities who apparently connected the maiden name on her passport with the well-known international criminal activities of Emil Starkloff. She was detained at Ellis Island and subjected to a strip search before she could go on to a temporary hotel roost in St. Louis.[11]

Meanwhile Marion, unchaperoned, was making the most of the time until Put's school let out. In May and June she was with Kropp, perhaps in Munich but certainly in Paris, where he had gone to do some buying for museums. Afterward she confided to Put that they had become lovers. But to a girl of her temperament the more lasting pleasure must have been the sense of momentous intellectual discovery—the feeling that serious, life-charged European thought was now her own. Before they parted, she had promised to translate Kropp's book into English and arrange for its publication in the United States.

Put arrived in Paris in June, while Kropp was on his way back to Munich to wrestle with prepublication tasks and prepare for a job at a vocational school in Dresden. Marion was full of thrilling sexual discovery and the greatness of the mission she was charged with, but not too full to kick up her heels a bit more. With one mind, she and Put took the $500 that their parents had earmarked for their American train fare, including a planned detour to Niagara Falls, and set out to do what they pleased. By the official itinerary they were to spend a month in Paris. Disdaining this tame notion, they hired a private limousine and took off for the château country of the Touraine. Their gloriously unauthorized joyride, which ended with the truly royal gesture of taking the limousine all the way to their ship at Cherbourg late in July, cleaned out every penny of the $500 but left Marion and Put with probably their happiest joint memory of each other's company.

Back in St. Louis, Marion eagerly described to all her friends the wonderful ideas of a man sure to rank among the great thinkers of the century, whose life's masterwork she would have the privilege of translating. John Becker, among others, was greatly interested. He was in the middle of his architecture studies at Washington University, and the currents emanating from Germany through the Deutscher Werkbund and the Bauhaus were breaths of keenest oxygen to students of his generation. He went on being interested even after the finished book reached Marion in November: *Wandlung der Form im XX. Jahrhundert* (Metamorphosis of Form in the Twentieth Century), published on behalf of the Werkbund. But in a short while everyone's raptures became somewhat muted.

Poor Marion had bitten off far too much for her years and experience. *Wandlung der Form* contained only a small amount of text to be translated, much of the argument resting on a large number of exquisite photographs of natural forms like shells. But it was the sort of book of which any translation would require a translation. The argument has the earmarks of an individual credo that has become a kind of crusade, and it is couched in a quasi-philosophical argot that defies easy summaries.

The gist of *Wandlung der Form*, if one can apply words like "gist" to so intricate a train of thought, is that twentieth-century life with its amplified, accelerated industrial heartbeat demands a new understanding of *Form*, meaning not just literal "form" but the intelligible expression of function. Kropp envisioned a precise fusion of hard, strong, streamlined structural *Form* based on modern technology and rhythmic ornamental motifs taken from natural phenomena—butterfly wings, seashells, exotic plumage. He had developed an extraordinarily idiosyncratic, semimystical vocabulary to codify the interplay of *Form* and ornament.[12]

Marion wrestled with all this like Jacob with the angel. People on whom she bestowed copies of *Wandlung der Form* politely said that it must be very profound. Kropp wrote frequently, never failing to inquire how she was getting on with it. From his end of the correspondence (all that survives), he does not seem to have been the easiest of admirers. Letter after letter painted a plaintive vista of aging loneliness, dwelt on his need for a *Kameradin* to be beside him in his crusade, and mentioned her miraculous fitness for the post—but he never worked up to actually proposing marriage, or even told her that he loved her. He was shortly wondering at her long silences and finding occasions for wintry reproach every time she did manage a letter. He continued to write at frequent intervals for more than a year and a half. But by 1928 he had more or less given up. "I have to assume that things are going so well with you, or maybe floating in seventh heaven, that your old friend Kropp has been forgotten. It is not pretty of you, but I won't get angry about it. . . . You will long since have thrown the translation of my book in the corner. Even that I won't be angry about."[13]

He was quite right, of course. Marion struggled for a long time with the translation of *Wandlung der Form* (John Becker offered to have a go at it and made no more headway than she), but at last she ceased to write to Kropp at all. But if Marion's grasp of a rashly embraced task had been superficial, her loyalty was not. She never ceased to think of

Ernst Kropp as one of the greatest people she had known, or to want to do something on behalf of him and his ideas. In her own mind, she remained committed to her promise until the day of her death.

In the meanwhile, she had picked up all of her old St. Louis friendships with undiminished enjoyment. She convinced Jin Becker (who often took up Marion's enthusiasms) to join her as a dance pupil of Lisbeth Hoops-Ebers, a transplanted veteran of the Bode School in Munich. She and the Becker siblings saw a great deal of each other, apparently without any special romantic designs on the part of John and Marion. All the Rombauers considered him practically family. John not only reciprocated the feeling but, around the time of receiving his architecture degree, commemorated it in a mock certificate. It appears that Irma (who often honored special events with one of her gorgeously iced cakes) had presented him with what he called "a gift of skilled craftsmanship and piercing sweetness." In return for this affectionate tribute John declared her "appointed to the honored office of AUNT, with all the rights, duties, and privileges appertaining unto such office." This gallant production, dashed off on "this 20th day of June 1927," does not suggest that at the moment "John Becker, Civil Nephew" had any idea of marrying the recipient's daughter.[14]

Even if his thoughts had been running along matrimonial lines, girls of Marion's education and social standing were not champing at the bit to marry as early as their mothers. On her return from Europe she was as confident as any male college graduate of finding her way in the world. Her parents proudly expected her to seek work (though they also expected that she would continue to live at home while single). It could be assumed that Miss Rombauer's eventual existence as Mrs. Somebody would never have to revolve around simply getting Mr. Somebody's dinner. It is true that her qualifications for a job—a double major in French and art history—were not exactly the ticket for a large range of well-paying positions. But in the prevailing climate of economic optimism it seemed as if anyone could make her own way.

Within a few months of coming back Marion had fallen into one of the new niches opening up for young women in just her situation. Stix, Baer and Fuller, one of the largest St. Louis department stores, now had a policy of recruiting for entry-level sales and buying positions among recent college alumnae who could eventually be polished into lower-administrative material. Marion found a job without difficulty and was placed in various departments before settling down in the personal-shopping bureau. She enjoyed it all hugely; enjoying experiences was one of her talents. To Ernst Kropp she grandly wrote that she was employed in a *Kunstgewerbehaus*, an establishment for the applied arts. She worked with china, glass, clothes, furnishings—all grist to the mill for one much occupied with aesthetic credos to light the path of everyday living.

The glamour of the job (at fifteen dollars a week plus commissions) had worn off after about a year, but Marion did not have to languish there long. Late in the summer of 1927 she was escaping the August heat at Bay View and struggling with *Wandlung der Form* when a friend about to be married telephoned long-distance—an almost unheard-of extravagance—to announce that she needed someone to fill in for her at the office while she was on her honeymoon. The job was St. Louis stringer for *Women's Wear Daily*. Marion, as she later recollected, was dubious:

> "But Jo, I've never reported for anything except the Mary Institute Chronicle."
>
> "That's O.K.," she said. "You just have to say *what when where* and *how* in the first paragraphs, and I told my boss you were a Vassar graduate so he's satisfied."[15]

Marion had managed not to hear the name of *Women's Wear Daily* in a year on her first job, but she was never daunted by her own inexperience. Unlike John Becker, she did not preen herself on her own gifts as a stylist; she simply followed Jo Goldstein's advice and put down the facts in order. The results seemed quite satisfactory. When Jo decided not to come back to the job, it was Marion's, at twenty-five dollars a week.

The St. Louis editorial headquarters of the parent Fairchild Company consisted of a dingy downtown office occupied by Marion and two male colleagues. The drawing part of her job was easy. The company supplied her with pads of "croquis"—presketched figures on which she had only to indicate details like cuffs, seams, and hemlines for the real artists who would work up the published drawings in New York. She already had a lot of department-store connections and some understanding of merchandising, and in most places she found that the *Women's Wear* name opened nearly any door she cared to knock at. One day a week she investigated clothes, shoes, and millinery in the wholesale markets; as the spirit moved, she attended any museum show or St. Louis Symphony concert and wrote up the fashion aspect of the event. One day she came into the office to be greeted by her two coworkers excitedly telling her that she had gotten a byline (an honor neither man had ever achieved) on a story about retail merchandise returned to stores, full of serious analysis and pie charts. Marion had to ask what a byline was.

In the spring of 1928 the New York office announced that it was assigning her to cover that year's Kentucky Derby, from which she was to file her first wire story. To her utter astonishment, her parents forbade her to go to the race unchaperoned. Considering the freedom she had had in Europe, Marion thought this decree odd. But she found a willing chaperone in Marguerite Martyn, the "wispy, rheumy, oldish, dowdy but friendly" society columnist of the *Post-Dispatch*.[16] The arrangement worked out perfectly, especially as regarded its sequel—Marion's flying visit from Churchill Downs to Cincinnati to see John Becker.

John's 1927 architecture degree had not led to any opportunities in St. Louis. At last he had landed a position at the firm of John Scudder Adkins in Cincinnati, where Adele, his mother, had a large contingent of shoe-business relatives. The city was a close match to St. Louis in point of Germanness but smaller and at first glance less interesting. "Every day or so . . . I wonder for an amazed moment what on earth I'm doing in this hilly ancient burg," he gloomily wrote to "Rom."[17] Missing the sophistication and bustle of St. Louis, he dabbled at a succession of arty leisure pursuits and sent Marion chatty, companionable letters about his somewhat becalmed existence. When she learned of her new assignment, they agreed that she would attend the Derby with Miss Martyn and file her story, then spend the night in Louisville with relatives of Adele Becker's and go on to Cincinnati the next day.

As she later recalled it, she arrived by the first train from Louisville. Her old friend met her and drove her out for lunch to a terrace restaurant on a high ridge looking toward Kentucky across the peculiarly gracious, Rhine-like sweep of the Ohio River. Whether it was the beautiful setting or the fact of meeting each other as independent adults far from the usual family associations, something happened on that day to make John and Marion stop seeing each other as mere chums. In the afternoon they wandered through the ramshackle but delightful Cincinnati Zoo. They found another river-view perch by a German monument in a spot called, appropriately enough, Eden Park, and sat talking until dark. "Hunger finally drove us to the Alms Hotel for supper—a magic meal that ended with baked custard and ripe strawberries. The midnight train took me exhausted but oh! so happy back to St. Louis."[18]

Marion and John went on falling in love for some months, without being able to see much of an immediate future together. He could not expect much from his parents in his father's reduced circumstances, and the profession he had chosen offered no ready sinecures. John thought of trying to transplant himself East on the chance of finding better prospects there. But in the end he returned to St. Louis (probably early in 1929) and moved back into the Longfellow Boulevard house with his parents.

Marion, meanwhile, had been offered another job. It was usually her luck to bounce from one half-accidental opportunity to another in a way common to educated women who begin the world with serious ideas and little practical training. The new opening was quite adventitious. She had taken to giving parties at the Rombauers' new post-Europe home, a big third-floor apartment on Waterman Avenue in the now-fashionable West End. It was a good place for having people over, and Marion had managed some rather elaborately planned affairs with shadow plays or charades.

Irma would usually contribute some of her famous "pinch pies," meringue shells filled with fruit and topped with whipped cream. Marion would decorate the place with her equally famous cutouts. With a pair of scissors and an assortment of colored papers, she would almost effortlessly cover the tall French doors to the sun porch with an array of fanciful, witty silhouettes and stylized motifs. People who saw her turn out these "murals" still recall the uncanny precision of her eye and hand—curiously, she was not especially good at drawing—and the charm of the results. After one of her parties the riot of figures was still up on the French doors when a younger Wednesday Club acquaintance of Irma's came by and not only marveled but asked Marion to demonstrate her unusual craft at the innovative private school where the visitor was teaching. One thing led to another, and before the summer of 1929 the young teacher, Caroline Risque Janis, had helped Marion obtain a position in her own department.

Miss Risque, as she usually preferred to be known at that time, was a much-admired sculptor, one of the most prominent artists in St. Louis. She was the head of the art department at John Burroughs School (named for the celebrated naturalist and essayist). Together with an elementary-grades counterpart, John Burroughs (for grades seven through ten, later twelve) was the recent creation of a group of progressive-minded St. Louisans who wanted to offer children a more loosely structured school experience than places like Mary Institute or Country Day.[19] Much later in life Marion described the school as "far-out," a term in which anyone who knew her would have recognized high praise. It was by no means unstructured or outré by later standards, but it was the kind of place where the children themselves helped dig the foundations of the workshop.

A chance for Marion to throw in her lot on the side of modern experiment was like a call to a Saint Joan. She promptly gave up the *Women's Wear Daily* job to spend the summer at Bay View preparing for her new responsibilities to young minds. She had been perfectly happy in her first two jobs, but since meeting Agnes Rindge and Ernst Kropp she had harbored a sense of lofty educational duty. But in the event, she had too much else to think about to accomplish all the summer reading and planning that she had envisioned. Not long before she left for Michigan, she and John Becker had become lovers.[20] John was glued for the time being to an uninspiring job with a St. Louis architectural firm. They spent the summer writing long, yearning letters that, as luck had it, record the Rombauers' last summer together as a family.

On the surface, everyone was in fairly good fettle. Irma seems to have been unwell before they left for the summer; she was starting to suffer from vague periodic ailments that sound like attacks of "nerves," a catchall description of the time. But in Michigan, according to Marion, she appeared wonderfully restored and, as usual, bent on a new bit of summer self-improvement:

> Mother is much better but still fervidly devoted to Italian, which she insists on reading aloud to me. Her latest "sight translation" ended with "mammals in heat," which with further vocabulary research proved to be "violets in flower," so I have been begging her to get a teacher and stop using her imagination.[21]

Edgar seemed in good spirits despite a disappointment earlier that spring. He had run unsuccessfully for a seat on the St. Louis Board of Education.[22] Considering his father's years of service to the School Board (as it had earlier been known) and the eighteen-year period of withdrawal from politics that had succeeded his term as Speaker of the House of Delegates in 1910–11, Edgar's decision to run cannot have been casual, or the rebuff a small one. But Marion (not at that time keenly aware of politics) does not mention the matter. From the sound of her Michigan letters, "Faz" (Father) was happily absorbed in doing nothing in particular.

Put stayed in St. Louis for most of the summer, working. On returning from Europe he had completely mutinied at the prospect of another second's education. Edgar undoubtedly could have found a business contact willing to provide some office-flunky position, but he elected not to intervene. Put himself found a job as a timekeeper with the newest Mississippi bridge project, to be built by the American Bridge Company at Chain of Rocks near the northern boundary of the city. Irma, though upset, eventually ceased to dream of Ivy League schools and made peace with what she had to recognize as a grown man's decision. She would not, however, have kept the peace had she known that by the summer of 1929, with the Chain of Rocks bridge nearly completed, Put, too, was involved in a romantic adventure. He had secretly married a St. Louis girl named Nita Fayles, and was not ready to spring the news on his parents. He showed up (wifeless) just in time for his twenty-second birthday, August 15, after an adventurous drive from St. Louis in an ill-starred jalopy. His new plan was to study photography.

In Bay View, the Rombauers had become acquainted with Al Callen, a portrait photographer with a summer studio in neighboring Charlevoix. Put had learned enough from him to think that with a little apprenticeship and application he could make a go of it. Callen planned to open a studio that fall in New York after the end of the Michigan season, and Put had arranged to follow him. Marion sadly reported to John that almost as soon as he appeared he and Irma were at each other's throats as usual: "He tries hard to behave—but Mother sees an unkempt, opinionated baby, and only one month to prepare him to 'meet the world.' "[23]

Put duly went off (with Nita, of whom his parents still knew nothing) to New York, and after several months of working with Callen felt ready to open his own studio. He joined what was at the time an influx of hopeful Northerners looking to start businesses in Florida, and set up a studio in Daytona Beach that winter. Marion survived the usual panic and exhaustion of beginning teachers to become confidently engrossed in the mission of liberating children's powers of self-expression, her new credo. She also brought into the John Burroughs curriculum a scaled-down version of what Vassar had given her, an amazingly ambitious survey of the world history of art that she worked at as fiercely as if it had been a college course.

Marion and John were now understood by their families to be as good as engaged, though his job prospects did not yet warrant their setting a date. Marion's skill with scissors and paper continued to attract local interest, and she found an occasion to pool her and John's joint talents for the Christmas program of a children's series, "The Story Hour," at the St. Louis City Art Museum. For this occasion John worked up a retelling of *The Love of Three Oranges,* the Carlo Gozzi comedy, which he probably had discovered through Prokofiev's dazzling opera. Before a few poster-sized backdrops and complex, colorful paper-cutout friezes, Marion (working as always freehand, with no template or sketch) proceeded to cut out figures and costumes for every episode of the story as it unfolded. It was a great success, and left the two of them with a body of material that seemed too good not to deserve some future use.[24]

That fall Irma had gratified one of her great interests by becoming president of the Women's Committee of the St. Louis Symphony Orchestra Board of Directors. Probably she had been a power in St. Louis musical circles for some time, though her name does not survive on many lists. The orchestra was a good one, and at different times Irma seems to have been rather deeply involved in orchestra politics. But in the season of 1929–30 her activities were cut short, because Edgar had suffered another breakdown.

Despite the timing, it is doubtful that the Great Depression, which overtook the country in the wake of the October 29 stock market crash, was the clue to this collapse. According to Put, he did have a good deal of money tied up in stocks that at once started a downhill slide, and he must have seen lean times ahead.[25] But Edgar was a business lawyer of such esteem in St. Louis that he undoubtedly could have kept his head above water through the rising tide of fiscal dismay. Most likely the severe private depression that seized him in November was essentially a new outbreak of his lifelong illness. Perhaps the spectacle of public calamity had played some contributing role; or he may have suffered a delayed reaction to his failure in the Board of Education election earlier that year. Put Rombauer (at that time still in Florida) believes that an additional factor was some recurring sign of the bladder cancer his father had suffered many years before. However, it must be noted that Health Commissioner Max C. Starkloff never alluded to such a circumstance, either at the inquest into his brother-in-law's death or in discussing the episode with his son Gene in later years.[26]

In any case, Irma once again attacked the problem through a rapid change of scene. As she had done long before in the aftermath of their first child's death, she took Edgar from the bleak St. Louis winter to a more welcoming climate—this time South Carolina, where they remained from December until the end of January 1930. They had hoped to visit Put in Florida but for some reason turned back a few hundred miles away. When they reached St. Louis, Edgar once more seemed close to a reasonable equilibrium. The route back had been difficult; the last leg of the trip was so impeded by snow and subzero conditions that they were obliged to leave the car in Evansville, Illinois, and go on to St. Louis by train. "Irma stood the strenuous trip remarkably well, and I marvel at her powers of endurance," Edgar wrote to Bay View friends on January 24, the day after their arrival. "I came home feeling better, although by no means a marvel and we are binding our energies on some way to solve the problems with which we are confronted"—what problems, he did not spell out.[27]

At eight-thirty on the morning of Monday, February 3, Irma set out from Waterman Avenue on a downtown shopping expedition. Marion must already have left for work. Edgar, according to Tuesday's *Globe-Democrat*, appeared "in good humor" and was remarking on the fine weather.[28] When Irma had gone, he went into the back bedroom and took out a Purdey double-barreled shotgun, the finest weapon of its kind that money could buy. He loaded only one barrel.[29]

"Know whether or not it was his personal property, this shot gun?" the coroner inquired of Max C. Starkloff the next day.

"Yes, I gave it to him fifteen, twenty years ago," the Health Commissioner said, and added, "His wife had no idea it was in the house."

Edgar sat down in a chair by the open window. He tied a string around his right foot. He tied the other end to the trigger and placed the muzzle of the weapon in his mouth. Some time later Elsie Holtman, the housemaid, who had paid no attention to a sound like a car backfiring, answered the phone. It was the downstairs neighbors, who had suddenly noticed blood dripping from the ceiling.

"I called and he didn't answer," she told the coroner, "and I knew he was ill and knew he was in the back room, and I knew something had happened, so I called Dr. Starkloff." Max hastily telephoned Julius Muench. The two brothers-in-law drove to Waterman Avenue and went into the unlocked bedroom. Dr. Starkloff saw at a glance that

Edgar was dead. They moved the body from the rocking chair (where it was plainly visible to horrified neighbors) to the bed, removed the discharged cartridge from the Purdey, and called the police. The inquest was arranged for Tuesday.

"Had he been sick or under a doctor's care recently?" was one of the coroner's first questions to Dr. Starkloff.

> A. I think he had been under a doctor's care. He had been sick with a mental condition for some period of time, off and on. He was suffering from a hallucination based upon the idea that his life was a failure.

> Q. Did you ever hear Mr. Rombauer say he would commit suicide?

> A. He stated to me several times that he didn't know how he was prevented from committing suicide before—when he had his first illness.

> Q. Did he ever attempt suicide before?

> A. No,—I do not know.

The funeral was held at the Church of the Unity on Waterman Avenue later on the day of the inquest. The St. Louis Bar Association was represented by seven men who had served with Edgar and the reform slate in the House of Delegates. The letter that arrived several days later from U.S. Senator Harry Hawes, a Democrat who had no special reason to remember Edgar as a political soul mate, surely expressed the opinion of many: "He was a very remarkable man, so straightforward, courageous, and patriotic, that I always felt that some day he would be able to serve his country or State with distinction in a political capacity."[30]

As often happens after a violent calamity, there is little direct record of the survivors' first reactions. If either Irma or Marion ever cared to describe those dreadful days in writing, no evidence remains. The one thing that seems plain is that both lashed out in despairing rage. When they telephoned Put in Daytona Beach, it was not simply to give him the news but to tell him that he was not wanted at home in this crisis—in effect, to put up an angry wall around their own grief and exclude him from the process of family readjustment.[31] Gene Starkloff, who was sixteen at the time, recalls a general impression in Commissioner Starkloff's household that Marion—passionately caught up in the idea that Edgar somehow "could have been saved by kindness"—apparently "just went off her rocker" in a torrent of "almost vicious recriminations."[32]

It appears that she never acknowledged to others, and perhaps not to herself, that her father had killed himself to end an unbearable mental suffering. His death would take a great toll on her bright young openness, so great that she went to her own death nearly forty-seven years later without ever having been able to tell either of her sons that Edgar had been a suicide. Decades after Edgar's death, Marion answered her favorite cousin Elsa Muench Hunstein's queries about the event by saying that she believed his illness had really stemmed from bad nutrition during his Chicago law-clerk days.[33] Irma was not given to this kind of bizarre rationalization. But she probably had a good deal to do with an impression, eventually very widespread in St. Louis, that Edgar had been suffering from an incurable cancer and had cared enough for his family and friends to spare them the agony of a prolonged illness. His decency and generosity of spirit were well enough known to make the thought more than plausible.

Gradually Irma and Marion returned to a rational acceptance of others' concern and sympathy, and were able to discuss their situation with Put. They faced something close to ruin. The true dimensions of the Great Depression were becoming clearer with every month of 1930. Marion had her salary at John Burroughs. Irma had little more than about six thousand dollars from their old bank accounts, the mortgage payments from the purchasers of the Flad Avenue house, the Bay View cottage lease, and a large parcel of stock (now almost valueless) in the American Metals Company, Edgar's largest corporate client. The Waterman Avenue apartment was far beyond their foreseeable means. One or both would have to find some other source of income.

John Becker was there, through thick and thin. He had helped Marion retrieve Edgar's car from Evansville in the first terrible days after the tragedy. Now he helped her get up an idea for a book based on their Story Hour performance at the Art Museum. They began sending children's book editors a manuscript of John's retelling of *The Love of Three Oranges*, with a complete set of Marion's colored-paper cutout illustrations. The proposal was rejected all around; among the naysayers was

Macmillan, later the publisher of *The Joy of Cooking*. (The children's book department head, Louise Seaman, thought the pictures "extraordinary" but the text not on the same level.)[34]

Irma also cast about for some plan. In another age, a woman in her situation would have found a job—indeed, might have used the remains of the estate to pay for a course of professional training or to start a small shop with a crony. Even in 1930, a woman of another background and temperament might have done either of these or, more modestly, might have asked a friend or relative to help her find a job. It is difficult to picture Irma Rombauer adopting any of these tactics. As early as 1907 her sister-in-law Bertha Rombauer was proudly listing herself in the St. Louis city directory as "Stenographer and Notary." It is safe to say that Irma, who to the end of her life disdained learning to use a typewriter, would not have been caught dead doing such a thing. But as her first summer of widowhood approached, she, too, took it into her head to write a book. It was not a terribly practical plan, but it matched her view of her position in society. The idea that gradually took shape in her mind was the simplest thing that could be jammed between a pair of endpapers by a woman of minimal formal education and little trained ability of any sort: a cookbook.

According to a later family report, her brother Max's household did not greet the widow's new career initiative with rapture. "Worst idea I ever heard of" was the consensus; and, "Irma's a TERRIBLE cook."[35] The more generous memories of some friends and relatives do not erase the fact that cooking never had been exactly the crown jewel among her attainments. As she began writing her book in 1930, she cannot have expected to produce much more than a pastiche of recipes donated by good-natured acquaintances who knew her situation, interspersed with a few versions of things that had always been served in the family.

4

The Birth of *Joy*

In the first year of the Depression, the Rombauer family painfully
regrouped under circumstances undreamed of twelve months before.
By the summer of 1930 Irma and Marion had moved from Waterman
Avenue to a smaller walkup apartment in the West End of St. Louis, at
5712 Cabanne (pronounced "cabinny") Avenue. Irma had placed the
American Metals shares in the hands of her nephew Max Muench—
Elsa and Julius's son, Marion's old playmate, now a stockbroker. He
could only report that dividends were headed down with no change in
sight. The prodigal Put, meanwhile, was off to new wanderings after a
brief pass through St. Louis. He had given up his idea of being a photographer and headed west from Florida in hopes of another bridge job
in Portland. When it fell through, he and Nita (of whose existence the
family at last learned that summer) took to picking hops and plums.
Irma had a hard time defending his secret marriage and menial occu-
pations to her prouder South Side and Indianapolis connections. But it
was a better time to be a resilient roustabout than an expensively educated would-be professional like John Becker.

John, at his wits' end watching local building projects being canceled and realizing that his parents—with a younger son still to put
through school—would soon have to give up their house, had decided
on a plan that he knew would cause fresh grief to Marion. He had

agreed to throw in his lot with a Cincinnati friend looking for architectural work in New York. In 1930 that was too far to visit more than once or twice a year, and long-distance phone calls were saved for once in a very expensive blue moon. The young couple's hopes of marriage seemed remoter than ever.

All of them fled from St. Louis that summer. Marion had suddenly been seized with an impulse to see Mexico, as powerful a contrast as could be imagined to the scene of her own loss. She managed to spend nearly four weeks there (mostly in and around Mexico City) in August, coming away with an abiding interest in pre-Columbian civilization and art. John and his Cincinnati crony set up an apartment in the Chelsea district of Manhattan and traipsed around knocking on putative employers' doors. The news was grim everywhere. At last he landed a job with the firm that had been hired to do the main designing for the Rockefeller Center project. Irma left for Michigan—not Bay View, where she had had to give up the Rombauers' cherished home away from home, but the nearby watering places of Tonawaytha and Horton's Bay. By now she was firmly set on the cookbook project, with which Edgar's old secretary Mazie Whyte had promised to help her. Irma's plan was to collect a respectable total of recipes, publish the results herself with some portion of her $6,000 legacy, and sell it either by direct mail or through bookstores and other venues.

She was not the first St. Louis matron to have thought of writing a cookbook. Gladys Taussig Lang, another product of genteel South St. Louis German circles, had achieved authorship in 1929 with a slender and tony volume titled *Choice Menus for Luncheons and Dinners*, published for a charitable cause.[1] Irma had given Put an acid description of this effort. It was filled with ideas like green turtle soup followed by cold lobster and spring lamb—la-di-da stuff at the best of times, and almost comically beside the mark in 1930. Irma thought herself much more equal to giving people something for their money.

Just what materials she started with is not known. There are various reports of recipes by Irma Rombauer in existence before her 1931 *Joy of Cooking*. All of these stories, however, date from long after the fact, and most rest on shaky or demonstrably incorrect memories. One frequent claim is that a little silk-tied booklet of mimeographed recipes used to be known in St. Louis, put together by or for Irma at the time of a cooking class she was supposed to have taught years before (no one knows when) for the Women's Alliance of the Waterman Avenue Unitarian Church. But some informants, including Marion, seem to have confused this with a separate mimeographed collection almost surely dating from *after* the first published *Joy* edition (see pages 97–98). No copy of an identifiably pre-1931 Rombauer recipe collection is now known to exist, although Put Rombauer reports that his mother got together a simple anthology of family favorites when he and Marion were leaving home and had Mazie Whyte type copies (since lost) for both of them.[2] He believes that this first little family collection became the seed of the 1931 cookbook. The chronology of this claim is problematic, since Marion did not leave home until *The Joy of Cooking* was in print and selling briskly. But it is possible that a small predecessor of the published book may come to light someday.

In any case, Irma let all her St. Louis connections (and many elsewhere) know of the new recipe project in 1930, and buttonholed people who looked like promising sources of material. Dorothy Merkel Alexander, a friend's granddaughter, much later recalled one of Irma's early recipe-gathering forays on the sublimely self-enclosed German South Side.

> One day Irma came by to visit and she said she was writing a cookbook and would Grandma Merkel [Mary Mueller Merkel, a boardinghouse operator and restaurateur with first-hand experience of what it took to survive widowhood] please give her some favorite recipes. Grandma and Irma talked. Grandma called in Aunt Clara and the three of them talked about what family recipes Irma might find useful. This was the Depression and people were trying desperately to make enough money to live. Writing and publishing a book could be costly. One did not dare fail and lose what little assets she had.
>
> When Irma came again some of the family recipes were ready for her, written out in Aunt Clara's careful Spencerian hand, in ink, on sheets of paper. . . .
>
> At the end of the planning, Grandma, despite her encouragement, said, "But, Irma, who will buy your book? All our friends *have* all those recipes."[3]

Mrs. Merkel was only one of many who advised or contributed. Irma could have counted on generous cooperation from Wednesday Club and church allies. Emma von Starkloff undoubtedly helped as well, and the Indianapolis contingent probably contributed some family dishes. Adele Becker donated some of her own recipes.

How far Irma had gotten with the project after her Michigan summer cannot be estimated, since no manuscript materials survive. But she returned that fall furiously geared up to the task of testing, culling, and finding more recipes. It was not a happy season for any of them. Her mother, who had spent part of the summer at a hotel in Bay View, had grown very frail, suffering now from a heart condition that left her few enjoyments beyond bridge in the evenings and baseball on the radio (she was a great Cardinals fan). The news from Indianapolis was sad. Irma's beloved uncle Louis Hollweg, who had suffered a stroke while the Rombauers were in Europe but recovered enough to carry on his business for several years, had weakened greatly in the last year and died in July of 1930. Despite her own shaky health, Emma had gone to Indianapolis to help Dada through the first shock, but Dada remained so shaken by the loss that in the end it seemed best for her to move in with Ina, the youngest of the Hollweg girls, now married to an Indianapolis businessman, Anton Vonnegut. Meanwhile, St. Louis was filled with what Marion (in one of the frequent letters to John in New York that furnish an invaluable window on Irma's work) called "tales of desperation" as one business failure succeeded another.

Marion, with the recuperative powers of youth, came back to John Burroughs School in September somewhat braced by the Mexican trip and a couple of weeks that she had managed to squeeze in with John in New York. After that, their letters were her lifeline. She was "Rom" to him no longer. Now she signed herself "Mary," the name that she had as a child somehow adopted for her family alone. Mary had been her name as daughter and sister, and would be her name as wife.

Given to cheery congeniality and great rushes of activity when all was going well, Marion discovered what serviceable props those commodities could be when it was not. "I barge about in an excess of enthusiasm about Mexico and a gladhanding that I trust disarms people," she wrote to John, uncannily prophesying the sort of behavior that would be her lifelong weapon against all adversity. She threw herself hectically into her teaching, her dance studies with Lisbeth Hoops-Ebers, the social doings of all the old South Side and Washington University crews. As far as she was concerned, the cookbook project served the same kind of purpose for Irma. She was surprised at her parent's single-mindedness as the endeavor went on. "Mother's hobby is beginning to embarrass me, she carries it to such lengths," Marion confided after the two of them had spent an evening with John's parents and the Becker family housemaid-cum-cook.[4]

John's New York adventure did not appear to have advanced the prospect of their marriage. His first job ended in wholesale company layoffs around October, and the Chelsea apartment arrangement had to be given up. His sister Jinny had come to the city a little after him and found a job in the theater department of the New School for Social Research. They managed to share an odd little flat in Greenwich Village while John scraped along with irregular freelance crumbs, enjoying the society of semibohemian New School types and a remarkable number of other exiled and broke St. Louisans (who, he told Marion, "multiply like the kings in *Macbeth*"). It was a settled thing that Marion would join him for Christmas—until some sort of rumor about their relationship surfaced in St. Louis and the trip had to be canceled. She was devastated, but no young woman of her upbringing could have openly acknowledged a premarital sexual liaison. She could only try to put together a better plan for the summer of 1931: to create a legitimate reason for being in New York on her own account. Accordingly, she signed up for a couple of courses at the Parsons School of Design, an affiliate of the New School.

According to the school records, both were noncredit courses that Marion failed to attend regularly.[5] But she did have a mission of sorts in New York. She had undertaken to test recipes for her mother, who appears to have virtually completed the main work on the cookbook by that time—though since the only evidence of her progress is the scattered mentions in Marion's and John's letters, few dates can be established with certainty.

While Marion tried out recipes in the kitchen of John and Jinny's tiny, tortuously angled apartment at Gay and Christopher Streets, Irma was doing some final testing of her own on the West Coast, where Put and Nita were her guinea pigs. Put had suddenly decided to seek a professional career after all—in Seattle, where he had settled permanently after some fruit-picking stints and more work on bridges there and in San Francisco. His idea was to sign up for some business college courses and use the credits in lieu of the usual requirements for admission to the University of Washington Law School. Where the money was to come from was quite unclear, but out of Irma's small means she promised to send him eighty dollars a month.[6] Buoyed by her Seattle trip and the prospect of closer ties with her prodigal son, she came back to St. Louis by way of Bay View, where Emma was staying with

Dada Hollweg and the Indianapolis regulars. From there Dada (apparently once more in spirits) dispatched a censorious German report on the whole St. Louis clan to her stepdaughter Julia—Irma's favorite cousin, now Mrs. Niles Chapman—in Indianapolis.

> I play bridge every evening whether I want to or not, but it is such a colossal pleasure for Tante Emma that I can't spoil it for her. Irma is amusing herself in her bohemian fashion, apparently quite satisfactorily, and sees everything she does on her mother's account in the rosiest colors. Putty has no job but is going to Business College! I think she is supporting him out of the little that she has. Marion is leading exactly the same kind of life in New York, and they all seem "blissfully happy" [in English], which is all that counts, of course.[7]

Dada's tut-tutting over these feckless relatives was premature. All would rapidly enter on a new period of hope and energy. Put proved to be in earnest about qualifying for law school. John opened the mail one August day to find a letter from a young architect in his old Cincinnati office who was now taking over the firm and, doubting his own ability to handle everything alone, offered John a partnership. On the strength of this news, he and Marion felt justified in announcing their engagement within their own families. Emma, writing to congratulate John, described Irma and Marion as "remarkably well," though "so very busy with School and Cookbook." In her view the trip to Seattle had done Irma much good: "she feels entirely different about Putty and his future now." Emma's hope for John and Marion, she told him, was that "I shall live long enough to see you happily united."[8]

Meanwhile, Irma's project had progressed from the 1930 fancy to an all-but-reality contained in a set of loose-leaf notebooks typed by Mazie Whyte. In the fall Irma, Mazie, and Marion set out to find a printer. Irma's friends had all heard of the project; Ethel Sprague, a mah-jongg- and bridge-playing acquaintance, suggested that she try the A. C. Clayton Printing Company. The president, Harold Hungerford, was Mrs. Sprague's nephew by marriage. The company was chiefly a printing business that did jobs for St. Louis shoe manufacturers (the more prestigious shoes were commonly sold with fancy printed wraps) and that had a contract printing labels for Listerine. Hungerford had never done a book, but he saw no reason not to accommodate a family friend.[9] The figure that he and Irma decided on, probably in late September, was about $3,000, or roughly half her cash assets.[10]

"How naive and straightforward was our approach to publishing!" Marion recalled in 1966.

> We simply called in a printer. I remember the Saturday morning he arrived, laden with washable cover fabrics, type and paper samples. In a few hours all decisions were made, and shortly afterwards we signed a contract for 3,000 copies, complete with mailing cartons and individualized stickers. Then came the new experience of galleys, proofreading and preparing an index.[11]

The contract in question has not survived, but probably it was only Irma who signed it. Mazie later stated in the course of a legal proceeding that it was she who prepared the index, and since she was responsible for several later ones, there is no reason to doubt her word.[12] Marion's main contributions were in the area of art and design. She had at least some slight knowledge of typefaces and page design, more than either of the others, and is likely to have steered Irma to the pleasant-looking format that was eventually adopted. She also, as she wrote to John, agreed to furnish another refinement: "chapter headings and a colorful jacket." The failure of their *Love of Three Oranges* project had not discouraged her from hope of finding some professional outlet for her abilities as an illustrator in her unusual medium. Though frantically occupied with filling in for the unwell Caroline Risque Janis and another art teacher at John Burroughs, she crowded in work on paper-cutout silhouettes for twenty chapter headings and the dust jacket (in addition to running errands to the printers) on weekends.

Irma worked herself into a great state at the first sight of the galley proofs. Indeed, she had been getting into a state at every moment of the book's homestretch. "Mother is tearful over the cook book, which appears in page form from the printers with countless mistakes—or so she thinks—in punctuation. I am really worried about her," Marion wrote to John in Cincinnati.

Mazie seems to have jumped happily and usefully into the business of dealing with the Clayton people. Marion reported that the typesetter who showed up at the Cabanne Avenue apartment to go over proofs "has fallen in love with her [Mazie] and Mother is hoping he will charge her less for corrections on that account." Mazie liked handling book logistics so well that she decided she had found a new métier, and confided to Marion that she planned to try her luck in the "printing" (i.e., production supervision) business, preferably teaming up with Marion as illustrator. In the end the trio (probably with a few commandeered friends) did a remarkably good job of proofreading the galleys through October and part of November—though not good enough to catch "2 cups baking powder" in a doughnut recipe that (along with a couple of other trifling errors) the collaborators had to correct laboriously by hand.[13] Irma arranged to copyright the work in her name, a piece of elementary prudence that they all would have cause to recall with bitterness in years to come.

Marion duly finished the chapter headings to Irma's satisfaction. She designed a label for the cardboard wrappers that mail-order copies were to be sent in. She designed the lettering and layout for the book jacket and chose the color scheme: sprightly green, blue, and black on an off-white background, with a stylized haloed figure standing over a heavily tusked monster, brandishing weapons that on second glance proved to be a broom and cooking pot. (This was the patron saint of cooks, Saint Martha of Bethany, the sister of Mary and Lazarus and in southern French legend the vanquisher of a sea monster called the Tarasque.)

Late in November the Clayton Company cleared its presses for a weekend run and delivered Irma's 3,000 copies to Cabanne Avenue. The date of publication listed by the U.S. Copyright Office is November 30, 1931, but copies were apparently on hand before that. (A December 4 article in the *St. Louis Star* mentions that the book is "barely two weeks old.")[14] The title was somewhat offbeat, suggesting the sort of perky cheerleading that had invaded the homemaking literature as servants had departed: *The Joy of Cooking: A Compilation of Reliable Recipes with a Casual Culinary Chat.* Many friends had already ordered copies, which Marion set out to deliver by hand (local children would later be enlisted for this service). The cardboard mailing wrappers arrived a day or two after the books.

One initial reaction survives, a letter written in German to "Liebe gute Irma" from Dada Hollweg, a woman not easy to please and previously a little snide about an occupation that she had seen as a bohemian diversion. The new author must have taken immense pleasure in her aunt's assessment of the cookbook as "marvellously attractive" and "artistically realized."

The execution of the whole book is original in the highest degree and would not find its equal in the whole world. I had no idea how comprehensive it would turn out to be. No wonder it cost you so much trouble and work!—but success will be the crown of your labors, and from now on you will be able to rest on laurels, since I am sure that you will enter now into a new literary sphere where you have long belonged.[15]

John Becker came down for Thanksgiving and undertook to deliver copies to Cincinnati connections and sound out a local women's exchange about selling the book on consignment. He sent Marion a rapid calculation of the probable local retail price, figuring in the sum per copy that each party ought to receive:

Publisher	$ .85
Irma	$1.17½
Other ladies i.e., the exchange	$ .22½
	$2.25[16]

It is a reasonable guess that the initial price in St. Louis was about the same. (Later it would be around $3.00—appreciably higher than the $2.50 price of Fannie Farmer or *The Settlement Cook Book* in the early thirties, but apparently no more than Irma had found the market would bear.)

From the start there was a fine response, aided at first by Irma's zeal in making all her friends sign up for copies. "Orders are coming in pretty fast, remarkably so, I think, considering that no one has seen the book," Marion wrote as the first copies ("better looking than I anticipated") arrived. "Cook book orders are swell," she mentioned a week or so later, and shortly after that, "The cook book continues to flourish. . . . I am designing a box cover and after Xmas [Mother] is going to go after the gift shop trade rather than the booksellers. It's an ideal gift and I think we'll just push it as that." Over Thanksgiving Irma had summed up the situation in a letter to her cousin Julia Chapman in Indianapolis: "I am very busy as I am enjoying a wild sale of the cookbook. So far every day has brought from ten to twenty orders and I *hope* that will keep up for a while. So far I have handled the St. Louis end myself but presently I shall put the book in various shops. . . . Sorry I cannot visit now. Too busy and too poor. I hope for better things!"[17]

She hoped with justice. All of the restless, scattershot, unschooled abilities she had previously fired into club politicking or milk-fund drives had suddenly come together in a positive genius for publicity and promotion. She had always had the ability to captivate complete strangers. Now she wrote to dozens of local gift-shop owners and book-sellers, or walked into their stores and charmed the living daylights out of them. She elicited names from friends in other cities and suggested her book at various women's exchanges. She talked to department-store buyers—Marion's old contacts were numerous and helpful—and called up any newspaper acquaintance she could think of. She persuaded Marion's old Derby chaperone Marguerite Martyn to devote more than three columns of a *Post-Dispatch* society page (just at the beginning of the Christmas season) to a feature article on her and the book headed "A Talented Hostess Writes a Cookbook."[18] She wangled another piece in the *St. Louis Star* loudly hailing her as living proof that "the activities of women in public work" were indeed compatible with dazzling mastery of home-front duties.[19] She remembered little gallery-owners and knickknack-sellers in the Michigan summer communities, and approached them with the shrewd guess that copies sold there had a good chance of finding their way anyplace in the country.

The sight of her mother's mounting energy was a relief to Marion, who knew that her own approaching marriage would leave Irma the solitary occupant of a household for the first time in her life. She and John had formally announced their engagement at the end of December. Some time before that she had broken her long silence to Ernst Kropp to send him the news. She received in reply his best wishes and a fervent exhortation to apply her teaching so as "to initiate the young people into living contemporary *Form*."[20] They never heard from each other again. Within a year *Die Form*, the Deutscher Werkbund–sponsored magazine of design and contemporary arts that she had discovered and subscribed to through him, would be on its way to becoming a vehicle of National Socialist propaganda, staffed by an entirely different crew, while the Werkbunders were driven into ignominy or exile.

Emma von Starkloff was not granted her wish to see Marion and John married. She died of heart disease on March 31, 1932, at the age of eighty-three. Luckily Irma had an object to focus on, and Marion had not only her teaching but the prospect of a new life in Cincinnati. But in the spring of 1932 John seems to have doubted that they could well afford to marry even now. He and his partner, Hubert Garriott, had gotten off to a cautious rather than brilliant start (their first commission after John's arrival turned out to be a stable for a polo club, hardly his idea of socially relevant architecture). For John and Marion to keep the pot boiling, she would have to work as well. Her mother's example of having a baby within ten months of the wedding was not an option for her. She ended up with another teaching position, though a tame one by comparison with her experience at the resolutely experimental John Burroughs. Her new employer, Hillsdale School, was far too sedate and society-oriented for Marion's taste.

With as brave hope as a woman of twenty-nine and a man of thirty could muster in those dark times, John and Marion were married on June 18, 1932. To the friends who witnessed the ceremony that hot, muggy Saturday afternoon they were the image of a briskly modern young couple. Four of Marion's John Burroughs students had volunteered to decorate the site of the ceremony—Phil and Adele Becker's living room in their Waterman Avenue apartment building, the next-door twin of the one Marion and Irma had left after Edgar's death. Irma, of course, had cooked or supervised all the food, including the tiered wedding cake made from a family recipe known to all Kuhlmann and von Starkloff connections as the invariable family almond torte. John's uncle William Dee Becker—the same William Dietrich Becker who had changed his name during the war, now a city court judge—read the marriage service and, Marion remembered, "radiated a charm, assurance of the good things in life and an inspiring confidence that great things lay ahead of us."[21]

After an evening reception the young couple went back to the Cabanne Avenue apartment for the night (Irma had arranged to stay with a friend). They set out the next morning—not on a honeymoon, which was beyond their touch, but back to John's struggling practice in Cincinnati. They crossed the river in Marion's Model A Ford and drove through the flat fertile fields of Illinois, then the narrow, rugged wooded hills of Indiana beyond Vincennes, down through the gorge of Aurora to the Ohio River, and on to a sublet apartment in the suburb of Wyoming. The home they were furnishing "after the modernistic mode," in the Post-Dispatch's lofty phrase, would not be available until after the summer.[22] Cincinnati society had not been prepared for the extreme plainness of John Becker's bride, but as one of the friends who met her in those days later observed, when you had been five minutes in her company, she was not at all plain.[23] Nonetheless, Irma never ceased wondering aloud what a man as handsome as John had ever seen in her uncomely daughter.[24]

If Marion had any qualms about leaving a widowed parent to grieve over the empty nest, they were baseless. Irma had in effect embarked on motherhood all over again. She did not lament the absence of her flesh-and-blood children, though she would have loved to have Put closer and sometimes made noises about moving to Seattle, a city she had loved at first sight. By the time Marion was gone her mother's attention was furiously occupied with a new goal—to nourish her little *Joy of Cooking* toward a mature incarnation as a commercially published book. It is even possible that the idea of a refurbished *Joy* had struck her by the time the first one was in print.

By the summer of 1932 Irma had made good progress toward selling her 3,000 copies. (Much later the very elderly Mazie stated in a court deposition that Irma's entire stock had sold out in six months, but enough other details of her recollections are manifestly mistaken to make this claim doubtful.)[25] She saw that readers cherished her book not just out of enjoyment but out of a sort of devotion seldom reserved for cookbooks. "It does not insult my intelligence," Marguerite Martyn had written in her 1931 article. An Indiana admirer, Benjamin W. Douglass, let May Lamberton Becker of the *Saturday Review* know that it was "unusual."[26] Irma had the presence of mind not just to think of having the original text reissued or filled out a bit but to plan on revising it in some drastically different manner. At some point in 1932 she hit on the idea that would form the basis of her appeal to publishers: a new way of writing recipes.

This real stroke of originality is one of the first hints of Irma Rombauer's sheer determination to succeed at her strangely chosen career. It cannot have looked like a career to anyone else at this point. Even Marion probably thought of her mother's labors as a project to occupy a new loneliness, not—as Dada Hollweg had suggested—as the passport to a deserved literary sphere. Irma's brainstorm about presenting recipes was not impressive-looking in its first stages, and may not have struck anyone else as a masterstroke.

The idea was simply to eliminate the list of ingredients usually placed before the directions (a convention that she had followed in the first 1931 *Joy*) and find a way of setting off each ingredient to the eye as it was introduced. The result, as she was presenting it to publishers between 1932 and 1935, looked like this:

GOLD CUP CAKES

About 12 two-inch cakes
An excellent recipe for using 4 odd egg yolks

Sift – – – – – – – – – – –	1/2 cup sugar
Beat until soft – – – – – –	1/4 cup butter
Add the sugar gradually	
Blend these ingredients	
until creamy	
Add – – – – – – – – – –	grated rind of
	1 orange or lemon
Beat in one at a time – – –	4 egg yolks
Add – – – – – – – – – –	1/2 teasp. vanilla
Sift before measuring – –	7/8 cup flour
	(1 cup less 2 tablsp.)
Resift with – – – – – – –	1 teasp. Bak. powd.
Add the sifted ingredients	
to the batter mixture in	
three parts alternating with	
thirds of – – – – – – – – –	1/4 cup milk
Stir in – – – – – – – – –	1/4 cup currants
	(optional)
Bake the cakes in	
greased muffin tins	
in a moderate oven, 375°	
Dust them with – – – – –	powdered sugar
or	
spread them with – – – – –	orange icing
	or other icing [27]

The example is from an undated mimeographed collection of Irma's recipes that her younger friend Elizabeth Goltermann found many decades later and had photocopied for Marion. All of the eighty-one recipes are cast in this format: ingredients given a right-hand column to themselves in an order corresponding to the directions on the left-hand side. Since the small booklet bore the name of the Women's Alliance of the Waterman Avenue Church of the Unity, Marion and Miss Goltermann assumed that it must have been the record of a cooking class that Irma was supposed to have taught there at an unknown date. The error of the assumption becomes plain at a closer look. That it was actually a sampling of recipes assembled after the 1931 *Joy of Cooking* and before the first commercial edition is easy enough to see from the title—"Unusual and Unpublished Recipes, by Irma S. Rombauer" ("unpublished" almost surely implies the existence of an earlier *published* book)—and the fact that though almost none of the recipes is in the 1931 *Joy*, they are all in the version she finally persuaded a publisher to issue in 1936.

As initially conceived by Irma and typed (undoubtedly) by Mazie Whyte, the innovation is primitive-looking. But its possibilities were eventually seen by a publisher. Its great advantage was that it enabled a recipe to get right down to the flow of the thing without the artificial dramatis-personae listing that conventionally occupies the space between the recipe title and the opening sentence of the directions in cookbooks based on the Fannie Farmer model (see pages 105–106). It was a rethinking of fundamentals remarkable for a woman who had paid no professional attention to recipes until she was fifty-three years old.

In 1932 Irma began to send around inquiries to commercial publishers. Bill Finneran, the sales manager who would energetically promote her book for many years, believed that Adolph Kroch, the celebrated Chicago bookseller, gave her her initial encouragement to approach publishers after his attention had been called to the book through some local orders, and that he actually tried to put her in touch with Simon and Schuster in New York.[28] Marion, in an account published in 1966, suggests that it was Irma who went to Kroch looking for advice.[29] In any case, her proposal was rejected wherever she took it, over a period of several years.

She kept no record of how many people she submitted her idea to. Some of her family were aware of her unavailing efforts, others apparently not. But her struggle and early disappointment came to the ears of Dada and the cousins in Indianapolis. The family there knew that there was a perfectly good publisher in town, the Bobbs-Merrill Company. They further knew that Anton and Ina Vonnegut (with whom Dada had lived since her husband's death in 1930) were socially acquainted with an officer of the firm, D. Laurance Chambers. Ina was accordingly delegated to invite Irma to a dinner and bridge party at their home, probably in the summer of 1932.[30]

The great scheme went off as planned, and in the course of the evening Chambers consented to have a look at his hostess's cousin's cookbook and the manuscript material for her projected revision. The course of the Bobbs-Merrill deliberations is at least partially preserved in the collection of the Lilly Library at Indiana University in Bloomington. Of course it was not divulged to Irma. But the result was clear enough: In late February of 1933, after months of suspense, Laurance Chambers returned Irma's manuscript with a polite letter of rejection.[31]

Put Rombauer insists that it was Bobbs-Merrill that pursued Irma, a theory that cannot be ruled out but does not fit easily with other known facts. What he is sure he remembers is hearing his mother describe how she opened her door in St. Louis one morning, with her hair in curlers, to be greeted by a trio of Bobbs-Merrill representatives announcing that they planned to make her book a competitor to Fannie Farmer, and seeing her at work furiously testing recipes for a Bobbs-Merrill–sanctioned project during a visit to Seattle.[32] But in fact she made several Seattle visits in the 1930s at times when she might have been testing recipes for one project or another, and nothing clearly proves that 1932—the year in which she first submitted *The Joy of Cooking*, and certainly a year when she did travel to Seattle for the summer—saw her working with any definite encouragement from Bobbs-Merrill on the score of a *Joy* revision. Unless the sales department actively aroused her hopes at first (something that Chambers is not likely to have countenanced) before the editors rejected the book, it is most probable that the enthusiastic-cheerleading visit by Bobbs-Merrill salesmen was an unrelated later event (February 2, 1936) and that Put's memory conflated a few different summers when Irma was testing recipes in Seattle. The only fact that is beyond dispute is that as of February 1933, the idea of coming to terms with Bobbs-Merrill seemed to have gone up in smoke along with other attempts to find a commercial publisher.

In later years Irma cheerfully gave all sorts of accounts of how her book had come to be, and sometimes sent reporters away with the idea that publishers had begged her for the privilege of issuing *The Joy of Cooking*—in vain, since she refused to let anyone touch it until she had revised it to her own satisfaction.[33] At the time, however, she was bitterly frustrated by her failure. Her modest success with the self-published 1931 *Joy of Cooking* had seemed to prove her talent for moving mountains. In fact she had moved only a tiny hummock. She was apparently just where she would have been if she had never undertaken her impetuous project: alone, unemployed, and broke. When she did achieve publication, she would confide to her editors that the prolonged shock to her early hopes had left her almost too numb to feel any pleasure in the accomplishment. Perhaps in those years she thought of Emma von Starkloff's initial comment on the little 1931 *Joy of Cooking*. During the first flush of sales Irma had breezily described her mother's reaction for Julia Chapman's benefit:

> The night she saw the cook-book for the first time she couldn't sleep. Marion asked why and Gran said, "Because it was so much better than I expected." "But Gran," Marion said, "what *did* you expect—Mother and I put forth our best effort." "Oh yes, child," she said, "but best efforts so seldom amount to anything."[34]

PART II

5

Chronicles of Cookery 1

Irma Rombauer and Marion Becker belong to the company of cookbook writers who, unlike the James Beards or Julia Childs of the field, essentially spent their professional lives working on a single book. This accident enables us to construct at least a partial "biography" of the book itself, both as a lively (if small) chapter in modern American publishing history and as a culinary record. Strange to say, few cookbooks have been deeply investigated from either point of view. But in truth they have ancestries, nourishing milieus, and stages of growth as crucial as those of flesh-and-blood biographical subjects.

Looking at cookbooks without this sort of reconstructive context can leave observers in a fog of misconceptions about "heirloom recipes" and the golden age when Grandmother ruled the kitchen. To understand Irma and the 1931 *Joy of Cooking* rightly we must set aside such notions. The real American heirloom recipes of the time—the common culinary accomplishments of a few generations back—will often turn out to be stuff that leaders of advanced taste now deplore. They may be mother lodes of condensed milk, cherry Jell-O, canned vegetables in thick white sauce, processed cheese, condensed tomato soup, canned fruit cocktail, or spaghetti cooked to the consistency of baby cereal.

Plastering retrospective snobberies over such foods because they are not chic today is purely silly. The fact is that all cultures form their own accommodation with the resources that their agriculture and technology make available to them. The attitudes that some of our grandmothers or great-grandmothers held toward the products of American know-how precisely parallel the attitudes of modern gourmetdom toward "boutique" olive oils or "artisanal" cheeses from keepers of the simple peasant heritage in Tuscany. Just as uncannily matched are the absorption of cookery writers then and now in a view of food basically shaped by other cookery writers, and the pleasure that a large readership takes in searching out what the authorities say is good. The difference is that the technology and economic trends of our day make quasi-peasant cheeses available almost exclusively to a small, affluent subculture, whereas canned fruit or chicken appeared sixty or ninety years ago to be an edible extension of modern democracy in action.

Many levels of taste—some suited to 1990s culinary marching orders, some quite irreconcilable—cheerfully coexist in Irma's 1931 book. One clue to its value as a record of cooking is that it was written with no thought of posterity. If it had been planned to represent what today's pundits think of as fine ancestral American traditions, it would have been like the old joke about the doctor proclaiming, "Gee, I just delivered Abraham Lincoln." Unsystematic lay documents like this preserve intricate, telling pictures that usually get smoothed over and blurred in professional cookbooks and women's magazines. They show accelerating or slightly dimming fashions, traditions displaced or still holding their own, ground gained by new products or equipment, arrays of preferences and opinions that speak volumes about the kitchen amateurs who held them. Not incidentally, they reveal dramatic shifts over time in people's ideas of what cookbooks or recipes are *for*. In Irma Rombauer's own lifetime the general raison d'être of household instruction had undergone profound changes, themselves the sequel to equally major changes during the lives of her mother and grandmother.

A convenient vantage point on some of those changes is furnished by two documents of 1896, when Irma von Starkloff, blithely ignorant of cooking, was leading the life of an eligible young society ornament recently returned from Europe. Our first exhibit is a recipe from one of Roderick and Augusta Rombauer's neighbors in the Lafayette Park vicinity of St. Louis at the time of the 1896 tornado witnessed by Edgar. It was published in a little string-tied compilation of recipes got up later that year by the ladies of the Lafayette Park Presbyterian congregation to raise money for rebuilding their demolished church:

BROILED OYSTERS.

Butter the size of a hickory nut in a hot skillet;
when browned, put oysters and liquor in and heat
thoroughly; arrange the oysters on hot buttered toast;
pour the liquid over them; season to taste.

MRS. WHERRITT.[1]

Miss Fannie Merritt Farmer, whose *Boston Cooking-School Cook Book* was published in the same year, went about cooking in quite another spirit. Probably she would have pointed out to Mrs. Wherritt that her recipe was really a version of panned (not broiled) oysters. Her own formula reads as follows:

Broiled Oysters.

1 pint selected oysters.   ¼ cup melted butter.
⅔ cup seasoned cracker crumbs.

Clean oysters and dry between towels. Lift with
plated fork by the tough muscle and dip in butter,
then in cracker crumbs which have been seasoned
with salt and pepper. Place in a buttered wire broiler
and broil over a clear fire until juices flow, turning
while broiling. Serve with or without Maître d'Hôtel
Butter.[2]

The remarkable thing about the unknown Mrs. Wherritt's recipe is how effortlessly it gets to the point. Anyone who knows how to cook can see the whole thing in a flash from her few words. Mrs. Wherritt clearly knew but found it unnecessary to state just how much butter she needed for how many oysters and when the skillet was hot enough, what the butter looked and smelled like at the right moment to add the oysters, just how soon the liquid should heat and begin to evaporate. Almost certainly, she had enough help in the buttered-toast department not to have to rush about the kitchen letting the oysters turn to leather. Beyond a doubt, she expected anyone reading her recipe to pick up on its rapid-fire cues like a skilled driver in traffic.

Just as clearly, Fannie Farmer's recipe tries to reproduce the outlines of a formal learning session for people who do not know how to cook. Its purpose is to impose the appearance of order on information either wholly unfamiliar to or only half grasped by the recipient. Its intended user would only be confused by swift cues. At the time, enlightened contemporaries would proudly have pointed to its exact measurements as proof that cooking had now become "modern" and "scientific." Its sentences brusquely marshaled the English language into an impersonal authority meant to conduct the recipe follower through sequential maneuvers with no distractions. Exactly like one of Miss Farmer's students at the Boston Cooking School in the 1890s, the housewife making her "Broiled Oysters" proceeded by executing one small subcommand at a time in an undeviating order. Even today, writers of culinary advice tend to hail the Farmer method as a self-evident improvement over the approach of a Mrs. Wherritt. In truth, it is an improvement only in a society where cookbooks are replacing cooking.

Contrary to popular misconception, more cookbooks filled with more precise formulas do not mean more cooking skills diffused throughout the land. Learning to cook from written recipes always has been an inefficient process at best. It takes only a minute's reflection to understand that the business of cooking predated the printed word by millennia. The two never have formed an especially satisfactory marriage. That we should expect them to is a measure of how far gone Americans now are in their need for remedial instruction to offset a dwindling (or at this point barely vestigial) knowledge of cooking. Cookbooks are the feeblest of substitutes for the true spurs to culinary understanding, which are long hours spent daily in handling the tools of the trade and constant reinforcement from other people engaged in the same work on the same spot. These irreplaceable teachers were well on their way out when Miss Farmer wrote.

Picture to yourself the wealthy bourgeois kitchen of 1845, when Irma's grandmother, Wilhelmine Minlos of Lübeck, married Carl Bernhard Kuhlmann and went to live in the small north German town of Eutin. Most of its crucial features would have been shared by English or American kitchens of the same period at all levels between moderate poverty and great wealth. It is a largish, wide, spread-out room by our kitchen standards. It would keep a single person running constant marathons in order to begin and complete even a single dish—but it is not ordinarily occupied by a single person. To get the day's meals on the table takes several people's hard physical efforts. The cook, an important live-in employee of the household, has one or two assistants (more in a large aristocratic home). The mistress herself, unless she is of extremely exalted rank, pitches in at especially busy times. So do any young daughters of the house, and probably the grandmother.

At a glance, the use of space and womanpower is quite foreign to us. There are no wall fixtures, built-in storage cabinets, or built-in work surfaces. The furniture consists of movable tables and dressers or hutches. The space has no structure except that conferred by the way the women have decided to break up the work. The only object approaching a fixture is a cast-iron stove that when lit can make the heat in that part of the room as brutal as an industrial foundry. Of course no perishable (and not much nonperishable) food can be kept any closer to it than the adjacent small room that is pantry or larder. The kitchen equipment, which would not fill much more than a shelf and a drawer in a modern American kitchen, probably includes more handmade than factory-made tools and cooking pans, though this will change drastically in a few years. There are at most a couple of built-in shelves or a few hanging hooks in the kitchen, unless it is quite elaborate. Food waiting for the cook's or scullery maid's attention is probably just sitting on the floor until someone can get to it.

What we see is an artisan's workshop operating by a personnel-centered concept of organization. People are sitting or standing in several parts of the room engaged in different parts of the effort, which is arduous even with skilled teamwork. Someone, or several people, must be there throughout the day. Most likely a manservant has lugged in the firewood or coal and a few buckets of water that will do for rinsing food to be cooked and for washing up after the cooking. By the united powers of the women, every ingredient must be not only cooked (with someone building the fire, then constantly judging and adjusting the heat without benefit of knobs or pushbuttons) but got ready to be cooked.

If anything is to be in puréed or fine-textured form, someone must make it so by manually forcing it through a sieve, pounding it in a mortar, or (hand meat grinders having yet to be invented) chopping it with a knife. Someone must pluck, cleanly disembowel, and behead poultry; scale and gut fish; rinse or scrub vegetables (which commonly arrive with the dirt of the garden and perhaps a few snails still clinging to them); pick bits of dirt and stone out of dried peas and beans; boil the hard loaf sugar to clarify it of scummy impurities and often insects;

crush or pound most spices; shell every nut; pick the stones from every raisin or currant (there are no asexual grape hybrids); and even blanch rice in boiling water—by the instructions of Henriette Davidis's *Praktisches Kochbuch*, published the year before Wilhelmine Kuhlmann's marriage—so that it will not curdle pudding-milk.[3]

Aside from the way such chores are flexibly distributed among different people at several scattered points of the available space, what is most striking about this kitchen to a time traveler from a century and a half later is that no cookbook is in sight. In fact, these two circumstances are related. Each woman in the room has learned (or, in the case of children, is in the process of learning) the rudiments of cooking just as any man of the period on a small farm or in an artisan's shop learns his job: by *doing,* in the company of older hands. The mistress (who surely can read) may perhaps consult a cookbook from time to time as a guide to planning the activity of the servants (who, if not illiterate, work quite independently of the written word). But what she expects to find there is not a detailed blueprint but a shorthand summary, or maybe a handful of cues to jog her memory on what she understands already. Painstaking written instruction would serve little purpose. It is the shared momentum of a collegial workshop and the unrelenting daily demands of the work itself that, in the world of 1845, frame a woman's education in household duties while leaving her little time or opportunity for other sorts of learning. If women were not glued to the kitchen and the sewing basket, the family would not eat or wear clothes.

Skipping across a few generations to a comparable American kitchen of the year in which *The Joy of Cooking* was published, we find a room based on drastically different perceptions of both human and spatial factors. It is true that "comparable" may be a slippery term, since the United States in 1931 is a vastly more heterogeneous society than either the United States or Germany in 1845 and a motley array of kitchen models may variously hold sway in different urban or rural areas. But if we choose the kitchen of a fairly well-off middle-class urban (or suburban) family who are following the new twentieth-century consumerist dream, we see at once that it cannot possibly be any sort of collegial workshop.

The new kitchen, as planned by time-and-motion experts and pioneered by appliance and utility companies in the first decades of the century, is a highly concentrated space perhaps half or a third the size of its 1845 predecessor. Anyone who still lives with a large kitchen in

1931 must by now be used to hearing that it is an inefficient relic of the past.[4] Most likely the fashionable kitchen is U- or L-shaped, to permit several built-in components (set directly against the walls) to face each other across the space of a few feet or to be closely placed at right angles to each other. Few or none of the larger furnishings are movable. Wall-mounted shelves and cabinets (also wall-mounted) of shelves and drawers hold the nonperishable food and most utensils. The higher ones may extend to the ceiling; the lower ones reach from the floor to not quite waist height, and one of these latter is roofed with a work surface or "countertop." The main work surface, however, may still be a movable table—a porcelain- or zinc-topped one, in families that can afford something better than oilcloth.

Everything is carefully aligned with regard to the two fixtures that govern the room: a sink with running water and a gas or electric stove. Both of these are also coated with easy-to-clean porcelain or zinc in up-to-date households, and the stove has the additional virtue—a function of the sheet-metal housing and insulated construction that are rapidly winning out over cast-iron stoves—of throwing very little heat from its efficiently contained heating elements into surrounding space. Thus it should ideally be able to stand right next to the storage chest for perishable food: an icebox or perhaps a mechanical refrigerator (both usually called "refrigerators"). The latter has not yet reached the vast majority of middle-class households, though Phil and Adele Becker (Marion's future parents-in-law) acquired a Norge model in 1930. But iceboxes in 1931 are by no means primitive. They, too, have benefited from great advances in the technology of heat insulation. The more expensive ones can maintain a 40°F interior temperature for several days even when situated barely at arm's length from the stove. And "at arm's length" is the operative principle in this kitchen. It has been designed so that a person standing at stove, sink, or countertop can reach out and pick up something in any part of the room without moving more than a few steps.

A room like this is essentially meant to plan your activity for you. Or, to put the matter differently, the streamlined kitchen of 1931 eliminates the main principle of culinary organization in the older household—deciding who among a small team of people in an otherwise undifferentiated space does what—and itself takes over the business of organizing all activities for one person who, whether maid or mistress, is expected to do everything. Three or four people working at once in such a room will fall all over each other, and even two may get in each other's way. The new kitchen achieves what it is meant to achieve when one woman works in it alone—and finishes in time to go do other things elsewhere. Indeed, it can be said to possess a certain self-emptying function, since one of its main purposes is to get her out of its confines as speedily as possible.

The 1931 kitchen embodies its own powerful assumptions about its chief user's knowledge and how she is to acquire it. At least one or two cookbooks, and probably more, sit on a shelf in permanent residence. They may be supplemented with a file of handwritten recipes on index cards, which the experts recommend instead of unsystematic jottings. The woman who runs or is run by this kitchen would be in trouble without such word-by-word guidance. Her mastery of cooking skills lies hardly at all in her fingers and brain; it consists mostly of the ability to read a manual. She has never been surrounded on a daily basis by the example of live instructors splitting up the meal making; at an age when her grandmother was considered old enough to help in the kitchen for several hours a day, she was spending most of the day in school. Nor has anyone ever expected her to devote the time to kitchen activities that is necessary to transform even the best live tutelage (let alone words on a page) into trained instinct. What she learns must be mostly learned in isolation in her one-person kitchen and applied through brief, self-contained episodes of activity that are all any reasonable observer could ask of her. After all, she has the rest of the house to take care of and perhaps a round of club and civic interests to rush off to like an Irma Rombauer.

The situation we have just described in 1931 is in many ways an informational void—often as much of a void for a servant charged with making meals as for a homemaker with no hired help. What developed to fill the void was written instruction. (There was actual classroom instruction as well, actively promoted by various public authorities from the 1870s on, but it could not reach as large and disparate an audience as the printed word.) Between the collegial 1845 kitchen with its personnel-centered operation and the highly structured 1931 space with its near absence of people lay many demographic dislocations and imperfect reorderings. As contributions to a vacuum of knowledge that finally became the accepted state of affairs, these developments provided a seldom examined stimulus to the flowering of modern cookbooks.

The crux of the matter is that the old space/womanpower equation fell apart during the nineteenth century long before the technological means existed to devise a new one. Inspired by the democratic promise that no one need remain a servant for life, the domestic help needed to get even a small family's meals on the table every day decamped to independent employment in great waves throughout the century. (The process was far slower in England and Europe, which explains some divergent attitudes toward cooking that developed on opposite sides of the Atlantic.) The size of the available kitchen workforce shrank, while kitchens themselves remained large in the absence of the one element that could have enabled them to be built more compactly: differentiated control of temperature for food storage and the orbit of the stove.

The built-in wrongness of the situation was not lost on the women who struggled with it. In itself, the gap between the demands of domestic work and the extant resources that could be applied to those demands gave a mighty shove to the business of dispensing household advice. As early as 1841 (by which time the "servant problem" was well advanced in the United States) the remarkable Catherine Beecher was wrestling (in her *Treatise on Domestic Economy*) with the limitations of domestic work space. By 1869 she and her sister Harriet Beecher Stowe, as coauthors of *The American Woman's Home*, were publishing actual diagrams of kitchens based on centralized, focused use of space.[5] But such suggestions could not for the moment be realized. Neither could most of the ideas offered nearly twenty years later by the author of *Quick Cooking: A Book of Culinary Heresies* (a volume once owned by the great feminist Lucy Stone). Styling herself "One of the Heretics," the clearly exasperated Flora Haines Loughead repeated the Beechers' advice to think of a steamship galley as the model of kitchen efficiency, devised dozens of recipes meant to take from ten minutes to an hour to complete, advised beleaguered home cooks to buy preserves from farmers' wives—"paying only a reasonable price for the labor expended"[6]—rather than try to put up their own, and exhorted women to get American business in on the act:

> It would require slight effort to induce dealers and manufacturers to take upon themselves for an almost inappreciable charge, many little tasks which now come upon our cooks. Whenever a steady demand arises for shelled peas, string beans, and Lima beans ready for the pot, fish ready cleaned, fowls thoroughly cleaned and trussed for the oven, our dealers will hasten to supply it.[7]

A few of Mrs. Loughead's heretical wishes would come true through the wizardry of commercial canning, but none of her hopes would soon be realized in exactly the form she envisioned. The changes that came were important but uncoordinated; extraordinary advances in food technology and household conveniences multiplied throughout the nineteenth century and into the first years of the twentieth without being able to make a dent in the central domestic labor crisis that faced all families except the very wealthiest. Many of these developments stand significantly lessened the burden of particular tasks. But insofar as they furthered the isolation of women trying to get meals in the home, they helped replace dependence on one's own experience and knowledge with dependence on what some expert had written.

At one end of the spectrum of household improvements were those brought by public engineering achievements such as municipal water systems serving private homes. This particular blessing generally happened in several stages, the early ones involving water and the later ones clean water. St. Louis, which had boasted some sort of waterworks since the 1830s, was not able to put in a reliable purification system until 1904, when the city launched a mighty rush job on a chemical clarifying works to improve the cosmetics of an illuminated cascade in time for the opening of the World's Fair. Before that, natives and visitors alike had regarded the St. Louis water supply with a certain awe.

"Every tumbler of it holds an acre of land in solution," Mark Twain observed in 1883. "I got this fact from the Bishop of the diocese. If you will let your glass stand half an hour you can separate the water from the land as easy as Genesis, and then you will find them both good—the one to eat, the other to drink."[8] Mayor Rolla Wells, in whose administration the purification plant was built, lyrically summed up the effect of the old water in his autobiography: "The clouds of a somber day had been compressed, as it were, with stray soils of many Northern, Eastern, and Western States into a muddy pack which was neither moisture nor solid, and this was our drink. We washed with it, we cooked with it, and survived of it, and, in a sense, were proud of it."[9] Not a St. Louisan of those times but would have known by firsthand conviction that the elixir in question was pure Mississippi River. But such everyday connoisseurship was vanishing fast in most cities by the mid-1890s, when someone asked Irma's cousin Julia Hollweg where Indianapolis water came from and she replied, "Out of a faucet."[10] This durable family story (which Marion passed on in the

1962 *Joy of Cooking*) eloquently testifies to one cost of more efficient communally applied technology: the growing isolation of urban Americans from the simplest facts of material life.

The same sort of gap between fact and popular understanding was becoming visible in other arenas of modern society. A proliferation of new foods overtook American kitchens after the Civil War. Some, as we shall see, were old foods in more convenient form. Many, however, were barely known or entirely unfamiliar products brought to the American table by a dawning global agribusiness dominated by U.S. enterprise. As modern industrial capitalism in a period of tremendous international expansion began transforming huge tracts of Latin America and Hawaii into early versions of the factory farm, the contents of city (and sometimes country) grocery shelves were also transformed. Foods once restricted in distribution became familiar, a development also hastened by the commanding growth of California agriculture and the advent of intensive plant breeding research in the last decades of the nineteenth century. The U.S. Department of Agriculture, ceaselessly experimenting with still more exotic products that might profitably be grown on domestic soil, from time to time in the first decades of the new century reported on the culinary possibilities of tropical fruits and root vegetables (some of which the United Fruit Company had also looked into in its foreign fiefdoms).

For virtually all American consumers from top to bottom of the social scale, these ventures heralded the advent of foods they had seldom or never heard of. Markets regularly began to offer items with no connection to anything most people had ever seen growing on a farm or in a home garden. Of course, people's opportunities to see even the most ordinary foods growing anywhere were simultaneously shrinking with the inexorable shift of population from the land into the cities. What was egregiously true of the new products became less conspicuously true of old ones as well: people needed to be told what they were and how to cook them. A city shopper who in 1860 had rarely seen any fruit except local ones in season might by 1890 encounter a pineapple or coconut, neither exactly a self-explanatory object. She (or he) would also grow steadily less able to measure even grapes or peaches against local standards, since a larger and larger proportion of them would no longer be grown locally after the turn of the century.

The old cooks had bought all but a few items of produce at a fairly close remove from their places of origin and knew all ingredients in terms of logical work processes. With the distancing of more and more consumers from their food supply came, in effect, a shift from lifelong familiarity with a language to dependence on the advice of translators—the cookbook writers, who reported alike on the commonplace and the exotic. The industrious Sarah Tyson Rorer of Philadelphia, whom Irma Rombauer might or might not have seen conducting cooking demonstrations at the St. Louis World's Fair in 1904, worked into the pages of the 1898 *Mrs. Rorer's New Cook Book* recipes using carob pods, breadfruit, taro root, guavas, mangoes, and tamarind—foods that most of her readers probably had never set eyes on.[11] She had grasped a mutation in our culture that would powerfully reshape Americans' ideas of cooking: the active pursuit of the unfamiliar.

Among the cultural gaps separating our hypothetical Depression-era kitchen occupant from her grandmother or great-grandmother, none is more remarkable than this. In the Lübeck or Eutin of the 1840s—as in Edinburgh, Lyons, or Philadelphia—hardly any mistress of a household great or small would have thought she was doing family or friends a favor by feeding them anything from beyond the confines of a well-understood, locally based cuisine. In ethnically unified societies people do not ordinarily *like* anything much different from the food they are accustomed to, a fact that in itself would eliminate the entire raison d'être of half the cookbooks sold today.

Even as late as 1845, with dramatic societal changes on the march in most Western countries, the pace of culinary change was slow enough that one novel ingredient had time to be absorbed into the commonplace before anyone had to have six more explained. The course of progress did not constantly assault the natural gastronomic conservatism of homogeneous cultures still dependent on small-scale local farming for most of the foods they knew. Nor did cookbook writers consider it their business to compose lessons on the nature and origins of new products. Until the late nineteenth century, many of them habitually ignored newcomers until they had become part of the woodwork; it is for this reason that earlier cookbooks give such remarkably scanty and behindhand evidence on just when people in the Old World began eating tomatoes or Irish potatoes. With a Sarah Tyson Rorer telling a national readership how to cook breadfruit in 1898, we obviously face the opposite problem in historical judgment of when which foods arrived: the food writer who serves as advance publicist for some item long before it is really available or acceptable to the intended audience.

By the time Irma von Starkloff married Edgar Rombauer in 1899, cookbook authors were increasingly primed to assume the mission of trailblazer for a troop of Cub Scouts, leaders who not just gave directions or formulas but virtually yanked people into the future or at least the front ranks of the present. They could not have succeeded in such a role if Americans had not begun to think of choices in their private surroundings—what they covered their sofas in, how they papered their walls, what they served for dinner—as the medium of adventure. Exotic ingredients were only bit players in this scenario. The turn-of-the-century food writers were also trying to introduce middle-class American homemakers to smatterings of foreign or immigrant cuisines.

Nearly a hundred years later these efforts do not loom large in the accounts of culinary historians. But in fact they point to significant changes in broader attitudes toward the good of cultural homogeneity or heterogeneity. An eagerness to sample what strangers were eating did not immediately sweep all circles, but a certain very cautious appetite for the exotic (or what at least sounded exotic) began to show up in print. What would have been unthinkable for well-meaning hostesses of sixty or eighty years before—showing guests special esteem by serving them something they had never tasted in their lives—began to be implicitly encouraged by the food writers.

Kitchen globe-trotting and cults of regional American cuisines are the gastronomic reflection of a hankering for armchair as well as real tourism that was an established cultural commodity in this country well before the end of the nineteenth century. The smorgasbord of European dishes offered to Stateside readers in Adelaide Keen's *With a Saucepan over the Sea* (1902) and the nostalgia for survivals of the slave-owning South gratified in Minnie C. Fox's *Blue Grass Cook Book* (1904) are early published examples.[12] (Both must have had at least mild success, for they were reissued respectively in 1910 and 1918.) The writers of all-purpose kitchen bibles did not all promptly rush to fill their pages with Continental or regional American specialties, but at least one of the sisterhood had already realized that not only these vogues but some of the ethnic cooking traditions now taking root on American soil offered immense opportunities for the expansion of cookbook turf. In 1898 *Mrs. Rorer's New Cook Book* presented lengthy sections of Jewish, "Spanish" (mostly meaning Mexican-derived Southwestern), Creole, and Hawaiian dishes. Like the breadfruit, some of these may have represented a premature evangelism. But any general culinary manual that served up such fare was in effect asking people to consult it as a cultural interpreter. No white Anglo-Saxon

Protestant housewife was going to have any ancestral clue to "Matzoth Balls for Soup" or "Chile Con-Cana" without a Mrs. Rorer to explain them.[13]

In addition to exotic new foods and new exposure to other cuisines, the age brought to American homes a remarkable stream of familiar but formerly rather costly, time-consuming foods in altered form that enabled a cook to circumvent once-laborious tasks with a wave of the hand. These included preshelled nuts, preground spices, seedless raisins, liquid extracts of flavoring ingredients that previously had had to be processed at home (or sometimes made up by an apothecary), and above all free-flowing refined white sugar—this last being the supreme example of how the new food-processing technologies of the post–Civil War era made cheap commodities out of expensive rarities.[14] Of course, the cheapness and plentifulness of sugar also depended on a rapid American corporate commandeering of tropical plantation sites around the world. But in any case, one result was the quite unprecedented vogue of cooking by children—children like little Irma and Elsa von Starkloff in the 1880s or Marion Rombauer a quarter of a century later.

Before their lifetimes the practice of letting children play at cooking on a regular basis with ingredients of their own choice had hardly been known. The demanding daily kitchen routine could not be casually interrupted. Not only was firing up a stove for a young nuisance's maiden efforts cumbersome and costly, but best-quality sugar could not possibly be spared to gratify the sweet tooth of the young through frequent do-it-yourself experiments. Indeed, until the eighteenth century sugar had been substantially reserved for preserving and confectionery, uses considered too august to be entrusted to anyone but the lady of the house. Well into the nineteenth, dwelling at length on candies or small cakes resembling our cookies marked a cookbook—for example, Eliza Leslie's 1828 *Seventy-five Receipts for Pastry, Cakes, and Sweetmeats*—as being addressed to refined and expensive tastes.

Until the new refining technology, working with sugar had entailed a somewhat complex knowledge that had to be acquired through experience of countless different batches. Now anyone could put this inexpensive, standardized ingredient in a saucepan (which also was more affordable than it had been of yore, and could easily be replaced if a novice burned the bottom off it while making candy) and proceed without all the ado of home clarifying and straining.

Soon cookbooks began to be filled with recipes reflecting a trend unknown to prior ages: a kind of recreational cuisine not connected with actual meals. Children and teenagers were its most conspicuous but far from its sole practitioners. It did not have to contribute anything to a usual breakfast, luncheon, or dinner; its reason for being was that it was a lark for everyone (especially the young) in the very cooking. Its essence was sugar-based snacks like cookies and candy, which swiftly multiplied in the cookbooks and were commonly used to teach children to cook. Unfortunately, they tend to be educational dead ends in the kitchen. Candy-making sheds absolutely no light on any other form of cooking; the new cookies that grew popular (as opposed to the small cakes that used to be produced for special occasions or religious holidays) often developed into no-work, anything-goes creations redeemed only by the all-justifying presence of sugar.

These fashions heralded what may be seen as a juvenilization of all cooking, whereby those who cooked would more and more be relegated to the role of perennial pupil following literal instructions. In this connection it should be pointed out that refined white sugar had a kind of synergistic effect with dramatic post–Civil War developments in flour milling and factory-scale wheat production. The giant Minnesota mills now supplied to American kitchens finely milled, almost wholly germless white flour at low prices that formerly would have bought you a product coarse and branny enough to scour the varnish off a chair. The new flour and sugar inspired a huge vogue of dessert (and especially cake) baking that was in many ways analogous to the American love affair with candy and cookies. The results could be more plausibly tacked onto meals, but their most satisfactory anchoring places turned out to be socially competitive feminine events like afternoon tea or, a little later, club or bridge luncheons.

From the 1870s on the proportion of ordinary cookbooks given over to candies, cookies, and cakes grew astonishingly, indicating an equal growth in the proportion of kitchen time and energy spent on recreational cooking or supplying informal opportunities to indulge a sweet tooth. It is significant that all of these (even the somewhat amorphous category of cookies) are somewhat self-enclosed endeavors that require careful adherence to measured formulas of the new, "scientific" sort on which a Fannie Farmer prided herself. One of their effects was to reinforce the supposition that all cooking consists of following detailed, quantified scripts rather than yourself getting to know what you are doing through hands-on apprenticeship with hardworking elders.

To some extent every invention that cut down on kitchen time and effort helped to weaken what may be called inner-directed as opposed to other-directed cooking. But the advance of "convenience" ingredients carried more implications for the regress of home-learned culinary knowledge and the triumph of cookbooks than almost any other factor. What was true of the new, "improved" flour and sugar was even more applicable to the myriad canned, bottled, and instantized products that during the same years began lessening people's dependence on perishable food while making erstwhile seasonal luxuries like fruit—an ancient symbol of privilege—into year-round pleasures equally available to plutocrats or working people.

These transformations had been given an enormous push by the demands of army suppliers and the answering efforts of industry during the Civil War. Industrial-scale canning of at least a few products achieved something approaching a rude assembly-line efficiency in the 1870s. From then on, canning and preserving technology grew at a furiously accelerating pace. It would complete the break with the individually mastered home work processes that at one time had been synonymous with cooking, and it would help to abolish the kind of recipe writing—already fading fast by the turn of the century—that assumed much independent judgment on the part of the user. To suppose that convenience foods like precooked cereals, canned condensed soups, instant puddings, and bottled condiments accomplished these feats simply because they eliminated a lot of work is not strictly accurate, for the work was still being done. It had been displaced to another sphere, not eliminated. The chicken for chicken soup still had to be drawn, plucked, cut up, and cooked—but en masse by assembly-line workers and machines, not in individual private homes. Even by 1900 or 1910 the home kitchen really could not compete with industry's ability to carry out such preparations speedily and cheaply.

When the component tasks of cooking had been done at home, women had perforce understood them from beginning to end. Now those who really understood what went into making soup were industrial engineers. In fact, what the cook was supposed to understand about the end product boiled down to two things. One was how to consummate the technological handling it had received at the factory by compatible handling in the home: "Follow directions on label." The other was how to buy it—a much more complex task, given the speed with which not just new products but whole new categories of products began to chase each other onto the store shelves. Learning about what was in the market became a solemn responsibility requiring much official coaching.

The cookbooks of the age show processed foods coming into currency in fits and starts. A "boughten" ingredient used with abandon in one book of the teens, late twenties, or early thirties may be nearly absent from another. In a general way, convenience foods made their way more speedily into the Wisconsin-based *Settlement Cook Book* (originally the product of an immigrant-settlement program at the Milwaukee Jewish Mission at around the turn of the century) than into the reigning classic, *The Boston Cooking-School Cook Book* (taken up after Miss Farmer's death by her sister, Cora D. Perkins, and then by Mrs. Perkins's daughter-in-law, Wilma Lord Perkins). But cookbooks certainly were not the primary source of information about canned and instantized foods. The new products rapidly spawned a huge promotional literature that moved into the erstwhile territory of the cookbooks.

Respectable authors like Sarah Tyson Rorer, Mary Lincoln of the Boston Cooking School, and Fannie Farmer herself (Mrs. Lincoln's successor as principal of the school) rushed to endorse particular brand names (which might be advertised in their books), while the largest food manufacturers began to hire home economists and cooks to dream up recipes using their products or learned-sounding explanations of why some novel item was better than the stuff people had always cooked with. The pace of change itself swiftly became a factor that all homemakers from the cleverest to the dullest-witted constantly had thrust on their awareness. Naturally enough, the praise of the unknown and unfamiliar sounded in everyone's ears so incessantly as to sink into staid commonplaceness.

One of the odder features of this scenario was that throughout the many decades while expectations of women's practical home-cooking skills were dwindling, the rhetoric surrounding women's all-important domestic mission was becoming almost ludicrously inflated. Whereas eighteenth-century cookbook authors frequently mentioned that their works might help you get your household into better order, their mid-nineteenth-century counterparts habitually enlarged the picture to include God, science, or both. The image of nurturing Christian homes as the foundation of the Republic figured largely in the Beecher sisters' urgings about systematized housekeeping. Their contemporary Sarah Josepha Hale, modestly defining woman's domestic mission as "promoting the health, happiness and improvement of her species,"[15] introduced the recipes of *Mrs. Hale's New Cook Book* (1857) with a treatise on metabolic principles. A generation later, when sheltered city girls might literally think that water came from faucets and cooking meant following recipes, feeding the family was regularly portrayed as a momentous achievement. (This certainly would not have occurred to many observers when the same achievement was chiefly carried out by servants.) By 1898, the preface of *Mrs. Rorer's New Cook Book* summoned the young cook to glory:

> I believe that every woman should know how to housekeep. Giving up entirely the moral influence of a good meal, I believe that all women should learn to cook as an aid to higher education. Cookery puts into practice chemistry, biology, physiology, arithmetic, and establishes an artistic taste. And if our motto is, "Let us live well, simply, economically, healthfully and artistically," we have embraced all the arts and sciences.[16]

The scientific aspirations here alluded to were a beloved theme of food writers throughout most of Irma Rombauer's pre-*Joy* career in the kitchen. Such ambitions would do a great deal to give preprocessed foods a competitive edge over the products of home labor—the burgeoning promotional literature from commercial manufacturers regularly dwelt on the superior sanitation and expertise of factories, though naysayers had arisen in some strength by about 1910. The appeal to science also tended to confirm the home cook's need for advice from professional writers; so many subjects outside women's own everyday knowledge now seemed to be entangled with cooking that without a comprehensive guide at their elbows they were doomed to inadequacy.

Even as women's role in the actual preparation of food shrank before the encroachments of industry, women were bombarded in magazines, newspapers, manufacturers' brochures, and cookbooks with the message that the welfare of the family hinged on their mastery of critical lore—for example, "food values," a crude concept that became somewhat more refined when the tools of chemical analysis improved around the turn of the century and the great vitamin discoveries began arriving after 1912.

One remarkably clear presentation of the issue appears in *Mary at the Farm* by Edith May Thomas, a half-novelized regional Pennsylvania cookbook of 1915 in which a young woman from Philadelphia prepares for her approaching marriage by spending a summer in rural Bucks County with her capable Pennsylvania German aunt. In one scene where Mary tries to convince Aunt Sarah that woman's place is not only in the home but in the yet unattained voting booth, the aunt argues that a modern homemaker should devote herself to studying critical domestic duties in all their impressive new dimensions. Mary, responding in what one suspects must have been the Irma Rombauer spirit, insists that today those duties are bound to take wives and mothers outside their own homes to tackle "the larger problems of municipal housekeeping." But the author makes sure that even in Mary's mind "municipal housekeeping" is securely tied to the stock theme of the exalted home-front mission:

> . . . the health, comfort and happiness of the family depend so largely on the *common sense* (only another name for effi- ciency) and skill of the homemaker, and the wise care and thought she expends on the preparation of wholesome, nutri- tious food, either the work of her own hands or prepared under her direction.[17]

Of course, the foods to which many of the advice-givers looked as the wave of the future were neither the work of the housewife's "own hands" nor "prepared under her direction," unless she bought into the popular supposition that the corporate kitchen was there to carry out every little wish of the female consumer better than she could have managed it herself. That Edith May Thomas did not subscribe to this notion is shown by her disdain for "cereals which come ready pre- pared."[18] But her book is plainly meant to record a vanishing country past a long way from the expectable domestic surroundings of any real "Mary Midleton" even as early as 1915. The heroine cannot have anticipated many opportunities to make her own strawberry vinegar or butter. Indeed, as a young kindergarten teacher headed for suburban bliss with a would-be engineer for the Philadelphia Electric Company, she may not have long cared to make her own soup stock or bread—or hot breakfast porridge, an article steamed by Aunt Sarah for at least two hours.

As time went on, the disparity between the lofty kitchen responsi- bilities expounded by authoritative manuals and the "Follow direc- tions on label" reality that millions of cooks opted for became obvious enough to shed a counteractive light on pious homilies about the awesome business of cooking for husbands and children. There emerged a longing for rewards beyond slogging away at "wholesome, nutritious food" in the efficient spirit of which prestigious cookbooks had sung. The food writer who tried to sound like an algebra teacher addressing a gaggle of earnest schoolgirls would cease to be a standard model. Irma Rombauer, who did not pay reverent attention to cookbooks during her married years, cannot have guessed that the most successful alternative would be her vivid and personable self.

The seeds of reaction against soberly constituted culinary authority are visible as early as the candy-cookie-cake vogue, which certainly accustomed people to following recipes in strict lockstep but also went against everything the experts preached about nutritional priorities. (The experts, as schizoid on these matters as their late-twentieth-century descendants, regularly inveighed against such indulgences but implicitly contradicted their own counsel by printing more and more recipes for them.) Given the chance, American women's culinary fancy rather swiftly turned to thoughts of gratification and pleasure, not the plain and healthful fare the cooking school authorities told them to concentrate on. By the time genuinely systematized kitchen design began to emerge between about 1910 and 1920, the homemakers who found themselves at least partly liberated from the unending tasks of the old cooking were ready to believe that the new cooking could be "artistic," amusing, even joyous.

One sign of the new mood is a greatly increased emphasis on visual factors, especially color. (Fanciful visual schemes with elaborate colored designs were not new in cookery, but until the late nineteenth century they were so laborious and time-consuming as to be reserved for specialized sorts of confectionery in lofty households; the availability of comparatively cheap and effortless means for "artistic" effects provided a great stimulus.) At around the turn of the century, cookery experts like Mrs. Rorer with her praise of "an artistic taste" began to go wild for color-coordinated menus, sometimes matched to seasonal themes but often just viewed as charming presentations in their own right, with all-white, pink, green and white, or other aesthetically chosen foods comprising the bill of fare.

A huge new vogue of salads was meanwhile springing up, based on the endlessly fruitful principle of arranging some different-colored ingredients next to each other and serving them with a dressing—or, in an allied development that would go on blossoming for another fifty or sixty years, in the surreal gleam of a bright-hued commercial gelatin matrix. The art of saladizing quickly rose to pictorial heights represented by Fannie Farmer's "Los Angeles Fruit Salad" (cutout orange baskets on lettuce leaves, garnished with canned pimientos, grapes, and parsley and filled with a mixture of cut-up marshmallows, skinned and halved seedless grapes, orange sections, pineapple cubes, walnut meats, and a whipped-cream dressing) or her "Monte Carlo Salad" (on a mayonnaise-masked and lettuce-bordered underpinning of grapefruit pulp with cut-up celery and apple, four rectangles of green mayonnaise denote "playing cards" with the different suits limned in truffle or canned pimiento shapes, the whole being garnished with "gold and silver coin" cut out from carrot and turnip slices).[19]

Elaborate visual schemes were also a main selling point for the newly voguish category of foods meant either to precede a meal or to be nibbled at in quasi-meals like afternoon tea. They went by a tangle of overlapping names; "canapé," the most clearly defined, usually referred to a tribe of small open-faced sandwiches comprised of fancy shapes of fried or toasted bread, bedecked with dainty toppings. At their most baroque, canapés might involve piped borders of some puréed mixture surrounding quadrants of other color accents and a final smattering of tiny garnishes.

The reasons for the popularity of such creations are not hard to fathom. In the first place, recipes for arranging three or seventeen ingredients on a plate and serving them with a dressing and an atmospheric title were as good as foolproof. They offered a kind of no-cooking cooking that (even when it involved using seven different kinds of fruit and spending some time on decorative niceties like peeling grapes) was much easier on both authors and home cooks than traditional kitchen labors. "Los Angeles Salad" provided more accessible and reliable instruction to people who had not grown up participating in the old collegial workshop than most written recipes for cooking dried beans or baking a loaf of bread—activities that canners and big commercial bakers were in any case making irrelevant for most households and that seemed to defeat the whole purpose of the efficient, meals-in-a-jiffy centralized kitchen. By 1920 mastery of the arduous processes that once had been the prerequisite to the simplest meal was not a goal that many beginning cooks measured themselves against, or that the most forward-looking cookbooks strove to inculcate. Easily copied designs with edible coloring materials seemed more suited to the modern version of culinary mastery. It was as if some breathtaking advance had freed the public schools to substitute amusing games with alphabet blocks for the useless tedium of reading.

A kinder way of looking at the new approach is to remember that during this period a gospel of self-expression through everyday resources was rapidly overtaking popular culture. Audiences for how-to advice began to look less for instruction than inspiration. Well-meant directions for "wholesome, nutritious food" and useful basic dishes did not lift the modern consumer's heart, while schemes for alternating red and green pepper strips with orange and grapefruit sections genuinely delighted women eager to believe that kitchen drudgery was a thing of the past. The essence of the higher cookery was *to combine ingredients*—not, that is, to marry them through any application of fundamental cooking processes, but to introduce them like guests at a party. In Irma's young matronhood, festive impulses and artistic sensibility were what distinguished today's from yesterday's cook.

Of course, manufacturers of kitchen equipment and processed foods did much to convince consumers that there were wondrous links between their products (whether color-coordinated appliances or instant puddings) and inner fulfillment through stylish cooking. But the new yearning cannot be put down only to corporate manipulations of the national psyche. Somehow a persuasion entered many female minds that simple home cooking can and should be made to represent mood, performance art, and fashion statement. This is the real message that glimmers through such early incarnations as the inadequate 1898 black-and-white photograph of a potato salad camouflaged under a Birnam Wood of parsley sprigs in *Mrs. Rorer's New Cook Book*.[20] It appears in far more aggressive form in the works of Ida Bailey Allen, a canny cooking-school instructor of the nineteen-teens who successfully repackaged herself after World War I as a purveyor of kitchen uplift via the airwaves. "Meals are dull—unless we make them gay," she told her audience in a 1926 spinoff of her popular radio program (*One Hundred Four Prize Radio Recipes*).[21] In that instance her proposed antidote to dullness was gelatin. *Ida Bailey Allen's Modern Cook Book* (1932) underlines the credo of artistic expression in home cooking through the swatches of free verse tacked onto most chapters. The poem that accompanies the salad chapter virtually crystallizes the notion of the kitchen as artist's studio. It portrays a "little woman" in her city kitchen at sunset, imaginatively transmuting her homesickness for the country vistas of her youth:

A blue plate "for sky."
Sliced tomatoes for the glowing red—
Yellow dressing for the gleaming light—
Lettuce and parsley—the background of trees.[22]

The search for exalted rewards and satisfactions through cooking never flagged after its turn-of-the-century beginnings, but it soon wandered into different paths. The elaborate constructions of the early salad fantasists and color-scheme proponents had begun to seem fussy and strained to some observers long before Mrs. Allen (a follower of established banalities rather than a pioneer of chic, in most of her pronouncements) painted her edible sunset.

Prohibition gave a helpful impetus to a breezier aesthetic. The Noble Experiment coincided with a vogue of debonair insouciance in most reaches of fashion. It also cemented a new relationship between eating and drinking, driving hard liquor from the male bastion of the saloon into the home and creating an urgent need for handy, smart foods to soak up booze—preferably filling foods with assertive flavors. The corresponding surge in new kinds of tidbits more or less swamped the abilities of culinary parlance to sort out the meanings of "appetizers," "cocktails," "hors d'oeuvre," and even the formerly better-distinguished "canapés." (The 1931 *Joy of Cooking* would show a general befuddlement about the application of such terms that was shared by most readers and writers.) But whatever you called them, the rapidly multiplying tribe of foods to drink with indicated another stage in the arrival of a recreational cooking—or perhaps more accurately in this case, recreational eating—connected loosely or not at all with meals.

Hostesses of the twenties did continue to serve little somethings as opening dinner courses. (In that application, they were most correctly called hors d'oeuvre.) But in drinking households where company had been asked to dinner, the hors d'oeuvre or appetizer course—which promptly mutated to include anything from a celery stick to a miniature lobster croquette—commonly became detached from the table service and was served with liquid refreshment in the living room, usually as finger food. This custom eventually became universal, even among nondrinkers.

Meanwhile, the new popularity of cocktail parties, whether powered by good bootleg liquor or bathtub swill, further boosted the popularity of cocktail tidbits and spurred the invention of easier spinoffs on the old canapé idea. In Fannie Farmer's day the toppings for canapés (like fillings for their cousins, tea sandwiches) had often involved someone's actually reducing ingredients like lobster, chicken, or ham to a fine spreadable paste with creamed butter and much elbow grease, and arranging them on neatly cut geometric shapes of fried bread. By the end of Prohibition in 1933, instant substitutes for the fussy underpinnings were widely available in the form of packaged potato chips, thin crackers, Melba toast rounds, and small pretzels. Cream cheese—virtually unknown for such purposes thirty years earlier—had become a quick all-purpose binder for "spreads" (also a new word in this context), while commercial mixtures like deviled ham helped anyone throw together ballast for an alcohol-fueled event by simply opening a jar or can. It was a revolution of sorts, enabling anyone with a bit of cash at hand to go to the store and launch a party almost on the spur of the moment. In this application, "convenience" foods were the soul of spontaneity, notwithstanding their other role as the soul of "scientific" housekeeping.

A vogue of snazzy impromptu entertaining; a hankering for colorful and undemanding self-expression through manipulation of food; the cult of the new and unusual; the presence of innumerable aggressively promoted "convenience" ingredients within the highly structured modern home kitchen; and underlying it all, a long-standing acceptance of culinary ignorance, isolation in the kitchen, and eagerness for remedial printed instruction—all of these developments helped to prepare the ground in which *The Joy of Cooking* would take root. Irma Rombauer might have been invented in order to sum up the age in which she first wrote. But she was not a creature of that particular moment. She possessed the inestimable advantage of having lived in the world more than fifty years before she ever thought of writing a cookbook. Throughout the career that she improbably carved out for herself after Edgar's death, she would always remain essentially what she had been before the 1931 *Joy:* a culinary amateur, quite uninterested in masquerading as a learned preceptor and frankly bored with a lot of the solemn stuff that the competition expounded under the guise of culinary education. It was the secret of her success, or a very large part of it.

The first, privately produced *Joy of Cooking* is not a document that 1990s gourmets are likely to browse through with delighted thoughts of rushing to the kitchen. It barely hints at what the book would later become. But anyone who wants to understand Irma Rombauer's eventual accomplishment must begin here, with a compact 395-page volume surrounded by uncertainties. Even the question of why Irma wrote a cookbook in the first place is more obscured than answered by her own preface. Her explanation was that putting together this collection had enabled her to ditch an inconvenient clutter of other cookbooks that she had previously had to carry around with her wherever she went.[23] (That might be a motive for copying recipes in a notebook, but it does not sound like much of a reason for spending $3,000 to have something published.) For her money Harold Hungerford had given her a demure gray-blue book (beneath Marion's striking Saint Martha dust jacket) of about 5¼ by 8 inches, handsomely printed on a much better paper stock than any that her later commercial publisher would ever deign to use. The lightly pebbled cover was semiwashable, a touch that not all first-time cookbook writers would have thought of. A professional with an eye to such things would have spotted many blunders in typography and copyediting, but the overall effect was unobtrusively appealing, given a modestly offbeat note by Marion's silhouette chapter headings. (These mostly took a literary or historical turn—e.g., a doubleted European accepting some object from a Red Indian in feathered headdress before "Vegetables," a Mexican woman grinding grain on a stone metate before "Breads," the Queen of Hearts pointing an accusatory finger at the Knave before "Pies.")

What Irma's qualifications might have been for going into the cookbook-writing business were left to the user's imagination, and even today are not easy to fathom. Both she and Marion would later indicate that she had arrived at matrimony in 1899 a complete dud as a cook. She could not possibly have deciphered most of the recipes in the 1896 *Tornado Cook Book*. Irma and Marion both relate that her first hands-on teacher was Edgar, an old hand with a campfire skillet.[24] There is more than a little plausibility to this story, for the sort of cooking Irma's friends most remembered from her was not dazzling culinary virtuosity but seat-of-the-pants improvisation. It was her nature to do most things in a blitz of energy, charm, and impatience to be doing something else. Cooking was no exception.

She must have managed to master enough of the received party dishes of the day to cut the sort of figure she wanted to cut in South St. Louis society, though undoubtedly she explained her wishes to a maid or maids more often than she marched into the kitchen herself to start dinner from scratch. She developed a great skill at decorating cakes, an accomplishment that Marion traced to a cooking course her mother—an inveterate pursuer of odd educational opportunities—had taken with a Mrs. Nannie Talbot Johnson of Paris, Kentucky, during one of the family's many summers amid the Chautauqua classes at Bay View. (From Mrs. Johnson's little 1912 compilation *Cake, Candy and Culinary Crinkles* it appears that her interests ran strongly to garnishes and ornamental effects.)[25] But the memories of latter-day survivors suggest that Irma was never among the reigning South Side mistresses of the culinary art. Cooking in itself had scant charm for her except as another expression of the social gift that she so intensely bent on her acquaintance. All who knew her cooking at first hand agree that her real talent was for contriving clever meals in no time flat out of whatever chanced to be hanging around the place. (Marion believed that the Bay View vacations had been the great nurturer of this gift.) If cooking can provide joy, she found it in what is called "whipping something up." She was the sort of woman who can breeze through a cupboard as bare as Mother Hubbard's and in the twinkling of an eye have guests sitting down to a spirited conversation over a dashing lunch—the first item rather than the second being the real point of the thing by Irma's lights.

Such cooking, when translated into written recipes, does not tend to wear well over a period of many decades. Today Irma's first venture into the cookbook line appears naively preoccupied with stuff that has proved ephemeral, even by the notoriously impermanent standards of cooking. She had managed to pull together the respectable total of about 1,200 entries. (Reckoning up recipe totals of cookbooks is uncertain at best, in that they usually contain many subvariants or negligible entries that hardly add up to separate dishes. But for purposes of comparison we may roughly estimate *The Settlement Cook Book* of the day [the eighteenth edition, 1930] to have contained 2,600 recipes.) But in 1931 she had only a hazy idea of how to make a cookbook into something more than a collection of dishes that happened to please her. She would learn to cover the bases more carefully in future. Still, the very artlessness of her first attempt provides an invaluable picture of what people like Irma thought about cooking. Examined with care, the book is an innocent self-portrait and a telling snapshot of a moment in early modern culinary history.

It is not hard to see that the first *Joy* is based on very spotty knowledge. Irma had made shift to duplicate some of the instructional features of the big kitchen bibles: tables of equivalent measures, charts of cooking times, definitions of culinary terms, suggested menus, lists of uses for leftovers. But she was not really conversant with all of this information, or with all of the subjects that professional food writers were now expected to master. When it came to nutrition she was far beyond her depth. She must, like any other newspaper and magazine reader, have absorbed the extensive publicity about vitamins that had begun in 1912 with Casimir Funk's isolation of the substance eventually dubbed vitamin B_1 (thiamine). She had energetically worked to get all the approved foods into her own young children—for example, tomatoes, which she did not know that poor Marion was allergic to. But she was not herself a product of the vitamin age, whereas Marion's generation was regularly lectured about protein and vitamins in the public schools. (The allergies had also stirred Marion to an early interest in food science.) Irma struggled to do right by nutrition in the book, without much idea of what it meant. To retain the "entire nutritive value" of ordinary white rice she suggested cooking a cup of it in *two quarts* of water until all the liquid was absorbed.[26] (This certain formula for waterlogged mush was not dropped from *The Joy of Cooking* until the nutrition-minded Marion became coauthor in 1951.)

She had dealt with basic cooking times for vegetables by getting "a teacher of Domestic Science" to work up a table, printed by Irma with the naive disclaimer that she herself as an "experienced cook" reserved the right to "differ about some of the amounts of water and the length of cooking." She prefaced the chart by repeating the new nutritional gospel that most vegetables should be cooked in "as little water as possible, so that when they are tender they will have absorbed all the moisture in the pan."[27] The amounts of water mentioned in the chart make this unlikely (e.g., four cups of water for enough green beans to serve four and five cups of water for enough spinach to do the same). The truth is that even the best-intending cooks found it hard to be consistent in reducing things to formulas.

Certainly there had been change since Fannie Farmer's 1896 *Boston Cooking-School Cook Book*, as can be seen by a comparison of that work's cooking times with the ones suggested by Irma's consultant: from 1 to 2½ hours for string beans in 1896 (versus 20 to 35 minutes in 1931), 25 to 30 minutes for spinach (4 to 5 minutes), 20 to 60 minutes for peas (20 to 45 minutes), 15 to 20 minutes for Brussels sprouts (9 to 10 minutes), 20 to 25 minutes for cauliflower (8 to 10 minutes), 35 to 60 minutes for cabbage (6 to 9 minutes, except for the red cabbage that

Germans loved to braise at length).[28] Miss Farmer apparently cooked these last two whole or cut in quarters, while Irma's expert probably expected the cabbage to be shredded and the cauliflower to be broken into florets. It should also be remembered that selective breeding of vegetables for tenderness—peas, for example—was not far advanced in 1896 and did not match all of today's consumer expectations even in 1931. But in any case, Irma was one of those who try to nod to supposed nutritional correctness while cooking pretty much as they please.

Her favorite treatments of vegetables in the 1931 *Joy* (and all of her subsequent editions) were tying them up in a sheet of parchment paper that could be immersed in boiling water and saved scrubbing a pot, or combining them with some sort of cream sauce. She clearly felt it her duty to mention that tomato skins contained "highly valued vitamins," but made it plain that she had trouble envisioning anything so "uninviting" as unpeeled tomatoes in polite company. ("A bit of tomato skin was once as out of place at a dinner table as a bowie knife," she wrote, leaving no doubt that she still considered it so.)[29] It was typical of her to let something that could pass for expert opinion cheerfully rub elbows with her own invincible prejudices, and there is something immensely likable in her matter-of-fact inconsistency.

This cavalier attitude about system was no bad thing. It expressed itself in the fey, scatterbrained quality that would always enliven her *Joy of Cooking*. In 1931 this appeared more inadvertent than deliberate, but Irma would learn to deploy it to nimbler effect in future. Proceeding by instinct rather than any sort of trained analysis, she went from one thing to another as her fancy took her and implicitly proclaimed her allegiance to the brisk tempo and bright effects of postwar living. Her idea of the perfect company dish was a soufflé—a creation surrounded by a rarefied mythos but in fact a simple, cheap, and nearly foolproof vehicle for all sorts of leftovers. Irma devoted an entire chapter to this branch of culinary showmanship. It was the essence of "whipping something up." (Marion's chapter heading showed airy dandelion heads blowing in the wind.) A little white sauce, a couple of beaten egg whites, a soufflé dish—and behold a few smatterings of yesterday's chicken or eggplant rapidly alchemized into a high, trembling golden puff. It united thrift and dispatch with flair in a manner irresistible to Irma. She had not the temperament to imagine such a thing as *slow* flair. Style and speed went together in her preferred approach to anything. Consequently she was the ideal audience for the "convenience" products of the day, in all their amazing multiplicity.

Canned condensed soups were one of her true loves. "Recently, the French Government conferred a decoration upon the cook who prepares Campbell's soup," she wrote. "It is regrettable that this distinction could not be made to include all the soup manufacturers who have brought to us this good and nutritious product at so low a cost."[30] She was also devoted to packaged and bottled products like bouillon cubes, Savita (a vegetable extract made by the originators of Kellogg's breakfast cereals), and food colorings. Irma had a good enough sense of proportion not to try to replace traditional versions of well-known soups and sauces with wholesale substitutions of commercial mixtures; she applied herself to some of the standard dishes like homemade cream of mushroom soup or stewed tomatoes in a fairly conscientious spirit. But much of the book's flavor comes from her hearty espousal of commercial shortcuts so ubiquitous by 1931 that they had almost ceased to register as shortcuts in the minds of most cooks.

These ingredients made up a language that Irma spoke fluently. Condensed tomato soup appears as the basis of a soufflé, a medium for poaching eggs, the liquid for thinning Braunschweiger sausage into a canapé spread, the tomato element in a seafood sauce for spaghetti, and the chief flavor accent in an aspic salad also involving cottage cheese, cream cheese, mayonnaise, and whipped cream with diced vegetables.[31] Condensed milk is another pervasive presence. Molded salads of the X-number-of-ingredients-set-in-gelatin ilk figure conspicuously. Frozen aspics were still much admired in the likes of Irma's circle; she recommends freezing a tomato-based mixture in cubes and serving it "topped with a dab of mayonnaise."[32] Without acknowledgment—she may well not have paid attention to sources—she borrows a jelled ginger ale concoction popularized by Fannie Farmer in 1912 and a *Settlement Cook Book* recipe called "Golden Glow Salad" involving shredded carrots and pineapple in lemon Jell-O. ("This is good in flavor and lovely in color," Irma noted.)[33] Though she did not subscribe to the more extreme visual-fantasy school of salad making, these sweetened medleys suited her taste well enough.

Then there are the little touches and accents from a panoply of bottles, standing for a whole new idea of what cooking means. Irma's directions for making pan gravy from roast meat drippings are a perfect instance. After telling the cook to make up a vegetable stock, baste the roast with it, strain off the juices at the end, and bind the sauce with a roux, she gets down to the business of making the gravy "good":

Add paprika, celery salt, catsup, (sparingly) beef cubes, or Savita, give it character. Having made it good, a great deal has been accomplished, but not enough, it must also look good. Keep a bottle of Kitchen Bouquet on hand. Add enough of this to make the gravy a fine color and it is ready to serve.[34]

This is an approach to cooking resembling nothing so much as suggestions for applying makeup, another watershed contribution of the young twentieth century. Irma had had enough exposure to old-fashioned roasts and pan gravies to acknowledge, very briefly, that "good gravy" did not need a lot of additions. But her heart was obviously in the more accessible skill of quick doctoring to make the home-cooked item resemble some communal idea of gravy best reflected by gravy from a can.

In fact, the advent of mass-produced convenience foods—often visually stamped on the public awareness through bright pictures on labels and color advertisements in magazines—had also ushered in widely shared new standards of both taste and appearance by which the products of home cooking from scratch might appear odd or dull. Everyone knew that apple jelly flavored with mint was *supposed* to be green, like the store-bought version. There was nothing in the nature of either apples or mint to make it so, but luckily the Burnett Extract Company and its competitors were there to minister to the oversights of creation. Furthermore, mass-produced foods based on all kinds of original products from apples and tomatoes to wheat and oats were carefully engineered (starting with very narrow choices of growing area and particular strain) to ensure that they would taste the same 365 days a year, in every state of the Union—something that could not be expected from batches of the crop in question grown in different regions or from different botanical cultivars.

Manufacturers had swiftly understood that unless one batch of a product was exactly like every other batch, it was scarcely worth putting their names on it. The public lessons of uniformity were profound. After a time, millions of people genuinely did not know that homemade beef consommé or tomato soup or mayonnaise, with all their built-in potential for differing from other people's versions, could be anything but clumsy imitations of more successful commercial models. Hence additions such as the salty, aggressive Savita, catsup, or bouillon cubes. They were like a final dab of lipstick and dash of eyebrow pencil without which a woman's face could never approach media-propagated standards of prettiness.

These smart little touches of creativity out of bottles are a million miles away from usual cooking approaches of a hundred years earlier. In 1831 or even 1881, results essentially depended on how you had worked with basic ingredients. Last-minute adjustments—aside from perhaps binding a sauce with egg yolks or some flour and butter—were seldom prominent features of a written recipe. (If you wanted to make the gravy browner, you had to caramelize sugar in a pan for the purpose.) But for Irma, whose career as a home cook had coincided with the increasing sway of preflavored, precolored foods, deploying extracts and colorings in this manner came as easily as breathing. When she wrote that there was "no excuse, except inefficiency, for whitish, lumpy, tasteless gravy,"[35] it clearly was her understanding that every modern cook could buy inexpensive instant counterspells against all manner of perceived faults. The flour-thickened gravy gussied up with bouillon cubes and Kitchen Bouquet and dashes of this and that embodied a sprightly *je ne sais quoi* that to her was synonymous with joyful cooking. Gourmet cooks of more recent upbringing may wince at the approach. But the perfectly natural fit between the convenience ingredients at Irma's command and her own temperament is one of the major truths about her book.

Quite irrespective of the fact that *The Joy of Cooking* and its author would at length become beloved and influential presences in American homes, the small 1931 volume also bears looking at as a sort of culinary time capsule. In dozens of particulars, this first *Joy of Cooking* reminds us that even in the comparatively modern, centralized kitchens that belonged to people like Irma Rombauer, there was much that we could not have taken for granted. We cannot, for example, assume that in 1931 Irma possessed a mechanical refrigerator rather than an icebox. Certainly she did not assume that her readers would.

Commercial ice had become so universally available in urban and suburban communities since the turn of the century that nearly anyone with or without a real refrigerator could count on efficient chilling for the wildly burgeoning tribe of gelatin-based salads and desserts as well as "icebox cookies" (very short, rich doughs chilled in order to prevent greasiness), "icebox cakes" (a custardy filling partly absorbed by some cake element), and "icebox rolls" (left to rise very slowly at a low temperature). The 1931 *Joy* includes all of these, equally achievable in the older or more recent appliance. Irma must have been aware that the new refrigerators did not always run smoothly or safely. Only months before she began to write her cookbook, her brother the Health Commissioner had been advocating a bill to require city supervision of mechanical refrigerators in St. Louis. (Several fires and explosions had been ascribed to them in Chicago in 1929.)[36] Still, anyone as bent as she on modernity would have felt bound to acknowledge them, as she did by giving alternate directions for hand-cranked freezers and mechanical refrigerators in the ice cream chapter.

In 1931 Irma knew about electric waffle irons[37] but apparently not about pressure cookers (which had reached *Settlement* by 1928 and *Boston* by 1930). She provided oven thermostat settings for the baking recipes, an up-to-date note that would have benefited people with new stoves possessing built-in thermostats and left everyone else estimating the temperature by the time-honored method of seeing how long the oven took to singe a bit of paper (or your hand). Ovens ready-equipped with thermostats were now widely available (the American Stove Company of St. Louis had been making them at least since 1925) but by no means universal. By 1930 *The Boston Cooking-School Cook Book* had adopted the new convention, which had reached *Settlement* in 1928. But plenty of cookbooks were still content with "low," "moderate," and "hot."

The specialized marketing wizardry of later generations had yet to touch some foods. In 1931, chicken was one of the more expensive meats—indeed, further out of reach for many households than it had been at the time of Herbert Hoover's 1928 "chicken in every pot" campaign speech. No corporate giant was differentially breeding "fryers," "broilers," or "roasters," or selling packages of this or that part. Of course the 1931 book has no recipes for chicken breasts or thighs. Chickens were bought whole, and when Irma got a "large" one for roasting, she figured on its being about 3½ pounds, compared to something like 6½ or more than 7 pounds for a large modern roaster.[38] (Possibly Irma was writing off the top of her head in this instance, because chickens of 4½ to 5 pounds were often recommended for roasting in other books.) If you wanted to serve chicken breasts—not an idea that would occur to many home cooks—you cut them off the bird yourself or got the butcher to do it. The poor man's substitute for this extravagance was veal, which cheap and oft-disdained fallback Irma suggests making into breaded cutlets "in preference to some more costly meat course."[39] Or the economy-minded might put canned tuna in a colander and pour boiling water over it, using the drained fish to make what Irma calls "Mock Chicken Sandwiches."[40]

Roast chicken, the company dish par excellence, receives a popular treatment of the time in the first *Joy of Cooking*. Roasting in the original sense—a dry-heat method requiring free circulation of air around meat on an open rack or spit before the heat source—had disappeared from American homes as enclosed ranges replaced open hearths in the course of the nineteenth century. An occasional diehard might still have remembered real roast chicken and beef, but for all practical purposes they were unknown. Now people imitated roasting in the enclosed range by putting the food in the oven at a high temperature to brown it quickly, then reducing the heat for most of the cooking time. The steam released by the food as its internal temperature rises, and the tendency of spattered drippings to smoke in the oven, give baked meats a very different flavor and texture from truly roasted ones. In effect, they cook in their own steam with a greater or lesser accent of fumes from the initial searing. But by 1931 virtually no one observed the nicety of even distinguishing between "roast chicken" and "baked chicken"; the latter was now called "roast chicken" without apology, and millions of cooks had taken to an even more thoroughly steamed version. This involved the self-contradictory "covered roasting pan," a device meant to be used with a lid in place and a small amount of water in the bottom of an insert.

Sarah Tyson Rorer, mentioning these vessels in 1898, had protested that "we cannot 'roast' in a covered pan."[41] But her view had not prevailed. Undoubtedly the popularity of the lidded pans, which braised rather than roasted, was another reason for the currency of Savita–Kitchen Bouquet "gravy," with some imitation of real roasting-juice savor supplied by bottled expedients. Apparently Irma did not care to oven-"roast" in anything but a covered pan; she gives no other method for either roast chicken or roast beef.

By 1931 women in her circles were also long removed from everyday knowledge of bread-baking. Both American living routines and American taste—aided by American grain-milling technology—had firmly rejected the sturdy-textured bread that had been familiar to everyone when wheat flour still contained most of the germ and making up the bread was a necessary part of the household schedule. The old bread at its plainest, commonest, and best had involved only flour, yeast (usually homemade until the last decades of the nineteenth century, and even later in rural homes), salt, and water.

The best flavor, a delicate tang of not-quite-sourness together with the satisfying smack of wheat, had depended on the cook's care in nursing along the dough through a preliminary stage of fermentation called the "sponge"—designed "to give strength and character to the ferment," in the words of the 1857 *Mrs. Hale's New Cook Book*—before the bulk of the flour was added.[42] But long before Irma Rombauer's first cookbook venture, the lengthy task of breadmaking had been largely displaced from the home except as a conscious exercise in pretty domesticity (and even in that case only in truncated versions). Well before the end of the nineteenth century, the general taste had begun to disdain any hint of sourness in bread, or any texture but the softest and finest.

From the evidence of her book, Irma knew no sort of homemade yeast bread except the soft-textured sweetish kind made with milk and sugar that had come into favor late in the nineteenth century along with the nearly germless whiter-than-white flour from the giant roller mills of Minneapolis.[43] Indeed, it would have been hard to find recipes for old-style yeast breads in any general American cookbook by 1931. But meanwhile, the wheat bran that at one time had been nearly useless except in livestock mashes had become a standard baking ingredient. Thirty years earlier a basic cookbook probably would not even have mentioned it except as a nasty nuisance. But Irma's very modest bread chapter managed to work it into four different recipes. The lowly substance was now one of the marketing success stories of the great milling companies. Its new stardom probably owed less to the nutritional evangelists who had been praising its laxative virtues for the better part of a century than to its introduction as a flour extender during the grain rationing of World War I.

By that time plain yeast breads, which become leaden and unpleasant with the addition of bran, were less popular home productions than were alkali-leavened quick breads and muffins. These hugely outnumber the yeast-based type in Irma's coverage of bread. Chemically leavened breads have a cakey crumb capable of supporting all sorts of additions from leftover Wheatena to peanut butter, and in the past few decades they had proved to be infinitely handy targets of what-the-hell invention. Bran could be piled into them in astonishing amounts (Irma's first bran muffin recipe had two cups of bran to the same amount of flour)[44] without much pain to anyone, especially when surrounded by further baggage like raisins, nuts, chopped dates, and a lot of sugar or molasses. In time, ordinary American eaters came to desire such bits of fillip in any sort of breakfast bread and many of the breads served at other times.

Among all the tantalizing fragments of historical evidence that the 1931 *Joy* provides about anything from the survival of an old Midwestern fondness for oysters to the state of pasteurized milk, none is more absorbing than the glimpses it gives of contemporary attitudes toward ethnic cooking traditions. Curiosity about how the rest of the world ate was now a journalistic staple. But curiosity in itself did not imply either a great knowledge of how other people actually did eat or a desire to go very far toward duplicating it. A certain cult of the foreign, a notable development in human history, had made qualified rather than unlimited headway against the much more natural instinct to give unknown customs a wide berth. We today, living in an age that treasures frequent collision with the outrageous as proof that we are all still breathing, may not find it easy to recognize that apparently innocuous, universally accepted elements of twentieth-century American cuisine once seemed deeply alien to many people.

It is easy to smile at our forebears' versions of kitchen globetrotting, but they were earnest and significant. A growing hunger for something more than dyed-in-the-wool Anglo-Saxon Protestant fare can be seen from the popularity of a 1930s radio program called *The Mystery Chef*, whose recipe offerings often included curiosities from faraway places like India and Romania.[45] At least one round-the-world cookbook of more than trivial understanding and insight had appeared a few years earlier: Ruth A. Jeremiah Gottfried's *The Questing Cook* (1927), which shows some actual familiarity with a few important features of Mediterranean and Far Eastern cuisines.[46] But we cannot naively expect to find our own ideas of ethnic authenticity—which, by the way, still remain trustingly dependent on the word of fashionable experts—in an earlier America's search for foreign adventure.

The adoption process for new culinary contributions was ragged and inconsistent. Some dishes—for example, rich yeast cakes with eggs and butter that in the German or other northern European past had been luxurious productions mostly associated with special religious occasions but that blossomed here into a secular profusion of "coffee cakes"—were so swiftly naturalized as to obliterate memories of their origins. Others remained stubbornly unassimilated, or crept into American use only in hardly recognizable versions with names like "Hungarian Goulash" or "Mexican Chicken."

In 1931 Irma Rombauer was not at the forefront of the quest for dazzling foreign discoveries. If she loved pursuing supposedly glamorous exotica, a task that would shortly be *de rigueur* for nearly all cookbook authors, she did not advertise the fact in her initial collection. In fact, she stuck quite closely to the sort of food she knew and sensibly avoided inventing pseudoethnic pedigrees in the vein of "Hungarian Salad" and "Spanish Lamb Chops," which two ornaments of recent Fannie Farmer editions had never been within three thousand miles of Budapest or Madrid. She did not even include such now-familiar borrowings as "chop suey" and "Spanish omelet," which had found their way into standard cookbooks but might refer to all sorts of mixtures made "Chinese" or "Spanish" by a wave of the soy-sauce bottle or a few tomatoes.

Probably the greatest single hindrance to exploring real Chinese or Spanish cuisine until the last decade before Irma wrote her *Joy* had been that most Americans genuinely did not understand the notion of cooking anything in oil.[47] We can hardly appreciate how wedded the descendants of English settlers and northern European immigrants were to the solid animal fats (butter, lard, rendered suet) that could be made at home, or at least locally, by simple processes that everyone understood. The technology for turning vegetable sources into refined oil, on the other hand, was not compatible with home production or small-scale manufacture by a neighborhood butcher or dairy.

Even the expensive imported olive oil, which epicures had always demanded for their salad, was subject to widespread adulteration with other substances fresh or rancid, and really was not a taste that most people cared to cultivate. The popular American (and English) substitute for oil-based salad dressings was the "boiled dressing," in which the fat was generally supplied by egg yolks with or without cream and the sauce might also be bound with flour. (Of the seventeen salad dressings in the 1931 *Joy of Cooking*, five are of the "boiled" type and two others are oil-free mixtures based on whipped cream.) But the idea of oil as a cooking medium was still less admissible than its use in salads. The extraordinarily foreign concept of "stir-frying" (as we now call it) finely cut-up ingredients over a high flame in a small amount of oil was not yet understood to be part of what made Chinese food taste different in Chinatown. The Italian concept of cooking food in olive oil was not much more accessible to a large contingent of cooks.

The indefatigable Ida Bailey Allen, as spokeswoman and recipe developer for the Corn Products Refining Company, probably changed many thousands of minds during the 1920s with her endorsements of Mazola oil, another beneficiary of the World War I patriotic drive to put underexploited foods to new uses.[48] Vegetable oils had also made some headway since about the turn of the century in the disguised form of hydrogenated shortenings designed to resemble the familiar and trusted lard.[49] For deep-frying, Irma may well have gone over (or expected many readers to have done so) from lard to Crisco or corn oil, since she mentions only "deep fat." But for sautéing or pan-frying purposes she is loyal to butter, or sometimes bacon drippings. This preference clearly colors her approach to the one foreign bailiwick (aside from German food) in which she shows more than a passing interest: Italian cooking.

Of the major immigrant groups, none except the Chinese had been more beforehand than the Italians in offering at least a distant version of their own cooking to the rest of America in the form of neighborhood restaurants. The English and northern European descendants went through all kinds of stratagems in trying to adapt this food to their own understanding. Irma, who patronized an Italian vegetable store and was on friendly terms with the owners, was one of those who hovered on the fringes of further comprehension. She had an idea of risotto (though not of its critical details) and baked stuffed artichokes.[50] She was alert enough to novelty to give three recipes for zucchini, a vegetable that had yet to make an appearance in *The Boston Cooking-School Cook Book* or *The Settlement Cook Book*. But though she carefully mentions that "in Italy they are usually sautéed in olive oil," she does not try this method herself. She gives zucchini a simple treatment universally applied to the familiar American vegetables, boiling them before combining them with melted butter or (more adventurously) "a little hot olive oil."[51]

Of her tomato sauces for spaghetti, one makes a gingerly venture into Italian territory by using a combination of tried-out bacon and olive oil to cook the other sauce ingredients (onion, ground round, green peppers, canned tomatoes, and canned or fresh mushrooms). The other, a fair sample of the hybridized approach under which spaghetti had won American citizenship, is a white sauce or béchamel mixed with a can of tomato soup and enriched with diced cheese and seafood.[52] Most likely Irma and her cronies were familiar with restaurant meals of spaghetti blanketed with a thick, concentrated tomato sauce that started with onions and tomatoes cooking in olive oil. But for home-cooking purposes, this example furnished only a loose model for discreet emulation or was happily ignored in favor of more intelligible approaches.

Needless to say, the idea of cooking Italian pasta al dente had not occurred to American cooks of Irma's generation—nor is there any reason that it should have. In the not-so-distant past, durum wheat pasta had been a luxury of the rich, who had cheerfully devised baked dishes and puddings of expensive imported "vermicelli" or "macaroni" to their own taste. (The name "macaroni" was at first applied to virtually all pasta. But by the time of Irma's marriage, it usually meant a long, tubular shape, "vermicelli" a thinner nonhollow equivalent. The word "spaghetti" arrived with an early wave of immigrants in the 1880s.) But by the turn of the century cheap American factory-made versions were beginning to attract a non-Italian public, just as store-bought egg noodles were beginning to attract a clientele beyond the Jews and Germans who had previously been the chief home noodle-makers and -eaters in this country.

Now it was the turn of middle-class and working-class people to take up pasta and noodles. Both were among the most convenient "convenience" products ever to reach the American table. They put competing starchy vegetable foods—potatoes, bread, rice, other cereal grains—to shame for ease of preparation. By the onset of the Great Depression they were a vast blessing to millions. Understandably enough, housewives did not fret over authentically "Italian" and "German" ways to treat these sturdy adoptees. Neither did most cookbook writers.

Irma's 1931 recipes show how non-Italian cooks of the day viewed spaghetti and macaroni. She did not produce anything as fanciful as the "Baked Macaroni with Peanut Butter"—a combination that looks as if it had gotten the nod from some sociologically minded nutrition expert—in recent *Boston* editions.[53] But she did not imagine that her readers would want their pasta to bite back. She cooked macaroni (which was still sold in long strands and had to be broken into pieces) "until it is tender—about 25 minutes" before draining and reheating it with milk, then serving it with a flour-bound tomato sauce. Or she turned it after cooking into the familiar baked macaroni and cheese, or a "loaf" bound with milk, eggs, and bread. Spaghetti in her judgment required about 20 minutes' cooking before it was tender enough to be served with her cheese–tomato soup sauce—though it might alternatively be cooked further with grated cheese (she suggested steaming it in a double boiler for an hour or baking it from 15 to 20 minutes) and then served with her ground meat–tomato sauce.[54]

Thus far we have not seen much to indicate why the first *Joy of Cooking* is of any intrinsic interest beyond its own day. In most respects it is an energetic but ingenuous attempt at cookbook writing that still can be mined for historical clues of different sorts without necessarily possessing much merit of its own. Any observer might justifiably wonder why it survived to triumph over the reigning cookbooks of the day. One of the reasons is apparent when we turn from something like Irma Rombauer's Italian recipes to her German recipes: she was infinitely lucky in her heritage, and she had striven to do her best by it.

Aside from the English colonists and their posterity, Germans made up the largest and close to the oldest ethnic strain in early twentieth-century America. World War I had extinguished a lot of their culture, and their general assimilation thenceforth would sadly deplete their cooking. But the same Irma who as a child had longed to shed her Germanness and become an "American" like her envied neighbors now seized the opportunity to affirm her roots in the culinary *Deutschtum*.

Of liver dumplings, she announced that as "the child of a South German," she felt obligated to include this worthy ("it has qualities") if not terribly handsome dish.[55] She proudly related that eating beef à la mode frequently reduced her to saying "in disappointed tones, 'Why it isn't anything like Sauerbraten.' "[56] She made sure to identify potato dumplings as "Kartoffel Kloesse" and yellow cucumber pickles as "Senf Gurken."[57] In all, she gave something like fifty-five or sixty German or German-derived recipes, from the nursery standby "Milk Rice" (*Milchreis*, a very simple rice pudding) and favorite homely side dishes like potato pancakes and braised red cabbage to the imposing herring-beet-apple salad that she always remembered from family Christmas dinners.

The largest groups of German recipes are in her baking chapters. Irma supplies good recipes for six *Torten*, including the invariable family-birthday almond cake ("This recipe must be starred as 'the' nut cake my friends so frequently ask for").[58] In the coffee cake department, one of the signal gifts of Germany and its northern neighbors to American cookery, she presents Christmas *Stollen* and two versions of *Kugelhopf*. She gives directions for her grandmother Kuhlmann's apple cake (a puffy, moist, soufflélike creation that in Germany probably would have borne the name of *Auflauf*); apple strudel; both yeast-raised and quick-leavened versions of apple, plum, or peach *Kuchen*. She gives more than a dozen of the German Christmas cookies that had been an invariable annual production in her own household as well as her parents'.

This plentiful tribute to the glories of German baking points to another crucial drawing card of the book. From Irma's first edition to Marion's last one, much the strongest and best material in *The Joy of Cooking* always has been in the realm of cakes, cookies, pies, and assorted desserts. These take up more than a third of the 1931 book and have a look of accomplished care and lively engagement that does not always pervade Irma's treatments of meat or vegetable dishes. *Mehlspeise*, as the Germans collectively call baked desserts, consti-tuted by far her favorite branch of cookery, a penchant that she would pass on to Marion.

In the arena of dessert baking and sweet things generally, Irma had contrived the happiest of marriages between the German St. Louis of her childhood in the 1880s and 1890s and the standard repertoire of "American" hostesses during the same period. In fact, their cooking had overlapped; both "American" and German dishes show up in the 1896 *Tornado Cook Book*, though the names of contributors or recipes may not always be recognizably German. The last decades of the cen-tury had been a national golden age for dessert bakers of all ethnic backgrounds in the first heyday of the new fine white flour and sugar.

Irma's tastes in cakes and the like had been firmly founded on cre-ations invented, or first made practical for everyday middle-class cook-ing, during this era—whether angel food cake or *Blitzkuchen*. With other kinds of food, she had been much quicker to take up new fash-ions and time-saving strategies: cheese spreads, canned-soup soufflés, hastily doctored gravies, canned vegetables, salads using Jell-O or amazing conglomerations of ingredients. (These last may also have appealed to her for their distant kinship with the jelled German *Sülze*—a term covering many aspiclike dishes—or disparate mixtures of sweet and savory ingredients like the north German holiday herring salad.) But in the case of desserts, she was not given to whiz-bang shortcuts and remained fairly choosy about new fads.

She did display an interest in the new "chiffon pies"—not the gelatin chiffon pies of a few years later, but fluffy predecessors with egg whites beaten into a custardlike base. She was willing to sacrifice quality for convenience so far as to recommend hot-water piecrust, which was much easier to mix than the traditional sort ("almost like magic," Irma wrote)[59] but ended up brittle and rather greasy. Nonetheless, the solid foundation of this material was food that Irma had known all her life. With some of the German Christmas recipes, she was clearly trying to pass on traditions in a form close to her own understanding of the original. She would not otherwise have specified the semiarchaic hartshorn salt (ammonium carbonate, one of the oldest alkaline leaveners) for versions of "German Honey Cakes" (*Lebkuchen*) and rosewater as a flavoring in "White Almond Wafers" (*Mandel Plaettchen*).[60] Broadly speaking, the baking material displays a heritage-minded rather than novelty-minded side of Irma's character as a cook, and has a great deal to do with her book's lasting appeal. Today any cook looking at the 1931 chapters on baking and desserts can see that they have suffered less from intervening vagaries of taste than anything else in *The Joy of Cooking.*

The final and most valuable ingredient in this unique mixture of elements was Irma Rombauer herself. From the first, she conveyed an impression of the book's being peculiarly *hers*—belonging to her in a way that cookbooks, which have most often tended to be an impersonal lot, do not usually belong to their authors. Her little preface did not give an absolutely factual picture of the book's origin, but it gave a picture beyond price of Irma Rombauer:

> Whenever I leave home and begin to move about, I am appalled to find how many people with a desire to write feel impelled to share their emotions with the general public.
>
> Time and again I have been told with modesty, with pride, or with both, that I was entertaining a literary angel unawares, until one day, recognizing the glint of authorship in a man's eye and anticipating his imminent confidence, I forstalled [sic] him by saying rapturously, "Oh, do you know, I am a reader?"
>
> And now, after all, I am a writer—of a kind.[61]

Indeed, she was a writer. She had never written anything before, except papers on historical or cultural subjects for the Wednesday Club. She was without formal higher education, spelled (in English, German, or French) as she saw fit, and knew nothing of how to put together any sort of factual description. Conveying technical information at any length would always terrify her. Yet she instinctively understood something that many accomplished writers never master: how to project her own personality.

It is true that the personality on the page resembled the Irma Rombauer of family memory rather as a kitten resembles a Bengal tiger. Nonetheless, she knew without being taught exactly how to make her readers feel that they were in the living presence of an uncommon companion—charming, civilized, irreverent, original, irrepressible. She met them, with a disarming smile, on some territory outside the ordinary confines of a cookbook, and invited them to share her amusement at the unlikeliness of an Irma Rombauer writing such a thing. She gave them a chuckle over the absurdity of (some) culinary writers by printing a small "miscellany" of directions she had found during her own research: "Take twelve eggs, if you have them," or: "*Pigs Feet.* Take your feet, wash them, scratch them, put them on the griddle, cook them to a turn and serve them."[62] She injected the odd bit of extremely uncommon common sense: "If onions were costly, surely they would be considered a great delicacy."[63] She rattled on with pretty feminine inconsequence:

> Those who have visited Hirschhorn in the sweetly romantic Neckar Valley and who have climbed the hill to the partly ruined castle that dominates the little village, will remember being confronted by a "Potato Monument" dedicated piously "To God and Francis Drake, who brought to Europe for the everlasting benefit of the poor—the Potato." Please don't say that Sir Walter Raleigh or Governor Lane imported the potato, for it really doesn't matter, does it?[64]

In some indefinable manner, she considered herself worth listening to not because of what she knew but because of who she was. Amateurish as was her first attempt, she had reserves to draw on that were miles beyond the understanding of most professionals. She would never claim that her mastery of cooking was encyclopedic, but her experience of eating placed her in a class of her own among the efficient recipe developers of the day. It had been no deliberate acquisition; it was simply part of herself.

Young Irma von Starkloff had spent five years of her adolescence in firsthand proximity to various European fin de siècle incarnations of the *grande cuisine,* at formal consular events in Bremen and elsewhere. She knew the great German-Austrian-Hungarian pastry tradition as represented on both European and American soil. But during the family's European sojourn she had also shared meals of pumpernickel bread with cheese or fish, *Stollen,* and "a ghostly, ghastly coffee well diluted with milk," in the kitchens of her uncle Georg Schroeder's parishioners in the coastal neighborhood of Wursten. She had sat peeling just-caught North Sea shrimp in the parsonage orchard when it boasted some twenty varieties of apple.[65] Fifty or seventy-five years before an improbable gaggle of creations called "quiche" descended on fashionable America, the nasty-tempered cook of her aunt Emma Rambert's boarding school in Lausanne had given Irma her first exposure to what the 1931 *Joy* calls "Cheese Custard Pie" (the Swiss *Käsewähe,* a version of a simple and satisfying dish known in all the former lands of the ancient Alemannic tribe).[66] In 1931 there cannot have been many first-time American cookbook authors with memories like these to draw on.

The first *Joy* shows Irma still feeling her way. She displays her own personality more tentatively and sparingly than she would in versions to come, when she more consciously understood what it was that she had to offer against the competition. While she trundled her idea of an expanded version around to uninterested publishers, she may well have doubted that her book had any future. But her eventual success was no accident. She, the self-deprecating amateur, had more to say to American cooks than whole platoons of cookbook authors who had spent their professional lives at the task.

It is worth noting that the other great competitor to Fannie Farmer during much of the twentieth century, *The Settlement Cook Book,* was also thoroughly amateur and chiefly German in its origins—though as the product of a German-Jewish "settlement house" run by the Milwaukee Jewish Mission at the turn of the century, it bore quite a different stamp. (Irma knew and admired the expanded editions that had blossomed from the first small recipe collection, and did the work the honor of casually borrowing some items from it for *Joy.*) But *Settlement* was not personable or fun, though it was not as starchily institutional as *The Boston Cooking-School Cook Book.* No other work matched Irma's ability to sound like a real person talking to other people. One need only compare a few pages of her writing with the would-be common touch of the relentlessly upbeat Ida Bailey Allen to see the essential phoniness of the latter and the unfeigned humanity of Irma.

This quality is inextricably linked to the mad inclusiveness of her culinary tastes. Irma Rombauer dearly loved to impress people, but along with her air-assuming tendencies went a curious and very strong streak of anti-elitism. The modern brand of food snobbery would have been thoroughly abhorrent to her. In her own life, she reserved a particular disdain for what she called "luxe de dentiste." When it came to food, she liked what she liked, with no apologies. She was equally happy eating canned asparagus soup or *Hasenpfeffer*. She was not without her own standards of right and wrong in cooking (they chiefly emerged in her approach to baking), but never thought of setting herself up as an arbiter of elegancies. When, in the 1931 *Joy*, she half jokingly calls a canapé "Deviled Eggs de Luxe" and adds, "(But no longer living up to their name since Woolworth has taken to selling caviar at ten cents a tin),"[67] she is obviously all for Woolworth's de-deluxing a symbol of swank.

In the makeup of her own culinary preferences, Irma would thus turn out to possess a great advantage. She would never presume to *lead* American taste; the existing state of taste was fine with her. She genuinely liked the American culinary Zeitgeist as it had developed in the course of her lifetime. She was naturally attuned to the popular idea of cooking as imaginative diversion and congenitally resistant to the lumbering pedagogy that had been for a time synonymous with cookbook writing—nor was she interested in a latter-day, sugar-coated version of that pedagogy. Her idea of how to make a cookbook, aside from a few excursions into what she considered the necessities of a basic manual, was to tell other people not how they should cook but how she cooked and what a bang she got out of it. It happened that American women in their new centralized, unexpectedly isolated kitchens, facing the solitary task of meal making with no more of the old communal knowledge than Irma had possessed on her wedding day, wanted nothing more than just such a radiant presence at their sides.

6

Rombauer and Bobbs-Merrill:
The Making of an Enmity

When Irma's Indianapolis connections helpfully tried to introduce her to a publisher in 1932, Ina Vonnegut considered the meeting of her two chief dinner guests an auspicious event. To her vivacious, dignified, slightly plump, immensely chic little St. Louis cousin she presented a tall, bespectacled man of fifty-three with a courtly air and a penchant for unlit cigars: David Laurance Chambers, vice president of the Bobbs-Merrill Company. She did not know that they were destined to become implacable foes.

Politely cornered over the dinner and bridge table, Chambers agreed to consider Mrs. Rombauer's book and some sort of revised manuscript material. He did not know a thing about cookbooks, and thus handed it all over to his right-hand woman, an associate editor named Jessica Brown Mannon. Mrs. Mannon secured three readers' reports, which today are preserved—with a revealing trove of other papers bearing on the early publishing history of *The Joy of Cooking*—in the Lilly Library of Indiana University at Bloomington.

One reader found the work "just another cook book" with no distinctive niche to fill.[1] Another (Mrs. Mannon's own sister) saw no great merit in the new recipe-writing method and pronounced the effort "awfully tame" by comparison with *The Palmer House Cook Book*, a tie-in with a famed Chicago restaurant that was one of the company's few recent forays into the cookbook field.[2] The most analytical of the three, a local high school home-economics teacher named Stena Marie Holdahl, was lukewarm. She complained about the title, was noncommittal on the new recipe format, and pointed out such lapses from received modernity as ignoring commercial presoaked hams. "It impresses me as a collection of the best of the recipes used in advertizing [sic] or so-called educational literature of food and equipment concerns," she wrote.

> The outstanding selling argument as I read is that the recipes have all the earmarks of being tried and retried and home table tested and pronounced good enough to publish by family and friends.
>
> Most of the material is legitimately filched as are the recipes and instructions in all cook books.
>
> I sum up my reaction to the book, certain changes considered, by saying that it is probably not necessary to the cooking population, but there are lots of good recipes between its covers.[3]

On February 23, 1933, Laurance Chambers sent Irma an elaborately polite rejection letter commenting on how well she had done with the book already and saying that "the book trade is in such a low state that we could not get any wider distribution for THE JOY OF COOKING than you are doing without our help."[4] It is not clear what happened next, except that she continued vainly trying to interest a publisher in her labor of love for at least two more years. But Jessica Mannon, a woman of patience and penetration, had tried a few of the recipes herself and retained some qualifications about the readers' opinions.

Whether she persuaded Chambers to have another look or Irma again approached Bobbs-Merrill, something had changed by the fall of 1935. Earlier that year, the company appears to have talked Irma into doing a revision on speculation (i.e., with no guarantee of either acceptance or reimbursement for expenses incurred in the work), based on yet another version that it had considered and pronounced not good enough. "Let's hope the third time proves the charm," Mrs. Mannon wrote to Irma on November 4, 1935, as Bobbs-Merrill began its study of the final version—a typescript prepared without pay by the loyal

Mazie Whyte, which filled fifteen volumes in notebook binders.[5] It was a complete recasting of the 1931 *Joy* in the new recipe format, together with a large number of new recipes, all supplemented by enough general instructional material to stack up creditably against the major all-purpose manuals.

Jessica Mannon and Laurance Chambers must actually have been primed to go ahead with the book before they had prevailed on the inexperienced author to finish getting it into acceptable shape at her own expense, because the editorial staff had word-count estimates in about a week. A contract signing was quickly scheduled. On December 5 Irma Rombauer and Laurance Chambers met at the company's Indianapolis offices to solemnize a professional marriage made in hell, or at least purgatory.

Irma did not then know much about Bobbs-Merrill, except that it was an old fixture of the Indianapolis business world. In fact, it was a great and remarkable house that had been a true pioneer of American publishing. No one could then have predicted the dismal decline that would more or less coincide with the rising fortunes of *The Joy of Cooking*.

Even in 1935 Bobbs-Merrill was something of an anomaly as the only major American publisher with headquarters in the Midwest.[6] It had sprung from a bookstore opened by Samuel Merrill in Indianapolis around 1851, and had gone through several mergers and reorganizations before taking on the name of "Bobbs-Merrill" in 1903. (Will Bobbs, who had then become a partner, had according to Marion been one of Irma's escorts in Indianapolis in her cousin Julia's debutante days.)[7] In the first decades of the century the firm's strength rested equally on three divisions: one for legal publishing (among other things, it was the publisher of record for the proceedings of the Indiana state legislature), one for school textbooks, and one for "trade books"—i.e., general fiction and nonfiction. Under an energetic executive named John Curtis, this last had become one of the most innovative trade houses of its day, not so much in the quality of what it put out (though that was not to be sneezed at) as in its marketing approach.

Even in the firm's last pre-Bobbs incarnation as Bowen-Merrill, the trade division had broken new ground by taking out a round of newspaper advertisements to call attention to its 1898 historical novel *When Knighthood Was in Flower*, by Charles Major. Historians of book publishing usually point to this event as the first modern book-advertising campaign in the United States, and to the book itself as the first nationally marketed best-seller. Later, John Curtis had rapidly seen the possibilities of movies as an extension of book-marketing resources. He had pursued Hollywood sales of likely properties and experimented with advertising tie-ins before anyone else in the field. During his tenure the company had also explored the then unusual idea of mapping out some likely elements for a best-selling novel and commissioning an author to slap down the thing on paper.

A prophet might have seen signs of stagnation and decline ahead, but Bobbs-Merrill was still one of the great powers in trade publishing. It had James Whitcomb Riley, Richard Halliburton, John Erskine's *The Private Life of Helen of Troy* (one of its star successes), Alice Tisdale Hobart, Mary Roberts Rinehart's "Tish" stories, the historical novels of Inglis Fletcher. Of innovative (or indeed serious) fiction it was no champion, but at one time its nonfiction lists were considered almost peerless in the field of American history. This was chiefly the doing of Laurance Chambers, himself an avid student of Civil War history who reputedly enjoyed the entire confidence of the most eminent scholars. The juvenile trade department, too, was remarkably strong. Its "Childhoods of Famous Americans" series was another successful offshoot of Chambers's interests, but its longtime bread and butter had been Frank Baum's *The Wonderful Wizard of Oz.*

Chambers, a Princeton alumnus who had risen through the ranks at Bobbs-Merrill in its finest epoch, is to this day regarded by some who worked for him as one of the giants of modern publishing, an editor to be ranked with Alfred Knopf or Maxwell Perkins. He had come to Bobbs-Merrill at about the time of the Bobbs acquisition, and had put down strong Hoosier roots by marrying the daughter of a well-known Indiana politician, U.S. Senator Tom Taggart. Most of the editors and many of the authors with whom he dealt viewed him with a respect bordering on reverence. But there were those whose admiration was at best qualified, and a few who frankly loathed him as a monster of sadism, arrogance, and even duplicity. In the late 1980s people still spoke with awe of Chambers's skill as a text editor, his uncanny ability to understand the possibilities of a manuscript and coax them to realization. He was widely thought to be the finest trainer of copy editors in the business. Most of his colleagues also considered him either a hardheaded businessman or a nearly pathological tightwad. In 1935 he was at the zenith of his power at Bobbs-Merrill, having become president in July of that year.

By now Irma Rombauer, proud of her early success with her little production, thought of herself as something of a businesswoman. But nothing in her history of Wednesday Club politicking and mailing out *Joy* copies to delighted St. Louisans had prepared her to read the motives and tactics of such a man. She had no notion of how to defend her own interests or even what interests she had to defend. She did not know that Chambers was an unsurpassed master of the critically staged browbeating scene. Those who worked with him recalled countless screaming rages that seemed as if they must end in apoplexy, controlled tantrums punctuated by adroit lapses into the mode of true-hearted commander of the ship. These hurricanes usually had a strategic purpose—in this case, to clear the ground of any inconvenient authorial claims before he acquired the property.

Irma arrived for the December 5 signing with no lawyer or agent and, the correspondence seems to indicate, was greeted with some sort of ultimatum accompanied by a typically inflamed and intimidating Chambers performance. She was unwell that day with indigestion (from which she suffered increasingly with age). She was ill for weeks after the scene at the office;[8] indeed, Chambers's behavior was such that Jessica Mannon, who understood him very well and served him with complete loyalty, saw fit to wangle an apology from him for having "appeared in a very bad humor."[9] But his well-timed fit of spleen had cost Irma Rombauer and her heirs hundreds of thousands (perhaps millions) of dollars. In her flustered and cannily exploited inexperience, and almost certainly facing Chambers's threatened refusal to publish her book, she had signed a contract assigning the copyright of the new edition *and the 1931 original* to Bobbs-Merrill.[10]

It was an incalculable blunder. In fairness to Laurance Chambers, his insistence on acquiring copyright to the work at hand was not in itself an outrageous swindle. For a publisher to register copyright in its own name on a compilation like a cookbook was not unusual in 1936 and is still an occasional practice today (an obvious example being the current Fannie Farmer edition). The joker was the inclusion of the 1931 copyright. Unfortunately, author-publisher relations would reach the stage of open war in only a few years, just as the extraordinary value of the property—a godsend to a company increasingly troubled under Chambers's leadership—was becoming apparent. At that point the 1931 copyright might have given Irma some legal leverage, or even an opening for taking *Joy* to another publisher. But in signing the 1935 contract she had surrendered any such option.

Most probably Chambers saw *The Joy of Cooking* as worth a modest initial risk rather than a great investment. He had no more regard for cookbooks than for any other kind of publishable trash. But when he decided to back a book, he did so with a will. When he decided not to, wild horses would not drag a cent of advertising money out of him. The 1944 success of Ayn Rand's *The Fountainhead*, which he had obstinately pegged as a work of too limited interest to justify ambitious promotion, at first struck him as rather an insult to his judgment.[11] But *Joy* was another matter. Though he was not yet ready for huge printings and all-out campaigns, he was willing to give it a chance to perform against the established manuals, possibly with a bigger push to be contemplated in future. Meaning to lose no time getting the book into the stores, he announced a publication date of March 26, 1936, and quickly set the wheels in motion for a fairly serious promotional effort. The first printing was set at the respectable if not gigantic figure of 10,000 copies.

At that time the work of Bobbs-Merrill was divided between two offices more than six hundred miles apart. It was a somewhat cumbersome arrangement in the absence of aids like photocopiers and everyday long-distance phone calls, but in 1936 the U.S. Post Office had the quaint habit of delivering much first-class mail overnight if not on the same day. In downtown Indianapolis, Bobbs-Merrill occupied a big warehouselike old building on North Meridian Street, the former site of an electric car showroom—there were still traces of battery acid on the floor—dating from the glory days of Indianapolis automobile manufacturing early in the century. This was editorial headquarters, where Laurance Chambers ruled over the process of judging and polishing actual words. The editorial staff might have their private views of his dictatorial temper, but in the first years of his presidency they felt real pride in working for a notable craftsman of modern publishing. The other, subsidiary establishment was in New York, the seat of actual manufacturing, most sales promotion, and some editorial work. A certain spirit of rivalry had developed between these power centers. Walter Hurley, the head of the New York office, ran a rather less rigid ship than Chambers, and from time to time the Indianapolis people felt looked down on by the crew among the bright lights.

None of them had much prior experience with cookbooks; *Joy* was the company's first serious entry into the kitchen-bible field. Bobbs-Merrill's idea of the property it was dealing with did not strike Irma as perspicacious. (According to Marion in *Little Acorn*, the firm vainly tried to throw out the title *Joy of Cooking*.)[12] Looking for pegs on which to hang the spring sales campaign, Chambers promptly assigned one of the Indianapolis editors to work up a comparison positioning *Joy* in regard to *The Boston Cooking-School Cook Book*, *The Settlement Cook Book*, and a recent success titled *The Mystery Chef's Own Cook Book*, an offshoot of the popular radio program that encouraged kitchen-shy people with professional careers to try their culinary wings.[13] Irma, who had never heard of *The Mystery Chef's Own Cook Book*, was more appalled than flattered by these comparisons and by being asked to provide attention-grabbing sidelights on the "uninterestingly blameless life" of such a one as herself, "an unknown ingenue grown old."[14] A few weeks later she was amazed to open her front door in St. Louis to be greeted by a bright young Bobbs-Merrill salesman (Ross Baker, later to be one of her perennial friends at the company) who, she wrote to her cousin Julia Chapman, "calmly informed me that mine was the best cook-book *ever written*." Irma did not believe such a thing for a minute. The checked washable blue and yellow fabric case samples he showed her, the fruit of someone's bright idea about giving a choice of colors to match buyers' kitchen decor, struck her as more "washed-out" than inspirational.[15]

Meanwhile, Jessica Mannon was trying to edit the recipes and instructional material into a planned 6-by-9⅛-inch volume of about 640 pages. (There had been suggestions about also including advertisements—then carried in many cookbooks—and photographs. Both ideas were dropped; Irma eventually persuaded Chambers to retain Marion's old chapter headings, which were not especially space-consuming.) Only a week after the signing Mrs. Mannon was suggesting that Irma's chatty comments and introductory paragraphs before recipes be judiciously pruned in order to save page space. Irma rose in all her dignity. She replied at once by telegram:

RATHER CUT RECIPES THAN PARAGRAPH INCENTIVE TO READ BOOK[S] BELIEVE IT OR NOT IT HAS BEEN CONSIDERED LITERATURE ESPECIALLY BY MEN AVERAGE COOK BOOK DEADLY MONOTONOUS EVEN FOR COOKS THINK THIS DISTINGUISHING FEATURE IMPORTANT WIDELY PRAISED AROUSES CURIOSITY CALLS ATTENTION TO RECEIPTES [*sic*] THAT WOULD NEVER BE TRIED OTHERWISE[16]

Jessica Mannon, the soul of thoughtfulness and sensitivity in her dealings with Irma Rombauer, took her at her word, then and always. Her response to the telegram was not to try to compromise or go through Irma's flights of fancy one at a time distinguishing between the stronger and weaker ones, but to back off entirely. She felt that there was something uniquely friendly and supportive in the way the book spoke to its readers, and did not care to risk alienating this unconventional author. Chambers did not presume to interfere with her editorial judgment in a field so far beyond his own competence. The Irmaisms stayed.

The New York office was starting to set the book in type by the end of December. Galley proofs began to arrive by mail in St. Louis, faster than Irma and Mazie Whyte (still giving her all without asking for a cent) could read and correct them. Now they could see the really remarkable visual transformation that Walter Hurley's production team had worked on Irma's clumsy, unfocused original design (see page 97) for the new recipe-writing method. It is not unreasonable to guess that Bobbs-Merrill had grasped what could be made of the new format before getting Irma to do her final unpaid revision work. Their version provided exactly what any new product needs in staking a first-impression claim against older competition: an unmistakable image.

An ignorant purchaser might well confuse a page of *The Boston Cooking-School Cook Book* with a page from any other cookbook in the standard ingredients-up-front format, but a page of *Joy* proclaimed its identity at once. Irma's original design, with each recipe splashed across the whole page, would have used up extravagant amounts of page space. The stroke of invention that made it possible to sell the book at a competitive retail price—$2.75, later reduced to $2.50—was to set the recipe directions in columns narrow enough to allow two columns to a page, with ingredients indented four spaces from the left-hand margin and marked off to the eye by boldface type.

Irma was no expert on typography or copyediting detail (as can be seen from the many technical inconsistencies of the 1931 production at right). But she entered into the task of correcting the galleys in an insistent spirit. She corresponded with Mina Kersey, the Indianapolis copy editor, on points of usage, and spilled much ink getting Jessica Mannon to overrule Miss Kersey's final "s" on the plural of "hors d'oeuvre." She argued about typographical minutiae such as the way of positioning the recipe titles and numbers of servings within each column, and would not be satisfied until the desired changes were made. Laurance Chambers reluctantly let her have her way on these, but it might have been better if he had not. The truth was that Irma did not really understand what was in her contract, or what went into making books.

CHOCOLATE PRUNE CAKE.

A delightful dessert. It may be served with whipped cream or pudding sauce. Remove the pits and cut into pieces:

1 cup cooked, lightly sweetened, well drained Prunes (page 263)

Sift:

¾ cup sugar

Beat until soft:

⅓ cup butter

Add the sugar gradually. Blend these ingredients until they are creamy. Melt, cool slightly and add:

1 ounce (square) chocolate

Beat well:

2 eggs

Reserve ¼ of the eggs. Add the remainder to the butter mixture. Sift before measuring:

1 cup and 6 tablespoons cake flour

Resift with:

2 teaspoons tartrate or phosphate baking powder or 1⅓ teaspoons combination type (see Baking Powder, page 301)
¼ teaspoon soda
¼ teaspoon salt

Add the sifted ingredients to the butter mixture in 3 parts alternately with thirds of:

⅓ cup milk

Beat the batter until it is smooth after each addition. Add the prunes and:

⅓ teaspoon vanilla

Bake the cake in two greased 8 inch layer pans in a moderate oven 375° for about 25 minutes. Spread the layers with:

Chocolate Butter Icing (page 450)

Make only ½ the amount given. That will be sufficient for the tops of this moderate sized cake. Put the left-over ½ egg in the icing.[17]

The contract was unremarkable, aside from the business of the copyright assignment and the absence of any cash advance against royalty payments for an effort in which Irma had already spent $1,000 of her own money; however, up-front payments were not as usual then as now in the publishing business. It provided a royalty schedule of 15 percent of the wholesale cost for the first 10,000 copies sold, 17½ percent for sales between 10,000 and 30,000, and 20 percent for anything over that. (A clause containing various exceptions for sales to outlets "outside the regular book-selling channels" pointed the way toward later controversy, but was for the moment harmless.) The contract also had the perfectly usual stipulation that any corrections Irma made in proof running to more than 15 percent of composition costs would have to be paid for by her as a deduction against royalties.[18]

The inclusion of this "AA's" (author's alterations) clause probably shows Bobbs-Merrill's inexperience with cookbooks, especially all-purpose culinary manuals like this one. Nobody would realize just what a trap the AA's proviso represented until the final printing was complete. It is unlikely that Chambers was trying to mislead Irma when at the beginning of the production process he undertook to pay about $175 or $180 toward the correction of errors in proof (representing his 15 percent) and left her to understand that this was a generous publisher's share. From her communications with Bobbs-Merrill about production matters she expected that the total charges for AA's would not come to anything near the $175.[19] But as she bustled about debating such details as indenting the number of servings or keeping them flush with the left-hand margin, she was unwittingly setting herself up for an unpleasant shock.

A pattern of unclear author-publisher communications and small misunderstandings had already set in by late winter. Irma was working the only way she could, in an absolute fever of untidy activities. Even as she and Mazie coped with floods of proof, she had stray remnants of the later chapters still to finish and could not resist asking Jessica Mannon to add occasional recipes that she had just discovered. Bobbs-Merrill in turn was always requesting her to cut or shorten things in proof in order to meet the 640-page limit, and had asked her to provide other odds and ends of material to make the manual more timely and complete. Mazie, who had done a working index for the last submission of the manuscript, had begged to be allowed to prepare the final version for the work.[20] (An index is usually commissioned by a publisher and billed to the author, so this piece of uncompensated generosity could be expected to save Irma a fair sum.) The two of them worked at breakneck speed with an eye to the March 26 publication date, under the impression that the actual printing would take no more than the couple of days that Harold Hungerford had spent putting out the 1931 edition. The company, which was budgeting about a month, had soon seen that the target date would have to be moved up to May 1. Somehow everyone assumed that Irma was abreast of the schedule, but no one actually explained it to her until the last week in March.

Without consulting Mrs. Mannon, Irma had meanwhile wangled another piece of local publicity from Marguerite Martyn at the *Post-Dispatch*, a feature article that appeared on March 25, a good six weeks before the book would be available. Proudly writing to Indianapolis to describe her coup, she was abashed to be rather crossly told that it had been a mistake. (Customers frustrated at the bookstore by premature notices often neglect to come back.) "I am crushed at having worked at cross-purposes when I thought I was furthering the publication," she contritely told Jessica Mannon.[21] But a worse mess erupted on April 18, when she received a letter from Mina Kersey announcing that the printer's bill for alterations in proof was in and that Irma's share of it was $221.10, to be deducted from her first royalty payment when it should be due.[22]

Irma was beside herself with rage. She had never understood that she was getting anywhere near the 15 percent threshold for AA's specified in the contract—and Chambers, though he had cautioned her that needless changes in proof might cost her something, had not furnished her with accurate estimates of what the total charges might be. Very likely he had not guessed rightly himself, and had allowed rosy-looking early projections to be sent to her because he knew so little about cookbooks. In hindsight it can be seen that Irma's insistence on altering details of the format had added up quickly because more of the text than she realized had already been set in type when she requested the changes. Bobbs-Merrill's insistence on getting her to do extensive cutting in proof had also been part of the mischief. But the most insidious source of AA's had been the cross-references.

At the galley-proof stage, there is no way to print cross-references with the final page numbers. The usual way of dealing with them is to insert the meaningless ciphers "00" or "000," calling attention to the fact that the real numbers are to be filled in when pagination is final. As can be seen from the sample recipe on pages 154–155, a general manual like *The Joy of Cooking* is simply crammed with cross-references. In fact, some publishers partly exempt cookbooks from the usual allowance for AA's, on the theory that in this branch of literature cross-references are too numerous to be handled in the usual fashion. Bobbs-Merrill, not experienced at producing cookbooks, had not gauged the problem rightly. The cutting in proof had thrown page references off even further.

On top of the misunderstanding about the publication date, this contretemps dealt a terrible blow to Bobbs-Merrill's relationship with its hopeful debutante. In her view, the company had put her and Mazie under intolerable pressure to finish their end of the work more than a month before they should have had to, and was responsible for a lot of textual errors that could have been avoided with less rush. The affair of the AA's struck her as a contemptible piece of meanness if not calculated deception—and to add insult to injury, many of the errors requiring correction in proof had in her opinion been made by the office and charged to her.

Bypassing Miss Kersey (who appeared immune to her charm), Irma wrote repeated appeals to the person she most trusted, Jessica Mannon. Of course Mrs. Mannon could do nothing. In any minutest detail of Bobbs-Merrill's fiscal affairs, everyone knew where final authority rested and what it would say. "Never has human hand squeezed a dollar bill tighter than Mr. Chambers's," the distinguished editor Hiram Haydn later marveled after a brief and embattled stint at Bobbs-Merrill in the early 1950s.[23] The president was not accustomed to atone for alleged faults, even in cases far clearer than this one, by shelling out any amount of money large or small. Nor could Irma, the ladies'-club Machiavelli, find any exploitable division of loyalties within the house. In that era there was no one in the Indianapolis office who, no matter what his private grievances, did not close ranks behind Chambers's leadership. All Jessica Mannon could do was to keep courteously saying that the firm considered the charges well within the limits of accepted publishing practice.[24]

By the time Irma ceased her impotent protests in mid-June, the seeds of an intense mutual dislike had been sown. She thought she had been misled and financially penalized for it; she would retain an image of an outfit that introduced editorial errors, did not bother to communicate reliably with its authors, and had to be watched lest it fleece them. Chambers, who thought she had been given enough information to keep track of accumulating charges, would in turn remember a troublemaking woman who had fussed and caviled at every stage over matters outside her own competence, and who had had the nerve to blame Bobbs-Merrill for the extra expense she had incurred through her own inefficiency. Marion Becker—who at about this time had a misunderstanding of her own with Bobbs-Merrill over the bill for fifty copies she had ordered—would never receive any impression but that her mother was dealing with sharpers of dubious editorial competence. But for the time being, the forms of civility prevailed thanks to the gentle and diplomatic Jessica Mannon, whom Irma always exempted from her growing disgust with Bobbs-Merrill.

Cheated and frustrated though she felt herself, Irma had nonetheless fallen on her feet in one regard. She could not possibly have found a house better equipped to turn her cherished book into a sales success. On her own, she could never have kept it in print for four years running, much less brought it to the attention of a national audience. No best-selling American cookbook except *The Settlement Cook Book* (which was handled in its best years by a private offshoot of the original Milwaukee settlement organization) has ever reached the public without the aid of either an established trade book publisher or a national service-magazine publisher. (*The Boston Cooking-School Cook Book*, for example, was in bookstores from coast to coast as a perennial part of the Little, Brown backlist at this same epoch, while *My Better Homes and Gardens Cook Book*—as it was then titled—had been advertised and sold since 1930 through the parent magazine.)

Bobbs-Merrill, long known as a pioneer in promoting books, meant to treat *The Joy of Cooking* as a banner of modernity showing up the obsolescence of such rivals as *Boston* and *Settlement*. Chambers had talked it up at the winter sales meeting in New York with Ross Baker and the rest of the salesmen; Baker had mapped out a strategy with Denhard, Pfeiffer and Wells, the advertising agency that handled the Bobbs-Merrill account. Together they had hit on the gimmick of a money-back guarantee to appear in print advertisements and on the dust jacket of the book: "Give this book a fair test for actual use. Try any dozen recipes. Then if you are not completely satisfied, return it and your money will be cheerfully refunded."[25] Anyone who has observed the infinite capacity of the human mind to misconstrue recipe directions will know this for the meaningless circus pitch that it is, but Bobbs-Merrill would continue to make much of it for the next half century while periodically assuring journalists that only some niggling handful of buyers had ever asked for their money back. The advertising copy dwelt heavily on Irma's up-to-date coverage of timely angles such as kitchenette cookery for the spatially challenged, recipes using electric mixers (which had been around since the 1920s but were still not addressed by the two big bibles), the new medium-temperature roasting method that meat packers had begun touting in the 1930s, and—Prohibition having been history for nearly three years—a handful of recipes for alcoholic cocktails. (Chambers, a teeto-taler, and Irma, who had scorned the Eighteenth Amendment and the Volstead Act with a fine South St. Louis hauteur, were equally eager to join the race for capitalizing on Repeal.) The ads and brochures also announced that Mrs. Rombauer was the first cookbook author to give "*the size of the pan* in which cakes are to be baked,"[26] something that the experts might tell you was a critical factor but that was not yet written into most recipes.

Chambers also assigned a young Indianapolis staff member, Angus Cameron, to carry out the actual publicity follow-up in terms of media contacts and promotional appearances. Cameron had a hard time at first getting Irma to go along with the latter. He appointed himself her constant pen pal and gently tried to enlarge her distinctly pre-twentieth-century ideas about when it is tasteful to blow one's own horn. As publication date neared, he also drafted a circular for book-sellers to demonstrate the superiority of Irma's recipe format through graphically juxtaposed examples of recipes from *Settlement, Boston,* and *Joy.*[27] Once the book was in the stores, Cameron sent off a huge fusillade of letters to newspaper women's-page columnists and book reviewers, and was soon rewarded with a deskful of glowing comments.

"If this book has too wide a circulation there will be little for us foods [sic] editors to do," remarked "Mary Meade" (Ruth Ellen Lorrien, later Ruth Ellen Church) of the *Chicago Tribune* in her note of thanks for a review copy.[28] A Detroit domestic-science school praised *Joy* as "a work of art—full of the finest recipes that we have ever been privileged to read."[29] The popular illustrator James Montgomery Flagg, a noted cooking hobbyist, claimed that Mrs. Rombauer "had written the first cookbook that could be called human."[30] Cameron did not fail to apprise her of her contribution to his own domestic happiness. "I was married last Thursday (week ago yesterday)," he wrote on May 8, "and my wife has said that she already has three reasons to be grateful to you and I agree with her. The three reasons were all delightful."[31]

With Cameron's tactful encouragement, Irma began to feel at home with publicity appearances, which he had had to urge on her at first.

She put the AA's humiliation behind her with a summer trip to the West Coast to see Put and Nita, intent on visiting all the Northwest Coast and California bookstores she could from a list Cameron had given her. She reported finding the book variously labeled—" 'America's greatest cook-book' (modest, that) and 'The cook-book to end all cook-books.' "[32] She was treated as a real celebrity, at least in her own circles, in St. Louis. In the spring the *Post-Dispatch* had offered her a column in its Sunday magazine. For a time she hoped to parlay this into a nationally syndicated column (the idea went nowhere and the original column was not long-lived, but it was a great boost to Irma's morale during the first kickoff season).[33] Initial sales of *Joy* were respectable, with the company's figures showing 6,838 copies sold in the first six months after the May 1 publication date—a more than honorable showing.[34] By then, Bobbs-Merrill was already planning a second 10,000-copy printing.

But in some ways Irma was still a Candide in big-time publishing. In the fall of 1936 she stumbled over one of the pitfalls that lie in wait for modern food writers. She returned from her West Coast trip to find a complaint (forwarded by Angus Cameron) from an advertising agency that handled the Rumford Baking Powder account, indignantly disputing *The Joy of Cooking*'s "unfair" explanation of the differences among various types and brands. Irma, horrified, begged Cameron to get a legal opinion on the issue while she tried to find some way to defuse the offending passage. When Mina Kersey notified her of the new printing and invited her to correct any errors she had found in the first one, it seemed like a providential chance to placate corporate wrath. Unfortunately, no one in Indianapolis had told Laurance Chambers of the whole affair when Irma innocently sent him a telegram about her proposed correction.[35]

At this the Great Baking Powder Keg blew sky-high. Cameron, who was at the moment out of town, had handed his file on the affair over to Colonel Robert Moorhead, head of the Bobbs-Merrill law-book division; so on demanding to be shown the file, Chambers found nothing. He promptly laid about him with a blitz of telegrams, phone calls, memos, and letters to make mad the guilty and appall the free. Irma was very angry at his high-handed theatrics, and this time said a thing or two sharply enough to win an apology of sorts.

The upshot probably was just what it would have been without the president's interference: a polite letter from the author to the Rumford representatives gently pointing out that she was "an amateur writing for amateurs"[36] and a new passage in the second printing carefully hedging on her earlier classification of "single-acting" and "double-acting" baking powders. Pesky technicalities were thickly insulated with a good dose of Irma:

> When confronted with the questions growing out of the use of the various forms of baking powder now on the market the puzzled layman is apt to sigh for the good old days, when this article was made at home, rather haphazardly, from a formula handed from one generation to the other.
>
> Had I died in 1933 baking powder would have been found written on my heart. [This—too good not to recycle—had been lifted from one of her frantic missives to Cameron.] Due to the complexity of the problem it became one of life's major issues.
>
> When William Beebe's nerves became overwrought due to the study of the personal relationships of birds, he turned from them to occupy himself with the habits of the less emotional fishes. I had no such outlet. I had to battle with many new things. . . .[37]

This experience confirmed Irma in her preference for steering clear of concrete scientific explanations and deflecting inconvenient factual issues into droll banter. She would never repeat the risk of venturing beyond protected amateur terrain in the guise of a serious instructor. It was certainly the wisest policy, for not only was she too old and science-shy to master such lore, but her chance for a national reputation rested not on chemical expertise but on the quality of humanity that James Montgomery Flagg had recognized.

After the initial burst of interest, sales of the supposed new classic fell off somewhat. Irma was not discouraged, nor were the growing circle of her fans at Bobbs-Merrill. By the time of the commercial edition's first anniversary, in May of 1937, Angus Cameron was telling her, "If you have any misgivings about the permanence of THE JOY OF COOKING, you may as well give them up. Without casting undeserved bouquets in our direction, I want to say to you that we have virtually accomplished the Herculean task of establishing a standard cook book. . . . Of course a standard cook book isn't made in a day—or a year—for that matter. We shall count on your continued and fine cooperation which we know will be forthcoming."[38] Within another year, Bobbs-Merrill was in the market for new ideas to harness the talents of Irma Rombauer.

The unlikely child of her middle years now occupied nearly Irma's whole thought. It was her idée fixe to see *The Joy of Cooking* not just a modest national success but a real reigning favorite. Apparently she worked on it virtually every day, seeking out more recipes, trying to get a handle on the latest products, always mentally projecting some grand reworking. The woman who had spent her entire life as someone's daughter, wife, or mother was at sixty an independent career personified. (It was characteristic of her particular brand of hauteur to describe herself as a "housewife.") The furious energy that once had had no focus beyond Wednesday Club intrigue and progressive charities was now bent on the future of her book.

Laurance Chambers was not ready to put more eggs in that basket. But he saw some sense in developing the company's most marketable cookbook writer to date. The correspondence suggests that Bobbs-Merrill indicated an interest in having her do another book, this time in the hurry-up-cuisine line. In any case, in July of 1938 Irma suddenly descended on the New York office, en route from a Maine vacation with the Chapmans to another sojourn with Put in Seattle, and unveiled to Ross Baker the idea that had come to her: a book of recipes for canned and packaged foods. Perhaps she had come in the hope of seeing Angus Cameron, who had recently relocated to the New York office, but he was gone, having just accepted an offer from Little, Brown.

The company was interested enough to ask for an outline. Irma could not work that way. Her style was to rush at a task and pummel it to the ground; she could neither draft nor follow careful blueprints. But she did have a very definite concept in mind: an inexpensive book or booklet of convenience-food recipes in all the usual menu categories, aimed at young people and others "who like to cook at home but who have small quarters and little time for complicated food."[39] It would be compact and catchy, and would have the extra advantage of eventually serving as an addition to the future revised edition of *Joy* on which her hopes were fixed.

Wisely or unwisely, Chambers and Mrs. Mannon gave Irma her head instead of trying to pin her down to well-outlined procedures. She galloped through the work in a matter of months, buoyed by the sense of having something to contribute that nobody had done before in quite the same way. She was right. Manufacturers' brochures and even brand-name recipe collections there were aplenty, but the particular mix of elements she was after could not be found in any one source.

She saw the general foundation as recipes cadged without much ceremony from commercial labels or promotional booklets. Of these Irma had a large collection that had already seen some service in preparing *The Joy of Cooking,* and she rightly figured that industry home economists would be more than happy to supply more. Marjorie Black of the National Canners Association and Eleanor Ahearn of Procter & Gamble (a Cincinnati connection of Marion's) were particularly helpful. Irma also naively thought of running a quick-recipe contest in a St. Louis newspaper and using the results, but Jessica Mannon prudently warned her not to build too much on this questionable tactic.[40] Instead, she gradually decided to allot some time to easy recipes for fresh produce and fish that met her idea of speed (thirty minutes from start to finish, sometimes hedged a bit) without necessarily resting on packaged convenience products.

Mrs. Mannon, though resigned to seeing the upshot of all this only when the manuscript should reach her, was nervous about the risk of copyright infringements on preexisting recipes. But Irma had consulted a lawyer on the point. She announced with confidence that recipes per se were not subject to copyright protection. To this day any copyright claimed on recipes is as good as useless, and the company's ignorance of the fact is another sign of its unfamiliarity with publishing cookbooks. As Irma cheerily explained:

> A slight change in wording or ingredients makes them the property of them who pirate them—excepted, of course, are lengthy passages from copyrighted books. It is a curious thing, the origin or popularity of dishes. A chiffon pie, an icebox cookie, a soup sweeps the country and there is scarcely a variance in a dozen publications. Muffins, waffles, cream puffs etc. seem to be standard recipes and anybody's property—at least so I am advised (and so I hope is the case).[41]

"Anybody's property" or no, she felt assured of her own essential originality. Like all who work with recipes for a living, she had come to appreciate how oddly they hover between the ethical (or legal) "mine" and "thine." It was quite clear to her that her book would bear a legitimately distinctive stamp. Collecting recipes from soup manufacturers troubled her no more than borrowing them from friends, since she invariably tried and adjusted them as she preferred. Nonetheless, she soon realized that her first idea of using brand names like Bisquick or Jell-O would bring her into dangerous proprietary waters and made sure to refer to them generically. Probably her original reason for thinking of brand names was that the composition and package size of some products—most conspicuously, canned soups—varied from manufacturer to manufacturer enough to make straightforward substitutions difficult.

The manuscript reached Jessica Mannon in mid-February. Once more she tried to feel out the author on the subject of being edited, and was answered with a perfectly Irma-like mixture of obstinacy, candor, and feminine attitude-striking. "Now you disapprove," Irma fluttered in response to one editorial objection, "and I shall never again know what is Hoyle or what isn't and shall lose the fun I have had in compiling nonsense."[42] Mrs. Mannon was not the woman to batter down Irma's resolution:

> I am conscious—keenly so—of being a second rate writer, but what bothers you about my phrases—is what best represents what I want to say. . . . Your disapproval of the bits I like best makes me shaky about writing—as I feel more commonplace and second rate than ever with them out. (To me it is putting a silk patch on a cotton gown.) Unless they are bad English (which I fail, alas, to recognize) please leave them in.[43]

Irma meant to be equally adamant about the new contract negotiations. Whether or not she yet understood the magnitude of her mistake on the original copyright of *Joy*, she was determined never to submit to another author's alteration charge. She announced to Jessica Mannon:

> As to the cost of the neccessary [sic] corrections I want it clearly understood please, that this time I bear no cost *whatever* in connection with neccessary or unneccessary corrections after the manuscript is turned over to you. It is not the money, (it was not the money in the first place) it is the bickering and the annoyance that I will not go through with again. I am not strong and the pressure put upon me last time was nearly my physical undoing.[44]

This time she had a lawyer in St. Louis to back her up: Paul Hoeffer, one of Marion's old chums. That Bobbs-Merrill would insist on holding copyright after the precedent of the first book was as unchallenge-able as the sum of two plus two, but the lawyer could and did chip away at Laurance Chambers on other issues. He inquired about reining the company in on discount sales until Chambers felt obliged to assert Bobbs-Merrill's sense of honor: "I take it you're afraid we may be tempted to use Paragraph 10 to the disadvantage of the author. We're pretty punctilious about that sort of thing, sir!"[45] The president agreed to omit the usual AA's clause—"a thing I have never known him to do before," Jessica Mannon marveled[46]—and gave way on the royalty arrangement. On this book, now titled *Streamlined Cooking*, royalties were to be calculated on the basis of the retail price (not wholesale, as in her *Joy of Cooking* contract). After some dickering Hoeffer secured a schedule rising from 10 percent to 12½ percent after the first 5,000 copies sold and 15 percent after the first 10,000 copies, an advance of $300 against royalties to be paid half on delivery of the manuscript and half on the date of publication (May 19, 1939), a speeding-up of royalty payments to thirty days rather than three months after each semi-annual statement, and a limitation of discount-royalty provisions to sales of more than 250 copies.[47]

From Irma's point of view, getting legal representation had been a sound move. Chambers, however, cannot have cared much for this turn of author-publisher relations. By his own lights he was a man of old-fashioned rectitude, straight and fearless in all dealings. He liked this to be recognized by his authors, and what he especially relished from them was *deference*. He got it—according to the sharp-tongued William Finneran, who joined the company in the early 1940s as a salesman—from "a lot of sycophant women" published by Bobbs-Merrill, of whom the best-known was the historical novelist Inglis Fletcher.[48] ("He was the greatest American editor who ever lived," she once told the *Indianapolis News*. "He taught me everything I know about writing."[49] She was not alone in these opinions.)

Finneran's diagnosis of the president's professional outlook as he encountered it was "At that time in his life he wasn't sure whether he liked a person or not unless he could control them."[50] Here, however, was a woman author whom he could not control. She considered her-self as much of an authority in her field as he was in his. She did not produce manuscripts that Chambers—unfamiliar with and disdainful of how-to books—could exercise his widely admired editorial talents on. She let him know that she thought herself ill-used and hired a lawyer to win unprecedented concessions on her contract. With each new stage of their dealings his distaste ripened toward active hostility.

The outcome of everyone's efforts with *Streamlined Cooking* was a terrible flop. Bobbs-Merrill as usual took pains over promotion, with good hopes for tie-ins with manufacturers in the wake of a favorable notice in the newsletter of the National Canners Association. Andrew Hepburn, Angus Cameron's successor as publicity coordinator, wanted to try the new medium of radio and got up a script for a two-minute spot that Bobbs-Merrill asked its salesmen to distribute to likely-looking corporate cosponsors around the country. It called *Streamlined Cooking* "as modern and up-to-date as the New York World's Fair," and stressed the marvel of turning out meals in thirty minutes. (Disbelieving straight man: "It can't be done!" Program anchor: "It can and it has and it is being done.")[51] Irma, by now an old hand at radio appearances on KMOX in St. Louis, visited an Indianapolis radio station to deliver a version of this pitch (as rewritten by herself) that she and Hepburn hoped would crystallize the interest of the Stokely Company, a large manufacturer of canned goods, in joint grocery-store displays of *Streamlined Cooking* and Stokely products.[52] But for some reason Bobbs-Merrill's courtship of such reciprocal back-scratchers was not especially successful. Nor did the general public flock to *Streamlined* despite the cheery blurb writer's litany of modern archetypes for whom it was tailor-made, from "the business woman who hurries home from the office to prepare the evening meal" and "the woman who has no maid" to "the camper, the trailer-dweller, the vacationist in a summer cottage," or "the husband who batches alone at home."[53] It was soon clear that the new book was not attracting any of these parties in substantial numbers.

No one ever knew quite why *Streamlined* failed to make a name for itself. Irma complained loudly about one batch of dust jackets that she pronounced "the acme of bad taste" and a strike against the book.[54] The retail price ($1.75, as opposed to Irma's original hope of a $1.00 book) may have been unattractive as well for a rather slight volume. Troubled times following a 1938 slump in the slowly recovering national economy may also have been a factor. (The publishing business had been hard enough hit to make Irma fear even for *Joy* sales, though they proved strong enough to warrant another printing in 1939.)

Alternatively, the new book may just not have been good enough to justify a long existence. Somehow Irma and Jessica Mannon, who got along famously as friends, never found the basis of constructive editorial give and take. Either Mrs. Mannon did not feel qualified to thresh out every sentence in a cookbook or she shrank from offending a writer whose gift she had instinctively recognized. It is by no means clear that every change she might have suggested for the 1936 *Joy of Cooking* would have been for the worse; in the event, she left in both charming jeux d'esprit and bits of chitchat verging on the feeble or pointless. *Streamlined Cooking* was much more heavily weighted toward the latter. It applied large swathings of bright banter to material that was relatively thin but distractingly disparate (as suggested by the subtitle, "New and Delightful Recipes for Canned, Packaged and Frosted Foods and Rapid Recipes for Fresh Foods"). The union of only half-marriageable elements—anything from canned French fries or a "soup" of scalded cream with catsup to pan-fried steak or apricot eggnog—was more crushed than cemented by Irma's coy and waggish introductory sallies:

> Did you know that Ghandi [*sic*] isn't bald? It's the way he cuts his hair—all a matter of taste, you see. A vegetable plate, unadorned, looks a bit bald too. Parsley adds to the scenery.[55]

> The Pennsylvania Department of Agriculture is now offering purple, red, pink, blue, yellow and white potatoes with red or blue eyes. Suit yourself and your color scheme, but red eyes might prove to be a blight on the party.[56]

In *Joy* her flights of fancy had been able to play entertainingly off a core of good solid instruction. *Streamlined*, by contrast, was an arbitrary and half-finished brainstorm. Even the dedication to Julia and Niles Chapman had a posturing air:

> This publication is the result of an indiscretion on my part. On a sleepless night the idea sprang (unlike Minerva from the brain of Jove) from a digestive disorder caused by an overindulgence in a Maine lobster dinner. I therefore dedicate it to my hosts, Mr. and Mrs. Niles Chapman, who tempted me, and hold them responsible for all consequences.[57]

Her maiden voyage in commercial publishing had been a work that hung together on its own merits (with the aid of an apt page design).

But this time she had fooled herself into thinking—and Bobbs-Merrill into hoping against better editorial judgment—that a bright idea adorned with enough Irmaisms could be a book.

Irma was loath to abandon her ambitions for *Streamlined Cooking*. As late as the spring of 1940 she and Bobbs-Merrill were hoping that an advertising agency's proposal to make room in the book for some direct plugs of the Dromedary Company's line of canned and packaged goods would convert failure into triumph.[58] But the idea fell through— surely a blessing in disguise, considering the importance that Marion Becker would later attach to her and her mother's independence of commercial ties—and Irma's attention was diverted to a new Chambers outrage.

Joy of Cooking sales had after all remained steady enough for a fourth 10,000-copy printing following the successful printings of 1936, 1938, and 1939. (In the light of hindsight, the 1940 printing may well have been a milestone in the company's thinking about the future of *Joy*.) This time Mrs. Mannon invited Irma to catch up on errors that had not been corrected in earlier printings, and quickly received a list that the author had been polishing up for three years. But unknown to Irma, production had actually begun when someone had had this afterthought. More than six weeks after her list had reached Mrs. Mannon, she was astonished to receive a bill of $15.20 for the printer's alterations, which had come in all to $30.40. The editor's accompanying note said, "I felt that the corrections you made helped the book and that we would also benefit by them, so we have been glad to assume one-half of the cost ourselves."[59]

Fifteen dollars was not by now a horrendous sum for Irma, but after two previous reprintings with no charges for any AA's (including the reconstructive surgery for baking powder), she was justified in being aghast. She was also troubled about the state of her royalty payments (not having grasped that the schedule was based on the wholesale cost of *Joy*). She wrote at once:

> I was so particular about the contract for Streamlined because I wanted to avoid my first mistake. Don't you appreciate my efforts to improve and keep my work up to date? After all this is a *joint* venture and Bobbs-Merrill have done much to make my end difficult. I am utterly discouraged.
>
> . . . I'd like to ignore it—but I cannot because I have to continue working with the firm. I appreciate their good qualities

and I like Mr. Hepburn very much—but I deplore the firm's pinch penny attitude. I feel that they do not want me as a friend.[60]

Mrs. Mannon, who had not understood that this was the first bill for alterations on reprintings, realized that the company had been sloppy in requesting corrections after part of the material was already in type. She was sufficiently impressed with the justice of the author's case to tell Laurance Chambers that she thought the charges had been a mistake. Amazingly, the bill was withdrawn.[61] This victory of fifteen dollars was perhaps Irma's last unequivocal triumph over Bobbs-Merrill.

The bulk of the Rombauer/Bobbs-Merrill correspondence in the Lilly Library breaks off not long after this episode, leaving unrecorded three important events of the next three years: Jessica Mannon left Bobbs-Merrill for family reasons in 1941 or 1942 and was replaced by her assistant, Rosemary Bretzman York; Irma Rombauer and Laurance Chambers stopped speaking or even communicating in writing on any but the rarest occasions; and *The Joy of Cooking* became a national best-seller. It is likely that someone at the company took pains to omit nearly all *Joy* records from the years—or more accurately, decades—of greatest controversy from the donation of Bobbs-Merrill archives to the library in 1967 (though some remarkable items slipped through in what did reach Lilly). Some of what happened can be reconstructed from later evidence, but the firm apparently did not want it reconstructed.

With Mrs. Mannon's departure any loyalty Irma had felt toward Bobbs-Merrill editors vanished. Rosemary York's colleagues mistakenly thought that she had a fine rapport with the author. It was, after all, she who finally presided over the great event Irma had dreamed of since 1936: the expansion and revision of *Joy* into a star property. But the price of the book's success would be the worst author-publisher battle yet—a melee that managed to be kept from public scrutiny, but that was drastic enough to leave Irma with a deep distrust of the genial, smiling Mrs. York's true motives.

This nearly undocumented drama was launched by Laurance Chambers's decision to abandon his previous cautious strategy for *Joy*. He had not tried to gamble on it as a blockbuster in 1936, but had given it a modest chance and quietly watched it perform year after year. The fourth 10,000-copy printing in 1940 was followed either by a larger one in 1941 or by successive 10,000-copy printings in 1941 and 1942, because a total of 52,151 copies are recorded as having been sold between 1936 and the end of 1942.[62] Bobbs-Merrill took the precaution of having the 1941 edition copyrighted (in its own name) as a separate edition—a step suggesting that the company was suddenly concerned to forestall even the smallest bit of potential leverage through which Irma might claim any post-1936 change or correction as copyrightable material of her own. By now annual sales were slowly but unmistakably inching upward, with a gain of about 1,000 in the calendar year of 1940. The evidence thus points to 1941 as the likeliest date of Chambers's first concrete plan for a sizable investment in an expanded *Joy of Cooking*. In December of 1942 the company drew up a contract describing a completed revision as then being in existence. Chambers and Mrs. York signed the agreement—but Irma did not. The two sides did not sign a final contract until May 27, 1943, less than two weeks before actual publication as listed in Copyright Office records (June 7).[63]

It takes no huge feat of detection to conclude that the affair of the 1943 contract caused Bobbs-Merrill down-to-the-wire uncertainties about being able to fulfill large advance orders on a major spring title and was the great outrage for which Laurance Chambers and Irma never forgave each other. In 1987 Patricia Jones, who joined the company as an editor in 1942, expressed a belief that the president felt his honor intolerably impugned when Mrs. Rombauer insisted on having an attorney go through every semicolon of the contract sniffing out any intent to rob.[64] (Paul Hoeffer having gone off to war, her St. Louis representative in this instance was her brother-in-law, the staid and diplomatic Julius Muench.) Chambers had been somewhat huffy about the legal vetting of the *Streamlined Cooking* contract, but whatever was said on this occasion must have been much worse. She emerged from the fray without having been able to make much of a dent on key provisions of the contract, but with a wholehearted appreciation of what she had lost in surrendering copyright.

The edition that produced the 1943 contractual wrangle was in itself a stroke of both sales intuition and luck. Irma had worked furiously in 1941 and 1942, knowing that this might be the chance she had sought for more than a decade.[65] As she had hoped all along (and as Chambers probably considered the key to the effort), the revision fitted together nearly all of *Streamlined Cooking* and the 1936 *Joy* on the gamble that their marriage would be a triumph. It also contained a fair number of new recipes and some other chunks of material that put up a good show against the competition. It made a hasty effort to address the food rationing instituted in World War II—a march neatly stolen on the latest (1941) *Boston,* which had just missed Pearl Harbor. Irma had also put together much new accessory information on such subjects as herbs, nutritional tallies for common foods, cooking terms, table settings, and the serving of wines.

It was soon obvious that the amalgamation of *Streamlined* and *Joy* had just the synergistic appeal that Irma Rombauer and Laurance Chambers had hoped for. The success story of the newest *Joy* is plain from the records of copies sold that Bobbs-Merrill periodically furnished to the author. By good fortune they can be roughly compared with the annual tabulations of printings that Little, Brown took to listing on the copyright page of *The Boston Cooking-School Cook Book.* We must keep in mind that the Little, Brown records do not—like the Bobbs-Merrill statements—represent copies actually *sold* (as opposed to *printed*) in a calendar year. Still, the numbers speak for themselves. In the period of 1936 through 1942, *The Joy of Cooking* sold 52,151 copies, topping 8,500 in 1940 and 1941 and 9,000 in 1942. In the same seven years 400,000 copies of *Boston* were printed, the smallest number being 20,000 in 1940 (the year before a major revision). But in 1943 *Joy* sold 61,428 copies, most of that certainly achieved in the seven months after the June 7 publication date of the revision, while Little, Brown printed 75,000 copies of *Boston*. In Irma's annus mirabilis of 1944 *The Joy of Cooking* surpassed its older rival, with 167,261 copies sold to 70,000 of *Boston* printed (and not necessarily sold).[66]

This turn of events must have given Angus Cameron at Little, Brown a certain Cassandra-like satisfaction. "You're going to have to watch *The Joy of Cooking,*" he had mentioned to the company president on his arrival at the firm in 1938. "Oh, no," replied the unperturbed Alfred B. McIntyre; "cookbooks come and go but Fannie Farmer outruns them all."[67] He was wrong. From 1944 until Miss Farmer's heirs got fed up and took the book to Alfred A. Knopf in the 1970s, *The Boston Cooking-School Cook Book* would be consistently, and at last overwhelmingly, outsold by *The Joy of Cooking*. In 1945 *Boston* rebounded to its largest printing ever for a single year, 190,000 copies. Total sales of *Joy* were 94,693. But the figures for the next year were 294,400 copies sold for *Joy*, 110,000 copies printed for *Boston* (both works, incidentally, being released in new editions that year).[68] The only subsequent year in which the Little, Brown book outperformed Irma Rombauer was 1951, when Bobbs-Merrill allowed its stock of the latest printing to run out while readying a new edition.

Joy's sudden ascendancy was the marvel of St. Louis. But it may not have been entirely due to the respective worth of the two books, though *The Boston Cooking-School Cook Book* was certainly in one of its less illustrious phases under the care of Wilma Lord Perkins. The rising fortunes of the younger book owed a great deal to Bobbs-Merrill's selling ideas (and as we shall see, to some accidents of wartime publishing). In Laurance Chambers's philosophy of bookmaking, economies of scale were the saving grace that allowed a publisher to turn a profit on the sorriest junk (a category in which he probably put cookbooks). "Gross volume," he would tell the less-than-convinced editor Hiram Haydn a few years later. "That's the answer: gross volume. You can't expect most good books to sell today."[69]

The handling of *Joy* was a truly amazing embodiment of this approach. The senior sales directors in charge of realizing it were Ross Baker and Bill Finneran. They mounted a tremendous campaign for advance orders in the winter and spring of 1943, and kept up the pressure ever after. Baker and Finneran's salesmen made lavish use of giveaway copies for the personnel in bookstores on their routes. Bobbs-Merrill also began aggressively recruiting partners for special sales arrangements in which, say, a department store would purchase a large number of copies at a steep discount to be offered as a premium or come-on in the cookware section. Another prominent weapon was periodic discount offers to bookstores: one free copy for every ten ordered by the store.[70]

These selling tactics, and the resultant bookkeeping, soon became a bone of contention between author and publisher. The reason can easily be found in the 1943 contract. The royalty schedule, based like that of *Streamlined Cooking* on retail price, was essentially 12½ percent—slightly better than in the rejected 1942 draft of the contract, but equally maddening in that both versions dangled a 15 percent rate in front of the author's nose if at any time after a certain sales threshold (30,000 copies, in the final version) "the cost of manufacturing of the said work (paper, press work, binding, jacket) is reduced to one-seventh of the catalogue retail price." The catch was that the royalty for discounted books was to be based on the discounted price rather than list price, while complimentary copies were subject to no royalty whatever.[71] Bobbs-Merrill's selling practices thus ensured that manufacturing costs would never—as officially tabulated on the books—fall below a seventh of the retail price, the qualifying point for the elusive 15 percent royalty.

The awful truth sank in together with Irma's first taste of true national celebrity. She was not one to depend on mere salesmen to promote her book. She made extraordinary efforts in her own way during 1943, working the St. Louis bookshops and letting no one in town forget the latest fruit of a native daughter's industry. This campaign produced a local triumph that she adroitly parlayed into the turning point of her career. When in July St. Louis sales of *Joy* surpassed those of the number-one nationwide best-seller, Wendell Willkie's *One World*, Irma seized opportunity by the forelock. She sent Willkie an autographed copy of *The Joy of Cooking*, with apologies for having beaten him on her own home turf.

The former Presidential candidate promptly replied with an autographed gift copy of *One World* inscribed, "With congratulations to the people of St. Louis, who show such discriminating judgment." Edith Willkie capped the exchange with a note thanking Irma for *The Joy of Cooking*: "I have scanned it carefully and think it is the most fascinating cook book I have ever read and the most practical."[72] The episode was picked up by the press, and *Time* magazine published a facetious little note on Mrs. Rombauer's hometown triumph. Deciding that the story was worth following up, the magazine then sent a reporter to Indianapolis and St. Louis to assemble a more detailed article on Irma and the book. It appeared on August 16, and admiringly reported that *The Joy of Cooking* was just as reliable as the Bobbs-Merrill guarantee indicated.[73]

While this publicity coup was spreading the Rombauer name from coast to coast, many East Coast editors and food pundits were examining the book with admiration. The timing could not have been better. *Joy* had been around long enough to be a vaguely familiar name, but it was young enough in comparison with the established bibles to seem fresh and unusual. The big selection of can-opener recipes from the 1939 *Streamlined* promised an awareness of modern realities not matched in *Boston* or *Settlement*; the sprinkling of suggestions for meatless or sugarless cooking was a critical wartime selling point. But it was the sense of blithe individuality leaping off the pages of the bulky (884 pages), impersonal-looking collection that piqued the curiosity of the New York food world. Irma began to receive calls from journalists, and even invitations (politely declined, for the nonce) to do newspaper and magazine articles. One unusually persistent representative of the Eastern press decided to make an appeal in person. A young journalist named Cecily Brownstone, then writing on food and nutrition for *Parents Magazine*, got on the train for St. Louis to spend a weekend meeting the new celebrity. The sixty-five-year-old cosmopolite and the energetic young ex-Canadian sat on a bench at the St. Louis Zoo and cautiously surveyed each other. "Did you vote for Roosevelt?" Mrs. Brownstone inquired. The answer was yes, and the two women (who had both become ardent New Dealers) would be friends for life.[74] From then on, Mrs. Brownstone was *Joy*'s constant advocate in New York, already the undisputed center of an ingrown but mightily influential culinary world.

Irma began to visit New York more often—probably at least once or twice a year from 1944 on—and to be lionized among Mrs. Brownstone's food-writer friends. She appeared repeatedly on Mary Margaret McBride's national radio show, attended "a 'wine tasters' party (very chic, I'm told),"[75] received invitations from manufacturers and public-relations agencies to attend events momentous or ridiculous. Pieces of entertaining publicity arose or were manufactured. A husband in a divorce case was said to have become glued to the book as his refuge from gastronomic desperation.[76] Billie Burke appeared on stage holding a copy in her latest Broadway play.[77] The National Father's Day Committee, according to the *El Paso Times*'s version of one widely reported item,

> ... asked Mrs. Irma Rombauer, author of the nation's best-selling cook book, "The Joy of Cooking," ... to plan a special menu for American fathers on June 18th. Mrs. Rombauer, conscious that father's own ideal of thick steak with French fries and lots of onions may not be easy to manage in these days of ration points and shortages, has answered with two dinner suggestions—the dream and the reality. [The newspaper did not record the details.][78]

At last Irma knew herself a star, and she adored it. Victorian-born though she was, she played the modern publicity game with rapidly mounting confidence.

Her wartime success held another particular meaning for the South St. Louis child who had repined at her German identity and longed to become an "American." To her astonishment and gratification, the book (and its author) became a minor but cherished mascot of American war morale. From all around the world, American servicemen wrote to thank her. "No doubt you are and have been accustomed to fan letters but I feel confident that none could be more sincere than this one," began one of her new correspondents.

> To begin with may I introduce myself? Primarily, I am the surgeon aboard this aircraft carrier, the U.S.S. INDEPEN-DENCE. . . . Of no less importance is my collateral duty, that of chairman of the Wardroom Mess Committee, and it is in this regard that I beg to express to you, on behalf of the one-hundred and seventy-five officers, our thanks for your price-less guidance via your book, "The Joy of Cooking." When the latest committee took over six months ago, it was when the going was the toughest, when the men were most tense, the supplies at their meagerest, and the food routine. To make matters worse none of us knew anything about cook-ing and our early sincere attempts merely brought the im-provements expected of a new broom. Not until someone found your book among the belongings of the Captain's Boy, did the remarkable happen. We thumbed hungrily through its pages bringing out, time after time, clusters of culinary gems. The criteria of a recipe's trial were just the presence of its ingredients in our larder, though some minor ones had to be imagined, the results were so perfect that before long even the pilots, who had always been thistles in our hair, were forced to admit the excellence of the cuisine. They soon learned to appreciate dishes never before tasted and to use the varied sauces that replaced the catsup, the vinegar, etc.; so that Lamb Terrapin or Bouillabaisse have become as familiar to them as have Croissants and Macédoine to the committee.[79]

Thanks poured in from humbler writers and people far worse off. From the Pacific theater a weary enlisted man wrote with sincere if incoherent appreciation:

> All though I am not a housewife I have a very [difficult] job to do and when you have twelve hungry Sailors to cook and bake for three times a day you just run out of ideas of what

to fix that is just what happened to me and then I found the new Joy of Cooking and I can tell you this that there isn't money enought [sic] to buy it if I could not get another one just like it.[80]

An American woman interned in the Japanese prison camp at Santo Tomas in the Philippines was sent a copy by her former cook. The food rations were scanty and dreary, but as she wrote, thanks to *Joy* she was able to turn the strange, lopsided supplies of ingredients into something actually appetizing.[81]

Irma's rise to best-sellerdom in time of national crisis thus took on patriotic dimensions that in view of her childhood yearnings and the anti-German nightmare of World War I must have been peculiarly sweet. She was no flag-waver. But she had quietly worked in a couple of notes that would not have been possible in the awful days of the first war, when the whole world of the St. Louis *Deutschtum* had seemed to be the target of a hysterical crusade and even to possess a name like "Rombauer" was to incur suspicion. The mood of World War II was entirely different, at least as regarded German-Americans (the hysteria this time was reserved for Japanese-Americans). In 1943 Irma proudly prefaced her recipes with the comment, "It has been a pleasure to compile this record of our American way of life. Tradition speaks to us in its pages, a tradition of plenty which should always be ours, and which will be, with the intelligent use of our mighty weapon, the cooking spoon."[82]

No German-American of her convictions and background could have summoned the morale for such a remark in 1917 and 1918—nor would many writers have dared to slip in the central watchword of German patriotism in a beloved new homeland that she and her South Side contemporaries had heard quoted at a hundred civic occasions from the 1870s until World War I:

> *Was du ererbt von deinen Vätern hast,*
> *Erwirb es, um es zu besitzen!*

All of the Rombauers' and von Starkloffs' old friends would have known those lines as well as other Americans know the first words of "The Star-Spangled Banner." Anyone of Irma's background would have recognized them at once even in the odd spot she had chosen to stick them, in English translation, at the end of a section on the "precious American heritage of hospitality" in the table-settings chapter:

> That which thy fathers have bequeathed to thee, earn it anew
> if thou wouldst possess it.[83]

With the 1943 book, Irma's dual German and American heritage reached the happiest fusion of her lifetime. But whatever her pride in her newfound American stature, it took on the smack of gall and wormwood when she contemplated her publishers.

Bobbs-Merrill's view of the matter did not entirely deny Irma's part in her own success, but Chambers and the salesmen thought that whatever got more copies circulating was the real key to that success. Sheer volume of sales crudely translated into at least some money for everyone, and if discount sales put more copies of the book in more households, that was all to the good. Irma contemptuously rejected this line of thinking, but there is a distinct possibility that the company was right. Would *The Joy of Cooking* have become "a staple like salt" (*Time* magazine's phrase of a few decades later)[84] for all manner of cooks and gotten into about a million American homes during the 1940s if the publishers had not flooded regular and irregular book-selling channels with bargain offers? The question is unanswerable, but at least thought-provoking. Irma knew only that the book was said to be selling beyond her wildest dreams but that there was something very peculiar about her royalty payments.

There was another significant factor in the success of the wartime *Joy of Cooking*, and it happens to shed some light on the justice of Irma's complaints. In the interest of national preparedness the federal government imposed quotas on paper supplies throughout World War II, driving the trade publishers to frantic stratagems for buying enough to print their seasonal lists and keep up with the demand for particularly successful books. It is entirely possible, although not verifiable, that Little, Brown could not find the paper to manage competitive press runs of *The Boston Cooking-School Cook Book* in 1944, when Irma Rombauer first beat it out. Bobbs-Merrill was lucky enough to farm out some of the *Joy* printing for 1945 and 1946 to the Blakiston Company of Philadelphia, a Doubleday subsidiary that published medical titles and had an unusually large paper quota.[85] Blakiston seems to have done its own shipping, selling (without discounts), and accounting for the book.

When in 1949 Theodora Zavin, an attorney at the New York legal firm of Greenbaum, Wolff & Ernst, examined some of the old *Joy* royalty statements in connection with Irma, Marion, and John's ongoing grievances, she noted that Blakiston's statements (for sales of its *Joy* printings totaling 73,173 in 1945 and 105,103 in 1946) "showed no resort whatever to the mass sales clause" and added, "Interestingly enough, the last statement which you received from Bobbs Merrill, just before the Blakiston Company took over the book [*sic*], shows that slightly more than 50% of their sales for the preceding period were made at more than a 50% discount."[86]

This astonishing observation is corroborated by a comparison of Bobbs-Merrill's own annual tallies of copies sold with a company record of payments to Irma Rombauer from 1936 through 1949 that someone rashly supplied to a law firm seeking ammunition for a wholly different proceeding in 1973. In 1944 *The Joy of Cooking* sold 167,261 copies. At a straight royalty of 12½ percent (the lowest figure in her contract) on a retail price of $2.50, that should have earned Irma about $52,000—a figure that obviously would have been higher if she had been allowed to reach the slippery 15 percent. What she actually got from Bobbs-Merrill was $28,010.44.[87] Of course, we do not know what advice she received from tax experts on arranging to stagger her income from year to year; other factors may have affected the recorded total in this or any other year. But that company sales practices drastically cut into her royalty earnings is clear.

Irma's anger grew with her fame. She would have no truck with the notion that the mass-sales discounts and giveaways actually solidified the book's foothold in the national market. Rightly or wrongly, she believed that the firm's continued reliance on such devices, now that *Joy* was nationally beloved on its own merits, was the sleaziest sort of hucksterism as applied to a fine and distinguished property that could be earning its author a 15 percent royalty on the list price. (The publisher would naturally have taken a more qualified view of the relationship between a book's own merits and its sales record.)

She took to asking booksellers she knew just what terms Bobbs-Merrill was offering during a particular season, and bitterly renewing her outrage. Each party impotently yearned to be free of the other. There is reason to believe that at one point Chambers began negotiating with "Mary Meade"—Ruth Ellen Church, whose column for the *Chicago Tribune* was nationally syndicated—for a projected kitchen manual, which he meant to hold over Irma's head as a threatened replacement for *Joy* if she became too obstreperous. Such was Bill Finneran's recollection, and it is borne out by the report of Joe Bettenmann, the son of old Missouri acquaintances and neighbors of Irma's, that in the 1940s she told his family that her publishers were trying to get rid of her as author of *Joy*.[88]

But if Irma was manacled by the 1935 contract, the publisher's hands were also tied. Authors are after all legally considered to have an interest in their own work even when copyright does not reside with them. Bobbs-Merrill could not have used a syllable of her text if it had broken with her as author. As for dumping a best-seller at the height of its fame and starting all over again with another all-purpose cookbook, that would have been sheer self-destruction for a company that many observers now suspected to be in deep fiscal trouble.

Bobbs-Merrill was thus condemned to live with her complaints. Irma was careful to display her finest brand of warmth and charm toward anyone she actually had to deal with in Indianapolis and New York; indeed, she genuinely liked Ross Baker and many of the sales and editorial staff. But she did not trouble to conceal her hatred of the person she held responsible for cozening and robbing her, Laurance Chambers. After a time, she did not trust Rosemary York (toward whom she was very sweet) any further than she could throw her.

Rombauer-handling strategies became a constant preoccupation at Bobbs-Merrill. No notes or letters passed to her that had not been scanned for legal ramifications. But in public, both parties successfully varnished over the fact that the company president and his best-selling author were not speaking to each other. No matter that in Finneran's words, "Chambers would have a look on his face as if he smelled something bad" at the mention of Irma Rombauer's name, or that when immobilized by an attack of some unpleasant illness (either ulcers or shingles, in Finneran's recollection) she dubbed the affliction "Mr. Chambers."[89] To her family she referred to him as "Old Dynamite."

This situation was not of concern to Irma alone. At every stage of her commercial success she had eagerly shared her good fortune with those closest to her. Her surpassing generosity was entwined with both a surpassing hunger for influence in others' lives and a strong sense of responsibility. It had been deeply satisfying to her to see her nearest and dearest basking in her largesse, but she knew that at her age she must be making other decisions involving their futures.

Even before the first Bobbs-Merrill arrangement she had used the 1931 book to help see Put through law school in Seattle. When royalties started coming in on the 1936 *Joy*, she enlarged her always generous gifts to both children and scrupulously acknowledged what she considered a boundless debt of gratitude toward Mazie Whyte—now Mazie Hartrich, having married a St. Louis businessman named Eugene Hartrich in the spring of 1936. In that year, when Irma's own income from Bobbs-Merrill was less than $1,700, she paid Mazie $900 as the least gesture she could make to recompense the years her friend had spent laboring on the book since 1931. Mazie continued to be her constant companion in the work, asking for nothing and being more than content with the modest sums (between $425 and $500 annually from 1937 through 1942) that Irma was able to spare from her own royalty checks.[90]

With true and lasting success came new opportunities for bounty. (According to Finneran, when he told Irma to anticipate a year's income many times what she had ever dreamed of, she said to him in pure delight, "Now I can do all the things I want for people I like.")[91] As soon as her first really large royalty payment arrived in December of 1943, she sat down and wrote out a check for $2,000 and a note to "Maizie" (as Irma always spelled the nickname):

Isn't this fun? It always gives me a thrill.

To think that we did it and that we are still friends![92]

She never lost her delight in what she called "this semi-annual, extracurricular Christmas."[93] Mazie since her marriage was well provided for in her own right, but that did not lessen Irma's sense of an obligation that also happened to be a pleasure.

She announced to her children that she was more than willing to cover (or handsomely contribute toward) expenses like mortgages, planting or landscaping, clothes, and medical bills. She still had a sense that they wanted looking after. Put had not lost what she considered his feckless ways, and it was plain that John and Marion would never reap more than a sort of tasteful semisolvency from the architectural practice of Garriott and Becker. Other uncertainties had to be figured in as well. She herself might suffer the awful fate of other elderly relatives, a disabling illness followed by years of expensive nursing care. And like anyone in an ongoing financial war, Irma lived with the thought that the enemy might after all contrive to ruin her (and others through her).

There were only two possible steps that Irma could take toward keeping the golden eggs coming in after the present flush of prosperity should be over and the next stage of the Bobbs-Merrill feud should be upon the house of Rombauer. One was to designate a successor. The other was to find a collaborator.

The first was accomplished in the bitter battle of the 1943-contract—Irma's only worthwhile victory in that otherwise frustrating struggle. To the list of obligations that the publisher agreed to assume she succeeded in adding:

> In case of the death of the Author or any disability preventing the Author from making or completing a subsequent revision, if called upon to do so, her daughter, Marion Rombauer Becker of Cincinnati, Ohio, is to be given first consideration in making such revision.[94]

This was something, but it was not enough. In 1943 it was far from certain that Marion would ever be interested in taking over the work. She had been only tangentially involved with Irma's culinary career (aside from having done another set of silhouette chapter-heading decorations for *Streamlined Cooking* in 1939) since the 1931 version of *Joy*. Besides, Irma, who liked having more than one iron in the fire, was perfectly free to find someone else as successor before the time of death or disability. Several difficult and contentious years went by in the turbulent orbit of Irma's personal relations before she was ready to make a formal commitment to the second step—in which, as we shall see, Marion might never have figured if other plans had not gone awry. When in the summer of 1948 she and Irma agreed to collaborate on the next edition of the book, Marion was at least partially sacrificing other priorities that had become very dear to her since she left her mother's St. Louis apartment sixteen years earlier and came to Cincinnati as the bride of John Becker.

7

Family Regroupings

"I divorced my kids when they were twenty-one," Irma once told a friend.[1] The two people in question would have been flabbergasted at that claim. But during the first decade or so after the 1931 *Joy of Cooking*, while Marion was putting down roots in Cincinnati and Put in Seattle, the three of them did get along in a state of both amity and partial independence. Put and Marion carved out their own paths at a healthy remove from their parent, who was now fairly well circumstanced (though not yet wealthy) and able to please herself without constantly invading her children's lives.

On the strength of the 1936 edition's modest success, Irma managed a long summer trip to Europe (including Hungary, which Edgar had never been able to visit). The war quickly put a stop to European tourism, and after 1939 she began occasionally visiting Mexico, a country for which she developed a great love. She went on with her St. Louis clubs and committees, though her generation was starting to fade from such scenes. Meanwhile, she was suddenly occupied with new people and priorities.

In the last years before the war Irma attracted a circle of much younger St. Louis friends—mostly cronies of John Becker's gregarious and witty younger brother, Philip—who were utterly captivated by her irreverent sophistication and grand joie de vivre. Some tongues wagged on the subject of a sixtyish woman palling around with a crew of bright young things. ("Well, you know Irma Rombauer—she doesn't love her children!" was one remark.)[2] But both sides found the relationship bracing.

Phil and his friends were too young to have learned German before the witch-hunts of World War I. Hankering to reclaim this part of the South St. Louis heritage, he asked her to give them lessons. Soon they were the "Thursday night children" of Irma, whom they christened "Frau Rom." Phil proved to have no aptitude at all for the tongue of Schiller and Goethe, and Irma had no idea of how to drill anyone in a grammar that she had never had to think about. (George Schriever, one of the charter members, once asked her whether something was dative or accusative. "You *horrible* man," said Irma, much miffed. "Such an impertinent question! *I* don't know.")[3] Consequently, the group called "The German Class" learned very little German. The curriculum soon wandered off into extemporaneous readings of Hyman Kaplan stories from the *New Yorker* punctuated by occasional Schubert *Lieder* recordings. Most of the "class" were wildflower or outdoor enthusiasts of some stripe, and they took to driving out on weekends to the rural vicinity of Antonia in Jefferson County, some thirty miles south of St. Louis. It was beautiful rolling country in the sub-sub-foothills of the faraway Ozarks. Like so much of America's erstwhile farmland, it had been abandoned in patches since the 1920s and presented a striking alternation of farm and scrub.

Irma had friends with extensive landholdings in the area, May and Charles Rice, who had introduced her to the Audubon Society and helped interest her in land-conservation causes. After a time the German Class began to talk of acquiring a little plot of their own. In late 1939 or early 1940, the Rices agreed to sell a five-acre parcel of their Antonia property to Irma and two of the German Class crew, Terry Nicholson and Ben Audrain. There was already a farmhouse near the road leading to the site, a hillside looking southeast toward the distant Mississippi and the Illinois side. It was their hope eventually to put up a cabin of some sort, letting out the farmhouse to a local family who acted as the Rices' caretakers.

"Frau Rom" and willing German Class volunteers came out on weekends from spring through autumn to begin clearing the tangle of growth that had half swallowed the land. But the coming war postponed and eventually rerouted their plans. Ben Audrain and Terry Nicholson decided to go into the infantry by way of the National

Guard well before Pearl Harbor, and made over their shares of the property to Irma.[4] Other "class" draftees or volunteers soon scattered to the ends of the earth. Most nonessential building was severely curtailed for the duration, but Irma kept on going out to the Rices' when weather and gas rations permitted, usually driven by Terry Nicholson's brother Craig (whose health had kept him out of military service) and the daughter of old South St. Louis acquaintances, Helen-Marie Fruth.

Irma's Jefferson County walks and building ambitions are one expression of a certain mother-daughter emulation that also took other forms during this period. Marion's life in Cincinnati had become a great source of vicarious pleasure and fulfillment to her mother. Irma went there several times a year (sometimes combining these visits with business trips to Indianapolis, a hundred miles away). "Marion has interests, Marion has *interests*," she would tell St. Louis friends in humorous exasperation at the young Mrs. Becker's furious range of activities. But in fact she was very proud to see her child blossom in pursuits hitherto open only to male forebears. "Marion will be too modest to say so, but her mother is not. She is making a place for herself in Cincinnati," Irma wrote to Julia Chapman after a 1945 forum in which Marion had taken part as "the only woman," "speaking on controversial matters" that Irma did not specify but that probably involved housing and race relations. "Like father Edgar and grandfathers Roderick and Max," the delighted parent described the heiress to a family civic tradition.[5]

The fact is that Marion almost from the day of her arrival in Cincinnati as a newlywed in 1932 had burst forth in a torrent of suddenly realized energies. (The three hundred fifty miles that separated her from her mother were a salutary though not impossible distance.) The position she had found teaching art at a posh and conventional private girls' school was a disappointment after the experimental atmosphere of John Burroughs in St. Louis; after four years, she gave up the Hillsdale School to start on a baby. But by then she was not only a known presence but a whirlwind force in civic affairs and other activities representing a whole complex of ardently held moral and aesthetic convictions. Unlike her mother, she had not had to content herself with auxiliary female versions of political involvement, but had marched into battle as matter-of-factly as her husband. Together they carved out a number of conspicuous niches in their adopted city, at that time one of the brighter hopes of American civic reformers.

While St. Louis sank deeper and deeper into filth, financial muddle, and racial ill will, Cincinnati in the early Depression years seemed to be addressing the future with some intelligence and hope. It resembled St. Louis in some ways—a strongly Southern-tinged character (the Cincinnati region had more in common with Kentucky across the river than with northern Ohio), a sturdy legacy of nineteenth-century German immigration, the peculiarly generous, leisurely, individualistic spirit of Midwestern Victorian architecture still visible in many of its sprawling residential neighborhoods. But the "Queen City" was sufficiently smaller (with a 1930 population of about 451,000 to St. Louis's 822,000) to give people more hope of making a difference. Rescued from decades of infamous bossism through a pioneering city-manager system pushed through by the reforming City Charter of 1924, it presented an optimistic spectacle of liberal initiative in the residual energy of the still thriving "Charter Party" or "Charter Committee."[6]

John and Marion lost no time taking up with the Charterites. In those first years the young Beckers' chief concerns were urban housing and regional planning, ideas that John repeatedly tried to hold up to the attention of architects and that then seemed to promise an end to all manner of community ills. Marion shortly became active in a lobbying organization called the Better Housing League that crusaded for slum clearance and affordable-housing construction in areas like the west end of Cincinnati, then filled with squalid tenements carved out of nineteenth-century mansions without benefit of electricity or running water. Together with the president of the organization, another Charterite type named Bleecker Marquette, she wrote and produced the Better Housing League annual reports for many years. She also rapidly became a power in the Regional Planning Council of Cincinnati and Vicinity, which sought to translate into concrete policies the still new concept of broadly based community planning strategies to coordinate the needs of transportation, public utilities, residential and business zoning, and the responsible use of land and water resources not just within city limits but throughout a larger environmental orbit.

It was probably such issues on which Irma heard her firebrand daughter speak, whether under the auspices of these organizations or other crusading alliances in which she was a leading light—the National Association for the Advancement of Colored People, the American Civil Liberties Union, the League of Women Voters, anti-Fascist groups of the era. That Marion had time for anything else is scarcely credible; but like Irma in young matronhood, she was a creature of galvanic, stupendous energy. She and John had also worked hard to forge ties with the Cincinnati arts community, becoming active in a group of collectors and connoisseurs called the Print and Drawing Circle and incidentally hobnobbing with wealthy patrons of the arts who had a finger in some of the same political pies as the Beckers. In consequence, they often moved in circles somewhat grander than might have seemed commensurate with John's rather modest architectural practice and Marion's teaching salary. At times, Irma hinted to acquaintances that she had qualms about their abilities as providers.[7]

But her admiration was great for John and Marion's example in many ways. In the quieter mode suited to one of her upbringing, Irma espoused their overall political views (all three had decisively deserted the Republican Party for Roosevelt) and entered into some of their interests. She could not go to a public forum and talk about slum clearance and racial troubles. But she could affirm her own commitment to such causes by becoming a founder of the People's Art Center, a WPA-associated project in St. Louis begun in 1942 in a predominantly black neighborhood and designed to encourage artistic talent among the disadvantaged. Like the "German Class" crew, John and Marion kept up her sense of being au courant. At Marion's taste in modern music— anything from Shostakovich to Webern—she drew the line. (Irma's idea of pure felicity was listening to Mozart.) But when it came to the world of growing things, mother and daughter outdid one another in happy discovery.

Plants and the outdoors in general became one of their great bonds. Within a few years of coming to Cincinnati, Marion had begun to realize that her real vocation and the grandest of all her grand political, moral, and aesthetic passions was gardening—not just sticking some pretty things in a patch of ground, but participating in the miracle of growth. Unfortunately she would never be able to make a professional career of this true love, but she began to arrange her whole world view around it.

Through her mother-in-law's family, the Dittmanns, she and John were introduced to Carl Krippendorf, the already elderly scion of another Cincinnati shoe-manufacturing family and the owner of a property called Lob's Wood some twenty miles southeast of the city.[8] On its two hundred acres he had created a magnificent nature preserve that also gratified his passion for all varieties of narcissus. Marion's first sight of the Lob's Wood daffodils in bloom, "flung like golden brocade on the forest floor," was an epochal revelation to her, like her first glimpses of modern art.[9] A vision of her own "wild garden" began to take shape in her imagination.

Meanwhile, she read and learned. She mastered botanical nomenclature, absorbed the gospel of organic gardening, cultivated the friendship of researchers, pondered the profound link between regional planning to manage community resources and the study of particular ecospheres. Lob's Wood helped concentrate her attention on the characteristic habitats of southwestern Ohio. The gardener's art was soon a cornerstone of all she believed about self-expression and an enlightened twentieth-century "design for living." It even mirrored the theories of natural ornament that she had tried to absorb from Ernst Kropp, whose book sat untranslated in her house.

She and John could not afford a spot that would be her own living laboratory. But they bought it anyhow in 1936, when Marion at thirty-three was pregnant with her first child and they were living in a city apartment on hilly Auburn Avenue not far from the University of Cincinnati campus. The site was an eight-acre patch of abandoned cornfield about fifteen miles east of downtown Cincinnati, in Anderson Township close to the Little Miami River. It was another textbook example of what had happened to once-thriving American farmland from New England to the Ozarks—a bald, eroded hilltop falling away steeply on one side to a small creek bed at the bottom of a gully.

In their present situation planning was not easy. Mark Becker arrived on January 16, 1937, safe and sound notwithstanding a car accident early in Marion's pregnancy when she was hurled from the moving vehicle, and despite a terrible flood—the worst in Cincinnati's history—that paralyzed the entire region shortly before she went into labor. (The lights went out partway through the delivery at Jewish Hospital.) However, it soon appeared that the child would have to undergo several operations. He had been born with a hernia that required corrective surgery while he was still quite small, and the doctors also recommended surgery for congenital varicose veins in his legs. Medical insurance was far from universal at this time. The young parents would have had a discouraging struggle to pay Mark's medical bills and start on a new house had it not been for the extravagant generosity of Irma, who also at length managed to talk them into a health-insurance policy.[10] She continued to suspect that these young idealists did not understand the practical priorities of life.

The house, whose progress she eagerly followed, was of course designed by John. Luckily they were able to start work in 1939 and finish well before the war. Irma came up from St. Louis in the summer of 1940 to help them move in and nourish her own hope for a country retreat. Mother and daughter spent most of the summer in a fury of landscaping and planning, of which Irma wrote delighted accounts to Jessica Mannon at Bobbs-Merrill. Marion's ambition was to work on the battered ex-cornfield like a living canvas, turning the ravine into a wild garden filled with both common and rare native plants of the region. She would let a presently forlorn-looking array of trees and shrubs selectively reclaim that corner, making a shady habitat for woodland flowers while screening the house from the secluded glen.

Around the house itself they planned more spacious and formal vistas, the eventual showpiece being a leisurely avenue of pines. These lined the driveway approach from what was then a country lane, framing the first glimpse of a modern Corbusierish edifice that both John and Marion considered a major aesthetic statement. From the road it presented a low, inconspicuous, almost windowless façade, all whitewashed cinderblock walls and austere, boxy, rectilinear surfaces. But a visitor came through the front door to find a long, airy, light-filled room with muted gray walls and floors, dominated by a row of windows that gave on the still-open southern slope of the former field. It was furnished with the absence of clutter and insistence on lucid, understated effects that were sacred tenets to husband and wife. Marion had found an estatelike sobriquet with which to ennoble their little dominion: "Cockaigne," known to medievalists as a land of storied plenty as well as the venue of a Middle English satire in which roasted geese flew through the air and goblets of wine transported themselves into the waiting gullets of non-self-denying monks.

In the year of their move to Cockaigne, Marion once again decided to take a job. Several local champions of modern art, including a couple of her old Hillsdale School pupils, approached her with an invitation to become the first paid director of a fledgling organization called the Cincinnati Modern Art Society (later to be known as the Contemporary Arts Center). In 1939 the CMAS founders had persuaded the hitherto hidebound Cincinnati Art Museum to make space available for an exhibition of modern works held by private Cincinnati-area collectors. It was at once clear that an eager audience existed for further activities. What Marion was asked to do was coordinate several exhibitions a year at the Museum and handle arrangements for a lecture series that the Society put on as an adjunct to the shows.[11]

Most of their more imposing presentations of the 1940s drew on the abundant contacts she had made in the New York art world through her old Vassar instructor Agnes Rindge as well as a network of Cincinnati enthusiasts; she was regularly in touch with people like Alfred Barr of the Museum of Modern Art, Peggy Guggenheim, and the gallery director Curt Valentin. Very soon Marion and the CMAS had made Cincinnati one of the few places outside of New York where the major dealers and curators found it worthwhile to exhibit modern art. Sometimes she developed entire exhibitions (with ancillary lectures) from initial concept through the final return of the artwork. She arranged for loan and transportation (including necessary packaging and insurance) of the objects to be exhibited, worked with the Art Museum staff on actual hanging, placement, and lighting, and for many years wrote and helped produce most of the catalogues. She and John also played host to visiting eminences, some of whom became great friends. It was through her eager evangelism on behalf of her mother's cookbook that The Joy of Cooking, peddled by its publisher as a cheap article of mass domestic life, also acquired a certain reputation in rather rarefied circles for craftsmanship and intellectual aptness. Among the friends on whom Marion pressed gift copies and who became long-term admirers of Joy were Herbert Read (whose family the Beckers kept supplied with children's hand-me-downs and gifts of food during the grim years of wartime and postwar rationing in England), Buckminster Fuller, and—by an odd coincidence—Siegfried Giedion, the exiled Swiss art theoretician, who at the time they met happened to be working on an extraordinary study of applied household technology called Mechanization Takes Command, which still contains some of the best historical accounts ever undertaken of cooking apparatus.

The CMAS job helped cement the Beckers' position as influential politickers on the Cincinnati art scene. John and Marion were people who would have scorned the role of grand string-pullers (even if they had had the wealth to support it), but who did like to see themselves in the thick of things. John had become a fixture in the local chapter of the American Institute of Architects and was also an active board member at the Cincinnati Art Academy, the school associated with the Art Museum. Both his activities and Marion's work at the Modern Art Society introduced them to a steady stream of faculty and promising students at the Academy. He also developed a deep commitment to a less glamorous cause, adult education. Never a teacher himself, he was genuinely engaged by the thought that educators could do more to realize the abilities of citizens in forums beyond the academic mainstream.

Marion and John's union appeared to many of their friends the perfect modern marriage, not only an obvious mutual devotion but a love built on shared intellectual foundations and deep mutual respect for one another's gifts. "You and John seem to me to add up to the relationship that I mean when I say marriage," her mother's old friend Edna Gellhorn wrote after a Cincinnati visit.[12] But not all their circle saw the situation in these terms. Nearly all regarded Marion as an extraordinary creature, a Renaissance woman, an inspiration. For those with whom she had forged some bond, she gave off a nearly tangible energy, radiance, and wholeness. Some of her friends also considered John a person of great substance in his own right; others thought him a handsome pose-striker who in terms of brains, knowledge, and accomplishment was not a patch on his wife.

People who found themselves on opposite sides of an issue from the Beckers often got a whiff of sanctimonious hauteur or impenetrable obstinacy. Husband and wife were extraordinarily close, thinking and speaking as one on all manner of issues. (Marion, who knew herself not to be the most naturally gifted of writers, almost always got his help in drafting or revising anything she had to write in critical battles.) Her allegiance to their shared beliefs helped reinforce an eager, crusading streak in her nature and a tendency to see any controversy she faced as a conflict between virtuous conviction and benighted error. Her finest qualities, a truth-seeker's earnestness and believer's ardor, might in some contexts look very much like officiousness and self-righteousness.

Irma, who vastly admired Marion's brains and zeal, could not keep away from the old sore point of her daughter's looks. Marion's close friends in Cincinnati knew that her mother had caused her great hurt on this score. Even casual observers often sensed that Irma's petite stylishness and Marion's plain, no-nonsense appearance were a clue to some more than superficial trouble between the two. When Marion was a grown woman, their St. Louis acquaintances would still hear Irma criticize her large hands and feet or wonder out loud how a man as handsome as John Becker could love anyone so poorly endowed in the department of good looks. When in 1945 Marion was expecting their second child, Irma did not scruple to call this late pregnancy a tactical blunder that would make the forty-two-year-old wife unattractive to her better half.[13]

She would have been happy to go to Cincinnati for Marion's confinement, but matters had been decided otherwise in the Becker household. John's mother, widowed that spring after Philip A. Becker had lost the struggle with a long, debilitating illness, had agreed to come. Marion, frantically occupied with the Modern Art Society job and her unpaid activist efforts, had discussed the situation with Put in Seattle and he undertook to invite Irma there.[14] That decision would prove one of the great disasters of the Rombauer family.

Put's domestic affairs had undergone a good deal of rearranging during the war, to the intense concern and curiosity of his mother. For a time he had given up the law for defense-related work in shipbuilding and then prefabricated-housing construction. He and Nita had been separated for some time when in the summer of 1942 Irma's uneasy queries elicited the news that he was in love with Margaret Varn Robinson, a divorcée with two small children. Put's divorce came through in the fall, and they were married in January of 1943.

Put had always been Irma's *Sorgenkind*, or "child of worry," the one who cost her the most anxiety and the sharpest pangs of love. She fretted endlessly over what she saw as the unstable muddle of his career and home life. Since he had gone to the West Coast in 1931 they had been on friendly enough terms, but with the new phase of both their lives beginning in 1943 Irma sought something more.

She traveled to Seattle in the summer of 1943—the first flush of her success—to meet Margaret, Judy, and Edward (who took the name of Edgar after Put adopted both children and gave them the surname of Rombauer). To Marion, Irma pronounced herself delighted with Margaret and the little ones and ecstatic at Put's newfound fatherhood.[15] He, too, had suddenly blossomed forth as a dedicated gardener. Missives of cheery domesticity passed back and forth among Cincinnati, Seattle, and St. Louis for the next two years. In February of 1945 Margaret gave birth to another son, Roderick.

The family had had a few changes of living quarters since the marriage, and Put, though he had returned to the law, seemed to be in a betwixt-and-between state about job plans. They were living in a trailer while having a house built on a spectacularly lovely site on Puget Sound looking toward the Olympic mountain range. Irma, for her part, was casting about for the best way of sharing her new wealth while still unsure that it would not prove a flash in the pan or that Laurance Chambers would not succeed in ousting her. It was in this edgy and unsettled situation that she arrived in Seattle during July of 1945. She went home about a month later, apparently in the thick of a battle that is not easy to reconstruct with much confidence. Most of the vital jigsaw clues as to the different parties' motives and intentions are now missing. However, it is a reasonable guess that Put and Irma reverted to a level of wrangling as mutually destructive as anything in his stormy childhood and that Margaret, who would become more and more emotionally frayed in the course of her marriage to Put, thought Irma had treated her insultingly if not plotted against her.

By Put's side of the story, Irma had been floating some political trial balloons about paying off one or both of her children's mortgages, and was now talking of coming out to live close to the Seattle family. She declared that she was fed up with Marion and John (who insisted on a frustrating hands-off-to-grandmothers policy with the progressively reared Mark), offered to bring Put rather than Marion in on the cookbook, and announced her intention of building a mother-in-law wing for their new house. He would have nothing to do with this agenda, and Irma captiously spent most of her stay in Seattle ignoring them (except for making much of little Roderick) and larking about on publicity events to which they were not invited.[16]

Irma apparently had plenty to say in refutation of this account, but no account of her own survives. It is true that she loved to play people off each other, making common cause with current favorites against whoever was presently in the doghouse, but that in itself does not prove or disprove any particular story.

At Cockaigne, Marion spent her last month of pregnancy resting and dispatching innocent tidings of Becker doings to Seattle. She gave birth to her second son, Ethan, on August 6, 1945, quite unaware of the news from Hiroshima. A week later, on August 14, she lay listening to the roar of the V-J Day celebration outside Christ Hospital,[17] not knowing that victory was provoking a fresh family clash on the West Coast. By Put's later report Irma, whom he and Margaret had expected to celebrate the historic moment with them, had made some excuse and gone off without notice to do her celebrating elsewhere.

Whatever the truth of the summer's events in Seattle, they kindled a blaze of resentment on both sides. Margaret was wildly upset by what she saw as her mother-in-law's criticisms and meddling during the visit[18]—and according to Put's later account, by an actual offer of money from Irma if she would accept a divorce and get out of the picture.[19] By the end of the year Marion was unhappily protesting that she could not make any sense out of what either Put or Irma was saying about the other. Put made his case in several phone calls that she found so upsetting as to request that he leave her out of the quarrel.[20] Whether Irma was more diplomatic or Marion placed more faith in her account, the upshot was a serious falling-out between brother and sister. Communications all but ceased for many years, and Put remained in John and Marion's black book as an irresponsible, unpredictable troublemaker.

Irma, though equally angry and distraught, made shift to keep up some semblance of communication, partly through her brother-in-law and nephew, Julius and Max Muench. She let it be known that she would continue to share her financial reward with the Seattle family on a fair and generous basis. She never visited Seattle again, or forgave Put for having—as she understood it—allowed "a third person, an outsider to influence him to believe ill of me."[21] But at odd intervals they wrote directly with holiday or Mother's Day greetings that carefully skirted their unresolved quarrel; at other times their dealings would be cautiously routed through Max or Julius.

On the whole Marion and Irma emerged from the debacle as allies, clucking over the latest disreputable tidings from the West Coast—the nearly instantaneous abandonment of Put and Margaret's new house; a year and a half spent by the whole family wandering through the United States by mobile home; their return to Seattle for the birth of another son, Jeffrey, in January of 1948; the gradual unraveling of the marriage amid mutual accusations of treachery and instability; Margaret's occasional pathetic appeals to Irma for help in her troubles. The falling-out of 1945 also helped push mother and daughter toward their eventual relationship as professional collaborators.

Within a year of this battle, Max Muench thought Irma alarmingly weakened and aged.[22] She was now nearing seventy, and had long since said goodbye to most vestiges of the last century's St. Louis. Her brother Max Starkloff had died in 1942; in the next year a terrible accident involving a local defense contractor's military glider prototype had killed a large number of civic luminaries, including the same Becker uncle (now Mayor William Dee Becker) who as a local judge had officiated at John and Marion's wedding. Irma's beloved Indianapolis cousins were fast approaching the status of feeble relics; her aunt Dada Hollweg was long gone, having died about six months after the appearance of the 1936 *Joy.* Irma herself would sometimes display an energy that amazed people half her age, sometimes appear close to the end of her strength. Repeating fainting fits and prostrating digestive upsets baffled the doctors, who spoke of a weak heart. The farm family who occupied the house by the entrance to her Jefferson County property, Jake and Lena Bettenmann, would see her forced to stop and rest several times in the course of a short walk,[23] a problem certainly not helped by her cigarette smoking. By now Irma had become a heavy drinker, of the sort who is slowly working through a glass of whiskey throughout much of the day.[24] Of course the strain of the Bobbs-Merrill situation—she lived with the knowledge that the official copyright-holders would love nothing better than to remove her as author of *The Joy of Cooking*—took an increasing physical and psychological toll.

The collapse of her relationship with the West Coast family at the height of Bobbs-Merrill tensions altered the balance of other plans and alliances. If Irma had been thinking of dividing her time between Seattle and St. Louis or even pulling up stakes from Missouri, the summer of 1945 certainly put an end to any such idea. She quickly proceeded with the building of the cabin in Jefferson County, underscoring the Cincinnati contingent's place in her affections by asking John Becker to design the house.

Ensuring the future of her book now entailed immediate choices. The field of potential sharers in that future was not large. Mazie would go on working as long as there was breath in her body, and Irma meant to guarantee her some income for life;[25] but Mazie was neither qualified for nor interested in any duty involving original responsibility for crucial material. Marion, who by the terms of the 1943 contract was to receive first consideration as successor, was several hundred miles away and up to her eyebrows in family, job, garden, and every progressive political cause Cincinnati had to offer. Besides, Marion when confronted with a task was quite unlike the more demure and gentle Mazie, who could stick firmly to an opinion but participated in a spirit of warm feminine camaraderie that brought out the same quality in Irma. Marion charged into things very seriously, eager to strike a blow for enlightened thought. With her, the work would be no tea party.

In the wake of the 1945 family fracas Irma edged closer to Marion—but also to another option. This was Jane Crawford Torno, the wife of a flautist with the St. Louis Symphony.

At around this time Jane and Laurent Torno became part of a circle that had grown out of the old "German Class," younger friends who went out to "Frau Rom's" Antonia property on weekends to help with the clearing and building. Irma's ties with them were if anything strengthened by her frustration with Put.

They all loved John's rough-and-ready stone cabin high on the hillside, as cool a spot as could be found in the area during the murderous eastern Missouri summers. It was a long, low-slung structure with thickly insulating walls of the local limestone; on one side the shallowly pitched tin roof extended to shade a stone-floored porch, running the length of the house, that looked southeast toward Illinois. The walls had been squared by Irma squinting down a broomstraw. The one-room interior had a fireplace with a crooked mantelpiece (the same technique had failed her here); a rudimentary kitchen that at first lacked stove, refrigerator, or any running water other than a pump hooked up to a cistern (the sum total of the indoor plumbing); and cots for Irma and any guests. The outhouse stood at a decorous remove. The chinks between the rough stone blocks of the walls and the edges of the beaverboard ceiling had been stuffed with hasty expedients like steel wool by her corps of volunteers.[26] It was this, and not a villa or a luxurious pseudocottage, that Irma had sought as the crown of her success—the expression of a hunger for the outdoors that was one of her husband's most treasured legacies to her. She loved the stone cabin more than she had ever loved anything except her family and her book, and it had cost her less pain than either.

The actual building—most of it done or supervised by her farmer neighbor Jake Bettenmann—had begun in 1946. The Tornos were often there pitching in, sometimes with their three young sons. They also saw Irma in town (she still kept a finger in St. Louis musical politics). By the time the cabin was habitable in 1947 Jane Torno, a knowledgeable amateur cook, was a promising candidate for new participant in the cookbook. In the spring of 1946 she and Irma had collaborated on a series of three articles for the food page of the *Post-Dispatch*.[27] During this period they also undertook a much longer piece for a juvenile audience, published as "Cooking Up Fun" in a parents-and-children serial compendium titled *Childcraft*. Meant to address youngsters from those just old enough to mix flavored gelatin powder and water to children capable of safely using the oven broiler for hot dogs, this ambitious entry bore a headnote identifying Irma Rombauer and Jane Crawford Torno as "co-authors of *The Cook Book [sic] for Girls and Boys*."[28]

The book in question had been the subject of planning and discussion at Bobbs-Merrill—highly illustrative of attitudes toward Irma—since

1943. In that year there had been in-house talk of capitalizing on the author's new best-sellerdom with a children's cookbook.[29] Irma's friendship with Cecily Brownstone—who had wangled her an article at *Parents Magazine* and introduced her to a lot of literary people in New York—may well have set her own mind and other people's thoughts on the track of writing for children. One of Irma's new East Coast friends was a children's book editor named Muriel Fuller, who knew all the leading lights of the field and apparently rendered her some sort of editorial or consultation service during the early years of her success. (Irma, though often requested by magazines to try her hand at an article, simply could not make it through a straightforward piece of description and exposition without a good deal of hand-holding and third-hand rewriting;[30] only in the peculiar framework that she herself had invented could she just spread her wings and write.) Just who steered her to Field Enterprises—the Chicago-based *Childcraft* publishers—is uncertain, but Miss Fuller as one of the unsung factotums of juvenile literature is surely a leading candidate. However the thing happened, Irma in the first glow of *Joy*'s national fame spent some time on the fringes of children's literature, and assorted minds at Bobbs-Merrill tried thinking up a mission for her.

The 1943 company brainstorming was not particularly productive. Rosemary York, all cordiality to Irma's face, skeptically commented, "Mrs. Rombauer is so difficult to work with that unless we have a definite step-by-step outline of what we want her to do, nothing can be accomplished."[31] (This condescending assessment is not necessarily wrong, but it painfully illuminates how little time anyone other than Jessica Mannon had devoted to wondering why Irma Rombauer was as marvelous as she was.) Two years later, when the project had at last reached a concrete stage, Mrs. York led the Indianapolis office in squashing a notion from the New York contingent that since "Mrs. Rombauer's is getting to be quite a household name," the book be titled something like "Mrs. Rombauer's Cookbook for Girls and Boys."[32] Mrs. York sent this on to Laurance Chambers with her own comment:

> They are nuts!
> Mrs. Rombauer's name is *not* a household word—at least not to the people of my acquaintance—though THE JOY OF COOKING is very familiar. To prove it, I asked Harry, Pat and Juanita [three of the Indianapolis staff] about their friends. They have found the same thing.

We all think it would be a mistake to use "Mrs. Rombauer" as part of the title of the children's cook book. Not only is it an unfamiliar name, but many people seem unsure how it should be pronounced. If adults find it a hard name, would not children find it doubly so?[33]

Laurance Chambers was delighted to back up this appraisal and put New York in its place. "I have nursed this publication from its first issue and know whereof I speak," he pronounced.[34] The question was not raised again.

The new work, in which Mrs. Torno was deeply involved, was planned to come out a short while after a purportedly new edition of *The Joy of Cooking*. In fact, the 1946 *Joy* was the 1943 edition—actually printed from the same plates—except that the war-rationing material had been deleted and a few more snippets from *Streamlined Cooking* added, along with brief suggestions on shopping for and stocking ingredients and a hasty smattering of new "quick method" cakes (mediocre or worse) that were based on emulsified shortenings and supposed to be mixable in a single bowl. Published on February 5, the new "edition" was the barest stopgap until a real revision could be prepared. Luckily most of the wartime material had been inserted in a fourteen-page chunk close to the end, so the necessary deletions and additions were relatively cheap to make. Indeed, there was no separate contract for this version, though of course Bobbs-Merrill made sure to take out copyright on the new material.

The children's cookbook was probably begun early in 1945, the contract being signed on February 28.[35] (All other contracts between the Rombauers and Bobbs-Merrill were for better or worse drawn up *after* the work had been completed.) Irma must have been working on it during her disastrous summer trip to Seattle, because a couple of discarded typescript chunks are still there in Put's possession. That Jane Torno was working with her on a regular basis in St. Louis is certain. But how much she did is not at all clear, for at the same time, Irma took the opportunity to strengthen the position of Marion. The contract named her, not Mrs. Torno, as the person to be given first consideration to complete any future revision of the children's cookbook if Irma could not. Some sort of difficulty arose over the pictures—just what, the surviving correspondence does not indicate, but Bobbs-Merrill (through Irma) ended up asking Marion to do a couple of dozen silhouette chapter headings in a great hurry over the summer of 1946.[36]

To reward this effort Irma requested that Marion receive a 50 percent share of the royalties from the work, which was published on November 7 as *A Cookbook for Girls and Boys*.[37]

The children's cookbook was one of the smoother author-publisher efforts in Irma's tangled marriage with Bobbs-Merrill. Perhaps it went the more easily because the manuscript was not part of the usual York-Chambers line of fire but was handled by Patricia Jones, the Bobbs-Merrill juvenile editor. (Irma also had advice from Cecily Brownstone and perhaps Muriel Fuller.)[38] Mrs. York, however, carried on at least part of the correspondence and may have thought that she had a potential ally in Marion, who tackled her mother—and prevailed—on the subject of a few editorial changes that the firm had been vainly requesting.[39] Anyone who knew John and Marion would also have heard their world views echoing through odd reaches of the book, such as a long anecdote about a Mexico City tortilla shop that concluded with a grand moralization on how progress was replacing nostalgic tradition for the "valiant" people of Mexico.[40] *Girls and Boys* quietly marks a stage of increased influence for Marion as a literary presence in her mother's work. Indeed, early in 1947 she was proposing to work with her mother as collaborator—but not on a cookbook. Marion longed to wrest from Irma's memory a scrapbook of Rombauer/von Starkloff reminiscences to be titled "Meet the Family."[41]

No part of the *Girls and Boys* royalties went to Jane Torno, nor did her name ever appear as coauthor of the work. But she remained very much part of the picture in Irma's thinking. By now *The Joy of Cooking* had some claim to represent the state of American cookery, and one sixty-nine-year-old woman with mounting health problems might justly fear to carry on the work alone. Merely gathering recipes, as Irma was always doing, could hardly address the deluge of culinary developments that had come along since she had first put pen to paper. Dedicated modernist though she was, she needed all the help she could get to follow—much less appraise—the gadgetry, specialization, and mass alchemy that were now dwarfing the equivalent innovations of Irma's youth. She could not simply continue the role of lighthearted, resourceful amateur without someone else there to interpret and summarize things beyond her ken. The work of testing also had become too massive to be managed by Irma or the willing Mazie running into the kitchen to try out something.

Cecily Brownstone in New York (now food correspondent for the Associated Press) became an important conduit of information, helping Irma skim the cream of the publicity events that clued in the trade press to new products and methods. In St. Louis she often called upon the knowledge of Merna Lazier, a local food journalist and former professional baker. But her mainstay in the next *Joy* edition was plainly going to be Jane Torno.

For a brief period after *Girls and Boys*, Irma's letters to Marion breezily record summer sojourns at the cabin with friends, including the Tornos, and stints of revision work with Jane and Mazie. (Irma and Jane Torno also collaborated on a 1948 promotional recipe-book called "Home Comfort" for the Wrought Iron Range Company of St. Louis, with material on freezing and canning capable of being transferred to the next *Joy* edition.)[42] Bobbs-Merrill, having smoothed over some of the rancor that had bade fair to erupt into open threats a year or two before, believed that the Rombauer-Torno team were progressing fast enough for publication in 1949, and was preparing to map out a production schedule accordingly.

All their expectations were abruptly ended in 1948. The work was sailing along when Irma began to find something strange and hostile in Mrs. Torno's behavior. After some baffling interval the cause became apparent: a severe mental illness, perhaps exacerbated by marital troubles.[43] She veered unpredictably in and out of the picture until at least December, apparently venting a lot of uncontrolled anger on the horrified Irma and leaving everyone in the dark about the status of work for which she had agreed to be responsible. At last she was temporarily committed to a mental hospital, leaving Laurent Torno to cope with three children and Irma with the unfinished manuscript. This drawn-out crisis coincided with another blow: Mazie's husband, Gene Hartrich, died on August 12. Her strength and good cheer would not be at Irma's disposal for a long time; even when Mazie was able to resume working, she was at first too dispirited to do much for either Irma's morale or the logistics of the effort.[44]

As the dimensions of the Torno disaster became manifest, Irma played her remaining card. At the end of July she wrote to Bobbs-Merrill requesting that Marion's position as successor be reinforced. Mrs. York wrote back on August 2, "Of course we shall be delighted to have Marion make the next revision of *The Joy of Cooking* [this clearly refers to the revision after the one presently in train] if and when there should be call for one. You have our full assurance on this."[45] At that point Bobbs-Merrill still expected the manuscript of the ongoing revision to come in without much further ado. Mrs. York had no reason to suppose that Marion would get into the current act in any major role.

"Our full assurance" was not enough for Irma. She (or her advisors, the Muenches) clearly thought she had better get something with the name of higher authority on it. On September 30, 1948, the August 2 representation was formally ratified by Irma Rombauer and Laurance Chambers, via a supplement to the 1943 contract that replaced the clause about Marion's being given "first consideration" in making any future revision in case her mother were dead or disabled with an unequivocal "her daughter, Marion Rombauer Becker of Cincinnati, Ohio, is to have authority to make or complete such revision."[46] Rosemary York would soon live to regret her cheery cooperation in this matter.

8

War Maneuvers

The notion of Marion as coauthor of *The Joy of Cooking* did not immediately enter anyone's mind when in 1948 she agreed to participate in the troubled revision. All was confusion for some time, and Marion's role might never have been officially pinned down on paper had it been left to her and her mother. Only when the Bobbs-Merrill war had shifted to a phase requiring new advisors would either think of putting both their names on the title page.

Like Irma, Marion had no brilliant qualifications for the job of cookbook author. Neither woman came to the work with a dazzling reputation as a cook; each was a community doer and mobilizer who fitted meals into her life with brisk efficiency rather than rhapsodic dedication. As wives and mothers, both by temperament adored the can opener as the best friend of any woman with the wit to use one. Marion, however, had lived to develop somewhat different priorities.

She had not had her mother's advantage of youthful exposure to either European tables or St. Louis German and "American" cooking in their Victorian heyday. But she had become curious about exactly the sorts of food that were *not* much in evidence in middle-class American households when she (or for that matter, Irma) was setting up her own kitchen. From her love affair with gardening in general she had graduated to an interest in organic gardening, biodynamic farming, whole-grain cookery, and various things then lumped together without much differentiation as "health foods." She became fascinated with fresh herbs and sought out unusual varieties for her own diligently tended herb garden. By the mid-1940s she was the sort of mother who writes to the H. J. Heinz Company inquiring just what is in her son's baby food.[1] She had qualms about the canned soups that she had always doted on (and continued to reach for with some regularity); she looked askance at advertising prattle about wonder foods and trusted as much as possible to the seasonal offerings of the Beckers' vegetable garden and neighboring small farms in still-bucolic Anderson Township. She tried to interest local women in the virtues of home-baked whole-wheat bread.[2] Undoubtedly her own lifelong food allergies had been a stimulus to exploration of roads less often taken, but at least an equal influence was her skepticism about the motives and methods of American business.

Marion's concerns made her a strategic foil to Irma, who had hardly ever been known to write a word in dispraise of convenience foods and popular trends (she did demur at the idea of marshmallows with sweet potatoes, but her tone suggested bemusement more than scorn).[3] Marion—or rather, the inseparably knit team of Marion and John—also brought other useful qualities to the business of writing. Irma wrote as she talked, in impulsive bursts of charm. Her quirky, untutored talent was surely the truest and best in the family, but it was not suited to explaining complicated facts. She was thoroughly unnerved by anything requiring sustained exposition. Marion, who had no particular gift of style, could and did sit down to put ideas on paper in prose good enough for the occasion in her lobbying and catalogue-writing work. Technical details and logical intricacies did not scare her. But when she cared about polish, she invariably got John to apply it. She considered him the *bel esprit* of the family. He was a great savorer of niceties and smoother of rough edges; rightly or wrongly, Marion trusted him to clothe her thoughts more elegantly than she could have herself. As a writing team, the two of them would never match Irma in natural flair, but they could tackle things that Irma quailed at.

To Bobbs-Merrill, Marion was an unknown quantity except as the artist for all three of her mother's cookbooks—and perhaps as a helpful presence in getting Irma to bend on some editorial suggestions regarding *A Cookbook for Girls and Boys*. The company cannot have foreseen her influence on the actual contents of *Joy* any more than she foresaw it herself when Irma drew her into the later stages of the Jane

Torno mess. For one thing, the company had seen very little of the revision at hand, and it is not clear what kind of shape the manuscript was in when Marion arrived on the scene in the fall of 1948. Rosemary York had a few pieces of completed text in her possession and—though no deadline existed—apparently thought that the rest was nearly ready for submission. So it may have been, but Mrs. York's expectations of seeing the whole thing within weeks (or at most a month or two) were about to be horribly dashed.

The revision effort was envisioned by all as a critical test for the continued future of the wartime smash hit, which was now selling rather less briskly. The contents of the old book essentially dated from 1936 and 1939. To market the next *Joy* as new and timely, author and publisher would have to inject more novelty than they had managed with the 1946 version. As to the substance, Irma was adding more general information on ingredients as they were introduced chapter by chapter, and would also provide entirely new sections on such subjects as home freezing, pressure cookery, high-altitude cookery, and the electric blender. She was also to update the existing material on canning, wines, herbs, and nutritional issues. As to the packaging, Bobbs-Merrill expected to revamp the entire design and commission a set of color photographs. For the latter job Mrs. York had suggested an Indianapolis photographer, Noble Bretzman, who happened to be her brother. Since he had never done any other food photography, Irma, Marion, and John understandably concluded that that was his chief qualification.

Marion's first entry into the affair in 1948 concerned the artwork—not unnaturally, since she had spent more than half a decade in the employ of the Cincinnati Modern Art Society and worked with Bobbs-Merrill on the pictures for *Streamlined* and *Girls and Boys*. In the second week of November she went to the Indianapolis office to meet with editor and photographer. She regarded their discussion as a chance to open up the entire question of the book's appearance, something that Irma had occasionally complained about in the past and that both the Beckers considered an immediate priority. Earlier that year, on March 23, Irma had managed to add to the existing 1943 contract a proviso that the publisher must submit any proposed changes in dust jacket or binding for her (or in case of her death, Marion's) approval.[4] Marion, who may well have been behind this agreement, meant to make the most of it. What she and John actually wanted was nothing less than the last word on all decisions regarding artwork and typography.

She showed up for the November 10 meeting with Irma's blessing for whatever position she chose to stake out on design matters, and with a large sheaf of pasted-up sample clippings and sketches to illustrate her ideas for the photographs. She also had a trial version of a new dust jacket, as roughed out by John. Mrs. York politely let it be known that Marion was needlessly complicating the job of her brother, Mr. Bretzman, as well as trespassing on in-house decisions that ultimately rested with the production department in New York. Marion returned to Cincinnati disgusted by what she saw as Bobbs-Merrill's utter lack of cooperation.

A general drawing-up of battle lines ensued. Marion wrote directly to Walter Hurley, chief of the production department, complaining that as far as she could see the company wanted *Joy* to look like all its run-of-the-mill competitors and had no notion of truly functional illustrations rooted in the letter or spirit of the book.[5] Laurance Chambers (who almost never himself communicated with the foe) at once authorized Mrs. York to deplore this blunt bypassing of herself, the firm's official Rombauer liaison, and tell the busybody Mrs. Becker that she did not understand the high mystery of book production.[6] Marion defiantly announced that she planned to address herself to appropriate authority as her concerns warranted, and that she would go on being the artistic conscience of the project.[7] Irma, meanwhile, was resolving to proclaim that she would no longer tolerate the discount-sales situation. At some point in the fall or early winter she conceived a new plan: to put Bobbs-Merrill's back to the wall on this and the photography issue by refusing to turn over the rest of the manuscript until the company had yielded on both points.

It was a good moment at which to raise a ruckus, for the plates used to print the 1943/1946 edition were now too dilapidated for Bobbs-Merrill to nurse them through more than a few future printings. Irma was very weary, and not looking forward to picking up the pieces of the work after Jane Torno's traumatic departure and Mazie Hartrich's bereavement. Marion and John—though still not expecting to participate in the actual revision—were a moral shot in the arm. Together they thought they could face down the enemy.

Noble Bretzman's photographs were duly shot and trotted out in early February of 1949 for Marion's reaction, which was predictable: "Not one single picture is representative of any good cooking."[8] His sister's wrath at this verdict was not tempered by the fact that Irma had authorized Marion to decide for both of them about the pictures.

Irma now apparently (the letter in question is missing) invoked or threatened to invoke last March's agreement requiring her approval of design changes.

On this signal Bobbs-Merrill unwisely prepared to join battle. Rosemary York wrote to Irma cuttingly dismissing Marion's judgment and claiming that the photographs were not covered by the agreement in question—but also announcing that the company was unilaterally canceling the agreement anyhow, as being unworkable with a loose cannon like Marion in the action. This barefaced welshing on a contract amendment that had been plainly signed by Laurance Chambers—Mrs. York's explanation was that the company had never received Irma's countersigned copy—must have struck the Rombauers as something like Hitler's way with inconvenient scraps of paper. The clincher, however, was the editor's threat that if Irma did not hand over the rest of the copy in a few weeks, Bobbs-Merrill would simply go ahead and print from the old plates with the addition of the Bretzman photographs.[9]

Here was the voice of Old Dynamite—himself incommunicado with the family—uttering his equivalent of "L'état, c'est moi." But it stimulated the appalled Irma, Marion, and John to think not of compliance but of a court injunction against the proposed printing.

Irma's New York friends were no strangers to the story of the author-publisher situation. Muriel Fuller, the editor and consultant whom she had met when the children's cookbook was being discussed, had proposed that she join the Author's League in order to qualify for representation by their legal counsel. Irma had not acted on the suggestion. But now she and the others decided that matters had gone beyond the powers of her St. Louis attorney, Julius Muench. Over the Washington's Birthday holiday of 1949 she, Mazie, Marion, and John assembled in St. Louis for a grand powwow. Alerted to the situation by Muriel Fuller in New York, the attorney she had recommended telephoned them on Friday, February 25, and suggested that they send him an account of the case. So with Marion manning one typewriter and Mazie another while everybody threshed out ideas, the four of them put together a description of everything they believed they had suffered at the hands of Bobbs-Merrill and mailed it off in two reports, one signed by Marion and one by Irma.

The lawyer would have had to be a dull sort not to be tantalized by Irma's opening gambit:

Dear Mr. Ernst:

Introducing the cast:

Irma S. Rombauer, housewife, 71 years old, author of "The Joy of Cooking."

She ran through the major dramatis personae, told the story of the picture debacle and the discount-sales policy, and described the latest atrocity:

> The publisher is now threatening to publish the current edition of the Joy of Cooking with the illustrations in question. He is issuing this threat because I have in my possession about three-fourths of the manuscript for the new edition [most likely, this far overestimates what Bobbs-Merrill had received] which I am withholding until my terms are met or some agreement is reached.
>
> You seem to be familiar with the character of this publishing house and undoubtedly know of their totalitarian tactics. Not wishing to threaten Bobbs-Merrill in return I have never written anything about the retention of the manuscript but am just sitting pretty.[10]

Marion recounted her own part of the battle of the illustrations and enclosed copies or transcriptions of the relevant missives to and from the enemy.

By Monday their reports were in New York on the desk of Morris L. Ernst, a name to command respect from anyone in the publishing business. Now a senior eminence in the firm of Greenbaum, Wolff & Ernst, he was a distinguished civil libertarian and something of a legend in his field, having represented Random House in the 1933 federal suit that cleared the way for U.S. publication of James Joyce's *Ulysses*. He was courteous, encouraging, and apparently very quick to begin making sense of the situation. On Tuesday, March 1, Irma was able to fire a decisive salvo in the form of a telegram to Mrs. York:

OBJECT TO ILLUSTRATIONS ON GROUND THAT THEY ARE DAMAGING TO MY REPUTATION AS A COOK AND NOT CONSISTANT [*sic*] WITH

MY WRITINGS AS AUTHOR PLEASE COMMUNICATE WITH MY ATTOR-
NEY MORRIS ERNST OF NEW YORK.[11]

There are gaps in the correspondence, but it is clear that the name of
Morris Ernst had the desired effect. Within a few weeks Rosemary
York had miraculously disappeared from the picture, the scheme of
reprinting the old plates with the new photographs had been summarily abandoned, the production department in New York had concurred
in rejecting Noble Bretzman's work for the new edition, and a more
diplomatic company-author liaison had been installed in the person of
Harrison Platt, who at that time held the post of production editor in
the Indianapolis office, supervising the coordination of editorial efforts
there with the work of actual production in New York. Even at Bobbs-
Merrill, there was some feeling that Mrs. York had steered everyone
very badly by bringing a family connection into a crucial battle over
the company's most important literary property.[12]

Greenbaum, Wolff & Ernst now sat down to study the affairs of the
famous cookbook. The Rombauers were strangers to them, but Bobbs-
Merrill's overall reputation was indeed clouded enough these days to
make Irma's disdainful reference to its "character" quite plain to her
audience. That the firm had a huge amount at stake was patent to all
observers in the publishing world.

Anyone with an ear to the ground knew that the venerable house
was said to be in dubious financial shape. Laurance Chambers, great
booksmith though he might be in his own fields of competence, had
more of a name for bad temper than good business judgment. Under
his leadership the trade department had become an unmendable hole
in the company pocket (though the law department, which he did not
meddle in, held its own).[13] In 1947 there had been an across-the-board
reduction in royalties paid to authors under new contracts.[14] Recalling
the president's declining years, the editor Hiram Haydn later saw his
stance as an impenetrable wall of embattled frustration:

> The older he grew the surer he became that he knew the
> answers, despite staggering evidence to the contrary. And
> the surer he became, the more tyrannical. It was the old
> story of a man trusting almost no one else. The more he
> came to doubt the adequacies of those who worked for him
> the more he insisted on being in total charge of the list. The
> less he was able to command the new writers the more he

indulged his prejudices. It became DLC against the world, and he would not relinquish the practices that had worked in the past.[15]

The New York office increasingly chafed under the seventy-year-old autocrat's rule, and even the Indianapolis loyalists knew that he could not last indefinitely. But with him or against him, everyone at Bobbs-Merrill now realized that during the 1940s *The Joy of Cooking* had become the single most reliable asset of the trade department, and that its future performance could mean the difference between survival and shipwreck. To have offered the firm's most popular author ammunition for a serious legal action was a blunder that Chambers—the real force behind all Bobbs-Merrill moves in the ongoing combat, though his name was not signed to any of the relevant missives—could not afford to repeat.

Having beaten back a shaky foe a few steps, Greenbaum, Wolff & Ernst did not anticipate any more irruptions in the crass-threat department but hesitated to bank on grander victories. Deciding that he could not handle all aspects of the messy business himself, Morris Ernst soon split it up with one of the firm's junior partners, Harriet F. Pilpel, a young attorney whose eminence in the field of publishing law would ultimately rival his own. Both lawyers rapidly saw that Irma and Marion were vastly confused about the implications of the 1943 contract and its later amendments.

Their muddle was the more unfortunate as Irma was making urgent (though, as it turned out, premature) noises about retiring from the work. On the same day as Irma's doughty see-my-lawyer telegram to Bobbs-Merrill (March 1), Marion had written to Morris Ernst passing on a message that was undoubtedly the upshot of the latest family council: her mother had been driven to near-collapse by the current affray, and "the moment of my taking over the bulk of revision is at hand. I am very anxious that the legality of my present status as revisor and my future status as heir to her rights be established."[16]

The moment of Marion's "taking over the bulk of revision" actually lay some years in the future; though Irma was often ailing as the quarrel lurched on, what she most wanted Marion to take over at present was the business of wrangling with Bobbs-Merrill. But as they placed their dilemma in the hands of Greenbaum, Wolff & Ernst, mother and daughter were implicitly edging toward a watershed decision: both of them were starting to see that Marion's responsibilities would finally have to extend to the fundamental contents of the revision, not just the artwork and design.

This implication of the case did not dawn on anyone at once. It was some time before the lawyers realized that Bobbs-Merrill's conduct of *Joy* affairs involved issues of more substance than the pictorial outrages that Irma and Marion kept clamoring over. At first the Rombauers appeared to be asking Ernst and Mrs. Pilpel rather than telling them what Marion's status was to be. It was in fact Mrs. Pilpel who first casually mentioned the possibility of coauthorship.[17]

Once the lawyers had sorted out Irma and Marion's chief complaints, they could not hold out dramatic hopes of remedying any of them. As Ernst wryly reported to Marion after one perusal—not his first—of the *Joy of Cooking* file, "I must say it ain't joy. As we have told you often, you are in bed with bad boys under an evil contract."[18] There was no undoing that contract, yet Irma and Marion eagerly dreamed that withholding the manuscript would drive Laurance Chambers to his knees on the questions of special discounts and tacky-looking page formats.

The lawyers, who saw no prospect of carrying either issue in litigation, unhappily suggested facing the facts of life under a bad contract and going on to realistic points of discussion. But their more experienced judgment could not dissuade Irma, Marion, and John from hanging on to the copy as an all-powerful weapon and preparing to fight it out on that line if it took all summer—to say nothing of fall, winter, spring, and most of the next summer. The family opinion, as expressed during the spring of 1949 in a telegram from Marion to Harriet Pilpel, was "THERE IS NO TRUSTING THEM ONCE THE MANUSCRIPT IS TURNED OVER."[19] The Bobbs-Merrill editors, utterly in the dark as to the state of the completed text, helplessly watched one potential publication date after another melt away while the Rombauers bravely waited for them to give in.

Tales of plots and counterplots circulated. Greenbaum, Wolff & Ernst revolved the issue of the new material and at times talked of taking it to another publisher, with Marion as author. On the whole, however, the risks of this scheme seemed to outweigh the benefits. The same must have been true of a plan Chambers was said to be considering, under which the company would commission a non-Rombauer revision of *Joy*.[20]

Trying to bring some order out of this chaos, the lawyers decided that any material "new" in the sense of actually having been developed from scratch might have different legal implications from text that essentially revised preexisting chapters of the old book. Matter representing a real departure from the last edition, they thought, could occupy a potentially useful limbo outside the provisions of the 1943 contract. Ernst and Mrs. Pilpel were dubious about the wisdom of withholding the text of the revised parts, but at least temporarily willing to see whether some leverage could be managed with the still incomplete new copy. But in any case, they urged the Rombauers to resume some sort of working relationship with Bobbs-Merrill.

After various feints by Greenbaum, Wolff & Ernst and the Bobbs-Merrill lawyer, Pincus Berner, the family agreed to hand over the revised (as opposed to new) sections and sit back to wait for the publisher's next move. With the help of Mazie, Marion, and even Bobbs-Merrill (which obligingly let her have back the few pieces of text that she had submitted before the latest hostilities broke out), Irma got together the final version of the revised material and prepared to hand it over. On the night of August 17 Marion set off by train from St. Louis with 136 pounds of manuscript, which she delivered to the Indianapolis office the next day along with a letter from Irma (dictated by Greenbaum, Wolff & Ernst) stating that in handing over this material she was waiving no right to future legal action.[21]

After studying the submitted text for a couple of months, Bobbs-Merrill horrified the Rombauers by announcing through Harrison Platt that Rosemary York, as the person best qualified to discuss *Joy* with its authors, was ready to enter the picture all over again and go over any suggested corrections with them at Indianapolis headquarters. (It is quite possible that Laurance Chambers had kept her secretly involved all along, waiting for a suitable moment to reintroduce her as the voice of the law.) Irma would have nothing to do with her.[22] Harry Platt, ignorant of cookbooks but elected by default to fill the hot seat, received them himself in November and again just before Christmas, having prudently snared the first-floor directors' room, which was well out of sight of Chambers or Mrs. York. So adamant were Irma and Marion about not running into Chambers that on their Indianapolis visits they would not use the Bobbs-Merrill ladies' room, which was next to his office, but went down the street to the Antlers Hotel.[23]

Their discussions were, of course, a charade, since the book would be as good as unpublishable without the still unsubmitted new material. Marion explained to Platt that she and her mother had complied with the publisher to the best of their abilities and that any more material would have to wait for significant Bobbs-Merrill concessions. Platt was not deputized to reply to this ploy. The higher-ups hung fire, letting occasional rumors trickle down through Pincus Berner to Harriet Pilpel about not publishing a revision at all.[24]

The standoff that had prevailed since the end of February went on, with faint bits of peripheral adjustment. Quite soon after the entry of Greenbaum, Wolff & Ernst, Bobbs-Merrill had hinted that it might be willing to set up procedures for at least notifying Irma about special sales often enough to let any objections be discussed in a timely fashion.[25] Irma was dissatisfied with this sop. What she wanted was some express restriction on discount arrangements. The lawyers, certain that no amount of threatening was going to produce anything close to her idea of reasonable limitations, gradually managed to prepare her for lesser gains.[26] They also thought that Marion ought to work with rather than against the Bobbs-Merrill production people on design issues, for no publisher on earth would (as she appeared to expect) give an author carte blanche on all choices of typeface and page format. Already in the spring of 1949 Marion had thawed so far as to begin communicating in a fairly friendly fashion with Walter Hurley and Ross Baker, who shared the somewhat vexed suzerainty of the New York office. Hurley, the production chief, had indicated that on a few areas—dust jacket, cover design, and the illustrative artwork—the company was willing to be guided by her opinion.[27] But this, too, was a fairly meaningless kind of progress as long as parts of the manuscript remained hostage and the discount-sales issue was unresolved.

All parties muttered, ominously hinted, and twiddled their thumbs for a brief eternity, while Harry Platt and the Rombauers politely pretended to discuss a manuscript that everyone knew could not be readied for production in its present form. At last in late February of 1950 Bobbs-Merrill—watching sales decline, and in the truly awful position of either having to have new plates made from the old text or committing itself to a new edition with only an incomplete basis for setting up a huge production schedule—proposed to limit discount sales to 35 percent of total sales.[28] That such a figure could have been trotted out with an air of magnanimity hints at what liberties had been taken in the past (as mentioned before, more than 50 percent of at least one year's sales in the mid-forties had been made at more than a 50 percent discount).[29]

Irma, smarting from years of frustration, wanted the lawyers to hold out for 20 percent.[30] But Harriet Pilpel doubted that Irma and

Marion's game with the manuscript would produce anything like that. Over the spring and summer they adjusted their sights sufficiently to start getting the new material into final form, in order to be able to produce it as soon as possible in case any offer that they could live with should arrive from Bobbs-Merrill. In mid-August Ross Baker relayed the firm's offer to come down to 32 percent on the discount-sales clause. After a few weeks' consideration the weary Rombauers accepted this less-than-whopping concession.[31]

Even now Irma might have held out for more had she not had to deal with two severe shocks in quick succession. In May her beloved cousin Julia Hollweg Chapman had suffered a stroke from which, it became clear over the summer, she would never recover consciousness. Early in September Julius Muench, while returning with Irma and a party of weekenders from the Jefferson County cabin, also had a stroke. Mercifully, he died within a few weeks. (Julia was not released from her helpless state until September of 1951.) Irma, who had been intermittently unwell throughout the whole legal fracas, was deeply drained by these losses. Unequal to the last throes of negotiations, she asked Marion to deal with Bobbs-Merrill on any remaining odds and ends.[32]

The lawyers swiftly drew up the new contract, which was ratified on October 14, 1950. It was a woefully small reward for the Rombauers' attempted siege of more than eighteen months. By far the most important new provision vis-à-vis the book's future was the recognition of Marion as coauthor[33]—but Bobbs-Merrill had never tried to block this step. The idea had been suggested by Greenbaum, Wolff & Ernst a few months after their entry into the case and not immediately comprehended by mother or daughter. Until then Irma had simply been sending Marion occasional sums (over and above the $3,500 to $4,000 apiece that she had been distributing to Marion, Put, and Mazie every year since sales took off during the war) as "consultancy fees." The lawyers had had to explain to them that this was quite an inadequate arrangement to ensure a recompense to Marion for her part in the present revision. As soon as Harriet Pilpel had raised the suggestion with Pincus Berner—in November of 1949—Bobbs-Merrill had cheerfully gone along with it.[34] The express (and this time noncancelable) right to be consulted in advance about changes in dust jacket, cover, or illustrations had been agreed to even earlier, when Marion first started dealing with Walter Hurley.[35] Almost nothing else had been gained through Irma and Marion's long holdout, except the paltry 32 percent clause. (It stated that the full royalty would be paid on discounted copies when they surpassed that percentage of total sales.)[36] Probably the same goals would have been reached by the summer or fall of 1949 if Irma had not pinned her hopes on summarily banning discount sales and Marion on acquiring final authority over design matters.

The royalty schedule otherwise remained essentially as it had been, with mother and daughter sharing the income on a 60–40 basis. The original evil of the alienated copyright continued unchanged. Harriet Pilpel had made no headway at all on a point that particularly irked her, a 50–50 split between authors and publishers for the sales or licensing of various subsidiary rights including categories like first serial rights and foreign editions, in which authors commonly receive a much higher share.[37] Just about the only other significant changes were that John "in consultation with the Publishers" was authorized to designate another revisor for future editions if both authors should be out of the picture and that in the event of a Bobbs-Merrill bankruptcy all rights should revert to the authors.[38] This proviso had been added at the instigation of Irma, who had heard dire rumors concerning the company's fiscal health. The 1950 contract also differed from its predecessors in having been drawn up under the laws of New York State. Ross Baker as head of the New York office signed for Bobbs-Merrill with Walter Hurley as witness, thereby saving Laurance Chambers the indignity of putting his hand to an instrument even faintly sullied by the wishes of the unmentionable Irma Rombauer.

The actual work of getting the greatly fragmented manuscript into production now commenced, with as much rancor as the latest scenes of the drama. It was necessary to handle the huge book one section at a time, with the first chapters being set in type in December, long before other parts had been adequately reviewed—or in some cases even written.

Speed was of the essence if the plates were to be got ready for shipping in time for publication in the spring of 1951. At first Marion was spending three days a week going over corrections with Bobbs-Merrill in Indianapolis, where the bulk of the manuscript was being kept in the company vault, and dispatching nightly queries to Irma about laundry lists of details. For all their efforts, estimating the total length of the manuscript was still an appalling chore. Some parts were simply pasted-up pages or sections of pages from the last edition with deletions and addenda marked in by hand; these were interspersed with both scattered pages and entire sections of new recipes and background material typed by Mazie Hartrich. The scope of the revision was great, perhaps greater than anyone at Bobbs-Merrill had bargained for. Making an informed but by no means infallible guess, the company set the length of the final book at 1,024 pages. From January on, Irma and Marion corrected galley proofs in a laborious arrangement that involved sending batches of galleys back and forth among St. Louis, Cincinnati, and Indianapolis. Harry Platt, in the name of "the House," kept imploring them to sacrifice whatever of this process they could, while Marion kept stubbornly saying that it was necessary for accuracy.

Other matters were even more trying. Early after the Noble Bretzman set-to, Marion—finally less than enchanted with the whole idea of photographs, no matter whose—had persuaded Walter Hurley that line drawings were an idea worth looking into. He had accepted Marion's own candidate: Ginnie Hofmann, a young artist who had been her secretary at the Modern Art Society. It was a decision that would contribute immensely to the eventual merits of the revision.

Mrs. Hofmann, now living in New Jersey not far from New York City, was able to get along well with both parties and acted as sometime courier between Marion and Hurley during the long standoff. After the October contract-signing, Bobbs-Merrill formally commissioned her to do more than a hundred fifty black-and-white line drawings that constituted one of the most ambitious attempts at illustration in any cookbook to date.[39] Through the winter and early spring of 1951 she worked along with Marion, stage by stage, as successive chapters of galley proofs were gotten into conclusive enough form to allow the cues for illustrations and charts to be inserted. It was an incredibly complicated and drawn-out process. For several months the pieces of the giant puzzle seemed to be coming together well enough, if not as fast as Bobbs-Merrill had hoped. But other issues kept turning into miniature wars.

By the terms of the contract the authors' wishes were to be law on the design of the dust jacket and cloth binding; Walter Hurley also made some attempt to listen to Marion's ideas on typographical matters that were really his to decide. She seized the opportunity to make all kinds of requests about the use of different point sizes, boldface versus lightface italics for certain cross-references, the vertical and horizontal lines marking off different blocks of type, and a host of other minutiae. Hurley could not or would not accommodate her on most of these. They also quarreled endlessly over the dust jacket, on which

Hurley had originally wanted a photograph or drawing of a pretty girl waving a copy of the book along with a copious blurb spelling out the stupendousness of the achievement. John Becker, whom his wife had deputed actually to design it, wanted and eventually got a clean, abstract look with strongly defined geometric relationships and an attention-commanding emblem or logo dominated by the word "JOY," with a large dot over the "J" and with the words "OF COOKING" fitted in underneath in a smaller L-shaped band. It was a major step in staking a first-glance claim (even before a browser had opened the book in a store) to a character quite distinct from the sweet vacuity of most contemporary cookbook jackets, and it has been at least the loose model for the logo of all subsequent editions. But the point had been carried only at the expense of much ill temper.

By the time the dust-jacket wrangle appeared to be ending in victory for the Beckers, Ross Baker, the head of sales, had entered the fray with the announcement that Bobbs-Merrill wanted this edition to be christened "The *New* Joy of Cooking," with attention lavishly called to the adjective so as to let every housewife in the land know what a radical departure the current revision was from all its predecessors. He and Hurley proposed not just putting this title on the dust jacket but stamping it all over the front of the cloth binding beneath the jacket.[40]

Unfortunately the change of title had been announced by the time John and Marion were able to react. They were appalled at the pure silliness of the idea. What, they wanted to know, was anyone going to come up with in the *next* edition to top "New"?[41] Angry telegrams flew back and forth while the first half of the book was already at the foundry. By now it was the second week of May, and the company—which on the signing of the contract had gone ahead with one of its largest promotional efforts ever—had already had to postpone the 100,000-copy first printing by about six weeks. Marion absolutely refused to yield. By the terms of the contract Bobbs-Merrill had no choice but to accept her fiat. "New" was accommodated on the dust jacket in a position clearly indicating that it was no part of the title proper, and the cover and title page continued to bear the name "The Joy of Cooking." The company, in extreme annoyance at Mrs. Rombauer's pigheaded daughter, obstinately went on plugging the book as "The New Joy," but this gesture carried no official force.

By this point the intricate fitting together of the text had hit a sudden snag. After nearly four months of routing the manuscript, galley proofs, inserted illustrations and charts, and page proofs, with constant pleas for speed and requests for last-minute cutting, Harry Platt summoned Irma and Marion to Indianapolis for an emergency conference the third week in April. He announced that thirty-one pages would have to be cut at once from the last hundred pages. The flabbergasted authors said that it was impossible. But it happened that most of the section in question was taken up with menus, suggestions for leftovers, and other material heavily larded with lists and charts. At a second look Marion and Irma realized that with a little adjustment of the layout—mostly changing one-column to two-column arrangements— the thing could be done with only a few pages of actual cutting.[42]

That Bobbs-Merrill hadn't thought of this themselves did not brighten Marion's opinion of Platt and his team. He in turn retained keen memories of an emergency involving Marion's chapter on nutrition, which had been submitted very late and had been described by several experts to whom he had separately shown it for their comments as full of awful, ignorant errors and distortions.[43] Though Marion would in later years produce extremely impressive coverage of the same subject in *Joy*, she had at the moment created another hitch in the tight production schedule (and risked real damage to the book's reputation). At Platt's instigation she agreed to trim the chapter back to little more than an outline and to remove or recast the questioned assertions.

The ordeal of production staggered to an end by about the middle of May. The first sections went to the foundry to be plated on May 7, while Irma, Marion, Mazie, and Ginnie Hofmann were still struggling with the last sections of proof and the final illustrations. By May 19 Marion was writing to Harriet Pilpel, "It seems very strange to be a mother again and a mere housewife and gardener and when I am a little less tired I know I shall love it."[44] There were bound copies by about June 25, and on July 15, one day before the official publication date as listed in U.S. Copyright Office records, Marion was reporting to Walter Hurley that she had seen the book in Cincinnati stores.[45] But even now the battle was not finished. There remained some outstanding production costs apparently incurred during the last-minute brinkmanship of the spring, and it was not clear who was to pay for them. There was also the new crisis of the index, which probably had not been a complete surprise but which the Rombauers apparently had had to put up with in order to avoid any further postponement of publication.

The eleventh-hour crunch had produced what was by far the worst index in any Bobbs-Merrill edition of *Joy* to date. Mazie Hartrich, who had prepared what she thought was an adequate version, had not been able to see it in proof. The editors seem to have cut it a great deal to save space, without much system. The result was amazingly short on cross-references, helpfully overlapping entries, and in some cases even primary entries. To find the drumstick-shaped veal-and-pork presentation called "City Chicken," you had to know enough about it to look under "Veal" (not, for some reason, under "Pork") or zero in on the bare reference "Drumsticks, Mock" under "Chicken," for the term "City Chicken" appeared nowhere in the *C*'s. The handling of variant formulas for general prototypes was wholly inconsistent, leaving the hapless reader to guess whether the rainbow's end for something like "Blueberry Muffins" was going to be in the *B*'s or the *M*'s. Helpful visual cues like boldface type for major categories or deep indentation for long sequences of recipe titles under headings like "Beef" or "Cookies" were generally missing.

Irma, Marion, and Mazie did not mean to live with this sloppy and frustrating reference tool—particularly since in the book's dedication Irma had elaborately singled Mazie out for praise as the compiler of "the admirable index" for each edition including this one.[46] They saw plainly enough that a good index is no trivial technicality but will make a tremendous difference over the long run to a cook who must use a big, complicated kitchen bible day in and day out. But their complaints seem to have gone unheeded over a period of many months. The reason was simple: the financial impracticality of fixing up the present index to any meaningful extent.

The book had been bound in "64's"—that is, in groups of 64 folded and gathered sheets prepared from the large original folio sheets. The existing text and index filled nearly all of the allotted 1,024 pages (sixteen × sixty-four), with only three blank sides at the end. To accommodate the index within the available space, it had been condensed into fifty pages, as compared with sixty-one for the *shorter* 1943/1946 *Joy of Cooking*. Any change involving more space than that would have meant resetting the entire book in another multiple of sixty-four pages, which would have been comparable to recalling a whole year's production of a new Ford model and replacing it with something else because a rearview mirror was badly designed. Even replacing the plates for the index alone, in order to do a better job within the limits of fifty pages, was an expense that Bobbs-Merrill refused to take on after the costly delays and mishaps that had plagued the whole enterprise for nearly three years. This time the company had had the foundry prepare plates of extremely durable and expensive nickel, meaning to have them last as close to forever as human effort could ensure.[47]

The surviving correspondence about this latest difference is fragmentary but indicates that it became fairly angry. A letter from Irma to Marion early in 1952 mentions having received from Bobbs-Merrill some hard-line message on the index, contained in a "vicious shaft, dictated undoubtedly by Old Dynamite":

> He cannot hurt us—but he can, and *is* hurting the book. Such a stiff-necked fool and totalitarian character. Where does it get him? I feel so sorry for his family for he must have horrid insides. As for Maizie, she is sunk. Please stress [Marion was now carrying on most of the more controversial correspondence with the firm] that she was never permitted to see proof on the index. And *please* don't let the B–M letters get you. That is what they are meant to do and I am determined to defeat their purpose.[48]

The matter might never have been resolved if Irma and Marion had not been serious enough about fixing the index to assume most of the cost themselves. The two sides did not reach agreement until the date of the third printing, which was dignified with a separate copyright (in the company's name, as always) by virtue of a very few emendations, including a bare handful of corrections in the index. On April 28, 1952, the official publication date of this "edition," Walter Hurley wrote to Irma and Marion spelling out the terms of an agreement whereby they were to pay $898.16 for these minor changes, cover most of the disputed 1951 production costs, supply a new index within six months, and pay for the privilege of having it set and plated to the tune of $9.30 per page plus the cost of author's alterations in proof (a nice twist of the knife, since Irma had hitherto carried her point on refusing to pay for AA's after the uproar of 1936).[49] It was a sort of blackmail that rankled, but they were determined to remedy a potential long-term handicap for the book.

The resulting new "edition" was published (and copyrighted in Bobbs-Merrill's name) on April 20, 1953. Mazie, with Marion's help, had been able to improve it only so much because of the insurmountable pinch of space (they had been given only two additional sides to work with). They had been forced to throw out or awkwardly truncate some existing entries to make room for others, and they could not always avoid inconsistency. But they had gallantly made the best of a bad situation in terms of providing usefully overlapping references to shorten the searching process and typographical cues to guide the questing eye through long columns of entries.

With the corrected index the disjointed soap opera of the first genuine postwar edition reached its ending—and in terms of the buying public's verdict, a happy ending. There was an awful crash in sales for 1951, when the old plates were retired before the new ones could be prepared and the book went out of stock; the official Bobbs-Merrill record furnished to the family for that year was 33,627 copies sold. But in 1952, the first full year of the Rombauer-Becker *Joy*, sales rebounded to 201,394, the highest figure since the banner year of 1946. For the next four years they would settle down at between about 82,000 and 90,000 a year, well below the pattern of the late forties but certainly suggesting a reliable future for the book.[50]

All parties could now be sure that the previous success under wartime circumstances had been no flash in the pan. Not only did press reception of the new edition range from polite to enthusiastic, but it conveyed the implicit assumption that *The Joy of Cooking* was a perennial staple, an American institution. The literary editor of the *Oakland Tribune* surprised readers of the regular book-review department by devoting a respectable amount of space to a cookbook.[51] A columnist for the *Indianapolis Times* burst forth in a sonnet titled "On First Looking into Bobbs-Merrill's Rombauer" that began:

> *Much have I squandered in the realms of food,*
> *And many costly chop and hash joints seen. . . .*[52]

A letter of inquiry arrived from *Pageant* magazine, shortly followed on Irma's doorstep by "a youngish man with his back teeth missing but some hair on the remaining ones."[53] He was the reporter Jay Kaye, whose airy profile in the January 1952 issue celebrating her as *Pageant*'s "Woman of the Year" roused the horrified subject to say that "it just escapes being *straight* fiction."[54] Still, it must have done plenty for sales. More to her taste was an article by Jane Nickerson that appeared in the *New York Times Book Review* on August 12, 1951. Though it did not go into great detail about the revision (or even mention the new coauthor), it chronicled the fortunes of *Joy* since 1943 so admiringly as to hold the work up as a culinary monument of the age.

Miss Nickerson, the paper's food news editor since 1947, tellingly suggested that the critical elements of the book's success had been timing ("Mrs. Rombauer summed up in her lively, intelligent approach to the table arts the New Deal of the American household"), "personality," and sheer scope of coverage: "When its enthusiastic users get together, they play an 'it even has' game" that "could go on forever, according to [the participants'] tastes, background, experience."[55]

The cachet of *New York Times* food coverage under Miss Nickerson was already considerable (though not so great as it would be under her successor, Craig Claiborne). In effect, this piece would be received by many as an authoritative announcement that *The Joy of Cooking* could stand as *the* American cookbook of its era. It heralded another development that would be greatly furthered by Marion's contributions: the emergence of *Joy* as a major source of information for other food writers.

But Irma Rombauer's new triumph offered only a temporary boost to the fortunes of her publisher. At most, *Joy* could help Bobbs-Merrill hobble along a little further. By the time the last dust from the indexing squabble settled in 1953, all observers in the publishing industry knew that large changes of uncertain import must come soon.

The eighteen years of Laurance Chambers's presidency, ironically coinciding with the eighteen years since Bobbs-Merrill had acquired *The Joy of Cooking,* had produced gradually dwindling profits in the trade division and an eventual decline in the overall reputation of the Bobbs-Merrill lists. In the summer of 1950 he had willingly or unwillingly agreed to try remedial measures by installing a new and very highly regarded editor in the New York office: Hiram Haydn, a well-known novelist and man of letters who was supposed to upgrade the trade list with aggressive new acquisitions. Haydn might have been the powerful company ally that the Rombauers never had had, if Morris Ernst and Harriet Pilpel (who greatly respected him) had chosen to drag him into the semilunatic turmoil of the moment. As it was, Irma did not meet him until the affair of the new contract was over, when she was delighted to find that his opinion of Laurance Chambers much resembled hers.[56]

But the appointment was a doomed effort. The autocratic old man literally could not bring himself to grant anyone the independent authority he had promised Haydn. After attacking the new editor's proclivity for—according to the later account in Haydn's autobiography, *Words and Faces*—Communists, Jews, Negroes, and works of "sexual obsession," he began a political tug-of-war that boded no long future for the relationship.[57] Haydn might have triumphed in the end, for in 1953 the moment of kicking the seventy-five-year-old president upstairs—the dearest wish of some at Bobbs-Merrill for half a generation—finally arrived. He was named chairman of the board of directors, a position in which Irma and Marion no longer needed to deal with him even through intermediaries. The head of the textbook department, company vice president Lowe Berger, succeeded Chambers as president, while Ross Baker of the New York office was named vice president.[58] But Hiram Haydn did not stay around to bring the trade department into better order under the change of command. He left in 1954 to help found a new publishing house, Atheneum. What new direction would emerge for the troubled company was anyone's guess.

The next revision of The Joy of Cooking seemed likely to be supervised by Harry Platt, now senior editor at Indianapolis headquarters. He and Berger were not the men to impose a dramatically new approach on the company's chief trade title (which in 1953 achieved the mildly lucrative distinction of being chosen as a Book-of-the-Month Club alternate selection).[59] But the scuttlebutt was that barring any miraculous resurgence, Bobbs-Merrill might well be sold in a few years—in which case Irma and Marion could find themselves faced with new orders from people more interested in reading the cookbook market and gambling on some emphatic switch of course. It did not make sense for either of them to do more than collect recipes and information in a general way while waiting to see how the Berger regime should settle out.

In the meanwhile, Irma's legal battles had impressed on her the need to get her own affairs into better order. Quite early on, Morris Ernst and Harriet Pilpel had tried to convince her and Marion of the need for some sorting out of the literary and other property. After a conference with the lawyers in New York during the fall of 1949, Irma had suddenly been seized with the impulse to make an up-to-date will and had hastily written one out in longhand, leaving 10 percent of the gross income from her books to Mazie, half of her holdings in stocks and bonds to Put, and everything else to Marion.[60] Mazie's future continued to occupy her conscience, so much so that at the time of the 1950 contract-signing she told the lawyers she wanted to draw up an agreement on the subject, to be binding on both herself and Marion. Her idea was to make over either $4,000 a year or (depending on the level of sales) one-third of Joy's net take for the year to Mazie, to be paid by the two of them on the same 60–40 basis as their income from royalties. Irma's express intent was that *The Joy of Cooking* should provide an income to Mazie as long as she (Mazie) should live, and in the original draft the agreement had applied to any edition of the book remaining in print throughout Mazie's lifetime.[61] But after consultation with Harriet Pilpel the terms were altered to apply only to the revision then in progress, so as to avoid confusion with the 1943/1946 edition, for which Marion bore no fiscal responsibility. The final version applied only to the forthcoming revision.[62] Marion had doubts about the arrangement[63]—which certainly could be read more than one way with regard to future contingencies—but on this subject her mother's wishes were not negotiable.

This step put Irma's mind at rest on the Hartrich score but left the task of arranging her personal property and literary estate, which embraced not just the current *Joy of Cooking* but *A Cookbook for Girls and Boys* and a small raft of copyrights now held by Bobbs-Merrill but destined under the 1909 Copyright Act to revert to Irma fifty-six years from their original registration dates. She, of course, would be long gone by then, but the potential import of the early *Joy* editions (together with *Streamlined Cooking*) had by no means ended when the company stopped printing them.

When the hurly-burly of proofreading and production had subsided in the spring of 1951, she made a more orthodox, lawyer-sanctioned will leaving all of her literary property as well as the household effects and Jefferson County real estate to Marion, with Marion and Put equally dividing the residue of the estate except for a small bequest to be distributed among her charitable and civic causes.[64] The instrument did not address the problem that various advisors apparently had been mentioning to her: forestalling a heavy future burden of inheritance taxes. That gap was filled about a year later, when the Bobbs-Merrill agreement about the index was being settled in 1952. At around the same time Irma converted the assets of *The Joy of Cooking* and *Girls and Boys* into a revocable trust with herself and Marion as trustees and John to replace either in case of incapacitation or death.[65]

With these arrangements Irma's affairs were buffered at least to her temporary satisfaction against immediate emergencies. Anyone who knew her would have guessed that many of the present decisions might be altered by future politicking, for if Irma had a certain streak of long-range fair-mindedness, she also took a keen pleasure in watching people dance to her tune at different moments. As the mood struck her, she might hint that some member of her close circle was her most indispensable mainstay or a sheer pain in the neck. There had been a degree of gamesmanship in her reliance on different people—Jane Torno, Mazie, Marion—at the several stages of the latest revision.

In later years Marion would say (and perhaps persuade herself) that when the weary unpleasantness of the 1951 revision was done, her mother had handed the reins over to her.[66] Indeed, in 1949 Irma had briefly let her think that the time for a transfer of responsibility was at hand. The book itself tells a truer story. Irma appears throughout the pages of the "New Joy" as "I." There was no question of Marion's being "I"—nor is there any reason to suppose that the situation would have been different if Irma had remained in reasonable health when the time approached for another revision.[67] She was not about to make room for two first-person presences. Septuagenarian though she was, she had not lost one jot of jealous love for *The Joy of Cooking.* She had not really been joking when during the last throes of the 1950 contract wrangle she had borrowed the tragicomic lament of the Widow Bolte in Wilhelm Busch's popular nineteenth-century verse yarn *Max und Moritz* to apply to her own heart's darling:

> *All mein Sehnen, all mein Hoffen,*
> *Meines Lebens schönster Traum,*
> *Hängt auf diesem Apfelbaum.*[68]

[All my longing, all my hope, my life's fairest dream hangs on this apple-tree.]

By now the work was her life. She could no more have given it up than she could have given up breathing, and she could not have shared the role of original begetter and proper custodian. It is true that (as we shall see) the revision bore the strong stamp of Marion's convictions, but at the same time it acknowledged her presence only in the third person ("Marion's children have always demanded a piece of their birthday cake for breakfast").[69] At one time Marion had been going to contribute a separate foreword of her own as coauthor, but in the end Irma had decided to act as sole mistress of ceremonies. Her foreword thanked Marion effusively and distributed smaller bouquets to Jane Torno and Ginnie Hofmann—but the most conspicuous acknowledgment of all went to Mazie Hartrich as the one dedicatee.[70] Nobody could doubt who was in control—and planned to remain in control.

Marion's claim that Irma decided to yield the conduct of *Joy* affairs to her after 1951 is accurate only in that her mother had happily resigned the burden of slugging it out with corporate officers at Bobbs-Merrill on matters of fiscal substance. Having brought in Marion to fight these battles for her, Irma was able to bask in the flattering side of the inevitable comparison—for over the years, she had managed to cultivate quite a fan club at the company outside the immediate sway of Laurance Chambers. The salesmen, led by Ross Baker and Bill Finneran, adored her; the secretaries and younger editors in Indianapolis exclaimed over her annual boxes of Christmas cookies and treasured the occasions when she would descend on the office, radiating wit and charm, and sweep them all off for lunch.

Marion, by contrast, quickly acquired a reputation at Bobbs-Merrill as the heavy, nor was her mother at all loath to let her appear so. Hypocrisy was quite foreign to Marion's nature. After listening for a dozen years to Irma's reports of company misdeeds, she had arrived on the scene believing open confrontation to be the only right course, and did not trouble to waste her own considerable charm on such a crew. A prudent observer might have guessed that an already dreadful author-publisher relationship was about to get worse.

PART III

9

Chronicles of Cookery 2

It is a truth just about never acknowledged that what contemporary Americans think of their neighbors' cooking bears the unsubtle stamp of class-linked snobberies and resentments. Of course we don't have a literal, fixed class system, but that stops no one from speaking a language of intricate value judgments about how other people spend their money and display their status. One of the main subjects of such verdicts is food.

Matters are thoroughly different in societies where there really *is* a class system dictating that, say, the nobility eat meat while the peasants, if able to find firewood, boil up a mess of roots. Our modern snobberies are the product of more broadly and flexibly distributed wealth, which gave rise in the course of the nineteenth century to a gaggle of counselors telling people how to spend it. Writers of household manuals or magazine articles on cooking had their share of this pulpit well before the Civil War. But it was not until the decade after World War I that the advisors themselves were held up to much scrutiny.

That was a watershed era, the time when male noncooks such as H. L. Mencken and Lewis Mumford started complaining in print about woman food authorities as "a vast and cocksure rabble of dietitians" or perpetrators of "aimless standardized hodgepodges" belonging to "the card-catalogue rather than the kitchen."[1] By the end of the 1920s some patterns had emerged that we now take for granted in American attitudes toward food as mirrored in different strata of journalism or "service" writing.

People who did not approve of canned soups and shortcut pies were vigorously deploring the debasement of popular taste by mass-manufactured expedients. Cultural arbiters were proclaiming the rediscovery of regional American cooking, and some of them were hoping to authenticate a national cookery as a magnificent patriotic possession. A nascent fellowship of purists and adventurers was starting to outline the terms on which food could be said to reflect sophisticated awareness, a vision that became loosely bound up with the label "gourmet." Even in fairly remote parts of the country, millions of people had been made aware of Chinese and Italian food through cheap local restaurants that forever altered ordinary Americans' gastronomic horizons. Meanwhile, the nation's food manufacturers went on inventing handy, streamlined products, to the unqualified approval of most shoppers and food writers and the increasing disapproval of an influential minority.

In other words, by 1930 American cooking and eating habits had begun to split up into competing levels of taste—the competition being not between thrift and expense, about which cookbook writers used to deliver virtuous sermonettes at least up to the turn of the century, but between styles of consumption that didn't necessarily translate into different price tags. Other factors contributed to a sort of fragmentation rapidly mirrored in the cookbooks. One was a great proliferation of novel products, whether literally new in the sense of just having been dreamed up by a gadgeteer, food chemist, or plant breeder or comparatively new in their accessibility to the American public—e.g., broccoli, which the brat in the celebrated "I say the hell with it" 1928 *New Yorker* cartoon reasonably enough tagged as spinach. At the same time, the tide of manufacturers' recipe brochures swelled impressively, becoming such a substantial part of the overall food literature as to inspire a 1928 anthology from a trade publisher (Morrow). The title speaks volumes: *The Blue Gingham Cook Book: A Complete and Widely Diversified Collection of Recipes Drawn from the Scientific Tests of Famous Food Manufacturers and Experts.*

It is not surprising that very soon the cookbook literature began taking a turn toward specialization. During the postwar period more and more published recipes were coming not from people working under plausible home conditions but from the staffs of organized test kitchens connected with major food manufacturers, home economics institutes, women's magazines, or (in some large cities) the food pages of newspapers. The test kitchens' main reason for being was what later came to be known as "recipe development," a pursuit that stands to cooking more or less as political image-grooming does to democratic discourse. It means thinking up things to do with ingredients and translating the results into recipe directions that even incompetents may be able to follow. Practiced alike by corporate kitchen staffs and supposedly independent food writers, this strategic skill did much to encourage a growing assumption that smart cooking meant inventing multiple roles for some particular ingredient to play.

The era was a difficult one for the big kitchen bibles, the all-purpose manuals meant to steer a great cross section of the female population through a lifetime's meal making. The bibles' old mission was breaking down with the disintegration of any coherent kitchen religion that could make sense to most people and its replacement by a crown of subspecialties and competing vogues. But after a time some observers decided that the ongoing shake-up of culinary culture and the growing prominence of cookbook publishing in general signaled a likely opportunity to launch a new all-purpose manual. The late 1930s and early 1940s thus saw a spate of new contenders to the title of foremost general American cooking manual. *The Joy of Cooking* was the only one ever to truly approach that status, and it also happened to be the only one that did not share certain prominent features.

All of the new would-be bibles except *The Joy of Cooking* looked like the work of committees, and were. They included *The Good Housekeeping Cook Book* (1942), the successor to much smaller *Good Housekeeping* recipe collections that had been revised under several titles since 1903; *Woman's Home Companion Cook Book* (1942); *America's Cook Book* (1937), which had been compiled for Scribner's by the Home Institute of the *New York Herald Tribune*; *The New American Cook Book* (1940), assembled by a large team of researchers and domestic scientists under the editorship of the prolific food writer Lily Haxworth Wallace and published by a New York book packager called Books, Inc.; and *The American Woman's Cook Book* (1938), an oft-retitled and repackaged work edited by another test-kitchen veteran, Ruth Berolzheimer of the Culinary Arts Institute in Chicago.

All of these works displayed blockbuster ambitions (each was at least eight hundred pages long) bolstered by the resources of major service magazines or other organizations. They involved staffs of home economists, researchers, and recipe developers assembling many hundreds of recipes and masses of background information on anything from teenage reducing diets to cleaning the stove broiler. They also called for complex teamwork by art directors, writers, and a battery of text and design editors. They were generally distinguished by handsome paper stock, copious photography (usually both color and black-and-white) with or without illustrative line drawings, and elaborate charts and tables of a kind that cannot be dreamed up and effectively presented on a page by amateurs. Their contents in fact tended to be so dense and disparate that sometimes the book began by explaining how to find your bearings via the index.

These encyclopedias in modified cookbook format testified in all respects to the complexities that had descended on the cookbook writer's job. Their recipes were as carefully chosen as planks in a party platform, to offer something to as many segments of the public as some student of consumer trends thought worthwhile.

True, they did not try to match the standards of the more fastidious gourmets and purists, those who harped on recherché touches or begged people to cook everything from scratch with good ingredients. (Rex Stout's fictional sleuth Nero Wolfe was a semicaricature of the first type; the New Yorker's regular food columnist, Sheila Hibben, who privately supplied some of the Wolfe books' culinary expertise, was the best-known real-life instance of the second.)[2] But they alertly responded to an emerging fact: the big industrial processors and the corporate recipe developers were inventing their own links with the gourmet bon ton, surrounding canned soup with the accouterments of elegance in magazine advertisements or presenting ready-to-serve versions of foreign dishes that gave millions of people their first taste of—to name just a few—borsch, minestrone, tamales, Italian-style tomato sauces, and chow mein. In a similar spirit, the new entrants in the all-American kitchen-manual sweepstakes carefully introduced varying doses of cosmopolitan-sounding recipes ("Finnish Eggs," "Mexican Salmon Chalupas") designed not to appear too outlandish or puzzling to a hypothetical average homemaker.

They weighed in much more heavily with the American fashions of thirty-odd years ago—fruit salads built on ornamental schemes, canapés and fancy little tea sandwiches, cream soups, all kinds of creamed vegetables and meats. These were now more popular than smart; lavishly decorated sweet salads in particular had become a butt of culinary reformers' derision by the mid-1930s. (Up-to-date hostesses who aspired to refinement made sure to serve tossed salads with herbs, a selection of interesting greens, and the very best olive oil.)[3] They took for granted shortcuts based on canned condensed soups, which arbiters like Sheila Hibben almost wholly avoided. They addressed budgetary constraints by way of the cheap vegetarian dishes beloved of Depression-era nutritionists—e.g., "Mock Sausage" of lima beans, or "Curried Cottage Cheese and Hard-Boiled Eggs in Rice Nests." All were conspicuously marked by the thinking of professional recipe developers, the ceaseless pursuit of novel vehicles and combinations that leapt from models like goulash or baked spaghetti to "Cheese Goulash" or spaghetti baked with sauerkraut, and that turned plain mayonnaise into mayonnaise with grated cheese, marmalade, marshmallow whip, pimiento cheese spread, or bananas and peanut butter.

In an age of vast confidence in packaging and marketing skills, these compilations represented educated guesses by high-powered talent about what was wanted to detach modern housewives from *The Boston Cooking-School Cook Book* or *The Settlement Cook Book*. Neither of the two older bibles had striven to spread themselves as thin as the new competitors. Both had remained shorter, plainer, and more straightforward, emphatically distanced from the encyclopedic aims and splashy visual elements of the latest arrivals. But in their choices about clinging to the past or moving toward the future, *Boston* and *Settlement* were now headed on contrasting courses.

At first *Boston*, always the more widely used in most areas of the country and representing something closer to a nationally understood cooking style, had been the more conservative. Under Cora D. Perkins (Fannie Farmer's sister and continuator) it had been rather slow to admit change. It was *Settlement* that had been the first to give actual oven temperatures for cakes and pies, discuss making ice cream with mechanical refrigerators, tell people how to use a pressure cooker, include post-Prohibition alcoholic cocktails, and record fashions like crêpes Suzette and the early versions of chiffon pie.[4] But slight signs of a role reversal appeared during the 1930s. With the *Boston* edition of 1930, Wilma Lord Perkins, Cora Perkins's daughter-in-law, began cautiously rearranging the chapter sequence of the old book and retitling, retooling, or even occasionally deleting venerable recipes. Her next revision, which came out in 1936 shortly after the first Bobbs-Merrill *Joy of Cooking*, inched a little further away from the Farmer model. What looked especially obsolete as time went on was the original lumbering treatment of food chemistry, hopelessly outmoded as early as 1920 and one of the first things the younger Mrs. Perkins tried to update and streamline. By 1941 she was paying more attention to new ingredients and gadgets, talking about putting "gaiety into housekeeping,"[5] discreetly nodding to the gourmets with an herb and seasoning chart and dishes like bouillabaisse, and even making American ethnic cooking a little more visible by introducing such melting-pot items as fruit kuchen under that name (rather than "coffee cake" or the like), spaghetti and meatballs, and sweet-and-sour tongue.

The Settlement Cook Book, meanwhile, began to look like something over which the cook in "The Sleeping Beauty" might have dozed off a hundred years before. Up to the mid-thirties it appeared fairly up-to-date in its coverage. To move into the present it had even started putting in an occasional canned-soup combination, and to make its own bow to exotica on our shores it had added one of the first descriptions of a proper smorgasbord in an American cookbook.[6] But very shortly the parent Settlement Cook Book Company, which apparently had worked to review and revise the contents several times a decade for some twenty years, seems to have stopped trying to march with the times. Changes grew smaller from edition to edition, and had virtually ceased by 1951. (In that year *Settlement* was still explaining how to make soap or take care of an icebox.)[7] The voguish dishes and gourmet yearnings of the thirties and early forties—curried meats, *omelettes aux fines herbes*, Swedish meatballs, sukiyaki, and beef Stroganoff all had their prewar following—left hardly a trace on the stubborn old cookbook. It was equally impervious to piecrust mix and instant pudding. Its turn-of-the-century origins were bravely but anachronistically obvious in its advice on housekeeping and taking care of a family, remnants of a time when cookery was understood to be an integral part of general household responsibilities rather than a stylish accomplishment.

In 1901 and 1915, the workers at the parent settlement in Milwaukee had been offering real, concrete advice to new immigrants (many of them household servants or struggling young mothers in unfamiliar surroundings) when they told them how to wash their hands, air and dust a room, or feed infants and invalids. The same material was still in the book in the late 1930s, even though the bulk of *Settlement*'s faithful audience by then consisted of second- or third-generation Jewish, German, and eastern European women—mostly though not exclusively Midwesterners—who did not need to have such things explained to them. In fact, large amounts of the family-and-household advice remained in the book even when the Milwaukee settlement turned the actual publication over to a commercial house, Simon and Schuster, in 1954; they were not removed until a major bowdlerization in 1965.

The enterprising observers who had suspected that these aging bibles might be assailable by younger contenders with new selling points were quite right. But they were wrong in their guess about what would appeal. Indeed both were vulnerable—*Settlement* for having ceased to read the current national scene, *Boston* for trying a half-hearted makeover without really having anything new to contribute. The competition rushed in en masse—and fell short of replacing either of the old books as treasured benchmarks of American kitchen life.

The New American Cook Book and the Scribner's–*Herald Tribune* effort had faded within a few years. The others displayed more staying power, but generally without setting the world on fire. *The American Woman's Cook Book*, distributed by the Culinary Arts Institute through many reworkings, remained in print until 1972; *Woman's Home Companion Cook Book* was published until 1970. *The Good Housekeeping Cook Book*, the most successful of the lot, is still in print after several major revisions. But part of the more durable works' success always rested on the marketing resources of a parent organization. They did not stand to be embraced or rejected on the same terms as Fannie Farmer and the trade cookbooks, for their sales performance did not depend on convincing a retail bookstore customer of their own identity. Consequently, nothing much softened their air of being large, impersonal publishing exercises. It was not what people really were looking for.

The 1936 *Joy of Cooking*, by contrast, was not based on experts' readings of the market and attempts to work in such-and-such merchandising advantages. The book certainly profited from the astute salesmanship of Bobbs-Merrill, but it could never have been dreamed up by salesmen. Unlike the other hopeful bibles, it never appeared to second-guess the degree of novelty or tradition, pretension or commonness, that would go over with someone's idea of the American woman. It rested very simply on the taste of one obscure person who had cooked for some thirty years without pausing to register the studied guesses of professional food writers about cooking as fashion statement.

Though Irma could be a thoroughgoing snob in many ways, when it came to cooking she was one of those who honestly regard the most amazingly diverse preferences as equals in the republic of taste. She had made no scientific study of what other all-purpose kitchen manuals did and didn't do. But she instinctively knew that she could do something else—something based on her matter-of-fact example, not consumer profiles assembled by Madison Avenue wizards. When in 1936 she tried to explain it to her editor, Jessica Mannon, she struggled for comparisons to suggest that she had provided an alternative to the intimidations of the big competitors while touching on most of their bases. She called *Boston*, like *Settlement*, "a reference book for collegians, while ours is a prep-school book many collegians will be glad to use because it does not tax their tired brains."[8] She had, she wrote, avoided "the rigid quality of a textbook" as well as tedious explanations that would only confuse beginners. She tried to point out that vastly different sorts of people seemed to tune in to the wavelength of her book:

> Domestics *love* it. (I hear that again and again.) A friend writes from Cincinnati, "My last summer's cook has paid your book the supreme compliment of stealing it." Beginners like the book. It appeals to their imagination by teaching them to be fearless. To quote a letter sent me by an experienced housekeeper, "Your book has taught me to use *my own brains*!"[9]

What Irma was trying to say almost leaps off the pages of *Joy* from even a perfunctory comparison of its opening with those of *Settlement* and *Boston*, in the editions in print while she was working on the 1936 *Joy*. *The Settlement Cook Book* began with what was exactly its weakest point in terms of up-to-date appeal to a perplexed bride, harassed career girl, or weary servant: the dogged mappings of woman's practical sphere titled "Household Rules" ("Never lick your fingers or wipe them on the dish towel"; "Do not blow on food to cool it") and "Feeding the Family" ("Every infant should receive cod liver oil from the second month on"). The first thing approaching a recipe was strained vegetables for babies. Aside from this material, the first recipe chapter proper was "Cereals," leading off with "Cereals or grains are seeds of certain members of the grass family. . . ."[10]

The Boston Cooking-School Cook Book commenced with the basics of nutrition—modernized and trimmed a bit from Miss Farmer's original account, but still pretty solemn going:

It is sufficient for the person not engaged in the study of dietetics to have an understanding of the elements which must be provided by food to build and repair body tissues and provide heat and energy, and also some knowledge of the characteristics and sources of vitamins, the so-called "accessory food factors" which play such an important part in the maintenance of health.[11]

After you got through that, you were treated to further pedagogy in the form of a chapter titled "Cooking Terms and Methods," defining words like "fricassee" and explaining how to measure butter or flour (also dealt with in the *Settlement* "Household Rules" along with instructions about table service and cleaning the sink). Then came "Beverages." The first real recipe was for tea, and the sentence that introduced it epitomized Miss Farmer's supple grace as a writer: "Tea is used by more than half the human race."[12]

A prospective buyer examining the beginning pages of other general manuals would find the basics of meal planning or a set of culinary definitions. The first chapter of the 1936 *Joy of Cooking*, however, wasted no time explaining anything. It started straight in on recipes—not "Cereals" or "Beverages" but "Cocktails." The first recipe, a tomato juice cocktail, had no other preamble than Marion's silhouette chapter heading (reused from 1931) showing a couple of roosters flaunting their tail feathers and the following saucy general headnote:

The chief virtue of cocktails is their informal quality. They loosen tongues and unbutton the reserves of the socially diffident. Serve them by all means, preferably in the living room and the sooner the better. They may be alcoholic or non. For the benefit of a minority serve the latter with the former.

To give this book the impression of sobriety and stability it deserves the alcoholic cocktails have been relegated to the chapter on Beverages. There they may blush unseen by those who disapprove of them and they may be readily found in the company of other good drinks by those who do not.[13]

No one who had peered into other all-purpose cooking tomes could mistake Irma's arch equivalent of "Phooey on the old fossils!" From the first, she knew how to mark her turf and throw down the gauntlet to the encyclopedias. If they wanted to be authorities lecturing people about the profound mystery of cooking, that was their business. Hers was simply to introduce people to reasonable formulas—in her eye-catching new recipe format—and keep reminding them, "Now, don't be snowed by the stuff they tell you about all this." She laughed at cookbooks; she laughed at her having written one. She waggled a finger through the frame of the picture labeled "Cookbook." Her idea of how to explain that many minds had applied themselves to certain topics with conflicting results was:

> These instructions are as clear as I can make them, but they are not infallible. (How can they be when one authority says: "Never destroy the flavor of wild duck by washing it;" and another says: "Always soak a wild duck in water for two hours"?)[14]

This turned the tables on the usual pupil-teacher relationship implied in a cooking manual. It also let Irma off the hook from making plain statements of culinary opinion with which some "authority" might disagree, a form of exposure that she shrank from. Again and again she disarmingly confessed nonauthority ("It is a relief to hear that everybody is ignorant, only on different subjects"),[15] allowed that she was as capable as anyone of being intimidated by some branch of cookery, or let the reader in on her completely unsystematic decision making about what to include in or leave out of the book.

She told people that recipes were not cast in stone. You could, if you wanted, thicken the gravy for one lamb dish by boiling it down, the "traditional" way. "Or be a Bolshevik and thicken it with: Flour (see Gravy, page 247)." She waved flighty historical asides under the nose of the reader—"Believe it or not, the original recipe [for Bordelaise sauce] called for a grain of asafetida! Why bring that up?"[16] She tweaked the sober conventions of recipe categories. Invoking "the author of a well-known opera guide" who remarked, of von Flotow's *Martha*, "that of course he knew it was German but he thought it ought to be French," she announced that she was *not* putting a recipe called "Oyster Celery" in the soup chapter: "I prefer to classify it as a luncheon dish for if I placed it among the soups it might be lost to fame and it deserves attention."[17]

It was obvious to her that everything in her book belonged there *because she liked it*. Irma liked a lawless assortment of dishes from mushrooms under glass to canned Welsh rarebit, and she stuck into her first commercially published work anything from offhand puns to romantic prattle about the origins of crêpes Suzette. The cement that kept everything in place was her own personality, displayed here much more freely than in the small 1931 original. No one foresaw what a powerful weapon her characteristic voice would be in a few years, when Laurance Chambers tried to treat her as a dispensable element in a work actually belonging to the copyright holder, Bobbs-Merrill.

Irma fretted and worried over other slickly produced contenders as they came along, surely recognizing that they called on reserves of talent that made one Missouri hostess look quite feeble. She could not have known how dull and unfocused they would later appear beside her.

Her limitations were many, and in 1936 her naïveté was great. But in addition to the canny exercise of her native charm, she had made some good decisions about expanded coverage. The enlarged *Joy of Cooking* astutely adopted certain selected purposes of the standard kitchen bibles while scorning their image.

Recognizing that the 1931 book had been too higgledy-piggledy and parochial, Irma had spent the years since working in modest-sized chunks of instruction on formerly scanted topics. In 1931 the best informational background had been on cakes and ice creams, particular favorites of hers, and many other areas had received only the paltriest excuse for general guidance. Now she had revised and filled out the basic directions for soup stocks and roast meats. She had rethought some earlier placement of recipes in particular chapters. The new book supplied more background facts about yeast-dough handling and deep-fat frying, explained some principles of candy-making in more careful detail, and greatly increased the number of basic formulas providing a general model for a concept like a standard soufflé so that you could then follow some less detailed variation. Yet she had not let any of these additions block the true Rombauer priority, which was to lead people through the steps of a dish without theorizing. Never as long as she remained in control of *The Joy of Cooking* would she dwell on lectures and explanations. Something told her that readers did not want to see the nuts and bolts of cookery analyzed—perhaps because she hated analyzing them. For her such stuff would have been as confusing as explaining inertia and angular momentum to people who just wanted to get in the car and drive.

The mixture of recipes in the new edition was neither conservative nor daring. The total was now something like 2,500 to 2,550 recipes, roughly doubled from the 1931 selection. Most of this came from fairly uniform additions in all areas, not sudden attention to a few. As before, cakes and other dessert baking formed the finest attraction of the work, and the selection of German recipes shone proudly. Irma had remedied the omission of some obvious fundamentals like chicken broth, chicken salad, clam chowder, succotash, puff paste, and fondant.

Adventurous foreign cooking was not lavishly emphasized, and—like other writers in the all-purpose bible field—Irma generally avoided anything calling for visits to the specialty grocers recommended by gourmet writers. With the exception of the genuinely exotic Dutch-Indonesian rijsttafel ("rice table"), most of the imports included for the first time in this edition were already known in the United States in more or less Americanized (sometimes canned) versions: borsch, chop suey, minestrone, Italian meatballs, polenta, goulash, crêpes Suzette, sukiyaki (rendered as "sakiyuki" in the first printing). She had no use for the pretentious pseudo-French monikers that had filled *The Boston Cooking-School Cook Book* for decades ("Belle Fermière Salad," "Halibut à la Rarebit"). Her French additions were few—chiefly soufflé potatoes, accompanied by a spirited recital of the dish's supposed invention in the reign of Louis XIV, and *omelette Poulard*, unfortunately in a nine-egg version that must have stymied many users and was dropped after 1946. She was also sparing with new additions based on the American regional vogue. Some, like New England boiled dinner and Boston brown bread, now really belonged to all parts of the country. The most noticeable among Irma's new regional entries had Southern, especially Louisiana, origins: beaten biscuits, duck pilau, chess tarts, transparent pie, several "jambolayas," and a few things given the popular designation "Creole" by virtue of some tomatoes or green peppers.

The revised version of the fish chapter furnishes a good clue to the 1936 *Joy*'s competitive strengths and weaknesses. The original ten recipes were now about fifty, and Irma had added a very brief guide to cleaning and handling, along with a one-page chart matching varieties or cuts with suitable cooking methods. She now addressed such varieties as salmon, mackerel, and red snapper, but a more prominent innovation was her new attention to anonymous, precut "fillets of fish," which were now proving a particularly attractive way to market fish to people who really did not like it but had heard it praised by experts as a cheap source of protein in hard times.

By comparison, the current Fannie Farmer edition displayed an unmistakable familiarity with a range of good ocean fish. Unlike *The Joy of Cooking*, it explained what to look for in buying a whole fish and told you how to fillet one yourself. It is not clear that Irma had ever fried a mess of smelts, or cooked bluefish or fresh cod. Her New England counterparts obviously had. Miss Farmer and her successors conveyed the essence of handling fresh fish; they provided not only recipes but succinct outlines of the main cooking techniques. In 1936 Irma could not compete with this, and perhaps did not want to. It was exactly the sort of methodology that she shied away from. Rather she demurred to the timider sort of cooks with recipes like one for fillets sprinkled with cornflakes that she called "a boon to the housekeeper who does not like to handle fish"[18]—but also, with one of those flashes of charm that convey real culinary illumination, mused, "Many centuries ago a Chinese sage said: 'If you would govern a country well, do it gently, as you would cook a small fish.' "[19]

Probably the greatest weakness of the revamped *Joy of Cooking* was no weakness at all in the eyes of Irma and those who responded to her peculiar spell: the overall organization. It had been somewhat tidied up from 1931, but still betrayed that she had no head for sorting culinary concepts into systematic categories. The "Fowl and Game" chapter ended with a messy assortment of recipes—gravies and sauces, poultry dressings, dumplings, stewed or dried fruit preparations—that seemed to be there because they could go with poultry, although some were obviously meant for meat or fish. Any canapés that weren't in "Canapés" had been shoved into "Hors d'Oeuvre." But the most unholy mess of all was a vast chapter called "Luncheon and Supper Dishes" that was, in Irma's eyes, the heart of *Joy*.

Hostesses of the 1930s distinguished more clearly than we do between dishes appropriately served as main courses at a proper dinner and ones best reserved for ladies' luncheons or catchall family suppers. But that does not go far toward explaining the rationale of what went into this sprawling chapter. It contained virtually all of the 1936 *Joy*'s recipes for eggs, noodles and other pasta, cheese, and cereals, which could perfectly well have had chapters of their own (and did in some other cookbooks). It went literally from soup—the aforementioned "Oyster Celery," a sort of oyster stew—to nuts—for example, rice croquettes with walnuts. Irma herself probably could not have said why certain dishes ended up in "Luncheon and Supper" while others were shunted elsewhere. Scalloped cabbage and baked mushrooms were among the chosen, while baked creamed cabbage with eggs and mush-rooms au gratin failed to be admitted. To add to this capriciousness, in the section of menus for different sorts of meals that Irma provided at the back of the book, some of the dishes from the "Luncheon and Sup-per" chapter turn up on dinner menus.

Yet the placement of the "Luncheon and Supper" contents was no arbitrary decision in Irma's own view. From the universal report of friends and relatives, there was something about putting together a clever little lunch or unpretentious supper that she reveled in more than any other sort of meal making. Quite simply, the chapter was an album of favorites whose specialness was so self-evident for Irma that it needed no explaining. She could not distance herself from her mate-rial sufficiently to parcel it out into logical divisions.

Her lack of system in regard to anything luncheon-and-supperish partly handicapped users trying to consult the book on certain funda-mentals. You could not learn to scramble eggs, boil spaghetti, or cook rice and cornmeal without going to "Luncheon and Supper Dishes." Since Bobbs-Merrill had maddeningly neglected to supply any sort of running heads at the top of pages to help readers figure out which chapter or part of a chapter they were in, novice cooks must have encountered severe navigational problems. Mazie Whyte had partly compensated by working out an index much improved from 1931, but no *Joy* user was going to be able to find crucial material with ease until she had just about gotten "Luncheon and Supper Dishes" by heart.

Dedicated users of any cookbook do eventually get an inner map of it by heart, so Irma's wayward organization never deterred those who fell in love with her overall approach. It must be pointed out that she had a genius for making inconsistency a virtue, and that this was one of the greatest secrets of her success.

Irma was more modern than most of her direct competitors, at moments—and more resolutely old-fashioned than any, at others. She cooked dishes that harked back to lovely old American or German tra-ditions, and others from which the more distinguished gourmets and American culinary patriots of the era would have recoiled in disgust. All sorts of incongruous preferences happily shared her affections, and she was occasionally willing to be a relic as well as an innovator.

She had, for example, gotten to electric mixers and the "modern" medium-temperature method of roasting beef ahead of the Fannie Farmer revisors. It did not stop her from also giving her own sear-and-steam roasting method, or recommending her favorite technique of beating egg whites on a platter—not in a bowl—using a flat oval whisk with crisscrossing wires—not a rotary eggbeater, which she loathed.[20] (This must have been a survival of something she had picked up very young.) She was eager to show that she kept abreast of the times by including a whole subsection of the new gelatin-based chiffon pies and various recipe developers' bright ideas like doughnut-shaped hamburgers or tomato-soup French dressing. Yet she let it be known that she retained great affection for things like an old-fashioned currant cake whose "fragrance is a reminder of the period when rose jars were in vogue."[21] She could unblushingly recommend a horrible vanilla sauce that was essentially a roux thinned with water. Yet in the same breath she fondly remembered the "delicate and good" flavor of real vanilla bean as opposed to the ubiquitous bottled extract.[22]

If this was inconsistent, it was inconsistent in the same ways as American cooking itself, the theater of loudly contrary impulses at least since World War I. Many decades later, a reader wrote to the food columnist Marian Burros of the *New York Times* to point out that "Mrs. Rombauer didn't purport to cover the American cooking scene. She *was* the American scene."[23] This is also to say that for all its oppositions of taste the scene still contained vestiges of something communal and central. The culinary public might be sorting itself out into many publics that did not much like each other's cooking, but for a time one shrewd and whimsical voice could talk to most of them without strain.

Hardly was the first Bobbs-Merrill *Joy of Cooking* in print when Irma was restlessly dreaming of a more ambitious version. Her first step toward this goal, the 1939 *Streamlined Cooking*, appeared at the time to be an unfortunate misstep. But with it she gained the means to stamp a still more advantageous distinction on *Joy* as compared to the rest of the field. By now she was studying other cookbook writers with greater awareness of choices to be made in what was covered or omitted; she had begun to broaden and update her understanding of what was going on in American cooking. She emerged with more savvy than she had brought to the first *Joy* editions, and with a still livelier commitment to the quick-cooking adherents, those who detested any extra time wasted in the kitchen.

For much of the *Streamlined* material she went to what she considered the horse's mouth: the test cooks and promotional spokeswomen of the big commercial food processors, who invented new products at an amazing rate and worked hard to explain them to people. Irma always had been the perfect audience for their efforts. An instance is the undemanding alacrity with which the 1931 *Joy* had echoed the 1920s promotional efforts of the pineapple distributors, happily passing along formulas for biscuits, scrambled eggs, French toast, baked stuffed tomatoes, and frozen cheese salad that featured pineapple or pineapple juice. In *Streamlined* she explored such territory with greater determination. She made no concession to the food writers who complained à la Sheila Hibben about commercial travesties of noble dishes, except to remark parenthetically, "(Even the Gods, I fancy, grew a bit tired of their eternal nectar and ambrosia.)"[24]

The number of "frosted" (frozen) meats, vegetables, and seafood varieties had grown tremendously since the start of the decade. (For retail purposes, commercial freezing really had not existed before 1930, the necessary technology having been developed in the late twenties.) The prepackaged quick-bread mix Bisquick now provided the biscuit recipe of choice for millions of cooks. Prepared pie fillings and cake-icing powders had invaded the market, and the test-kitchen elves had successfully gotten across the idea of using instant puddings as pie fillings almost as soon as they had been invented. Canned fruit and vegetable juices had multiplied wildly, encouraged by the still reverberating vitamin discoveries and a new California-led health craze. (In 1931 Irma does not seem to have known canned tomato juice, though it appears in the 1936 book.)

Canned ready-to-serve dishes, as we have seen, had taken a turn for the more international, and it would be impossible to overstate how adroitly the corporate recipe developers had been able to parallel at least the aura of the higher fashion, lending can-opener cookery its own claim to be a sort of gourmet cookery. World traveling at table was an idea that had filtered down even to modest middle-class families to some degree; for those who could not make the leap to confronting a true foreignness in cooking materials or methods, canned enchiladas or ravioli might be an exciting enlargement of culinary horizons. As with industrially processed foods in general, the canned versions came to taste better to a large segment of the public than the equivalent dish made from scratch.

If Irma had any quarrel with this mentality, she managed to conceal the fact pretty well. There really is no reason that she should have quarreled with it. She was utterly devoted to the mix-and-match games that the industrial test kitchens had initiated with canned products, turning condensed mushroom and tomato soup into ingredients in other dishes as well as finished dishes in their own right and continually baptizing canned-soup combinations with names like "Dutch Consommé" or "Onion Soup Creole." What she saw in the modern culinary landscape was a wonderful richness and variety. She did not particularly distinguish between commercially packaged items and other evidences of progress, from odd-colored potato varieties to the remarkable abundance of fresh fruit out of season:

> Formerly we had a short, intensive strawberry season. Now, like poor relations, they are always with us. No longer a thrill, just an everyday "happenstance" that leaves us unmoved.[25]

It was all grist to the mill of the truly ingenious cook. She managed to intimate that "convenience" foods were a delightful creative challenge:

> Used with discretion, frosted, packaged, and canned foods are a household blessing and the wealth of these foods is amazing—as amazing as the time and effort saved in producing a like effect with fresh materials. It is up to you (and me) to make them acceptable and interesting.[26]

Irma did not mention that it was the work of industry brochure editors and flacks that generally pointed the way to "you (and me)."

One new development that helped smooth the path of convenience foods to quasi-gourmet esteem was a vogue for herbs and seasonings (usually out of bottles, though there was some attempt to encourage real home herb gardens). Garlic in particular quickly became synonymous with gastronomic sophistication. It is no accident that Irma first discussed the uses of herbs and aromatics in a book on hurry-up cuisine, for they were being discovered by the recipe developers as a splendid means of uniting self-expression with haste. One read a chart, heated some condensed soup for a sauce, and decided whether to raise it to the plane of gastronomic novelty with curry powder or a pinch of this or that dried herb. Something similar had happened with wine almost before the ink was dry on Repeal at the end of 1933; dozens of self-appointed experts had rushed to educate the public in a new mystery called "cooking with wine and spirits." The herb craze, however, penetrated further into American kitchens.

In *Streamlined Cooking* Irma discoursed aptly enough on the fact that "less fashionable gardeners" than the present cheerleaders had grown herbs for centuries "with far less fuss" than now. But the context of this remark was a discussion of picking up the flavors of canned goods, especially vegetables, with a dose of herbs or garlic. Begging readers not to "dismiss canned food as inadequate until you have tried out its possibilities," she recommended assorted remedies:

> Combined herbs (the French call them a bouquet) add a wonderful something to stews, sauces and soups and combined herbs are marvelous in the salad bowl. Add one or more of your favorite herbs (dried) to your pantry shelf, also a choice of Worcestershire, A, A-1 or Tabasco sauce, catsup, poultry seasoning, horseradish, the various new mustard combinations, French dressing, etc., and you are ready for any emergency.[27]

Certainly Irma had always found some place for garlic and herbs in her own cooking, but what propelled them to her attention now was their usefulness to cooks who wished to apply flavors to quickie dishes in the true hurry-up spirit. In her mind the slow alchemy of flavor blending achieved through, say, the traditional approach to soup stock with its simple but critical seasonings did not have the same dashing appeal—or relevance to a modern cook's wants.

Interestingly enough, Irma never applied to *Streamlined* the claim she had privately made that *Joy* was popular with "domestics," the maids who still handled part of a day's meals for many people in her circles. Her preface intimated that she was addressing "businesswomen" or "[their] equally busy housewife sister on maid's day out."[28] It would have been horribly rude in 1939—nor are things much different now—to tout any cookbook in public as offering any particular benefit to hired servants or working-class families. The usual sales pitch of convenience products was above such mundane considerations. Advertisements for canned soup commonly showed not frazzled women grabbing for the can opener but persons of aristocratic mien looking gratified over the soup course. *Streamlined Cooking* did not parade such crass pretensions. It staked out a slightly different territory. The fare presented here did not represent the meals anyone expected the maid to cook or a dinner party of the town's most distinguished citizens to eat, but a kind of cookery involving minimal drudgery and maximum creative flair—an approach fitting for the nation's Irmas and her social peers when they had to get an everyday meal for themselves. The uplift she had sought to confer on the subject did not prove terribly marketable in this particular book, but she had not guessed entirely wrong.

Streamlined Cooking failed miserably on its original terms as Irma's attempt to carve out an abiding monument to haste. But its contents looked quite different when she painstakingly interwove them with the 1936 *Joy of Cooking* to create the best-selling 1943 version. Now *Joy* had a claim that unmistakably set it apart from the two major kitchen bibles, *Settlement* with its sclerotic shell of a vanished identity and *Boston* with its hesitant search for a newer image. Neither had anything like the emphasis that *Joy* placed on convenience-ingredient cookery. Irma had also surpassed the newer would-be bibles in this area—even *The Good Housekeeping Cook Book*, which was especially strong on canned soups and other jiffy stratagems.

The huge mass of quick-cooking recipes from *Streamlined Cooking* must have been one decisive reason for the sudden success of the wartime *Joy of Cooking*. Bobbs-Merrill, of course, had contributed greatly with its giant selling effort and had had a stroke of luck in regard to the paper rationing. Yet these factors were only the beginning in an extraordinarily sound repositioning.

Irma had striven to respond to needs of the cooking public beyond speed and sprightliness. She had gone further in the treatment of herbs, repeating her general remarks from *Streamlined* and adding a one-page herb chart prefaced by a more detailed introduction. Here she dryly observed that "the cultivation of herbs has become a cult" and expressed some exasperation at the intimidating snobbery of "epicures" about "wedding the right herb to the right dish."[29] She had worked in a few more American regional dishes, again chiefly Southern—Maryland fried chicken, Jefferson Davis pie, fried pies, Brunswick stew. She had significantly expanded the number of foreign or vaguely foreign dishes. These now included duck bigarade, *pot de crème*, potato gnocchi, beef Stroganoff, vichyssoise (a French-American hybrid popularized by Louis Diat at the New York Ritz-Carlton), guacamole, egg foo young, Dobos torte, chicken cacciatore, Swedish meatballs (in two versions, under the name "Beef à la Lindstrom"), ravioli, and bouillabaisse. (The last two, like Brunswick stew, had recently been circulated in canned versions.) She gave a version of French bread that would win no prizes for good and authentic detail today but demonstrates that a French-bread cult among American gourmets already was expanding breadmaking notions; it is an interesting recipe using the old technique of floating a ball of starter in lukewarm water to develop before the bulk of the flour is worked in.

Irma also had found room to introduce items of produce that food writers had made better known during the thirties: fennel, chayote, "dasheens" (taro root), "celtuce" (a lettuce variety cultivated in China for its fleshy stem, not yet mentioned in other kitchen bibles), the mustard-dandelion-kale group of greens, and soybeans (in the vegetable chapter as well as the wartime rationing section). She enlarged her attention to broccoli, which had not been universally familiar to either shoppers or cookbook authors until the 1930s. She dealt for the first time with venison, one of the perennial gourmet symbols that had received a bare mention in the 1936 *Joy*.

Surely these additions to the 1943 edition were a strong selling point. But they did not necessarily make the difference between a temporary sales peak and a lasting place among American cookbooks. The new status of *Joy* probably owes much to another factor. Irma had managed to infuse into the book something even more engaging than the display of her own personality: the sense of a real, solid friendship with her readers.

This was no figment of anyone's imagination. It was exactly as she described it in the preface to the wartime edition:

> ... I now feel a close kinship with many thousands of persons. I hear from them constantly, through telephone calls, letters, messages and articles, and I am greeted as an old friend in the most unexpected places.
>
> My daughter says that when my book is praised I purr like a cat. Perhaps I do. I can't help it for I am a fortunate woman.
>
> After middle age, my family duties ended, my brood scattered, my civic and social interests (properly) in younger hands, many familiar doors seemed closed to me. Suddenly a new one flew open. It has led to a multitude of human contacts, experiences and gratifications. I feel *useful* once more, far more useful than I ever expected to be. Who wouldn't purr? Thanks to you, my friends, known and unknown, for your many manifestations of approval and appreciation. I have tried out a number of recipes you sent me, some of which you will find in these pages. I regret that all could not be included.[30]

She was as good as her word. She proudly introduced the begetters of new recipes—"an English woman living in Massachusetts," "a Maryland man," "an unknown Seattle friend whose family has used this rule for many years"[31]—to her other readers like someone bringing new friends into a comfortable circle. It conferred a uniquely participatory, welcoming quality on the now-enormous cookbook. Moreover, it cemented Irma's own place as center of the circle, the life of the party giving her friends a good chuckle even at her own expense:

> A colored cook in St. Louis objects strenuously to following this or any other cook book. [Even very earnest liberals of Irma's generation in St. Louis rattled off humorous references to "colored" people without the slightest embarrassment.] Outright rebellion came at the suggestion that apple be added to cabbage. When her mistress insisted that the rule be followed, she left the room mumbling darkly: "That ole Mrs. Rombauer! Ought to run *her* out of town, that's what *we* ought to do!"[32]

This note of camaraderie was underlined by new recipes with titles like "Rombauer Rice Dish" ("Freely varied each time it is made but in such demand that I shall try to write a general rule for it")[33] and "My Favorite Soup" (a good tomato-vegetable soup with noodles), mingling with the allusions to new *Joy* friends. With the Bobbs-Merrill war now at its height, Irma had mightily strengthened her hand by infusing a sincere and inimitable author-reader companionship into the work.

Less atmospheric but probably extremely helpful to the 1943 book's success was the greater degree of order that had been imposed on the contents. It had grown to a dense 884 pages, with a total of roughly 3,350 recipes (versus about 640 pages and perhaps 2,500 recipes in 1936), but it was easier to use. Bobbs-Merrill had chosen a smaller, squarer page trim with a more compact effect, and this time had supplied running chapter heads to help you find your place. Additional running heads marked off some messy subsections like all the baggage at the end of the "Poultry and Game" chapter. Author and publisher alike had seen the sense of improving on some of the reference material. A meager, amateurish-looking laundry list titled "Cooking Terms and Helpful Hints" and a jumbled page of measuring equivalents (for example, how many cups of cocoa make a pound or how many teaspoons make a tablespoon) had each been sorted out into arrangements that were both plainer on the page and richer in detail.

Irma's main improvement, a stunning feat for a woman as impatient as she with facts and figures, had been reorganizing much of the basic culinary information within chapters while adding new kinds of information—still, however, retaining her breezy conversational tone and reassuring distance from officialdom. A chaotic sequence of introductory material at the beginning of the meat chapter had been taken apart and put together far more lucidly. The instructions on handling poultry now included new material on drawing it and removing crop, oil sac, and feet—information clearly added not by necessity, since all of this was usually done by the butcher rather than the purchaser, but for the sake of old-fashioned completeness.

"Luncheon and Supper Dishes" was even huger than it had been before, having received dozens of additions from *Streamlined Cooking*. But its subsections now had more reasonable boundaries marked by prefatory comments on matters like the general method of cooking cereals. Irma had meanwhile gotten the courage to put together a few facts on the dismal science of nutrition, an expansion of a tiny stab she had made at the subject in *Streamlined*. That had been a twenty-line "Health Chart" giving recommended servings of the major food groups; this time she provided a more detailed version of the same advice together with a chart of vitamin sources, a list of caloric values for modest portions of common foods (source uncredited), and the National Research Council's recommendations on caloric intake.

The war emergency apparently had spurred Irma to efforts with "service" information that she might not otherwise have taken pains with—for example, on vegetable protein sources and particularly soybeans, or the unrationed sweeteners like honey and corn syrup that people were trying to bake with as a result of sugar rationing. She also obviously had gone much deeper than before into the subject of home canning. This had benefited from improved technology and marketing efforts during the thirties and was promoted when war began as an adjunct to the Victory Gardens campaign. Irma, who does not seem to have discovered pressure cookers until she was working on the 1939 *Streamlined Cooking*, now provided detailed instructions for the use of a pressure canner. She also covered several other popular canning methods such as open-kettle. In contrast to her timorousness about technicalities in the matter of the baking-powder controversy, she had been extremely scrupulous in her presentation of safety factors, carefully citing a government bulletin on home canning and choosing her words with an awareness that mistaken advice could be a great danger.

This kind of effort with information indicates the growth of Irma's ambitions for *Joy*. In 1931 she had neither wanted to nor known how to focus on much beyond her own favorite recipes, and certainly had wasted little time on things she didn't cook herself. In 1936 she had protested that her book was an *alternative* to the standard manuals with their heavy freight of knowledge, not intended to be one itself. She had shied away from matters of scientific fact; when she encountered conflicting advice from the authorities on some point, she would nervously recite both approaches with as little sign of choosing sides as possible.

Now, however, she met the necessity of exercising real intelligence to help readers sort out some questions—for example, talking about how to handle old-fashioned country hams, instead of just accepting a big company's claim that they were a thing of the past. In 1936 she had been content to say that "modern methods" of producing hams had done away with the old bother. In 1943 she carefully distinguished between smoked and "New Processed" hams, giving directions for both and special instructions for cleaning and soaking one of the Smithfield-type country hams that the American-epicure movement loyally championed against the commercially tenderized variety.

She could now see the sense of including recipes she herself might detest—like red devil's food cake, whose striking color came from a somewhat soapy-tasting combination of chocolate, baking soda, and baking powder. ("Generally popular—but not with me, which is not to be taken as a criterion," she commented, before printing a version more or less swiped from *Settlement*.)[34] This time round she rose more directly to the matter of "modern" and "old-fashioned" meat-roasting methods; the latter now went all but unmentioned in the latest Fannie Farmer. Irma, however, refused to consign her preferred approach to the dustbin.

> This [the medium-temperature method] is today the generally accepted manner of roasting meats and fowl. As there are a few people who fail to advance with the times or who, being otherwise progressive, hanker nostalgically for the roasts that mother used to make, a chart for roasting by the old-fashioned method is appended.[35]

This was not just coy flutter, but a hint to the wise that "generally accepted" culinary doctrine wasn't everything.

With the combined *Joy/Streamlined* edition of 1943 Irma lastingly altered the competitive stature of the book. Her sprightly, irreverent alternative to the kitchen bibles now *was* a bible, and deserved to be. It is true that the book had not magically become a systematic course of instruction. It still had a wayward quality that could let down readers searching for general knowledge. Sections like the fish chapter remained short on good information; some fairly slapdash material still testified to *Joy*'s half-accidental origins. But she had given it a whole new foothold on existence, and she had given herself something like an objective command of cookery in many branches. She could now legitimately consider herself one of the "collegians."

In its former incarnation, *The Joy of Cooking* could never have moved to the forefront of American cookbooks. Irma's idea of a lightweight recipe collection with a limited scope had been appealing, but it also would have meant sticking to a limited audience. The 1936 *Joy* had not seemed likely to crack a sales limit of 8,000 to 10,000 copies a year. Yet somehow she had moved it into serious-manual territory without falsifying its insouciant charm. At the age of sixty-six, this untutored woman had lifted herself to a higher plane of responsibility and authority as a writer of genuine instruction. Remarkably, she had done it while also fitting in all of her can-opener favorites from *Streamlined Cooking* and establishing a bond of author-reader comradeship unique among American cookbooks.

As we have seen, this first taste of national glory was embittered for Irma by her antagonism with Bobbs-Merrill. Even had all been well with the publisher, the head that wore the new crown would have lain uneasy at the knowledge that American cooking had begun to change at a wilder pace than ever before. Food writing was more than ever a map of fragmentation. Cookbook authors much younger than Irma might well stare in bewilderment, unable to keep track of half the novelties that whizzed past their noses and wondering how to define their own market amid the confusion.

One bewildering new factor was that specialty cookbooks were starting to claim a much greater share of attention than they had even in the busy thirties. Many books were now devoted to individual foreign cuisines, an admirable example being the 1945 *How to Cook and Eat in Chinese* by Buwei Yang Chao. Pearl Buck, who was married to Richard D. Walsh, the publisher of the John Day Company, had persuaded him to issue this remarkable work. It gave you the wherewithal to start "learning" Chinese cookery as you might learn a new language, as opposed to mouthing a phrase-book sentence or two. Ten years later book buyers would be able to select from among several contending trade cookbooks about—among other choices—Chinese, Italian, Mexican, or Swedish cooking as matter-of-factly as 1955 city dwellers could decide which ethnic restaurant they wanted to visit that night. Not all, of course, were equally good. But eventually they would put new pressure on the standard kitchen guidebooks to improve the recipes they had formerly offered as "Mexican" or "Chinese."

Kitchen technology was another contributor to the specialty literature, and another moving target for the big bibles to try to keep up with. In the prosperous aftermath of the war a great many appliances and gadgets—including some that had gotten their first commercial start in the Depression but had then had limited market potential—came into being in millions of middle-class households. A new generation of electric stoves and refrigerators with larger freezing compartments appeared in American kitchens. Home freezers became a fairly widespread luxury, eventually supplanting the rental spaces in community freezer lockers that had been available in some areas during (and for a few years after) the war. Electric mixers, blenders, and pressure cookers reached a wider demographic spectrum of purchasers. All of these commonly came with manufacturers' directions, including recipes or preparation charts, and all would become the subject of entire cookbooks.

The proliferation of foods processed into new forms or tailored to new marketing opportunities continued unabated after the war. Chickens sold in cut-up parts had become a familiar though not yet universal sight before 1950; precooked rice appeared at about the same time. The manufacturers of frozen foods were making ready to branch out for the benefit of the nation's freezer owners, offering not just meats and produce but, according to the 1949 *Good Housekeeping Cook Book*, cooked dishes like baked beans and chicken à la king.[36] In the same year James Beard, in *The Fireside Cook Book*, mentioned the availability of "excellent" frozen French fries and "very acceptable" piecrust.[37] Packaged mixes had been developed to make fudge, ice cream, yeast rolls, and apple pie (you put the filling mix into the piecrust mix).

Meanwhile, the war years had if anything brightened the luster of the gourmet movement and helped it find diverse expression. Even before Pearl Harbor, the coincidence of the 1939 New York World's Fair and the outbreak of German aggression had left a lot of high-powered European talent camped on American shores, from the staff of the French pavilion (which rapidly became "Le Pavillon" restaurant) to the resourceful cooking-school founder Dione Lucas. Celebrity spots with cosmopolitan menus shone glamorously in New York, probably the most illustrious being the Colony restaurant. It was a heady time for the city's corps of food journalists, whom Irma first regularly began to be introduced to at this time.

Nothing illustrated the promise of the cooking-and-dining cult in these years better than *Gourmet* magazine, which swiftly earned a devoted following despite having started publication in the year of Pearl Harbor. Its founder and publisher, Earle MacAusland, had previously worked at the Butterick Publishing Company and *Parents Magazine*, both of which sponsored a lot of recipe development. Rightly guessing that there would be a reliable market for a national magazine pulling together some of the many culinary enthusiasms that had developed in the 1930s, he and his editor—a veteran of the New York food scene named Pearl Metzelthin—started with a cleverly judged mixture of approaches.

For one thing, MacAusland had grasped the fact that in the past ten or fifteen years the kinds of food writing people were interested in reading with or without recipes had developed mightily. Gastronomic reminiscence was starting to blossom as a genre and had even won a certain literary recognition (in 1936 the American Booksellers Association had chosen as the "most original book" of the year Della Thompson Lutes's culinary memoir of a farm childhood in southern Michigan, *The Country Kitchen*).[38] From the start, *Gourmet* looked out assiduously for food writers who were something more than food writers.

MacAusland was lucky at once to reap a smash hit in Samuel Chamberlain, a well-traveled artist who under the pseudonym of Phineas Beck (a pun on *fin bec,* French slang for a connoisseur of food) genially related the adventures of "Clémentine," the cook who had come back to Massachusetts with the Chamberlains after their long sojourn in France. Every month *Gourmet* readers turned to Clémentine's story with the eagerness of Dickens fans picking up on the latest installment of *Our Mutual Friend,* and in the recipes accompanying the articles they received a truly pleasant idea of the *cuisine bourgeoise.* Latching onto a far more elegant rising talent, MacAusland also introduced *Gourmet* readers to the writing of M. F. K. Fisher, who posed a catholic array of more or less gastronomic subjects before the easel of her own fastidiously self-absorbed prose without attempting to set herself up as a *cooking* authority.

The title *Gourmet* itself and features like a monthly quiz on obscurely named French dishes suggested the aura of admission to an elite. At the same time, a regular report on new products by Clementine Paddleford of the *New York Herald Tribune* gave a more sophisticated spin to the kind of consumer information commonly provided in newspapers and women's magazines. And from the beginning, *Gourmet* gave prominent attention to American cooking, from Maryland to Washington State. It did not disdain sweet salads and canned-soup sauces, which many of its readers genuinely liked. One can read this tolerance as a sign of wishy-washy standards or a fear to offend potential advertisers, but it also suggests that the magazine cared as much about what people really were cooking as about gilded images of what they were cooking.

This atmosphere of inclusiveness did not last. The air of *Gourmet* ten years after its founding shows the epicurean audience having become more extreme in its epicureanism. Uncouth "convenience" ingredients were much rarer in *Gourmet*'s recipes by 1951, and it now seldom cared to address people who liked packaged gelatin salads and other wrong-side-of-the-tracks cookery. Clearly the magazine had rethought its market with a more rigorously defined focus. So, in another manner, had *Good Housekeeping*. The 1942 *Good Housekeeping Cook Book* had extended a cautious arm toward readers who might yearn for a little gourmet globe-trotting—bouillabaisse, "Armenian Rice," "Genoese Spaghetti," "Eggplant Roma," recipes for leeks and fennel. All were eliminated in the 1949 edition, while the already extensive coverage of instant mixes and other commercial convenience foods was stepped up several notches.

The authorities who spun the wheels of food fashion were busier than ever, on their several levels. In elegant circles, modish dishes like wild rice amandine and melon with prosciutto would be introduced on some eminent advisor's say-so, while other fads made the rounds among friends who clipped recipes for something combining cake mix and pudding mix. Women's service magazines and newspaper food columns often picked up the latter formulas from manufacturers' publicity handouts. But the fancier writers also could sometimes be found recycling recipes that had reached them from promoters.

So far the most obvious challengers to the standard American cooking manuals had been newcomers that laid strong claims to the quicker and humbler end of the market. But after the war a new breed of cookbooks appeared that combined kitchen-bible and gourmet elements in an unprecedented way. Clearly some observers were betting on loftier styles of cooking counting for more in Middle American kitchens.

The Gold Cook Book (1947) by Louis P. de Gouy was the first of these, a weighty 1,256-page tome addressed to all imaginable segments of the cookbook market. De Gouy, an Escoffier pupil and a chef of wide experience, had been the first food editor of *Gourmet*, where MacAusland and the staff happened to be planning their own weighty tome. De Guoy, however, beat them to the punch by incorporating into *The Gold Cook Book* (and copyrighting in his own name) slews of material from his work for *Gourmet* since 1941, either borrowed word for word or partly reworked. A war would surely have ensued had he not died of a heart attack the very week the book was published. *The Gold Cook Book* outdid any of the bibles in breadth of "service" information; it was also peppered with entertaining bits of erudite fancy, and contained an extraordinary array of pompously French-titled recipes and ones claiming other international parentage, along with a liberal selection of others for cooks who were quite happy with gelatin salads or cornbread made with evaporated milk. Turning through its 2,000-odd recipes at random, you might come on pompano en papillote, champagne sherbet, peanut-butter sandwich filling, or "Frankfurter Crown Roast." In its ambitious, indeed loopy mixture of goals and preferences, *The Gold Cook Book* would stand as the most catholic and encyclopedic American kitchen manual until the 1962 *Joy of Cooking*.

A more selective attempt at a kitchen bible for the fashionably enlightened came in 1949 from James Beard, the not particularly famous forty-six-year-old author of a handful of specialty-subject cookbooks. *The Fireside Cook Book*, packaged in an elaborate oversize format by the publisher, Simon and Schuster, was probably the best general American cookbook of its time in terms of efficiently summarized culinary information and cooking that showed what it meant to work with ingredients rather than shove them into recipes. It had a good foundation of meat-and-potatoes American cookery along with a lot of the international-but-not-too-unfamiliar dishes well known to urban gourmets in 1949: veal Parmigiana, Swiss cheese fondue, salade niçoise, pot-au-feu, sorrel and potato soup, steak tartare. Beard had well judged his audience as the sort of home cooks who aspire to something approaching gourmet knowledge and sophistication but have their feet firmly planted on the ground and remain loyal to a few convenience ingredients.

The Gourmet Cookbook, published in 1950 under the auspices of the magazine, was an enormous and expensive volume that announced itself as a way of life rather than any sort of teaching tool. MacAusland's preface mistily intimated that anyone from beginner on up could use "the world's recipe file" as here presented to advance his or her skill in "the art of Gasterea, the goddess of gastronomy."[39] In fact, *The Gourmet Cookbook*'s editors had decided even more firmly than Irma Rombauer not to get dull stuff like explanations of cooking principles into the act. Each chapter plunged straight into an imposing sequence of recipes, hardly pausing to discuss what you were supposed to be doing. Every recipe was meant to be as self-contained as possible, without the usual cross-references to basic preparations like beef stock or techniques like clarifying; there was nowhere to look up pieces of knowledge that could be applied in different contexts, such as the way to beat egg whites. The book did not address people who wanted to have such things explained, as it did not address those who cooked with canned soup and lime Jell-O. (It admitted a few fruit salads, but they were simple and fresh, far from the extravaganzas that Ogden Nash, in the mid-thirties, had called "a month of sundaes"; there were also a few jelled salads, but they used unflavored gelatin, which in 1950 was a less déclassé ingredient than the presweetened kinds.) The complete absence of instruction on cooking procedures or the nature of ingredients was no mere omission. It rested on a concept of cooking as a gallery of great dishes and talismans of distinguished sensibility dwelling in a kingdom of their own. Household responsibilities did not exist in this realm, nor did the building blocks of knowledge.

For the two chief general manuals, *Boston* and *Joy* (*Settlement* had abandoned any attempt to stay current), the appeal of such works plainly indicated that they would have to work in stronger gourmet claims. How Irma originally meant to cope with this and the myriad other directions being taken by American cooking will never be known, because her initial revision efforts were first derailed by the illness of her helper Jane Torno and then long delayed by the threat of a legal showdown with Bobbs-Merrill.

Irma's and Bobbs-Merrill's nervous awareness that immediately was not soon enough to get started on postwar image-remodeling is evident in the version of *Joy* that was rushed into print in 1946 as a "new edition," a claim as accurate as calling your old car a new car after replacing a taillight. The plates of the 1943 edition were used intact except for a forty-page stretch toward the end and the necessary changes in the index. In the reset pages the wartime rationing suggestions were replaced by the material that would have been there in the first place if not for the national emergency: summaries of the *Streamlined Cooking* advice on stocking canned time-savers and planning jiffy menus. The sloppiness of the supposed update is evident from the fact that the "new" information on the pressure cooker was repeated verbatim from the vegetable chapter. More legitimately new were four pages that listed essential kitchen equipment, staple ingredients, and amounts to buy (e.g., a pound of meat for four people) and three pages of "Quick Method Cakes."

If the new cakes represent Irma's guess about what direction to take next in *Joy*, they were not a very good guess. Their real source was the General Mills test kitchens, which had invented a "double-quick cake" technique that required only one mixing bowl. The new cakes, which required hydrogenated shortening and cake flour along with precise stopwatch-timed mixing, were Irma's first sacrifice of old-fashioned standards to commercial "progress" in the area of cake baking, where she had hitherto been true to butter and (with rare exceptions) traditional mixing methods. She had also neglected to credit General Mills and its fictitious "Betty Crocker" for "these marvelous rules." (The omission was remedied in the 1951 *Joy*.) It certainly looked as if Irma planned to go even further in the commitment to quick-cooking strategies that had helped reposition *Joy* among American cookbooks in 1943. Whether her coworker Jane Torno meant to back up this orientation or counterbalance it with other kinds of cooking cannot be guessed, because no manuscript evidence remains of their early efforts.

Irma's other work of 1946, *A Cookbook for Girls and Boys* (on which Jane Torno also worked to an undetermined extent), gives a much more complicated picture of her thinking about the future. It was not entirely endearing as a first cookbook for the young, striking an uneasy balance between the companionable and condescending and not always paying attention to critical points of instruction. The bread recipe, for example, does not explain how correct temperatures affect the action of yeast; "French Fried Potato Chips" gives dangerously insufficient guidance on handling a kettle of hot fat.

Most of the recipes had been taken directly from *The Joy of Cooking* with some rewriting for extra clarity. Irma had done an excellent job of mapping out the overall coverage among really substantial concepts like roasting meats (here she mentioned only the medium-temperature method, perhaps thinking alternative suggestions too confusing); fairly demanding executions like angel cake, cherry pie, soufflés, and fondant; and fun-in-the-kitchen dishes on the level of milk shakes, "Tuna Fish Fondue," and chocolate waffles.

A Cookbook for Girls and Boys is a curious work—not quite a pickup, not quite a book in its own right—but probably no children's cookbook has ever bettered Irma's guesses about the several kinds of cooking that children want to be and should be exposed to. As a clue to how she was reading the larger culinary scene, it has some distinct surprises suggesting that even an Irma Rombauer might be ready to retreat a step from the endorsement of quick cooking. What undoubtedly gave her second thoughts on this score was modern nutritional advice—especially that coming from her own daughter.

The children's cookbook, which one might have expected to be filled with canned and packaged simplifications of real cooking, actually gave short shrift to salads of preflavored gelatin, weddings of canned soups, and instant mixes. These did appear, but not in the profusion that Irma's previous career would have suggested. Very little of her beloved *Streamlined Cooking* material made its way into *Girls and Boys*. Fresh vegetables and fruits were distinctly emphasized over canned versions. For a change, the chapter on cakes was shorter than the ones on meats and vegetables. Canned preparations, though used in many recipes, stood in an obviously subordinate position in the soup chapter. All of these choices reflect a plain consensus on the part of influential nutritionists that children should be exposed to vitamins and minerals through milk, cereal, several kinds of vegetables a day, and fruit in fresh or dried form. Sugar was seriously frowned on as spoiling the appetite for better foods. Here, too, the war had been a large factor for change, giving rise to educational campaigns on the patriotic worth of good nutrition for all Americans from the cradle.

Where did Irma get her ideas on the subject? Jane Torno, who collaborated with her on the *Childcraft* article "Cooking Up Fun" in 1945, had young children of her own and surely was concerned with expert advice. But the article had exactly the emphasis on sugary shortcuts that does *not* appear in *Girls and Boys*. (It led off with the "magical" experience of "flavored gelatin mixtures.")[40] A likelier influence is Cecily Brownstone's contacts at *Parents Magazine* and in children's-literature circles. And in the light of hindsight there is little doubt that the strongest influence of all was Marion.

Of course Marion herself was now a mother, and had ventured at least some bits of editorial intervention in *Girls and Boys* as well as doing the illustrations. Glimpses of her progressive convictions on politics and "the right human relations" crop up in the book, sometimes to very peculiar effect. Marion as a grown woman had a charismatic ability to catch up other people in her fervor for truth and enlightenment. Irma, though she could be the captious and carping mother, also could be carried along by her daughter's faith.

This faith included one feature of the American culinary landscape that Irma had hitherto ignored: the new health crusaders' credo. By 1946 "Thoroughly Modern Millie" (as her son Mark once called Marion) had made a sharp swerve from certain thoroughly modern convictions of her youth. Gardening and the study of natural ecosystems had introduced her to minds who profoundly questioned what twentieth-century technology had done for food. She had become increasingly skeptical about some of the industrial marvels that her mother most adored, and in her change of heart lies the key to how *The Joy of Cooking* converted a bright but uncertain flash of popularity into lasting eminence.

This story begins in the 1930s with the stirrings of American organic gardening and a new religion of nutrition. In Cincinnati Marion had been introduced to the "biodynamic farming" theories of the Swiss Ehrenfried Pfeiffer, first published in this country by J. I. Rodale (a disciple of a Pfeiffer-influenced theorist in England) and more or less akin to what Rodale subsequently popularized as "organic gardening." The idea behind biodynamics was that certain strategic details in the planting, raising, and harvesting of food tend either to block or to channel into it the life-enhancing energies of the earth and other elements. The link with Rodale's organic gardening was the claim that compost and manure were the only fertilizers that didn't amount to nutritional despoilment of any crop grown with them (and long-term damage to the soil). Gardeners who had studied this approach believed that most of the food commercially grown in America was horribly depleted of the health-giving qualities it ought to have and frequently tainted with dangerous chemical residues.

Meanwhile, a closely related attack on the sins of American food was gathering from another direction. With the first great spurt of vitamin discoveries that followed the isolation of vitamin A in 1913, the former crude understanding of the major nutrients (proteins, fats, carbohydrates, and a few obviously present elements like sodium, potassium, and calcium) was refined by the realization that a tremendous role in human physiology was played by chemical elements or compounds present in food only in tiny amounts (i.e., "trace elements" or "micronutrient elements" and vitamins). This crucial medical breakthrough opened up a Pandora's box of popular delusions and earnest obsessions, occasionally accompanied by some sense.

A vitamin craze blossomed in the 1920s, popularizing raw fruits and vegetables (whose unique benefits had not been grasped in Fannie Farmer's time) while making canned fruits, vegetables, and juices national commercial staples. California shortly became a particular hotbed of health-food cults. On West Coast trips that took her through the state in the 1930s Irma found restaurants there replacing sugar with honey and vinegar with lemon juice in "unusual combinations of hashed fruits and vegetables," while the signs on juice bars proclaimed, "Drink your salad."[41] The general understanding was that vitamins were "protective," which was true in that they prevented the great deficiency diseases like scurvy and pellagra.

One wing of opinion took up a latter-day version of a belief that had been preached in other contexts by nineteenth-century nutritional evangelists like Sylvester Graham: that unnatural debasement of food was having a terrible effect on just about everybody. The kernel of truth on which this idea rested is that nearly all fruits, vegetables, and grains retain more of their original vitamins the less they are interfered with. Already it had been repeatedly and conclusively demonstrated that peeling, degerminating, overcooking, and various sorts of processing from bran extraction to pickling cause loss of vitamins. By the late 1930s a dietitian named Adelle Davis was moving toward the conclusion that a general nutritional impoverishment had overtaken American food. She also decried the use of chemical preservatives in commercial processing (something that had aroused the suspicions of pure-food advocates as early as the first decade of the century). Among those who subsequently discovered her ideas was Marion Becker.

Marion's involvement with the organic-gardening movement, dating from at least 1939 or 1940, predisposed her toward an interest in what were called "natural foods." She had always been as glad a believer in can-opener cuisine as Irma herself; a combination of condensed mushroom soup and bouillon in *Streamlined Cooking* and the 1943 *Joy* bears the name "Marion's Soup," and she probably contributed more. But by the time of Ethan's birth in 1945 she was dubious about the contents of commercial baby food.[42] She owned and scribbled comments in a copy of Adelle Davis's 1947 cookbook *Let's Cook It Right*. ("She makes some good if unappetizing points" is written on the flyleaf. For Marion, what was "appetizing" often performed a certain tug-of-war against what was enlightened.)

Irma had observed recent nutritional trends with a layperson's uncertainty. She did not care to know more about such affairs than the stock advice on eating a balanced diet with selections from different food categories—vegetables, fruits, milk, meat, etc. The technicalities of the subject bored and intimidated her, but she deferred, if sometimes skeptically, to Marion's learning and zeal. When Marion agreed to work with her on *Joy*, it was a foregone conclusion that the culinary priorities laid down in earlier editions would be drastically rearranged. *Let's Cook It Right* was a concrete influence.

Adelle Davis, who in recent years has sometimes been portrayed as a nut case pure and simple, must on the contrary have been a genuinely interesting mind, a mixture of keenly commonsensical insights and half-baked idées fixes cemented by a powerful personal fervor. The gist of her teaching was that all sorts of health problems from colds to cataracts were in effect deficiency diseases, just as traceable as rickets or beriberi to failures of preventive nutrition. The remedy was massive doses of protein, a battery of vigor-giving supplements in pill or powdered form, and proper cooking to conserve natural nutrients. She was a supporter of a cause that had adherents among a sizable cross section of food experts: the use of whole-grain flours containing the original thiamine, niacin, folic acid, and other B vitamins, in preference to the "enriched" flours introduced during World War II that replaced some of the nutrients lost in modern milling.

Less widely shared were Miss Davis's enthusiasm for a sort of saturation-bombing approach in which every meal was supposed to cram in the last possible milligram of protein along with every vitamin and mineral, and her oft-repeated credo that that cooking is best which cooks least. In her opinion, the more nearly cooking approximated rawness, the better it was for you. The idea of real broiling or roasting was anathema to her. She was also severely opposed to forms of cooking that involve marinating, curing in dry mixtures or pickling solutions, or even rinsing vegetables and most other foods for more than an instant, lest water-soluble nutrients like vitamin C be leached out. She wanted to see more breads raised with yeast rather than baking powder or other chemical leaveners, which she believed interfered with the B vitamins in flour. Of course canned and highly processed foods of all kinds appeared to Adelle Davis to be a form of nutritional assassination.

Marion was a swift convert to the organic gardeners' and vitamin evangelists' arguments that what most people ate had been gravely compromised in nutritional worth by the commercial growers and processors. She was the more inclined to ponder the links between food and illness because of her own multiple allergies, and the more inclined to distrust the food available to most people because of her and John's overall political beliefs, which were roundly New Deal (later liberal Democratic) and anti–big business. The first area of cookery to which her new convictions drew her was bread-baking; at some point in the late forties she was trying to interest her Newtown Township neighbors in whole grains and get up a small local home-baking movement.[43] In 1948, the first year from which one of Marion's appointment calendars survives, she was consulting mail-order catalogues that offered vitamin supplements, organically grown grains and flours, and books like the Rodale Press's *Natural Bread*. It was also in this year that she first began working seriously on *The Joy of Cooking*.

Many years later Marion would appreciate that general-interest cooking manuals must exercise great caution in printing any health advice likely to be perceived as controversial. But now she rushed in where most cookbooks feared to tread. The results were sometimes ludicrous, sometimes uncommonly trenchant.

In the 1951 Rombauer-Becker *Joy of Cooking* nearly every reference to cooking vegetables in salted water had been deleted because of Marion's Davis-inspired concern over vitamin loss. The vegetable chapter now recommended the quickest possible precooking preparation, to minimize destruction of nutrients through oxidation, and the use of "stainless steel or plastic knives,"[44] which were less likely to react chemically with the food. It severely cautioned against reheating vegetables—you were advised to eat leftovers cold when possible—and tried to sidestep double-cooking methods through such labored suggestions as starting with raw rather than cooked potatoes in an entirely new recipe for hashed brown potatoes.

The salad chapter warned against adding salt and vinegar, "even in wilted salads," too far in advance (as all kinds of soaking and marinating were considered nutrient leachers from the Davis standpoint), and apologetically defended a wilted cucumber salad as "very good, even if it has lost some of its food value through soaking."[45] The leaching effect might, however, be desirable when the object was soup stock made from beef or other bones: "If you wish to extract extra calcium from the bones add 2 tablespoons of vinegar to 1 quart of water."[46] The general remarks on sauces suggested increasing the nutritional value of "highly flavored sauces like those with tomato" by adding powdered milk and debittered brewer's yeast, which were among Adelle Davis's prime weapons in the unending struggle to pump enough protein and B vitamins into the family. Presumably, strong accents like tomato would drown out the distractions of the other two.[47]

Marion had not dared to follow the Davis lead all the way on roast meats. *Let's Cook It Right* advocated "roasting" in a 250°F oven, an approach that most health authorities thought insufficient to kill dangerous bacteria. As in the last *Joy* edition, the "modern" recommended temperature in this one was 300°F or in some cases 350°F, with Irma's covered-pan version of the searing method still remaining as an "old-fashioned" option. But now a diagram graphically warned you about shrinkage of the meat with high-temperature roasting. In line with Adelle Davis's general thermophobia, the broiling instructions mentioned no setting higher than 350°F. A method called "Broiled and Roasted Meats" sought to modify the ultra-low-temperature approach by browning the meat next to the oven heat element at a 350°F setting, then baking it at "250° to 300° until done."[48]

For the first time in *Joy of Cooking* history, large numbers of old recipes had been deleted. Some were probably victims of a general triage that sacrificed items of marginal interest to make room for timelier ones; additionally, some closely overlapping variants had been condensed into single formulas, the result of a campaign to save page space that had also inspired much rewriting of sprawling old recipes in tighter form. But the overall recipe deletions show a very clear pattern that is not merely a matter of saving space: much pruning of convenience-ingredient formulas and sweet or molded salads, which Marion had come to distrust on nutritional grounds. Sizable amounts of the *Streamlined Cooking* material added in 1943 were now conspicuously missing.

Even an incomplete recital of the discarded luncheon-dish and main-dish recipes speaks volumes: "Canned Roast Beef," "Canned Creole Rice," "Ham Loaf with Tomato Soup," "Canned Hominy,

Shrimp and Mushroom Soup Dish," "Canned Luncheon Tongue and Peas Creamed," and so forth. The salad chapter had lost "Cider Aspic," "Frozen Pineapple Cheese Salad," "Molded Cheese Mayonnaise," and "Frozen Tomato Aspic" (among others). Irma's hymn to canned soup, which had celebrated the availability of "this good and nutritious product at so low a cost," had been toned down to "this good and often nutritious product."[49] Marion was not sure that the cost of such things was really low compared to cooking from scratch, and had misgivings about assuming that they were always nutritious. "Catsup Cream Soup," an Irma favorite composed of the two elements in the title, was gone. So was "Marion's Soup" (though it had been replaced by a similar mushroom soup/bouillon idea).

A few new quick-fix dishes and Jell-O salads had been added, but such cooking now occupied a smaller proportion of the book. Not the woman to judge nutritional progress solely by how much discredited stuff she had removed, Marion had also worked hard to replace it with other kinds of material. Her most important additions had been in the areas of grains generally and bread-baking in particular. In earlier *Joy* editions cereals as such had come in for little attention, and Irma understood so little about flours that since 1936 she had been meaninglessly writing "bread flour" in all kinds of recipes (puddings, cake fillings, etc.) that did not in the least call for the special properties of bread flour, an ingredient that many of her readers would have had difficulty finding anyhow. The only choice most shoppers had was between "cake flour" and "all-purpose flour." Bread flour (made from high-gluten strains of wheat that help a loaf rise more springily, though this does not in itself create the best texture or flavor) was not universally known in 1946, when Irma got around to replacing it with all-purpose flour in the recipes of *A Cookbook for Girls and Boys*, possibly at Marion's instigation.

The 1951 Irma-Marion edition saw careful changes in nearly every mention of grains, cereals, and flours. The section on cereals now lamented the ills of "modern processing."[50] The guidance on basic cooking of cereals was much more detailed. Gone was Irma's unfortunate suggestion about cooking rice to absorb eight times its volume in water. The chief method in the new edition involved two cups of water to a cup of rice. Former mentions of rinsing or draining rice either before or after cooking had mostly yielded to severe cautions against such practices as a robbery of nutrients. Brown rice was now praised over white as "richer in taste and a far better buy nutritionally."[51]

Almost every recipe using cornmeal now specified the water-ground grain, "which retains the germ."[52] Legumes also came in for some attention, and Marion had contributed one of the earliest recipes for bean curd ("soybean cheese") in any American cookbook. Unfortunately it was quite unusable, since she had not grasped the fact that soybean milk coagulates on different principles than cow's milk.[53]

The bread chapter now began with a sort of call to arms:

> French bread, biscuit, tortillas, pumpernickel, corn pone, scones, rice cakes and so forth—the very names conjure up old cultures that produced breads as characteristic as their makers. Will our characteristics be judged by the pallid commercial bread loaf in general use today? What a heritage for our children! Let's see what we can do about it.[54]

Here Marion must have been influenced by the brilliant historical survey of milling and baking technology in her friend Siegfried Giedion's *Mechanization Takes Command*, which had been in preparation early in their acquaintance. Giedion had expressed the hope that a reaction "against all artificiality in food" would "outlive the dictatorship of production."[55] Marion addressed an allied goal in her own way. The 1951 *Joy of Cooking* was alone among the general-interest culinary manuals of its day in pointing out the historical primacy of unbleached, germ-containing flours until very recent times and spelling out just what was lost in modern milling (illustrated by Ginnie Hofmann's accurate diagram of an actual wheat kernel). "Compared to whole grain flour 'enriched' flour is still impoverished," Marion wrote, sardonically noting how "our miraculously mechanized but standardized economy" had reduced the usual choice of flours to "cake" or "all-purpose."[56] It was an unprecedented sort of comment for an all-purpose cooking manual, a genuine attack on one of the much-vaunted achievements of the American food industry.

Marion had added invaluable new general information on the action of yeast and the business of mixing and kneading; she described many nonwheat flours and meals. Some dozen new recipes for yeast breads and rolls had been added to the chapter. Bread makers of the 1990s will search in vain for much on nursing doughs through several fermenting or rising stages, though the sourdough method was admirably represented by "Myrna's Rye Bread," the contribution of Irma's St. Louis acquaintance, the unfortunately misspelled Merna

Lazier.[57] But Marion's overall coverage of the subject was unequaled in any comparable kitchen bible of the day. The latest Fannie Farmer gave a very little information on nonwheat flours and vaguely extolled homemade bread over the bakery equivalent, "particularly if you use unbleached flour and enrich the bread further with soy flour and wheat germ."[58] *The Good Housekeeping Cook Book* offered the muddled thought, "Now that flour is being enriched, there is more reason than ever to use it frequently in yeast breads."[59] Marion, however, had gone at many intertwined questions with a probing curiosity and polemical ardor that would influence the thinking of millions.

She had also added a new chapter on nutrition that turned into an awful debacle. With grains and breads she had had some reputable opinion on her side. But in attempting to pronounce on nutrition in general, she was far beyond her depth, though she would know more in future. When Harrison Platt showed the now-lost original draft of the chapter to several readers for expert opinions, they turned emphatic thumbs-down on it. The excerpted criticisms that he passed on to her noted that she had written "hydrocarbons" when she meant "fats," offered shaky claims about losses of nutrients in food under various conditions, and asserted that the nutritional value of milk is seriously impaired by pasteurization.[60] (Pasteurization does alter the structure of milk in a manner to affect some products made from it, but changes in vitamin content per se are negligible from the standpoint of human nutrition.)

Marion had failed to understand the difference between a work like *Let's Cook It Right* that is defined by its controversial intentions and a kitchen bible that, even when it ventures to address disputatious matters, has a responsibility to a large, miscellaneous public. This episode must have been a stinging lesson to her. There was nothing for it but to trim the nutrition chapter back to something simpler and more general. But Marion still stubbornly managed to squeeze in some of her original intent in the new two-and-a-half-page version.

She removed the questioned material about pasteurized milk and a suggestion (vetoed by Platt's experts as impractical) that readers try to find out what sort of soil the produce in the local market had been grown in before buying it. Yet she did not surrender various articles of her nutritional faith. She warned about the undesirability of "pickled, salted, or highly processed" meats compared to fresh, the damage done to some proteins by "too great heat," and the dangers of "excess carbohydrates." (Marion would always remain a child of the era in which elementary school classes were taught the principles of nutrition through skits featuring a cast of characters led by "Captain Protein.") She insisted, "Natural foods are usually our best sources for complete nourishment," and would never surrender a conviction that the complexities of nutrient content in food as it comes from the soil can be only crudely mimicked by "enrichment." Though she stuck close to the standard explanations of proteins, fats, carbohydrates, and the best sources of vitamins, her essay sounded a note of challenge quite unlike the passive little summaries of received nutritional wisdom in the other kitchen manuals:

> During the last fifty years a great change has taken place in the processing and preserving of foods. We have drifted into assuming that sanitary and keeping qualities are synonymous with nutritive values, but preservatives and purifying processes frequently tend to be destructive of vital elements in food.

> Seasonal foods, which automatically give us menu variation, are usually higher in food value and lower in cost. Whole-grain cereals are no more costly than highly processed ones. Fresh fruits are frequently less expensive than canned fruits loaded with sugar.[61]

She would return to these themes in future editions with a more mature blend of keenness and evangelism, and would help inspire other mainstream cookbooks to move closer to what had been seen as the sole territory of health cranks.

Marion left another mark on *Joy* that at the time caused endless arguments with Bobbs-Merrill but that would decisively set the book apart from its peers. In league with John, and backed up by Irma, she battled for critical changes in the book's physical appearance—a huge factor in the experience of anyone, tyro or veteran, who uses a work of how-to instruction on a daily basis.

The great war of the 1951 edition began with the company's unwise attempt to put color photographs into the book and continued with a lengthy squabble between Marion and the production chief, Walter Hurley, over the dust jacket. The jacket of recent editions had featured a vapid little drawing of a pert female wearing a doll's grin and an apron; Hurley hoped to replace this with a photograph or drawing of a trim, modishly clad young woman holding aloft a cherry pie or copy of the book. The trial shot he commissioned flawlessly mirrored the postwar cult of domesticity embraced by all the popular media, which relentlessly reminded everyone that woman's place was really in the home, being *feminine*. Marion had no great quarrel with this assumption, but she did not want to see an inane visual embodiment of it telling people what *The Joy of Cooking* was all about.

What she fought for and eventually got on the dust jacket was strikingly out of the usual cookbook mold: the attention-focusing *Joy* logo originated by John and laid out by him as the centerpiece of a simple abstract design with forceful sans serif type. At the same time Marion had unsentimentally agreed to throw out her own chapter-heading silhouettes, a feature of all editions since 1931. In their place she had introduced Ginnie Hofmann's copious line drawings, the most genuinely informative artwork to be found in any cookbook of the time.

The accomplishment is evident from a few comparisons with other cookbooks. The 1951 *Boston Cooking-School Cook Book* is a more attractively designed volume in many ways. But what most rapidly gives away its age is Jeannette Klute's color photographs, quite a cut above the vapid work in service-magazine compendiums like *The Good Housekeeping Cook Book* but inescapably more dated than the contents. Barbara Corrigan's instructional line drawings convey little about work processes and sit rather woodenly on the page. Time has been still unkinder to Eileen Gaden's photography for the 1950 *Gourmet Cookbook,* to say nothing of the now primitive-looking color reproduction in the finished volume. Today these ninety-three elaborately styled pictures suggest not anything tempting and elegant, but the quaintness of what people once found tempting and elegant. As for the 1949 *Fireside Cook Book*, filled with an extravaganza of quasi-humorous tinted line drawings and colored lithographs scampering over every page in deliriously inventive layouts, the chief message now conveyed by the physical book is how tirelessly a dedicated team at Simon and Schuster worked to plaster over James Beard's text with huge doses of triviality.

By contrast, Ginnie Hofmann's illustrations for the 1951 *Joy of Cooking* still look the way they were meant to. Her simple, graceful line drawings certainly match a perky sugar-and-spice style much favored at the time, but have not come to look jarringly quaint by comparison with the text. Nearly forty-five years later they strike just the note Marion wanted—clean, deft, understated. Mrs. Hofmann went unerringly to the business of communicating actual pieces of information—from how to punch down risen yeast dough to suggestions for table decor—without embroidering on essentials. The drawings are straightforwardly rather than "cleverly" placed in the text, and invariably seem to open up the page, not clutter it up with arch little touches.

Mrs. Hofmann, a young and inexperienced cook, was not beyond culinary errors—for example, a drawing in the pie chapter giving a mistaken notion of the direction in which the dough should be rolled out.[62] But her intelligent execution of Marion's ideas helped give the entire volume a pleasingly functional effect, sharply defined but free of quickly dating gimmicks. Marion's contributions to the new edition had their strengths and weaknesses, but the work done by Mrs. Hofmann under her direction was an unalloyed strength, surely the best-realized of Marion's ideas for remodelling the old book. The Hofmann illustrations would be a critical element in the affection of fans who did not consciously notice such things.

No matter what Marion's influence on the latest *Joy of Cooking*, Irma's influence remained the defining one for most readers. She did not hatch any new campaigns or designs. She simply went on being Irma, exercising the force of her own charm even more determinedly to fasten together everything that was now in the book. Anyone who had not noticed the two names on the title page might still have assumed that the work had only a single author, for Irma made no attempt to enlarge her well-loved first-person-singular presence to the plural. "I" would never be "we" in her view of *Joy*:

> Frequently when I sing the praises of my pressure cooker I am asked: "How dare you use it? Why, it frightens me to death." Then I explain that there is nothing complicated about pressure cooker technique, that mastering a few simple rules insures safety. Aldous Huxley found the Mexicans "anti-mechanical." So am I, but I use my pressure cooker daily with ease.[63]

> I'm tired of writing definite rules, so this [Deviled Egg and Crab Casserole] is going to be a beautifully indefinite one. If an imagination is not exercised, doesn't it become atrophied? I've never given mine a chance to relax, so I don't know.[64]

If anything, her proprietary grip on things was more zestful and convincing than ever. Once again flippant asides bounced off the page at recipe hunters: "A definition of eternity: A ham and 2 people."[65] Once again she managed to intimate her disdain for the clumsy ways of *other* cookbooks:

> The expectant [high-altitude] cake baker is sometimes presented with a graph. Can you read a graph? Among the fairies that stood at my cradle the mathematical one was conspicuously absent—or on a binge—for I struggle helplessly with graphs and assume that others are similarly afflicted.[66]

With airy spontaneity Irma alluded to her favorite authors (Jane Austen, she observed, would have pronounced a cottage pudding "only moderately genteel") or radio comedies ("To quote Archie of Duffy's Tavern, 'Leave us not shilly-dally.' ")[67] Maeterlinck and Willa Cather were invoked in the introduction to the salad chapter, and the comparative seductions of pie and ice cream in American life were summed up with a borrowing from Edgar Bergen: "Here, like Charlie McCarthy, we are torn 'between vice and versa.' "[68]

No one else could begin to suggest the delight of good cooking and eating with the effortless touch of Irma Rombauer:

> Chill well before serving [Mont Blanc].
> You may cover the top of the cream with
> a grating of:
> > **Sweet chocolate**
> And then, as my dear old French
> friend would have said: "I'd be so
> pleased I would not thank the King to
> be my uncle."[69]

She had reinforced the previous *Joy*'s sense of drawing readers into an intimate circle. Now a number of recipes bore the name of their begetters ("Clara's Pearl Tapioca Pudding," "Posie's Custard with Whipped Cream") or were credited to some acquaintance in the headnote. These latter attributions might just obliquely mention an "Adele" or a "Jane" (Marion's mother-in-law, Adele Becker; the abruptly retired Jane Torno) without explanation. But this very casualness helped sustain a genial family-and-friends atmosphere unique among the serious national manuals.

More recipes from *Joy* readers in different parts of the country had been welcomed into the fold, and these underscored a sense of nationwide culinary scope even when they were not identifiably "regional." Irma cemented the loyalty of her coast-to-coast audience and produced an aura of communal representation that would have been the despair of any imitator by her deft introduction of people like the "fan from Montana" whose apple pie suggestion combined two separate *Joy* recipes in a new way, "a Maine correspondent" who had shared her own added touch with lobster stew, and the adoptive Marylander who at first "threw the natives into fainting fits" before learning their method of cooking crabs.[70]

What Irma and Marion did separately in the first mother-daughter edition is matched by the importance of what they did together. They were an odd couple indeed, the mistress of capricious badinage and the earnest truth-seeker. The struggle they must have had to fit both their aims into one book is obvious as early as Irma's one-page introduction. (She had scotched the idea of Marion's doing another introduction of her own.)

> "Mother," said Marion, "the book needs an introduction."
> "Why?" I said. "Will cooks ever read it?" She replied: "Perhaps they will read it if you tell them a story, for if they do not, how will they know that an ingredient in parenthesis [*sic*] means 'optional' and 'chocolate' means the bitter kind unless otherwise stated?"

The promised story (which involved a wooden leg and a near brush with extinction) concerned misplaced priorities, and the moral was doggedly driven home:

> How good is your sense of values? What is your first thought when you prepare a meal? Is it of a decorated cake or a fancy salad? It should be of the nutritional value of the food you plan to serve, not only for the one meal but in relation to the whole day's intake. Gastronomy and nutrition are not synonymous—so don't confound them. Your thought should be of the correct preparation, cooking and timing of the food. It should be an attempt at variety in ingredients, textures and flavors.[71]

Already this adjustment of maternal and filial approaches sounds a little like the more ragged reconciliations of the Democratic Party. There were other moments when Irma must have had to swallow hard or Marion must have been brought up sharp against parental rebellion:

> My conscience—or is it Marion?—compels me to make this statement: From the nutritional standpoint the boiling of fish is objectionable, for, unless watched carefully and never permitted to go beyond the simmering point, it destroys flavors and nutritional values that are less apt to be lost in the steaming of fish. The latter is a highly recommended method. Sorry, "boiled" fish is one of my favorite dishes.[72]

But usually the collaborators were able to pull together elements of the old *Joy* and the new educational mission with some plausibility—for example, taking an earlier drollery of Irma's about vegetables that all too often have "been drained of the life force and despairingly surrendered to the inevitable," and using it to preach respect for the "life force" through proper cooking.[73]

Their united talents had unfortunately failed to do anything about the book's organization, which retained all its previous drawbacks together with great gobs of new material as hard to fit in as the children of the old woman who lived in a shoe. You never knew just where you might encounter one of these wayward progeny. The new directions for separating an egg, for example, were in the already swollen "Luncheon and Supper Dishes," miles from the *beating* of eggs in "Cakes."

Some of the new material had also been gathered into more or less orderly chapters of its own. It was these that Irma and Marion had deliberately held up during the latest author-publisher war, knowing that Bobbs-Merrill especially wanted to tout them in its selling of the "new improved" book. Some of the material in the new chapters may date back to the Jane Torno days. (In 1948 she and Irma had collaborated on a treatment of freezing and canning for a brochure—now apparently not to be found—published by a St. Louis stove manufacturer, and Irma had requested permission to use some of this work in the *Joy* revision. Probably Marion had reworked or replaced much of it by the time the book appeared.) Most of it was fairly thin stuff.

There was a section on high-altitude baking that summarized material from "the blessed publications" of industry sources and state agricultural experiment stations, and that reprinted eleven recipes picked up from a Colorado A&M College publication and six from a General Foods booklet specifying Swans Down cake flour and Calumet baking powder. (Brand names now also appeared in the previously uncredited one-bowl cakes developed at General Mills and in a new section of "chiffon cakes" devised by the same source.) There was a blender chapter consisting of about a dozen unsystematically chosen recipes and one of Irma's eager tributes to a new gadget. (Blenders were a prewar introduction that had recently taken off in spectacular fashion.) A new pressure-cooker chapter interspersed a good deal of solid advice with a rather random-looking array of recipes that seemed only sometimes to draw on the real advantages of the machine.

The 1951 freezer chapter, on the other hand, was nearly a small manual in its own right. While blenders and pressure cookers had won a following as gadgets or time-savers, home freezers had rapidly developed into a major tool of household management for those who could afford the space—a modern wrinkle in the old-style concept of a self-sufficient larder. The new chapter, the most thorough treatment of freezing in any of the current general manuals, exhaustively discussed how to freeze and thaw a great range of fresh and home-prepared foods—though it is a shock to find a reference to freezing stuffed poultry for later roasting, a dangerous practice already warned against in the 1951 *Boston*.[74] Virtually nothing was said of commercial frozen foods. The omission savors more of Marion the industry distruster than of Irma, who had been welcoming packaged frozen items since *Streamlined Cooking*.

The new edition contained greatly expanded coverage in a few other conspicuous areas, one of the most striking being "Entertaining and Table Service" (formerly just "Table Setting"). In 1943 Irma had provided some commonsensical remarks on serving a meal to guests and a few diagrams of place settings. This kindly and practical advice was far from the spirit of the revised chapter. Now you were told that "it is well to know how a semi-formal meal should be served" and led through "dignified and simple current practice"[75] in three pages of detailed scenarios clearly requiring a maid or waiter. Marion, who liked to give advice on aesthetic matters, probably was responsible for various suggestions about suitable centerpieces and admissible decorative schemes. The changes were a clear sign of social demands accompanying the new glorification of domesticity and the extension of old snobberies to a larger spectrum of American homes.

An entirely different message is suggested by other sorts of material woven into the 1951 *Joy of Cooking*. A side of Marion that emerged more plainly year by year was a real attraction to the kind of cooking knowledge wanted in desert-island situations that pitted a modern man or woman against fairly primitive conditions. During the war *Joy* had on occasion held out a lifeline to people literally dependent on internment-camp rations. Irma herself now spent considerable time in the Antonia kitchen, which was not just countrified but rudimentary. Between them they now sought to address needs far removed from comfortable, up-to-date households. An obvious example is the new edition's directions for pasteurizing milk at home, an issue of interest to very few *Joy* users but of critical importance to those. The freezer chapter and the expanded, more technically precise coverage of home canning point in the same direction; both gave painstaking information about putting up freshly butchered poultry, game, and meat (sometimes in large quantities) in your own kitchen. In years to come, *The Joy of Cooking*'s reputation as the book to turn to in contingencies not addressed by any other supposedly all-purpose manual would rest on just such material.

It was a modest but important augury of a mission that became firmer the longer Marion was involved with the book: to represent not just modern methods or enlightened nutrition but also the endangered species of culinary tradition. Irma, whose roots were Victorian, sometimes clung to a quaint touch or habit. But Marion, despite her own shorter culinary memories, actively worked to reclaim the old and vestigial for modern cooks. Almost surely it was she who added to the "New Joy" recipes for almond milk (made by steeping pulverized almonds in water, and not just old-fashioned but positively medieval) and "panade" (a version of the bread-thickened soups that had vanished from the English table centuries before).[76]

As a further reclamation of the past, basic preparations that Irma's readers of twenty years ago might have thought ridiculously bothersome were now treated as important parts of cooking. The shortcut cooking that both she and Marion had learned and loved had now fallen into enough disesteem in high culinary circles to be scaled back for reasons of fashion as well as nutrition. Making painstaking dishes from scratch stamped a hostess as up-to-date in certain coteries. Accordingly, the new edition had *Joy*'s first recipe ever for a simple veal stock meant to provide the aspic for a jelled salad. The fish chapter had acquired a fumet; the main section on sauces explained the principle of a roux, by name. An unthickened gravy, a simple pan-deglazing with some tarragon, staked its claim to attention with the comment, "These [flourless sauces] are such a welcome change after the monotonous flour-thickened type."[77]

The reasons behind things, which Irma had generally refrained from poking into, were more prominently addressed. The meat chapter now discussed the uses of different cuts with the aid of diagrams and a reminder of why anatomy was destiny in matching cooking methods and cuts. The meat cooking timetables (from the National Livestock and Meat Board) now had a note alerting the reader to the limits of precision:

> It is impossible to give an absolutely accurate timetable for roasting meat, as too many factors are involved, such as the lean and the fat, the shape, the size and quality of the roast. Lean meat cooks more rapidly than fat. The degree of aging also affects the time of cooking.[78]

Writing like this presupposes readers who are interested in getting beyond formulas to build their own knowledge and judgment.

The achievement of this first mother-daughter *Joy* formed a startling contrast to *The Boston Cooking-School Cook Book*, which also had been reinventing itself over the years under Wilma Lord Perkins. *Boston* had edged away from the role of reference manual precisely when the blithe, antitextbook *Joy of Cooking* had been edging toward it.

Already in 1930 Mrs. Perkins had been toning down the lecturing air of the old book. Since then, very likely inspired by the success of the lighthearted Irma Rombauer, she had been throwing out things that smelled of the lamp and reaching after an image both cozier and smarter. By the time of her 1951 revision she had discarded many general discussions of basic procedures—for example, a detailed treatment of soup-making. She had progressively given up on trying to make much sense out of nutrition and food chemistry for readers, and by now was telling people not to get too bothered about such considerations: "Watch government bulletins and magazine articles for the latest information but do not allow concentration on food values to destroy your interest in planning menus with imagination."[79]

In her coverage of fish and seafood, Mrs. Perkins had gradually dismantled another of the old *Boston*'s great strengths. In 1936 *Joy* clearly had been the weaker of the two in this area. But by 1951 it had made determined strides. Irma and Marion's new fish chapter began with an allusion to the delights of fishing and nearly five pages of basic information laid out in leisurely sections, with Ginnie Hofmann's helpful illustrations. For the first time the authors told you something about shopping for fish—more, indeed, than the current *Boston*. The latter had now dropped most of Miss Farmer's voluminous information on particular fish and shellfish (nutritional composition, seasonal availability from the waters they were fished in, the best ways of cooking them). The coverage of lowly fare like oyster crabs—which Irma and Marion had just recognized for the first time in 1951—and smelts was much skimpier. Eel had vanished from *Boston* just as *Joy* introduced its first eel recipe.

Probably a real fish lover comparing the 1951 seafood chapters in the two works would have found both divided between good basic dishes and undistinguished shufflings of ingredients (some of which had been in *Boston* even in Miss Farmer's time). But they had reached their present condition from opposite prior directions. Mrs. Perkins had added a number of casseroles and other vehicles for leftover or canned fish, and replaced old-fashioned dishes like tripe and oyster ragout or oysters on milk toast with more modish entries like oysters Rockefeller or "oven-fried oysters." The Rombauers in turn gave a lot of undistinguished fillets-of-something recipes aimed at people who wished they weren't eating fish—but had also worked in much more "service" detail on fish generally and paid new attention to many kinds of shellfish that had been dealt with more vaguely or (like mussels and abalone) not mentioned at all in earlier editions. The New England book had partly surrendered one of its great regional advantages, while the Midwestern one had worked to overcome a geographical handicap. Seafood would never be one of the highest attractions of *The Joy of Cooking*, but the new chapter showed the authors' ability to recognize and remedy a weakness.

A prospective buyer wondering which of the rivals was more up-to-date would have found no clear-cut answer—partly because there was no obvious consensus on what it meant to be up-to-date in 1951. The Rombauers, however, were further ahead on the back-to-basics movement. They could be found recommending that cooks seek out old-fashioned vanilla bean, which Irma had only nostalgically commented on in 1943 and which Mrs. Perkins didn't mention at all. They had left her behind on such matters as culturing your own yogurt, hunting out wild greens, making up fresh sausage patties, or spending several days on sourdough rye bread. Both books had worked hard to bring in more adventurous international dishes or recently naturalized ones. New in both books in 1951 were beef bourguignon, aioli, a truer approximation of Swiss-style cheese fondue than either had yet published, and pizza (which Irma and Marion called "Vegetable Shortcake or Pizza Napoletana"). Quiche was not exactly new in either book, but the name was. Mrs. Perkins rebaptized her "Alsatian Cheese Tart" of the 1941 edition with the name "Quiche Lorraine"; Irma and Marion added a similar recipe under the same title next to Irma's 1931 "Cheese Custard Pie." *The Joy of Cooking* had scooped *Boston* on gazpacho, coq au vin, pot-au-feu, blintzes, cock-a-leekie (minus the traditional prunes), "Sicilian Spinach" made with olive oil, garlic, and anchovies, and Florentines, which they described as a postwar import made by European refugees. Wisely enough, neither book had tried to explore the slowly unfolding mysteries of Chinese cooking, but the Rombauers did pointedly abjure all claim of authenticity for their "Chicken Chop Suey" and suggest, "Read Mrs. Buwei Yang Chao's delightful 'How to Cook and Eat in Chinese' for real Chinese dishes."[80] Meanwhile, Mrs. Perkins was discreetly inching toward the "convenience" territory that *Boston* had generally shunned. She had at last admitted canned-soup recipes (though a mere handful compared to *Joy*) and a few of the quick one-bowl cakes.

What Wilma Lord Perkins could not inject into her surgery on the durable Farmer book was any sense of positively redefining it. She had chopped out a lot of purposeful old material and replaced it with scattered thises and thats, while the Rombauers had tended to delete ephemera and make way for more solid instruction. The stiff-sounding approach of the old *Boston* was gone, all right, but the effect was of subtraction rather than addition, undermining what had been most characterful in Fannie Farmer. The 1951 *Joy of Cooking*, if not exactly a seamless melding of mother-daughter concerns, had faced concrete changes more intelligently. It now added to the bold individuality of Irma's writing an equally bold claim to the role of challenging, original teacher.

Of these gambles, it was the Rombauers' that would pay off. The 1951 *Boston* edition lasted until 1959, when the next revision appeared. The Little, Brown printing tabulations recorded on the copyright pages add up to 188,500 copies printed throughout the life of the edition, 1951–58. A Bobbs-Merrill summary of copies sold during the same years shows sales of *Joy* (not total printings, which were certainly higher) at 732,004 copies.[81] *The Joy of Cooking* now had no challenger among the trade manuals. Its only real competition in the general-cookbook field came from mass-market works partly sold outside the normal trade channels and backed by the muscle of giant corporations or service-magazine publishers (e.g., *The Betty Crocker Cook Book* and *Better Homes and Gardens Cook Book*).

Every edition of *Joy* had represented some sort of breakthrough for its author or authors. This one, Irma's last and Marion's first effort at cookbook writing, lasted until 1962 and is still cooked from today by a handful of aging users. It points firmly toward both past and future. A culinary historian examining its pages for survivals of vanished ways will find plenty, including some that were speedily becoming anachronistic in 1951. Irma and Marion still wrote of "top milk," though even then most fluid milk was sold homogenized, and mentioned "clabbered milk"—naturally soured to a thick consistency—as a well-known kitchen resource, though it was probably unfamiliar to most of their readers. They clearly expected more frying and sautéing to be done in solid fats than cooking oil. Margarine goes almost unmentioned (Irma had routinely written "butter or butter substitute" in *A Cook Book for Girls and Boys,* but pulled back from this concession in the "New Joy").

Their treatment of spaghetti and other pasta made only a small nod toward new fashions like cooking it al dente and dressing it simply with butter and chopped herbs. Most of their remarks on the subject were printed unchanged from 1943 and reflected the general understanding of spaghetti as a "largely inspirational"[82] free-for-all—particularly suited to bachelors who prided themselves on winging it with any kind of meat or condiments in the house—that had followed its translation from ethnic to all-American status in the early decades of the century. Lamb chops, the reader was firmly informed, "are not served rare,"[83] and few were the culinary authorities who would have said otherwise. The National Livestock and Meat Board, from which the *Joy* timetables were taken, probably had never heard of an American taste for rare lamb.

A searcher for clues to new developments on the horizon will find these in good supply, too. The discovery of cultured sour cream by a clientele much larger than the Jewish and eastern European cooks who had always relied on it is obvious in the 1951 *Joy of Cooking* recipes, and a new formula titled "Sour Cream Hollandaise" suggests one reason for its wider acceptance: "This rule became popular during butter rationing."[84] Sour cream was also tailor-made for the new habit of plunking some "dip" and convenient dunking items like crackers or cooked shrimp on the cocktail table by way of an appetizer; the hors d'oeuvre chapter nods to this vogue with a handful of new "dipping sauce" recipes. A noisy national concern about inflated meat prices, a fly in the ointment of overall postwar prosperity, lay behind the authors' suggestion that housewives try to sneak some of the cheaper "variety meats" into family meals despite an already intractable general prejudice. ("The following is a hush-hush section," they whispered coyly, " 'just between us girls.' ")[85]

The newly popular custom of "roasting" meats in aluminum foil made its *Joy* debut in this edition; "the wonderful spinach packaged in cellophane bags" was hailed as a breakthrough. Household plastic bags were mentioned for the first time.[86] Monosodium glutamate, "the mysterious 'white powder' of the Orient," probably at its height of favor in the United States during this period, appeared in the herb chapter as a useful flavor enhancer for all sorts of meat and vegetable dishes.[87] (According to Ethan, it was a standby ingredient in his mother's kitchen at this time, though she had sharply retrenched before the 1962 edition.) A fad that had arisen in the late 1930s along with the green-salad renaissance was prominently endorsed: the unwashed wooden salad bowl, which was supposed to become "seasoned" with frequent use.[88] (This, too, had lost favor with Marion by the time of the next edition.) One sign that some of the better gourmet precepts were reaching an expanded audience is the frequent mention of freshly ground pepper and nutmeg—actually, Irma had first commented on the superiority of just-grated nutmeg in *Girls and Boys*. In 1951 *Joy* first admitted the mixture now universally known as tuna salad, though an earlier aspic of Irma's also remained under that name. Marion's nutritional priorities appear in the admonition to use the oil from the tuna fish can—a way of conserving valuable nutrients, from her point of view.[89]

Gone were Irma's old recipe for boiled coffee—anathema to the new generation of epicures—and most of the former references to "cooking wine." A vanishing institution vanished a little further as the word "Icebox" was excised from any recipe title and uniformly replaced by "Refrigerator." And a sign of larger change in Irma and Marion's America was quietly imposed on the new edition: most of Irma's would-be-humorous stories about "colored" people, now painfully unwelcome to Marion's sensibilities, had had any reference to race deleted.

The authors added their own small token of interracial goodwill in the new headnote to a 1943 tamale pie recipe, pointing out that "Freda de Knight has assembled the traditional recipes of the colored people in her interesting book 'A Date with a Dish' " and mentioning some of that work's variations on the cornmeal-mush pie idea.[90] The age was departing in which it could be taken for granted that any black woman using a cookbook like *The Joy of Cooking* was a hired servant cooking for a white household rather than a homemaker cooking for her own family. The work stood on the verge of being able to address a larger cross section of American society than anyone could have thought possible when the first version was obscurely launched in Depression-era St. Louis.

Irma, nearly seventy-four when the first collaborative edition struggled into print after a long lawyer-ridden battle, had lived to see herself arguably the most beloved cookbook author in America. The new edition's sales were less spectacular than those of the wartime and immediate postwar editions, but they were solid enough to tell her that *The Joy of Cooking* would remain a fixture of the national kitchen at least until the next edition, which she soon began thinking about with her usual proprietary instinct.

Probably she would have scoffed at the notion that in her twenty years' efforts as a cooking expert she had made a genuine contribution to a part of twentieth-century culture. Marion might have entertained such a thought. Irma had no patience with grandiose claims about food. The secret of her influence was in her unaffected appetite for the world as she found it, not as some wise person might have wished it to be.

It would take some nerve to claim that Irma had forever changed American cooking; evidence-gathering tools do not exist to show that she changed it at all. What is certain is that she changed American cookbooks. She had not exactly meant to do so, though she had put her finger on something very important when she wrote to Jessica Mannon making the apparently contradictory claims that her book taught people to use their own heads but did not tax their tired brains (tired, that is, from the dull task of following other manuals). Hers was the kitchen bible that had recognized an audience of frustrated cooks bored or intimidated by cut-and-dried, lecturelike cooking instruction, and that had tempted them to form a literate companionship of free spirits. This was an invigorating achievement, but it was only the vehicle of another achievement: her cookbook brought together as fans and equals all sorts of Americans who would positively have hated each other's cooking.

Probably such a thing would not have been possible for an author much older or younger than Irma, and certainly it would not have been possible for a trained food professional. Her good luck in being an amateur cannot be overstated—and it was Marion's good luck as well, though Marion worked at the business of mastering culinary lore longer and harder than her mother. To the end of their days both would remain accidental cookbook authors, people who had wandered into the field by inadvertence. Years later, trying to explain how she and her mother had unaccountably become successful cookbook writers, Marion tellingly observed, "All through her life—and, as I have found, all through mine—the most unlikely enthusiasms, the most far-fetched experiences, have, after long dormancy, suddenly burst into applicable attitudes."[91] Irma (and later, Marion) spoke to the cooking public out of inner reserves that belonged to them intrinsically, not professionally. If we can attribute their success to one factor above all, it was some friendly impulse that the professional food writers could only have feebly imitated. For this reason they were able to bridge chasms of taste that earlier cookbook authors had not had to deal with.

In her own personal experience or through glimmers of older tradition that were still strong in her St. Louis childhood, Irma von Starkloff Rombauer spanned the generations of women who cooked by trained instinct, the self-consciously modern years when women were reducing cooking to solemn pseudoexact formulas for the benefit of ignorant sisters, and a quite different order of competing "lifestyle" preferences. Perhaps she would not have had the confidence to address the last situation had it not been for her links with the first two.

By the time the 1931 *Joy of Cooking* was in print, American cookery had taken on fashion overtones unknown in Irma's childhood, and was being busily dissected by weighty social commentators. Its much-ballyhooed achievements of the Fannie Farmer era now had chic and eloquent detractors. Thus the professional service journalists had started to be conscious of currents and countercurrents to be navigated. Defining their audience was becoming almost as important as knowing anything about cooking. They had to decide just whom they would address or ignore as the American culinary public began to sort itself out into many publics, with troubling overtones of status-chasing and social boundary-drawing. Millions of people came to look down on each other's cooking preferences as cheap and junky or laugh at them as ridiculously bothersome. But still a sturdy residue of home cooks remained who did not particularly notice gaps or incompatibilities of taste, and Irma had the good fortune to be one of these. She began her cookbook-writing career without the least notion of professionally second-guessing national market segments. There is a genuineness about her unselfconscious juxtaposition of doctored-up gravy, frozen fruit salads, and old German Christmas cakes in the 1931 *Joy* that cannot be found in books by more careful and sophisticated cooks.

The growth of *Joy* from one woman's "Compilation of Reliable Recipes, with a Casual Culinary Chat"—the original subtitle, finally retired in 1951—to a major American kitchen bible coincided with a still greater fragmentation of taste, to the point where even a born ransacker of all modes like Irma had to be at least marginally aware of doing a balancing act. The extremes of the gourmet and can-opener schools drew apart yet further from each other. Never had it been harder for a general-purpose cookbook to address a real cross section of American cooks than it was when Irma girded her loins for the 1951 revision. In the affluent consumer climate that succeeded the war, divisions of taste became still more socially tricky and culturally loaded—even politically sensitive, in the case of "natural foods" preferences like those determinedly injected into the book by Marion. Yet Irma's capacious embrace even now managed to enfold any imaginable sort of cooking.

Every one of her decisions to enlarge the scope of *The Joy of Cooking* had been a gamble. They had paid off because she had had the perfect resolution of any incongruity in herself and her instinctive rapport with all sorts of readers. She was the first cookbook writer who had been able to give the disorderly spectacle of modern American cooking some coherence through sheer force of personality, and she would be the last. Her final gamble, the choice of Marion as coauthor and successor, would prove the masterstroke of all long beyond their own lifetimes, but it would forever alter the clear and individual voice in which Irma Rombauer had addressed a nationwide circle of friends.

10

Indian Summer Interrupted

When the first Rombauer-Becker *Joy of Cooking* was at last well launched and Bobbs-Merrill had agreed to let the index be corrected, Irma settled down to comparative happiness and prosperity. The moment was probably the pinnacle of her career. With Marion's help she had decisively routed those who had threatened to destroy her as author of *Joy*, and she had lived to see herself, only twenty-odd years after her first amateur publishing venture, accepted by millions as a timeless feature of the American landscape.

This last impression owed much to the efforts of her younger friend Cecily Brownstone, now food editor for the Associated Press and able at least sometimes to set the tone for other journalists. From about 1951 on, she drew Irma and Marion into a circle of food-writer friends who saw a good deal of each other in (and out of) the line of duty. Among the regulars whom she introduced to the celebrated Mrs. Rombauer and her daughter were the *New York Times* food columnist Jane Nickerson (the author of the admiring *Times Book Review* piece) and the cookbook writers James Beard and Marian Tracy. Perhaps Irma's favorite among the group was the much-traveled, multilingual Helmut Ripperger, who by a pleasant coincidence had been American vice-consul in Bremen some years after she had spent half her teens there as the consul's daughter. (He was also an art historian and researcher of provenance who quickly discovered much in common with Marion.) The author of a set of glib little cookbooks on specialty subjects like cheese and herbs, "Rip" was now preparing to tackle a more ambitious project, a manual of French cooking for Americans intended as a team effort with a pair of Frenchwomen named Simone Beck and Louisette Bertholle who needed an American collaborator.[1]

Irma's periodic visits, usually in company with Marion, came to be eagerly awaited by Cecily's friends. She did not so much greet them as hold court for them with every bit of cosmopolitan verve at her command, and they regarded the small white-haired woman as a rare being, a figure from another era. Marion was much liked on her own merits, but for the group her mother was the star of stars. These people did much to burnish the image of Irma Rombauer as one of the eternal verities of American cooking. They helped ensure that the recipe-reading public would encounter her not just through her own work but through deferential mentions by other well-known food authorities at such regular intervals that she came to seem like a lodestar that had always been fixed in the sky.

Irma and Marion often combined their stays among the Brownstone-Beard crowd with visits to corporate functions at which they would be lovingly courted by promoters. (In fact, there is a story of a well-tanked executive once carrying the courting so far as to make amorous advances to Irma under the table at what Marion used to call the "Banana Congress," the annual fall conference sponsored by the United Fruit Company.) Marion could never feel quite at home amid this kind of public hoopla. She knew very well how to exercise her warmth and charm on people when she could meet them one on one. But the idea of promotional appearances and snapping cameras was agony to her. Nearly everyone—certainly every woman—who regularly saw her and her mother together in New York had some glimmer of her sensitivity on the score of appearance. Heavy and middle-aged now, she had mastered the art of dressing in very simple tailored clothes with strong accents of simple, imaginative modern jewelry—the most becoming self-presentations she could have contrived, but not good enough for Irma, who made a point of deploring the space shoes that her daughter had taken to for the sake of comfort. Marion kept the shoes and avoided the spotlight. She was content to observe Irma's pleasure in being fêted.

Irma had not been born in an age of public self-promotion by respectable women, but her strange late-in-life career had brought out a sturdy gift for well-bred hustling. She could always sparkle for an audience, in the knowledge that doing so was to *Joy*'s practical advantage. The medium of television did not yet offer many opportunities for an author in her position, but she might come away from her New York visits with an AP feature by Cecily Brownstone to be picked up in newspapers around the country, or a charming photograph like the one showing her studiously preparing a New Year's Eve menu that accompanied a Jane Nickerson article in the *Times* late in 1952.[2] These tokens of her success were very sweet to her, though she was no longer able to cram in as many activities on a visit as she once had been.

Irma was certainly slower and less resilient than she had been a few years earlier. Still, she was not ready to consider herself feeble. When the first financial good tidings arrived after the appearance of the 1951 edition, she was strong enough to embark on a fling: a visit to Europe over the summer of 1952 in the company of her fifteen-year-old grandson, Mark Becker. Their plan was to rent a chauffeured car in Paris and wind from Normandy and Brittany through the Loire and Dordogne valleys and along the French Riviera to Italy and perhaps Switzerland, at a pace suitable to Irma's limitations.[3]

Germany, she had made it clear, was out of the question. Though she and Marion continued to help the last Kuhlmann cousins in Hanover, she had no wish to see the land of her father and mother in its present disgraced and mutilated state. She had been invited to stay with George Schriever (of the old German class) and his wife in Bremen, where he was working for the State Department, but she refused with some asperity.[4]

While waiting in Paris for the mills of French bureaucracy to straighten out a snafu over the paperwork for the car they were to travel in, Irma looked up Helmut Ripperger's French colleague Louisette Bertholle. It was over lunch at Mme. Bertholle's that she was introduced to an American woman living in Paris—Julia Child, for whom Simone Beck and Mme. Bertholle would shortly ditch Ripperger. (The only evidence of the earlier Bertholle-Beck-Ripperger collaboration is a tiny spiral-bound collection of recipes published in 1952 by Ives Washburn under the title *What's Cooking in France.*) Mrs. Child later recalled the famous author as "suffering from slight digestive troubles" and much exercised about the ongoing index-revision squabble with Bobbs-Merrill.[5]

Irma, who had no reason to suspect that she was in the presence of culinary history, did not mention the event in her abundant letters to

Marion and the St. Louis contingent. She was too busy venting her fury over the automobile mix-up and sadly comparing postwar Parisians with those of the 1890s and 1920s:

> How casual and grubby most people look! Where are the elegance and the distinction of the past? Uncombed men and women, horribly dyed hair, bare legs, sloppy shoes, etc. A well dressed, even a clean, trim person stands out on such a back-ground. An occasional boulevardier is a lone wolf.[6]

Mark, a born questioner of all authority and a hippie before his time in matters of dress, rebelled endlessly and very articulately against Irma's ideas of supervision. By the time they showed up in Rome for lunch with Robert Isaacson, the son of a Jefferson County neighbor of Irma's, and his lover, the poet James Merrill, they clearly had polished the art of mutual vexation to a fine gloss. ("I'd never heard anyone take an elephant gun to a child," Isaacson later remarked of her reaction to being cut off by the brash youngster at the start of an anecdote.)[7] But they were able to maintain a fairly companionable truce for good stretches of the trip.

The Italian lake country was the high point of the adventure for Irma. "If I were a poor person I would want to be an Italian," she commented rather mistily while watching a street fair in progress by Lake Lecco.[8] The Swiss Alps, by contrast, roused her not to nostalgia for her girlhood but to thoughts of Mark Twain's remark that "in Switzerland even the glaciers had more cleanly habits."[9]

Of their dining adventures she wrote little to Marion and her friends "because it always strikes me that what people eat and drink is a personal matter, not fit for general conversation. At least accounts of gustatory enjoyments always bore me."[10] But she did cobble together a letter on French food for the *Post-Dispatch* food department, undoubtedly penned with a view to securing a tax write-off for the trip. Far from the exalted palaver that readers of fifteen or forty years later would have expected, her unsystematic glance nonetheless shrewdly identified some of the critical distinctions between French and American home cooking as the higher proportion of both salaries and time that Frenchwomen habitually devoted to meal making and their inclination "to eat what the district offers or to do without." She concluded with one of those indelible touches that flash out here and there from even her flimsiest efforts:

France gives you much food for thought as well as for the gullet. But in the end, the excellence of all cooking may be summed up in the words of a famous hotelman, (now long dead) who would periodically announce to his guests: "Eat of this, monsieur, for I have put my hand to it." The "hand" is what counts for it gives you the ability to make the most of materials offered, to give to what you do an individual touch and to bring to your task an attention and an affection that gives a rich return.[11]

The European trip was a considerable physical strain for Irma. She had been forced to stop and rest at frequent intervals, and declined to take part in Mark's more ambitious explorations. The ill-defined symptoms and bouts of extreme fatigue that had intermittently troubled her for a long period were becoming more and more of a handicap. On her return she was in no hurry to undertake any serious exertion. As her ailments gained on her, she sought help from a new quarter: Dr. Murray Israel, who had a considerable geriatric practice in New York City and on Long Island and who became one of the chief reasons for her numerous stays in New York. Having married a girl from the old South St. Louis set, "Judy" (Marian) Judell, he had known and wholeheartedly admired Irma (to him, she was always "The Queen") for years before she became his patient.

Through Dr. Israel, Irma was introduced to one of the earliest systematic attempts to manage arteriosclerosis (which she surely had at this time, in a fairly advanced stage) by controlling serum cholesterol. The Israel treatment involved a stringent low-fat diet in conjunction with a course of pills and injections containing B vitamins and—a sledgehammer measure meant to break down cholesterol faster in the bloodstream by speeding up the entire metabolism—thyroid extract and other metabolic agents. Whether this regimen helped Irma or hurt her, it gave her new problems with the mine-strewn business of getting through the day's meals. Already prone to taxing gastric upsets if she strayed far from very bland, simple fare, she now found that almost anything she still enjoyed eating was officially prohibited. When in 1954 Marion tried to interest her in the Adelle Davis approach to diet, Irma simply threw up her hands in exasperation. As she told Marion, Murray's verboten list ruled out half the Davis suggestions, and besides:

My intestinal tract says—

> no whole grains
> no hully things (dried legumes)
> no fresh fruits, seeds or peels
> no cheese
> no salads

(Reads like Ethan's report card.)

In a frustration that millions of elderly people then and now might have echoed, she concluded, "I know I am improperly nourished but don't know how to be better nourished with all these restrictions."[12] It was a maddening disability for one supposed to be a world-class *fin bec* and authority on making the most of food.

Except for these discomforts—fairly minor considering her age—Irma had reached an agreeable Indian summer with few pressing concerns. She was indeed thinking of the next *Joy of Cooking* revision, but with little urgency about particular decisions. Her letters for the few years following the 1951 *Joy* record a round of unremarkable private doings. St. Louis grew grimmer and more racially divided, and she began to think of giving up the now less-than-idyllic neighborhood of Cabanne Avenue as well as the climb to and from her third-floor walkup. She still kept a finger in St. Louis cultural and social affairs, sponsoring the occasional debutante party or appearing at functions of the Missouri Historical Society (to which she had donated various of the old Rombauer and von Starkloff valuables). She had the satisfaction of at least a gingerly rapprochement with Put, whose marriage to Margaret ended in divorce in 1954 and who shortly came to St. Louis to introduce her to a new bride—his former secretary, the much younger Marjorie Dick. She joined the television age, acquiring a set in the spring of 1954 and surviving her initial dismay at "too much *Mord und Totschlag*" (blood and gore) to become riveted to the sight of the Army-McCarthy hearings. She was not up to another European trip, but she did manage a couple of lengthy stays in Mexico City to escape the merciless Missouri summer, in 1953 and 1954. (For the first of these Helen-Marie Fruth—now working at the *Post-Dispatch*—contrived to wangle her a paid assignment, an article about Mexican food that Irma herself characterized as "drivel" but that once again was useful for income-tax purposes.)[13]

She received an unexpected message from the very remote past in the fall of 1953, in the form of a letter from a young scholar working on a biography of Booth Tarkington (who had died in 1946). The researcher, James Woodress, happened to be a St. Louisan with a good memory for names and had put two and two together when he came on the mention of Irma von Starkloff among the Tarkington papers at the Princeton University Library.[14] Irma wrote back at once with a succinct account of the ill-fated romance and readily consented to an interview during the Christmas holidays. She entertained Woodress with cookies, good Scotch, and much charm, sending him on his way with a box of brownies for his wife.[15]

Whether by coincidence or impelled by this stimulus to memory, Irma actually began to write the story of her life or at least some part of it. It was a step that Marion had been urging on her for some time, though what Marion intensely craved to see was a kind of family memoir. She had always been spellbound by her mother's tales—from all accounts, Irma was an utterly dazzling raconteur—of assorted Rombauers, von Starkloffs, Kuhlmanns, and the beloved contingent in Indianapolis, a city that Marion had first imagined through Irma's childhood memories of a glamorous realm presided over by the "Santa Claus" figure of her uncle, Louis Hollweg. She had not only begged her mother to capture this wealth of material on paper but, at one point before the Jane Torno crisis threw all Irma's plans into chaos, had been going to help her write an account to be titled "Meet the Family."[16]

It is not likely that either of them thought of an audience beyond the immediate family. Irma hated putting together serious consecutive accounts of anything for public consumption. Her confidence in her powers as a writer extended only to the little free-form *mots* or vignettes that were her trademark. At different moments of her life she had wished to shine in a more orthodox literary sphere, but little evidence remains of any effort except an unpublished short story titled "Estergom" that probably dates from shortly after her European trip of 1937. It concerns a party of American tourists bamboozled into visiting a nonexistent Hungarian village festival, and though it is a slight effort at best, it contains enough agreeably acid flashes to make one wish that she had tried her wings again.[17] That she did not work at some kind of more extended writing is a great loss, for plainly she had gifts that are only partly hinted at in her published work and were never developed through systematic effort. In the unselfconscious surroundings of her letters to family and friends, unremarkable stretches alternate with casual brilliance and a more trenchant sort of wit than she permitted herself in public. The fragmentary autobiography, "My Little World," is the longest piece of descriptive writing that she is known to have attempted, and shows to immense effect the qualities that she might have had to offer as a writer of something other than cookbooks.

The roughly seventy-page manuscript is now in the possession of her grandson Ethan Becker in Cincinnati. It is accompanied by several dozen scraps of paper containing miscellaneous jottings in English and German that were evidently notes she meant to refer to. The intended audience was Marion, who is repeatedly addressed (not by name, but it is clear who was meant) in casual asides. The opening event is Irma's "first hurtling into reality," the terrifying crash of the ice breaking up on the river near her home in Carondelet one night around 1880 or 1881. The story runs along swiftly and fluently up to the beginning of the von Starkloffs' stay in Bremen when she was twelve, then abruptly breaks off.

The most striking feature of her account is her skill at characterization. The figure who probably has the best of it is her father, to whom Irma returns again and again trying to capture his particular mixture of resonant, kindly German dignity, volatile temper, and exasperating but lovable self-absorption:

> I can see him now—immaculately attired [in Civil War uniform, prepared to make one of his Camp Jackson Day addresses]—as beautiful as a man can be through cleanliness and health, in new white kid-gloves, a roll of white paper tied with a white satin ribbon in his hand (unfortunately he read his many clear and concise speeches, but they were lollapaloosas for fire and moral indignation). He would revolve for my inspection and ask—quite certain of the answer—"Mein liebes Kind, kann ich so erscheinen?" [Dear child, can I be seen in public like this?][18]

> In temperament he was always given to storms, and he was possessed of a fine moral indignation with a low boiling point that overflowed readily into ink. After writing a denunciatory letter—usually political and I fear personal—he would read it aloud to mother and wind up with a triumphant "Und den steckt er nicht hinter den Spiegel!" [We won't hear him crowing about *that!*][19]

No one else is described in as luxuriant detail, but the rest of Irma's "little world" is re-created with equal deftness and verve. She set down a thoughtful, finely touched portrait of her mother; an edgily revealing reflection on her relationship with her half-admired, half-resented sister; a tantalizing glimpse of the fascinated revulsion she felt for the "menacing and noxious" shadow of her dashing swindler half-brother Emil Starkloff; a myriad of razor-sharp details of life in the leisured old Carondelet and St. Louis *Deutschtum*.

In her own past and the dramatis personae of her family, as presented for her daughter's private scrutiny, Irma had finally found the motivating power to conquer her usual diffidence about pulling together a subject. Here was precisely what she needed to unlock an innate gift for marvelously sustained narrative. The result cannot now be dated with much assurance. But several details like glancing references to people or events inconclusively suggest that "My Little World" was written after the appearance of the 1951 "New Joy." This guess is reinforced by the clear impression the manuscript conveys of having been written rapidly and with unhesitating concentration, not dabbled at over intervals of months or years. Irma is unlikely to have had the time or energy to devote to such a project before the 1951 *Joy* was finished. Another clue may come from the fact that the manuscript breaks off literally in midsentence just as the story reaches the first appearance of a major character (Wilhelmine Kuhlmann, Irma's grandmother), indicating if not proving that the project was not abandoned but interrupted in full flow by some unforeseen circumstance. This at least potentially points to the spring of 1955.

That year had begun disastrously for the family. Irma and Marion had been preparing for one of their New York trips at the end of 1954 when Marion discovered a lump in her right breast. Apparently there was some period of uncertainty over the diagnosis and the best medical course, because she was not immediately operated on. Her desire to keep the truth from her family as long as possible may have contributed to the delay; according to her son Ethan, she did not tell John that she had an illness requiring an operation until the day before she went into the hospital, when she already knew that the growth had been diagnosed as malignant.[20] Her first radical mastectomy took place on February 11, 1955, and when the surgeon had finished, he had chopped away so much skin that he had to perform a skin graft several days later to close the three-inch gap he had produced.[21] When she had regained some strength, the doctors started her on a long and cruel course of radioactive cobalt treatments.

Marion's steady recovery throughout the spring was one of the last happinesses of her mother's life. Irma had spent the winter waiting for medical bulletins while pursuing her long-standing goal of finding an apartment in a better neighborhood and a more modern building. She was just in the process of moving to an elevator building on Lindell Boulevard (somewhat more convenient to downtown) when the still convalescing Marion received an emergency telephone call from St. Louis. On the morning of May 26 Irma's masseuse, arriving for a scheduled appointment, had found her lying unconscious in the bathroom at Cabanne Avenue. She had been rushed to St. Luke's Hospital, where the doctors diagnosed a cerebral thrombosis.[22] It is possible that this was the event that ended her work on "My Little World."

The stroke was not life-threatening. But from that moment, Irma's own accounts of things become less and less reliable as a guide to what was actually going on. Indeed, the charm and self-possession of her letters even from much earlier years often belie seething tempests and angry campaigns that were then occupying her but that she affected not to notice. This truth stands out in much sharper relief after the onset of her illness. Almost at once her family found themselves plunged into a series of explosions that go serenely unmentioned or glossed over in Irma's correspondence.

The stroke had been mild (resulting in some quickly improving left-side paralysis), and Irma's mental acuity was not at all impaired. She made at least the beginnings of a good recovery and was well enough to leave the hospital by June 9. By then she was also strong enough to have begun heaping demands and accusations on everyone around her. It was soon clear that she was a crisis incarnate, requiring constant attention.

The first problem to become apparent had been in the making for many years, but was not fully obvious to others until a day or two after the stroke, when Put arrived from the West Coast in a state of great concern to find his mother brightly sitting up in bed and greeting him with "Son, how would you like a drink?" It developed that while Irma's doctors were busy telling Marion, "No liquor," with severe emphasis, the patient had stolen a march on them. She had awakened in her hospital room at some remote hour of the night and at once telephoned Arthur Jones, the quietly efficient black St. Louisan who had been looking after her apartment for the past twenty years. He had duly smuggled in her request, a bottle of whiskey, which she had secreted at her bedside.[23] Soon they all realized that Irma, who never appeared drunk, had worked up over the years to a serious dependence on alcohol. When deprived of it she became extremely difficult to deal with. In her weak and frustrated condition, she began unleashing on her caregivers the sort of fury that throughout most of her life had been reserved for her family.

Marion herself was in no shape for much exertion, but she was willy-nilly obliged to make the arrangements for Irma's convalescence. She and John completed the move from Cabanne Avenue during her mother's hospitalization, only to be rewarded with a barrage of complaints about the condition of the Lindell Boulevard apartment—a sublet—and some muddled threat about withholding the rent in retaliation for real or imagined offenses. Put, Marion, and their cousin Max Muench (now Irma's chief St. Louis financial advisor, to whom she had assigned power of attorney more than ten years previously) had to mend fences with the subletter.[24] They were actually discussing the matter of Irma's legal competency at the same time that she was writing a delightful and wholly lucid letter to James Woodress thanking him for a copy of the just-published Tarkington biography, which she had read in the hospital.[25] Irma's treatment of the nurses Marion had hired was unpredictable and at times outrageous.

By degrees Irma gained strength. Though she remained mostly housebound, she was quickly able to resume a semblance of normal social behavior with some of her friends. But those who bore the most responsibility—Marion, Irma's loyal Wednesday Club friend Laura Corbitt, Max, and his daughter, Irma's devoted great-niece Elsa Muench Hunstein—were on occasion treated to uncontrolled outbursts or accounts of scenes from others. The inner changes wrought by frustrating immobility and dependence were not always obvious to an observer. At times she could mask them very well, as when Judy and Murray Israel came by on a St. Louis trip and were delighted to find that she had "retained her spirits admirably, and all of her keenness"—though, as they also pointed out to Marion, "her biggest problem (as you well know) is malnutrition" and "she is taking that extra amount of alcohol that removes the appetite."[26] At other times she could not keep up the mask at all. She would quarrel with one of the nurses and send her packing, or get a bee in her bonnet about the apartment and refuse to pay the rent, then childishly insist to Max Muench that she *had* paid it when she could produce no receipt or check stub. When she was not complaining about her attendants, she might take it into her head to present one of them with some valued possession, leaving the family to discover the loss and try to remonstrate with her. Within about six months of the stroke she had become so incensed at Max that she transferred power of attorney to Marion.[27]

Against all odds, Irma strove to pick up the pieces of her life's work. Even now, when greatly weakened and made miserable by chronic nausea, she thought constantly of *The Joy of Cooking*. That her intellect was perfectly alert and her faculties composed enough for the work is clear from the fact that it is not always possible to tell whether some undated letter or scrap of manuscript does or does not precede the "cerebrovascular accident," as the doctors called it. The surviving papers unmistakably show that she continued working on *Joy* with Mazie Hartrich to the limit of her strength, discussing revision plans and reviewing the fan mail. What is more, she tried to go on with the work of recipe development. It is impossible to guess how many recipes in the next *Joy of Cooking* are attributable to Irma's poststroke efforts; the total is not likely to be large. But Elsa Hunstein clearly recalls "Ginger Thins" (page 707 of the current 1975 *Joy of Cooking*) having been developed with the help of Irma's nursing attendants, who would regularly bring them out for the Hunstein children when they visited; while Cecily Brownstone possesses Irma's own longhand version of the cookies that eventually appeared in the book as "Molasses Crisps Cockaigne" (1975 *Joy*, page 716).[28]

As she had done before when she was out of town or extremely preoccupied, she did from time to time ask Marion to deal with some of the correspondence.[29] But in no way was she ready to resign the reins to her. There was no question of Irma's letting anyone else be the "I" at the center of her all-important relationship with her audience.

Irma's will to recover was greatly boosted early in 1956 by the surprise of a letter from Washington University, claiming her as a long-lost alumna (though in fact she had never received a degree) and asking her to a Founder's Day award ceremony on February 23.[30] She looked forward to the event with great pleasure; attention was a tonic to her. By now the weather was becoming pleasant and she was starting to get out with the aid of Helen-Marie Fruth and Craig Nicholson, hoping for a spring and summer of peaceful stays at the beloved Jefferson County cabin. But this brief resurgence was thwarted on February 15, when Marion arrived expecting to celebrate her mother's improvement and found that Irma had just suffered another stroke.[31]

Once more Irma fought back to some approximation of herself. But this time the damage was worse and the improvement shorter-lived. Her speech was more obviously impaired, and the right words did not reliably come when she tried to put pen to paper. Still she sought to continue working on *The Joy of Cooking;* a few garbled notes scrawled on the back of a bank slip testify that she clung to her intention of carrying out a revision at least as late as January of 1957.[32] But her efforts at communication became more and more futile. Within months of the 1956 stroke she was well on her way to the horror she had often told friends she dreaded above all things: to lie imprisoned in the useless husk of a body. She would live that nightmare to the full, and she would not be spared the wretchedness of knowing it.

All who knew her agree that Irma's mind continued to function through nearly every agony of her long illness. But from 1956 on, words increasingly failed her. Soon she could read only outsize printing. Her own speech and writing became like botched telegraphy in some half-mastered code. The anger that had always been part of that small human force-field took on a terrible life of its own, freed from earlier inhibitions.

Nearly everyone who came in contact with her was at some time the victim of incoherent—or worse, coherent—abuse. More strokes followed over the next several years. The time came, well before 1960, when Irma not only could not bear to be seen by most of her old friends but drove them away in a rage. Even then—the most frightful of her torments—she did not completely lose the knowledge of who and where she was.

The most regular object of her wrath was Marion, who kept having to fly or drive to St. Louis every time Irma called to complain of imaginary maltreatment by her attendants or they called to say that matters were out of control. Sometimes her mother would be sitting up ready to make cheerful and more or less intelligible conversation. Sometimes she would start trying to discuss plans for the cookbook, plainly indicating that she considered herself in charge. Or she might turn on Marion like a crazed animal, scratching her face and pulling her hair in screaming fury and repeating the old story of her ugliness.[33] Again and again Marion rehired nurses whom Irma had just fired, or sadly acknowledged that they had better not come back and started looking for someone else. It is not pleasant to imagine what sort of experiences lie behind documents like the letter of one recently fired maid in September 1956, thanking Marion for "your wonderful humanity and kindness to me, while working for your Mother."[34]

No one ever saw Marion behave toward the wreck of her mother with anything but dignity and love. How she had the strength to keep on was a wonder to those who knew the situation, for she was in great pain herself for years after her operation. Her recovery had been handicapped not only by Irma's illness but by a traumatic course of radiation therapy that added to the original disfigurement of the mastectomy the further disfigurement of severe burns and scarring over her entire upper torso. Though the doctors assured her that the outlook was good for complete recovery with no recurrence of the cancer, she also had to cope with lymphedema, a frequent complication of radical mastectomy. In this condition lymph is unable to drain normally from the affected limb, which gradually swells to monstrous size from the accumulation of fluid. By the end of 1956 Marion was at times unable to use her right arm or even put on a normal dress or blouse over it.

The lymphedema was not only unsightly and horribly painful but dangerous, because a limb engorged to such a degree is prone to infection from the slightest scratch or bump. She was shunted from doctor to doctor. No one was able to suggest anything more practical than keeping the arm elevated. This involved a ridiculous traction arrangement that Marion was obliged to wheel around like some medieval punishment, and another over her bed.

It was virtually a Pavlovian reflex with Marion to smile in the face of mental or physical pain. She was no Pollyanna, but she shrank compulsively from letting any other human being see her in genuine distress. It was impossible for her *not* to conceal suffering. Her closest family never knew her to appear like anything but a cheerfully healthy person. Her idea of adjusting to illness was to go out and work harder. Given her instincts, it is not really surprising that as her difficulties increased, she seemed to take on an awesome stamina.

The situation certainly called for someone with more than ordinary staying power. After the last odds and ends of the previous revision had been mopped up, Marion and Irma had had each other's strength to count on (with Irma as ultimate authority) at some not very clearly foreseen stage of the revision work, in the comfortably distant future. But by the beginning of 1957 all bets were off. Marion, silently struggling with the lasting effects of her own illness, had no Irma to look to for either culinary or editorial counsel in approaching the next *Joy*. Instead of a deliberate transition between her mother's and her own supervision of the great cookbook, there had been a sudden and catastrophic end to one party's involvement. Though Irma still lived and breathed and longed to command the effort, never again would she be able to write a word toward the dearest purpose of her life. Meanwhile, the vague reports that occasionally came in from the Bobbs-Merrill front suggested that at any moment in the next few years, some new executive might arrive wanting to get on with the next edition straightway.

In other words, Marion would swiftly have to invent a new role for herself, under the worst of circumstances. It was bound to involve reinventing *The Joy of Cooking* to a greater or lesser extent, and she had no way of knowing whether her act of reimagination would succeed with either publisher or readers.

11

The Last Battle

Even apart from Marion's and her mother's illnesses, the Becker family had not had the easiest of times since the 1951 *Joy of Cooking*. The deadline for the revised version of the disputed index was nearly at hand in October of 1952 when Marion had to drop everything after the seven-year-old Ethan—who had been playing in nearby Clough Creek downstream from a discharge of raw sewage—came down with polio. She was at his bedside for weeks, armed with every bit of information she could find about the disease and spiritedly analyzing therapeutic options with the doctors. (Mazie Hartrich finished getting the manuscript of the new index to Bobbs-Merrill.) Ethan was one of the lucky patients who would completely get over the initial paralysis, but his recovery was not certain for months.

John and Marion were meanwhile wrestling with the educational future of Mark, a born nonconformist whose erratic performance in the three Rs had perplexed Irma as well as themselves. He had managed to get into the George School, a distinguished Quaker boarding school in the Philadelphia area, and later Haverford College. At both, however, he seesawed dizzily between acceptable and awful grades, and had flunked out of Haverford by 1956. His parents were thoroughly nonplussed.

With a streak of the same countercultural stubbornness that had run in the family since old Roderick Rombauer, Mark refused to limp back to Cockaigne for further parental analysis of his failings. He decided to do some exploring on his own. In St. Louis, the resourceful Helen-Marie Fruth helped him find a job as a copy boy at the *Post-Dispatch*. After a while he drifted west in the wake of a girlfriend who was going to college in Oregon. Mark went through some short-lived jobs in the Portland area, defensively fielding puzzled and unhappy letters from home and making a few abortive attempts to get back onto the college track, before finding work with a marine biology station on the coast.

That an evidently bright young man might not get through a rite of passage like college was a thought completely bewildering to his parents. John saw little in Mark's adventures but fecklessness. Marion, who liked to think that she appreciated people who marched to different drummers, was hurt and frustrated. Both had nourished hopes that *The Joy of Cooking* would continue in the family beyond their own day. Now it seemed that what Irma had begun might end with their own generation—another discouraging note in a work situation already rife with trouble and uncertainty.

Bobbs-Merrill was in no happier state than was Marion as she began work on the edition that would end in the most shattering author-publisher Armageddon of all. Much of the blame for the disasters that ensued can be laid to a virtual interregnum at the company after Laurance Chambers was booted upstairs in 1953 and to the manner in which the reins were eventually taken up by others.

The firm's leadership marked time for several years in the mid-1950s with little idea of what might come next. But on November 11, 1957, Bobbs-Merrill ended years of rumor by announcing that the principal stockholders—Chambers, company president Lowe Berger, and Colonel Robert Moorhead of the legal publishing division—had sold their interest (amounting to 60 percent of the stock) for $1 million. The purchaser was not any of the New York companies that had been thought likely contenders but an unheralded hometown candidate, Howard W. Sams, Inc., of Indianapolis.[1] Its founder, the sixty-one-year-old Howard Sams, had been quick to divine a market for technical books after World War II and had carved out a large niche in the technical-manual field as publisher of numerous guides to telephone installation, home and commercial wiring, television repair, and applied electronics.

Sams was, however, a stranger to trade publishing. He quickly announced that he did not plan to disturb the internal affairs of Bobbs-Merrill trade books aside from injecting a hefty dose of capital (apparently much needed, since the trade division had operated at a loss in 1957). The only major change he contemplated was installing a new company president. Lowe Berger, seriously ill, resigned on completion of the sale; Sams thereupon assumed the role of vice president in charge of sales and acting president while promoting the company treasurer, Leo Gobin, to vice president and general manager.[2] To the publishing trade Sams now proclaimed a talent search to select a new president.

Marion received assurances of Sams's good intentions through a form letter addressed to "Mr. Becker."[3] Despite this gaffe he seemed inclined to be helpful, agreeing to put more money into advertising *Joy* and (at least in her belief) giving the nod to what she told him of her revision plans. But it is uncertain just how much he or anyone at Bobbs-Merrill really understood of Marion's ideas, which were too intricate and far-reaching to be easily conveyed to anyone not already immersed in the subject.

The already confused chain of command at Bobbs-Merrill fell into worse disarray with the appointment of the new president in March of 1959. He was M. Hughes Miller, vice president of American Book–Stratford Press and a former executive of Charles E. Merrill Company, where he had worked on the highly successful *My Weekly Reader* program for schoolchildren. At forty-six, he probably looked like new blood to a company that had not had much for some time.[4]

Miller's arrival augured not only renewed discord between author and publisher but epic-scale conflict within the house. From the memories of people who survived his ill-fated stint at Bobbs-Merrill, he was as obstinate and fond of nasty showdowns as Laurance Chambers. Chambers's worst enemies, however, would have agreed that he possessed learning, editorial judgment, and after his own fashion courtliness. Miller's new colleagues do not seem to have been struck by such qualities. Furthermore, Chambers had prudently left some parts of the organization to mind their own business when that seemed the better part of valor. Miller combined interventionist zeal with a talent for alienating people.

Instead of entering on an era of saner and more orderly relations with the publisher, Marion soon saw that she would have worse corporate chaos to deal with. Bobbs-Merrill staffers began leaving almost as soon as the new president had warmed up his chair. Within six months of his arrival Miller had succeeded in driving out the old New York mainstays Walter Hurley and Ross Baker, thereby removing a vital component of the firm's judgment in sailing the treacherous waters of *Joy of Cooking* affairs. Baker's place as head of the sales department was taken by the scrappy Bill Finneran, who detested Marion as a pushy, inadequate substitute for her delightful mother. Marion did not know it, but Finneran and Miller hoped to press the discount-sales approach to new extremes.

Under Sams and Miller, Bobbs-Merrill soon embarked on a campaign of expansion and diversification. Both the law and education divisions began buying smaller companies in their fields. The trade division started a new paperback imprint. The children's department acquired the "Raggedy Ann" books.[5] More painfully for the old guard at the trade division, the overall editorial and production setup was thoroughly revamped. The great Hoosier publisher was Hoosier no more, for Miller lost no time transferring editorial headquarters to New York. Indianapolis was designated as the new seat of manufacturing and little else, though the board of directors remained there. In both cities, Bobbs-Merrill's existing offices were scheduled to be relocated to larger quarters.

The remaining veterans did not cheer all of Miller's initiatives, nor did everyone care for his level of editorial taste. This swiftly proved itself to be several notches below old Bobbs-Merrill standards, which the Beckers had never thought lofty. The spring list for 1959, a last echo of the former regime, had prominently featured Robert Dahl's serious autobiographical account of recovery from mental illness and Jules Dubois's biography of the newly renowned Fidel Castro (a work that had cost its editor, Harrison Platt, a short stint in a Havana jail in a case of mistaken identity).[6] In 1960 the corresponding list led off with *God Is a Good God* by Oral Roberts and *Once upon a Dream*, the autobiography of Patti Page.[7]

The Miller shake-up at Bobbs-Merrill intensified a pattern of inadequate communication and unresolved issues that had long predated his appearance on the *Joy of Cooking* scene. A major invitation to misunderstanding already existed and now further flourished with the turnover of personnel: the absence of a contract. Since Bobbs-Merrill had talked Irma Rombauer into revising her manuscript on speculation in 1935, all *Joy of Cooking* contracts had been drawn up only *after* a manuscript had been submitted and accepted. There had never been so much as a contractual deadline or a stipulated advance against royalties.

The only saving grace in this situation had been that everyone was familiar enough with everyone else to ensure a fairly orderly transition from Mazie Hartrich's typescripts to the printed page. Besides, the framework of the first Bobbs-Merrill *Joy* had remained intact in every revision through 1951, meaning that no editor had been called on to debate ticklish points of editorial judgment with the author during the throes of composition. The team in Indianapolis and New York simply waited for Irma to accomplish her familiar magic, in the intervals of quarreling over accusations of chicanery.

Even after Marion appeared on the scene, editor-author discussions were few and not terribly productive; since Jessica Mannon left, no editor had enjoyed either Irma's or Marion's confidence. The noneditors Walter Hurley (in the production office) and Ross Baker (as head salesman) were more in Marion's counsels than was Harry Platt, who was expected to oversee the editing of the next revision. It was they, and not Platt, to whom she had confided some of her ideas in the fall of 1957 and from whom she thought she had received definitive official encouragement. Their departure left Bobbs-Merrill heavily dependent on the canny, cool Platt, who had never dreamed of making judgment calls against Irma in regard to anything more serious than grammar but had no such scruples about Marion. He had no great opinion of her powers, and might have seriously locked horns with her if matters had fallen out differently. But Miller's arrival soon changed his plans. Platt sized up the new regime and decided to leave Bobbs-Merrill early in 1960. He and the company agreed that he would continue to supervise some projects, including the *Joy* revision, on a freelance basis—a dubious arrangement in that no senior editor familiar with the old book remained on staff.[8]

Through this unlucky train of circumstances, Marion and "the NEW Bobbs-Merrill" (as it had called itself in a splashy *Publishers Weekly* ad)[9] arrived at the stage of fixing a semiofficial deadline without really having consulted each other about what was to be in the book or how the work was to be carried out. Platt probably knew more than anyone else at Bobbs-Merrill, but he did not immediately have much to go on in evaluating Marion's progress and was not eager to represent either side's thinking to the other. Howard Sams was not particularly qualified to evaluate the importance of anything she may have told him in his few months as acting president. As for Miller, he promptly started quarreling with the Beckers without having gotten a good handle on what they were doing.

Marion had first inquired about a deadline toward the end of the Bobbs-Merrill interregnum, and had been given a date in May—later changed to mid-June—of 1960. But long before then Hughes Miller had missed the opportunity to direct her efforts to any good purpose.

By 1956 or 1957, while the firm was rudderless, she had arrived at a plan for revising *The Joy of Cooking* that meant a stunning break with its past. Marion herself may not have comprehended the degree of change implied by her ideas, and she did not understand just how much the Sams-Miller crew did not understand. Her serious work of information-gathering seems to have begun in 1958. Her rethinking of the old book, however, went back at least two years earlier. Her conclusions were so penetrating that in the end they more than doubled the life span of what her mother had founded and tended. But her design for concretely realizing these ideas was divided between strokes of well-aimed invention and naive contrivances that no publisher would have agreed to.

Early in 1956 Marion decided on a work plan that meant pasting up the entire contents of the last edition, together with all new material as it was developed, on a series of color-coded 4-by-6-inch index cards that could be switched around in boxes of chapter files. Her mother and Mazie Hartrich had rejected an earlier version of this idea in 1954, but in 1956 Mazie agreed to prepare the first tool she needed to implement it, a set of cards containing the entire contents of the 1951 "New Joy" as cut from the pages and pasted up to Marion's specifications. No such shortcuts as photocopiers were then available to most people, and the job took Mazie several months.[10]

Marion's plan was to keep inserting additional cards in the categories delineated by the different colors as new recipes and other material were approved for inclusion, while periodically reviewing the older ones and pulling the cards on anything scheduled for deletion. The card index in its final form would then be submitted to Bobbs-Merrill *as the completed manuscript.* This system seemed perfectly practical to her, John, and her part-time secretary, Jane Brueggeman, who had worked for Marion since early Modern Art Society days and enjoyed absolute rapport with her. She was sure that Bobbs-Merrill had understood and approved it.

The truth is that no publisher could have considered such an arrangement remotely acceptable as the final manuscript of an intricate 800- to 1,000-page book. Even if Marion had been ready to present Bobbs-Merrill with a complete and faultless manuscript in index-card form—which was never the case from beginning to end of the debacle—working with multiple boxes of cards would have been intolerably laborious and confusing for everyone at all stages between examining the manuscript for a page-space estimate and sending it to the printers. But in the great disarray preceding and especially following Hughes Miller's appearance, no one in a position of responsibility ever sized up the approaching crisis and allowed time for the obvious solution: insisting that Marion have her card-file index completely and carefully transcribed to an orthodox 8½-by-11-inch typescript and that she review it thoroughly before she submitted it for final acceptance.

Marion's work plan had rather quickly evolved to exclude Mazie. In January of 1958 she asked Harriet Pilpel to summarize what she was and was not bound to by the 1950 agreement her mother had insisted on making to ensure a proper reward for Mazie's long service to the book. No one at Greenbaum, Wolff & Ernst could give conclusive answers to her questions except to point out that the document applied only to the 1951 "New Joy," not any subsequent edition.[11]

Given the great complexity of the approach that Marion had determined on, she had no wish to work with Mazie three hundred miles away when she had at hand a helper—Jane Brueggeman—who understood everything she meant almost like a second self. She quickly let Mazie know that her services would not be required for the ongoing revision work and tried to feel her out about granting a little leeway on the present fiscal arrangements. As her own and Irma's medical bills continued, Marion had come to find the annual Hartrich payments ($4,000, shared 60 percent–40 percent between mother and daughter) a considerable financial burden. Knowing now that her mother could only have some handful of years left with no hope of recovery, she suggested that Mazie accept some partial deferment of payments until after Irma's death.[12]

Mazie emphatically refused to permit any change in the schedule of payments and, though Mazie herself had not been a party to the 1950 agreement, Marion did not dare breach it. Their conversation (late in February of 1958) must have been fairly acrimonious, because Marion ended by requesting a statement of Mazie's services rendered to date on the new edition, with a view to paying them off and having a free hand in at least that regard. Mazie at first refused, but matters did not come to a complete break. The two women continued to exchange polite messages about the twice-yearly payments sent by Marion (who by now had to write the check on Irma's account as well as her own) for, as they called it, Mazie's "consultant" services on the last edition, and eventually Mazie did agree to submit some statement of charges that cleared the decks in regard to the revision in progress.[13]

Whatever the ethical overtones of Marion's eagerness to be done with the Hartrich obligation, her wish to map out her own course with her own people makes eminent sense. She may not have begun in 1956 with the deliberate intention of dismantling *The Joy of Cooking* in order to re-create it along new lines, but that was what her labors would amount to in the end. Unknown to the Miller team at Bobbs-Merrill, she was feeling her way toward a book that would be the most exhaustive, far-ranging culinary teaching manual presented to the American public in her lifetime. The freedom to explore and experiment was not just a practical advantage but a sine qua non in her gradual visualization of the goal.

Already in the 1951 joint edition Marion had managed to confer a more directly informational slant on the book within Irma's old framework. Since then she had become still more concerned with the sorts of things that readers seemed not to know, and more bent on chasing down the knowledge that made the difference between walking through a formulaic script and applying real judgment.

How determined she was to get down to fundamentals is shown by the importance she placed on merely measuring ingredients accurately, a problem at the root of many cake or pastry failures reported in readers' letters. Her attention had been called to the issue by a version of *Joy* rather raggedly adapted for British use, published in London since 1946 by J. M. Dent and Sons. Sales of this edition had always been insignificant, and Marion found one reason in the uselessness of American measurements for British purchasers. (The difference between U.S. fluid ounces and those derived from the Imperial pint is small but cumulatively disastrous, and the two nations' teaspoons and tablespoons are also slightly at variance.) She would have loved to have a set of American measuring cups and spoons given away or sold with each copy. Indeed, at one point she tried to interest Bobbs-Merrill in doing the same thing with the next U.S. revision.[14] Though the idea was scotched, she insisted on devoting at least half a dozen pages to different ways of understanding how much of something you are using. The whole question would never have troubled cooks a few centuries back, when seat-of-the-pants skills were the rule rather than the exception, but for modern audiences it was no foolish technicality. The amount of time Marion spent on it points to her growing curiosity about the basic problem of *how to use a cookbook*.

Irma had addressed the matter of using cookbooks by her own irreverent lights and come up with her novel recipe format—but she had not sought to go beyond this spark of invention. She was not, like Marion, a knowledge addict burning to take people on written voyages of discovery. Irma had never been terribly interested in the wherefores of cooking; her approach was simply to write down the formulas as reliably as possible and keep applying doses of sparkling, encouraging companionship.

Marion, who would never be able to match her mother's natural aptitude for forging a bond with readers, instinctively went about turning *The Joy of Cooking* into a unique learning tool, a mission that simply could not be accomplished within the existing framework. In the past everything—even large dollops of information added at her instigation in 1951—had somehow got fitted into a set of chapters that had remained generally recognizable for twenty years. Venturing into ground not broken by her mother's or any other general kitchen manual, Marion stood the old organization on its head. What she wanted was a better organization that would still leave room for the spontaneity and informality beloved by longtime users of *Joy.* Even such familiar landmarks as the beginning chapter on cocktails were displaced in her shake-up, the miscellany of drinks and predinner tidbits that had been lumped together under that name now being retitled and reassigned to several different chapters. She was not an inspired organizer, and her index-card system did not serve her well for developing a coherent overall structure. But with instinctive perseverance she kept cramming in the kinds of things that usually get cropped from the edge of the picture in straightforward recipe books.

Large chunks of such material went into a new chapter on cooking processes in their own right, "The Foods We Heat." Here Marion sought to convey the sense behind different methods from sautéing to parboiling, with painstaking attention to factors like choosing kinds of cooking vessels, gauging variables in timing, supervising the temperature of fat for deep-frying, and just simply moving from a familiar to an unfamiliar situation:

> For years, we made magnificent hollandaise in a stoneware
> bowl that fit the base of an aluminum double boiler. It was a

completely effortless procedure. Then the bowl broke and the magic fled.[15]

A longer and more disorderly chapter called "Know Your Ingredients" served as an enormous lumber room of material on different culinary components ranging, in Marion's phrase, "from butter to weather." This was the final repository of the measuring information. It also told you how to beat eggs, identify a panoply of herbs and spices, purify contaminated water, melt chocolate, and make a lot of basic preparations from soup stocks to cottage cheese to chili vinegar. But Marion still had huge motley caches of material to fit in. Most things that did not seem to have any other resting place were put into what she called the "Abouts": capsule essays or free-form clumps of descriptive text inserted throughout all of the recipe chapters and anchored as plausibly as possible to some general subject ("About Boning Fowl") or group of recipes ("About Steamed Puddings"). There were literally hundred of "Abouts" of any length between three or four lines and the better part of a page. They added tremendously to the depth of the overall coverage, but also had the less welcome effect of lengthening the book a good deal more than anyone realized.

Other aims of Marion's also meant increased length. She had been greatly impressed over the years by readers' letters from remote corners of the globe describing how *Joy* had seen them through thick and thin, and she had decided to make it even more of a desert-island mainstay—a resource from which people in the most improbable circumstances could figure out how to use a breadfruit or dig and outfit a hole for pit-cooking. She went out of her way to define any cooking term that she could imagine anyone, anywhere, wanting to look up for any reason, from "allumette" to "matignon." She crammed in information on mangosteens, fenugreek, cherimoyas, wild mushrooms, sorrel, the nearly forgotten "martynia" (whose seed pods used to be pickled like capers), the cooking of whale or bear.

Marion did know that the length of the text might be getting to be a problem and had tried in her own way to address it while further sharpening the already distinctive visual identity of the book. She conceived that hundreds (or thousands) of words and phrases might be replaced throughout the whole volume by a set of visual cues—stylized symbols introduced early on by a key. One of the planned symbols had already been used in 1951: parentheses ( ) to denote optional ingredients in recipes. To forestall confusion it had been necessary to avoid the use of parentheses for any other purpose anywhere else in the book, but Harry Platt and the copy editors apparently had not found this restriction hard to observe in 1951. The other symbols, worked out amid fluctuating Bobbs-Merrill support or opposition mostly before the change of leadership, were a snowflake ❄ to indicate freezing or the use of frozen ingredients, a triangle ▲ for high-altitude directions, a star ★ for Christmas specialties, a backyard grill ▤ for outdoor cookery, a stylized pressure cooker ⊗ and blender ⊼ to indicate the use of those machines, and an arrow-shaped pointer ◗ to alert readers to particularly critical information in both descriptive text and recipes. (Another helpful idea eventually agreed on by all—it is not clear whether it came from Marion or Bobbs-Merrill—was a pair of red grosgrain ribbon markers to help users keep their place while looking up something elsewhere.) No one foresaw how badly Bobbs-Merrill would handle the complexities of copyediting and setting added by all of these.

Lengthening by yards and trying to condense by inches, Marion had committed herself to another effort that would dramatically increase *Joy*'s appeal for thousands or millions of readers but also swell the total bulk of a manuscript whose length the publisher had not yet gauged. She had decided to add a large number of recipes reflecting the spectacular 1950s boom in ambitious cosmopolitan hobby-cooking. Already Irma and Marion had been conspicuously beforehand with this sort of coverage in 1951. Marion's reading of the situation was that even greater adventurousness was justified now—that an all-purpose manual for American housewives not only could but should count on their being interested in cassoulet, couscous, stuffed grape leaves, salade niçoise, navarin printanier, enchiladas, fish quenelles, and turkey mole.

Of course she was right. By now the epicurean cults and culinary globe-trotting that had been long established in certain strata of American culture were trickling down to middle-class households more visibly than they had before the war. All prior gourmet vogues were as nothing compared with the ongoing one nourished by a global-consumer or bourgeois-connoisseur mentality in which all Americans above abject poverty were now invited to share. It received ever-loftier expression in magazine and newspaper food coverage; housewives from coast to coast were relentlessly encouraged by journalists to see themselves as a sophisticated leisure class seeking enlightened self-fulfillment from a world-spanning smorgasbord of goods and services.

Men were meanwhile the main beneficiaries of a new wave of expensive, elaborate, and occasionally very good restaurants spawned by the early heyday of corporate expense accounts and dedicated to gastronomic wanderlust. During the 1950s these mutually reinforcing trends helped boost the popularity of cooking courses, a phenomenon that Marion noted with interest.

By the time of the Sams takeover in 1958 Marion, as a perennial power at the Cincinnati Town and Country Garden Club, was trying to push the group in the direction of the wilderness-conservation and ecological-awareness projects that were now a central mission for her. She and John had developed close friendships with two much-admired Cincinnati chefs: the Alsatian-born Pierre Adrian of the celebrated Maisonette and the young James Gregory, fresh from the dining room of NATO headquarters in Belgium, who had made a splash at the fashionable Camargo Club. Always one to marry separate interests wherever she could, Marion helped convince Town and Country to finance a major wilderness-area purchase in conjunction with the Nature Conservancy, and further talked the club into raising funds for the purpose early in 1959 through a series of four or five cooking lessons by Gregory, Adrian, and other local chefs.[16]

The first two sets of demonstration lessons, comprising the "Continental Cooking School" for stylish international dishes and the "Bride's Cooking School" for more rudimentary teaching, were a big enough success to be repeated in one form or another for several years in a row. Marion's close involvement with this actual culinary instruction project during the busy intermediate stages of *Joy* revision added insight and conviction to her approach.

All observers who have seriously tried to compare even the most perfunctory live cooking demonstration with a written recipe for (supposedly) the same thing must be awestruck at how hard it is to translate complex action into a handful of signals. Nothing is simple, automatic, or ever wholly successful about articulating the information gleaned by watching practical hands at work in order to make the culinary result systematically reproducible by all manner of clever or foolish people—the forlorn mission of recipe writing. Marion's work with the Town and Country cooking courses certainly helped strengthen her commitment to the material that would aid people in using recipes: the "Abouts" and the new informational chapters. Indeed, these would be a much greater factor in the lasting success of her effort than the glamorous new foreign recipes. Her reach sometimes disastrously exceeded her grasp in introducing other cooks to the wonders of assorted cuisines; the garblings in her notions of tamales or shrimp teriyaki are painful, and she lavished much time on pretentious performances like a turkey galantine quite inappropriate for home cooking (and atrociously seasoned with Worcestershire sauce and monosodium glutamate). The remarkable staying power of her first solo revision—which remained in print in paperback until 1997—is mostly owing to her initiative in trying to set down kinds of knowledge for which recipes are inadequate.

A further spur to this mission was a culinary discussion group that took shape around 1958 as an informal Monday lunchtime roundtable at La Maisonette. Jim Gregory supplied expertise along with the *patron*, Pierre Adrian. The lunch-meeting crew usually included "Lee" (Lolita) Harper, who as "Ann Holiday" was chief home economist and consumer representative for the Cincinnati Gas and Electric Company. Marion had retained her as a consultant for *Joy* on general "service" and home-economics matters. Eleanor Ahearn, a retired Procter & Gamble contact of Marion and Irma's, was another sometime member of the group who on occasion helped out with the same kinds of questions. A Maisonette regular who had become Marion's consultant on menu making was Luella Schierland, known to the Beckers as a hostess of repute with a solid knowledge of the currently received "serious" cooking. Jane Brueggeman was a frequent participant. Marion and John were at the core of the group, often pointing the conversation to some area that they happened to be investigating or seeking to analyze some classic dish from several informed perspectives.

The lunch-group agenda—and sometimes the menu—loosely reflected the course of Marion's revision efforts. Pierre Adrian might prepare something for them all to sample and discuss, or a food professional with a knowledge of a specialized area such as baking might show up for a few visits. These conversations sharpened Marion's interest in getting to the reasons behind things, and deepened her conviction that she was certainly on the right track in making the revised *Joy of Cooking* not only a storehouse of facts but an invitation to readers to join in an exhilarating quest for knowledge.

The actual research, testing, and preliminary drafting of material developed into a team effort involving some of the same people on a formal or informal basis. The bulk of the recipe testing was carried out by the Beckers' part-time cook-housekeepers, Odessa Whitehead and (somewhat later) Isabell Coleman. The mainstays of the writing were

Marion as framer and ultimate codifier, Jane Brueggeman as sounding board and follower-through on anything from major ideas to minor logistics, and John as Marion's alter ego and the editorial mastermind.

It would be impossible to overstate John's contribution to the ongoing effort. Not at this period having overwhelming calls on his time from the architectural practice, he devoted virtually full-time attention to *The Joy of Cooking*. Marion and Jane saw him as not only the stylistic eye and ear of the writing process but the continuator of something resembling the welcoming, chatty persona of Irma. He had helped Marion thresh out the whole concept of the new revision. He read along with her or listened to her descriptions of new gleanings from culinary history and food technology, batted around ideas with the Monday lunch regulars at La Maisonette, joined her at meetings with Platt and Miller. He toned down forbidding chunks of factual exposition and wove in anecdotes, asides, or offbeat metaphors in a painstaking (though not always convincing) approximation of the Rombauer voice. Replacing Irma's first-person singularities with the editorial "we," he often managed to be very funny:

> Always in the back of our minds, spurring us on [to greater adventure in the drinks department], is the memory of a cartoon which depicted a group of guests sitting around a living room, strickenly regarding their cocktail glasses, while the hostess, one of those inimitable Hokinson types, all embonpoint, cheer, and fluttering organdy, announces, "A very dear old friend gave me some wonderful old Scotch and I just happened to find a bottle of papaya juice in the refrigerator!"

> We would like to spare you the ordeal of an old friend of ours, whose enthusiasm for outdoor grilling is repeatedly dampened by his wife's low-voiced but grim injunction: "Remember, Orville, medium-burnt, not well-burnt!"[17]

Marion, whom her friends thought inhibited about trying to be funny, regarded him as the life and soul of the writing. Not everyone saw it the same way. The English-born Dorothy Wartenberg, whom the Beckers knew through Cincinnati cultural affairs and who was now helping out in assorted research for the new American edition while adding some improvements to the English counterpart, found the "rather mandarin kind of style" in which he tended to rewrite everything more of an irritant than a pleasure.[18] This view was widely shared at Bobbs-Merrill. But John was a tremendous moral and practical support to Marion as she strove to shape the complex project against the constant backdrop of physical pain and impairment that was now her medical situation.

Marion did not believe in being sick and maintained a resolute pose of health. But by 1957 her right arm would sometimes distend to nearly the size of a girl's waist if not held in traction over her head, and the fingers would swell so badly that she could neither type nor hold a pen. Often her helpers had to take dictation while Marion lay in bed with the arm propped up. But she did not let this roadblock slow her down on drafting work in progress for her own purposes. Without batting an eye, she picked up the pen in her left hand and forged ahead by repeating the mirror-writing trick of her childhood. (Most of her longhand correspondence from 1957 and 1958 is written on thin onionskin sheets that the often surprised recipients could hold up to the light to read in reverse.) She was forced to handle the bulk of the revision work by this peculiar method until late in 1958, when after years of bootless medical advice she found a glimmer of hope. Dr. "Feri" (Ferdinand) Donath, the Beckers' family physician and by Marion's lights the gold standard of intelligently focused medical attention, at last found a clinic in Cleveland that was fitting patients for an elasticized device known as the Jobst sleeve.

Marion's improvement was quick and dramatic. Once fitted with the sleeve, she was able to work for reasonable periods without the elephantiasis-like swelling that she had endured since 1955. Even so, she would never be free of discomfort and unpredictable bouts of inflammation. It was fortunate for her that she could conduct most of the revision effort from her own home, surrounded by family and friends and integrating much of the recipe testing (through Mrs. Whitehead and Mrs. Coleman) into the private household routine.

She had decided early on that large amounts of material would have to be cut from the old book. It was a step for which thousands of readers never forgave her, but one would be hard put to think of anyone better qualified to face the inevitable revisor's dilemma: to retain talismans for which an older cadre felt a proprietary loyalty or to make room for the interests of younger cooks convinced that *their* preferences were timeless. Marion did not solve the problem with seamless grace. Still, it is difficult to imagine any other person doing half so good a job. Marion had, after all, grown up with and loved the cooking that Irma had put on record in 1931 and 1936. She could claim to have been present at the creation (as illustrator, recipe tester, and production supervisor), but she could also apply a measure of independent judgment to things that Irma could not have borne to part with.

Knowing that she was treading a fine line, Marion made a diligent effort to conflate and condense rather than delete outright. Wherever possible, she used the new informational segments (e.g., "About Croquettes") along with a prototype recipe to supply general insight while eliminating some of the separate formulas ("Sweetbread Croquettes," "Egg Croquettes," "Macaroni or Spaghetti Croquettes"). But some culinary categories were still pruned very heavily, especially the canned-soup combinations and jelled sweet salads that had already been trimmed to some degree in 1951. A good many quickie items that had been added to the 1943 edition from *Streamlined Cooking* disappeared for good. Marion also lost no time in scuttling the quick-mix one-bowl cakes introduced in 1946; she severely retooled and shortened the section of chiffon-cake recipes that had appeared in 1951, and coldly noted that their selling point was unsaturated fat, not excellence. Many other individual entries throughout the book fell to her ax as well, taking with them some whiff of outmoded fashion (lobster and grapefruit cocktail, frozen marshmallow-pecan mousse) or a more substantial savor of the past (pickled peaches, oyster pie).

What she had done would always appear to some observers to be an act of betrayal. People who did not like her, like Bill Finneran of the sales department, were not slow to decide that "Marion was jealous of her own mother" and consequently "tried to write out her mother" from the book.[19] This opinion was not shared at all by Cecily Brownstone—the greatest friend Irma had made in food-writing circles, and the one person aside from Marion and Mazie Hartrich who understood what Irma had put into the original *Joy of Cooking*. She believed that Marion's decision to recast the book from the foundation up was legitimate (indeed, necessary), and had willingly helped and supported her in finding new material. She saw what many would not: that Marion had made heroic efforts to retain the flavor of Irma's individual taste and personality and, in grafting on other material, to link Irma with the continuation of the enterprise.

That Marion was willing to impose radical changes on *The Joy of Cooking* did not in the least weaken her almost obsessive sense of the book as a faithful private record, a sort of album first inscribed by her mother. Mementos of people and things mattered to her much more than to Irma, who was now beyond being consulted about mementos in any case. A crucial goal of Marion's was to work in many little tokens of both their lives. Without making a great noise about it, she asked the contingent of their food-writer friends who had added such pleasure to her mother's last active years to contribute a favorite recipe each to the revision. (The results are still in the book: the venerable American–East Indian hybrid called "Country Captain" from Cecily Brownstone, Helmut Ripperger's buttery Roquefort cheese spread, Jim Beard's ricotta cheesecake, Jane Nickerson's way of making a shortcakelike dessert of Irma's with fresh guavas.)[20] She added bits of family lore like the story of Julia Hollweg identifying faucets as the source of Indianapolis's water,[21] along with an occasional detail that their friends would have known harked back to Irma:

> We all enjoy red and white radish garnishes and, if we've read Pepys, we know he ate them buttered at William Penn's—worth trying, too, especially with black radishes.[22]

A similar impulse was behind another of her innovations: adding the name of "Cockaigne"—for her own home—to identify Rombauer-Becker favorites among the recipes. This gesture had been spurred by the many fan letters inquiring what dishes the authors themselves most loved. It probably never had its intended effect because large numbers of her readers did not think to read her explanation of it in the foreword; people still write to culinary advice-givers for definitions of "Cockaigne." Nonetheless, this idea of Marion's is a fair clue to an eager hunger for personal sharing—one of her most conspicuous qualities in private life—that would give her revisions of *Joy* a sufficient inner energy to keep engaging the loyalty (above and beyond the merely dutiful attention) of new readers for thirty-odd years.

As all these decisions about the course of the revised *Joy* took shape in Marion's mind, the project grew in both size and intricacy to something that would have daunted any editor. She was not in close communication with anyone at Bobbs-Merrill during the time of her most intensive thinking—nor, as we have seen, was the company in any condition to supervise the effort coherently either before or after Hughes Miller's arrival. The June 1960 deadline for submission of the manuscript soon evaporated. Marion was nowhere near completion of the work by then, but Bobbs-Merrill was very likely to blame as well, having thrown a large monkey wrench into the schedule by contriving to lose all of the originals of Ginnie Hofmann's artwork for the 1951 edition.[23] By the end of 1960 Marion and the company were already quarreling and trading accusations about what had and hadn't been agreed to in the revision.

At this stage Marion showed some portion of the revision work to Harry Platt. He pronounced it an awful mistake, and passed his criticisms on to Miller. From the matter of the 1951 nutrition chapter he had arrived at a view of the troublesome Mrs. Becker as an incorrigible lecturer with a poor grasp of her subject. In his judgment Irma Rombauer—canny, artless, down-to-earth, and grandly sophisticated in one inimitable package—had simply gotten people to the stove with a minimum of fuss and irresistibly pulled them into the *hows* of cooking without long preliminary harangues on the *whys*. He was not the only Bobbs-Merrill veteran, and would not be the last reader of *Joy*, to disdain the daughter as an interloper who couldn't wait to get her hands on her mother's work.

Marion was enraged at his response ("violently derogatory and completely destructive," as she later described it)[24] but not at all shaken in her intention. She would have girded her loins to face down Platt and argue her own case to Hughes Miller, but once again general corporate chaos intervened. The company had fallen behind on paying Platt, who now decided to wash his hands of the project altogether. At some point not long after his report on Marion's revision efforts he apprised Irma (whom he regarded as an old friend worthy of a courteous goodbye, even in her present state) that he was severing the freelance connection with Bobbs-Merrill and taking up other commitments. He was in no great hurry to tell Miller that he was bowing out, though he did spread the word elsewhere. In consequence Marion knew of his withdrawal long before the discomfited administration learned of it and notified her.[25]

By now it was the summer of 1961, and Miller was hard at work formulating a new production schedule based on an entirely unrealistic idea of what Marion was doing or what would be required to translate it into print. He had been seriously worried by Platt's criticisms, but neither of them had fully comprehended just what traps the company and Marion had already set for themselves in the handling of the still incomplete book.

In 1959, already realizing that her barrage of changes would ultimately increase the size of *Joy*, Marion had asked Howard Sams and then Miller to be allowed to make the new edition somewhat longer than the last one.[26] Miller had cautiously agreed—but without realizing that he and Marion were actually agreeing to quite different things. The trouble was that several separate production and layout issues were under discussion at the same time. The Beckers came away with an understanding about length based on the total number of pages, Bobbs-Merrill with an idea of the situation based on the overall character count—the number of picas (the basic typesetter's units) that would fit on the pages under a slightly different layout. Given the demands of the crowded two-column page arrangement with Irma's typographically complicated, narrowly constricting recipe format, a discrepancy of even a few lines per column was bound to be vast in its cumulative effect.

Happily ignorant of this iceberg waiting to intercept the ship, Miller prepared to bustle into production as soon as possible. In July of 1961, with no manuscript in hand and no in-house editor to whack things into shape, he decided to commit the company to a large first printing the next spring. Of course the amounts of paper to be ordered and the specifications to be requested for the cases (hardback bindings) and dust jackets depended on the actual length of the book, but Miller was confident that he had everything under control. In an act of sheer folly, he elected to sacrifice the all-important step of looking at the manuscript in its entirety before starting to set it in type.

Marion's manuscript was at that stage a highly incomplete arrangement of index-card files. Deciding that the key to speeding things up was to hire someone who would simultaneously turn this unusable affair into a standard 8½-by-11-inch typescript and edit the result for production, Miller prepared to turn the enormous mess over to a freelance editor. Marion, with her usual capacity for believing what she wanted, had grandly proffered John's services and talked herself into thinking that Bobbs-Merrill would go along with the suggestion. John's qualifications for the job existed chiefly in her fantasy—but the candidate Miller eventually picked was if anything worse.

Alice Wilson Richardson, a New York fashion-magazine editor and former advertising copywriter, was in Miller's eyes a fully accredited cookbook editor by virtue of having once written a cookbook. Marion had perused this very small effort, *Just a Minute*, and found it ridiculous. (It was essentially a noncookbook for noncooks trying to serve chic meals in a hurry; the caliber of the instruction may be judged by the fact that the recipe for sabayon never says anything about *cooking* the egg mixture.)[27] Still, she might have managed to work with Miss

Richardson if she had been permitted to finish up her one-of-a-kind manuscript to her own satisfaction and then survey a complete typed copy for accuracy before it was sent off to the typesetters. But the Miller-Richardson plan—which was really as much of a disservice to Bobbs-Merrill as to Marion—called for the hired editor to funnel separate segments of the text into production, a handful at a time, as fast as they could be pried loose from the balky author.

Miss Richardson flew out to Cincinnati to be introduced to Marion late in August, and stamped herself on the Becker party's admittedly jaundiced memory as having had several Martinis before lunch and gone to sleep afterward. Against her better judgment, Marion let the editor take several chapters of index cards back to New York to start editing and transcribing. The technology of photocopying still being in its infancy, she could not simply run off a few sets of duplicates from the cards. But she did take the expensive precaution of getting one set made by the new Eastman Kodak "Verifax" process, to the tune of about two hundred dollars. The images were not very good, but she would be glad of them later.

By this time Marion's attention was chronically divided between the Bobbs-Merrill situation and her mother's worsening state in St. Louis. Since 1958 or 1959, Irma's mental acuity had declined steeply. For a time she had been at least half able to follow Marion's dogged updates on the progress of revision. Though her eyesight was so poor that she could not read for herself and she was too deaf to understand all of what was said to her, she managed to communicate with visitors (when she did not go into a rage at their mere presence) by scrawling clumsy notes if they could not make out her speech. But by two or three years after the second stroke her good days were few and far between.

Despite the irrational spleen she had shown toward her nephew Max Muench since he had first been forced to keep tabs on her check writing and record keeping in the early days of her illness, he went on trying to look after her affairs until his sudden death from a heart attack in July of 1959. The burden of caretaking chores then fell on his daughter Elsa Muench Hunstein and Irma's old Wednesday Club chum—eventually to be executrix of her will—Laura Corbitt, an accountant and insurance agent who tried to pick up some of the fiscal threads from Max.

When Hughes Miller shoved Alice Richardson into the revision effort, Irma was rapidly going downhill. She had had a series of strokes that further distorted her speech and at last left her almost completely paralyzed on the left side. No hint of Irma's true condition reached the public, journalistic reticence still being thought more decent by people like Jane Nickerson and Cecily Brownstone than plastering a celebrity's misfortunes over the newspapers. But she was long beyond competently discussing *Joy* affairs with Marion (who tried to make the effort even when her mother was extremely feeble). By 1960 she was sometimes lucid, often confused, but perpetually capable of fearsome wrath. Marion came often to St. Louis, always dreading some ghastly attack, and would return to Cincinnati utterly drained. It was Elsa's belief that the special fury Irma poured on her daughter was a passionate, impotent jealousy at seeing *The Joy of Cooking* in the hands of another.[28]

Marion did not discuss her St. Louis visits with most acquaintances. But not long after Max's death she sat down to write a sealed letter to "my three men"—John and their sons—begging not to be kept alive "should I be stricken as Mother is so the future holds no promise of recovery and no real enjoyment of the present." She could imagine nothing worse for herself than being reduced to the useless, devouring "greed for life" that she now saw in her mother.[29]

While Marion was struggling with what she thought the last stages of her card-file manuscript after Platt's exit in 1961, Irma had suddenly seemed to take a turn for the worse. She was hospitalized for several weeks in June and July in a state of extreme unresponsiveness that the experts tentatively attributed to some red blood cell abnormality. "As alert as she ever is" was her doctor's glum assessment of her condition on release.[30]

Marion was getting over this crisis when another sort of jolt arrived from Oregon, where Mark had become extremely interested in a girl named Jennifer Chapin. Late in August, while Marion was hopelessly tied up with the manuscript and her first response to the Richardson editing plan, they suddenly announced their intention to get married and drove off on August 26 to the nearby elopers' paradise of Stevenson, Washington, with just a handful of friends and Chapin relatives in attendance.

Wearily and warily returning to the *Joy* imbroglio, Marion saw it swiftly blow up to proportions undreamed of during the 1949–50 standoff over the "New Joy." The problem was, as the Beckers saw it, editorial incompetence on an officially sanctioned rampage—a contingency not remotely addressed in the previous contract.

Under ideal conditions the manuscript would have progressed through a certain number of stages in good order before emerging as a finished volume on the bookstore shelves. For one thing, it would have been completely submitted before anyone tried to do anything more with it, and the publisher would have refused to accept it in any form that could not be directly prepared—as one consecutive text, from beginning to end—for production. It would have been carefully copy-edited, and Marion would have examined the resulting text in its entirety. Bobbs-Merrill would meanwhile have made accurate space estimates based on the submitted manuscript, not guesswork by an author who was really talking at cross-purposes with their people. The manuscript would next have been set in type as "galley proofs," which at that time were formidable sheets of consecutively set text two or three times the length of a regular page. (Modern reproduction technology has since enabled publishers to do the first setting in something close to the size of the finished volume.)

Author and editors alike would have proofread the galleys and discussed any necessary changes, which would have been only a minor problem at that stage unless they were really frequent and drastic. Everything would then have gone on to the far more expensive and irrevocable stage of "page proofs," where the copy is broken into blocks of type corresponding to the final pages, with page numbers and running heads. Ideally nothing much should have been left to fix by this stage; corrections in page proofs can be horrendously expensive, especially if they mean altering page breaks and then having to renumber everything that comes afterward. Had the copy been adequately handled before it reached page proofs, it would have been ready to roll off the presses with little more ado.

This scenario is some distance from what actually happened. In the first place, Marion had originally thought that she could turn most of the card manuscript over to Miller by the end of July of 1961 and finish the rest shortly thereafter, but her estimate was wildly optimistic. Not entirely through her own fault, she took until March of 1962 to submit all the major portions of the text, and even then gaps remained to be filled. At all stages of the tragicomedy, everyone was working with different chunks of a ragged and incomplete manuscript.

Marion began to object to the handling of her text almost at once and probably would have had a knockdown fight with Miller before the end of 1961 if not for two catastrophes that forced the furious president to abandon his plan of spring publication at all costs: late in

November Marion broke a leg and only about a week later Monroe Stearns, the managing editor, joined the growing parade of Bobbs-Merrill refugees looking for work elsewhere. When everyone had partly recovered from these setbacks, the demented Keystone Kops routine that had begun to establish itself after Miss Richardson's arrival took over in full force.

The pattern was roughly as follows: Alice Richardson would receive certain chapters of Marion's index-card manuscript, go over them to arrange the text to her own satisfaction, have the results typed, and send the new version back to Marion, who would be laboring frantically on some other section. Marion would at once discover that the editor had introduced dozens or perhaps hundreds of unwarranted changes, many of them pure errors. She would drop whatever she had been working on and set to work restoring the text to its first state with the help of the original cards when she could pry them loose from Miss Richardson and the barely readable Verifax copies when she couldn't. Hughes Miller would demand to know what the delay was—publication was now officially set for July—and Marion would complain about his hireling's mistakes. Meanwhile, some previously disputed batch of copy would be making its way into galley proofs, carefully re-restored to the Richardson rather than Becker version.

Such was the state of affairs when the new managing editor and later editor in chief, William Raney, was dispatched to Cincinnati on March 18 to cope with the latest Becker insurrection. (John and Marion had now decided to call in both Harriet Pilpel and their local lawyer, James L. Magrish.) Raney, a highly respected publishing veteran best known in book circles for having edited Norman Mailer's *The Naked and the Dead* at Rinehart and Company, listened to the desperate author with alert attention. Marion thought she had acquired an ally. He professed himself horrified at what the Beckers showed him: the first galleys, with all the Richardson mistakes that they had erased reinstated and a number of *new* mistakes added. The cues Marion had inserted in the original text to indicate the placement of illustrations had in many places been completely removed or misplaced. The disaster was all the worse because since the previous fall Miller had imperiously been telling Marion that any mistakes she might be inclined to bellyache over in the Richardson typescript could be fixed up at the galley-proof stage; now the galleys themselves looked so awful that Marion did not see how she and Bobbs-Merrill could go on to page proofs.

Raney announced that he deplored this mess as much as the Beckers and would go back to try to argue their case with the truculent Miller, who all along had blamed every difficulty on Marion's intransigence rather than the bizarre handling of the copy to which he had committed Bobbs-Merrill. He also promised that no unauthorized editorial tampering would be permitted with the remaining parts of Marion's card manuscript.[31] The Beckers thought that Alice Richardson had as good as been given her walking papers.

But Raney was in a situation of which Marion knew nothing. Eventually she learned to distrust him, but she never had a chance to confirm the dismaying picture revealed by a handful of papers that turned up years later as exhibits in an unrelated legal action commenced by Mazie Hartrich: Miller had ordered Raney to lie to the Beckers, systematically and repeatedly, about the actual handling of the manuscript by Alice Richardson, who was still editing and re-editing the copy with the president's blessing. Raney, wretchedly protesting that he foresaw nothing but disaster from this course, nonetheless did as he was told.[32]

Of course Miller was in an awful bind. His presidency was on the line. After two and a half years of his blustering presence, it was not clear to observers in the publishing trade whether Bobbs-Merrill was actually making money—the company, after changing hands in 1958 for the sum of $1 million, representing more than half its stock, was now in the middle of a five-year plan that was supposed to boost projected sales volume to $12.5 million—or just losing it on a bigger scale. He had expected that by now Bobbs-Merrill's new $2.5 million manufacturing plant in Indianapolis (a state-of-the-art showpiece of the Sams-Miller regime, supposedly to be justified by success stories like the new *Joy of Cooking*)[33] would have finished a mammoth first printing. He had had to postpone this along with a blockbuster spring sales campaign for *Joy*, much to the disgust of the salesmen under Bill Finneran (who later summed up his opinion of Marion with an angry "Becker was a son of a bitch").[34] The rest of the Bobbs-Merrill spring season had been woeful, since the trade list had been cut to nearly half its ordinary size in order to free up press time and sales efforts. Vast orders of paper and binding materials had had to be rejuggled. Miller simply could not permit the same thing to happen all over again in July. He was ready not only to take any shortcut necessary for getting books to ship but to make up the pages out of the telephone book if he couldn't get them from the dreadful Mrs. Becker.

Marion thought she had carried her point. Raney, who was not about to disabuse her, had given her permission to recruit more people to help read the vast amounts of galley proof that were coming in. She promptly hired Jane Brueggeman and Dorothy Wartenberg to spell her and John in the close reading for sense and consistency, with a few other readers coming in at intervals for the less skilled work. Jim Gregory, though much occupied with his forthcoming wedding and a planned move to New England, agreed to spend several days a week going over the text for culinary accuracy; having helped shape the course of Marion's thinking from the beginning of the project, he was the person she most trusted to judge the fitness of the whole. She was convinced that Bobbs-Merrill had been remiss in not hiring someone with a sound knowledge of cooking to do what she now asked Gregory to do (and added this to the list of general grievances she had built up against the Miller regime).

Matters thus proceeded fairly quietly for about seven weeks in March and April, with Alice Richardson busy editing the remaining copy, by Miller's instruction, for $1,000 a month, while the Beckers continued under the impression that she had been dismissed. This peculiar idyll was shattered when the Indianapolis production office finally saw enough of the text in consecutive form to understand the gigantic mistake made in the summer of 1961, when Marion and Bobbs-Merrill had last discussed the length of the book. What the production people had planned and bought paper for was 832 pages by the new layout specifications as they understood them. The actual manuscript, now that everyone could see it in most of its entirety (minus a few still-to-be-submitted scraps and patches), was clearly headed beyond the 1,000-page mark by the same methods of estimation.

Bobbs-Merrill now embarked on at least internal discussions of a course of action far surpassing any chicanery of which the Rombauers had ever accused Laurance Chambers. No memo survives to indicate just when Hughes Miller conceived his next design, but it must have been quite soon. Speed was of the essence; the July publication date had now collapsed in ashes, but it might be possible to salvage things in time for the fall season by a simple plan: if Marion raised any more obstacles, Miller would take the existing copy, no matter what shape it was in, and print it without her knowledge or consent. This stratagem, for obvious reasons, was never made plain to all of the Bobbs-Merrill staff or executive higher-ups. Howard Sams was in the know. So was Bill Finneran, impatiently waiting to fulfill deferred sales commitments and delighted to do an end run around Marion. The likeliest explanation of Bill Raney's conduct is that he went along with the scheme in mounting dismay, hoping against hope that matters would not come to the worst. He did, however, contrive to leave a paper trail of in-house memos recording the duplicity in which he had been forced to collude, and by pure luck two of them made their way long after his death to the Hartrich legal file in St. Louis.[35]

When the production office had absorbed the enormity of the discrepancy in length, Raney wrote to Marion early in May to break the news that more than two hundred pages would have to be cut at once. He knew that the only hope of averting some horrendous action on the part of Miller was to get straight down to the task. The simplest thing was to cut whole recipes. Raney (though he had overseen an edition of *The Good Housekeeping Cook Book* at Rinehart) did not know enough about cooking to pick the most expendable ones, but he tried to convince Marion that between them they could accomplish a lot.[36]

Perhaps her alert antennae sensed the fact that Raney was lying about something, without understanding just what. In any case, Marion first hesitated to cooperate with him, trying to persuade him to talk over the problem with Cecily Brownstone in the naive hope that possibly this expert could abolish mathematical fact, and then convinced herself that the horrible-sounding space estimates were nothing but a piece of gross incompetence on the part of Bobbs-Merrill. (She must have remembered another last-minute space emergency in 1951 that had turned out to be mostly imaginary.) While she was trying to sort out the truth of the alleged overrun, she received stronger corroboration that something was terribly fishy in the company's handling of the copy. The supposedly corrected version of the originally disputed galley proofs began to arrive in Cincinnati, further marked up to remove Marion's intentions *for the third time* and restore mistakes that in some cases dated back to the first stages of the Richardson typescript. There was an excellent reason—or rather, a very bad one—for this: Miller had instructed Raney that in Raney's own words, "Alice Richardson is to edit the Beckers' edited galleys, but the Beckers are not to know about this."[37]

The handling of the artwork meanwhile appeared more and more out of control. Long before, the company had lost all of Ginnie Hofmann's original drawings used in the 1951 edition. As a result, she had been commissioned to redo those of the old illustrations that for some reason couldn't be effectively reproduced from the older edition or that needed changes, while several dozen more illustrations were to be supplied by an artist with a similar but blockier style, Beverly Warner. Marion had carefully indicated where all drawings were to be placed when they came in. Not only had many of her cues disappeared, but on surveying the latest chunks of galley proof she could not ascertain whether anyone in Indianapolis or New York was keeping track of placement or printing specifications. Of the available photostats that she had tried to paste up next to the relevant portions of the text, some were unaccountably missing. In addition, whole recipes seemed to have vanished without explanation.

On June 15 Raney flew out to Cincinnati to announce that the number of pages Marion would have to cut was now estimated at close to *three* hundred. She showed him the galleys.

"It will be a miracle if this book is ever published," said the wretched man. He used to return from his Cincinnati visits in an agony of spirit that some of the Bobbs-Merrill staff attributed to the Tartar-like disposition of Mrs. Becker. In fact, the strain of deception told on him more and more. In sheer desperation he gave Marion, John, and Jane a dark hint of Miller's plan to take matters into his own hands and warned them that he would deny it on a stack of Bibles if it ever came out.[38]

From this moment on, the whole affair slid into utter chaos. Rather than taking Raney's gesture of candor as an invitation to cooperate on getting the text into mutually acceptable form before Miller seized some surreptitious initiative, Marion made up her mind that whatever the company said about space was simply untrue. While Raney, returning to his double game, sought to discuss the length of the manuscript and the condition of the galleys in a businesslike and friendly tone, Marion dug in her heels and struck back doughtily at every move of his. Throughout the next six weeks she demanded that Bobbs-Merrill review its figures and acknowledge its error on the space issue. Blind to the possibility that the error might be hers, she refused to participate in further work on the galleys until the company backed down.

The summer of 1962 went by in a crazed succession of crises, with Marion's attention frantically divided between sequential *Joy of Cooking* catastrophes and the situation in St. Louis, where Irma continued her snail's crawl toward death. Just how angrily overwrought Marion was during this reign of malign disarray can be gathered from the episode of Irma's "conversion."

One morning at the end of May Elsa Hunstein went to see Irma, who began conversing fairly lucidly but unexpectedly veered off to start talking about getting married to someone, a Catholic. Connecting this notion with a recent visit by the devout Mazie Hartrich and another recent remark of Irma's about needing to be converted and baptized, Elsa wondered whether Mazie had been seeking to bring her into the church.[39] Marion, already wound up to an extreme emotional pitch over the nightmare of the galleys, promptly took this suggestion at face value and started a terrible quarrel over Mazie's supposed attempt to take advantage of Irma in her present infirmity.

Mazie replied with great dignity and good sense, denying that she had ever done anything but try to decipher one of Irma's more obscure meanderings that seemed to contain a religious allusion, and pointing out that Irma could not just "be dragged unwillingly into the Church. She couldn't be accepted as a member without a great deal of instruction to make sure that she had a very clear understanding of all its dogmas and a firm belief in everything the Church teaches. . . . I have as much respect for another's religion as you have."[40]

Marion calmed down enough to offer an apology of sorts, and the quarrel was patched over with an exchange of friendly notes. Yet what Marion retained in the Cockaigne files was not Mazie's explanation but her own letter of accusation. More than ten years later, in a court deposition, she was still hinting darkly at this personal grievance.[41]

Her judgment cannot have been improved by the dreadful state of Irma (who had been hospitalized with acute bronchopneumonia in April and seesawed more and more pitifully between semiclarity and wandering) and the continuing Bobbs-Merrill imbroglio. At the time of the conversion scare the company, which had decided to brazen out some of the promotional commitments made when Miller really expected the new version to hit the stores in or before July, had gotten up a twenty-four-page brochure with recipes from the book, to be handed out at a *"Joy of Cooking* Week" celebration at the J. L. Hudson's department store in Detroit.

Harriet Pilpel and her colleagues were furious over this uncompensated use of their client's work in progress. Marion was outraged at the fact that Hudson's had arranged the affair as a tie-in with the Farberware cookware company and actually advertised it as "Our 'Joy of

Cooking with Farberware' Week," a highly improper suggestion of some concrete relationship between Farberware and the book. But what rankled most was that some hundred *Joy of Cooking* recipes had been demonstrated in the store between June 3 and 9 by none other than Alice Richardson, shamelessly billed as "editor of The Joy of Cooking."[42]

The Beckers were getting ready to raise a ruckus about the Hudson's promotion when an embarrassingly similar contretemps occurred with one of their own team. Jim Gregory had celebrated his wedding (at the Beckers') and gone off to a restaurant in western Massachusetts, where he had lined up a summer job for the eighteen-year-old Ethan. It turned out that Gregory's employer, Cane Ridge Gallery, had put out a flyer proudly identifying him as "co-author of *The Joy of Cooking.*" This was far worse than any claim in the Hudson's business, though Gregory himself did not seem to have been the culprit. (He later attributed the embroidery to an overzealous publicist.)[43]

With some difficulty, the lawyers got Cane Ridge to retract the claim. But the Beckers felt that they had laid themselves open to exploitation from a quarter they had had faith in. They were distressed enough to think that Ethan had better come home, though he could only hope to straggle sadly through the summer in a houseful of angry, distracted people. Mark and Jennifer came to the rescue, suggesting that he fly out to Oregon and have a few months with them. The Becker-Gregory relationship never returned to its first state of confidence.

It was against this background that Marion confronted the Bobbs-Merrill plea for drastic cutting of the text. Had she been less harassed on all fronts, she might have been able to admit that Raney had some reason on his side, or to take in the implications of what he had briefly let slip about the president's inner counsels. As it was, she would not listen either to what he said or to the signals he was trying to send through the battle smoke to let her know that this was the last possible moment for them to cooperate before being overtaken by force majeure. In righteous hauteur she got Harriet Pilpel to insist that the 297-page cutting estimate was "in gross error."[44] She hired a compositor in Cincinnati to make her own official space estimate based on an exceedingly complex set of assumptions and fired off peremptory missives to Raney full of simplistic assertions about the original space allotment, convoluted arguments about the consequences of the new page format, and claims that it was all Bobbs-Merrill's own fault anyhow for not having made a proper space study in the first place.

The company, which according to Raney had "eight carloads of paper" on hand at the Indianapolis warehouse and urgently needed to schedule "some 350 hours of presstime" in "one continuous run" in order to proceed from the hopelessly mangled galley proofs to page proofs and the final printing, waited in mounting anger and desperation.[45] At last the Becker and Bobbs-Merrill lawyers between them managed to pry loose from the production office some relevant data about the basis for Bobbs-Merrill's space calculations. After a look at these figures in late July, Marion unbent enough to try to bargain for 896 pages, which she thought she could manage through drastic cutting. This proposal was useless for the simple reason that the 150,000 hardback bindings sitting in the warehouse had been ordered with an 832-page length in mind.

Probably Marion's discussions with Raney had become wholly irrelevant to Miller's true plans by or not long after the first week of August, when the Beckers agreed to a conference in New York. It consisted of one of Miller's well-known yelling fits, followed on the next day by a constructive-sounding debate on cutting options led by Raney in the "good cop" role.[46] Judging by later events, their joint performance may well have been a charade, since Marion had held things up too long to permit any orthodox preparations for a fall release date. The Beckers, of course, had no way of judging the good or bad faith of anything said to them. It appeared that Miller might be willing to give them 864 pages if thinner paper could be substituted for part of the job, and this might be justification for tentatively cooperating on some part of the immense cutting task that apparently remained ahead of them. With some hesitation they decided to proceed with the cutting and correcting. Harriet Pilpel and the Bobbs-Merrill lawyer in New York, Paul Gitlin, began discussing page space with the zeal of veteran production editors. John and Marion went back to Cincinnati to tackle the galleys in earnest, and at once the dreaded message came from St. Louis.

Irma had suffered a series of "Jacksonian seizures," a type of localized convulsion that probably signified advanced hardening of the arteries shutting down some areas of brain function. She was admitted to St. Luke's Hospital on August 10. The condition did not seem life-threatening; the seizures were easily controlled with phenobarbital.

But no sooner had Irma been discharged than a graver danger developed. In a week she was back in the hospital with a high fever from some infection in her long-paralyzed left leg. It was gangrene. A heartbeat irregularity also secondary to failing brain function had discharged a clot into an artery.[47]

Marion and Put (to whom she talked in Seattle) could not think of putting a frail eighty-four-year-old woman through the torture of an operation. But the hospital juggernaut had foreclosed their options. Before Marion could reach any of the high-powered doctors among the Starkloff connections and ask them to intervene, the leg had been frozen to stop the spread of sepsis; there was no choice but to amputate it. Irma's fever had at one point gone as high as 110°, and as Marion wrote to Mazie Hartrich, "it is hard to know what if anything is left of her mind."[48]

Pleased with the results of the operation, the doctors at first told the family that Irma could go home in a couple of weeks. But the wound became infected and failed to heal. It took another month of treatment to bring the condition under control. During that time Irma, heavily drugged to dull the pain and prevent any agitated outbreaks, apparently never regained enough awareness to understand that the leg was missing—or so the agonized daughter hoped. Marion thought that Irma knew her and John, but it was hard to be sure. She had deteriorated so badly in the course of the infection that now there was no thought of her going home. With Elsa Hunstein and Laura Corbitt, Marion arranged to have her transferred by ambulance to the Barnard Nursing Home on September 29. The doctors now feared an embolism in the other leg.

Put, her lifelong joy and torment, had been told that there was no point in coming, since his mother would no longer be able to recognize him. He flew in from Seattle nonetheless, and when he stood by Irma's bedside, she clasped his hand in a steadfast grip and did not let go of it for forty-five minutes.[49] With John and Marion, he went through the bleak task of breaking up her Lindell Boulevard apartment, in which she had hardly spent a day as anything but an unwilling invalid. There was little Marion could tell friends and well-wishers except that Irma did not seem to be suffering.

Marion could not stay on hand to deal with the crisis, but had to shuttle back and forth between St. Louis and Cincinnati to try to keep abreast of the bewildering course of Bobbs-Merrill machinations in the latest phase of the *Joy* disaster. She had been proceeding on the dubious assumption that the company needed the cut and corrected galleys, but now the Becker party scented some change—and not for the better. There were hints of a strange vacuum on the other side of the hitherto high-pressure argument. An unnatural silence seemed to have fallen over the higher realms at Bobbs-Merrill. It could not presage anything good, but Harriet Pilpel had a new stratagem in mind that Marion was struggling to comply with.

Mrs. Pilpel's idea, a countercharade to whatever was going on in Miller's camp, rested on the fact that Bobbs-Merrill had let the previous edition go out of print. This had happened by accident rather than design, since the company had expected to be printing the new version six months ago. But by a strict construction of the last contract all rights were to revert to Irma and Marion if, on written notification from them after the last version should go out of print, the publishers failed to issue a new edition within thirty days.[50] Mrs. Pilpel planned to invoke this clause by presenting Paul Gitlin, her Bobbs-Merrill counterpart, with a version of the corrected galleys cut to correspond to the 864-page length that Miller had indicated he might accept, telling him that this was an official submission of the manuscript, and announcing that the thirty-day clock was now ticking.

Between hectic visits to Irma's bedside in St. Louis Marion and John, together with Jane Brueggeman, managed to get the horribly jumbled galleys into shape to do duty as the "manuscript." On September 17 one of the Greenbaum, Wolff & Ernst lawyers appeared at Gitlin's office with this document and the official notice of submission.[51] It was a mere feint, but it might afford them a chance to study the opponent's feints. The Becker party guessed that Miller's intrigues had gone on to a new phase, a surmise bolstered by a *Publishers Weekly* article reporting that advance sales already (as of September 24) amounted to 95,503 copies and that Bobbs-Merrill expected to ship finished books "at the end of September."[52] It was physically impossible that the messy affair submitted on September 17 could have been transformed into bound books by then. Either *Publishers Weekly* was completely at sea on the real date or a version of *The Joy of Cooking* had materialized without the knowledge of Marion, the author.

If villainy was afoot, there was nothing she could do about it now. The official Becker position as stated by her lawyers was that the complete manuscript had been legally submitted and must now be acted on by Bobbs-Merrill. Marion could only wait to hear Miller's reaction to the latest ploy.

Meanwhile, the shock of what was happening to her mother penetrated Marion's thoughts more devastatingly than ever as at last she found a certain leisure for reflection. The hospital vigils and the ordeal of breaking up Irma's apartment had filled her with a flood of memories—memories that seemed to be some sort of urgent personal responsibility now that Irma was resigning her part in them. As always during moments of intense feeling, Marion terribly wanted to sit down and release on paper a store of remembrance that was beyond words—"some sort of résumé, an accounting," as she put it. Once more she wished that Irma could have written her story herself. Marion had no time, however, for anything more than an undated one-page outpouring of pity and grief for the "wispy, frightened frustrated and confused" creature that had been Irma Rombauer.[53] On Sunday, October 14, she went out to spend a day with friends in the country, and came back that evening to a phone call from Elsa, who had been trying to reach her all day. Irma had died that morning in the nursing home. It was the sixty-third anniversary of her marriage to Edgar Rombauer.

Marion flew the next day to St. Louis. Hughes Miller's telegram of "my personal as well as company condolences" arrived at Cockaigne some hours later.[54] With Elsa and Laura Corbitt, she arranged for a private cremation, burial of the remains in handsome and august Bellefontaine Cemetery, and a memorial service at the First Unitarian Church on Wednesday. The minister, the Reverend Thaddeus Clark, had not known Mrs. Rombauer in her days of health, and people who knew the family thought that his summing-up had been rather stringently dictated by Marion. In any case, it went to the heart of the matter as Marion saw it, Irma's relationship with *Joy of Cooking* readers and the sense in which even a cookbook can be seen as a microcosm of human striving:

> Irma Rombauer touched and transformed many whom she had never seen nor met. She made one of the ordinary and daily necessities of life into something more than ordinary. She gave many persons, often subdued by drudgery and dullness, a vision of the manner in which the ordinary could be transformed into an act of beauty and an achievement for the human spirit. . . . Suddenly one was in her presence and felt the personality that came through the pages, and his life was transformed, or if not something so exalted, it was lifted up one level higher.

. . . Our genius, if ultimately we reveal that we have something to contribute to the ongoing of mankind, will be revealed in the manner in which we deal with the practical, the common sense, the necessary, and the ordinary materials of daily life. Irma Rombauer has very possibly made more of a contribution to this stream of our history than we know.[55]

They returned from the church to Laura Corbitt's home. There Marion was greeting the mourners when a woman came up to her and sociably announced, "Your book is in the store."[56] At once she sent someone out to bring back a copy, and found herself staring at a brightly jacketed volume saying *Joy of Cooking* and bearing the names of Irma Rombauer and Marion Rombauer Becker—the fruit of a rush job carried out behind her back, to which Miller and Raney probably had committed themselves in August while she was occupied with her mother's illness.

For all the hints of sinister dealings that Marion had been receiving over the last four months, nothing could have prepared her to see the brazen proof at this moment. It was the culmination of every wrong or affront that Irma had endured at the hands of the hated company since Laurance Chambers did her out of the copyright; it was the worst piece of bullying that Hughes Miller had shoved down the Beckers' throats. In her first fury Marion could think of nothing but wiping her mother's and her own name—to say nothing of *The Joy of Cooking*'s—clean of a defiling mockery. She would have destroyed every copy if she could.

On the day of Marion's horrible discovery in St. Louis, Paul Gitlin as Bobbs-Merrill counsel in New York had a copy of the book formally delivered to Harriet Pilpel. She and Marion were not immediately able to confer at length, but she did receive Marion's authorization for a threatening telegram that she launched to Gitlin at once and that was confirmed in telegrams to Miller and Howard Sams the next day by James L. Magrish, the Beckers' lawyer in Cincinnati.[57] Mrs. Pilpel decided that the moment had come for the battle of battles: a motion to file for an injunction to stop the printing and distribution of the bastard *Joy*, and a suit for breach of contract and copyright infringement. Bobbs-Merrill of course planned to claim copyright (which was formally registered on October 20), but doing so without benefit of any prior agreement signed by the author was an awful risk on the firm's part. She thought that they had several kinds of good ammunition for at last recovering copyright, as Irma and Marion had impotently wished for twenty-seven years. The Beckers were as ready for all-out war as she. They started getting up a plan to call a press conference repudiating the unauthorized version before a battery of newspaper and television reporters, while asking readers across America to hang on to their old copies of *Joy* rather than purchase an imposture.

The press conference never took place, nor did any injunction or lawsuit ever materialize. Instead of an epic showdown, the shocks of October 17 heralded an amazing outbreak of peace. The war probably had been forestalled—though none of the parties could yet know it—by the end of October.

Exactly how the worst crisis of *Joy*'s history was converted into reconciliation is hardly recorded at all. The Becker files of the event are extremely fragmentary, and no record of Bobbs-Merrill's inner counsels is likely ever to see the light of day. But much can be pieced together from later events. Unmistakably, the executive higher-ups at Bobbs-Merrill were startled into a drastic reassessment of their president's conduct.

The fact is that Miller had *published a book without a contract*, an act of stunning recklessness that left the receipt of income from sales something like the receipt of a live bomb. In the absence of an understanding jointly ratified by author and publisher, the new copyright's status was more dubious than that of any predecessor. That the 150,000-copy first printing was sold out in a matter of weeks only underscored the degree of risk inherent in collecting moneys without a signed agreement for paying the author.

The Beckers cannot have guessed the degree of internal dissension at Bobbs-Merrill. But Miller had finally overreached himself there. At the original Indianapolis headquarters Laurance Chambers had maintained a cohesive editorial team with enough esprit de corps and local patriotism to back him up in spite of any private reservations. Miller, by contrast, had high-handedly broken up the old headquarters and cobbled together a far more uneven, accidental editorial force around himself in New York, leaving Indianapolis as the seat of the printing plant and the board of directors. These were not measures to consolidate his ties with all sectors of the organization, especially considering the great pother of acquisitions that had marked his tenure along with dizzying entrances and exits of personnel. Consequently Miller did not have deep reserves of corporate loyalty to back him up on the *Joy of Cooking* affair.

The Becker party was separately rethinking its position. Marion's rage at the subterfuge that she had discovered almost literally at the moment of her mother's death never wholly cooled, but within days or weeks of the double blow something seems to have at least provisionally shifted in her outlook. Though she would have loved nothing better than to let Harriet Pilpel wreak retaliation on the ungodly, she began paying attention to two trusted advisors who did not see things that way.

Jim Magrish seriously doubted Mrs. Pilpel's assessment of their chances in a lawsuit. Indeed, Marion's position was far from unassailable. One result of an injunction might be a suit by Miller alleging loss of revenue through her actions. Proceeding to trial on the basis of copyright infringement or breach of contract probably would have had the Becker lawyers constructing elaborate arguments involving the reversion-of-rights clause of the last contract and the supposed official "manuscript" submitted from the galleys in September, while the opponents sought to convince the jury that the company had almost completely met Marion's terms for preparing the new book and that nearly 100 percent of the words added to it were hers. But the argument of Magrish's that most struck home with Marion was that her crusade might be harming rather than defending the book's good name: "I fear that there will be lasting damage to the public image and reception of 'The Joy of Cooking,' if litigation occurs, especially at this time."[58]

This was exactly what Cecily Brownstone had thought when Marion tried to enlist her support for the Beckers' planned public denunciation of the unauthorized *Joy*. Mrs. Brownstone had never cared for Irma and Marion's eagerness to turn over *Joy* affairs to the adversarial skills of Greenbaum, Wolff & Ernst instead of getting themselves a seasoned literary agent who spoke the language of practical accommodation, not legal jousting. She now used every bit of conviction she could muster to insist that Marion was making a terrible mistake in dragging *The Joy of Cooking* into a public circus for the sake of some perceived holy right.[59]

Marion might not have been ready to listen to such opinions before the cataclysms of the summer and fall. But once she stood in the position of heir rather than partial custodian, some critical change occurred in her evaluation of moral showdowns versus continuing responsibilities. She now reacted to the advice of Magrish and Mrs.

Brownstone by pulling back from any more into-the-breach bravado—and for good. It is likely that her instinctive abhorrence of personal publicity had been awakened by the prospect of reporters nosing out human-interest angles in the story of the author-publisher fracas, "especially at this time"—a moment when the book might lastingly be stamped in the public mind with lurid associations coinciding with the testimonies to Irma Rombauer that were turning up in print everywhere. Keeping the story under wraps was really more in character for a woman as intensely private as Marion than marching up to make loud revelations before a battalion of cameras. That the whole sorry business hadn't gotten out was perhaps one silver lining to the strike that had shut down the New York newspapers that fall.

In the end, Marion swapped the hope of confounding her mother's and her enemies for the chance to bring *The Joy of Cooking* into the future unencumbered by soap-opera distractions in the media. Rightly or wrongly accepting Cecily Brownstone's argument that calling the world's attention to everything wrong with the present version would only harm *Joy* over the long run, she authorized Jim Magrish to look for other ways out.

Magrish quickly set out to explore means of averting litigation. He must have been a rare diplomat, for the famous Harriet Pilpel—who had been pleading with Marion to go ahead without delay—willingly agreed to let him try his hand at negotiating. Unknown to the Becker side, Bobbs-Merrill was glad of the chance to do likewise. The two sides were soon tentatively outlining guidelines for further discussion.

Hughes Miller was not at the forefront of the effort. His chief interest was still to forge ahead with the book as it was. He had offered Marion a carrot in the form of a check for $50,000, along with terms of which no one now seems sure except that she was to shut up and let later printings of the garbled text proceed.[60] "She'll throw it right back in your face," predicted Leo Gobin, vice president and general manager in Indianapolis. It scarcely needs saying that he was right. Gobin had formed some idea of her character in his years as Bobbs-Merrill treasurer, and he viewed the threat of a copyright-infringement suit as quite realistic.[61] Apparently Howard Sams and the board of directors were close enough to the same opinion to encourage Gobin and the firm's Indianapolis counsel, Harold Bredell, to take over a good part of the *Joy* negotiations from Miller and Gitlin.

The second printing had critical implications for both sides. Openly going ahead on it without Marion's consent might aggravate any injury that a court found to have been done to her in the first place. But she was inclined to countenance it because of an ardent hope that it could be used to get at least some corrections into print, which she thought virtually a moral necessity. This view is not hard to fathom when one looks at the book.

The new edition as she had seen it after her mother's funeral was exactly what the endeavor seems to have been at every production stage since Alice Richardson had gotten the first parts of her typescript into the company's hands: the product of desperate efforts by editors, copy editors, and proofreaders working at a frantic pace with no opportunity to view the text in its entirety and with Hughes Miller breathing down their necks. Throughout all phases of the work they obviously had been reduced to wild guesses informed by little or no cooking expertise. Bill Raney could perhaps have salvaged a decent version from the wreckage with Marion's cooperation, but all hope of that had vanished when Miller decided to go ahead without her.

The first mistake occurred in the key to Marion's symbols printed on the endpapers. Here the parentheses ( ), meant exclusively to mark optional ingredients, had unaccountably become a circle ○. By the foreword this had turned into a solid circle ●. The text was strewn with minor typos like "Is is" for "It is" and major obstacles to understanding like "Roll into stacks" for "Roll into sticks" in a gnocchi recipe.[62] "The preceding description" (of the Chinese stir-frying method for vegetables) had become "the following description," though no description followed.[63] Scores of cross-references gave wrong page numbers or referred to wrongly titled or nonexistent recipes, some probably victims of the summer's cutting frenzy. The goose confit recipe directed you to the suggested accompaniment of "Home Fried Potatoes, page 299," which turned out to be a complete dead end.[64] Someone had confused baked meringues with meringue topping for pies, mistakenly pointing readers to the latter as a vehicle for "Angel Pie" (a custard filling in a meringue shell) or chocolate ice cream.[65] Then there was the menu section, which had simply been picked up from the 1951 book despite the fact that many of the recipes mentioned there had been dropped from the new edition. Bobbs-Merrill had adroitly solved that problem by omitting page references for all the missing dishes.

Recipes had been mangled throughout in a variety of ways, from pasting together fragments of two curry-sauce variants as one recipe to breaking off the Dutch-Indonesian rijsttafel without having got to the rice for which the dish is named.[66] The beginning of a recipe for broiled spring chicken had been transposed to the end.[67] The last part of "Sour Cream Rolls" was missing, though a mind reader could have discovered it tacked onto the ending of "Overnight Rolls."[68] "Quick Seafood Tureen" concluded not with the simple serving suggestion "Buttered Toast or French Toast" but with a mishmash of eight ingredients that had somehow wandered over from *three separate lists* in a discussion of soup garnishes on the next page.[69] Two quite separate recipes for *ossi bucchi*—one misspelled "*bucci*"—appeared with no explanation thirty pages apart, each telling you to add "gremolata" without translating or cross-referencing the term, which was not explained anywhere in the book.[70]

Mauled foreign terms were everywhere. "Pâte" (dough, paste, pastry) and "pâté" were unimaginably mixed up, as were "glace" (ice, ice cream, glaze) and "glacé" (the past participle meaning glazed, iced, or frozen). *Truite au Bleu* was "Trout au Beu."[71] The section on dessert cheeses contained three misspellings in as many languages ("Coulomniers," "Gemmelost," "Provelone").[72]

As Marion had foreseen, her wishes about the placement of illustrations had gone by the board much of the time. A drawing meant to suggest some uses of choux paste appeared without explanation at the end of the puff-paste illustration sequence.[73] The instructions for making an omelet had you shaking a skillet and swirling a fork in the direction of arrows that someone had managed to omit from the accompanying sketch.[74] Her set of symbols had also shared in the general disarray, particularly the convention for the use of parentheses, which had been honored when anybody remembered it and ignored the rest of the time.

All other failures had been as it were distilled and perfected in the index, which had been the final task in Bobbs-Merrill's surreptitious last-minute scramble. It had been printed annoyingly small, with no typographical distinctions to help a reader sort out kinds of entries or go straight to major headings. In fact, it was harder to read than the 1951 index that Marion and Irma had insisted on replacing. Wrong page numbers abounded; at moments alphabetical order disappeared. The *M*'s ended not with "Mutton" but with "Mantua, Sauce" (a mistake for "Nantua"). "Chopper" (which was supposed to be "Copper") was between "Cookouts" and "Coq au Vin." "Saffron" appeared as "saffrow," "brioche" as "briochi"; the Hungarian stew called "pörkölt" was indented under the heading "Pork." The luckless rijsttafel had been further tortured into "Rysttafel Table."

The dreadful quality of the false *Joy* paradoxically had the effect of making Marion more desperately eager to get some halfway decent alternative in print. Reports of spectacular sales and good initial reviews only made her bitterly ponder how easy it is to puff a cookbook without evaluating its long-term reliability. She believed that every copy in the hands of an unsuspecting buyer represented a threat over time to the twenty-six-year-old national reputation of her mother's durable monument. In the first heat of the expected battle she and John had set to work listing all identifiable errors—it was something like counting locusts in a Scriptural plague—in order to document their claim that the current edition was damaging to the reputation of the work and its authors. The sheer scope of garbling that they uncovered helped shift her goal from issuing a true version containing what she had written in the first place to rushing an acceptable fix-up into production.

It seems fair to say that by the end of October each side had scared itself into a more prudent course. With Magrish negotiating for the Beckers, the company agreed on November 8 to put a few corrections in the second printing, and Marion undertook to provide them.[75] It was a legally significant concession for her, because—even though nobody was yet ready to move to a contract—she was implicitly approving publication of the bad text in almost its original badness. The company agreed to limit the second printing to 50,000 copies, thus minimizing the damage that could be done by the hundreds of remaining errors.[76] Bobbs-Merrill also indicated a willingness to work out some sort of deferred-royalty arrangement that would partly defuse its receipt of income possibly involving infringement. (The author, of course, could not now consent to receive a cent on the disputed book without compromising any claim that it was illegitimate.) But though Marion had already spent a lot of her own money on the revision effort, she was less concerned with getting paid than with what she regarded as a great point won: Bobbs-Merrill would discuss how to get "further changes and corrections" into the book.[77]

Though everyone's representations thus far had been "without prejudice," meaning that each side was still reserving the option to bring an action at any time, Marion now poured everything into the task of revamping the text for a third printing. (The second appeared early in

December.) It was not a long process, for the list of mistakes was ready to go and for the first time in more than a year she was able to work without emergencies in St. Louis or angry threats at Bobbs-Merrill headquarters. Marion had also consented to restrictions that shortened her task. She had agreed to use the existing book (in the barely modified second printing) as her model, limiting herself to the same total length of 864 pages and also making most individual chapters conform to the number of pages they took up in the bad edition.[78] It was a tremendous sacrifice of her original objective. But in the interest of getting the hated 1962 version behind them all as soon as possible, she resigned herself to never seeing the book in print in the form she had originally envisioned.

Throughout November and part of December Marion and John worked through the text of the second printing at great speed, transcribing corrections and ruthlessly ignoring pieces of the original that they might otherwise have fought to save. Marion also pasted up a "dummy"—i.e., a schematic model, with specifications, showing the layout of each page—of the entire book. This was necessary to undo the botched placement and sizing of the illustrations. The index was a separate matter, unsalvageable as it stood. They meant to lengthen it by about a third (cutting as necessary elsewhere to save on the page total) and completely redesign it both typographically and in the degree of cross-referencing. Jane Brueggeman compiled the actual listings and worked with her to restore it to at least the usefulness of the previous index as finally thrashed out in 1953.

When Marion had finished, it was obvious that despite her agreement to make no unnecessary changes, what Bobbs-Merrill had on its hands was not a third printing but a complete resetting job. There was virtually no page whose layout remained intact. Marion seriously doubted that the company would accept the new version. Her fears were confirmed when she once more started trying to deal with Raney as editor. At once she began to sense hedgings and evasions about just what changes Miller would agree to. She came away from a meeting with Raney on December 28 miserably convinced that "we are again dealing with people who can't be trusted and even if Raney really wants the book to be right he will knuckle under to Miller or whoever wants him to at BM," and looking ahead to worse battles in 1963.[79]

It was a good guess. Nothing would change the president's mind on the uselessness of trying to please the Beckers. But if Marion's tremendous cutting and rewriting job was too much for Miller to consider printing, Miller himself had now become too much for some at Bobbs-Merrill to stomach. A final internal convulsion was going on at the company even as she despaired of making anyone there see reason. With the suddenness of a fairy tale the Beckers found everything turned around for themselves and *The Joy of Cooking.*

On January 22 Howard Sams announced, without further particulars, that Hughes Miller had resigned as Bobbs-Merrill president. The *Publishers Weekly* squib on the event some three weeks later gave the date of his resignation as January 1. Leo Gobin was named to the new position of executive vice president. Once more Sams himself agreed to serve as interim president. This time nothing was said about talent searches.[80]

The old order, as far as the dazed Beckers were concerned, was gone. Its passing had been conclusively marked on January 12, when Laurance Chambers died (on his eighty-fourth birthday) at his home in Indianapolis, having outlived his old enemy by not quite three months. Bobbs-Merrill would never again be ruled by an editor of such stature. But the gods began to smile on *Joy of Cooking* affairs as never before.

Miller had hardly finished moving out of his office when Bobbs-Merrill let the Beckers know that the newest version submitted by Marion was going to be published with all deliberate speed, no matter what the cost. "I suppose that after a meeting such as the Beckers, you and I attended in Indianapolis yesterday, we can ask whether we are dreaming," Jim Magrish wrote to Harriet Pilpel on February 13. Apparently the company had agreed to junk the plates of the old text, assume the full cost of resetting the book from beginning to end to accomplish Marion's changes, and throw in some particular compensation to her as well.[81]

The contract could not be drawn up on the spot, for there was a good deal of legal fallout from Irma's death that would involve complicated representations on Marion's part to address a whole new set of copyright issues (see pages 347–348). But the negotiations proceeded with an air of courtesy and rationality quite outlandish by historic *Joy of Cooking* standards. The decisive factor, aside from Jim Magrish's desire to seek pacific solutions, seems to have been the chemistry between Marion and the new de facto company head, Leo Gobin.

For some reason she liked and trusted Gobin at once. He in turn understood perfectly why she had staked so much on her radically altered version of her mother's success story; as he put it later, "She wanted to have something of importance. She wanted it to be something that was worthwhile, not just a shirttail revision."[82] Unlike many at Bobbs-Merrill, he unhesitatingly dealt with Marion Becker on her own merits, not just as a poor excuse for Irma Rombauer. In a businesslike, undemonstrative way, he was prepared to offer respect and cooperation in return for her tireless and intelligent hard work. In Gobin she would have a friend in power—no chum, but a reliable coworker—to the end of her life.

The amazing dream of having the company accede to her corrections at its own cost was no dream. On April 5 a new contract certifying that promise was signed and put into effect. Despite Bobbs-Merrill's about-face on the corrected edition, the agreement was in many respects a drastic giveaway on Marion's part. Indeed, she had already sacrificed her own interest to a degree explainable only by her passionate wish to retire the 1962 text from circulation at the earliest possible moment—and perhaps her fear of losing all claim to a work that she knew to be morally Irma's and hers. The saving grace was that the new company leadership rightly valued her great concessions and her sincere concern for the book, and was willing to behave in a certain spirit of mutual indebtedness for the shared aim of getting a reasonable text in print.

The most unpalatable pill in the contract was a provision requiring Marion to recognize the 1962 surreptitious rush job as a legitimate edition—effectually resigning any chance to use Miller's crass gamble as the occasion of any copyright-infringement or breach-of-contract suit in future.[83] No step since Irma's original surrender of the copyright had so conclusively shut the door on the authors' options in that direction. Harriet Pilpel did not endeavor to stop her. The lawyer did try to get Marion to hold out for some dramatic improvements in the royalty schedule, but she was content with the small gain that Magrish recommended accepting: 14 percent (as opposed to the prior 12½ percent) as the basic rate, the same 15 percent (Mrs. Pilpel had wanted 17½ percent) for the elusive top rate if manufacturing costs should fall to a seventh of the retail price. The percentage of sales at reduced royalty rates permitted on special discount arrangements remained at the vexing 32 percent that she and Irma had not been able to crack during the last war.[84] The royalties already accrued on the disputed edition and Marion's expenditure of time and money in producing a better one were dealt with through a $55,000 disbursement comprising $40,000 for royalties and $15,000 in consideration of her extraordinary efforts. In order to reduce her tax burden in future, royalty disbursements for any six-month period thereafter were to be limited to $25,000, any surplus being credited to a deferred account.[85] Future impasses, everyone hoped, might be avoided through a new clause in the contract requiring that author-publisher disputes be submitted to arbitration.[86]

It was not a particularly advantageous contract for Marion, but after the blowups of the previous October she was done with risky confrontations once and for all. As she had trusted, Leo Gobin was as good as his word on getting out the new edition at Bobbs-Merrill's own expense as soon as possible. The company decided to wait out any shortages or gaps in stock that might occur before the corrected book appeared rather than outrage Marion all over again with yet another reprinting of the disputed edition. In response to Marion's urgent pleading, a form letter was devised offering polite apologies and a free copy of the emended version to purchasers of the bad one who wrote in complaining about mistakes. Meanwhile, an efficient and unflappable Bobbs-Merrill/Becker liaison had materialized in Indianapolis: Bill Finneran's lieutenant Marian Israel (no relation to the Beckers' friend Marian Judell Israel), who began handling most of Marion's queries and messages on day-to-day *Joy of Cooking* affairs. Finneran was no fan of Marion's, but his assistant proved to be exactly the sort of composed, civil presence that had been wanting for many years.

The corrected *Joy* was copyrighted on August 31, without fanfare. The company was not about to bring this implicit admission of past failures to anyone's attention. Marion, mindful of Cecily Brownstone's appeal to keep the good name of the book paramount, refrained from saying anything publicly about the significance of the event. (In private, she could never hear of any new acquaintance owning the 1962 *Joy* without vehemently dissociating herself from it and promptly sending this victim of error a copy of the corrected book.) Food writers and cookbook reviewers—to say nothing of the general public—mostly remained unaware that the 1963 text was anything more than a slightly corrected reprint of the book published the previous fall.

Marion had now seen into print the serious and original contribution to American food writing that she had meant to make. She could not, under the circumstances, expect a chorus of praise across the land. But she knew that she had produced something well beyond the existing limits of the cookbook genre. In effect, she had created new expectations for the whole field of all-purpose kitchen manuals. While resolutely preserving the sturdy original German elements and making at least a game attempt to retain the spontaneous charm that was her mother's unique contribution, she had drawn in a range of new aims that stamped her presence on the book as honestly and lastingly as Irma had stamped her own. She had found a novel and challenging way to interweave concrete teaching through recipe formulas—at all levels from scrambled eggs to croquembouche—with enlightenment through painstaking descriptive forays into kinds of knowledge seldom found outside specialized manuals for food professionals.

In a summary of issues prepared (though not sent) the previous December when she was trying to impress on Bill Raney the need to publish her corrected version, she and John had set down some of the realizations that she had come to as she labored along through the many crises of the last seven years. This memo furnishes a key to the guiding ideas of her work. Dismissing any talk of favorable reviews proving that the company had after all known what it was doing, she had insisted that the true record of this edition's achievement would be read not in the present but in a long-term future dependent on "the impression it makes on the person who buys the book, and who uses it, page by page, day-in-day-out in the kitchen."[87]

As Jane Brueggeman once said of her old friend and employer, "She did nothing on the surface";[88] the qualities she had fought to get into the book were ones that she guessed would emerge for readers through years of use and would keep its reputation growing over a long period, not the features to ensure a quick splash. There was no doubt in her mind that *Joy*'s fitness for the long haul resided in its being "far more than a collection of recipes," "a book which, in addition, teaches the reader how to cook." Where her priorities lay is revealed in her offhand mention of the "seemingly casual and ingratiating style" in which this was accomplished (that "seemingly" sums up every reason that Marion Becker could never be Irma Rombauer) and the analogies that she reached for to get her point across: "More than with any other 'general' cookbook, 'The Joy' is basically, like a guide to contract bridge, or a manual on carpentry, a technical book."[89]

The struggle to translate her concept into reality had nearly cost her—and posthumously, Irma—everything. Probably Marion felt more than a glimmer of vindication when the only living person who knew her mother's *Joy of Cooking* as well as she herself did replied to a gift of a new (corrected) copy with a simple but significant acknowledgment. Mazie Hartrich wrote from St. Louis:

> The "Joy" has at last reached full maturity—its scope is tremendous.
>
> Since it came I've read it very carefully and find that it covers everything—a real encyclopedia of cooking. Many thanks for the autographed copy.
>
> How proud your mother would be of you if she could have lived to see this book![90]

PART IV

12

Little Acorn and *Wild Wealth*

The 1963 *Joy of Cooking* inaugurated a time of greater mutual respect than authors and publisher had ever known. Minor skirmishes never ceased, but with the death of Laurance Chambers and the sudden exit of Hughes Miller the real wars were over. In the April 1963 contract the reconciled parties not only arrived at mutually agreeable terms of payment but jointly applied themselves to wrapping up some legal consequences of Irma Rombauer's death.

Her will as probated on April 21, 1963, named Marion as the heir to the literary property. Marion also received the Jefferson County place and all of her mother's household belongings. The estate otherwise went to Put: some $112,000, mostly in stocks and securities.[1] At first he feared that he (through the estate) might be in for an awful tax burden. But Leo Gobin and the Bobbs-Merrill accounting department extended some cooperation to him in sifting through the relevant figures to establish that the actual tax liability was comparatively slight. Put was grateful for this timely assistance—but Bobbs-Merrill had reason to be helpful to Irma's heirs, for certain loose ends concerning copyright could not be tied up without them.

In legal fact Bobbs-Merrill's control of copyright for all *Joy of Cooking* editions was *assigned* rather than *original*. In every contract since 1935 the author or authors had "assigned and transferred" all rights to the publisher and explicitly agreed that Bobbs-Merrill might copyright the book in its own name. As the law then stood, every *Joy* copyright would expire twenty-eight years after its first registration. If not renewed *by the authors* for a further twenty-eight-year term, it would then fall into the public domain. A stipulation had therefore been written into all contracts that Irma (in 1950, Marion as well) should apply for renewal of any copyright before its first term expired, of course assigning the renewed copyright to Bobbs-Merrill. This had been done with the 1931 copyright in 1959.

But that did not exhaust the issue. The authors were considered to have a potential interest in all copyrights, and this interest was an inheritable asset that might conceivably be invoked in future by Put, Marion, and their spouses or children.

Bobbs-Merrill was thus eager to eliminate any imaginable uncertainties about the numerous *Joy* copyrights that it now held. Luckily for the firm, Marion had made up her mind not to rock the boat on copyright. In the 1963 contract and elsewhere, she consented to various measures intended to make the publisher's claim as watertight as possible. John, Mark, and Ethan all signed representations making over any putative interest of theirs to Bobbs-Merrill, and Marion agreed to use her "best efforts" to persuade Put to do likewise.

Both parties must have considered him potential trouble. But when after much nervous delay Marion—still viewing him as the family loose cannon—finally broached the delicate matter of copyright interest, Put promptly signed the necessary forms surrendering any claim and sent them back by return mail, generously observing that it was a matter of plain family justice to allow her to arrange *Joy* affairs as she saw fit.[2] Brother and sister, who had entertained very cool opinions of each other since Put's epic falling-out with Irma in 1945, now returned to a state of tolerable if not gushing friendship.

The latest *Joy of Cooking* now entered on a period of unprecedented triumph. The prior sales pattern—a natural one with any cookbook—had always been a steep increase on the release of a new edition, followed by a gradual decline in a few years. Instead, the new edition started climbing in popularity year by year. It was a stunning vindication of Marion's gamble in radically re-creating the beloved book. The Bobbs-Merrill sales tallies furnished to the Beckers showed 91,010 copies sold in 1962, 109,984 in 1963, 145,639 in 1964 (when a separate copyright was registered), and 209,603 in 1965. Only in 1952 had the previous version, the "New Joy," outsold the present one on an annual basis or even come close. In fact, sales would continue to increase yearly, almost without exception, until 1974, when the next edition was in preparation.[3]

Meanwhile, other lucrative possibilities were being examined. Inquiries sporadically came in about deals on subsidiary rights—instructional films based on materials from *Joy*, a large-type edition, translations into Spanish and Serbo-Croatian. None of these particular schemes was realized, but the field of possible spin-offs and foreign editions held obvious promise. The popularity of *Joy* was even reported to have produced pirated versions in the Far East, and a Taiwanese company was seeking Bobbs-Merrill's approval for a licensed photo-offset issue of the book as a countermeasure.

The magnitude of Marion's triumph had not been foreseen by anyone during the battle of the 1962 edition. It propelled John and Marion not only into a new tax bracket but into a new realm of decisions about the future of themselves, their children, and their golden egg.

John retired from his practice at Garriott and Becker in the mid-1960s, expecting to divide his time between helping Marion with the cookbook and writing projects of his own. He and Marion had sounded out the two boys about collaborating with them on *Joy* with a view to eventually taking over the book. But no clear hope had emerged there. Ethan, who possessed the Rombauer genes for resistance to usual forms of schooling, was still too young to be held to lasting promises. He had variously thought of bacteriological research—perhaps a legacy of the polio ordeal—or some sort of intelligence work; he might or might not eventually gravitate toward the particular discipline of *Joy*.

Mark's future was still more unsettled. He had been working at a marine biological research center in the Portland area, but the atmosphere would become strained when his parents tried to ascertain whether this was a permanent career. When first asked by them to consider coming in on *Joy* he brusquely turned down the idea. Marion had better luck with her new daughter-in-law, a slight, gentle girl who liked and admired the older woman without exactly being swept up in the same raptures as many of Marion's art and gardening friends. Jennifer at first went along with Mark's decision. But in the fall of 1963 she agreed to begin working on *The Joy of Cooking* on a one-year trial basis, from the young couple's new home near another branch of Mark's research laboratory at Depoe Bay on the Oregon coast.

Marion was radiant with hope. In her eyes *Joy* was not just a family business but a sort of sacred family altar. She began a voluble correspondence filled with mentions of helpful gift subscriptions and recipe-testing equipment, and was extremely pleased with Jennifer's conscientious evaluation of the current *Joy*'s strengths and weaknesses. But their collaboration ended before it had properly begun, with a terrifying phone call from the West Coast in March of 1964 apprising her and John that Mark was very ill. After what had seemed an initial period of energetic enterprise at the Depoe Bay site, something had gone wrong enough to be an obvious psychiatric emergency. Marion and John rushed to Oregon to help Jennifer. Mark was hospitalized for several months in a state of extreme depression, undergoing the therapy of choice, electroshock and Thorazine.

The family response to this crisis seems to have been terrified muddle worsened by poor communication with the doctors in charge of the case. Though Jennifer, John, and Marion were told that the prognosis was good for recovery, they did not feel that they really knew what had happened or was happening. Marion could not bring herself to speak of what must have been her real fear, the link with her beloved father's psychiatric history. It is a reasonable guess that the Rombauer family had some genetic predisposition to manic depression. But Marion could not bear such guesses. She was so secretive on the subject of Edgar's suicide that Ethan did not learn the truth until after her own death; Mark found it out only through a chance remark dropped by Cecily Brownstone. To her and John's already tense relationship with Mark was added a new reluctance to broach subjects that might upset anyone's equilibrium.

By fall Mark's recovery was well advanced. But in another abrupt swerve of events, Jennifer found that she was pregnant. Among other implications for the future, she certainly would not be able to return to the trial arrangement for a couple of years unless in the most desultory way. By the time of Joseph Becker's birth on May 12, 1965, Marion had retreated from at least immediately trying to pin down the boys on any role in the next revision.

Over the next few years the situation remained murky. Ethan wandered into and out of college and tried his hand at a couple of ventures including a rock-and-roll recording studio and a company that designed and installed security systems. Mark decided to become a schoolteacher and went back to complete his degree at Portland State University. His relationship with his parents remained thorny, and they had come away from some further discussion of work on the cookbook with seriously crossed wires. Marion and John believed that Mark and Jennifer had again declined any substantial role in *The Joy of Cooking*. What Mark thought they had said no to was an invitation to move back to Cincinnati and join some predetermined program of revision as foot soldiers under his mother's direction.

It is a great pity that the Becker family was not able to bring its collective intelligence to bear on the future of *Joy* at this juncture, for the rising sales of the latest edition meant a more urgent need to get a grip on the business side of Marion's success. She understood hard work, but she did not understand money nearly as well as Irma had. John was no better than she at these things, though sometimes he would draft imperious-sounding memos for her about fiscal grievances against Bobbs-Merrill. Discount sales, still a sore point between the parties, had become if anything more unintelligible to the family than in Irma's time. The Book-of-the-Month Club contract was particularly galling to them. It involved four different categories of sales on a slender royalty schedule. After many complaints from the Beckers, Bill Finneran finally negotiated some concessions in August of 1968.[4] But they remained puzzled and not well satisfied with the many different sales arrangements that the firm continued to adopt.

Harriet Pilpel might have been able to steer them toward some constructive ideas of the future, but the Beckers seem to have sought her advice only sporadically during this period. In the late 1960s they turned for help to Thomas W. Itin, toward whom they stood almost as second parents. He had grown up in the Beckers' neighborhood and worked for them after school as a yard boy. John in particular had taken an interest in this smart and willing lad, who wanted to go to college and make something of himself. John had helped see Tom through Cornell University, from which he went on to a New York University MBA program. He enjoyed a rapid rise to responsibility at Mobil Oil, where he soon became head of personnel for Middle Eastern operations. (A recipe for a version of couscous contributed by his wife, Shirley, while they were living in Libya entered *The Joy of Cooking* in 1962.) From Mobil he had moved to a Midwestern securities firm, then struck out for himself as an investment broker and financial consultant.[5]

At only slightly more than Mark's age Tom Itin had a plateful of accomplishments that might well have been seen as an implicit reproach to Mark. The young businessman behaved toward John with more filial deference than the real son, who dug into any argument with tactless obstinacy and clearly meant to stay two thousand miles away from the parental orbit. The difficult father-son relationship very likely helped solidify a place for young Itin in his benefactor's confidence.

At some point in 1967 or 1968, John and Marion asked Itin to help manage their assets. With his advice they began looking into advantageous ways to arrange their income and potential tax shelters. They started spending vacations with the Itins at Great Traverse Bay in Michigan (about fifty miles from Marion's childhood Eden at Bay View) and contemplating an investment in a vacation-condominium property of Tom Itin's in Traverse City. From this time on, a good deal of their money began to be tied up in speculations meant to maximize their long-term return from *Joy*. They were not themselves conversant with such planning, but preferred to go along with Itin's superior expertise.

In the first flush of the latest *Joy*'s success, it had been a novelty to them to be able to spend money on themselves. Both John and Marion were genuinely indifferent to many of the things that money could buy, though they had always managed to hobnob with moneyed families and display their own cultivated taste. They did not now treat themselves to many material luxuries beyond more expensive cars. Their one major indulgence on the strength of success was a modest spate of world travel during the 1960s. As soon as Marion had gotten the corrected 1963 edition to bed and signed the contract certifying a new peace with Bobbs-Merrill, they took off to visit a project that she had a particular interest in: the American Farm School at Thessaloníki, Greece, intended to bring some benefits of modern agricultural education to bear in an impoverished region. In 1965 they joined a Garden Clubs of America tour of English gardens—for Marion, probably the most glorious of all their travels. They went to Morocco and other parts of the Mediterranean; they arranged a long Far Eastern visit that was supposed to be the culmination of Marion's lifelong love of Heian Japanese civilization, a passion nourished through countless rereadings of *The Tale of Genji*.

This last trip unfortunately coincided with the 1968 pandemic of Hong Kong flu, which felled both the Beckers almost as soon as they stepped off the plane in Tokyo. After that they could barely drag themselves through what had been meant to be a thrilling pilgrimage. It did, however, have a seriocomic footnote. Leo Gobin had suggested that Marion and John stop in Taiwan to check out the status of the photo-offset *Joy* that Bobbs-Merrill had agreed to license, in an edition of 500 copies, for Far Eastern distribution in an attempt to stake a claim against pirated versions. They were most agreeably entertained at Mei Ya Publications, Inc., which was selling its *Joy* at $100 in Taiwanese dollars—the equivalent of $2.50, and a steal compared to the current U.S. price of $6.95. They departed with only a faint suspicion that their pleasant hosts were not planning any mere 500-copy run. It eventually developed that Mei Ya was itself getting ready to print and distribute thousands of unauthorized copies. The Beckers never did learn just how much they had lost in royalties.[6]

This same period saw Marion beginning to think about another sort of fulfillment that she had never made time for before: writing for her own pleasure. She would have loved to be turned loose to do various books other than *The Joy of Cooking*, the family bread and butter but not the love of her life. She dallied with thoughts of several projects that would please her whether they ever made a cent or, indeed, saw the light of day beyond her own closest kin.

The project that people in the Beckers' own circle would have most readily guessed was a book on gardening or ecosystems. In everyday life her energies were ceaselessly occupied with the living canvas and plant sanctuary of Cockaigne, as well as environmental and farming issues that she had been attuned to for close to twenty-five years, long before "ecology" was the stuff of headlines. She was the friend and learned amateur colleague of forestry experts, botanists, students of climate and geology. Here and there she had managed to work into *Joy* some token of this other, unofficial life's work—for example, a tiny reference to the new understanding of so-called "primitive" agriculture that her friend Edgar Anderson, later recognized as a founding father of ethnobotany, had arrived at through both genetic and practical observation of crops.[7] A Marion writing today could explore such concerns more directly and fully in a cookbook; at the time they would have smacked of eccentricity. She had no real forum for sharing her knowledge of plant life in print, though in Cincinnati she worked on one far-reaching project after another connected with the preservation of habitats and restoration of degraded ecosystems.

Another recurrent idea of Marion's was a family memoir, something she always wished her mother could have written. Many of Irma's memories—and of course her matchless gift for recounting them—had gone with her. "Meet the Family" as Marion had proposed it to her nearly twenty years before would never be written. But the notion of some similar work began to visit her more often, along with an impulse to jot down stray thoughts, perceptions, or bits of her current reading in intermittent "chapbook" or "commonplace-book" fashion. Though she was not yet ready to begin on her own equivalent of Irma's memoir, certain fragments found together with a more sustained later attempt apparently date from this time.

She also wished that she could tell the world something about *The Joy of Cooking* as she had been privileged to see it. What she loved above all was the fan mail as a record of *Joy*'s vital link with American cookbook users for more than a generation. Like Irma, she held the fans in grateful esteem as actual friends. In 1958 she had asked Harriet Pilpel's advice on a project to be called "My Mother's Wastebasket": an anthology of letters received from readers over the years that would in effect tell *Joy*'s story in terms of the author-fan bond. The lawyer had explained that obtaining the necessary permissions would be next to impossible, but Marion had never wholly abandoned the idea.[8]

Her eagerness indeed grew year by year as she pored over letters from every part of the globe. She felt that the latest *Joy*'s strengths were in a sense the doing of the readers, whose questions and comments were always showing her something new to be done. Best of all were the replies to her replies, evidence of a tangible connection with all sorts of people. At least two of her correspondents eventually became important friends, though never to be met in person. One was Julia Todd Forbes, an adoptive New Zealander who along with her design-engineer husband had taken up the quintessential "alternative lifestyle" on the outskirts of Auckland. As an independence seeker raising virtually everything they ate, she felt a keen sympathy with the book's remarkable coverage of do-it-yourself basics, and was delighted to discover her general convictions about the politics of food shared by her new pen pal. Marion's other favorite correspondent was a New Englander retired to Florida, Helen Beattie Leech, a devoted user who had formed the ambition of cooking her way through the entire *Joy of Cooking*. As she reported her progress the two women took to swapping family news and opinions on books or issues. Rewards like this struck Marion as more than accidental; they pointed to something unique about the book.

For the sake of the fans, she would have liked to collect at least some of the more presentable bits of *Joy*'s history, from any antecedents of Irma's first published version through different stages of growth on up to the present. The problem was that by the mid-sixties almost no one was left who really remembered the earliest days. Marion herself had not at the time observed everything with strict repor-torial attention. She wanted clearer documentation of *Joy*'s begin-nings, and had found an interested St. Louis friend in Elizabeth Goltermann, now part owner of Irma's Jefferson County cabin.

Miss Goltermann and her friend Elinor Hayward, both employees of the St. Louis school system, had rented the cabin during the last years of Irma's illness and had inquired about buying the property shortly after her death. It was a happy arrangement for all, for the two women plainly saw Mrs. Rombauer's house and grounds in the light of a living memorial. They were also "wild gardeners" after Marion's own heart, and quickly joined the list of gardening correspondents who exchanged news with her on their local growing seasons.

Miss Goltermann had collected every *Joy of Cooking* edition, and kept an eye out for bits of treasured Rombauer memorabilia. She and Marion had discussed the rumored *Joy* prototype, the little mimeo-graphed collection that had been sold as "Unusual and Unpublished Recipes" for the Women's Alliance of Irma's Unitarian congregation in St. Louis. Neither, however, owned a copy.

As we have seen (pages 97–98), the work was almost certainly a suc-cessor rather than precursor to the 1931 book. But the bibliographic details were now hazy in all memories, including those of Marion, who conceived that a facsimile of this supposed *Ur*-version could be of interest to contemporary *Joy* fans. She thought it might be distributed as a bonus or giveaway and had a new title picked out: "Little Acorn." Miss Goltermann eventually did manage to track down a copy of "Unusual and Unpublished Recipes." But when Marion had had a chance to examine the text, she suspected that this very slight work might not enhance *Joy*'s reputation among 1960s cooks. She decided that an account of the work's origins and history was a better idea.

She was dealing now with a new Bobbs-Merrill editor in chief. In October of 1964 the gifted but unhappy Bill Raney had locked himself into a New York hotel room and swallowed a lethal dose of pills. His successor, Robert Amussen, a newcomer to the firm, had no war-epoch associations with the Beckers and was impressed with Marion's intel-ligence and energy. In July of 1965 the two of them began discussing schemes to mark the thirtieth anniversary of the first Bobbs-Merrill *Joy* in 1966. By November they had agreed on a retrospective in the form of a sixty-four-page booklet containing a smattering of sales statistics, family pictures and memorabilia, press reviews, fan letters, and biographical facts, the whole to be presented with an introduction by Cecily Brownstone. It was to be finished early in 1966 and distributed as a Bobbs-Merrill giveaway at the American Booksellers Association meeting in Washington, D.C., that June.[9]

The resulting work was completed by Marion in a few months' eager exertion and duly unveiled at the ABA convention under the title *Little Acorn*, which originally had been intended for the other project. A few parts of the original proposal had been altered (the Brownstone introduction became an afterword; any attempt to give concrete sales figures was abandoned), but it was essentially as Marion and Bob Amussen had discussed it. Today it stands as the first line of investigation—notwithstanding some vagueness or actual errors concerning dates and facts—for anyone interested in the story of *Joy* or the Rombauers. It labors, however, under a few severe handicaps. One is that though Marion innocently thought it a work of great importance, for Bobbs-Merrill it was a modest freebie ranking fairly low on any scale of priorities.

Little Acorn more or less proclaimed "Giveaway Item" at first sight. It was a pretty if flimsy little booklet in a square 8-by-8-inch format, printed in shades of brown charmingly suggesting an old-fashioned sepia-toned album—but also completely devoid of such details as page numbers or the title and author's name on the cover; the only surface clue to the contents was a photograph of an acorn. Marion, no judge of publishing ways, had supervised the design without suspecting that it was not exactly consonant with the serious record that she had had in mind. The degree of editorial attention that Bobbs-Merrill bestowed on *Little Acorn* may be gauged from the fact that no one had caught the misspelling of Laurance Chambers's name as "Lawrence," or demurred at a picture caption calling John Becker "present editor" of *The Joy of Cooking*.

Marion thought that there could be real retail opportunities for *Little Acorn*, perhaps in an enlarged version. This time she meant to hold copyright herself so as to make her own decisions on the book's future after its immediate purpose. That Bobbs-Merrill agreed indicates the slight importance of the project in the publisher's view. There was an absurdity in the situation that she failed to register. The simple fact is that she and the company could not possibly have cooperated on a true history of *The Joy of Cooking*. The one she had written carefully whitewashed a war-torn past into a capsule account objectionable to nobody—indeed, so obviously guarded and indirect as to have no real future beyond its limited promotional purpose. She had painted herself into a corner with *Little Acorn*, and did not have the experience of the book trade to see how little evidence the work in its ABA form gave of retail promise.

Surely Marion did not think in such terms as "whitewash." It is evident, however, that getting together with the longtime Rombauer adversary—even under the friendly Gobin regime—to publish an account of *The Joy of Cooking* involved peculiar constrictions that abetted her worst tendency as a writer: a fondness for subtle, studiously arranged, factually muzzy little glimpses rather than plain statements. (John, who did much polishing and editing of the text, probably contributed abundantly to this effect of decorative poses.) But considering that *Little Acorn* is inescapably equivalent to a Hatfield account of the family saga told so as not to offend the McCoys, what Marion managed to accomplish is remarkable.

In four brief chapters she outlined her mother's and her own lives, the career of *Joy* through successive editions from 1931 to the present, the perspectives of commentators, and the fan mail. There was a certain apt motif running throughout much of this, especially the personal history and the account of the ongoing dialogue with readers. *Little Acorn* is firmly imbued with the concept of the *Lebenskunst*, which Marion in fact invoked to sum up her mother's life through the family story of Dada Kuhlmann exclaiming, "Ach, du bist eine treue Lebenskünstlerin!" to a very small Irma. "The epithet is largely untranslatable," she wrote; "the art all-embracing." In her belief the spirit of the "life art" belongs to *The Joy of Cooking*, running "all through its pages, like sunlight through living leaves."[10]

It was a way of setting apart *Joy*, which Marion genuinely viewed as a sacred trust, from the greedy and impersonal hucksterism that she found largely dominating the American food scene. She did a lovely job of recounting cherished trivia of the family's life, all contributing to the implication that *The Joy of Cooking* was the beloved institution it was because it embodied inner values staunchly treasured by generations of Rombauers, Engelmanns, and von Starkloffs from the barricades of Frankfurt in 1833 on up to the present. Her own part in this legacy, she announced, was symbolized by a resolve to keep the family cookbook "personalized, critical, detached, uncommitted"—"Of the multitudinous ingredients in *Joy* the uniquely priceless one is its makers' integrity."[11] (According to Ethan, during the preparation of the 1962 edition she had turned down a Procter & Gamble offer of a million dollars if she would mention some company products in the new book.)

In the chapter on the fan mail—the closest she could come to the anthology of letters that she still longed to publish—she struck a similar note. She treated her and Irma's happy exchanges with *Joy* friends as an enlightening contrast to author-reader relationships involving anonymous corporate symbols. The consumer representative of one firm, doomed to life under some cozy pseudonym, had once mournfully told Marion that the lawyers at her firm wouldn't even let her answer customers' letters. Obviously this woman could never experience *Joy*'s chief joys as seen by Marion: "warm, person-to-person expressions of gratitude"; "a reward of unbelievable satisfaction, full payment for the hours of struggle that *Joy* constantly demands";[12] a kind of partnership in the task of defining new directions for future editions. *The Joy of Cooking*, rooted in a family's interests and values, naturally spoke to a larger family.

Marion did not hammer away at these implications, but let them emerge through her obvious pleasure in writing of the gracious old St. Louis *Deutschtum* and the current *Joy* fellowship. Perhaps the happiest part of *Little Acorn* is her evocation of her childhood world's rituals and furniture—the contrasting atmospheres of Sunday dinners with her severe Rombauer and genial von Starkloff grandparents; the four-mile walk from their Flad Avenue home to downtown punctually shared every weekday morning by her father and three friends; a gloriously garish painting near the Art Museum entrance, indelibly stamped on her youthful memory, that featured "the scum of Paris" hopefully awaiting an interesting Revolutionary atrocity. To portray Irma was a more difficult challenge, and one to which she rose with more loyalty than completeness.

What is conspicuously missing from Marion's account of her mother is any mention of Irma's fierceness and pride, her brilliantly focused and all-consuming charm. She fell back on a little anthology of journalists' descriptions and gentle mentions of such traits as generosity, "constant, impulsive considerations" for people, gifts for bringing out unknown strengths in others, and "buoyancy" even through grief. But there are moments of priceless detail, like the memory of how "Mother almost always took to her bed to write":

> My mind retains an early morning vignette: Mother, generously propped up with pillows, determinedly scribbling, surrounded on three sides not only by notes for constructive future use but by a great litter of torn paper. For she had a

habit, once she had extracted information, of tearing the pages on which she had found it into very small bits, as if with this gesture she could free herself, once and for all, from a tyranny of prescription.[13]

Marion had great hopes for *Little Acorn,* and might have found a practical sales niche for it if she had been willing to hire a literary agent to advise her on marketing a revised version. But it was destined to remain almost unknown except among the hundreds of friends and acquaintances to whom she gave copies. Its debut as a company giveaway at the 1966 ABA meeting made scarcely a ripple in cookbook or other circles. The talk of the gathering was the news that had rocked the publishing trade several weeks earlier: on May 13 the entire constellation of Howard W. Sams holdings, including Bobbs-Merrill, had been bought by the International Telephone and Telegraph Corporation.[14]

An age of mergers and takeovers had begun that dwarfed the 1958 Sams purchase of Bobbs-Merrill. "Information companies" were the growth industry of the hour, and no organization better symbolized the galloping advance of the electronics barons in the 1960s than ITT under Harold Geneen. By now, engulf-and-devour trends in other business sectors had liberal types like Marion Becker listening to the young Ralph Nader and talking about ancestors on the barricades. In the publishing world, the same sort of acquisitions might appear to offer temporary protection for a respectable, somewhat overextended old firm like Bobbs-Merrill. More astute observers saw them as an omen of harsh corporate bottom-line thinking applied to books.

It was not the time for Marion to expect much Bobbs-Merrill interest in launching a marginal fribble like *Little Acorn* as a retail title. Understanding little of publishing beyond a small window furnished by the quite atypical *Joy of Cooking,* she did not know how to prod Leo Gobin or Bob Amussen on a commercial release or to look for another publisher. But the matter was rudely pushed from her attention by other events.

John's mother, by now very frail, declined badly over the summer of 1966, and the family had been coping with this strain for several months when in late October Marion noticed a strange puckering of her left nipple. She was swiftly referred for diagnostic surgery, which found a golf ball–sized malignant mass in the armpit and evidence of cancer in ten of the twelve lymph nodes. Her second radical mastectomy was performed at once, on November 4.[15] The degree of involvement (made known only to a few, but much worse than in 1955) was a terrible augury for the future.

John desperately shuttled back and forth for several weeks from Cincinnati to St. Louis, where Adele Becker died on November 22. Marion, as close to exhaustion as she would ever be, wrote to Bob Amussen that she was "for the present intimidated about assuming direct responsibilities."[16] There was a complication late in December, a blood clot on her lung that necessitated a course of blood-thinning drugs. But this time she was spared the ordeal of lymphedema in the affected arm (though the other one intermittently continued to give her trouble).

This small mercy helped Marion meet the illness by assuming the air of normal health almost before her loved ones had had a chance to take in the situation. Only a few days after the operation Ethan—at the time a student at Michigan State University in Oakland—had arrived home full of dismay and concern to be greeted by the patient, fully dressed, walking calmly down the stairs and telling him that she would get him some lunch. The astonished young man began to protest that she belonged in bed. "Oh, I'm fine," said Marion. "I've been working in the garden all morning." She had the purest horror of invalid behavior, and from her husband and sons to the chancest contacts, no one ever saw a speck of it from her.

She mentioned to no friend the great mental suffering that she described in writing only years later. In fact she felt herself walled up in the incredible loneliness of illness, submitting to the well-meant but somehow evasive, impersonal dictates of caregivers who did not understand the human dimensions of what they decreed. She was started on another round of the painful, disfiguring radioactive cobalt therapy that she had been through nine years before. In the end the ordeal overcame her strength, and she refused to complete the full course of treatments.[17] Even so, her already scarred body was still more cruelly burned.

When she was able to think connectedly about business, Marion made a further attempt to launch *Little Acorn* as a retail book. Bobbs-Merrill had originally printed 5,000 copies, of which a sizable stock remained on hand with no further plans for distributing them. She attempted to convince Amussen and Gobin to use the book in bonus or piggyback arrangements on special *Joy of Cooking* deals, or to test-market it in its own right in some selected area. Receiving only vague encouragement, she eventually persuaded the company to ratify a second formal letter of agreement regarding the work. The first, executed on February 25, 1966, and meant to cover the ABA release, had given her a flat fee of $3,000 and control of copyright. The second approached the status of an orthodox book contract, establishing a royalty schedule on a retail price of $2.25 (later raised to $2.95) and providing for another 5,000-copy printing.[18] It appears that the first printing was eventually exhausted and that a second one was completed in 1968, but the company never did commit itself to any serious distribution plan.

By the time of the second *Little Acorn* contract (December 8, 1967) it seemed inevitable that the next *Joy of Cooking* revision would soon require too constant attention to allow much further effort on *Little Acorn* or other projects. Marion and Jane Brueggeman had been quietly getting some of the necessary groundwork in place since the 1963 contract that had buried the hatchet with Bobbs-Merrill. The chapter files were set up. John had from time to time collected whimsicalities for the "Irma" grace notes, while Marion had kept track of food trends and research. They felt fairly well prepared for the stage of serious effort— and this time everyone at Bobbs-Merrill had full confidence that Marion knew exactly what she was doing with *Joy*.

The company's attitude had undergone a thorough turnaround since the Rombauer-Chambers and Becker-Miller donnybrooks of other eras. The nature of the last edition's success, a sustained and still-ascending height rather than a sudden pinnacle, was a mighty persuader that Marion Becker deserved to stand at the head of the cookbook-writing profession through solid authority rather than glancing appeal. At the same time, *Joy*'s position among competitors had been subtly altered by the fact that the star author did not especially want to be a star.

Irma, through all Bobbs-Merrill wars, had been an inventive self-promoter and darling of the press. But with her death and the latest armistice Marion had more or less withdrawn from the orbit of the New York food world (except for her friendship with Cecily Brownstone), leaving the public at large to suppose that *Joy*'s present excellence was entirely owing to Irma Rombauer. As time went on, many of the younger writers had almost no idea who Marion Becker was. A sort of mythos grew up around the book, suggesting that the magnificent Mrs. Rombauer's *Joy of Cooking* had suffered a sorry decline in modern times.

Since the same food writers who repeated this legend were often too young to have followed the real textual changes in any detail and routinely quoted the current version as an authority without troubling to look up whether any piece of information dated from Irma's or Marion's watch, the supposition did nothing to discourage sales. Marion did not care to argue the matter with most of the present commentators; even if she had not painfully shrunk from the limelight, she would have thought that personal glory seeking could at this stage only trivialize rather than enhance *Joy*'s self-evident worth. She was right. The near invisibility of the venerable cookbook's current author on the noisy and ephemera-ridden food scene tended to set it apart from the parade of trends and gossip.

But there was a potentially unpleasant obverse to the coin, as Marion found out somewhat later when she picked up the November 9, 1969, *New York Times Book Review* to find her editor, Bob Amussen, quoted in an article titled "What We Need Now Is Another French Cookbook." The author, Marcia Seligson, had taken some well-judged potshots at rubbishy cooking instruction and singled out *Joy* as a rare exemplar of excellence. But in the same breath she had managed to bring Amussen's name into an invidious comparison of the current *Joy* with "the original"—that is, the 1931 book, which she apparently knew nothing about. In her airy summary of the matter, "After Mrs. Rombauer died the project was taken over by her daughter—who, in what may have been a burst of Oedipal malice, deleted the homey asides and several of the best recipes."[19]

This crude little squib was possibly the nastiest public insult ever dealt to either author of *The Joy of Cooking*. Since Amussen had consented to be interviewed for the piece, it was not an unreasonable guess that he had countenanced its opinion. In truth, he was as appalled as Marion herself and lost no time informing the writer that her irresponsible garblings of accurate information given in good faith had damaged "a personal relationship that matters to me."[20] But casual smears like the "Oedipal malice" remark have a sticking power beyond the reach of reason, and the whole affair went on rankling in Marion's mind long after Amussen's angry reply to Marcia Seligson.

Nothing could have been further from Bobbs-Merrill's wishes than wanton gibes at the respected Marion Becker. Leo Gobin saw well enough that her real contribution transcended glib observers' fashion ratings. It was both simple justice and good policy to extend every possible courtesy to her—though the firm was not in one of its most lustrous editorial eras and some gestures meant as courtesies were not very systematically carried out. That had been the case with *Little Acorn*. It was also the case with the project that she was engaged in at the time of the Seligson affair, a much greater Bobbs-Merrill favor to the star author in that the company had actually permitted her to adjust the *Joy of Cooking* revision schedule to make time for a passionately cherished ambition.

The project began shortly after the signing of the second *Little Acorn* contract, when Marion was still trying to develop plans for that work. In January of 1968, however, she was approached by an old friend with what Marion considered a still more important idea.

Frances Jones Poetker, a Cincinnati florist, was one of the Beckers' original Modern Art Society allies. A nationally known figure in her chosen profession, she was the author of a syndicated newspaper feature called "Fun with Flowers" and numerous magazine articles. Marion and she had many bonds; not only were they both Vassar graduates married to architects and active in local art politics, but the florist had been one of Marion's early mentors in "wild gardening." Mrs. Poetker was no mere flower seller. She was a trained botanist who had earned a master's degree at the University of Cincinnati for a study of local plant habitats, and she had introduced Marion to a cluster of ecologically minded scientists in different disciplines at the university.

Mrs. Poetker's idea involved one of her old professors who had gone on to Yale: the distinguished botanist Paul Bigelow Sears, whose 1935 *Deserts on the March* was and is the most famous general study of the Dust Bowl disaster. She proposed that the three of them apply their joint talents to a book on wild plants, chiefly focusing on the flora of the upper Ohio Valley. Sears would develop the concept of ecosystems and habitats; Mrs. Poetker would write about using wild plants in flower arrangements. Marion would address the creation and maintenance of "wild gardens" through her experience at Cockaigne, a concrete lesson in the reclamation of degraded agricultural land and encouragement of mixed growth.

To her unspeakable joy Bob Amussen consented to listen to their proposal, and after some consideration of deadlines and priorities Bobbs-Merrill decided to allow her to complete the project before the cookbook revision. By their best guess the plant book might be finished some time in 1970. After that she and John would go ahead with the all-out push on the next *Joy*, which probably would take at least two years. Supposing that she began on revision in 1971, the next edition might be published in 1973 or more likely 1974.

Marion probably knew or half knew that the plant book, eventually titled *Wild Wealth*, was a very expensive present to her that could never have justified itself to Bobbs-Merrill as a marketable book in its own right. She did not know that it would turn into a singularly messy and contentious present. Two major problems attended the ambitious work throughout its creation, leaving all-too-clear traces in the large and beautiful illustrated volume eventually published in October of 1971. One was that Bobbs-Merrill's editorial handling of the project seems to have been mostly hands-off. The other, which was closely related, was that *Wild Wealth* involved four separate contributions—the three authors' and the illustrator's—which were allowed to fall into place in an extremely disjointed manner. In the acknowledgments of *Wild Wealth* the authors would later thank Bobbs-Merrill "for allowing us to pursue our visions of text, layout and presentation untrammeled."[21] "Us" mostly meant Marion and Frances Poetker, and what they saw as an absence of trammels contributed greatly to an absence of harmonious common efforts.

The work was even more of a shining hope for Marion than *Little Acorn*. She saw it as the fulfillment of a life's ambition, and it is easy to understand why. *Wild Wealth* is a splendid volume filled with important ideas and arresting images; it contains the distillation of three plant observers' lifelong experience and insight in their individual areas of concern. Long out of print, it is still treasured by some gardeners and bibliophiles as a singular and lovable masterwork. Unfortunately, it struggled rather than sailed into print.

The writing in itself went quite smoothly: each author's contribution was well in hand in a fairly short time. Paul Sears's section, the most elegantly written, was also much the shortest. Sears, who was in the process of retiring from Yale and moving to New Mexico, was actually little involved with the work's execution. It was clear to all that Mrs. Poetker and Marion were the real impresarios. At a good remove from their busy efforts, he presented them with a lucid three-part essay introducing lay readers to the nation's major ecosystems, the environmental backdrop of geology and climate in the upper Ohio Valley, and the region's most important vegetative patterns within the fluid context of ecological succession. It was a polished, effortless-looking world-in-a-grain-of-sand synopsis by one of the signal shapers of modern ecological studies.

Frances Poetker's part of the book, though carried off with equal skill and address, does not seem to belong to the same mental world. It was meant to introduce readers to the particular rewards and requirements of indoor arrangements using wild plants, the bulk of the space being taken up with a gallery of illustrated sample arrangements that ran a canny, roughly seasonal gamut from fairly programmatic "theme" presentations to simple, free-spirited assemblages of materials. The whole thing was clearly the performance of someone used to delivering snappy, no-nonsense, very intelligent how-to advice to a large general readership.

Marion's section took up the center of the book and was by far its longest part. It was meant—though this was not particularly spelled out for the reader—to link the other two contributions through the unifying idea of Cockaigne: the small ecological laboratory in which the broad concepts enunciated by Sears could be shown in action, and the source of most of the plants used in the Poetker arrangements. The idea worked, up to a point. What Marion had produced was an ardent, staunchly individual gardening treatise built around her three decades' experience in manipulating a soil-based canvas. As she saw it, her woods at Cockaigne were a living lesson in the sensitive juxtaposition of native Ohio Valley wild plants and judiciously chosen hardy exotics. In four chapters marking the progression of the seasons, she moved eagerly between the outlines of a moral-ecological philosophy and various practical tools for translating it into action, the goal in all cases being to work with rather than against nature.

Marion's contribution to *Wild Wealth* was the longest connected piece of expository writing she ever produced. It was rich, wide-ranging, and challenging, but the abundance of information it contained was not easy to extract. She did best when bent on some tangible matter such as the advantages of mulching in an unpredictable, drought-ridden climate like that of Cockaigne, or evaluating varieties of her beloved daffodils and colchicums. Elsewhere the writing sometimes tended toward a kind of hyperaesthetic sprawl in which detachment and system would be fogged over with contrived effects ("the mauve taupes of the white oaks cried out to sing a duet with the pale golds of the tulip trees").[22] To grasp the complexly interwoven detail of these essays takes repeated rereadings—though that is a testimony to the wealth of Marion's ideas as well as the undeniable foibles of her writing. Indeed, her part of the book might have made a substantial book by itself with only slight reorganization.

The three authors' efforts, disparate as they are, could well have been made to function as one coherent whole with some elementary machinery that apparently did not occur to Marion or Mrs. Poetker and was never insisted on by any editor. *Wild Wealth* lacks a table of contents, an overall preface explaining how the book came to be and how its three main sections are related, introductions to any of those sections, subheadings to mark divisions in the rambling course of chapters (especially Marion's), or any plain identification in the text of the oft-invoked name "Cockaigne." The two principal begetters, Marion and Frances Poetker, must have pinned much on the unifying power of the one great element that had not been decided on when Bobbs-Merrill agreed to the project: the illustrations.

From the beginning the fourth cornerstone of the whole plan had been a wealth of richly detailed interpretive drawings given pride of place in a spacious format—not literal scientific renderings of plants, but a visual approach that would generate its own excitement. The chief authors decided that they had found exactly what they wanted in the Cincinnati-based artist Janice Rebert Forberg, who had no botanical training but whose pen-and-ink work appeared to them to possess a lovely sympathy with growing forms. Even a brief examination of the finished volume suggests the qualities that attracted them. The Forberg drawings contained a great profusion of stylistic approaches, but all had in common a thrusting asymmetry that made the plant appear to be *going* somewhere; one could imagine the pen or pencil traveling the same course as the living sap toward the end point of stem or leaf. But the same examination also shows that something went wrong. With no warning or explanation, a browser may page from one of these energy-charged images to a soberly literal drawing that looks like the work of another hand, and is. Behind this clash of modes lies the story of a first-class war.

The trouble in brief was that the two chief collaborators believed themselves to be the art directors of the project without understanding certain legal responsibilities and limitations. At the outset they had sent off the artist to make her own contract with Bobbs-Merrill, expecting that all the authors' contracts could be wrapped up separately at a later date. Friction gradually developed between Marion and Mrs. Forberg, who was drawing live specimens in situ at Cockaigne (or occasionally at her studio) as they came into bloom or leaf throughout the growing season. Her particular pen-and-ink technique placed great importance on the the way a slightly porous paper physically took up the ink from a certain type of pen nib as her hand moved. For this reason she disliked doing corrections on finished drawings, preferring to start all over again and draw off what she saw at a single sitting. Marion, however, kept having further suggestions about drawings that she had initially said were fine, or ideas about adding another species to a finished grouping. She expected to see the artist keep working until she had executed the idea to Marion's satisfaction.

The situation grew more and more vexatious to Janice Forberg, who at that point was the only one of the four contributors with any contractual standing. She was thus in a legal position to force the issue of how many alterations could reasonably be required of her. To Marion's great annoyance, the artist went to a lawyer and won a stipulation restricting Marion's authority to demand changes or redrawings of any picture once she had formally accepted it.[23]

From this first blowup Marion and her ally Mrs. Poetker proceeded to a severe legal blunder: an arrangement with a second artist, a scientific illustrator named "Bettina" (Elizabeth) Dalvé. It had been agreed on all along that another artist might be brought in for certain supplementary material such as maps and charts. But the two chief authors made the mistake of asking Mrs. Dalvé to draw several other subjects. It does not appear that they meant to request a substantial body of plant drawings from her. But they had no contractual authority to do anything that impinged on the status of the official illustrator, Mrs. Forberg. What came to her ears was a report that Mrs. Dalvé had been hired to do important work—beyond mere maps and charts—for *Wild Wealth*.

By now two growing seasons had gone by and Bobbs-Merrill was waiting to start discussing the next *Joy of Cooking*. The time was at hand to draft the *Wild Wealth* authors' contracts and any other necessary machinery for establishing the mutual obligations and rights of all parties. The Forberg-Dalvé controversy was an obstacle that the principal authors had not foreseen. Rather than hold up production of the book—now scheduled for 1971 publication—they agreed in December of 1970 to a hydra-headed tangle of contracts.[24] When the ink was dry on everything they found that Bettina Dalvé could be credited in the finished book only in the most limited manner, and that a maze of restrictions surrounded anyone's possible reproduction of the Forberg drawings (e.g., for slides to illustrate a talk).

Marion was filled with fury. After a time she took to cutting the artist dead when one had work to deliver to the other's door. But for the moment she could not surrender to her rage, for much work remained to be done. Bobbs-Merrill had astonishingly failed to consider the art specifications until the last minute; Mrs. Forberg and Mrs. Dalvé had worked with no idea of how large or small any drawing would be printed in the finished book. In fact, the company had arrived almost at the beginning of the production process with no layout—either through general lackadaisicalness or because the authors had led Amussen and the production chief, William Bokermann, to understand that they would take care of it. Marion and Janice Forberg suspended hostilities sufficiently to seek help close to home. Both were good friends of the well-loved Cincinnati artist Charles Harper, who did not work in anything remotely resembling Mrs. Forberg's style but had a great familiarity with natural-history subjects. He listened to their account of the situation and sat down with Mrs. Forberg to go through the drawings one by one. Remedying the omissions of the publisher, they managed almost at a single sitting to decide the placement and size of reproduction for each. The result was extraordinarily stimulating and even witty, lending every image an air of having just materialized in an appropriate spot.

The great visual richness of the finished book was widely noted by reviewers in the fall of 1971. It was an imposing 11-by-9-inch volume printed in a small, muted, but interestingly nuanced palette of colors attuned to the 1970s vogue for "natural" or "earth" tones. In the spring of 1972 *Wild Wealth* would fulfill Marion's proudest hopes by winning an award ("Top Honor Book") at a prestigious book designers' exhibition, the Chicago Book Clinic. The designers credited with the achievement were Marion, Janice Forberg, Charley Harper, and Bill Bokermann.[25] It was surely the private pinnacle of Marion's career as an author, a thousand times more significant in her eyes than any fame that might have come to her through the cookbook.

But even this triumph was qualified by fresh grievances against Janice Forberg, whom Marion had come to regard as an ingrate and the mean-minded saboteur of another artist. *Wild Wealth*'s release was tied in with the publication of excerpts and illustrations in two estimable periodicals, the *Explorer* (the publication of the Cleveland Museum of Natural History) and the *Morton Arboretum Quarterly*. Not only did both mistakenly credit Janice Forberg as the only illustrator, but the *Explorer* actually printed one of the Dalvé drawings (credited to Mrs. Forberg) as the cover illustration.[26] This happened to be the only picture in which the methodical, self-effacing scientific illustrator spread imaginative wings in a manner to compete with Mrs. Forberg. It was perhaps the single most powerful image in the book: a magnificent drawing of a white oak in winter, a towering, sinuous structure that seemed fit to hold up the sky like the World Ash Tree of Norse myth. For some reason the authors did not insist on any printed correction crediting Mrs. Dalvé. The consequence of this ill-timed mistake became clear when they later sought permission to reproduce both artists' work in another form, as a set of greeting cards. They had to give up on the idea, for Mrs. Forberg's lawyer was able to use the *Explorer* and *Morton Arboretum Quarterly* precedents to block full and correct attribution of the supplementary artist's pictures.[27] It was a horrible travesty of justice, but Marion and Frances Poetker were helpless.

Despite this rancorous footnote to the achievement, Marion had great hopes for *Wild Wealth* in commercial as well as higher terms. She usually shunned public appearances like the plague, but for this book she would have faced lions. She consented to interviews that she probably would never have done on behalf of *Joy;* she spoke to gardeners' groups and showed up for book signings. Bobbs-Merrill, meanwhile, contributed modest rather than all-out promotional efforts. The company did issue a handsome *Wild Wealth* calendar as a lame-duck effort for 1971 and a timelier one for 1972 (when it was distributed at the spring meeting of the ABA). The publicity office, getting up some well-meant releases, managed to arouse Marion's ire with a piece of promotional copy calling her "the woman who has kept her mother's book, THE JOY OF COOKING, alive through the years."[28] "If keeping Joy alive is all I've been doing God help Bobbs-Merrill," Marion fumed in a draft memo.[29]

She had a new editor in chief to give a piece of her mind to. Bob Amussen had left the company over the summer and been replaced by Eugene Rachlis, a veteran magazine writer and book editor most recently at Prentice-Hall. Marion fiercely let him know that "this vision of me nursing an invalid volume is not my version of my efforts these last twenty years. . . . With promotion like [the offending remark] who needs competition!"[30]

Rachlis and Leo Gobin were not disposed to quarrel with her, for a vision of *Joy* nursing an invalid company would have been more to the point. The good graces of its author were assiduously (if sometimes sloppily) sought by all. Gobin had now granted two of her dearest wishes, publishing *Little Acorn* in token fashion and *Wild Wealth* as an impressive coffee-table book. Marion fervently believed in the general appeal of both. But the little commemorative volume was never put into more than marginal distribution, and the plant book was a short-lived succès d'estime. It had been extremely expensive to produce, and the retail price was accordingly fixed at a level ($17.95 as a special pre-Christmas offer, $20.00 thereafter) that placed it in the gift-season splurge category. Despite lavishly laudatory reviews in botanical journals here and abroad and admiring notices in the general press, the bookstores were soon returning unsold copies. Marion was bitterly disappointed, but fair-minded enough to be grateful to Gobin for giving her the chance to realize an impassioned dream. He knew perfectly well that she would reward him with a heroic effort on the next *Joy of Cooking*, though he did not imagine how heroic.

13

Marion's Last Years

True to her understanding with Bobbs-Merrill, Marion turned from the grand ambitions of *Wild Wealth* to pragmatic planning for the next *Joy of Cooking* with hardly a pause. She expected to devote most of 1972 and 1973 to the main body of the revision work, clearing the way for publication in 1974.

She and John made an energetic beginning early in 1972, happy in the knowledge that Ethan at twenty-six had at last decided to work on *Joy.* When he told them that he wanted to participate in this revision on a serious though not necessarily full-time basis, they promptly conceived the idea of sending him to the Cordon Bleu school in Paris, on the theory that it was time some Rombauer or Becker acquired real professional culinary training. Thus he was some 4,000 miles away from the main effort in Cincinnati when Marion received news amounting to a death sentence.

Late in May a sharp pain on the left side of her chest sent her to Holmes Hospital expecting to hear that she had pneumonia, which she had suffered with like symptoms several times in the past. What the doctors found was inoperable, metastasized cancer, already well enough entrenched in her left lung to be causing fluid to accumulate in the pleural cavity.[1] She was told that with a new series of cobalt treatments—the ordeal she had refused to see through to the end after her second mastectomy—she could probably measure her term of survival in years rather than months.

Virtually all of Marion's work on her final *Joy of Cooking* was therefore done in the knowledge of her advancing illness. Every version that she had been involved with since 1948 had been completed against some dismaying backdrop of legal, editorial, or physical troubles. This edition, however, was literally a race against death.

She could not bear to report the ghastly truth to Ethan in France, so he did not learn of her condition until he came back to Cincinnati some three months after the doctors had broken the news to her. Not at all secretive about most matters, she had an almost pathological instinct to conceal real suffering from those she loved best. But she would not have deceived Bobbs-Merrill about the facts of the case. She believed that she could live to finish the book, and so did Leo Gobin when she had explained the situation to him.

When Marion returned to the revision work in June, she also quickly attempted to review her affairs. She and John began by revising their wills and seeking a tax valuation of *Joy*, preparatory to converting the literary property into a trust with the two of them as trustees. The new trust arrangement, intended to replace the previous trust created by Irma and Marion in 1952, was meant to allow John to function in effect as part owner of *Joy* during Marion's remaining span and unquestioned successor after her death. There was also a provision for Ethan to succeed as trustee should both be dead or disabled.[2]

The instrument was drawn up without the help of their trusted Cincinnati lawyer Jim Magrish, who had suddenly died of a heart attack that same summer. For some reason they did not ask the opinion of Harriet Pilpel, their old legal bulwark in New York, about committing themselves to the new trust. Their main advisors in their current sorting-out of income and property were Morse Johnson of Magrish's old law firm and Thomas W. Itin, the young Michigan-based financial consultant who had already begun taking a hand in their fiscal planning.

Marion's remaining powers now had to go into the long haul of the revision. The fiery warrior of prior author-publisher battles was long gone. Almost from the moment of her mother's death Marion had turned away from brinkmanship in the conduct of *Joy* affairs. She was not always happy with Bobbs-Merrill's actions—it seemed to her that the firm had not done enough for either *Wild Wealth* or *Little Acorn*—but at this point she could waste no strength or courage on matters that she might have lustily contested in the past. It was obvious to all that a transfer of authorship was approaching under even more difficult circumstances than those Marion had faced when she took over the author's role. The instability inherent in the alienated copyright meant more to her as an elderly cancer patient than it had a quarter of a century earlier. This time around she was at pains not to get into distracting altercations with Bobbs-Merrill, which luckily was as intent as she on cooperation.

Consequently, her last revision effort was a miracle of author-publisher harmony by previous *Joy of Cooking* standards. It did not hurt that Eugene Rachlis, her new editor, formed a high regard for both the Beckers as people of intellectual poise and determined ability. (He had reached his own conclusions about Bobbs-Merrill's original acquisition of copyright, which he thought a scandalous injustice, but he never succeeded in impressing this view on his superiors.)[3] Marion in turn placed enough confidence in his judgment to accede without argument to various decisions. Undoubtedly at his request, she agreed to submit the manuscript this time as a proper typescript rather than a disjointed card-file arrangement. She reviewed production and layout ideas with Rachlis and the production supervisor, Bill Bokermann (later succeeded by John Van Biezen), and easily reached agreement on an overall look that would be a strong departure from any previous edition. The cramped-looking page of the 1962 and 1963 versions was to be replaced by a strikingly different design featuring a clean-looking sans serif typeface and a larger page size to accommodate wider margins and a generally brighter, more spacious appearance. It displayed Irma's trademark recipe format to more attractive effect than previous layouts, and represented the belated success of John and Marion's pleas over the past twenty years to introduce more space and lightness into the page design.

Both parties soon decided that the change in visual concept was going to demand some rethinking of the artwork. The problem was technical: Ginnie Hofmann's otherwise ideal illustrations contained too much solid black to be reproduced without appearing too heavy and intense for their new typographical surroundings. It took some time for Marion and Bobbs-Merrill to conclude that they could not solve the matter by simply reshooting the old drawings through a screen and commissioning a few new ones from another artist. Finding both Bettina Dalvé (the supplementary artist for *Wild Wealth*) and Charley Harper (who had provided timely assistance on that work's design) unavailable for the job, Marion walked into the downtown studio of a former Harper pupil and came out with a very promising idea of the young man, Ikki Matsumoto. His style was reasonably compatible with the Hofmann approach, though essentially sturdier and richer in decorative exuberance. Bobbs-Merrill ended by hiring him to redo almost every line drawing in the book, substituting cross-hatching for the solid black areas. Marion insisted on retaining a tiny handful of Ginnie Hofmann's pictures so that the title page might continue to credit the original illustrator's great contribution to *The Joy of Cooking*.

Still smarting from her attempts to harness Janice Forberg's powerfully independent vision in *Wild Wealth*, Marion was overjoyed to work with an illustrator who did what she wanted with simple fluency. Her main innovation in the artwork this time was decorative chapter headings meant to prefigure ideas or materials in the ensuing text—abler, less stylized counterparts of her own primitive cutout chapter headings for the earliest editions of *Joy*.

Bobbs-Merrill and she were quick to agree on the art and most other issues, but the company declined to pick up on a suggestion that would have relieved Marion's mind greatly: to have John explicitly recognized as what she considered him to be, the real editor of *The Joy of Cooking*. Gene Rachlis probably would have gone along with the idea. He thought that John (who was authorized in the last contract to select a revisor in case of Marion's death) might well end up having to complete the book in any case.[4] But it appears that Rachlis rated the husband's talents more highly than most people at Bobbs-Merrill. Leo Gobin, who had had longer to appreciate Marion's tenacity, did not doubt that she would survive to finish the new edition and saw no reason to confer any further official status on John. He thought that they could not do better than to leave Marion to her own devices.[5]

Gobin had rightly judged her strength, stamina, and capacity to maintain the central responsibility for the enormous project. The job was perhaps the easier in that Marion planned to keep the chapter structure of the last major revision fairly intact rather than try to invent a new framework. But there was no part of the text that she did not minutely review and amplify, correct, replace, or delete as she thought necessary—down to such details as setting right a botanical boner in the 1963 description of nectarines or adding a new picture to show that well-stretched strudel dough is literally translucent.[6]

As before, John was the chief polisher of everyone else's efforts, virtually an extension of Marion's mind and in her view a matchless judge of prose style. The coverage of sauces was one of his particular responsibilities, and he planned to write the chapter on drinks and wine. He also kept a quarry of bons mots and little anecdotes from which he furnished Irma-like drolleries at apt moments—a tactic that perhaps explains the somewhat manufactured quality of his humor compared with Irma's airy spontaneity.

Jane Brueggeman was nearly as close to mastery of the entire contents as John and Marion, but because of painful and crippling rheumatoid arthritis she could manage only brief stints of typing or dictation. She concentrated on the thinking and organization with Marion, while most of the secretarial work was taken over by a young woman named Nancy Swats who had answered a newspaper ad placed by the Beckers. She found Marion at seventy a "pretty young thinker" and a rare sort of boss, personally concerned about troubles like sick children and genuinely delighted to initiate a new member into the unique enterprise.

The old think tank of *Joy* friends that had shared working lunches at La Maisonette during Marion's research for the last edition had been partly broken up by deaths and career moves, but Lee Harper, Marion's old consultant from the Cincinnati-area utility company, was still available to help with "service" information and occasional recipe troubleshooting. She was joined by another veteran home economist, Lydia Cooley, a retired director of home economics at Procter & Gamble. At Cockaigne, Isabell Coleman again carried out a great amount of the day-to-day recipe testing. Ethan, dividing his time between the revision work and a new business venture making a line of mountain-climbing equipment, was put to work on any task that came to hand and specifically assigned to go over the coverage of outdoor cooking and dealing with game—a natural enough bailiwick for him as the family's most dedicated camper and hunter.

The Beckers had converted their garage into an office–cum–reference library that accommodated most of the labors of themselves, Jane, and Nancy Swats. They had been able to pick up from the chapter files of the last edition (maintained and updated by Marion and Jane over the intervening decade) quite smoothly, but even so the tentative 1974 publication date had had to be pushed back to 1975 after Marion's diagnosis. The cancer progressed inexorably, but not yet aggressively enough to cast any doubt on the completion of the work. She had had to be hospitalized twice early in 1973 to have the accumulating fluid drained from the pleural cavity, along with nitrogen mustard injections to try to stop the recurrent pleural effusion. It hardly broke her stride for a day's worth of writing and editing. Ikki Matsumoto and Nancy Swats, meeting her for the first time at around this period, had no sense of dealing with a sick person. Her energy amazed even those who did not know of her condition and was nearly incredible to those who did. Even when she had to work from her bed, she refused the role of invalid, the more determined to assume command as her physical self weakened.

It was not entirely an act. There is some evidence that during the early 1970s Marion—true-blue atheist though she was—experienced a kind of heightened spiritual awareness, patchily inferrable from the autobiographical musings that she began to set down more often. Her sporadic impulses to pour out feelings on paper crystallized into a desire to say something to her own posterity, which at that time consisted of the very young Joe Becker. Probably she had no very clear blueprint of what she wanted to write, except that it would introduce her kin and herself to Joe and other descendants yet to be born. A first idea of some memoir came to her just as he was starting school in 1971.[7] She made a number of scattered attempts to continue in 1972, very likely impelled by her awareness of living on borrowed time after the diagnosis of her condition.

But at this stage Marion was not given the chance to proceed further with any autobiographical exploration. The year 1973 overwhelmed the Beckers with unforeseen events that would have left the healthiest person scrambling just to keep up with the course of developments.

The happiest of these bolts from the blue was the prospect of Ethan's marriage, or remarriage. (In the summer of 1971, while Marion was struggling with the furor over the *Wild Wealth* artwork, he had suddenly announced his engagement to Ann Ransom, a young artist's model, and embarked on a union that fell apart in a few months.) In France he had met an American exchange student from Oregon, Joan Woerndle, whom he decided to see more of. Early in 1973, after a Colorado trip in connection with the mountain-climbing-gear business, he went on to the West Coast to renew their acquaintance. That spring they set up housekeeping together at Ethan's apartment in the semibohemian Cincinnati neighborhood of Mount Adams. When he presented her to his family, Joan and Marion fell in love at first sight.

Marion had usually been able to captivate people she liked, but seldom so completely as she captivated Joan. She seemed to radiate confidence, welcome, kindness, tact, and firsthand understanding of unmarried involvements. Ethan's girlfriend also found Ethan's mother the liveliest of company, more fun to be with than any peer. Like Nancy Swats and Ikki Matsumoto, she could not think of Marion as a sick person. What she saw was an ageless strength.

After some months of life in the Mount Adams apartment, the word "engagement" was ambiguously mentioned between Joan and Ethan. Joan did not think anything momentous had transpired until, at their next meeting, she found Marion advancing to wrap her in a mighty embrace. It was not only on her own account that Marion rejoiced (though her friends thought she had always wanted a daughter), but on that of the cookbook. Joan knew nothing of cooking, but Marion hastened to welcome her to the existing revision team, assuring her that nothing was more valuable to them all than a willing novice to help them gauge how well the basic instruction spoke to real beginners. Soon she had Joan involved with actual testing. Her true hope, of course, was for an eventual husband-wife collaboration on *The Joy of Cooking* like her own partnership with John.

Shortly before Joan's arrival another apparently happy surprise was already in train: plans for a paperback issue of *Joy*. The deal had been informally hammered out in negotiations between Bobbs-Merrill and New American Library during February and March. By the terms of the last contract Marion was entitled to half the proceeds from any sale of paperback rights. "Are you sitting down?" Leo Gobin wanted to know when he telephoned Marion to tell her what was going on. It was a good precaution. She was about to receive three-quarters of a million dollars.

The $1.5 million on which Gobin had just shaken hands with the NAL representatives was the largest sum ever paid up to that time for paperback rights to any one title. The actual contract between the two publishers had not been ratified when the *New York Times* broke the story on April 3 in a piece soon carried from coast to coast by member papers of the New York Times News Service.[8]

It was some consolation for the Marcia Seligson affair. The reporter, Eric Pace, had interviewed Marion (among others) and provided a fairly accurate summary of *Joy*'s history, incorporating this into a wide-ranging article on the ongoing cookbook boom. He portrayed the book as well worth the $1.5 million. A sidebar by the paper's restaurant critic, Raymond Sokolov, praised "the trusty text book, primer for brides and standby for old hands," and insisted that contrary to the claim of some, the current edition most certainly had not thrown out what was treasurable in past versions. With this tribute the editors had included one of Marion's favorite recipes, an unusual and dense-textured spiced loaf cake made with rye flour and honey. The ordinarily publicity-shy Marion was so pleasantly surprised by the way the *Times* coverage had turned out that she wrote to thank both authors, mentioning to Pace her pleasure in "the congratulatory letters and calls which are pouring in from all over" as friends in different parts of the country caught up with the story.[9]

Three weeks later a distinctly uncongratulatory letter arrived from a lawyer in St. Louis. There Mazie Hartrich's family had read the Pace story in the *Post-Dispatch* with great interest and pen in hand, marking some of the factual claims for later investigation and underlining the lofty answer Marion had given when the reporter asked what she planned to do with the loot: "We're not people who are terribly interested in material things."[10] Convinced that Mazie was being wronged, they had persuaded her to talk to the lawyer, Thomas E. Wack. His letter demanded that Marion immediately remit at least $40,000 unless she wanted "costly, time-consuming, and embarrassing litigation."[11]

Like most laypeople struck by a legal thunderbolt, the Beckers reacted with floundering bewilderment and urgent messages to lawyers. Since Wack intended to bring action in St. Louis, Marion retained the services there of Hugo Walther, an attorney and old von Starkloff family connection who had acted for Put in the settling of Irma's estate. Together with Harriet Pilpel in New York and Morse Johnson in Cincinnati, he began trying to assemble the relevant facts. Marion, grimly seeking to focus what physical and emotional strength she possessed on the demands of *Joy* revision, kept having her concentration broken by the grinding of the legal machine.

On July 5 Wack obtained a summons upon a plea in the Circuit Court of St. Louis County. Both sides soon agreed on a removal to the U.S. District Court for the Eastern District of Missouri, and Wack moved ahead with dispatch. In August he fired off five pages of "interrogatories"—a sequence of questions involving an intricate reconstruction of many circumstances over several decades—and requests for any and all documents pertaining to them. He also announced that he would subpoena a mass of records from Bobbs-Merrill and take depositions from Mazie, Marion, and a Bobbs-Merrill financial officer.[12]

The Hartrich complaint chiefly rested on the 1950 agreement that Irma had conceived and gotten Marion to sign while the first mother-daughter edition was in preparation.[13] It required the two of them to pay Mazie, out of the proceeds from that edition, either $4,000 annually or (if income from the book failed to exceed $12,000) a third of the year's take. During Irma's lifetime she and Marion had split the Hartrich payments on a 60–40 basis; the responsibility was thereafter to be binding on Marion as Irma's heir and the sole living author. Nonetheless, she had stopped all payments after her mother died in 1962. The gist of Wack's argument was that the 1950 agreement had justly recompensed Mazie's important contributions to *The Joy of Cooking*, and that Marion had flouted a lawful obligation while continuing to profit from those contributions as sales soared and lucrative deals were arranged. (The examination of Bobbs-Merrill's accounts was intended to establish just how much wealth she had raked in at Mazie's expense.)

It was a plausible-sounding claim that certainly caused great alarm and confusion to the Beckers, but it was dead wrong on two important matters of fact. In the first place, the 1950 instrument was no longer in effect, not because Marion had abrogated it but because it had been deliberately written to apply only to the so-called "New Joy" of 1951, which was now out of print. That the "New Joy" had ceased to exist as an income-producing work literally at the moment of Irma's death was a horrible coincidence, but only a coincidence. In the second place, Marion had so drastically revised the contents of *Joy* for the edition now in print that Wack would have had great difficulty establishing that she had filched or presumed on any work of Mazie's. A third issue that he does not seem to have paid great attention to was the need of proving that anything Mazie had done on the book in Irma's day had represented real editorial contributions as opposed to typing and general friendly support.

But probably the most self-defeating thing about the Hartrich side of the suit was the obvious presumption of "laches"—in law, a negligent delay in seeking redress for supposed injury. Wack's complaint alleged that Mazie had protested the breaking-off of payments when it occurred. His firm's surviving file on *Hartrich* v. *Becker* shows not one piece of evidence to back up this assertion. The suit did not mention that—as we shall see—Mazie had actually continued to send friendly messages to Marion after the end of the latter's fiscal obligation under the 1950 agreement. No document exists to suggest that Mazie legally acknowledged any grievance during or after 1962, at least not until 1973, when she was extremely frail and elderly and the Hartrich relatives noticed Eric Pace's article in the *Post-Dispatch* mentioning the $1.5 million.

It is plain that the legal advantage in the ill-advised Hartrich suit belonged to Marion. It is equally plain that the moral high ground did not. Needless to say, the high ground did not come into the legal dispute. But the facts deserve to be set straighter than they were at the time by either party.

Irma's correspondence clearly documents that she believed Mazie to have borne some real responsibility for *Joy*'s success and indeed its very existence. Both Marion and Mazie had helped produce the little 1931 version with no thought of pay. But in the crucial years between Marion's marriage in 1932 and her decision to join the revision work in 1948, she had been only slightly and sporadically involved with *Joy*. During the same years Mazie had given her all to the effort as Irma's loyal secretary and beloved confidante. She had typed, applauded, criticized, proofread, indexed, and probably on occasion tested. That interval—for part of which Mazie had happily worked without pay—had seen the transformation of *Joy* from obscure vanity book to national best-seller.

As soon as Irma could make even a token repayment for this selfless help she eagerly did so. There is every reason to suppose that she intended to continue some form of compensation for the remainder of Mazie's life.[14] The 1950 document meant to ensure this was unfortunately flawed. Its terms were supposed to "lapse with Mary Whyte Hartrich's death," not before, but it was written to apply only to the "New Joy" so as to avoid confusion with income from the prior (1946) edition.

Irma had not foreseen a *Joy* edition in which Mazie Hartrich would not be seriously involved. That contingency, however, developed after she herself became too ill to work on the book in 1955 or at the latest 1956. When Marion then undertook a tremendous restructuring of the contents, she reasonably enough wanted to work with Jane Brueggeman in Cincinnati rather than Mazie in St. Louis. By 1958 she had begun pondering what the 1950 understanding did or did not hold her to, and had let Mazie know that the agreement would lapse with the next edition.[15] Meanwhile, she fell into the habit of talking (and probably thinking) about the cookbook's history as if she had supplied valuable editorial contributions without interruption from 1931 on, while Mazie had been a mere secretary. She also later gave people to understand that her mother had handed over sole responsibility for the work to her after 1951, thus dismissing or denying Irma and Mazie's continued work relationship in the early fifties.[16]

Marion's wish to be done with an obligation that had been none of her making is understandable. But thwarting her mother's honorable intent by failing to offer even a small annual recompense to Mazie under subsequent editions was one of her least magnanimous actions. She was surely capable of distinguishing between the letter and the spirit of what Irma had tried to do in 1950; it was the former that she chose to observe.

The Hartrich and Becker lawyers were concerned with quite another set of facts, all of which boded much better for Marion than Mazie. If Thomas Wack had not seen the weaknesses of Mazie's case by the time he deposed her on December 3, he must have had misgivings about continuing to trial afterward. The deposition is a pathetic document that shows the eighty-three-year-old plaintiff muddled and tremulous under even gentle questioning. She related an account of the supposedly contemptuous treatment she had received from Marion that may have had some dim connection with a few facts, but that also seemed to change in circumstantial details every time she tried to tell it. To the questions of Marion's attorneys about why she had not bothered to complain before the news of the $750,000 windfall, she could offer only a childish rationalization about not having wanted to add to Marion's expenses.[17]

This performance did not augur well for Mazie's ability to testify in a courtroom under hostile questioning. Nor did any of Wack's inquiries into Bobbs-Merrill's financial records turn up a smoking gun with Marion's guilty fingerprints. (There was a completely unrelated smoking gun, a few papers from the affair of the unauthorized edition eleven years earlier that had somehow migrated into the file of subpoenaed Bobbs-Merrill documents and that contained damning evidence of Bill Raney and Hughes Miller's actions, but these were never seen by anyone who would have understood their import.)[18]

Marion could not have realized how doubtfully the other side's case was shaping up. For all she knew, she would have to face a grueling federal trial on charges of defrauding an old friend when she should have been husbanding her physical and mental strength for the current *Joy* revision. But she did not for a minute mean to yield to what she considered blackmail. She was determined to go on with it when, in a matter of weeks, the fabric of the world collapsed around her.

On December 19, leaving a Christmas party to which she and John had driven in separate cars, she saw him walking strangely, then realized that he was headed in the opposite direction from where he had parked his car. He seemed to reorient himself almost at once. But Marion, watching closely, noticed a slight dragging of one leg over the next few days. A couple of days after Christmas he volunteered that he might have had a slight stroke. At first the neurologist to whom they were referred seemed to agree. But over a wavering several weeks, John's walking became so much worse that the doctors soon knew a far graver brain condition was involved.

It was under these circumstances that Marion appeared for the deposition of January 10, 1974—luckily, Wack had agreed to come to Cincinnati—and met the attorney's first background queries with her own affirmation of what it meant to be Marion Rombauer Becker.

Q. And what is your principal business or occupation, Mrs. Becker?

A. Life artist.[19]

Her deposition was a marathon performance that lasted all that day and until noon on the eleventh. It was clear that for all her physical ills Marion would make a far stronger trial witness than the flustered Mazie. Wack could not shake her on any critical point. With a layman's ignorance of what goes into cookbooks, he stumbled badly in attempting to show that she had helped herself to Mazie's work. At every attempt to prove some use of supposedly Hartrich-derived material, Marion irrefutably explained why her treatment in the current edition was new and original. She carefully avoided any direct imputations against Mazie, limiting herself to relating various of her own contributions to *The Joy of Cooking* while repeatedly stating that she had no firsthand knowledge of her mother's specific financial or other arrangements with Mazie through the first few commercial editions.

She had another important card to play. Hugo Walther and Morse Johnson, who were on hand to intervene when Wack tried to lead her into dangerous shoals, produced an important document that more or less annihilated the notion of Marion's having just swiped anyone's work. It was an estimate that Leo Gobin had furnished to Put during his 1963 efforts to sort out the tax liability of Irma's estate, stating that by Gobin's calculation approximately 80 percent of the 1962 edition had been Marion's own contribution. And as she and her lawyers explained to Wack, virtually anything else had been minutely reviewed and reintegrated into the whole during the course of revision.[20]

Backing up the argument of laches that her lawyers were preparing to develop when the case came to trial, she insisted without hesitation that she did not remember receiving any message whatever from Mazie since Irma's death. Marion's memory was at fault here, since Mazie had written her at least three times during that period—but the letters in question would only have strengthened her case and helped sink Mazie's. Far from making known any grievance about the cessation of payments when or after it occurred, Mazie had sent a kind note (now missing) on the appearance of the 1962 *Joy* revision and a cordial thank-you on receiving a gift copy of *Little Acorn* in 1966.[21] Still worse for any claim of having considered herself wronged was her letter of congratulation to Marion on the 1963 *Joy of Cooking*. Had Marion remembered its existence she surely would have brought it to the lawyers' attention: "The 'Joy' has at last reached full maturity. . . . How proud your mother would be of you if she could have lived to see this book!"[22]

Even without that bit of reinforcement, Marion had acquitted herself triumphantly in the deposition. Though this part of the ordeal ended with both parties supposedly prepared for litigation, Wack was not long in feeling out Hugo Walther on an out-of-court settlement. By January 31 Marion was reporting to Harriet Pilpel that he had asked for $24,000 to call off the suit.[23]

Meanwhile, John's baffling symptoms continued. He was now barely able to walk with a cane. He and Marion had meant to escape to Arizona for a hasty working vacation. But it was obvious that he would not be able to leave Cockaigne—not even for Ethan and Joan's wedding, which was to take place in Portland on Joan's birthday, Saint Valentine's Day. In the end Marion flew out to Oregon and back on her own. The newlyweds took over the Tucson hotel reservation for their honeymoon.

John's mind was clear, but the evidence now manifestly suggested a brain tumor. Because of the neurologist's schedule, there was an agonizing delay in admitting him to the hospital for surgery. By the time of the operation on March 8 he was almost unable to walk on his own.

There were two tumors. Only one could be removed; the biopsy determined that it was malignant.[24]

By then Marion had already decided to accept a settlement with Mazie. At any other time she might well have held out against so crassly opportunistic a bid for extortion. But in her own physical struggle she could not think of anything except helping John—she still grasped at hopes of his partial recovery—and finishing the revision. Walther and Johnson had beaten down Wack to $13,500, which Marion accepted. On March 6, two days before John's operation, Mazie signed a release agreeing to dismissal of the suit "with prejudice"—i.e., relinquishing any right to reinstate it in future. Marion was to assume court costs of about $500.[25] If the two women ever again held any sort of communication, no evidence of it remains.

The paperback bonanza had proved to be a poisoned apple. The only real pleasure it gave Marion was a brief interlude of showering presents on people and causes, just as Irma had done in the heady early days of best-sellerdom. Old friends received gifts sufficient to send them round the world. A young woman of her acquaintance who had decided to abandon a musical career for medicine was quietly enabled to attend medical school. Worthy environmental projects received generous donations. One of the most unusual of these, a study of bird-migration patterns in Tunisia, had been suggested by the Rombauers' friend Marian Judell Israel, who was in North Africa with the Peace Corps following the breakup of her marriage to Murray.

Most other sequels to the New American Library sale were at best troublous. A large tax burden loomed down the road, though Tom Itin had undertaken to direct money into suitable shelters and supervise the overall cash flow while the $750,000 was being paid out in installments over the next several years. NAL's handling of the paperback version turned into a long series of headaches. The first printing managed to omit Marion's key to the special symbols. NAL then started planning discount offers and giveaways on a scale that made Bobbs-Merrill look restrained. Marion was soon at odds with them over premium sales, on which she had developed an emphatic policy.

Her declaration of independence from food-industry payola in *Little Acorn* had been no idle boast. She had had written into the last *Joy of Cooking* contract a clause requiring both her and Bobbs-Merrill's approval for commercial tie-ins. She was not a party to the Bobbs-Merrill–NAL deal, but Leo Gobin—knowing his author—had added a similar provision to that contract. Premium sales of the paperback book required the consent of Bobbs-Merrill and Marion, "such consent not to be unreasonably withheld."[26]

By now Gobin and Rachlis had some idea of the service she had done the book in refusing to let it be mixed up in promotional campaigns for other products connected with cooking. NAL had no such delicacy. The president, Herbert K. Schnall, thought *Joy* was a natural magnet for all kinds of corporate compadres in search of promotional tie-ins. Marion must have been an awful shock to him. She decreed that the book could be used as a come-on for other products or services only when they were so unrelated to food or cooking as to eliminate all appearance of an endorsement. A bank was fine. A cake mix was not. Even nonfood products from a corporation with food-manufacturing divisions were questionable.

If he grasped such distinctions, Schnall did not think much of them. The first gold mine Marion Becker cost him, something he had considered a done deal, was an order of a quarter of a million copies—later raised to half a million—from the firm of Thomas Lipton, late in 1973.[27] Other pitches of the same sort followed, and were rejected. NAL could have raised the issue of unreasonably withheld consent, except that Bobbs-Merrill backed her to the hilt. Bright ideas from Schnall or the NAL director of premium marketing were routinely funneled through Rachlis, who politely passed on her replies and declined to exert any further influence. It did not escape Marion's gratitude that he and Gobin were as best they could shielding her from a great nuisance during nearly insupportable crises.

By the time she agreed to buy off Mazie, Marion was having trouble holding her own physically. John was now scheduled for cobalt therapy, and the two of them ended up being hospitalized together in early April. Again she received nitrogen mustard treatments to inhibit the ongoing seepage of fluid from the lung, but this time they caused a fearful setback. She suffered such intense nausea and vomiting that she had to be placed on intravenous fluids for several days. The pleural effusion recurred at once. She was not discharged until April 24, still far from strong.[28] She had tried to keep up some sort of work schedule through everything, but the right arm was once again painful, sometimes driving her back to the left-handed mirror writing.

John's mind had remained alert through his illness. But his speech and writing were now nearly gone, and soon the doctors had to insert an indwelling catheter. He was trying to learn to walk again with the help of a therapist, but the outlook was at best clouded. Marion saw that he would require round-the-clock nursing care beyond anything that she could have provided had she been in good health herself.

At this juncture—it was the first week in May—one of Judy Israel's buoyant letters arrived from North Africa, mentioning that she did not know exactly what she would do when the current Peace Corps stint was up. Marion went to the phone and called Tunisia. She explained the situation as adequately as she could and asked Judy to come and join the writing and editing effort at Cockaigne. Judy agreed at once. She thought she could wind up her duties in time to be in Cincinnati by mid-June.[29]

Marion had not said so, but in essence what she needed was another John Becker to give her a few months' push in the terrible race. The greater part of the work was at least roughly in shape, but a huge amount remained still to be done. No one else now working with her— the bright but inexperienced Ethan, the still more ignorant Joan, the devoted but painfully crippled Jane Brueggeman—could match exactly what John and now Judy had to offer, which was birthright citizenship in the St. Louis *Deutschtum* combined with humor and intellectual panache. Judy had known Irma—the beloved "Frau Rom"—since childhood and been a chum of the old German Class regulars. She was also an experienced home cook, an ex-academic (she had taught college French for several years) acquainted with methods of research, and an irrepressible wit with the sort of offbeat curiosity that *Joy* fans always had responded to.

The general revision was probably about two-thirds complete when Judy arrived on June 12. Several chapters were already in good enough shape to go on to Rachlis and the Bobbs-Merrill copy editor, Gladys Moore. The Matsumoto drawings were close to finished, requiring only some corrections and filling-in of gaps. But great sections remained to be reviewed and substantial pieces of text to be written before the manuscript could even approach an acceptable state. Gene Rachlis came out to confer with Marion on July 10, and she pledged to have just about everything in his hands by October 15. This, however, would still leave them several months of work afterward reading proof and supplying textual odds and ends.

Judy's addition to the marathon effort proved just what Marion had hoped, an infusion of new energy and morale. Her first assignment was to put herself in the position of a dumb-bunny bride reporting on what she could or couldn't understand in the last *Joy*. She moved on to John's usual concerns—overall continuity, flow, and readability. She also took over the chapter that he would have written on drinks and wine. She neither expected nor wanted to claim authorship of any particular passage (indeed, no such claim could be very meaningful in view of the pains Marion took with every detail of the text). But she did much to inject the sort of ebullient whimsy that readers had come to associate with *The Joy of Cooking*. Irma Rombauer herself might have enjoyed the manner in which the introduction to wine, as sketched out by Judy, insouciantly roved among the opinions of Art Buchwald (who claimed to like champagne "because it tastes as though his foot's asleep"), Voltaire ("Beauty to the toad is the she-toad"), and Rabelais ("Fays ce que vouldras," aptly rendered as "Do your own thing").[30]

With the reinforcement of Judy Israel, Marion and her associates managed to maintain remarkable cheer throughout the desperate summer of 1974. They howled over a widely printed wire-service account of a St. Louis Catholic girls' school receiving twenty-five copies of *The Joy of Sex* from a book supplier who had been asked to send *The Joy of Cooking*.[31] Marion's resolve and grace never failed to astonish those who worked with her during those grueling months. One beautiful morning she made her early way out to her cherished herb garden and had miniature corsages of lavender and sweet herbs ready for the rest as they arrived. Week after week, she contrived to make the experience of working in the same house as two mortally ill people almost happy for everyone else. Some time afterward she wrote that a private beacon of courage for her in facing the illness was a radio interview that she had heard with a survivor of a Nazi concentration camp.[32] Whatever the source of her strength, it was somehow communicated to the sharers of the effort.

The crew on duty most of the time consisted of Jane (obliged to rest at frequent intervals because of her chronic pain), Judy, and Nancy Swats. Ethan and Joan, now living in a nearby subdivision, were there most days. Marion wrote in a small office down the hall from the main office or upstairs in bed, depending on her state. She slept erratically most nights and would usually awaken at three or four in the morning. Sometimes she would write haiku in the night watches.[33] But mostly she used this time to get through her best work of the day, secure against the later distraction of telephone or doorbell.

Once or twice she tried to bring John into the main work room to follow the others' progress, for he was still interested and perfectly aware of what was going on around him. But despite speech therapy he was nearly unable to communicate. As the condition progressed, he could express himself only with his eyes. It was agony for Marion and Ethan to see this most verbal of men robbed of what had given him such pleasure.

Mark, who came for several visits with Jennifer and the nine-year-old Joe, seemed to know better how to reach the dying man. John had not been able to walk for many months, but Mark got him into a garden cart and trundled him about the paths at Cockaigne to see the summer's growth. For some reason Joan was best able of all to communicate with him, while Marion felt insuperably cut off, almost paralyzed by the sense of his loneliness. "My own grief and helplessness," she later wrote, "seemed to build a barrier to speech which could only be bridged by physical contact."[34]

After John's operation she had at first tried to persuade herself that he might at least partly recover. But over the summer she finally understood that there was no hope. The only kindness she could offer now was to spare him the last indignities of a hospital and let him die, probably within a few months, in the house he had built. For the first and only time in the ordeal, Judy Israel saw her burst into tears and cry out, "What am I going to do?"

Always before she had been confident that if something happened to her, *The Joy of Cooking* would be carried on by the nearly equal skill and knowledge of John. The 1972 *Joy of Cooking* trust arrangement had been drawn up under that assumption. Now it looked like a less-than-ideal means of conveying her interests. She must try to provide for the book's future—but in the present frantic exertion to finish the new edition, she could manage little more than a hurried signal to her most trusted advisors that they had better put their heads together.

The signal consisted of a meeting that she convened at Cockaigne on July 24. Those present, besides herself, were Ethan, Harriet Pilpel, Morse Johnson, Tom Itin, and Jim Walter of the accounting firm Coopers and Lybrand, which Itin had brought in several years earlier to help with tax matters.[35]

Marion presided over the discussion with an aplomb and clearheadedness that put Harriet Pilpel in mind of Kipling's "If."[36] But the truth of her situation was daunting, and she was deeply daunted. Her main goal in calling the meeting had been not to make a lot of far-reaching decisions but to assemble in one room the people who would have to take over *Joy* affairs from her and elicit from them a general agreement to keep in touch with each other through a round-robin arrangement.

Several of those present thought it was time to tackle Bobbs-Merrill on some concessions to be demanded in the next *Joy* contract. Mrs. Pilpel, for one, would have loved to hold out for a higher basic royalty rate. But Marion simply did not have the nerve to ask the company for anything controversial. At this stage she was unsure of how to arrange the transfer of trusteeship and authorship to Ethan, and she desperately wished to be able to appeal to Leo Gobin's good graces in case she had to draw funds at short notice.

This priority had nothing to do with greed for money. It was dictated by the investment strategy of Tom Itin, from whom she had gathered that flexible cash-flow options for their small portfolio would help them negotiate the minefield of tax liability in the next few years. Marion, to whom a mere phrase like "cash flow" was impressively scientific, was fearful to disturb the good will of Bobbs-Merrill in any way that might threaten the family interests.[37] Knowing John to be at death's door and herself not far behind, she would not authorize any participant in the meeting to proceed with more than cautious initiatives on any score.

After this hasty and inconclusive gathering of advisors, Marion and the revision team gathered themselves for a final mighty push. In the next two months they finished virtually all of what Rachlis had asked to have by mid-October. At the end of September the job was close enough to completion for Marion to hand herself over to the doctors and submit to what was likely to be literally a kill-or-cure measure: a new sequence of cobalt therapy.

The first treatment was scheduled for October 7. On October 1 Marion wrote a note to Morse Johnson and the children enclosing a message that she wanted sent to her friends after her death. Three days later she drafted a long memo to Mark and Ethan summarizing her wishes for various items not covered by her will. But as it turned out, the cobalt therapy worked this time, up to a point. Marion got through the course with at least slightly renewed strength and without the punishing side effects she had suffered in the spring. She had been granted a partial reprieve, but now John began to slip away fast. For the first time she understood the phrase "the smell of death." He had been comatose for several days when Marion finished the last cobalt treatment. In the evening of the next day, October 22, he died.

A strange scrap of paper in John's handwriting survives among the tangle of letters and documents at Cockaigne. It contains the closing lines of William Butler Yeats's poem "To a Friend Whose Work Has Come to Nothing":

> Bred to a harder thing
> Than Triumph, turn away
> And like a laughing string
> Whereon mad fingers play
> Amid a place of stone,
> Be secret and exult,
> Because of all things known
> That is most difficult.

The date and purpose of this carefully printed excerpt cannot now be guessed; John may or may not have meant to draw any connection with his own life. But the career he had made for himself had come to much less than the ambitions that had floated before him as a bright young aesthete trying his hand at short stories or—as he had done in 1930—proposing himself for architecture critic of the *New Yorker*.[38] In Cincinnati he had actually ended by carving out a modest living designing projects like banks, firehouses, plants, and schools, with a few charming private homes as his chief personal satisfaction. His most lasting work would prove to be several decades of thoroughly unsung contributions to his mother-in-law's and wife's cookbook.

Marion's friends entertained widely varying opinions of her handsome husband. Some of them believed that he was a singularly civilized and clear-thinking human being. Others were convinced that most of the real ability and purpose that he and Marion had between them belonged to her. In the eyes of their son Ethan, theirs was a true union of equals who melded like halves of an extraordinary whole, remaining "almost indecently in love" to the very end. But there were those who saw the marriage in less ideal terms, as resting on Marion and John's shared assumption that he was a creature of superior gifts, a gem always to be displayed to best advantage.

It had been understood that when John retired he would be able to devote himself to his own writing. In 1970 the moment seemed to have come, when their friend Geoff Vincent, an old St. Louis neighbor of Irma's and a veteran editor at the *New York Times* and *Louisville Courier-Journal*, invited him to write a regular column titled "Places and Spaces" for the Sunday *Courier-Journal*, on urban affairs and housing in their human and environmental dimensions. The plan collapsed after three articles when John took offense at one piece's having been postponed for some reason.[39] In the last few years his family and friends believed that he was writing a book that would be some sort of philosophical summing-up, a distillation of his life's thought. After his death Marion and the children searched for the manuscript but found nothing that could have been John's book, though at one time an outline had been in existence.[40] Either it never had been begun or he had destroyed the manuscript at the onset of his illness.

Marion would have scorned any funerary fuss for herself, but for John nothing was too good. She bought an expensive plot in Spring Grove, a Cincinnati landmark that was both a nondenominational cemetery and one of the handsomest independent arboretums in the United States. As quickly as her own condition would permit, she arranged a memorial for about a hundred guests at Cockaigne on Saturday, November 2. Morse Johnson, who delivered the eulogy, had taken as his text a bit of Japanese calligraphy that Marion had turned up in a St. Louis odds-and-ends store and later found an expert to translate: "Sometimes on a beautiful day like this, I like to walk in the true way with my friends." Luckily the brilliance of the fall afternoon matched the thought. Marion got through the day with the help of her grandson, Joe, who held her hand throughout the program and, she later wrote, "gave me the courage to control my grief." When it was all over, her mind returned to the long-deferred plan for a family memoir.[41]

She had not tried to go on with that project since 1973. But the idea had only been set aside, not forgotten. On some undated occasion she actually drew a crude image of the concept as it had formed itself in her mind: a tangle of connected loops signifying "links" or "the link." What it meant to her was the interlocked destinies of the family, past, present, and future. She had unveiled the same idea to Joe when she first started putting down memories on paper for his benefit in 1971, explaining that she wanted him to glimpse "the many links that bind us to each other" as a family.[42] John's death seemed to make the task more imperative.

In November she was obliged to turn back to the immediate demands of the current *Joy*, which she was now starting to read in proof. But as soon as she could she made a stab at bearing witness, an act that she felt as a kind of moral obligation. Early in January of 1975—she did not note the exact date—she sat down and wrote at the top of a piece of paper, "LINKS: The Life of a Family."

What followed was an account of John's memorial service—the old Cincinnati civic and arts allies who had turned out in force, the strength she drew from Joe's presence, the playing of Beethoven's second Razumovsky quartet by the four longtime Becker friends who were the members of the La Salle String Quartet. The moment that most resonated in her memory had come at the end of the day after the guests had gone, when the immediate family with Tom and Shirley Itin—"almost family" in the Beckers' affections—had sat with her over some hot soup in the office and watched all tokens of the event being cleared away from the premises while the sunset faded outside. "This experience was ours as a family," she wrote, "and it is for this intimate audience alone that I try to ressurect [sic] the links from the past that make us what we are as we carry on into the future."[43]

Early on Easter Sunday, March 30, Marion wept as she wrote her second "Links" entry of the year, recording that the last of the *Joy* revision work had been completed the previous evening. Probably this meant that she had conquered what she considered the last major tasks (proofreading, fitting in some final jigsaw bits) before Bobbs-Merrill prepared to print the finished book, leaving only small and more or less mechanical details to be checked. The final stint had remained on schedule despite two unlooked-for events. One was Judy Israel's departure at the end of January, with Marion's delighted blessing. On an East Coast trip to see her first grandchild in a hospital maternity ward Judy had encountered Murray, and they were remarried within about a week. A much graver threat to the Bobbs-Merrill timetable had come when Marion suddenly discovered that the copy seemed to be some ninety-six pages over the allotted length. Without missing a beat, Leo Gobin looked over the situation and told her that there was nothing to worry about. In a decision that saved the production schedule but left the huge book rather less than ideally legible, he simply reduced the type size by a point.[44]

The submission of the text had been nearly 100 percent complete by February 12; the contract was signed, with little controversy over any provision, on March 14. Marion's lawyers had had the agreement drawn up this time between Bobbs-Merrill and herself as trustee under the 1972 trust, Ethan being named to succeed her in future revisions after her death by virtue of his position as successor trustee.[45] She had sought no further concessions on any matter of substance, letting the royalty schedule and most other important provisions remain as they had been in the 1963 contract. Trying to joust with Bobbs-Merrill on her own account was the last thing she wanted in her state of illness, grief, and deeply felt vulnerability over the ancient wrong of the copyright. She did, however, separately redress another injustice that had come to her notice at about the same time. When Ikki Matsumoto had first discussed the illustrating job with Bobbs-Merrill, he had naively submitted a bid far lower than what the work probably was worth. Marion, at last learning what the company had actually paid him, thought it so scandalously low that she insisted on paying him several thousand dollars more out of her own pocket.[46]

This time Bobbs-Merrill (undoubtedly remembering the ludicrous scramble of 1962) had prudently decided to get a large stock in print well before the scheduled publication date of September 15. The actual copyright date is June 1; the company had a 150,000-copy first printing on hand shortly before that, in time to display finished books at the American Booksellers Association meeting in Washington, D.C., during the last week of May. Gene Rachlis was able to buttonhole Julia Child at the event in an attempt to enlist her good will. Over the summer the company kept up a sprinkling of advance publicity meant to heighten the publishing trade's and cookbook-buying public's anticipation of a blockbuster release. For the first time in several decades of *Joy*'s history, the event proceeded without a hitch. The results were everything Marion or Bobbs-Merrill could have desired.

What they had on their hands was the most tremendous success in the annals of *The Joy of Cooking.* Two 150,000-copy printings had been completed when books started being shipped to the stores at the end of August, and the pace of advance orders suggested that another one would be needed soon. Favorable press coverage appeared everywhere, though Marion refused all personal publicity efforts and no journalist had a glimmer of the excruciating story behind her triumph.

Knowing that the 1975 book was her farewell to *Joy*, she had for the first time provided a special page of acknowledgments recognizing those who in her view had made the work possible. It was a supremely Marion-like document, somewhat less than scientific in its generosity. She offered a chilly nod to Mazie Hartrich solely for "technical assistance" on the privately published 1931 book, and treated as present fact the "constant and unstinting effort toward *Joy*'s enrichment" given by John, whose death she could not bear to mention to the readers. Not caring to differentiate between the relative involvements of Ethan and Mark, who had now decided to work together on the next revision, she cited them equally as contributors to this one.

To Leo Gobin, whom she thanked in this official summing-up for having "guarded for us great freedom in our work," she thought she also owed a more private farewell salute. On May 26 she wrote him begging off from any sort of publicity appearances and interviews in view of her limited physical stamina, and took the opportunity to tell him how she valued their "long happy" association despite the shadow of inherited author-publisher enmities:

> I do thank you heartily for the great good sense and steadiness you have shown as we worked up together the content and production standards that *Joy* now embodies due to our co-operative efforts—and I want to repeat my gratitude for the complete freedom you gave me to develop my potential.[47]

The edition that Gobin had shepherded into print hewed more faithfully to Marion's intent than any other *Joy* version she had worked on. It would prove remarkably durable, surviving through at least twenty years of particularly spasmodic and unnerving shifts in culinary fashion, food marketing, kitchen technology, and nutritional theory. Not only would it chime with the Zeitgeist in 1975, but in some ways it would go on ringing bells more significantly than any of the other kitchen bibles for a long while. The reason is that it pursued certain convictions and hobbyhorses that had been Marion's for half her life, and that these had taken on great meaning for the American public. Her last edition happened to coincide with a crucial stage in the adoption of radical culture—at least, assorted bits of it—into mainstream culture.

In the 1951 *Joy* Marion had vigorously sought to introduce some of her own notions of healthful eating; she had pulled in her horns a little in the next revision in order to concentrate on something closer to the gourmet fashion. She had not then known that young visionaries throughout the land would start rejecting the contents of the supermarket shelves and launching quests for food that they considered more natural, nutritious, and socially responsible. When it happened, she was delighted, though skeptical of many fads that passed for the new truth.

The campaigns of Ralph Nader (one of Marion's heroes) to denounce possibly harmful additives in processed foods as the result of corporate malfeasance point to an important development of the late sixties and early seventies. In the rapidly fragmenting arena of New

Left politics, the subject of food had started to acquire social and moral implications so fast that it hardly seemed possible to be a true progressive without wanting to overthrow the despotic sway of agribusiness and industrial chemistry at the nation's table. What was even more critical to the long-term success of the 1975 *Joy* was that these same implications would subsequently shed some of their New Left links and remain in the awareness of consumers through many giddy ins and outs of political fashion well into the 1990s.

Marion could not know this. But she did see that by 1975, beliefs like hers on the relationships between food and health, land use, and good citizenship looked like very sensible ideas to a large spectrum of the American public. She was emboldened to direct *Joy* more emphatically to issues that she had first noticed decades before. In the new book she commented on the impoverishment of soil through overexploitation or crude dosing with chemical fertilizers, the troubling environmental repercussions of "chickens fed in batteries, pigs and cattle concentrated in feed lots," the discovery "that many of our lakes and estuaries have become nearly incapable of supporting life," the "galaxy of pollutants such as viruses, nitrates, heavy metals, pesticides, and asbestos and other carcinogens" in our drinking water.[48] In consequence, her last version struck an eager chord with millions of home cooks who had started to absorb toned-down versions of the "natural foods" credo broadcast to the under-thirty generation a few years earlier by segments of the radical counterculture. This response would not die away, but would go on resonating for a long time.

Twenty-some years have not left this remarkable document looking freshly minted in all ways. The recipe selection, as in 1963, tried to include some new ethnic smatterings (e.g., Greek taramasalata, Chinese firepot, a peanut soup from Ghana and a beef stew attributed to West Africa, a version of a Spanish potato omelet) based on extremely incomplete knowledge. Marion, who never claimed to be a prophet, surely failed to foresee the recent gigantic shake-up of the American ethnic mix, and paid no attention at all to large clusters of cuisines that are now thoroughly entrenched in the United States. But it is patently unfair to complain about the absence of Vietnamese or Cuban dishes in the 1975 *Joy*. If there is any fault to be found with her emphasis, it is that she did not make even more room for her own convictions at the expense of what she still thought *Joy*'s real drawing card for "serious" cooks, the coverage of French food.

In Marion's own everyday scale of values, responsible farming and eating were much more important than someone's idea of Frenchified culinary elegance. But in her reading of cookbook buyers' interests, she continued to assume that what would mean most to the real cognoscenti was the highly publicized vogue of haute cuisine that had been swept in some fifteen years before with (among other influences) Julia Child's popular television series *The French Chef*. The very idea of sending Ethan to the Cordon Bleu indicates that Marion still expected the most enlightened, up-to-date *Joy* users to see opulent, elaborate French dishes as the height of culinary attainment. That fashion might be fickle regarding even the supreme worth of certain "classics" was beyond most food writers' imagining.

Marion's coverage of French cuisine had been naive and spotty in the last edition, and remained so in this. It was a subject that caused her to genuflect before icons she really knew little of. In the light of hindsight, her continued obeisance to the talismans of Gallocentric uplift helped date the book much faster than her allegiance to environmental causes. The French haute cuisine model would shortly be passé or genuinely forgotten by many of the younger cookbook audience, who would have been more impressed by a bigger selection of vegetable main dishes from cuisines with long-standing vegetarian traditions—something that would have neatly reinforced her remarks about the wastefulness of modern meat production and the need to conserve the earth's resources.

Even in the fairly circumspect treatment that she limited herself to, the new edition's plain sympathy with "health food" enthusiasts and back-to-the-soil pioneers gave it a real future advantage over most of the all-round cooking manuals. Another lucky stroke was Marion's expanded attention to the botanical exotica that she had always loved exploring—carambola, feijoa, durian, passion fruit, genip, the still-novel kiwifruit. Twenty years later, when most would be regularly available in hundreds (at least) of American groceries, her last *Joy* would still outclass all other general American kitchen bibles in this area of coverage.

Two other important decisions reflected Marion's idea of the degree to which the book should take note of timesaving new kitchen technology. Irma had nearly always rushed to embrace "advances," but Marion had become quite cautious about some of them. She forbore to mention food processors, which had attracted a certain amount of press after the first licensed American version of the French Robot-

Coupe appeared in 1973 but still did not look like anything more than an exotic toy to all observers. Marion's guess, though obviously premature, was not altogether a disadvantage for the book. Several years after the revision was published many food writers would be enthusiastically translating any sort of formula from scrambled eggs to French bread into food-processor directions, and several years after *that* many of the resulting recipes would look very silly.

Microwave ovens, by now too important to ignore, posed a more complex dilemma. Marion experimented at length with the device, which had been widely available for more than half a decade, and turned an emphatic thumbs-down on it. Reminding her readers that "heat is a subtle medium that for best results will always demand intelligent human attention," she dwelt severely on the inferior "eating quality or appearance" of most microwave-cooked foods and the elaborate measures necessary to offset the machine's limitations.[49] This verdict was mild compared with her private opinion. She had come to suspect (though erroneously) that exposure to microwaves might denature proteins to the point of impairing the protein value of food. Her distrust of—as she saw it—a phony advancement on real cooking was so great that she actually wrote to Ralph Nader in February of 1973 expressing her fear "that a great hoax is being lavishly perpetrated on the American public" and suggesting "a full-scale microwave oven report from one of your agencies."[50] No record exists of a reply.

For better or worse, Marion retained the general *Joy of Cooking* framework that she had arrived at in the 1963 revision. Even then the design had not been easy for anyone to grasp on first picking up the book and trying to use it: three prominent chapters on nutrition, cooking methods, and ingredients interspersed among chapters devoted to orthodox menu categories, with nearly every chapter presenting a constant alternation between recipes and the chunks of background explanation that she called the "Abouts." Marion had just about carried off this complicated scheme before. This time the material came closer to defeating the organization. Any piece of information might end up crammed into any available corner of the work; there are people who have owned and continuously used it for twenty years without knowing that some particular subject is even mentioned in it.

Marion herself was aware enough of the many mazes confronting a reader to write a small preface to the often baffling sixty-five-page index explaining how to use it and concluding, "Meanwhile, happy hunting!"[51] She knew that at least the superdedicated users would eventually learn their way around any big bible as instinctively as cats around a row of backyards. The stunningly overburdened organization of the latest *Joy* proved no obstacle to longtime popularity. Certainly it did not hinder the work's immediate reception.

The critical praise heaped on the 1975 *Joy* was virtually unanimous. Various reviewers approvingly noted Marion's sturdy skepticism about some of the wonders confronting modern consumers and her pleasure in championing older home methods and country skills. With its emphatic consumerist stance, the newest version struck many observers as representing homespun cloth in a polyester age. This impression helped a few prestigious observers decide that something was lacking in an ambitious new rival, *The Doubleday Cookbook* by Jean Anderson and Elaine Hanna. It was a massive compilation that aspired to almost equal scope with *Joy* and was hailed by several reviewers as the finest book of its kind. But two influential roundups of the season's cookbooks curtly dismissed it by comparison with the reincarnated *Joy of Cooking*. In the *Washington Post* (and its syndicates), William Rice pronounced that *Doubleday* "has less personality and is less rewarding" than the older rival, while Raymond Sokolov in the *New York Times Book Review* used *Joy* to damn "such paradigms of faceless commercialism as the gigantic new DOUBLEDAY COOKBOOK."[52]

Voices of dissent were few. Several reviewers justly complained about the small type, but not many essayed a genuine evaluation of the work's overall advantages and disadvantages. One of the few exceptions was Julia Child's assessment in the October 1975 issue of *McCall's* magazine. The reviewer, who had coined the horrible phrase "Mrs. Joy" for both Irma Rombauer and her book and milked it for all it was worth, praised the new revision generously but not fatuously. She mentioned that by comparison with earlier versions *Joy* now seemed to be trying to cover too much ground for consistent excellence, and tactfully suggested that as the book expanded its "all-embracing" notion of American food, "that large embrace" had gathered "bits of chaff" such as some seriously garbled French recipes.[53] Marion, who heard the piece read over the phone by Cecily Brownstone as soon as the new *McCall's* issue was out, chose to ignore its criticisms and dwell on its handsome praise. She was quite delighted by Mrs. Child's recollections of briefly meeting Irma in Paris in 1952, though she and Cecily did a double take at the description of her mother's "unassuming and gentle manner."[54]

Between her final effort to complete *Joy* and the book's triumphal launch in the fall, Marion had nearly collapsed and somehow pulled herself together to start planning the next goals of her life. By the second week of May she had been hospitalized twice for an extreme shortness of breath that pointed to further deterioration of the lungs, and had been sent home with the oxygen supply and nasal plugs that would be her constant companions through the rest of her long battle.[55] She was a great deal weaker now, and inescapably tethered to the oxygen tank. Most of the time she could not even drive herself from Cockaigne to a meeting. The familiar trees and paths came to seem to her like a prison, if a beautiful and cherished one.

The oxygen did make a difference to her breathing. In the late spring and early summer of 1975 Marion rebounded with extraordinary mental and flickering physical energy. She believed she saw signs that the lung damage—which one pulmonary specialist who had examined her thought had been caused less by the disease itself than the aggressive radiation therapy—might be at least partly reversible.

As often happens with women widowed after long marriages, her personality subtly altered with the new shape of her life. Ethan, Joan, and Jane Brueggeman observed with surprise that she had developed a real relish for humor, something that she had never permitted herself to yield to very heartily. (John had always been the wit in the family as far as she was concerned, and the judge of what was funny.) Joan and Ethan thought she might literally die laughing at *Monty Python and the Holy Grail*, to which they took her and the oxygen tank.

She became a devoted Woody Allen fan, roaring with pleasure over *Lovborg's Women.* She had never had a greater curiosity about what was new. She pondered national events (which were at best rancorous in the aftermath of Watergate) with heightened interest, and established a family ritual of listening to *All Things Considered* on National Public Radio every evening when Joan and Ethan joined her for dinner. She had also eagerly returned to the writing of "Links." It was actually only one of *five* projected books that she set her sights on in the first surge of hope when she thought her health was at least half returning.

The other four were an updated version of *A Cookbook for Girls and Boys* to be written with Joan, a revival of her old idea for an anthology of *Joy* fan letters, an illustrated book of flower arrangements by Town and Country Garden Club friends to be introduced with an essay by Marion on the art of making simple impromptu arrangements with well-chosen containers, and her unfulfilled obligation to Ernst Kropp—the translation and American publication of *Wandlung der Form im XX. Jahrhundert,* to which she had promised to see nearly fifty years before. She still had the book, an old photograph of her lover, and a bundle of his letters. She also had at hand a far more capable translator than herself: Dorothy Wartenberg, who had been variously involved with the 1963 *Joy* revision and had just finished writing a Ph.D. thesis on Brecht for the University of Cincinnati German studies department.

None of these five projects would ever be completed. The flower-arranging book was not meant for commercial publication and could be picked up or put aside with no deadline pressure. Marion worked on it intermittently in 1975 and 1976 with the chosen illustrator, Doris Burton, a Cincinnati Art Academy graduate whom the Beckers had gotten to know after frequenting her husband's gas station. It got as far as a draft of the introduction (based on a talk Marion had given to Town and Country) and several dozen Polaroids of Doris Burton's drawings, but apparently did not reach the stage of a definitive blueprint.[56] "The Junior Joy," as they planned to retitle the revised children's cookbook, was to be recast by Joan and Marion with a new ecological emphasis. At one point they actually began discussing a tentative draft contract with Bobbs-Merrill, but they never went on to a concrete outline or schedule.[57] Marion was serious enough about "My Mother's Wastebasket," the collection of fan letters, to have a large sheaf of material retyped from her files of reader correspondence, but did not ultimately have the ingenuity, or perhaps the time, to figure out a way around the legal barriers that Harriet Pilpel had warned her of many years before.

Wandlung der Form might well have come to fruition if Marion had not hit a dead end in ascertaining the legal status of the work. As far as Mrs. Pilpel and her colleagues could determine, nothing was known of Ernst Kropp's fate after the advent of Hitler, and the publisher, Hermann Reckendorf, had also disappeared after 1933.[58] While the lawyers were trying to find out whether any party remained with a claim on the book rights, Dorothy Wartenberg accepted a position in Washington, D.C., with the National Endowment for the Humanities. Even now Marion believed that Kropp's ideas on the relation of natural and technological forms deserved the American audience that he had wanted to secure for them in 1926, but the project had to be shelved temporarily—as it turned out, permanently.

The one book that Marion did manage to concentrate her energies on over a substantial period was "Links," intended as a parting legacy to her family, present and future. "My time to accomplish the many things besides *Joy* in which I am interested is short," she had told Leo Gobin in May, when the company started to prod her about publicity appearances, "and I must turn what strength I have to those priorities and values which are important to me."[59] Of her various hopes, the memoir was the one for which she most persistently conserved that strength.

As we have seen, the origins of "Links" go back to scattered auto-biographical jottings from much earlier. Like other epochal passages of her life, the loss of John during the past October had been a trigger to her memoir-writing impulse. She made her first systematic start in January with the description of his memorial service, and signaled her determination to go on with the project on Easter Sunday, the day after the task of revision was complete in her eyes. She began the writing of "Links" in earnest during May, and worked on it as best she could literally up to the time of her death.

It was an enormous project that remained not only incomplete but fragmentary enough to make reconstructing the overall design somewhat difficult. Though Marion explained something of the plan to the children, no one except herself had a detailed mental map of it. However, the materials that remain enable us to deduce that her general purpose was a sprawling, leisurely pastiche or collage forming a documentary history of the family in its multifarious branches—Minloses, Kuhlmanns, von Starkloffs, Engelmanns, Koerners, Rombauers, Beckers. She would have assembled, in somewhat but not strictly chronological order, a treasury of cullings from family letters, pictures, diaries, and some published accounts (newspaper and magazine articles, secondary historical works, the autobiographies of her grandfather Rombauer and great-grandfather Koerner). She meant to provide some sort of commentary or perspective cementing all of these, not strict historical annotations but musings or reminiscences in many different veins set down as her mind roamed associatively over any particular moment or general subject from an old clipping to the U.S. bicentennial.

The ambitious scheme meant sorting through a vast welter of stuff—including what remained of Irma's papers—that she had assembled through the years with the instinct of a compulsive pack rat but without plan or system. She had done something similar when she was working on *Little Acorn* a decade earlier; probably she transferred some of the documents she had collected then to the jumbled cartons of "Links" materials that she was now getting together. Of course Marion did not think to stick explanatory labels on most of what she had dug up, and she never got to the stage of formally cataloguing a final selection of particular documents destined for "Links." There are items that are now quite unidentifiable. But though the preliminary gathering of souvenirs never progressed to a completely decipherable arrangement, Marion did somehow manage to spell out a great part of the message that she wanted to leave: a feeling that there was honor in bearing witness to the past for the sake of future links in the chain, and wonder at how she had ended up being "what I am for better or worse."[60]

The documentary materials that Marion piled into her "Links" cartons now furnish some of the best historical quarrying for any reconstruction of the old St. Louis *Deutschtum* and her parents' early lives. At the same time, the sketches and reminiscences that she wrote to fill in another dimension of the family story bring her to life in a way that her published work does not.

Her autobiographical entries were obviously set down in haste without much polishing. This is on the whole an advantage, for the spontaneous flow of thought does not get covered over as it generally did in the years when John fastidiously rearranged most writing of hers that was meant to be seen by others. She was no born stylist, but for this purpose she wrote volubly and freely, not stopping to fuss with the prose but simply getting down some idea or emotion as directly as possible. She seems to have worked in rapid bursts, probably meaning to revise the text later when she came to put the whole thing in final order. If she had to break off some vignette or train of thought in the middle of writing, she merely left it unfinished and went on to something else in the next entry.

Marion worked on "Links," at intervals, for more than eighteen months. Between May of 1975 and December of 1976 she compiled some fifty entries, ranging in length from two or three small pages of her favorite pale-gray Eaton stationery to twenty-five or thirty pages. She had already written a precursor entry in the form of a letter to Joe in 1971 and seven more entries in 1972, in addition to various earlier chunks of reminiscence or introspective commentary that she kept with the "Links" manuscript.

The subjects and approaches seem to have been chosen on the spur of extremely miscellaneous moments. Marion might set herself a topic such as "collectors and collecting" that enabled her to range through different memories, from her childhood habit of accumulating little hoards of miniature commercial samples or the bits of ersatz Turkey carpet that came with her father's cigarette packs, on up to her and John's friendships with art collectors and dealers, with descriptions of their own most cherished art holdings.[61] On occasion she related her current reading, whether a biography of Beatrix Potter or Robert Pirsig's *Zen and the Art of Motorcycle Maintenance*, a work that fired her up (at the age of seventy-two) to thoughts of rearranging her life's purposes more clearly and coherently.[62] Sometimes world events captured her imagination, most profoundly the dramatic rescue of the hostages at Entebbe airport in Uganda during the summer of 1976.[63] Or she might simply record household doings at Cockaigne or what she called the "va-et-vient" (comings and goings) of guests, in casual diary fashion. Some entries skate briskly over the surface of her current activities; others show her looking into herself with a sort of bewilderment, "still wondering at this late date how one individual of no particular gifts can or does leave a significant trace."[64]

She had let the children know that she planned to write very frankly about many things—frankly enough that she did not want any part of "Links" published until after their deaths. But Marion's idea of frankness really did not extend to criticizing any member of her family on paper or describing her own greatest hurts and disappointments. She was both instinctively guarded about revealing pain and instinctively given to honoring those she loved rather than holding them up to the bar of her own or anyone else's opinion. Often her words appear to have been painstakingly minced for the benefit of posterity, and it is most unlikely that she would have treated her father's suicide or her relationship with her mother in anything but the most oblique manner.

The most productive period of her work on "Links" was the early summer of 1975, when she was usually making entries several times a week and sometimes almost daily. But she could not keep up this pace. Her early optimism about regaining some of the lost lung capacity faded as muggy weather and unhealthful temperature inversions settled over the Cincinnati area. She did not want to admit that she was growing weaker rather than stronger month by month, but by fall and winter her "Links" entries were having to be fitted in more infrequently amid other demands on her dwindling energy.

In the early flush of hope that she would manage to return to something like normal activities, Marion was able to contemplate death with a certain wry detachment, quoting Woody Allen's "I just don't want to be there when it happens."[65] She met setbacks with bravely concrete plans—for example, having a small swimming pool built in the basement at Cockaigne in the hope that the exercise might help reduce the swelling in her hands and feet caused by advancing heart and lung insufficiency. She could still summon her powers to help lead cherished gardening or environmental projects, as long as her part could be mostly carried out from Cockaigne.

She had gotten the Town and Country Garden Club involved in a plan to install a medicinal herb garden at the plaza of the new University of Cincinnati Medical Center Building.[66] She also helped pull together a much more complex effort in honor of the 1976 national bicentennial, an outgrowth of a long campaign she had helped spearhead to add the nearby Little Miami River to the system of Federally protected "scenic rivers" closed to unauthorized development. The bicentennial spin-off of the Little Miami project was especially dear to her as an example of modern technology applied to conservation purposes: a set of sectional maps of the whole river watershed from above Yellow Springs to Cincinnati, and a computer tracking system to keep systematically updating information on the entire mapped area.[67]

The main duty that had to share her attention with "Links" and her other interests was estate planning. To reduce the later tax burden on Ethan, she sold him the house for a nominal fee and leased it back from him as both residence and office. (The assessor who looked over Cockaigne for a tax valuation told them that the kitchen was not at all up to snuff—an unsurprising find, since Marion had always preferred to conduct her cooking experiments in a very modestly equipped kitchen with the same limitations that many of her readers probably faced.) Meanwhile, it was necessary to do something about the ill-advised trust arrangement drawn up in 1972 when it seemed plain that John would outlive her.

Unfortunately, the instrument was irrevocable, and locked up income from the literary property in a structure that could not be significantly amended to fit altered circumstances. With the help of Harriet Pilpel (not at all pleased about their failure to consult her on the 1972 trust) and Tom Itin, Marion set out to recast her affairs more flexibly. In June of 1975 she created another trust—this time revocable, and better capable of being reshaped in case of unforeseen contingencies—with herself and Ethan as trustees.[68] The instrument covered various non-*Joy* assets, chiefly investments to which Itin had steered the Beckers when he began helping them manage the unprecedented revenue from the 1963 revision and later the paperback windfall. About a year later Marion drew up her final will, which turned the second trust into an escape hatch from the first. It transferred all the assets of the 1972 trust to the newer one, along with all of Marion's residuary estate except for personal and household effects.[69] This piggyback arrangement freed her to make desirable adjustments from time to time—for example, adding more trustees. The final roster of trustees consisted of herself, Ethan, and their two chief advisors, Harriet Pilpel and Tom Itin.

As she strove to put her affairs in order, Marion was puzzled to find herself apparently poorer rather than richer in terms of ready money. John's sister and brother, Virginia Becker Furness and Phil Becker, were now in poor health, and she badly wanted to help them, but her finances now looked more straitened than she had expected. The reason appeared to be the amount of money consumed by both taxes and tax shelters. She hoped that things would be easier after 1977, when taxes on the remaining installment from the paperback sale would have been safely paid off and some more cash could perhaps be spared for her own wishes.

The success of the cookbook was not at issue. Printing after printing sold out in rapid order; the first eighteen months after the copyright registration (June 1, 1975) saw the work through six printings, with 236,443 copies recorded as being sold in 1975 and 334,483 in 1976.[70] It is a measure of Marion's devotion to *The Joy of Cooking* that even now she kept carefully reading through the text in order to spot any small corrections that might be made in future printings. If someone pointed out a larger error she was not insulted but appreciative. When the soybean-product experts Akiko Aoyagi and William Shurtleff wrote to explain that the directions for homemade soy milk and bean curd were seriously muddled, Marion, grateful for this sign of the seriousness with which her work was taken, conscientiously sent in the necessary changes in time for the printing of August 1976.[71]

Her relations with the publisher remained cordial despite a brief blowup in the fall of 1975, when the *Ladies' Home Journal*, to which Bobbs-Merrill had granted first serial rights, printed excerpts from the new edition in two issues along with a lot of splashy colored photographs. Marion not only considered these hideous but thought that Bobbs-Merrill never should have authorized the use of photographs under any circumstances. (It was necessary to read the credits with great attention in order to tell that they were not part of the real book.)[72] Gobin and Rachlis, probably realizing that they should have respected her close-to-moral certitude on the subject of *Joy*'s visual presentation in any form whatever, hastened to make peace with their most important author. Bobbs-Merrill's estimate of her achievement never had been higher. Perhaps there were a few veterans of the Chambers era who looked at Marion's work and saw a clumsy bastardization of her mother's original. Gobin and Rachlis saw the most uncompromising standards applied down to the last detail, a simply boundless determination to improve on something that was already in a class by itself.

Even now she was not recognized in the smartest food-writing circles as much more than a name on a title page, but she did receive a scattering of tributes in other venues. The most publicized of these was one of the "Great Living Cincinnatian" awards presented annually by the Cincinnati Chamber of Commerce. She was the first woman to receive the honor. Marion, who did not at all consider herself a Chamber of Commerce type, suspected that the committee, looking for a female candidate who would not sound too Woman's Libbish, had not bothered to notice her real politics.[73] Nonetheless, she cheerfully cooperated with a film crew preparing a short biographical montage to be shown on the great occasion and a reporter researching a tie-in article for *Cincinnati* magazine. At the ceremony on February 3, 1976, she gave a brief speech hailing Cincinnati as a nurturer of sturdy originals, some of whom she had been privileged to work with on civic or other causes. Her voice was weak almost to the point of vanishing and she could not have managed the evening's exertion at all without the oxygen tank, but the official photographs of the evening caught her in intent midsentence, radiantly oblivious of the tubes that fed her breath.[74]

Closer to her scheme of values was the "Oak Leaf" award that the Nature Conservancy bestowed on her in the spring of 1975.[75] It honored her long and dedicated conservation efforts at least since 1958, the year in which she and a group of Town and Country Garden Club allies had organized a series of cooking classes in order to help finance the Conservancy's pioneering purchase (since enlarged by later acquisitions in the same area) of Lynx Prairie. Probably the most satisfying of all was the recognition offered by the old Modern Art Society, now rechristened the "Contemporary Arts Center" and occupying headquarters of its own instead of depending on the Cincinnati Art Museum for exhibition space. In December of 1975 the organization invited Marion, as the Society's first professional director, to speak on the occasion of its thirty-fifth anniversary. The honor reaffirmed a standing that she was infinitely prouder of than her veiled eminence among cookbook writers. "It's nice to talk about art," she remarked with some wistfulness in the hearing of a *Cincinnati Enquirer* society columnist. "I'm usually asked about hollandaise sauce."[76]

In this most triumphant season of her life, Marion had begun to fail inch by inch. Her heart and lungs were more enfeebled than ever, and the swelling of the extremities was only partly controlled by diuretics. Increasingly exasperated with her caregivers, she felt the disillusioned patient's natural instinct to try to assert some control over her condition. Stoic and resilient though she was, as she saw her reserves waning she was at last driven to issue a fiat to the doctors in charge of her case. She wanted them to call in Murray Israel—in her opinion, a prophet without honor—and carried her point in March of 1976. After a few days of observing her in Holmes Hospital in consultation with Murray, they unenthusiastically agreed to adjust her medications to include some form of his thyroxin-and-vitamin regimen, in which she believed so firmly that she had helped pay some of the legal expenses for his unsuccessful battle to win FDA approval for an injectable version called "Cothyrobal."[77]

Marion was convinced that the new approach was helping and that she could slowly fight her way back to a more stable physical plateau. Believing herself much improved, she ventured to leave Cincinnati for the first time since John's illness. In the second week of May she drove with Joan and Ethan (and an ample oxygen supply) to a Garden Clubs of America meeting in Louisville. Pleased with this evidence of progress, she showed up on May 17 for one of her regular checkups with William Altemeier, her surgeon, and at once found herself being clapped in the hospital. He had recognized at once that what Marion thought an inconvenient slight hoarseness was a serious symptom.

The trouble turned out to be a paralyzed vocal cord, perhaps caused by scar tissue pressing on a nerve somewhere. This was Marion's worst hospital experience yet—as she described it to a friend, "a week of tests and asides of 'Who is she?' and 'She' and 'She' being bandied about in my presence by internes as though I were a piece of merchandise—and an old and useless one at that."[78] Having pronounced that there were now several areas of bone cancer, the doctors turned her over to an oncologist and scattered to their various summer travels, leaving her in a state of angry and despairing impotence.

Marion appealed by phone to Murray Israel and derived some improvement—or certainly relief of pain—in areas of bone invasion after a few weeks on the calcium and magnesium supplements he recommended.[79] She was still trying to think of constructive measures and future plans. She managed another energetic spate of "Links" entries in June and July, and hit on the idea of enlarging her local travel horizons by buying a mobile home with room for a large supply of oxygen. But her strength was going too fast for her to get more than a month or two's real use out of it.

Early in September she inserted into "Links" a long and passionate commentary on situations like hers. It was couched as a letter to a doctor friend, Jerome Berman, for whom Jane Brueggeman had sometimes worked as a secretary-receptionist in fallow periods between *Joy* revisions. He was interested in collecting materials on the doctor-patient relationship as help or hindrance toward recovery. Since Marion's voice was not up to much actual conversation, she swiftly dashed off her ideas on paper. It was her fiercest effort in months and perhaps the most striking single entry in "Links," the sort of document that patients wish could be required reading for all doctors.

On this subject she justly thought herself a connoisseur. She was old enough to have seen physicians like the two Max Starkloffs, her grandfather and uncle, who "devoted every breath to the welfare of their patients not only as patients but people."[80] She had survived to be placed in the hands of experts who routinely subjected those in their care to great physical and mental suffering with no thought for making the experience more human. She knew with absolute certainty what the worst thing was that a sick person had to endure: "that frightful loneliness that strikes with illness regardless of how loving and physically affectionate one's family or how concerned one's friends or how confident the patient in the skill of the surgeon or the competence of the doctor."[81] She also had a firm idea of what enabled some physicians to break through the inward prison of illness: a true desire to hear the patient express his own thoughts, openness to suggestions from any source, and "an almost blind optimism that transfers itself to the patient in the form of hope."[82] She had found these qualities in the Beckers' old friend Feri Donath (who had died at about the time of her second mastectomy), and she found them now in Murray Israel. Her other doctors might view his ideas with unveiled skepticism. But he possessed the great gift of making the doctor-patient relationship a courageous one—an obvious goal of medical care that she saw being stunningly ignored or trampled on by most of the medical machine.

From this point on, both the "Links" entries and Marion's letters to friends show a marked shift in tone as the walls of illness closed in. For some time she had dwelt much on a book new to her: Cyril Connolly's *The Unquiet Grave,* a "word cycle" whose strange, dreamlike sequence of aphorisms and musings on the twin themes of cultural and individual malaise struck some deep response in her. Her thoughts turned repeatedly to irreducible human loneliness.[83]

Marion's endurance was further sapped by another loss: John's brother Phil, who had been diagnosed that spring with cancer of the esophagus, died in early September after a dreadful gauntlet of operations and cobalt treatments. The second anniversary of John's death found her spirit "locked up in a sort of misery by physical disabilities I can't seem to pull out of."[84] She would still strive to put an optimistic spin on the case for the benefit of friends and family, but the bleakness of her private thoughts appears in a passage she wrote down from a Japanese novel of the *Genji* period, summing up the incommunicability of human perceptions:

> I remember a clear morning. . . . As it became sunnier, the dew gradually vanished from the clover and the other plants where it had lain so heavily; the branches began to stir, then suddenly sprang up of their own accord. Later I described to people how beautiful it all was. What most impressed me was that they were not at all impressed.[85]

Knowing now that she was not likely to finish "Links" or even be able to review the overall shape of the project for the children's benefit, she wrote to Harriet Pilpel suggesting they talk about legal ways of putting constraints on the use or accessibility of the material.[86] She also began planning a meeting with Gene Rachlis and an ITT executive (Stan Sills, who was being detailed to handle Bobbs-Merrill affairs for the parent corporation) to ponder the next phase of *Joy* plans. What might have been broached in either discussion will never be known. After November 30, the date of her note to Mrs. Pilpel, events rapidly lurched beyond her control.

For some reason Marion had become uneasy about the financial advice she was receiving from Tom Itin. The Beckers had never felt themselves able to follow all his reasoning on the handling of their assets, which had meant sinking major (for them) sums of money into an assortment of ventures as limited partners. (Itin himself was a principal in some of the companies to which he had steered them.) These tax shelters always seemed to have them digging deeper into their own pockets than they had expected. Even John had once complained that holding an interest in one Itin real estate venture was "a lot like holding the Red Queen's baby," which "changed with unnerving rapidity into a pig, a hedgehog, a flamingo etc. etc."[87] In 1969 Marion had put her foot down at a proposal of his for mortgaging the house in order to invest in an oil-exploration scheme.[88] But most of the time John—and after his death, Marion—had accepted Itin's recommendations for keeping substantial amounts of money in play, applying for bank loans or calling on Leo Gobin for cash advances to the trust in order to sink more capital into one or another part of the portfolio as he advised. Early in December she came to a sudden mistrust, under circumstances that remain obscure.

It is certain that Itin had not committed any illegal action in managing the Beckers' money, and there is no reason to believe that he had done anything unprincipled. But Marion's actions in December suggest that she thought he had done something disastrous. After eight or nine years in which he had worn several hats—Becker family advisor, broker collecting commissions, corporate principal—she abruptly concluded that she and the trust were on the brink of financial ruin. Apparently she found reason to believe that the general partners of nearly all the companies involved were close to insolvent, that the firms' actual assets were a puny shadow of their paper assets, and that in addition to a monstrous burden of contingent liabilities facing all the limited partners, the *Joy* trust would be obliged to pay out all the taxes that the shelters had been meant to spare it.

That Tom Itin could even inadvertently have brought serious trouble on the Beckers was a thought not to be borne by a woman who considered him "almost family" (her phrase in "Links") and who generally maintained that family could do no wrong. He was "almost family" no more. On Friday, December 10, she wrote to him to dissolve the relationship: "To me there is nothing more devastating than the loss of a deeply felt friendship—so it is with the greatest sense of deprivation that I must tell you that ours has come to an end." Unfortunately for the sake of later reconstruction, she declined to learn his side of the story: "I know you will want to be heard but I feel nothing but heartache can result for either of us."[89] To Joan and Ethan, it appeared that her will had been crushed.

In Michigan, Tom Itin greeted Marion's letter of dismissal with a disbelieving shock undoubtedly intensified by the fact that she had left him no opportunity to defend himself. At once he began frantically trying to reach anyone who might know what was going on. But all was confusion in Cincinnati.

Marion, by now very weak, had spent the weekend after her termination of Itin's services entertaining house guests—not feeling much heart for the task, as she indicated in her last "Links" entry, on Monday morning, December 13. She was now being started on a new hormone, diethylstilbestrol. Early in the week she suffered a bad reaction, with severe nausea, weakness, and respiratory difficulty. She was admitted to Holmes Hospital on Wednesday in critical condition, while agitated phone calls over the Itin situation flew between Cincinnati and New York.[90] Marion believed it a matter of the utmost urgency to remove him as a *Joy of Cooking* trustee. Harriet Pilpel, who had been out of the country when Marion's suspicions crystallized, had returned to New York just in time to acquiesce in this step. On the day Marion entered the hospital she signed an amendment replacing Itin with the respected Cincinnati attorney William T. Bahlmann, who had been assisting in the conduct of trust affairs for some time.[91]

Marion's lungs became swollen and congested, and her blood sodium fell to a dangerous low. After a few days of heart stimulants the doctors detected some improvement. She was able to resume discussing trust affairs, though there was no thought of her talking to the horrified Tom Itin.

Ethan and Joan, who had seen her rally from setbacks apparently as serious and apply her great strength to encouraging those around her, expected that this crisis probably would end like so many before. But the edema of the lungs soon recurred and worsened. Over the next week the overburdened heart gradually failed. Marion died on the afternoon of Tuesday, December 28, five days before her seventy-fourth birthday. She was cremated the next day (with typical practical-ity, she had long before pointed out the name of a good funeral home to the children). Her ashes were placed beside John's at Spring Grove. At her request there was no memorial service.

Several weeks later her friends received the message she had composed in the fall of 1974 and asked Joan and Ethan to send out after her death.

> *Think of me as I think of you*
> *—My Family and My Friends—*
> *grateful for the gift of communication between us—for the unique contribution each of you has made to enriching my life by your understanding, affection and by your cooperation in the achievement of those goals which have drawn us together and that made for me a life of incredible satisfactions—balanced only by the realization of the scope of unfulfilled potentials.*
>
> *I leave life with regret that it took me so long to glimpse its creative wholeness.*
>
> *May greater insights linked with bolder actions be our common future.*
>
> *Hail and farewell,*
> *Marion Rombauer Becker*

Epilogue

The two *Joy of Cooking* editions overseen by Marion remained in print and continued to sell strongly for many years after her death. The 1963/1964 edition was issued in various one- or two-volume paperback formats by New American Library under several imprints. History repeated itself in 1982, when Bobbs-Merrill and NAL renegotiated the sale of the paperback rights for $2.5 million—once again, the highest amount ever paid for paperback rights to a single title up to that time. By NAL's estimate some 5 million copies of the 1963/1964 *Joy* were sold between 1973 and 1997—when, as we shall see, the book entered another incarnation. Meanwhile, the 1975 revision was to last longer and sell better in hardback than any of its predecessors. By 1997, more than 3.5 million copies had been sold, bringing the total hardback sales of Irma and Marion's versions since 1931 to more than 9.3 million.

The furor over Tom Itin's conduct of the Becker finances, greatly distressing to both parties because of the coincidence with Marion's death, produced a great deal of acrimony but no legal action. In the end Ethan agreed to a redistribution of the assets originally acquired at Itin's instigation, swapping more troubled for more secure holdings. The initially ominous-looking financial position of the estate was greatly improved by the tremendous success of the 1975 book and the new paperback sale.

The herb garden that Marion had suggested as a Town and Country Garden Club project was completed and opened at the University Medical Center in downtown Cincinnati in 1977 as the Marion Rombauer Becker Medicinal Herb Garden.

Marion never knew that she had been named as a recipient of one of the 1976 Governor's Awards presented by the State of Ohio. Joan and Ethan accepted the honor on her behalf at a ceremony in Columbus on February 10, 1977.

The children honored Marion's wish to omit any sort of formal memorial. But they decided to invite her friends to walk in her woods at the height of the next spring wildflower season, on April 23 and 24, 1977: "Pause with us," they wrote, "to think of Marion and to enjoy the beauty of the garden she had sown."

After Marion's death Joan and Ethan moved into the premises at Cockaigne. Their son, John Alexander Becker, was born on March 25, 1979.

Marion's hope that all of the next generation might collaborate on a future *Joy* was not realized. Joan and Ethan separated and were divorced while John was still a baby. For a time Mark and Jennifer attempted to work with Ethan, but after several years they all amicably agreed that Ethan would assume sole responsibility for the next edition of *Joy*.

The preparation of a revised version was unsettled by several upheavals in the American publishing world. Despite the vast success of the 1975 *Joy*, Bobbs-Merrill continued to decline and was publishing only a handful of titles a year when it was acquired—along with the *Joy of Cooking* copyrights—by the Macmillan Publishing Company (a U.S. company with no ties to the British firm) in April of 1985. Macmillan (already comprising a diverse stable of formerly independent publishing houses) promptly dissolved what remained of Bobbs-Merrill, although for a short time the name was kept as an imprint used solely for *Joy*. The new publisher and Ethan Becker soon began to disagree on the course of revision, and reached a state of extreme antagonism that lasted several years. But their differences were rendered moot after Macmillan itself became the target of various takeover attempts.

In 1988 Macmillan was bought up by the flamboyant British millionaire Robert Maxwell. After his mysterious death in 1991, the fate of Macmillan was the subject of many guessing games not resolved until 1993, when the Macmillan complex was acquired by a still more gigantic complex, Paramount Publishing. When the dust had settled from a number of enormous acquisitions, Macmillan and its former stable of subsidiaries had been absorbed into Simon and Schuster under the larger aegis of Paramount Communications, which in turn belongs to Viacom.

Simon and Schuster quickly began a thoroughgoing shake-up of the Macmillan holdings. *The Joy of Cooking* was assigned to the Scribner imprint, which was all that remained of the once celebrated firm of Charles Scribner's Sons. Plans were soon drawn up for the completion of the next *Joy of Cooking* revision, which had been in limbo for several years.

In the fall of 1997, Scribner brought out the long-awaited new *Joy*. Overseen by the well-known cookbook editor Maria Guarnaschelli, the 1997 *Joy* comprised contributions from dozens of professional food writers. Scribner shortly launched a series of spin-off cookbooks with both black-and-white and color photography (*All About Grilling, All About Soups and Stews,* etc.), as well as a "multimedia set," which includes both the book and a CD-ROM. The new revision was an instant success, with 1,575,000 copies in print as of this writing (October 2002). In addition, Scribner continues to publish the 1975 hardback *Joy of Cooking* and also delighted *Joy* fans in 1998 by reissuing Irma Rombauer's original 1931 *The Joy of Cooking,* with an introduction by Edgar R. Rombauer, Jr.

Mr. Rombauer died in Seattle on September 3, 1999. Joan Becker, who after her divorce from Ethan studied nursing and began a career as a visiting nurse, now divides her time between Portland, Oregon, and Tucson, Arizona. Their son, John, is married and living in Asheville, North Carolina. Mark and Jennifer live in Moscow, Idaho; Joe is in Sand Point, Montana.

In 1997, Ethan married Susan Cope in a simple ceremony at Cockaigne, where they now live. Ethan and Susan are working with Scribner on a new *Joy of Cooking* edition that they hope to complete in time for the book's seventy-fifth anniversary in 2006.

Marion Becker, who always considered herself more of a gardener than a cook, would have been delighted to know that her love of plants has earned her a small footnote in the annals of botany. In 1970 she donated cuttings of a particularly hardy and dense boxwood strain (one she had been growing for years at Cockaigne after discovering it in Michigan) to a garden being planned at the Missouri Botanical Garden in St. Louis in honor of her friend Edgar Anderson. Marion's gift so impressed the boxwood enthusiasts who later formed the Boxwood Society of the Midwest that they decided to register it with the American Boxwood Society under its own designation. It now bears the official name *Buxus sempervirens* Joy—evergreen boxwood *Joy*.

NOTES

ABBREVIATIONS: COLLECTIONS

BPC: Becker Papers, Cincinnati (Cockaigne).
LL: Lilly Library, Indiana University, Bloomington, Indiana.
MHS: The Missouri Historical Society, St. Louis.

ABBREVIATIONS: SHORT TITLE FORMS

"My Little World": Irma Rombauer. Unpublished autobiographical manuscript.
   (BPC)
1931 *Joy:* Irma S. Rombauer. *The Joy of Cooking: A Compilation of Reliable
   Recipes with a Casual Culinary Chat.* St. Louis: A. C. Clayton Printing
   Company, 1931.
1936 *Joy:* Irma S. Rombauer. *The Joy of Cooking: A Compilation of Reliable
   Recipes with a Casual Culinary Chat.* Indianapolis and New York: The
   Bobbs-Merrill Company, 1936. (New copyright 1941.)
Streamlined: Irma S. Rombauer. *Streamlined Cooking: New and Delightful
   Recipes for Canned, Packaged and Frosted Foods and Rapid Recipes for
   Fresh Foods.* Indianapolis and New York: The Bobbs-Merrill Company,
   1939.
1943 *Joy:* Irma S. Rombauer. *The Joy of Cooking: A Compilation of Reliable
   Recipes with an Occasional Culinary Chat.* Indianapolis and New York:
   The Bobbs-Merrill Company, 1943.
1946 *Joy:* Irma S. Rombauer. *The Joy of Cooking: A Compilation of Reliable
   Recipes with an Occasional Culinary Chat.* Indianapolis and New York:
   The Bobbs-Merrill Company, 1946.

Girls and Boys: Irma S. Rombauer. *A Cookbook for Girls and Boys.* Indianapolis and New York: The Bobbs-Merrill Company, 1946.

1951 *Joy:* Irma S. Rombauer and Marion Rombauer Becker. *The Joy of Cooking.* Indianapolis and New York: The Bobbs-Merrill Company, 1951. (New copyrights 1952 and 1953.)

1962 *Joy:* Irma S. Rombauer and Marion Rombauer Becker. *Joy of Cooking.* Indianapolis and New York: The Bobbs-Merrill Company, 1962.

1963 *Joy:* Irma S. Rombauer and Marion Rombauer Becker. *Joy of Cooking.* Indianapolis and New York: The Bobbs-Merrill Company, 1963. (New copyright 1964.)

Little Acorn: Marion Rombauer Becker. *Little Acorn: The Story behind The Joy of Cooking, 1931–1966.* Indianapolis and New York: The Bobbs-Merrill Company, 1966. (Reissued under new copyright in 1981 as *Little Acorn: Joy of Cooking: The First Fifty Years, 1931–1981.*)

Wild Wealth: Paul Bigelow Sears, Marion Rombauer Becker, Frances Jones Poetker, and Janice Rebert Forberg. *Wild Wealth.* Indianapolis and New York: The Bobbs-Merrill Company, 1971.

1974 deposition: Deposition of Marion Rombauer Becker in the matter of *Mary Whyte Hartrich* v. *Marion Rombauer Becker,* January 10–11, 1974. (BPC)

1975 *Joy:* Irma S. Rombauer and Marion Rombauer Becker. *Joy of Cooking.* Indianapolis and New York: The Bobbs-Merrill Company, 1975.

"Links": Marion Rombauer Becker. Unpublished autobiographical manuscript. (BPC)

1. THE GOLDEN AGE OF ST. LOUIS

For the early history of Irma von Starkloff's family and nineteenth-century St. Louis, I have drawn extensively on "My Little World"; James Neal Primm, *Lion of the Valley: St. Louis, Missouri* (Boulder, Colo.: Pruett Publishing Company, 1981); and "Die Familie von Starkloff" (an unpublished genealogy of which Elsa Hunstein kindly lent me an original copy and Ethan Becker a typewritten transcript apparently prepared for the family at a later date). The von Starkloff genealogy is my source for dates of family births, deaths, and marriages, where not otherwise noted.

1. T. S. Eliot, letter to Marquis Childs quoted in *St. Louis Post-Dispatch,* October 15, 1930; T. S. Eliot, "American Literature and the American Language," address delivered at Washington University, June 9, 1953, published in *Washington University Studies,* New Series: Literature and Language, no. 23 (St. Louis: Washington University Press, 1953), p. 6.
2. 1974 deposition, p. 2.
3. *Little Acorn,* n.p.
4. "My Little World," p. 8; details of von Starkloff family history also taken from "Die Familie von Starkloff." See entry "Starkloff, Hugo M.," in *Encyclopedia of the History of St. Louis: A Compilation of History and Biography for Ready Reference,* ed. William Hyde and Howard L. Conard (New York, Louisville, and St. Louis: The Southern History Company, 1899), vol. 4, pp. 2126–2127.
5. "My Little World," p. 9.

6. "The City of St. Louis," *Mississippi-Blätter* (*Westliche Post* weekend supplement), November 6, 1859, translated by Steven Rowan in *Germans for a Free Missouri: Translations from the St. Louis Radical Press, 1857–1862* (Columbia, Missouri: University of Missouri Press, 1983), pp. 89–90. This collection provides a detailed picture of St. Louis German antislavery activity in the years leading up to the Civil War. Primm, *Lion of the Valley*, gives the best general picture of the city at the time of Max von Starkloff's arrival.

7. R. E. Rombauer, "The Life of Hon. Gustavus Koerner," in *Transactions of the Illinois Historical Society for the Year 1904* (Publication no. 9 of the Illinois State Historical Society), pp. 286–307. Koerner's career is recounted by himself in *Memoirs of Gustave Koerner, 1809–1896: Life-Sketches Written at the Suggestion of His Children*, 2 vols., ed. Thomas J. McCormack (Cedar Rapids, Iowa: The Torch Press, 1909).

8. For the story of Camp Jackson, see James Neal Primm's introduction to *Germans for a Free·Missouri*, pp. 15–19; Primm, *Lion of the Valley*, pp. 248–276; Audrey L. Olsen, *St. Louis Germans, 1850–1920: The Nature of an Immigrant Community and Its Relation to the Assimilation Process* (New York: Arno Press, 1980), pp. 171–173; entry "Turners" in *Encyclopedia of the History of St. Louis*, vol. 4, pp. 2314–2318.

9. Selwyn Troen, *The Public and the Schools: Shaping the St. Louis System, 1838–1920* (Columbia, Mo.: University of Missouri Press, 1975), p. 86. Troen misidentifies the attorney as Robert Rombauer.

10. Ibid., pp. 103–104; Primm, *Lion of the Valley*, p. 342. Among those who endeavored to assist me in finding some trace of Emma Kuhlmann's connection with the kindergarten were Martin Knorr, Library Director of Harris-Stowe College, St. Louis (letter to Elizabeth Goltermann, November 27, 1985), Margaret Hilliker (telephone interview, December 9, 1985), and Sarah Van Ausdal (letter, November 26, 1985). I am indebted to Elizabeth Goltermann for her efforts in this matter.

11. Obituary of Hermine von Starkloff, *St. Louis Daily Globe*, March 30, 1875.

12. Emil Starkloff's dossier at the U.S. Penitentiary in Atlanta for 1916–1917 indicates a long prior career of fraud; this is corroborated by his nephew Dr. Gene Starkloff (interview with Elsa Hunstein, Dr. Gene Starkloff, and Alice Gerdine, December 12, 1985) and by Irma in "My Little World," pp. 39–41. Emil is listed as a postal clerk in the St. Louis city directory for 1879.

13. "Die Familie von Starkloff," p. xxi (p. 18b of typescript); "Kuhlmann genealogy" (unpublished genealogy compiled by Richard Vonnegut), p. 22.

14. "My Little World," p. 31.

15. Ibid., p. 1.

16. Ibid., p. 30 (passage partly crossed out).

17. *St. Louis Post-Dispatch*, October 27, 1883, and October 30, 1883.

18. "My Little World," p. 35.

19. Ibid., p. 33.

20. Ibid., p. 48, pp. 34–35.

21. *Current Biography: Who's News and Why 1953*, ed. Marjorie Dent Candee (New York: The H. H. Wilson Company, 1953), p. 544.

22. "My Little World," p. 32.

23. Ibid., p. 50, pp. 32–32a.

24. *St. Louis Republic*, June 30, 1889; see also *St. Louis Post-Dispatch*, June 30, 1889, and *St. Louis Globe-Democrat*, July 2, 1889.
25. "My Little World," p. 51.
26. Ibid., p. 63.
27. Ibid., p. 4.
28. Ibid., p. 68.
29. Ibid., p. 58.
30. Ibid., p. 63.
31. *Little Acorn*, n.p.
32. "My Little World," p. 63.
33. From a sheaf of undated, unnumbered notes that apparently furnished cues and aide-mémoire for "My Little World." (BPC)
34. Some records of Dr. von Starkloff's consulship, including several of his reports to the U.S. State Department during the cholera epidemic, were provided to me by Dr. Muller, Archivdirektor, Staatsarchiv Bremen (letter of February 18, 1986, with Dr. Muller's own summary of consular records). See also Richard Bartholdt, *From Steerage to Congress: Reminiscences and Recollections* (Philadelphia: Dorrance and Company, 1930), p. 112.
35. Ina Vonnegut to Marion Becker, undated (early 1966). (BPC)
36. Obituary of Dr. Max C. Starkloff, *St. Louis Post-Dispatch*, January 16, 1942; entry "Starkloff, Maximilian C.," in *Encyclopedia of the History of St. Louis*, vol. 4, pp. 2127–2128.
37. "My Little World," p. 41.
38. Rombauer, Edgar R., Sr., unpublished autobiography, pp. 92–94. (BPC)
39. Ibid., p. 98.
40. Primm, *Lion of the Valley*, pp. 361–362.
41. Telephone interview with Elsa Hunstein, March 13, 1986.
42. Irma Rombauer to James L. Woodress, undated ("Friday," possibly October 23, 1953). (Copy supplied to me by James L. Woodress; Professor Woodress also kindly sent copies of two other undated letters written to him by Irma Rombauer, probably close to New Year's Day, 1954, and late June 1955.)
43. Newton Booth Tarkington to Irma von Starkloff, December 19, 1897. (BPC)
44. See above, n. 42 (undated "Friday" letter).
45. December 19, 1897, Tarkington to Irma von Starkloff.
46. Irma von Starkloff to Booth Tarkington, December 22, 1897. (The Booth Tarkington Papers, Manuscripts Division, Department of Rare Books and Special Collections, Princeton University Libraries. Cited by permission of the Princeton University Libraries.)
47. Irma von Starkloff to Newton B. Tarkington, March 9, 1898. (Tarkington papers; cited by permission of the Princeton University Libraries.)
48. Booth Tarkington, *The Gentleman from Indiana* (New York: Doubleday and McClure, 1899), pp. 70–71.

2. BEGINNINGS AND ENDINGS

Unless otherwise credited, my sources for dates of family births, deaths, marriages, and other vital passages are "Die Familie von Starkloff" (see p. 418); Gertrud Baecker and Fritz Engelmann, *Die Kurpfälzischen Familien Engel-*

mann und Hilgard (Ludwigshafen am Rhein: Richard Louis Verlag, 1958), pp. 84–85; Paul Riecker and Emil Rombauer, *Nachkommen von Dr. Joh. Christoph Elhard* (Brassó, Hungary: Buchdruckerei Victor Schlandt, 1900); and Edgar R. Rombauer Sr., "Memorial Sketches of the Lives of Those Members of the Engelmann Family Whose Remains Lie in the Engelmann Family Cemetery near Shiloh, Illinois" (unpublished, undated typescript) (BPC).

1. The Rombauers' last years in Hungary and American beginnings are related in Roderick E. Rombauer, *The History of a Life* (privately published, 1903), pp. 7–19. See also entries "R. E. Rombauer" in *The National Cyclopaedia of American Biography*, vol. 25 (New York: James T. White and Company, 1936), pp. 334–335, and "Rombauer, Roderick E.," in *Encyclopedia of the History of St. Louis: A Compilation of History and Biography for Ready Reference*, ed. William Hyde and Howard L. Conard (New York, Louisville, and St. Louis: The Southern History Company, 1899), vol. 4, pp. 1935–1936.
2. Rombauer, *History of a Life*, p. 45.
3. Diary of William B. Napton, March 30, 1870, MS pp. 254–255. (MHS)
4. "My Little World," p. 11a.
5. Rombauer, Edgar R., Sr., unpublished autobiography, p. 38. (BPC)
6. Ibid., p. 45. Roderick himself had adopted virtually the same regimen during his first two years in St. Louis; see *History of a Life*, p. 20.
7. Edgar relates the course of his first breakdown and the offer from the sealing-rights tribunal in his autobiography, pp. 68–70.
8. Edgar's courtship of Irma is told in the autobiography, pp. 82–84.
9. Undated scrap of paper in Irma Rombauer's handwriting, found with some autobiographical fragments and possibly dating from early 1947: "grateful for having had an exuberant husband." (BPC)
10. Telephone interview with Elsa Hunstein, June 5, 1984.
11. Edgar R. Rombauer Sr. autobiography, p. 84.
12. Edgar describes his second breakdown and sequent events in the autobiography, pp. 87–91.
13. Marion describes aspects of her early childhood in *Little Acorn* (n.p.), "Links," March 30, 1975, and a draft of a letter to Cecily Brownstone, December 7, 1963 (BPC). Some additional details appear in manuscript passages deleted from the final version of *Little Acorn* (BPC).
14. Edgar R. Rombauer Sr. autobiography, p. 99; letter from Lydia Rombauer Brown, January 1, 1987. Edgar relates his and Irma's subsequent problems with Rod in the autobiography, pp. 99–102.
15. "Links," March 30, 1975.
16. That cooking held no paramount place in Irma's scale of social and intellectual priorities was made clear to me by virtually everyone who knew her in earlier years. That she was not one of the most renowned cooks of her set was suggested by—among others—Alice Gerdine (interview with Elsa Hunstein, Dr. Gene Starkloff, and Alice Gerdine, December 12, 1985) and Patricia Egan (interview, March 12, 1987). Marion points out in *Little Acorn* (n.p.) "that Mother, to the very end of her life, regarded social intercourse as more important than food. The dinner table, in our childhood, frequently suggested a lectern rather than a buffet. What I remember better than the dishes it upheld—which, I must admit, constantly improved in quality—

was the talk which went 'round it, talk which burst forth from our richly multiple interests."

17. "My Little World," p. 37.

18. Dr. Gene Starkloff, in December 12, 1985, Hunstein/Starkloff/Gerdine interview.

19. Charlotte Eliot's public-spirited zeal and literary ambitions were strongly stamped on the memory of her son T. S. Eliot; see Lyndall Gordon, *Eliot's Early Years* (New York: Oxford University Press, 1977), pp. 2–6.

20. Cited in Peggy Lamson, *Roger Baldwin, Founder of the American Civil Liberties Union: A Portrait* (Boston: Houghton Mifflin, 1976), p. 31.

21. The Wednesday Club declined to cooperate with my requests for information on Irma Rombauer's club activities. Some early membership lists and assorted other records are preserved at the Missouri Historical Society. See membership listings for 1901 and 1911, program listings for 1915–17.

22. Interview with Merna Lazier, June 8, 1984.

23. *Little Acorn*, n.p.

24. The arrest of Starkloff and Post was reported in the *New York Times* on May 20 and 22, 1910, and the story filled the Philadelphia papers for several days in May. Emil's dossier at the Federal penitentiary in Atlanta mentions his ordering the Spanish and violin-method textbooks. I have found no record of what happened to Emil after 1922, when he and Post were the subject of a custody squabble between the law-enforcement authorities of New York City and Dunkirk, New York (*New York Times*, April 8 and 9, 1922).

25. "My Little World," p. 40.

26. Rolla Wells, *Episodes of My Life* (St. Louis: W. J. McCarthy, 1933), p. 156.

27. *St. Louis Post-Dispatch*, February 4, 1930.

28. Marion mentions her father's evening readings-aloud to the family in *Little Acorn* (n.p.); she describes his attentiveness to the children in the December 7, 1963, letter to Cecily Brownstone (see above, n. 13) and in an undated manuscript fragment beginning, "My wonderfully sharing father was dead. . . ." (BPC)

29. Interview with Edgar R. Rombauer Jr., May 21, 1993.

30. Marion Becker, manuscript fragment, August 1, 1972. (BPC)

31. Without prompting, a great number of acquaintances commented to me that the physical contrast between Irma and Marion as grown women seemed to be the cause of some unresolved trouble between them. Marion's brother, sons, and several close friends went further, all declaring that her mother had deliberately humiliated her since childhood on the score of her appearance.

32. Marion describes her lifelong fascination with dance in "Links," July 2, 1976.

33. Marion describes the train of events that led her from eye doctors to allergists in "Links," September 4, 1976.

34. For Irma's acquisition of cooking skills from her husband, see *Current Biography: Who's News and Why 1953*, ed. Marjorie Dent Candee (New York: The H. H. Wilson Company, 1936), p. 544, and *Little Acorn*, n.p.

35. *Little Acorn*, n.p. For a history of the Bay View Chautauqua, see Keith J. Fennimore, *The Heritage of Bay View, 1875–1975* (Grand Rapids: William B. Eerdmans Publishing Company, 1975).

36. James Neal Primm, *Lion of the Valley: St. Louis, Missouri* (Boulder, Colo.: Pruett Publishing Company, 1981), pp. 434–441, describes rising racial animosities in St. Louis; see also Audrey L. Olsen, *St. Louis Germans, 1850–1920* (New York: Arno Press, 1980), pp. 129–130.
37. The People's Art Center, which arose out of a Depression-era Works Progress Administration program, was incorporated as a nonprofit foundation in 1942. See *St. Louis Post-Dispatch*, May 5, 1963.
38. German and "American" antagonisms in St. Louis in the decades leading up to World War I are described in David W. Detjen, *The Germans in Missouri, 1900–1918: Prohibition, Neutrality, and Assimilation* (Columbia, Mo.: University of Missouri Press, 1985). The *Bund*, which gradually regrouped after World War I, later acquired a frankly pro-Nazi cast.
39. The "Naked Truth" affair is described in Carolyn Hewes Toft and Jane Molloy Porter, *Compton Heights: A History and Architectural Guide* (St. Louis: Landmarks Association of St. Louis, 1984), pp. 30–34; see also obituary of Dr. Hugo Maximilian von Starkloff, *St. Louis Republican*, November 1, 1914.
40. "Dr. H. M. von Starkloff's Andenken geehret," *Mississippi-Blätter*, November 22, 1914.
41. "St. Louis Physicians Honor Dr. Starkloff," *St. Louis Post-Dispatch*, January 31, 1934.
42. Philip R. Becker to Virginia and Richard Furness, March 4, 1975: undated comments by Virginia Becker Furness written in margins of her brother's letter. (BPC)

3. THE ROMBAUERS AFTER THE WAR

In reconstructing the lives of the Becker family I have drawn on an interview with A. William J. Becker III (February 3, 1986), a telephone interview with Anne Stern (December 3, 1987), an unpublished Becker genealogy drawn up by Philip R. Becker (BPC), and contemporary letters among John and Marion's circle of friends in the years before their marriage (BPC).

1. Wednesday Club membership listings for 1921–25. (MHS)
2. Letter from Julian Hill, November 1, 1985. I have also drawn on an interview with Polly and Julian Hill and Charles Van Ravenswaay (January 8, 1986), as well as interviews with Emma K. Fischer (March 22, 1984) and Frances Jones Poetker (February 17, 1986).
3. *Little Acorn*, n.p.
4. Interview with Edgar R. Rombauer Jr., June 2, 1984, and May 22, 1993; telephone interview with Edgar R. Rombauer Jr., September 27, 1987.
5. Mary Whyte's two-volume transcript of Edgar's letters (BPC) is the chief record of the family European trip. I have also drawn on the June 2, 1984, Rombauer interview and another interview on May 21, 1993.
6. Charles Van Wyck Brooks gives an account of the Gindler teaching in *Sensory Awareness* (New York: Viking, 1974), pp. 229–231. Marion's notebooks (in German) from the Gindler classes at the Bode School are still among the Becker papers at Cockaigne.
7. *Little Acorn*, n.p.

8. Irma Rombauer to Marion Becker, undated (probably June 24, 1952) (BPC). Marion kept a snapshot of Kropp with his letters (BPC).

9. For the history of the Deutscher Werkbund see Joan Campbell, *The German Werkbund: The Politics of Reform in the Applied Arts* (Princeton, N.J.: Princeton University Press, 1978); entries under "Deutscher Werkbund" in *Encyclopedia of Modern Architecture*, ed. Gerd Hatje (London: Thames and Hudson, 1963), pp. 84–87, and *Encyclopedia of 20th-Century Architecture*, ed. Vittorio Magnago Lampugnani (New York: Harry N. Abrams, 1986), pp. 80–83.

10. *Girls and Boys*, p. 140.

11. Reported by Elsa Hunstein in interview with Elsa Hunstein, Dr. Gene Starkloff, and Alice Gerdine, December 12, 1985.

12. Ernst Kropp, *Wandlung der Form im XX. Jahrhundert*. Bücher der Form im Auftrag des Deutschen Werkbundes, herausgegeben von Dr. Walter Riezler, fünfter Band (Berlin: Verlag Hermann Reckendorf, 1926).

13. Ernst Kropp to Marion Rombauer, May 2, 1928 (my translation). (BPC)

14. Mock "Certificate of Relationship" in John Becker's handwriting. (BPC)

15. "Links," June 29, 1975.

16. Ibid.

17. John Becker to Marion Rombauer, October 21, 1927. (BPC)

18. Marion Becker, autobiographical manuscript dated "Derby Day, 1972" (May 6); she also describes the visit in the June 29, 1975, "Links" entry. (BPC)

19. See Martin L. Perry, *A Way of Life: The Story of John Burroughs School, 1923–1973* (St. Louis: John Burroughs School, 1973).

20. The beginning of the relationship is clearly alluded to in the first two letters (undated) of a series that John wrote to Marion at Bay View in the summer of 1929. (BPC)

21. Marion Rombauer to John Becker, undated (first letter of a series that she wrote to him in St. Louis in the summer of 1929). (BPC)

22. *St. Louis Post-Dispatch*, February 3 and 4, 1930.

23. Marion Rombauer to John Becker, undated (probably late August 1929). (BPC)

24. The presentation is described in two undated, unidentified St. Louis newspaper clippings at Cockaigne: "Art Museum Party for Children Saturday" and "Illustrates Fairy Story with Paper Cutouts." Mary Powell to Marion Rombauer, January 2, 1930, expresses the Museum's thanks for the performance. (BPC)

25. September 27, 1987, Rombauer telephone interview; interview with Edgar R. Rombauer Jr., June 3, 1984.

26. Dr. Gene Starkloff specifically stated that he had never heard his father mention Edgar's having had bladder cancer (December 12, 1985, Hunstein/Starkloff/Gerdine interview).

27. Edgar R. Rombauer Sr. to Ralph and Jessie Maxson, January 24, 1930, enclosed in Marion Becker to Edgar R. Rombauer Jr., December 4, 1943. (Copies kindly supplied to me by Edgar R. Rombauer Jr.)

28. *St. Louis Globe-Democrat*, February 4, 1930.

29. Details of Edgar's suicide from transcript of the inquest (Coroner's Office in the City of St. Louis, Inquest on body of Edgar R. Rombauer at 9 o'clock A.M. Feb. 4, 1930, case no. 204).

30. Harry B. Hawes to Irma Rombauer, February 8, 1930. (BPC)
31. Interview with Edgar R. Rombauer Jr., June 4, 1984, and several subsequent conversations.
32. Dr. Gene Starkloff, December 12, 1985, Hunstein/Starkloff/Gerdine interview.
33. Elsa Hunstein, December 12, 1985, Hunstein/Starkloff/Gerdine interview.
34. Louise Seaman to Marion Rombauer, April 9, 1930. (BPC)
35. Interview with Patricia Egan, March 12, 1987.

4. THE BIRTH OF *JOY*

The letters of Marion Rombauer to John Becker in 1930 and 1931 (BPC) furnish most details for my account of the 1931 *Joy of Cooking*'s production and early distribution. Unfortunately, nearly all are undated and few can be certainly ascribed to any period more exact than within the space of a month or two. For this reason I have not attempted to annotate most of the passages I quote in this chapter from Marion's letters about the 1931 *Joy*.

·1. Gladys (Taussig) Lang, *Choice Menus for Luncheons and Dinners* (St. Louis: Court-Usher Printing Company, 1929). Mrs. Lang followed this up with *"More Menus" for Luncheons, Dinners, Etc.* (St. Louis: Court-Usher Printing Company, 1933), and eventually wrote a longer work for a commercial publisher, *The Complete Menu Cook Book* (Boston: Houghton Mifflin, 1939).
2. Interview with Edgar R. Rombauer Jr., May 21, 1993.
3. Letter from Dorothy Merkel Alexander, December 22, 1985; I am indebted to Julia Child for putting me in touch with Mrs. Alexander.
4. Marion Rombauer to John Becker, undated (probably late October 1930).
5. Letter from Daniel J. Giannini, April 22, 1986, with copies of Marion Rombauer's records from the Parsons School of Design.
6. May 21, 1993, Rombauer interview; telephone interview with Edgar R. Rombauer Jr., September 27, 1987.
7. Dada Hollweg to Julia Chapman, July 31, 1931 (my translation). (BPC)
8. Emma von Starkloff to John Becker, September 30, 1931. (BPC)
9. Interview with Cynthia Gibbons, October 31, 1994.
10. The fee of $3,000 was independently recollected by Edgar R. Rombauer Jr., Ethan Becker, and other acquaintances on repeated occasions.
11. *Little Acorn*, n.p.
12. December 3, 1973, Hartrich deposition (see below, p. 449, n. 17), p. 7.
13. 1931 *Joy*, p. 202. Hand corrections were also made on "Hazelnut Cakes," p. 282, and "Orange Paste with Nuts," p. 370.
14. *St. Louis Star*, December 4, 1931.
15. Dada Hollweg to Irma Rombauer, undated (probably November 1931; my translation). (BPC)
16. John Becker to Marion Rombauer, undated (probably early December 1931). (BPC)
17. Irma Rombauer to Julia Chapman, undated (possibly November 26, 1931). (BPC)
18. *St. Louis Post-Dispatch*, December 3, 1931.
19. *St. Louis Star*, December 4, 1931.

20. Ernst Kropp to Marion Rombauer, December 29, 1931. (BPC)
21. "Links," June 18, 1975.
22. *St. Louis Post-Dispatch,* June 19, 1932.
23. Interview with Emma K. Fischer, March 22, 1984.
24. Marian Judell Israel (interview with Helen-Marie Fruth and Marian Judell Israel, January 7, 1986).
25. December 3, 1973, Hartrich deposition, p. 6.
26. *Saturday Review,* December 31, 1932, p. 356 and February 25, 1933, p. 455; Irma Rombauer to Jessica Mannon, May 9, 1936. (LL)
27. Irma Rombauer, "Unusual and Unpublished Recipes," mimeographed booklet (St. Louis: Church of the Unity, 5015 Waterman Avenue, n.d.), n.p. (Photocopy of original supplied to Marion in 1971 by Elizabeth Goltermann.) (BPC)
28. Telephone interview with William Finneran, November 11, 1987.
29. *Little Acorn,* n.p.
30. Ina Vonnegut to Marion Becker, undated (probably early 1966); letter from Richard Vonnegut, January 30, 1984.
31. Laurance Chambers to Irma Rombauer, February 23, 1933. (LL)
32. Interview with Edgar R. Rombauer Jr., June 3, 1984, and many subsequent conversations.
33. For an egregious example see the *St. Louis Post-Dispatch* article on Irma's outselling Wendell Willkie (July 21, 1943, "Sends Willkie a Copy of Her Cook Book") that helped launch her national celebrity. She is quoted as saying, "Then, a few book publishers got copies of it [the 1931 *Joy*] and they pestered me to let them publish it, but I refused because I was at that time revising it for a second edition."
34. Irma Rombauer to Julia Chapman, undated (probably November 26, 1931).

5. CHRONICLES OF COOKERY 1

1. *Tornado Cook Book: Compiled in Behalf of the Lafayette Park Presbyterian Church* (St. Louis, 1896), n.p.
2. Fannie Merritt Farmer, *The Boston Cooking-School Cook Book* (New York: Weathervane Books, 1973; facsimile of 1896 edition published by Little, Brown in Boston), p. 163. This and subsequent editions are hereafter referred to as "1896 *Boston,*" "1914 *Boston,*" etc.
3. *Henriette Davidis' Praktisches Kochbuch für die gewöhnliche und feinere Küche,* bearbeitet nach der Originalausgabe von Roland Gööck (Munich: Wilhelm Heyne Verlag, 1983; somewhat modernized redaction of 1844 edition with details from other early editions), p. 20 ("Reis zu reinigen und zu blanchieren"). This instruction appears in subsequent Davidis editions at least as late as 1903.
4. Georgie Boynton Child's *The Efficient Kitchen* (New York: McBride, Nast and Company, 1914) is an illuminating treatment of "modern" kitchen arrangements.
5. Catherine E. Beecher, *A Treatise on Domestic Economy* (New York: Marsh Capen Lyon and Webb, 1845), pp. 317–322; Catherine E. Beecher and Harriet Beecher Stowe, *The American Woman's Home* (New York: J. B. Ford and Company, 1869), pp. 32–35.

6. [Flora Haines Loughead], *Quick Cooking: A Book of Culinary Heresies, by One of the Heretics* (New York: Putnam's/The Knickerbocker Press, 1888), p. 15. The copy owned by Lucy Stone is now in the Schlesinger Library of the History of Women, Radcliffe College.

7. Ibid., p. 14.

8. Mark Twain, *Life on the Mississippi* (New York: Avenel, 1986; reissue of the 1962 Oxford World's Classics edition), pp. 156–157.

9. Rolla Wells, *Episodes of My Life* (St. Louis: W. J. McCarthy, 1933), p. 156. Wells also cites the above passage from *Life on the Mississippi*, clearly a standing joke to more than one generation in St. Louis.

10. Mentioned in 1963 *Joy*, p. 493, and 1975 *Joy*, p. 519. One of Irma's draft notes accompanying "My Little World" supplies the naive young lady's identity (in the book she is simply called "an 1890 debutante cousin from Indianapolis").

11. Sarah Tyson Rorer, *Mrs. Rorer's New Cook Book: A Manual of Housekeeping* (New York: Crown Publishers for the *Ladies' Home Journal* Cook Book Club, n.d.; facsimile of 1898 edition published by Arnold and Company in Philadelphia), pp. 360, 694, 698, 701.

12. Adelaide Keen, *With a Saucepan over the Sea: Quaint and Delicious Recipes from the Kitchens of Foreign Countries* (Boston: Little, Brown, 1902 and 1910); Minnie C. Fox, *The Blue Grass Cook Book* (New York: Fox, Duffield, 1904; New York: Charles Scribner's Sons, 1918).

13. *Mrs. Rorer's New Cook Book*, pp. 670, 681.

14. An important treatment of sugar in Western society over the past five hundred years is Sidney W. Mintz, *Sweetness and Power: The Place of Sugar in Modern History* (New York: Viking, 1985).

15. Sarah Josepha Hale, *Mrs. Hale's New Cook Book* (Philadelphia: T. B. Peterson, 1857), p. xxxvii.

16. *Mrs. Rorer's New Cook Book*, p. 5.

17. Edith M. Thomas, *Mary at the Farm and Book of Recipes, Compiled During Her Visit among the "Pennsylvania Germans,"* 2nd ed. (Harrisburg, Pa.: Evangelical Press, 1928), pp. 31–32.

18. Ibid., p. 309.

19. Fannie Farmer, *A New Book of Cookery* (Boston: Little, Brown, 1912), pp. 208–209; 1912 *Boston*, p. 341.

20. *Mrs. Rorer's New Cook Book*, illustration facing p. 458.

21. Ida Bailey Allen, *One Hundred Four Prize Radio Recipes, with Twenty-four Radio Home-Maker's Talks* (New York: J. H. Sears and Company, Inc., 1926), p. 91.

22. Ida Bailey Allen, *Ida Bailey Allen's Modern Cook Book: 2500 Delicious Recipes* (New York: Garden City Publishing Company, Inc., 1932; reissue of 1924 *Mrs. Allen on Cooking, Menus, Service*), p. 564.

23. 1931 *Joy*, Preface, n.p.

24. *Current Biography: Who's News and Why 1953*, ed. Marjorie Dent Candee (New York: The H. H. Wilson Company, 1953), p. 544; *Little Acorn*, n.p.

25. Nannie Talbot Johnson, *Cake, Candy and Culinary Crinkles* (Louisville, Kentucky: Pentecost Publishing Company, 1912). This was a companion to *What to Cook and How to Cook It*, a wider-ranging compilation published by the same house in 1899 and reissued by G. P. Putnam's Sons in 1923.

26. 1931 *Joy*, p. 44.
27. Ibid., p. 94.
28. 1896 *Boston*, pp. 32–33; 1931 *Joy*, p. 95.
29. 1931 *Joy*, p. 172.
30. Ibid., p. 19.
31. Ibid., pp. 82, 35, 7, 40, 180.
32. Ibid., p. 174.
33. Ibid., p. 177; see Farmer, *A New Book of Cookery*, p. 209, and Mrs. Simon Kander, *The Settlement Cook Book*, 20th ed. (Milwaukee: The Settlement Book Company, 1934), p. 309.
34. 1931 *Joy*, p. 153.
35. Ibid., p. 153.
36. *St. Louis Post-Dispatch*, January 24, 1930.
37. 1931 *Joy*, p. 65.
38. Ibid., p. 145.
39. Ibid., p. 154.
40. Ibid., p. 11.
41. *Mrs. Rorer's New Cook Book*, p. 44.
42. *Mrs. Hale's New Cook Book*, p. 421.
43. Nineteenth-century changes in American breadmaking have been repeatedly and illuminatingly treated by Karen Hess. See especially Mary Randolph, *The Virginia House-wife*, facsimile of 1824 edition with historical notes and commentary by Karen Hess (Columbia, South Carolina: University of South Carolina Press, 1984), pp. 272–274, and Karen Hess, "The American Loaf: A Historical View," *Journal of Gastronomy*, vol. 3, no. 4 (winter, 1987–88), pp. 2–23.
44. 1931 *Joy*, p. 190.
45. "The Mystery Chef" was John McPherson, and a collection of his recipes was published in 1934 as *The Mystery Chef's Own Cook Book* (New York: Longmans, Green Company, 1934).
46. Ruth A. Jeremiah Gottfried, *The Questing Cook: A Bundle of Good Recipes from Foreign Kitchens* (Cambridge, Mass.: Washburn and Thomas, 1927).
47. A 1903 observer remarks on "the use of animal fats . . . for many purposes for which the inhabitants of other countries largely employ vegetable oils" and "a somewhat inexplicable prejudice against the use of vegetable oil for cooking purposes" as being distinctively American traits; see excerpt from Charles M. Daugherty, "The Industry in Oil Seeds," USDA Yearbook, 1903, reprinted in *Agriculture in the United States: A Documentary History*, ed. Wayne D. Rasmussen (New York: Random House, 1974), vol. 2, p. 1792.
48. See Ida Bailey Allen, *The Modern Method of Preparing Delightful Foods* (New York: Corn Products Refining Company, 1929). Advertisements for Mazola appeared prominently in her other cookbooks.
49. Daugherty, "The Industry in Oil Seeds," p. 1792.
50. 1931 *Joy*, pp. 45, 119.
51. Ibid., pp. 120–121.
52. The recipes for spaghetti with tomato sauce are on pp. 40–41 of the 1931 *Joy*.
53. 1924 *Boston*, p. 100; 1930 *Boston*, p. 92.
54. See 1931 *Joy*, pp. 40–42, for the main macaroni and spaghetti recipes.

55. Ibid., p. 143.
56. Ibid., pp. 129–130.
57. Ibid., pp. 151, 356–357.
58. Ibid., p. 260.
59. Ibid., p. 211.
60. Ibid., pp. 279–280, 283.
61. Ibid., Preface, n.p.
62. Ibid., p. 378.
63. Ibid., p. 114.
64. Ibid., pp. 95–96.
65. "My Little World," pp. 66, 67; *Girls and Boys*, p. 73.
66. 1931 *Joy*, pp. 60–61. Marguerite, the evil-tempered cook whose version of a savory cheese pie Irma first tasted in Switzerland, is named in the draft list of people and circumstances she meant to include in the unwritten Swiss section of "My Little World." (BPC)
67. 1931 *Joy*, p. 15.

6. ROMBAUER AND BOBBS-MERRILL: THE MAKING OF AN ENMITY

My reconstruction of Irma Rombauer's early relationship with her publisher draws on the Bobbs-Merrill papers in the Manuscripts Division of the Lilly Library of Indiana University at Bloomington and on the following conversations with former Bobbs-Merrill employees: interviews with Angus Cameron (January 30, 1986, and March 29, 1988), Harrison Platt (May 29, 1986), Leo Gobin (November 6, 1987), Marian Israel (November 7, 1987), Patricia Jones (November 10, 1987), and Elizabeth Bragdon Easton (March 10, 1986); telephone interviews with Leo Gobin (March 4, 1986), Harrison Platt (March 10, 1986), Guernsey Van Riper (November 6, 1987), Judith Cross-Henley (November 10, 1987), and William Finneran (November 11, 1987, and March 15, 1988). A useful overall history of Bobbs-Merrill up to Irma's early years as one of the firm's authors is Jack O'Bar, "A History of the Bobbs-Merrill Company, 1850–1940, with a Postlude through the Early 1960s" (Ph.D. dissertation, Indiana University, 1975). For a vivid if splenetic portrait of D. Laurance Chambers see Hiram Haydn, *Words and Faces* (New York: Harcourt Brace Jovanovich, 1974), pp. 32–57.

All passages from the Bobbs-Merrill *Joy of Cooking* and other Rombauer files are quoted by permission of the Lilly Library.

1. Undated reader's report by Nancy Poston. (LL)
2. Jessica Mannon to Laurance Chambers, January 28, 1933. (LL)
3. Undated reader's report by Stena Marie Holdahl. (LL)
4. Laurance Chambers to Irma Rombauer, February 23, 1933. (LL)
5. Jessica Mannon to Irma Rombauer, November 4, 1935. (LL)
6. For accounts of Bobbs-Merrill's early initiatives in marketing and promotion, see Charles A. Madison, *Book Publishing in America* (New York: McGraw-Hill, 1966), pp. 258–260; John W. Tebbel, *A History of Book Publishing in the United States* (New York: R. R. Bowker Company, 1975), vol. 2, pp. 157–158, 509; Alice Payne Hackett, *Seventy Years of Best Sellers, 1895–1965* (New York: R. R. Bowker Company, 1967), pp. 95–97.

7. *Little Acorn*, n.p.
8. Irma Rombauer to Julia Chapman, February 3, 1936. (BPC)
9. Laurance Chambers to Irma Rombauer, December 6, 1935. (LL)
10. December 5, 1935, *Joy of Cooking* contract, paragraph 2: "... agrees to assign to the Publishers the copyright in the previously published, briefer form of the said work entitled THE JOY OF COOKING." (BPC)
11. Haydn, *Words and Faces*, p. 33.
12. *Little Acorn*, n.p.
13. Anne Ross, undated editorial memo (probably January 3, 1936), commented on in Irma Rombauer to Jessica Mannon, January 5, 1936. (LL)
14. Irma Rombauer to Jessica Mannon, January 13, 1936. (LL)
15. Irma Rombauer to Julia Chapman, February 3, 1936; the eager salesman's visit had occurred the preceding day. (BPC)
16. Jessica Mannon to Irma Rombauer, December 13, 1935; telegram from Irma Rombauer to Jessica Mannon, December 13, 1935. (LL)
17. 1936 *Joy*, p. 385.
18. December 5, 1936, *Joy of Cooking* contract, paragraphs 3, 5(a)–5(e). (BPC)
19. Irma Rombauer to Mina Kersey, December 30, 1935; Irma Rombauer to Jessica Mannon, May 13, 1936. (LL)
20. Irma Rombauer to Mina Kersey, January 26, 1936. (LL)
21. *St. Louis Post-Dispatch*, March 25, 1936; Irma Rombauer to Jessica Mannon, March 30, 1936. (LL)
22. Mina Kersey to Irma Rombauer, April 17, 1936. (LL)
23. Haydn, *Words and Faces*, p. 33.
24. Jessica Mannon to Irma Rombauer, May 4, 9, 30, and June 24, 1936. (LL)
25. 1936 *Joy*, jacket blurb.
26. Sales announcement for 1936 *Joy*. (LL)
27. January 30, 1986, Cameron interview; frequent Cameron–Rombauer letters appear in the files in February of 1936. (LL)
28. Ruth Ellen Lorrien to Angus Cameron, July 28, 1936. (LL)
29. Quoted in Angus Cameron to Irma Rombauer, July 21, 1936. (LL)
30. Quoted in Angus Cameron to Alice Walsh (of the *Detroit News*), July 14, 1936. (LL)
31. Angus Cameron to Irma Rombauer, May 8, 1936. (LL)
32. Irma Rombauer to Angus Cameron, September 10, 1936. (LL)
33. I have been unable to locate copies of any of Irma's 1936 *Post-Dispatch* articles, which appeared in a weekend supplement and not the regular newspaper. She first reports the invitation in a letter to Cameron dated "Wednesday" (probably April 1, 1936) and mentions to him on May 7, "My column is doing wonders" (for book sales). On August 5, when she writes to Cameron about the prospect of lining up a syndicated column, she claims to have a number of columns (presumably already published) on hand to show as samples (LL). Apparently the *Post-Dispatch* column had been abandoned by the time of her return from Seattle to St. Louis that fall. She was still trying to pursue the syndicated-column idea at least until the fall of 1937.
34. Bobbs-Merrill accounting statement furnished to Irma Rombauer, November 1, 1936. (LL)
35. The Rumford affair first surfaces in the files on September 14, 1936 (J. W. Atherton to Bobbs-Merrill Company), and crops up intermittently for

some weeks until Irma's telegram to Laurance Chambers, November 11, 1936. (LL)

36. Irma Rombauer to C. A. Collins, November 27, 1936. (LL)
37. 1936 *Joy* (second printing), p. 301.
38. Angus Cameron to Irma Rombauer, May 7, 1937. (LL)
39. Irma Rombauer to Jessica Mannon, July 25, 1938. (LL)
40. Jessica Mannon to Irma Rombauer, August 3, 1938. (LL)
41. Irma Rombauer to Jessica Mannon, August 12, 1938 (LL). Even now anyone can evade copyright on any recipe by switching ¼ to ½ teaspoon or playing with the wording a little bit.
42. Irma Rombauer to Jessica Mannon, February 22, 1939. (LL)
43. Irma Rombauer to Jessica Mannon, February 13, 1939. (LL)
44. Irma Rombauer to Jessica Mannon, November 12, 1938. (LL)
45. Laurance Chambers to Paul Hoeffer, December 30, 1938. (LL)
46. Jessica Mannon to Irma Rombauer, November 17, 1938.
47. I have not seen an executed copy of the *Streamlined Cooking* contract, but the substance of the negotiations is clear from the exchange of letters between Chambers and Hoeffer in December 1938 and the undated copy of the contract (probably December 1938) signed by Chambers and Jessica Mannon (BPC). The actual contract probably was executed around January 8–10, 1939.
48. November 11, 1987, Finneran telephone interview.
49. *Indianapolis News*, October 8, 1963.
50. November 11, 1987, Finneran telephone interview.
51. Andrew Hepburn, undated radio broadcast script meant for WCFL, Chicago; probably a general prototype aired on many stations in May and June 1939.
52. Andrew Hepburn to Irma Rombauer, June 7, 1939. (LL)
53. *Streamlined Cooking* publicity blurb. (LL)
54. Irma Rombauer to Andrew Hepburn, June 1, 1939. (LL)
55. *Streamlined Cooking*, p. 79.
56. Ibid., p. 58.
57. Ibid., Preface, n.p.
58. Jessica Mannon to Irma Rombauer, April 10, 1940. (LL)
59. Jessica Mannon to Irma Rombauer, May 23, 1940 (following up on Irma Rombauer to Jessica Mannon, April 7, 1940). (LL)
60. Irma Rombauer to Jessica Mannon, May 27, 1940.
61. Jessica Mannon to Irma Rombauer, May 28 and 29, 1940. (LL)
62. The sales tabulation for *The Joy of Cooking*, 1936–37, is taken from a general summary of sales furnished by Bobbs-Merrill to Marion Becker in March 1968. (BPC)
63. May 27, 1943, *Joy of Cooking* contract and unexecuted draft of December 1942. (BPC)
64. November 10, 1987, Jones interview.
65. Irma's intense concentration on work, and the importance of the forthcoming revision, are mentioned in several letters to Put in 1942 and 1943, but she does not comment on the Bobbs-Merrill situation.
66. For Bobbs-Merrill's sales figures on *Joy*, see n. 62; tabulation of total *Boston* printings taken from copyright page of 1959 edition.

67. January 30, 1986, Cameron interview.
68. For *Joy* sales and *Boston* printing figures, see above, nn. 62 and 66.
69. Haydn, *Words and Faces*, p. 57.
70. November 11, 1987, and March 15, 1988, Finneran telephone interviews; November 6, 1987, Gobin interview.
71. May 27, 1943, *Joy of Cooking* contract, paragraphs 12, 13. (BPC)
72. Inscribed copy of *One World* sent by the Willkies; Edith Willkie to Irma Rombauer, July 16, 1943 (BPC). See *St. Louis Post-Dispatch*, July 23, 1943.
73. *Time*, July 12, 1943, p. 84; *Time*, August 16, 1943, pp. 102–103.
74. Telephone interview with Cecily Brownstone, January 22, 1994.
75. Irma Rombauer to Julia Chapman, undated (probably 1944). (BPC)
76. Mentioned in Marian Judell Israel to Irma Rombauer, May 18, 1944. (BPC)
77. Billie Burke to Irma Rombauer, June 8, 1944 (transcript by Bobbs-Merrill publicity office). (BPC)
78. *El Paso Times*, May 28, 1944.
79. Marine Corps Lieutenant Leon Littman to Irma Rombauer, September 27, 1945. (BPC)
80. Seaman First Class August Willard Solomon to Irma Rombauer, April 15, 1944 (transcript by Bobbs-Merrill publicity office). (BPC)
81. Mrs. William Burke Jr. to Irma Rombauer, undated (transcript by Bobbs-Merrill publicity office) (BPC). The contents are cited in slightly different form in the *St. Louis Star-Times*, September 28, 1945.
82. 1943 *Joy*, Preface, n.p.
83. Ibid., p. 784.
84. *Time* obituary of Irma Rombauer, October 26, 1962, pp. 64–66.
85. November 6, 1987, Gobin interview; March 15, 1988, Finneran telephone interview.
86. Theodora Zavin to Marion Becker, August 3, 1949. (BPC)
87. File of *Hartrich* v. *Becker* (see below, p. 448, headnote), Plaintiff's Exhibit No. 11 (Bobbs-Merrill schedule of income paid to Irma Rombauer, 1936–49). Since the totals for the years 1946–49 also include royalties on *A Cookbook for Girls and Boys*, the real figure for *Joy* is even smaller than it appears.
88. Interview with Joe Bettenmann, December 9, 1985; March 15, 1988, Finneran telephone interview.
89. November 11, 1987, Finneran telephone interview.
90. Memorandum by Mary Whyte Hartrich of payments to her by Irma Rombauer, 1936–49. (MHS)
91. November 11, 1987, Finneran telephone interview.
92. Irma Rombauer to Mary Whyte Hartrich, December 19, 1943. Quoted by permission of the Missouri Historical Society.
93. Irma Rombauer to Mary Whyte Hartrich, January 26, 1945. Quoted by permission of the Missouri Historical Society.
94. May 27, 1943, *Joy of Cooking* contract, paragraph 7. (BPC)

7. FAMILY REGROUPINGS

Documentation of *Joy* history and Irma's life in the 1940s is extremely sparse and unsystematic. A number of letters from Irma, Marion, and other family members, kindly copied for me by Edgar R. Rombauer Jr., shed light on some events, as do a small collection of letters to Mary Whyte Hartrich in the Missouri Historical Society and a random assortment of letters still at Cockaigne.

Materials from Bobbs-Merrill files donated to Indiana University are again quoted by permission of the Lilly Library.

1. Reported by Merna Lazier (interview, June 8, 1984).
2. Reported by Marian Judell Israel (interview with Helen-Marie Fruth and Marian Judell Israel, January 7, 1986).
3. Reported by George Schriever (interview, March 7, 1984).
4. Telephone interview with Terry Nicholson, November 2, 1985.
5. Irma Rombauer to Julia Chapman, January 27, 1945. (BPC)
6. A useful brief history of Cincinnati, by an old political ally of Marion Becker's, is Iola Hassler Silberstein, *Cincinnati Then and Now* (Cincinnati: The League of Women Voters of the Cincinnati Area, 1982). See pp. 185–194 for the early history of the Charter government.
7. Irma's less-than-perfect faith in John and Marion's practical abilities was hinted to me by several former Bobbs-Merrill employees.
8. See Elizabeth Lawrence, *Lob's Wood* (Cincinnati: Cincinnati Nature Center, 1971); interview with Abby Dittmann Wise, December 14, 1983.
9. *Wild Wealth*, p. 74.
10. Irma Rombauer to Edgar R. Rombauer Jr., September 26, 1942.
11. See *The Modern Art Society: The Center's Early Years, 1939–1954* (catalogue of 1979 retrospective exhibition, Cincinnati: The Contemporary Arts Center, 1979); interview with Peggy Frank Crawford, April 2, 1988. I have also drawn on the large collection of Modern Art Society materials and letters from Marion and John's friends in the arts community that still remains at Cockaigne.
12. Edna Gellhorn to Marion Becker, undated (probably early or mid-1940s). (BPC)
13. Reported by Emma K. Fischer (interview, March 22, 1984).
14. Telephone interview with Edgar R. Rombauer Jr., April 2, 1988.
15. Irma Rombauer to Marion Becker, undated, forwarded by Marion to Julia Chapman, August 4, 1943. (BPC)
16. Interview with Edgar R. Rombauer, May 21, 1993; April 2, 1988, Rombauer telephone interview.
17. Marion Becker, autobiographical manuscript fragment, August 6, 1972. (BPC)
18. Julius Muench to Irma Rombauer, August 15, 1946. (BPC)
19. May 21, 1993, Rombauer interview.
20. Marion Becker to Edgar R. Rombauer Jr., December 28, 1945.
21. Irma Rombauer to Marion Becker, undated ("Sunday," probably June 1947) (BPC). Irma had made shift to write Put in cautiously friendly fashion at least by August of 1946, but usually expressed herself to Marion with some bitterness.
22. Max Muench to Edgar R. Rombauer Jr., April 5, 1946.
23. Interview with Joe Bettenmann, December 9, 1985.
24. Reported by Edgar R. Rombauer Jr. in April 2, 1988, telephone interview and on several other occasions; corroborated by Irma's later history during her illness.

25. Irma Rombauer to Mary Whyte Hartrich, undated (apparently 1940), states that her income from *Joy* "in the four years of its existence" (i.e., as a modestly successful Bobbs-Merrill book) has been $8,400 and that she wants Mazie "to have at least $4,000 from the Joy." (Quoted by permission of the Missouri Historical Society.) By Mazie's own calculation Irma paid her a total of $2,225 in those four years, 1936 through 1939 (memorandum by Mary Whyte Hartrich of payments to her by Irma Rombauer, 1936–49 [MHS]). After the book's sudden 1943 leap to prominence Irma began sending Mazie larger sums in twice-yearly installments, and later events make clear that she meant this arrangement to continue for Mazie's lifetime. See pp. 180–181 and 222–223.

26. December 9, 1985, Bettenmann interview.

27. The Torno-Rombauer *Post-Dispatch* articles are "How to Conserve Wheat in Your Kitchen" (March 26, 1946), "Uses for Leftover Foods" (April 10, 1946), and "Vegetables in Leftover Dishes" (April 16, 1946).

28. *Childcraft* (Chicago: Field Enterprises, Inc., 1937–49), vol. 8, pp. 193–209.

29. The files at the Lilly Library record some internal Bobbs-Merrill discussions of a children's-cookbook project, with several exchanges between Rosemary York in Indianapolis and various people in the New York office.

30. Telephone interview with Cecily Brownstone, March 28, 1988.

31. Rosemary York to Ross Baker, November 4, 1942. (LL)

32. John L. B. Williams (editorial head of the New York office) to Laurance Chambers, March 28, 1946. (LL)

33. Rosemary York to Laurance Chambers, March 30, 1946. (LL)

34. Laurance Chambers to John L. B. Williams, April 8, 1946. (LL)

35. February 28, 1945, contract for "The Junior Joy of Cooking" (later retitled *A Cookbook for Girls and Boys*). (BPC)

36. Rosemary York to Marion Becker, August 7, 1946; several letters from Irma to Marion during August comment on the annoyance of the rush job and Bobbs-Merrill's ineptitude. (BPC)

37. Irma Rombauer to Laurance Chambers, September 28, 1946; ratified by Chambers, September 30, 1946. (BPC)

38. Irma's letters to Mazie also mention help on the children's book manuscript from "Vivien," perhaps another *Parents* editor. (MHS)

39. Rosemary York to Marion Becker, August 12, 1946. (BPC)

40. *Girls and Boys*, pp. 128–130.

41. Marion Becker to Julia Chapman, undated (probably January or February 1947). (BPC)

42. I have found no copy of the 1948 "Home Comfort." The Rombauer-Torno freezing and canning chapters are referred to in B. B. Culver Jr. (of the Wrought Iron Range Company) to Irma Rombauer, January 13, 1949. (BPC)

43. Telephone interview with Laurent Torno Jr., March 24, 1988.

44. Even at a much later stage, an undated letter from Irma to Marion probably written in late 1950 or early 1951 describes Mazie as so "cheerless" and discouraged since her husband's death as to make their common efforts on *Joy* difficult. (BPC)

45. Rosemary York to Irma Rombauer, August 2, 1948. (BPC)

46. Supplement to May 27, 1943, *Joy of Cooking* contract, executed September 30, 1948. (BPC)

8. WAR MANEUVERS

With the vexed history of the 1951 *Joy of Cooking* we reach a period represented in Marion's files at Cockaigne by rich but very erratic documentation; episodes that are almost redundantly attested to alternate with frustrating gaps. Marion's 1949–53 correspondence with Greenbaum, Wolff & Ernst and Bobbs-Merrill—including many papers of her mother's that Marion also salvaged for her own files at some unknown point—forms the backbone of my account. In piecing together the rest of the story I have drawn on interviews with Harrison Platt (May 29, 1986), Elizabeth Bragdon Easton (March 10, 1988), and Marian Israel (November 7, 1987) and telephone interviews with Harrison Platt (March 10, 1986) and William Finneran (November 11, 1987, and March 15, 1988).

1. Rowland T. Jones (of the H. J. Heinz Company) to Marion Becker, July 25, 1946, replying to a query of hers about the content of baby food. (BPC)
2. Undated, untitled clipping from Cincinnati-area newspaper, headed "Newton [sic] Woman's Bread Recipe Is Proved Best," apparently from late 1940s. (BPC)
3. 1936 *Joy*, p. 169 (comment on marshmallows and sweet potatoes repeated in several later editions).
4. Laurance Chambers to Irma Rombauer, March 23, 1948 (BPC). Apparently Irma's countersigned copy was not properly returned to Bobbs-Merrill.
5. Marion Becker to Walter Hurley, November 11, 1948 (incomplete copy). (BPC)
6. Rosemary York to Marion Becker, November 17, 1948. (BPC)
7. Marion Becker to Rosemary York, undated longhand draft replying to the above letter. (BPC)
8. Marion Becker to Rosemary York, February 9, 1949. (BPC)
9. Rosemary York to Irma Rombauer, February 15, 1949. (BPC)
10. Irma Rombauer to Morris Ernst, cover letter enclosing several transcripts of Rombauer/Bobbs-Merrill exchanges, February 25, 1949 (BPC). The file or files assembled for the purpose of reporting the case to Ernst furnishes a general (though incomplete) chronology of the war up to that point.
11. Telegram from Irma Rombauer to Rosemary York, March 1, 1949. (BPC)
12. Telephone interview with Harrison Platt, March 10, 1986; interview with Harrison Platt, May 29, 1986.
13. Hiram Haydn, *Words and Faces* (New York: Harcourt Brace Jovanovich, 1974), p. 47.
14. Jack O'Bar, "A History of the Bobbs-Merrill Company, 1850–1940" (Ph.D. dissertation, Indiana University, 1975), p. 98.
15. Haydn, *Words and Faces*, p. 57.
16. Marion Becker to Morris Ernst, March 1, 1949. (BPC)
17. Harriet Pilpel to Marion Becker, May 13, 1949. (BPC)
18. Morris Ernst to Marion Becker, July 11, 1949. (BPC)
19. Telegram from Marion Becker to Harriet Pilpel, April 8, 1949. (BPC)
20. Harriet Pilpel to Irma Rombauer on April 5, 1949, suggests threatening to have the undelivered portion of the manuscript published elsewhere. A notion to get the radio hostess Mary Margaret McBride to do a joint cook-

book with Marion using the new material is mentioned in Morris Ernst to Irma Rombauer, April 8 and 21, 1949, and Harriet Pilpel to Marion Becker, May 3, 1949. (BPC)

21. Harriet Pilpel to Irma Rombauer and Marion Becker, August 15, 1949; Irma Rombauer to the Bobbs-Merrill Company, August 18, 1949. (BPC)
22. Harrison Platt to Irma Rombauer, October 11, 1949; draft version of Irma Rombauer to Harrison Platt, October 20, 1949. (BPC)
23. March 10, 1986, Platt telephone interview.
24. Harriet Pilpel to Irma Rombauer, November 16, 1949, and to Marion Becker, November 23, 1949. (BPC)
25. Harriet Pilpel to Irma Rombauer, April 5, 1949, and to Marion Becker, May 13, 1949. (BPC)
26. Harriet Pilpel to Irma Rombauer, May 3, 1949, and March 1 and March 9, 1950; and to Marion Becker, May 13, 1949, and March 22, 1950. (BPC)
27. The Becker files indicate that several friendly exchanges on design matters took place between Marion and Walter Hurley in the months following an initial meeting in April 1949. (BPC)
28. Harriet Pilpel to Irma Rombauer and Marion Becker, February 21, 1950. (BPC)
29. See above, p. 179 (Theodora Zavin to Marion Becker discussing *Joy* sales record).
30. Telegram from Irma Rombauer to Marion Becker, February 23, 1950. (BPC)
31. The actual 32 percent offer is not extant in Marion's files but is referred to in Marion Becker to Theodora Zavin, August 21, 1950. Marion Becker to Harriet Pilpel, September 14, 1950, plainly indicates that the Rombauer side is preparing to accept the latest Bobbs-Merrill terms. (BPC)
32. Marion Becker to Harriet Pilpel, September 14, 1950, with accompanying draft of Marion Becker to Ross Baker, September 14, 1950. (BPC)
33. October 14, 1950, *Joy of Cooking* contract, preamble. (BPC)
34. Harriet Pilpel to Irma Rombauer, November 16, 1949 (BPC). Ross Baker, the Bobbs-Merrill head of sales, seems to have made verbal overtures to Marion about her appearing as coauthor as early as July 1949, when she mentions his suggestion in an undated longhand draft letter to Greenbaum, Wolff & Ernst (BPC).
35. Harriet Pilpel to Irma Rombauer, April 5, 1949, and to Marion Becker, May 13, 1949. (BPC)
36. October 14, 1950, *Joy of Cooking* contract, paragraph 13. (BPC)
37. Harriet Pilpel to Irma Rombauer, April 5, 1949. (BPC)
38. October 14, 1950, *Joy of Cooking* contract, paragraph 16. (BPC)
39. Ross Baker to Marion Becker, October 26, 1950, refers to negotiations with Ginnie Hofmann as artist. (BPC)
40. There is voluminous correspondence on the proposed change to "New Joy," including Walter Hurley to Marion Becker, March 14, 1951, and telegram from Ross Baker to Marion Becker, May 10, 1951. (BPC)
41. John Becker to Walter Hurley, April 30, 1951. (BPC)
42. Marion Becker to Harriet Pilpel, April 22, 1951. (BPC)
43. March 10, 1986, Platt telephone interview and May 29, 1986, Platt interview; Harrison Platt to Marion Becker, including excerpts from consultants' opinions, April 9, 1951. (BPC)

44. Marion Becker to Harriet Pilpel, May 19, 1951. (BPC)
45. Marion Becker to Walter Hurley, July 15, 1951. (BPC)
46. 1951 *Joy*, Preface, n.p.
47. Ginnie Hofmann to Irma Rombauer, May 21, 1951. (BPC)
48. Irma Rombauer to Marion Becker, undated (probably January or February 1952). (BPC)
49. Walter Hurley to Irma Rombauer and Marion Becker, April 28, 1952 (BPC). Since the 1950 contract, like all since *Streamlined* in 1939, had required Bobbs-Merrill to pay for alterations in proof with a stipulation that the author would make no unnecessary changes, Irma and Marion must have considered the improvement of the index vitally important to the book's future.
50. For Bobbs-Merrill sales figures, see above, p. 431, n. 62.
51. *Oakland Tribune*, July 29, 1951.
52. *Indianapolis Times*, undated clipping, 1951.
53. Irma Rombauer to Marion Becker, undated (probably August 1951), enclosing *Pageant*'s letter of inquiry, Laura Bergquist to Irma Rombauer, August 15, 1951. (BPC)
54. Irma Rombauer to Cecily Brownstone, undated (probably November 1951), referring to advance copy of Jay Kaye, "She Gets Most Joy from Cooking," *Pageant* magazine, January 1952, pp. 24–29. (BPC)
55. Jane Nickerson, "They Wanted to Cook Like Mother," *New York Times Book Review*, August 12, 1951, p. 6.
56. Irma Rombauer to John Becker, undated (probably October 1950) (BPC). Irma clearly had political hopes for Haydn.
57. Haydn, *Words and Faces*, pp. 49–51, 53–56.
58. O'Bar, "History of the Bobbs-Merrill Company, 1850–1940," p. 228.
59. The 1968 Bobbs-Merrill sales summary (see above, p. 431, n. 62) lists 10,500 copies sold through the Book-of-the-Month Club in 1953, out of a total of 91,133. (BPC)
60. Irma Rombauer to Marion Becker, October 5, 1949 (mentioning an urgent need to revise her will to "protect Maizie"); Irma Rombauer, signed and witnessed longhand will dated October 13, 1949. (BPC)
61. Irma Rombauer to Marion Becker, tentative draft of letter of agreement concerning Mary Whyte Hartrich, November 10, 1950. (BPC)
62. Harriet Pilpel to Irma Rombauer, October 26, 1950; Marion Becker to Harriet Pilpel, November 28, 1950 (BPC). Other queries about the agreement concerning Mazie, and at least one other trial draft, were circulated at about the same time and were mentioned in subsequent legal proceedings (*Hartrich* v. *Becker*; see below, p. 448, no. 15). The actual agreement was signed by Marion in its final form on December 28, 1950.
63. Marion Becker to Harriet Pilpel, January 7, 1958, mentions Marion's earlier doubts about the Hartrich agreement. (BPC)
64. Irma Rombauer, executed copy of will dated June 14, 1951. (BPC)
65. Trust Agreement between Irma S. Rombauer as Settlor and Irma S. Rombauer and Marion R. Becker as Trustees, May 2, 1952. (BPC)
66. See p. 381. Marion's claim that Irma had transferred all *Joy of Cooking* affairs to her after 1951 is explicitly affirmed in *Little Acorn* and the 1974 deposition.

67. Several undated letters to Marion from January and February of 1954 (BPC) show Irma seriously trying to evolve a general plan for the next *Joy of Cooking* revision and considering how to match selling points of the latest Betty Crocker or *Better Homes and Gardens* offerings. She continued to make private comments on other food writers' work in the manner of a current, not retired, colleague. I have found no evidence that Irma ever explicitly turned over the responsibility of revision to Marion or anyone else.

68. Scribbled in Irma's hand on the last page of a letter from Hugo Muench (September 26, 1950) that she passed along to Marion. (BPC)

69. 1951 *Joy*, p. 538.

70. Ibid., n.p.

9. CHRONICLES OF COOKERY 2

My treatment of culinary developments draws heavily on various editions (though by no means the complete run) of the two chief competitors to *The Joy of Cooking:* Fannie Merritt Farmer, *The Boston Cooking-School Cook Book*, as revised by her successors Cora D. Perkins and Wilma Lord Perkins; and Lizzie Kander, *The Settlement Cook Book* (hereafter cited as "1924 *Boston*" and "1927 *Settlement*"). The earliest Rombauer/Bobbs-Merrill letters are once more cited by permission of the Lilly Library.

1. H. L. Mencken, "Victualry as a Fine Art," *Chicago Tribune*, June 13, 1926, reprinted in *The Bathtub Hoax and Other Blasts and Bravos from the Chicago Tribune by H. L. Mencken*, ed. Robert McHugh (New York: Octagon Books, 1977), pp. 269–273; Lewis Mumford, "Back to the Table," *New Republic*, August 15, 1928, p. 332.

2. John J. McAleer's *Rex Stout: A Biography* (Boston: Little, Brown, 1977) reports that Stout paid Mrs. Hibben, a longtime friend, $2,000 to supply the recipes for *Too Many Cooks* in 1938.

3. Mary Grosvenor Ellsworth gives a painstaking introduction to the "new" salad-making in *Much Depends on Dinner* (New York: Alfred A. Knopf, 1939), pp. 163–170.

4. I cannot attest to the contents of all *Settlement* and *Boston* editions during this period. But the 1927 *Settlement* includes a treatment of pressure cookers (pp. 21–22) and ice cream frozen in iceless refrigerators (p. 388), and often though not universally mentions oven temperatures for baked desserts; the 1934 edition has alcoholic cocktails and custard-based chiffon pies. I first find mentions of some oven-temperature settings and ice cream making with mechanical refrigerators in the 1930 *Boston*. The book barely mentions pressure cookers in 1930, first describing them in detail in 1936. The custard type of chiffon pie appears in 1941, as do some alcoholic punches; a smattering of other alcoholic cocktails is admitted in 1951.

5. 1941 *Boston*, p. 21.

6. A "smorgasbord" is described in the appetizer chapter of the 1934 *Settlement*, p. 317.

7. See 1951 *Settlement*, pp. 12–13.

8. Irma Rombauer to Jessica Mannon, January 7, 1936. (LL)

9. Irma Rombauer to Jessica Mannon, January 5, 1936. (LL)
10. 1936 *Settlement*, pp. 5, 27, 43.
11. 1930 *Boston*, p. 3.
12. Ibid., p. 20.
13. 1936 *Joy*, p. 1.
14. Ibid., p. 235.
15. Ibid., p. 191.
16. Ibid., pp. 215, 255.
17. Ibid., p. 68.
18. Ibid., p. 149.
19. Ibid., p. 142.
20. Ibid., p. 369. Irma Rombauer to Andrew Hepburn, June 2, 1939 (LL), mentions her dislike of the so-called "Dover beater."
21. 1936 *Joy*, p. 378.
22. Ibid., p. 491.
23. Quoted in Marian Burros, "De Gustibus," *New York Times*, March 16, 1985.
24. *Streamlined*, p. ix.
25. Ibid., p. 179.
26. Ibid., p. ix.
27. Ibid., p. 82.
28. Ibid., p. ix.
29. 1943 *Joy*, p. 763.
30. Ibid., Preface, n.p.
31. Ibid., pp. 128, 114, 534.
32. Ibid., p. 264.
33. Ibid., p. 107.
34. Ibid., p. 542; cf. "Devil's Food No. 2" in the 1934 *Settlement*, p. 450. Irma Rombauer to Jessica Mannon, February 1, 1939, replying to a query from a Bobbs-Merrill staff member about why red devil's food is not in the 1936 *Joy*, confesses, "I *hate* it," but acknowledges that she ought in future to be less wedded to her own prejudices. (LL)
35. 1943 *Joy*, pp. 304–305.
36. *The Good Housekeeping Cook Book*, ed. Dorothy B. Marsh (New York: Rinehart and Company, 1949), p. 813.
37. James A. Beard, *The Fireside Cook Book: A Complete Guide to Fine Cooking for Beginners and Experts* (New York: Simon and Schuster, 1949), pp. 264–265.
38. Obituary of Della Lutes, *New York Times*, July 14, 1942.
39. *The Gourmet Cookbook* (New York: Gourmet, Inc., 1950), p. 8.
40. Irma S. Rombauer and Jane Crawford Torno, "Cooking Up Fun," *Childcraft* (Chicago: Field Enterprises, Inc., 1937–49), vol. 8, p. 194.
41. *Streamlined*, pp. 149, 29.
42. Rowland T. Jones (of the H. J. Heinz Company) to Marion Becker, July 25, 1946, replying to a query of hers about the content of baby food. (BPC)
43. Undated, untitled clipping from Cincinnati-area newspaper, headed "Newton [sic] Woman's Bread Recipe Is Proved Best," apparently from late 1940s. (BPC)
44. 1951 *Joy*, p. 262.

45. Ibid., pp. 451, 459.
46. Ibid., p. 41.
47. Ibid., p. 427.
48. Ibid., pp. 335, 338.
49. 1931 *Joy*, p. 19 (comment retained in all later editions through 1946); 1951 *Joy*, p. 40.
50. 1951 *Joy*, p. 99.
51. Ibid., p. 103.
52. Ibid., p. 500.
53. Ibid., p. 192.
54. Ibid., p. 499.
55. Siegfried Giedion, *Mechanization Takes Command: A Contribution to Anonymous History* (New York and London: W. W. Norton, 1969), p. 207.
56. 1951 *Joy*, pp. 499–500.
57. Ibid., p. 532.
58. 1951 *Boston*, p. 67.
59. 1949 *Good Housekeeping Cook Book*, p. 428.
60. Harrison Platt to Marion Becker, April 9, 1951. (BPC)
61. 1951 *Joy*, pp. 931–933.
62. Ibid., p. 562.
63. Ibid., p. 876.
64. Ibid., p. 90.
65. Ibid., p. 370.
66. Ibid., p. 899.
67. Ibid., pp. 724, 85.
68. Ibid., pp. 451, 761.
69. Ibid., p. 746.
70. Ibid., pp. 569, 61, 249.
71. Ibid., Introduction, n.p.
72. Ibid., p. 237.
73. *Streamlined*, p. 56, and 1943 *Joy*, p. 245; cf. 1951 *Joy*, p. 262.
74. 1951 *Joy*, p. 868; 1951 *Boston*, p. 813.
75. 1951 *Joy*, pp. 920–921.
76. Ibid., pp. 709–710, 52.
77. Ibid., p. 426.
78. Ibid., p. 335.
79. 1951 *Boston*, p. 47.
80. 1951 *Joy*, p. 142. See Buwei Yang Chao, *How to Cook and Eat in Chinese* (New York: The John Day Company, 1945).
81. Comparative figures on *Joy* sales and *Boston* printings are from a general summary of sales furnished by Bobbs-Merrill to Marion Becker in March 1968 (BPC) and the copyright page of the 1959 edition of *Boston*, respectively.
82. 1943 *Joy*, p. 93; 1951 *Joy*, p. 92.
83. 1951 *Joy*, p. 338.
84. Ibid., p. 430.
85. Ibid., p. 376.
86. Ibid., pp. 404, 313, 860.
87. Ibid., p. 834.

88. Ibid., pp. 451–452.
89. Ibid., p. 468.
90. Ibid., p. 156.
91. *Little Acorn*, n.p.

10. INDIAN SUMMER INTERRUPTED

1. The blurb of the Bertholle/Beck/Ripperger *What's Cooking in France* (a tiny spiral-bound paperback volume of only sixty-three pages; New York: Ives Washburn, Inc., 1952), states, "In preparation by these same authors is a larger volume of French cooking from which these recipes have been selected." Marion comments on the failed collaboration in "Links," September 30, 1975, mentioning not Mme. Beck but Louisette Bertholle, with whom Ripperger apparently had a falling-out.
2. *New York Times*, December 26, 1952.
3. Irma's 1952 letters from Europe, which Marion sent on to other friends, are still among the Becker papers at Cockaigne.
4. George and Placide Schriever to Irma Rombauer, May 27, 1952 (BPC); interview with George Schriever, March 7, 1984.
5. Julia Child, "How Good Is the New 'Joy of Cooking'?" *McCall's*, October 1975, pp. 63–66.
6. Irma Rombauer to Marion Becker, June 18, 1952. (BPC)
7. Interview with Robert Isaacson, March 9, 1988.
8. Irma Rombauer to Marion Becker, undated (probably August 15, 1952). (BPC)
9. Irma Rombauer to Marion Becker, undated (probably August 25 and 26, 1952). (BPC)
10. Irma Rombauer to Marion Becker, August 27, 1952. (BPC)
11. Irma S. Rombauer, "Our American Regional Cooking Compares Favorably with French," *St. Louis Post-Dispatch*, July 31, 1952.
12. Irma Rombauer to Marion Becker, undated (probably December 1954). (BPC)
13. Irma S. Rombauer, "Some Taste Treats from Mexico," *St. Louis Post-Dispatch*, October 23, 1953; Irma Rombauer to Marion Becker, October 24, 1953. (BPC)
14. James Woodress to Irma Rombauer, October 16 and October 24, 1953. (Copies kindly forwarded to me by Professor Woodress along with copies of Irma's replies, probably October 23, 1953, and circa New Year's Day, 1954.)
15. Letter from James Woodress, January 31, 1984.
16. Marion Becker to Julia Chapman, undated (probably January or February 1947). (BPC)
17. "Estergom" (named for the Hungarian town of Esztergom, some thirty miles northwest of Budapest on the Danube) is preserved as a nine-page typescript among the Becker papers at Cockaigne.
18. "My Little World," pp. 9–10.
19. Ibid., p. 29.
20. "Carcinoma of the breast" is listed as the *preoperative* diagnosis on the Christian R. Holmes Hospital record of the mastectomy, February 11, 1955. (Marion Becker's hospital records kindly furnished to me by Holmes Hospital.)

21. Holmes Hospital operative records, February 11 and 16, 1955.
22. Telephone interview with Elsa Hunstein, March 13, 1986; St. Luke's Hospital treatment record, June 9, 1955. (Irma Rombauer's hospital records kindly furnished to me by St. Louis Regional Medical Center.)
23. Interview with Edgar R. Rombauer Jr., June 5, 1984; telephone interview with Edgar R. Rombauer Jr., April 2, 1988. Other observers independently commented on Irma's craving for alcohol in her enfeebled state.
24. Edgar R. Rombauer Jr. to Marion Becker, Max Muench, and Thomas J. Snowden (the official tenant and subletter of the Lindell Boulevard apartment), June 13, 1955. (BPC)
25. Irma Rombauer to James Woodress, undated (probably mid- or late June 1955; copy kindly furnished to me by James Woodress).
26. Marian Judell Israel to Marion Becker, undated (circa New Year's Day, 1956). (BPC)
27. Max Muench to Marion Becker, November 30, 1955. Irma assigned power of attorney to Marion on December 7, 1955, and also February 7, 1956. (BPC)
28. March 13, 1986, Hunstein telephone interview; telephone interview with Cecily Brownstone, January 22, 1994.
29. In an undated letter to Marion apparently from November 1955, Irma complains of being "swamped by daily correspondance [sic]" in Mazie's absence, and announces, "I shall shunt some of it onto you for really, I cannot do it all." Several months later, in an undated letter to Marion probably written around mid-February 1956, Irma refers to having met with Mazie about "the revision"—presumably, to discuss some proposed division of efforts among the three of them—and found her "amenable." (BPC)
30. Ethan A. H. Shepley (Washington University chancellor) to Irma Rombauer, January 27, 1956. (BPC)
31. Marion Becker to Edgar R. Rombauer Jr., February 15, 1956 (copy kindly furnished to me by Edgar R. Rombauer Jr.).
32. By April of 1956 Irma was instructing Mazie to reply to a fan letter (BPC). A marked-up copy of the 1953 "New Joy" in the possession of Edgar R. Rombauer Jr. contains many notations in Irma's hand obviously dating from a time of partial impairment in handwriting but essentially lucid thought processes. The bank ticket—Irma had an inveterate habit of scribbling down things on unused checks or other handy pieces of paper—is a deposit slip dated January 7, 1957, stuck into the same 1953 *Joy*, containing various notes on baking results for cookies.
33. Interview with Edgar R. Rombauer Jr., June 3, 1984. That Irma visited virtually demented rages on Marion at intervals was reported by, among others, Elsa Hunstein, Ethan Becker, and Frances Jones Poetker.
34. "Eliza" to Marion Becker, September 19, 1956. (BPC)

11. THE LAST BATTLE

The affair of the unauthorized edition presents the same problems of documentation as the events leading up to the 1951 *Joy* (see chapter 8): variously superabundant or nonexistent materials in Marion's files; usually tending to back up her views of the case and omitting most evidence to the contrary. In attempting to construct a fair picture of highly tangled controversies, I have drawn on interviews with Dorothy Wartenberg (January 6, 1986), Jane Brueggeman (February 21, 1986), Harrison Platt (May 29, 1986), Leo Gobin (November 6, 1987), and Marian Israel (November 7, 1987) and telephone interviews with Cecily Brownstone (on multiple occasions), Leo Gobin (March 4, 1986, and July 1, 1993), Harrison Platt (March 10, 1986), Grace Shaw (April 3, 1986), James Gregory (April 30, 1986), and William Finneran (November 11, 1987, and March 15, 1988).

1. *Indianapolis Times*, November 12, 1958.
2. *Indianapolis Star*, November 19, 1958.
3. Howard Sams to Marion Becker, November 20, 1958. (BPC)
4. *Publishers Weekly*, March 9, 1959, p. 34.
5. Charles A. Madison, *Book Publishing in America* (New York: McGraw-Hill, 1966), pp. 453–454; *Publishers Weekly*, July 4, 1960, p. 164, August 8, 1960, pp. 36–37, and November 28, 1960, p. 22.
6. *Publishers Weekly*, March 30, 1959, p. 37, and May 11, 1959, pp. 37–38.
7. *Publishers Weekly*, January 25, 1960, pp. 213–214.
8. May 29, 1986, Platt interview.
9. *Publishers Weekly*, February 2, 1959, p. 18.
10. Several undated letters from Irma to Marion apparently written early in 1954 mention the card-file idea as one that Irma and Mazie did not care for; Mary Whyte Hartrich to Marion Becker, March 13, 1954, gives the same verdict (BPC). But Marion's determination to carry on with the card plan a couple of years later is documented in Marion Becker to Mary Whyte Hartrich, January 23, February 3, and June 9, 1956 (MHS).
11. Harriet Pilpel to Marion Becker, January 27, 1958; John Becker to Harriet Pilpel, March 27, 1958; also Greenbaum, Wolff & Ernst internal memos from Morton Goldberg to Harriet Pilpel, January 24, February 14, and April 11, 1958. (BPC)
12. Marion's suggestion about deferring some of the payments due to Mazie under the 1950 agreement, and Mazie's refusal to accept this idea, are referred to in the April 11, 1958, Goldberg memo and mentioned in Marion's appointment calendar for February 28, 1958 (BPC). On this occasion Marion told Mazie that payments to her would cease with the next edition of *Joy*.
13. Marion Becker to Mary Whyte Hartrich, September 2, 1958 (mirror-written letter, MHS; see page 313), refers to a statement of expenses submitted by Mazie.
14. An undated draft memo by Marion on *Joy* promotion ideas, probably written in 1960 or 1961 and meant to be discussed with Bobbs-Merrill, discusses the measuring-tool scheme at length. (BPC)
15. 1963 *Joy*, p. 132.
16. The cooking course is mentioned in two undated mirror-written letters (see page 313) from Marion to Irma (probably written in 1959) and in the citation for the Garden Club of America award (the Amy Angell Collier Montague Medal) presented to Marion in 1961 for civic achievements including the conservation project in question, the Nature Conservancy's purchase of Lynx Prairie in Adams County. (BPC)
17. 1963 *Joy*, pp. 36, 138.
18. January 6, 1986, Wartenberg interview.
19. November 11, 1987, Finneran telephone interview.

20. See 1963 *Joy*, pp. 472, 708, 612, 606; the same recipes are in the 1975 *Joy*, pp. 428, 756, 660, 661.
21. 1963 *Joy*, p. 493.
22. Ibid., p. 300.
23. Marion Becker to William Raney, May 2, 1962. (BPC)
24. Marion Becker to Harriet Pilpel and James Magrish, June 16, 1962 (longhand draft for general chronology of the troubles). (BPC)
25. Ibid.; Hughes Miller to Marion Becker, July 28, 1961 (BPC); May 29, 1986, Platt interview.
26. Marion Becker to Harrison Platt and Dave Rosenberg (at that time Bobbs-Merrill production supervisor), January 25, 1960, discussing space and layout and mentioning a decision made in December to increase the number of pages by thirty-two. (BPC)
27. Alice Wilson Richardson, *Just a Minute: A Book of Quick Cookery* (New York: Procyon Press, 1947), p. 99. The book was later reissued as *The Just a Minute Cookbook* (New York: Prentice-Hall, 1952).
28. Telephone interview with Elsa Hunstein, March 13, 1986.
29. Marion Becker to John, Mark, and Ethan Becker, Labor Day (September 4), 1961. (BPC)
30. St. Luke's Hospital discharge summary, July 4, 1961.
31. Marion Becker to Harriet Pilpel and James Magrish, March 19, 1962. (BPC)
32. William Raney to Hughes Miller, May 2, 1962, and August 31, 1962. These are respectively numbered Plaintiff's Exhibit to the Defendant's Deposition No. 35 and Plaintiff's Exhibit No. 79 in the *Hartrich* v. *Becker* file (see headnote on p. 448).
33. See the *Publishers Weekly* articles "Bobbs-Merrill's Sales Volume Reaches New Peak," August 8, 1960, pp. 36–37, and "Sams, Bobbs-Merrill Push-Button Plant Is Ready for the Future," June 13, 1962, pp. 70–74.
34. March 15, 1988, Finneran telephone interview.
35. See above, n. 32.
36. William Raney to Marion Becker, May 2 and May 9, 1962. (BPC)
37. Raney to Miller, May 2, 1962 (see above, n. 32).
38. Marion reports the details of the June 15 meeting with Raney in a long memo, extant in several versions, that she prepared for Harriet Pilpel and James Magrish, November 10, 1962. (BPC)
39. Elsa Hunstein to Marion Becker, June 1, 1962. (BPC)
40. Mary Whyte Hartrich to Marion Becker, June 16, 1962. Quoted by permission of the Missouri Historical Society.
41. 1974 deposition, pp. 137–138.
42. J. L. Hudson's advertisement in *Detroit News*, June 3, 1962, p. 6-A; Harriet Pilpel to William Raney, June 26, 1962. (BPC)
43. James Magrish to Morton Goldberg, June 28, 1962 (BPC); April 30, 1986, Gregory telephone interview.
44. Harriet Pilpel to William Raney, June 26, 1962. (BPC)
45. William Raney to Marion Becker, July 4, 1962. (BPC)
46. Marion Becker to James Magrish, August 9, 1962, and to William Raney, August 10, 1962. (BPC)
47. St. Luke's Hospital discharge summary, August 15, 1962; attending physician's surgical consultation report, August 23, 1962.

48. Marion Becker to Mary Whyte Hartrich, August 24, 1962. Quoted by permission of the Missouri Historical Society.

49. Interview with Edgar R. Rombauer Jr., May 21, 1963.

50. October 14, 1950, *Joy of Cooking* contract, paragraph 14. (BPC)

51. Harriet Pilpel to Paul Gitlin, September 17, 1962. (BPC)

52. *Publishers Weekly*, September 24, 1963, p. 33.

53. Marion Becker, undated autobiographical manuscript fragment beginning, "A month ago my poor mother suffered the added indignity of an amputation due to an embolism." (BPC)

54. Telegram from Hughes Miller to Marion Becker, October 15, 1962. (BPC)

55. Transcript of memorial service for Irma Starkloff Rombauer, First Unitarian Church, St. Louis, October 17, 1962. (Copy kindly furnished to me by Elizabeth Goltermann.)

56. Reported by Elsa Hunstein, March 13, 1986, telephone interview.

57. Telegrams from Harriet Pilpel to Paul Gitlin, October 17, 1962, and from James Magrish to Hughes Miller and Howard Sams, October 18, 1962. (BPC)

58. James Magrish to Harriet Pilpel, October 26, 1962. (BPC)

59. Telephone interview with Cecily Brownstone, March 23, 1993.

60. Hughes Miller's attempt to buy Marion's compliance was mentioned to me by Dorothy Wartenberg (January 6, 1986, interview) and Jane Brueggeman (February 21, 1986, interview), and acknowledged by Leo Gobin (November 6, 1987, interview).

61. November 6, 1987, Gobin interview.

62. 1962 *Joy*, first printing, pp. 475, 180.

63. Ibid., p. 262.

64. Ibid., p. 488.

65. Ibid., pp. 627 and 732, both cross-referenced to the meringue topping recipe on p. 696.

66. Ibid., pp. 185–186.

67. Ibid., pp. 479–480.

68. Ibid., pp. 575–576.

69. Ibid., pp. 170–171.

70. Ibid., pp. 435, 466.

71. Ibid., p. 376.

72. Ibid., p. 723.

73. Ibid., p. 607.

74. Ibid., pp. 200–201.

75. James Magrish to Marion Becker, November 9, 1962, enclosing copy of telegram sent to him by Ernst, Cane, Berner and Gitlin (Bobbs-Merrill attorneys in New York) on the evening of November 8. (BPC)

76. November 8, 1962, telegram (see previous note).

77. Ibid.

78. James Magrish, memo apparently intended to be sent to several parties, November 23, 1962. (BPC)

79. Marion Becker to James Magrish, December 29, 1962. (BPC)

80. *Indianapolis News*, January 22, 1963; *Publishers Weekly*, February 11, 1963, p. 100.

81. James Magrish to Harriet Pilpel, February 13, 1963; by then Bobbs-Merrill had indicated its willingness to pay the resetting costs and compensate

Marion independently of the royalty schedule in a tentative draft contract submitted to Magrish by Harold Bredell (Bobbs-Merrill counsel in Indianapolis) on January 23, 1963. (BPC)

82. March 4, 1986, Gobin telephone interview.
83. April 5, 1963, *Joy of Cooking* contract, paragraph 2. (BPC)
84. Ibid., paragraphs 7(a), 15, 16.
85. Ibid., paragraph 8. The deferred-royalty account, which proved less advantageous than the Beckers had supposed, was abolished by an amendment to the contract on June 8, 1968. (BPC)
86. April 5, 1963, *Joy of Cooking* contract, paragraph 26.
87. Draft memo (unsent) from Marion Becker to Bobbs-Merrill, December 14, 1962. (BPC)
88. February 21, 1986, Brueggeman interview.
89. December 14, 1962, draft memo (see above, n. 87).
90. Mary Whyte Hartrich to Marion Becker, September 10, 1963. (BPC)

12. *LITTLE ACORN* AND *WILD WEALTH*

In reconstructing the history of *Wild Wealth* I have drawn on interviews with Frances Jones Poetker (February 17, 1986), Marian Israel (November 7, 1987), and Janice Rebert Forberg (October 13, 1993).

1. *St. Louis Post-Dispatch*, April 27, 1963; Last Will and Testament of Irma Starkloff Rombauer, March 17, 1963 (copy sent me by Probate Division, St. Louis Circuit Court).
2. Edgar R. Rombauer Jr. to Marion Becker, March 9, 1964; copyright interest assignment executed by Edgar R. Rombauer Jr., March 9, 1964. (BPC)
3. Sales totals through 1967 are from a general summary of sales furnished by Bobbs-Merrill to Marion Becker in March 1968; after 1967 I have relied on the semiannual Bobbs-Merrill royalty statements furnished to Marion (BPC). The totals reported in the last eleven years of Marion's authorship are 201,005 in 1966, 210,078 in 1967, 237,203 in 1968, 262,859 in 1969, 250,586 in 1970, 281,186 in 1971, 248,223 in 1972, 292,893 in 1973, 188,264 in 1974, 236,443 in 1975, and 334,483 in 1976.
4. Lester Troob (Book-of-the-Month Club) to William Finneran, August 29, 1968. (BPC)
5. Entry for Thomas William Itin in *Who's Who in the Midwest, 1992–1993*, p. 337.
6. Contract between Bobbs-Merrill and Mei Ya Publications, Inc., signed by Leo Gobin, August 17, 1967; Marion Becker to Leo Gobin, November 20, 1968. (BPC)
7. 1963 *Joy*, p. 26; the reference is to Edgar Anderson, *Plants, Man and Life* (Berkeley and Los Angeles: University of California Press, 1967), p. 127.
8. Marion Becker to Harriet Pilpel, May 19, 1958; Harriet Pilpel to Marion Becker, May 26, 1958. (BPC)
9. Marion Becker to James Magrish, November 26, 1965 (draft version); Marion Becker to Robert Amussen, November 30, 1965; the early chronology of plans for *Little Acorn* is summarized in Marion's draft of a letter to Robert Amussen, January 22, 1966. (BPC)

10. *Little Acorn*, n.p.
11. Ibid., n.p.
12. Ibid., n.p.
13. Ibid., n.p.
14. *Publishers Weekly*, May 26, 1966, pp. 54–55.
15. Holmes Hospital operative record, November 4, 1966, and surgical pathology record, November 5, 1966.
16. Marion Becker to Robert Amussen, November 15, 1966 (draft version). (BPC)
17. "Links," September 4, 1976. Marion's appointment calendar for 1967 contains what apparently was a summary of information that she drew up before deciding not to go on with the radiation treatments, attached to the page for April 12. (BPC)
18. Letter of understanding on untitled promotional booklet: Leo Gobin to Marion Becker, February 25, 1966; letter of understanding on *Little Acorn*: Leo Gobin to Marion Becker, December 8, 1967. (BPC)
19. Marcia Seligson, "What We Need Now Is Another French Cookbook," *New York Times Book Review*, November 9, 1969, pp. 8–12.
20. Robert Amussen to Marcia Seligson, November 7, 1969. (BPC)
21. *Wild Wealth*, Acknowledgments, n.p.
22. Ibid., p. 182.
23. October 13, 1993, Forberg interview.
24. There are three final *Wild Wealth* contracts, all dated December 11, 1970: between Janice Forberg and Bobbs-Merrill, among the three authors and Bobbs-Merrill, and a "supplementary agreement" (of which only an incomplete copy is extant) among the authors and Janice Forberg. (BPC)
25. Catalogue of Chicago Book Clinic exhibit, May 2, 1972. (BPC)
26. *Morton Arboretum Quarterly*, vol. 7, no. 4 (winter, 1971), pp. 45–52 and inside back cover; *Explorer*, vol. 13, no. 3 (fall, 1971), pp. 4–12 and front cover.
27. Marion Becker to Lois Stewart (director of permissions for Bobbs-Merrill) and Leo Gobin, September 3, 1972 (draft versions) (BPC). Janice Forberg also recalls that at one point Marion and Frances Poetker wanted to use Bettina Dalvé's drawing of the white oak on the front of the dust jacket in later printings of *Wild Wealth*, another idea that they were legally forced to abandon (October 13, 1993, Forberg interview).
28. Bobbs-Merrill promotional release from Catherine Hartman, November 9, 1971. (BPC)
29. Marion Becker to Catherine Hartman, November 13, 1971 (draft version). (BPC)
30. Marion Becker to Eugene Rachlis, November 14, 1971. (BPC)

13. MARION'S LAST YEARS

For Marion's last revision of *The Joy of Cooking* I have drawn on the Becker papers at Cockaigne and the following conversations: interviews with Eugene Rachlis (October 23, 1985), Dorothy Wartenberg (January 6, 1986), Helen-Marie Fruth and Marian Judell Israel (January 7, 1986), Jane Brueggeman (February 21, 1986), Nancy Swats (April 15, 1986), Leo Gobin (November 6, 1987), and Joan Becker (May 16, 1993); and telephone interviews with Leo Gobin (March 14, 1986, and July 1, 1993), Ikki Matsumoto (December 17, 1993), and Marian Judell

Israel (March 2 and 3, 1994). For the threatened lawsuit by Mazie Hartrich, the most important sources are the Hartrich papers in the Missouri Historical Society; the file on *Hartrich* v. *Becker* (U.S. District Court for the Eastern District of Missouri, Eastern Division, No. 73 C 544[A]) now possessed by Armstrong, Teasdale, Schlafly and Davis in St. Louis and kindly copied for me by Edwin L. Noel; and Marion's 1974 deposition (see above, p. 418) with accompanying exhibits. I have also drawn on a telephone interview with Eugene A. Hartrich (January 26, 1994) and mentions of financial arrangements in several letters written by Irma to the West Coast family between approximately 1943 and 1946 (copies kindly furnished to me by Edgar R. Rombauer Jr.).

1. Holmes Hospital discharge summary, June 9, 1972.
2. Instrument of Trust between Marion Rombauer Becker, Grantor, and Marion Rombauer Becker and John W. Becker as Trustees, December 27, 1972. (BPC)
3. October 23, 1985, Rachlis interview.
4. Ibid.
5. November 6, 1987, Gobin interview.
6. 1975 *Joy*, pp. 139 (cf. 1963 edition, p. 118) and 648.
7. Marion Becker, incomplete undated draft (apparently early September 1971) of letter to Joe Becker beginning, "You are beginning school." (BPC)
8. Eric Pace, "Record $1.5 Million for Paperback That Revels in the Joy of Cooking"; Raymond Sokolov, "It's Plain, It's Fancy—and It Works"; "Honey Cake a Favorite of Beckers," all in *New York Times*, April 3, 1973.
9. Marion Becker to Eric Pace, undated draft. (BPC)
10. Marked clipping from *St. Louis Post-Dispatch*, April 4, 1973. (MHS)
11. Thomas E. Wack to Marion Becker, April 27, 1973. (BPC)
12. *Hartrich* v. *Becker*: Plaintiff's Interrogatories, August 20, 1973. (BPC)
13. Letter of agreement: Irma Rombauer to Marion Becker, signed by Marion Becker on December 28, 1950, copy accompanying summons issued to Marion Becker by Circuit Court of St. Louis County, July 5, 1973. (BPC)
14. On October 5, 1949, Irma informed Marion that she wanted Mazie "to have at least 4000 annually for life" if book sales permitted, and asked her to see to it "should I be unable to carry out this wish" (BPC). On October 13, 1949, she wrote out a will in longhand leaving 10 percent of the gross income on the literary property to Mazie (BPC). By October of the following year she was talking with Harriet Pilpel about a more formal measure that became the December 28, 1950, letter of agreement. Earlier, two letters to Put (April 29, 1945, and August 9, 1946) indicate that in the wake of the wartime edition's success she began sending equal amounts of money to Mazie, Marion, Put, and Max Muench (who had helped her financially in the past). This may be the "unbusinesslike business arrangement" that Irma referred to in a letter to Mazie on July 30, 1945, saying that she had told Put and Marion of it in "a lengthy memorandum" that is now lost. (Quoted by permission of the Missouri Historical Society.) See also above, p. 181 and pp. 222–223.
15. Harriet Pilpel to Irma Rombauer, November 16, 1949, and to Marion Becker, November 23, 1949; Irma Rombauer to Marion Becker, October 5, 1949 (mentioning an urgent need to revise her will to "protect Maizie"); Irma Rombauer, signed and witnessed longhand will dated October 13, 1949; Irma Rombauer to Marion Becker, tentative draft of letter of agree-

ment concerning Mary Whyte Hartrich, November 10, 1950; Harriet Pilpel to Irma Rombauer, October 26, 1950; Marion Becker to Harriet Pilpel, November 28, 1950; Marion Becker to Harriet Pilpel, January 7, 1958, mentions Marion's earlier doubts about the Hartrich agreement. (BPC)

16. In *Little Acorn*, Marion's treatment of the period following the 1951 *Joy* conveys the manifestly mistaken impression that Irma had given up any active role in the cookbook.

17. *Hartrich* v. *Becker:* Deposition of Mary Whyte Hartrich, December 3, 1973, pp. 91–92 (Armstrong, Teasdale file).

18. See above, pp. 322–324 and p. 444, n. 32.

19. 1974 deposition, p. 2.

20. Ibid., pp. 107–114; Leo Gobin to Edgar R. Rombauer Jr., July 1, 1963. (BPC)

21. Marion wrote Mazie to thank her for a note about the 1962 revision on November 27, 1962 (MHS). Mazie thanked Marion for a copy of *Little Acorn* on July 10, 1966 (BPC).

22. Mary Whyte Hartrich to Marion Becker, September 10, 1963. (BPC)

23. Marion Becker to Harriet Pilpel, January 31, 1974. (BPC)

24. "Links," June 20, 1975 (the main chronology of John's illness); Marion Becker to Hugo Walther, March 11, 1974. (BPC)

25. *Hartrich* v. *Becker:* notarized release statement by Mary Whyte Hartrich, March 6, 1974, and stipulation for dismissal. (BPC)

26. Agreement between New American Library and Bobbs-Merrill, May 30, 1973, paragraph 7(b). (BPC)

27. Herbert K. Schnall to Eugene Rachlis, October 8, 1973. (BPC)

28. Holmes Hospital discharge summary, April 24, 1974.

29. For Judy Israel's part in the 1975 *Joy* revision, my main sources were the January 7, 1986, Fruth-Israel interview and the March 2 and March 3, 1994, Israel telephone interviews.

30. 1975 *Joy*, pp. 56, 54, 53.

31. *New York Times*, June 16, 1974 (UPI item carried in many newspapers).

32. "Links," June 18, 1975.

33. Reported by Jane Brueggeman (February 21, 1986, interview).

34. "Links," June 20, 1975.

35. Memo of July 24, 1974, conference. (BPC)

36. Harriet Pilpel to Marion Becker, July 25, 1974. (BPC)

37. Marion Becker to Harriet Pilpel, September 7, 1974. (BPC)

38. John's application to the *New Yorker*, and the magazine's rejection, are mentioned in two undated letters from John to Marion, apparently written in November and December of 1930. (BPC)

39. Interview with Geoffrey Vincent, January 12, 1986. John's three articles were published in the *Louisville Courier-Journal* on March 15, April 26, and June 28, 1970.

40. May 16, 1993, Joan Becker interview; Marion mentions the outline of John's book in the October 4, 1974, letter to "Dear Kids" (see p. 389).

41. "Links," undated entry in January of 1975.

42. See above, n. 7.

43. "Links," January 1975.

44. November 6, 1987, Gobin interview; July 1, 1993, Gobin telephone interview.

45. March 14, 1975, *Joy of Cooking* contract, preface and paragraph 8. (BPC)

46. December 17, 1993, Matsumoto telephone interview.

47. Marion Becker to Leo Gobin, May 26, 1975. (BPC)

48. 1975 *Joy*, pp. 4, 394, 519.

49. Ibid., pp. 160–161.

50. Marion Becker to Ralph Nader, February 27, 1973. (BPC)

51. 1975 *Joy*, p. 850.

52. *Washington Post*, December 14, 1975; *New York Times Book Review*, December 7, 1975.

53. Julia Child, "How Good Is the New 'Joy of Cooking'? " *McCall's*, October 1975, pp. 63–68.

54. Ibid., p. 66; "Links," September 30, 1975.

55. Holmes Hospital discharge summaries, April 25 and May 6, 1975.

56. Several drafts of Marion's text for the flower-arranging book are preserved in a loose-leaf notebook at Cockaigne, along with assorted notes. (BPC)

57. As of February 20, 1976, Harriet Pilpel sent the "round robin" group (see above, p. 388) a proposed contract for "The Junior Joy," but only her cover letter now exists along with an earlier draft and several references in the correspondence. (BPC)

58. Jeremy Nussbaum (of Greenbaum, Wolff & Ernst) to Marion Becker, August 19, 1975, enclosing letters from the Deutsches Literaturarchiv and the Berliner Verleger- und Buchhändlervereinigung; Harriet Pilpel to Marion Becker, August 28 and November 18, 1975 (the November letter enclosing letter from Franz-Wilhelm Peter). (BPC)

59. Marion Becker to Leo Gobin, May 26, 1975. (BPC)

60. "Links," March 30, 1975.

61. "Links," June 12, 1975.

62. Marion Becker, autobiographical manuscript fragment, August 1, 1972; "Links," September 25, 1975.

63. "Links," July 5, 1976.

64. "Links," March 30, 1975.

65. "Links," June 20, 1975.

66. Letter inserted into "Links": Marion Becker to △ (her private symbol for Mark, Jennifer, and Joe), July 13, 1965.

67. Ibid.; Marion Becker, draft memo, June 4, 1976, on Garden Clubs of America Bicentennial Committee plans. (BPC)

68. Trust Agreement between Marion Becker, Grantor, and Marion Becker and Ethan Becker, Trustees, June 6, 1975, with several later amendments. (BPC)

69. Marion Becker, Last Will and Testament, June 21, 1976. (BPC)

70. See p. 446, n. 3.

71. Bill Shurtleff and Akiko Aoyagi to Marion Becker, November (undated) 1975 (BPC). See 1975 *Joy*, fifth and subsequent printings, p. 535.

72. Letter of agreement between Anna Cosman (Bobbs-Merrill permissions department) and Mary Beth O'Connell (*Ladies' Home Journal*, May 12, 1975) (BPC); excerpts printed under the heading, "The (new) Joy of Cooking," *Ladies' Home Journal*, September and November, 1975.

73. "Links," January 20, 1976.

74. A draft version of the "Great Living Cincinnatian" award speech was inserted into "Links" on or about January 25, 1976; see also *Cincinnati Enquirer*, February 4, 1976.
75. *Cincinnati Enquirer*, April 26, 1975.
76. *Cincinnati Enquirer* "In Society" column, December 20, 1975; a transcript of the Contemporary Arts Center lecture (given on December 16, 1975) was forwarded by Marion Becker to Stephen Friedman (*Cincinnati* magazine) and Van Cottongim (editor of the film montage) on January 13, 1976. (BPC)
77. Holmes Hospital discharge summary, March 21, 1976; various correspondence took place on the "Cothyrobal" hearing early in 1976, several letters still being preserved at Cockaigne.
78. Marion Becker to "Adelaide" (perhaps Adelaide Farney), June 1, 1976. (BPC)
79. "Links," July 4, 1976.
80. Letter inserted into "Links": Marion Becker to Jerome Berman, September 4, 1976.
81. Ibid.
82. Ibid.
83. "Links," August 29, 1976, and November 7, 1976. Marion had earlier bought dozens of copies of *The Unquiet Grave* to present to friends, and marked many passages, perhaps meaning to include some in the "chapbook" part of "Links."
84. "Links," October 23, 1976.
85. "Links," November 30, 1976.
86. Letter inserted into "Links": Marion Becker to Harriet Pilpel, November 30, 1976.
87. John Becker to Tom Itin, June 25, 1969 (draft version). (BPC)
88. John Becker to Tom Itin, November 1, 1969. (BPC)
89. Marion Becker to Tom Itin, December 10, 1976. (BPC)
90. Holmes Hospital patient history, December 21, 1976; Richard Ader (of Greenbaum, Wolff & Ernst) to Marion Becker, December 10, 1976. (BPC)
91. Amendment to June 16, 1976, trust agreement signed by Marion, notarized December 15 and 16, 1976. (BPC)

SELECTED BIBLIOGRAPHY

Allen, Ida Bailey. *Ida Bailey Allen's Modern Cook Book: 2500 Delicious Recipes.* Garden City, N.Y.: Garden City Publishing Company, Inc., 1932.

———. *Mrs. Allen's Cook Book.* Boston: Small, Maynard and Company, 1917.

America's Cook Book. Compiled by the Home Institute of the *New York Herald Tribune.* New York: Charles Scribner's Sons, 1937.

Beard, James A. *The Fireside Cook Book.* New York: Simon and Schuster, 1949.

Becker, Marion Rombauer. *Little Acorn: The Story behind The Joy of Cooking, 1931–1966.* Indianapolis and New York: The Bobbs-Merrill Company, 1966.

Beecher, Catherine E. *A Treatise on Domestic Economy.* New York: Marsh Capen Lyon and Webb, 1841.

Beecher, Catherine E., and Harriet Beecher Stowe. *The American Woman's Home.* New York: J. B. Ford and Company, 1869.

Berolzheimer, Ruth. *The American Woman's Cook Book.* Garden City, N.Y.: Garden City Publishing Company, Inc., 1947.

Campbell, Joan. *The German Werkbund: The Politics of Reform in the Applied Arts.* Princeton, N.J.: Princeton University Press, 1978.

Child, Georgie Boynton. *The Efficient Kitchen.* New York: McBride, Nast and Company, 1914.

Cummings, Richard Osborn. *The American and His Food: A History of Food Habits in the United States.* New York: Arno Press, 1970. (Reissue of second edition, University of Chicago Press, 1941.)

Davidis, Henriette. *Henriette Davidis' Praktisches Kochbuch für die gewöhnliche und feinere Küche.* Bearbeitet nach der Originalausgabe von Roland Gööck. Munich: Wilhelm Heyne Verlag, 1983. (Based on 1844 edition with some modernization and occasional details from other early editions.)

————. *Praktisches Kochbuch für die Deutschen in Amerika, nach der 36. Auflage des deutschen Kochbuches der Henriette Davidis* bearbeitet von Hedwig Voss. Milwaukee: Geo. Brumder's Verlag, 1897.

Davis, Adelle. *Let's Cook It Right: Good Health Comes from Good Cooking.* New York: Harcourt, Brace and Company, 1947.

De Gouy, Louis P. *The Gold Cook Book.* New York: Greenberg, Publisher, 1947.

Detjen, David W. *The Germans in Missouri, 1900–1918: Prohibition, Neutrality, and Assimilation.* Columbia, Mo.: University of Missouri Press, 1985.

Ellsworth, Mary Grosvenor. *Much Depends on Dinner.* New York: Alfred A. Knopf, 1939.

Ewan, Stuart. *Captains of Consciousness: Advertising and the Social Roots of the Consumer Culture.* New York: McGraw-Hill, 1976.

Farmer, Fannie. *The Boston Cooking-School Cook Book.* New York: Weathervane Books, 1973. (Facsimile of first edition, Boston: Little, Brown, 1896.) Revised edition by Fannie Farmer, 1906; revised editions by Cora D. Perkins, 1918, 1923; revised editions by Wilma Lord Perkins, 1930, 1936, 1941, 1946, 1951, 1959.

Friedman, Stephen. "The Joys of Marion Rombauer Becker." *Cincinnati Magazine,* March 1976, pp. 36–41.

Germans for a Free Missouri: Translations from the St. Louis Radical Press, 1857–1862. Selected and translated by Steven Rowan, with introduction and commentary by James Neal Primm. Columbia, Missouri: University of Missouri Press, 1983.

The Good Housekeeping Cook Book. New York: Farrar and Rinehart, Inc. (distributed for International Readers League), 1942.

The Good Housekeeping Cook Book. Ed. Dorothy B. Marsh. New York: Rinehart and Company, 1949.

Gottfried, Ruth A. Jeremiah. *The Questing Cook: A Bundle of Good Recipes from Foreign Kitchens.* Cambridge, Massachusetts: Washburn and Thomas, 1927.

The Gourmet Cookbook. New York: Gourmet, Inc., 1950.

Hale, Sarah Josepha. *Mrs. Hale's New Cook Book.* Philadelphia: T. B. Peterson, 1857.

"Harland, Marion" (pseudonym of Mary Virginia Terhune). *Common Sense in the Household: A Manual of Practical Housewifery.* New York: Charles Scribner's Sons, 1889. (First published in 1871.)

Haydn, Hiram. *Words and Faces.* New York: Harcourt Brace Jovanovich, 1974.

Hess, Karen. "The American Loaf: A Historical View." *Journal of Gastronomy.* Vol. 3, no. 4 (winter, 1987–88), pp. 2–23.

Hibben, Sheila. *American Regional Cookery.* Boston: Little, Brown, 1946.

————. *A Kitchen Manual.* New York: Duell, Sloan and Pearce, 1941.

————. *The National Cook Book.* New York: Harper and Brothers, 1932.

Johnson, Nannie Talbot. *Cake, Candy and Culinary Crinkles.* Louisville, Ky.: Pentecost Publishing Company, 1912.

————. *What to Cook and How to Cook It.* Louisville, Ky.: Pentecost Publishing Company, 1899.

Kander, Mrs. Simon (Lizzie Black Kander). *The Settlement Cook Book.* Milwaukee: The Settlement Book Company, 1927, 1928, 1934, 1936, 1941, 1949, 1951. (These are representative editions of a work first published in 1901.)

Kropp, Ernst. *Wandlung der Form im XX. Jahrhundert.* Bücher der Form im Auftrag des Deutschen Werkbundes, herausgegeben von Dr. Walter Riezler, fünfter Band. Berlin: Verlag Hermann Reckendorf, 1926.

Lawrence, Elizabeth. *Lob's Wood.* Cincinnati: The Cincinnati Nature Center, 1971.

Lincoln, Mary J. *Mrs. Lincoln's Boston Cook Book: What to Do and What Not to Do in Cooking.* Boston: Little, Brown, 1883.

[Loughead, Flora Haines.] *Quick Cooking: A Book of Culinary Heresies, by One of the Heretics.* New York: Putnam's/The Knickerbocker Press, 1888.

[MacPherson, John.] *The Mystery Chef's Own Cook Book.* New York: Longmans, Green and Company, 1934.

Madison, Charles A. *Book Publishing in America.* New York: McGraw-Hill, 1966.

Marchand, Roland. *Advertising the American Dream: Making Way for Modernity, 1920–1940.* Berkeley and Los Angeles: University of California Press, 1985.

Mintz, Sidney W. *Sweetness and Power: The Place of Sugar in Modern History.* New York: Viking, 1985.

O'Bar, Jack. "A History of the Bobbs-Merrill Company, 1850–1940, with a Postlude through the Early 1960s." Ph.D. dissertation, Indiana University, 1975.

Primm, James Neal, *Lion of the Valley: St. Louis, Missouri.* Boulder, Colo.: Pruett Publishing Company, 1981.

Rombauer, Irma S. *A Cookbook for Girls and Boys.* Indianapolis and New York: The Bobbs-Merrill Company, 1946.

———. *A Cookbook for Girls and Boys.* Rev. ed. Indianapolis and New York: The Bobbs-Merrill Company, 1952.

———. *The Joy of Cooking: A Compilation of Reliable Recipes with a Casual Culinary Chat.* St. Louis: A. C. Clayton Printing Company, 1931.

———. *The Joy of Cooking: A Compilation of Reliable Recipes with a Casual Culinary Chat.* Indianapolis and New York: The Bobbs-Merrill Company, 1936.

———. *The Joy of Cooking: A Compilation of Reliable Recipes with a Casual Culinary Chat.* Indianapolis and New York: The Bobbs-Merrill Company, 1941. (Reprint of 1936 edition.)

———. *The Joy of Cooking: A Compilation of Reliable Recipes with an Occasional Culinary Chat.* Indianapolis and New York: The Bobbs-Merrill Company, 1943.

———. *The Joy of Cooking: A Compilation of Reliable Recipes with an Occasional Culinary Chat.* Indianapolis and New York: The Bobbs-Merrill Company, 1946.

Rombauer, Irma S., and Marion Rombauer Becker. *The Joy of Cooking.* Indianapolis and New York: The Bobbs-Merrill Company, 1951.

———. *The Joy of Cooking.* Indianapolis and New York: The Bobbs-Merrill Company, 1952. (Reprint of 1951 edition.)

———. *The Joy of Cooking.* Indianapolis and New York: The Bobbs-Merrill Company, 1953. (Reprint of 1951 edition, with new index.)

———. *Joy of Cooking.* Indianapolis and New York: The Bobbs-Merrill Company, 1962.

————. *Joy of Cooking*. Indianapolis and New York: The Bobbs-Merrill Company, 1963.

————. *Joy of Cooking*. Indianapolis and New York: The Bobbs-Merrill Company, 1964. (Reprint of 1963 edition.)

————. *Joy of Cooking*. Indianapolis and New York: The Bobbs-Merrill Company, 1975.

Rombauer, Irma S. *Streamlined Cooking: New and Delightful Recipes for Canned, Packaged and Frosted Foods and Rapid Recipes for Fresh Foods*. Indianapolis and New York: The Bobbs-Merrill Company, 1939.

————. "Unusual and Unpublished Recipes." St. Louis: Church of the Unity, 5015 Waterman Avenue, n.d.

Rombauer, Roderick E. *The History of a Life*. Privately published, 1903.

Root, Waverley, and Richard de Rochemont. *Eating in America: A History*. New York: William Morrow and Company, 1976.

Rorer, Sarah Tyson. *Mrs. Rorer's New Cook Book: A Manual of Housekeeping*. New York: Crown Publishers for the *Ladies' Home Journal* Cook Book Club, 1970. (Facsimile of first edition, Philadelphia: Arnold and Company, 1898.)

Sears, Paul Bigelow, Marion Rombauer Becker, Frances Jones Poetker, and Janice Rebert Forberg. *Wild Wealth*. Indianapolis and New York: The Bobbs-Merrill Company, 1971.

Tebbel, John W. *A History of Book Publishing in the United States*. 4 Vols. New York: R. R. Bowker Company, 1952.

Thomas, Edith May. *Mary at the Farm and Book of Recipes, Compiled during Her Visit among the "Pennsylvania Germans."* 2nd ed. Harrisburg, Pa.: Evangelical Press, 1928. (First published in 1915.)

Tornado Cook Book: Compiled in Behalf of the Lafayette Park Presbyterian Church. St. Louis, 1896.

Van Ravenswaay, Charles. "Missouri Cookery." *Bulletin of the Missouri Historical Society*. Vol. 3, no. 2 (January 1947), pp. 53–59.

Wallace, Lily Haxworth. *The New American Cook Book*. New York: Books, Inc., 1942.

Wilcox, Estelle Woods. *Buckeye Cookery and Practical Housekeeping*. St. Paul: Minnesota Historical Society Press, 1988. (Reprint of 1880 edition; the work was first published in 1876.)

Wolcott, Imogene. *The Blue Gingham Cook Book: A Complete and Widely Diversified Collection of Recipes Drawn from the Scientific Tests of Famous Food Manufacturers and Experts*. New York: William Morrow and Company, 1928.

Woman's Home Companion Cook Book. New York: P. F. Collier and Son, 1942.

Woodress, James L. *Booth Tarkington: Gentleman from Indiana*. Philadelphia: J. B. Lippincott Company, 1955.

SUGGESTED READING

Those interested in reading more about nineteenth- and twentieth-century cooking in relation to household arrangements, domestic fashion, and sociological change may wish to look for the following works:

Clark, Robert. *James Beard: A Biography.* New York: HarperCollins, 1993.

Cowan, Ruth Schwartz. *More Work for Mother: The Ironies of Household Technology from the Open Hearth to the Microwave.* New York: Basic Books, Inc., 1983.

Dining in America, 1850–1900. Ed. Kathryn Glover. Amherst and Rochester: The University of Massachusetts Press and the Margaret Woodbury Strong Museum, 1987.

Giedion, Siegfried. *Mechanization Takes Command: A Contribution to Anonymous History.* New York and London: W. W. Norton and Company, 1969. (First published in 1948.)

Levenstein, Harvey. *Paradox of Plenty: A Social History of Eating in Modern America.* New York and Oxford: Oxford University Press, 1993.

———. *Revolution at the Table: The Transformation of the American Diet.* New York and Oxford: Oxford University Press, 1988.

Shapiro, Laura. *Perfection Salad: Women and Cooking at the Turn of the Century.* New York: Farrar, Straus and Giroux, 1986.

Strasser, Susan. *Never Done: A History of American Housework.* New York: Pantheon Books, 1982.

Sutherland, Daniel E. *Americans and Their Servants: Domestic Service in the United States from 1800 to 1920.* Baton Rouge and London: Louisiana State University Press, 1981.

Williams, Susan. *Savory Suppers and Fashionable Feasts: Dining in Victorian America*. New York: Pantheon Books in association with the Strong Museum, 1985.

Woloch, Nancy. *Women and the American Experience*. New York: Alfred A. Knopf, 1984.

An interesting work that appeared too late for me to make use of it is Sylvia Lovegren, *Fashionable Food: Seven Decades of Food Fads* (New York: Macmillan, 1995).

INDEX

writing ability of, 54, 313, 385; mother's generosity toward, 181, 188; mother's illness and, 294–97, 319; mother's relationship with, 53, 55, 183, 185, 187, 191–95, 272–73, 285, 296–97, 319, 403; mother's will and estate and, 222–23; "My Little World" and, 290–92; nicknamed "Mary," 52–53, 88; nicknamed "Rom," 67, 88; older culinary traditions as concern of, 275–76; as original illustrator and designer of mother's cookbooks, 91, 92, 127, 153, 198–99, 203, 204, 260, 269; paper-cutout work as skill of, 77, 80, 83–84, 91; personal writing ambitions of in 1960s, 353–54; personality of, 52–53, 66–67, 88, 191, 195, 399; physical appearance and demeanor of, 53, 55, 95–96, 191–92, 285, 296; power of attorney assigned by mother to, 295; pregnancies and childbearing of, 188, 191–92, 193; publicity and promotional appearances avoided by, 1, 285, 361–62; resistance of invalidism, 297, 313, 360, 372, 376, 377, 387; Rombauer grandparents and, 36, 42, 358; von Starkloff grandparents and, 42, 358; Streamlined and, 204, 262; travels of (1960s), 352–53; unfinished book projects of, 399–400; will and estate of, 372, 389, 404–5; at Women's Wear Daily, 75–76, 78; writing style and ability of, 3–4, 191, 203, 303, 316, 357, 365–66, 402. See also Bobbs-Merrill Company; Joy of Cooking, The; "Links"; Little Acorn; Wild Wealth

Becker, Mark (Marion and John's son), 193, 260, 299–300, 319, 327, 348–52, 393, 415; birth of, 188; education of, 299, 300, 350; father's last illness and, 388; Irma's European trip with (1952), 286–88; Tom Itin and relationship with father, 351–52; "Links" and, 401, 403; marriage of, 319; as possible Joy participant, 300, 349, 350–51, 393, 414; psychiatric crisis of, 350

Becker, May Lamberton, 96

Becker, Philip August (John's father), 56–57, 65, 66, 77, 109; death of, 192

Becker, Philip Robert (John's brother), 183–84, 405; death of, 409

Becker, Virginia (John's sister). See Furness, Virginia Becker

Becker, William Dee (formerly William Dietrich Becker), 63, 95, 194

Marion Rombauer Becker Medicinal Herb Garden (Cincinnati), 404, 413–14

Beecher, Catherine, 11, 119

Bellefontaine Cemetery (St. Louis), 331

Berger, Lowe, 222, 300, 301

Berman, Jerome, 408

Berner, Pincus, 211, 212, 213

Berolzheimer, Ruth, 231

Bertholle, Louisette, 285, 286

Bettenmann, Jake, 195, 196

Bettenmann, Joe, 180

Bettenmann, Lena, 195

Better Homes and Gardens Cook Book, 279

Better Housing League (Cincinnati), 186

"Betty Crocker" (General Mills fictional spokeswoman) and *The Betty Crocker Cook Book,* 258, 279

Bicentennial, U.S. (1976), 404

Biodynamics, 260

Black, Marjorie, 164

Blakiston Company, 178–79

Blenders, electric, 204, 253, 274, 309

Blow, Susan, 15–16

Blue Gingham Cook Book, The, 230

Bobbs-Merrill Company, 98–99, 147–82, 235, 247, 298, 299, 400; acquired by Macmillan, 414; acquired by Howard Sams, 300; decline of (1930s–50s), 149, 150, 180, 208–9, 214, 221–22; early history of, 149–50; *Girls and Boys* and, 196–99, 203, 204; Hartrich affair and, 322, 324, 378, 379, 381, 383; *Joy* copyright acquired by, 151; *Joy* copyrights reassigned to, 347–48; *Joy* refused by (1933), 98–99, 147–48; *Joy* subsequently accepted by (1935), 148–49; leadership crises of (1950s–60s), 300–303, 305, 315, 316, 322, 333–34, 340; legal fight of with Irma and Marion (1949–50), 206–14, 257; legal fight of with Marion (1962), 321, 327–28, 330, 332–39; *Little Acorn* and, 355–57, 360–61, 363, 370, 372; Marion's last illness and, 372, 385, 394; 1936 *Joy* and, 148–63; 1943 *Joy* and, 170–74, 178–82, 198, 204, 205, 249, 252; 1946 *Joy* and, 198, 204, 205, 258; 1951 *Joy* and, 199–225, 273, 284, 286, 299; 1962/63 *Joy* and, 300–344, 347; 1975 *Joy* and, 361, 363, 367, 370, 371–74, 386, 389, 392–94, 405–6; paperback *Joy* and, 377–78, 384–85, 413; replacement author of *Joy* considered by, 179–80, 195, 210; separate Indianapolis-New York offices of, 152, 197, 302, 333;

"German Class," 184–85, 195–96, 386
German cookery, 22; in *Joy*, 141–43, 240, 343
Germany: postwar, Irma's avoidance of, 286; Rombauers' sojourn in (1925–26), 69–72; von Starkloffs' sojourn in (1889–94), 23–27, 144–45
Giedion, Siegfried, 190, 266
Gindler, Elsa, 70
Gitlin, Paul, 328, 330, 332, 335
Gobin, Leo, 301, 347, 352, 383, 389, 401, 410; *Little Acorn* and, 357, 359, 360, 363, 370; Marion's relationship with, 340–41, 362–63, 369–70; 1963 *Joy* and, 335, 340–41, 342; 1975 *Joy* and, 374, 392, 394, 406; paperback *Joy* and, 377, 384–85; *Wild Wealth* and, 362–63, 370
Gold Cook Book, The (de Gouy), 256
Goldman, Emma, 48
Goldstein, Jo, 75
Goltermann, Elizabeth, 97, 355
Good Housekeeping, 255
Good Housekeeping Cook Book, The, 231–32, 235, 247, 253, 255, 267, 269, 324
Gottfried, Ruth A. Jeremiah, 137
Gourmet, 254–55, 256, 257
Gourmet Cookbook, The, 257, 269
Gourmet movement, 230, 253–57; influence of on postwar kitchen bibles, 256–57
Governor's Awards (Ohio), 414
Graham, Sylvester, 261
Gravy: approach to in 1931 *Joy*, 131–33
"Great Living Cincinnatian" award, 406
Greenbaum, Wolff & Ernst, 179, 207–8, 209–14, 305, 330, 334. *See also* Pilpel, Harriet F.
Gregory, James, 310, 311, 323, 327
Guarnaschelli, Maria D., 415
Guggenheim, Peggy, 190

Hale, Sarah Josepha, 119–20
Ham: *Joy* coverage of (interim post-1931 version), 148; (1943), 251
Hanna, Elaine, 398
Harlan, John Marshall, 37–38
Harlan, John Maynard, 37
Harper, Charles, 368, 373–74
Harper, Lolita ("Lee") ("Ann Holiday"), 311, 375
Harrison, Benjamin, 23, 27
Hartrich, Eugene, 181, 200
Hartrich, Mary Whyte ("Mazie"), 68–69, 199, 200, 295, 303, 329, 393; Irma's

"conversion" and, 326; Irma's 1949 will and, 222; Irma's 1950 agreement with Marion concerning, 222–23, 305, 379, 380–81; legal action against Marion brought by, 322, 324, 378–83, 384; loyalty and devotion to Irma, 154, 195, 380; 1931 *Joy* and, 86, 87, 90–92, 96, 380; 1936 *Joy* and, 98, 148, 154, 156–58, 242; 1951 *Joy* and, 205, 206, 211, 215, 217–20, 224, 299; 1962/63 *Joy* and, 304, 305–6, 344, 380–81; payments to, 181, 222–23, 305–6, 378–83; settlement with, 384
Haverford College, 299
Hawes, Harry, 82
Haydn, Hiram, 158, 173, 208–9, 221–22
Hayward, Elinor, 355
Health foods, cult of in 1930s and 40s, 260–62, 263; renewed interest in during 1970s, 394–95, 396
H. J. Heinz Company, 203
Hepburn, Andrew, 167, 170
Herbs, 1930s vogue of, 245; suitability of to convenience-food cookery, 245–46; in 1943 *Joy*, 247; in *Streamlined*, 246
Hibben, Sheila, 232, 233, 244
High-altitude baking, 1951 *Joy* coverage of, 204, 272–74
Hillsdale School (Cincinnati), 95, 185, 189
Hoblitzelle, Fanny, 22
Hoblitzelle, Nellie, 22
Hoeffer, Paul, 165–67, 171
Hofmann, Ginnie, 215, 217, 224, 266, 269–70, 277, 316, 324–25, 373, 374
Holdahl, Stena Marie, 148
Hollweg, Ferdinand (Irma's cousin), 30
Hollweg, Ina. *See* Vonnegut, Ina Hollweg
Hollweg, Julia. *See* Chapman, Julia Hollweg
Hollweg, Louis (Irma's uncle), 20, 88, 290
Hollweg, Louise Kuhlmann ("Dada") (Irma's aunt), 10, 19–20, 23, 88, 90, 92–93, 96, 98, 357; death of, 194
Hollweg, Norma (Norma Hollweg Haerle) (Irma's cousin), 23, 30
Holtman, Elsie, 81
Home canning, 1943 *Joy* coverage of, 250–51; 1951 *Joy* coverage of, 275
"Home Comfort" (Rombauer and Torno), 200, 273
Home freezing, 1951 *Joy* coverage of, 274, 275
Hoops-Ebers, Lisbeth, 74, 88
How to Cook and Eat in Chinese (Chao), 252–53, 278

J. L. Hudson's (Detroit), 326–27
Hungerford, Harold, 90–91, 127, 157
Hunstein, Elsa Muench (Irma's great-niece), 40, 83, 294, 295, 318, 319, 326, 329, 331
Hurley, Walter, 152, 154, 205, 212–17, 219, 268–69, 302, 303

Ice cream freezers, hand-cranked, 134
Iceboxes, 109, 234, 280; and proliferation of chilled dishes, 133–34. *See also* Kitchen appliances and equipment
Ida Bailey Allen's Modern Cook Book (Allen), 124–25
Indianapolis Times, 220
Industrial processing, effect of on staple foods, 116–18
International Telephone and Telegraph Corporation (ITT), 359, 409–10
Isaacson, Robert, 287
Israel, Marian (Bobbs-Merrill employee), 342
Israel, Marian Judell ("Judy"), 288, 294, 384, 388; participation of in 1975 *Joy,* 386–87, 392
Israel, Murray, 288–89, 294, 384, 392, 407, 408, 409
Italian cookery, 138, 230; Irma's idea of (1931), 139–41
Italy: Irma's trip to (1952), 287
Itin, Shirley, 351, 392
Itin, Thomas W., 351–52, 372, 384, 388–89, 392, 404–5; dispute over fiscal management of, 410–11, 413

Jackson, Claiborne, 13
Janis, Caroline Risque, 77, 91
Jefferson County, Mo.: Irma's property and cabin in, 184–85, 195, 196, 223, 295–96, 347, 355
Johnson, Morse, 372, 378, 382–83, 384, 388–89, 391
Johnson, Nannie Talbot, 128
Jones, Arthur, 293–94
Jones, Patricia, 171, 199
Joy of Cooking, The (general): alienated copyright, significance of, 151, 165, 171, 180, 214, 373; as asset critical to Bobbs-Merrill's future, 151, 180, 208–9, 221, 322; author-reader bond in, 2–4, 248–49, 252, 270–72, 331–32, 358; authorship succession of, 182, 193, 195–201, 202, 209–10, 213, 224–25, 283, 297–98, 300, 349–51, 372–73, 377, 388–89, 392; British edition of (J. M.

Dent), 306; as cementer of diverse preferences, 4–6, 235–36, 238–39, 242–43, 281–83; "Cockaigne," meaning of, 315; fan mail for, 176–77, 354, 357, 358, 399, 400; idiosyncrasies and inconsistencies as strength of, 4–5, 130, 146, 238, 242–43; as informational resource for other food writers, 221, 362; Irma's presence in, 3, 143–46, 153–54, 248, 270–71, 343; Marion's history of (*see Little Acorn*); Marion's particular stamp on, 3–4, 260–68, 307, 342–44; mother-daughter relationship in, 1–2, 272–73, 314, 316, 362; projected 1997 revision of, 415; recipe format devised for, 96–98, 148, 154–55, 160, 307, 317, 373; trust arrangements for, 223, 372, 388–89, 392, 404–5, 411; "vanity-book" quality of, 2, 4; younger writers' later preconceptions of, 361–62
Joy of Cooking, The, copyrights for: assignment of, 151, 347–48; assorted, 223, 414; potential infringement of, 332–35; **1931,** 92, 151; **1936,** 151, 156, 165, 341; **1941,** 171; **1943,** 171; **1946,** 198; **1951,** 217; **1952,** 219; **1953,** 219; **1962,** 332; **1963,** 342; **1964,** 348; **1975,** 393
Joy of Cooking, The, editions of: summarized, xiii, 455–56; **1931,** 2, 96, 99, 100, 147–48, 151, 154, 157, 239, 240, 244, 251, 283, 362, 380, 393, 415, culinary analysis of, 103–4, 126–46, writing and publication of, 84, 86–94; **1936,** 161, 168, 169–70, 183, 251, 252, 355, culinary analysis of, 237–43, preparation and publication of, 148–49, 150–58, promotion of, 152–53, 159–61; **1943,** 198, 205, 218, 223, 258, 274, and breakdown of author-publisher relationship, 170–71, 173–74, 178–82, culinary analysis of, 247–52, as Irma's breakthrough, 172, 174–78, Marion's evangelism on behalf of, 190; **1946,** 172, 198, 204, 205, 218, 258, 380; **1951,** 258, 284, 286, 292, 299, 306, 307, 309, 316, 324, 330, 336, 337, 379, · 380, 394, Bobbs-Merrill allows to go out of print in 1962, 330, Bobbs-Merrill/Rombauer standoff over, 204–16, culinary analysis of, 263–83, early work on, 199–200, editing and publication of, 214–17, Marion as co-author of, 202–20, 224, 262–70, 272–81, 283, proposed to retitle "New Joy," 216; **1962,** 381, 383, Bobbs-Merrill's principal handling of text and produc-

tion, 315–18, 320–25, 327–28, Bobbs-Merrill's surreptitious preparations for publication of, 323–24, 325, 327–28, 330, 332, and culinary developments of 1950s, 309–10, as drastic departure from prior editions, 304, 306–9, length problems of manuscript of, 308, 316–17, 323–28, Marion's index-card manuscript of, 304–5, 307, 317, 320, multiple flaws of, 336–38, and 1957–62 Bobbs-Merrill corporate changes, 300–304, 316, 320–21, repair of author-publisher relationship after unauthorized publication of, 333–35, 338–41, **1963,** 338–44, 347–49 (*see also* 1962 *Joy*); **1975,** 295, 363–64, 367, 414, and culinary developments of 1960s and 70s, 394–97, early work on, 361, 371, 374–76, 377, and Judy Israel, 386–87, Marion's commitment to continual improvement of, 405, 406, publication and reception of, 393, 398, 405, repeated medical crises and, 371–72, 375–76, 382–84, 385–86, 389, work on interrupted by Hartrich affair, 378–84

Joy of Cooking, The, paperback issue (1973), 377–78, 384–85, 405; (1982), 413

Joy of Cooking, The, rumored precursor of 1931 version, 86–87, 97–98, 355

Joy of Cooking, The: AA's quarrel and (1936), 156, 157–59, 169–70; "Abouts" in (1962/63), 308, 310, (1975), 397; acknowledgments page of (1975), 393–94; altering emphases of on time-saving strategies (1931), 130–33, 142–43, (1943), 247, (1951), 264, 265, 275, (1962/63), 314 (*see also Streamlined Cooking*); American servicemen's appreciation for (1943), 176–77; anachronisms in (1951), 279; attention to cooking techniques in (1962/63), 307–8; attention to culinary tradition in (1951), 275–76, 277; authorial control of design decisions as issue for (1951), 205–10, 212, 213, 215–16; as authority addressing wide spectrum of contingencies, 251–52, 274–75, 308; color photographs proposed for (1951), 204–208, 268; contributions of Irma's food-writer friends to (1962/63), 315; correction of errors in (1936), 161–62, 169–70, (1975), 405; decisions to delete recipes (1951), 264–65, (1962/63), 313–14; dedication of (1951), 218;

discount-sales arrangements for (1943–46), 173, 178, 179, (in 1951 *Joy* negotiations), 205, 207, 210, 212–14, 302, (1963), 341, 351, (paperback version), 384; dust jacket for (1931), 91, 92, 127, (1951), 204, 213, 215–16, 268–69; editing of (1936), 153–54, 155, 168, (1962), 303, 317–18, 319–25, 336–37; ethnic and foreign foods in (1931), 138, 139–43, (1936), 240, (1943), 247–48, (1951), 278, (1962/63), 310–11, (1975), 394–95, 398; Far Eastern distribution of (1963), 352–53; gathering of recipes for (1931), 87; German elements in (1931), 141–43, (1936), 240, (1962/63), 343; grains, cereals, and flours discussed in (1951), 265–66; health credos and (1951), 260–68, (1975), 394–95, 396; illustrations and artwork for (1931), 91, 92, 127, 153, (1951), 204–8, 215, 216, 217, 268–70, 277, (1962/63), 316, 324–25, (1975), 373–74, 386, 393; increasing seriousness of Irma's approach in (1936), 239–40, (1943), 247–48, 249–52; index for (1936), 156–57, 242, (1951), 217–20, 284, 286, 299, (1962), 337–38, 339, (1975), 397–98; introduction of (1951), 272; Irma's absorption in revision of 1936 version, 163, 243; Irma's generosity with profits from (1936, 1943), 180–81, 188, 192–93, 194; Irma's irreverent tone in (1936), 237–38; Irma's plans and efforts toward post-1951 revision of, 289, 295, 296, 297–98; Irma's search for publisher in early 1930s, 98–99, 145, 147–49; John's contributions to, (1951), 203, 216, (1962/63), 312–13, (1975), 375; "Luncheon and Supper Dishes" chapter of (1936), 241–42, (1943), 250, (1951), 273; mainstream adoption of health-food beliefs and (1975), 394–95; Marion's increasing emphasis on information in (1951), 265–67, 275, 306–7, (1962/63), 306–8, 310; Marion's interest in history of, 354–59; marketing and promotion of (1931), 93–94, (1936), 152–53, 159–61, 235, (1943), 173–75, 178, 179, 247, (1951), 216, (1962), 326, (1975), 393; measuring information in (1943), 249–50, (1962/63), 306–7, 308; meat coverage of (1951), 276, 279, 280; media and public response to (1931), 92–93, 96, (1936), 160, 161, (1943), 174–75, (1951), 220–21, (1975), 398;

Reckendorf, Hermann, 400
Reedy, William Marion, 47
Refrigerators. *See* Kitchen appliances
Regional American cooking, 230; in *Joy*, 240, 247
Regional Planning Council of Cincinnati and Vicinity, 186
Rice, cooking of, 129, 265
Rice, Charles, 184
Rice, May, 184
Rice, William, 398
Richardson, Alice Wilson, 317–18, 319, 321–22, 323, 324, 327, 336
Rindge, Agnes (Agnes Rindge Claflin), 66, 67, 70, 78, 190
Ripperger, Helmut, 284–85, 286, 315
Roasting meats and fowl: coverage of in successive *Joy* editions, 135, 251–52, 259, 264, 280; Adelle Davis's opposition to, 262, 264
Robinson, Margaret Varn. *See* Rombauer, Margaret Robinson
Rodale, J. I., 260
Rodale Press, 263
Rombauer, Augusta Koerner (Edgar's mother), 35, 36, 47, 61
Rombauer, Bertha (Edgar's grandmother), 34
Rombauer, Bertha (Edgar's sister), 39, 43, 44, 84
Rombauer, Edgar Roderick (Irma's husband), 28, 29, 33–44, 56–57, 76, 183, 185; birth of, 35; as camper and outdoor enthusiast, 36, 57, 127, 196; childhood of, 36; courtship and wedding of, 39–40; culinary skills of, 57, 127; European sojourn of (1925), 68–69; family background of, 34–36; family biographical sketches written by, 63–64; as father, 51–52; illness with bladder cancer, 63, 68, 80–81, 83; law career of, 36–39, 40, 51–52, 69; mental illness of, 38–39, 41, 51, 52, 62–63, 68, 80–83, 350; as nephew's guardian, 42–43, 56; personality of, 39, 52; physical appearance of, 39; political career of, 39, 49–51, 59, 60, 78–79, 80, 82; sense of failure of, 52; suicide of, 2, 52, 81–83, 350, 403; wife's relationship with, 39, 41, 51–52, 68, 81
Rombauer, Edgar Roderick, Jr. ("Put") (Irma and Edgar's son), 80, 81, 86, 87, 96, 99, 161, 415; birth of, 43; childhood of, 43–45, 51–58, 61, 63, 65, 68–69, 71, 72; early job adventures of, 55, 79, 85,

89; education of, 54–55, 65, 68–69, 79, 89–90, 180; European sojourn of (1925–26), 68–69, 71, 72; father's suicide and, 82–83; first marriage and divorce of, 79, 85, 192; law career of, 89–90, 180, 192; mother's declining health and, 194–95, 293, 294, 329; mother's generosity toward, 180–81, 192–93, 194; mother's relationship with, 54–55, 79, 183, 192–94, 196, 289, 329; mother's will and estate and, 222, 223, 347, 348, 378, 383; 1945 quarrel with mother, 192–94, 196, 348; physical appearance of, 55; second marriage and divorce of, 192, 289; sister's relationship with, 194, 348; third marriage of, 289
Rombauer, Edward (later Edgar) (Put's stepson), 192
Rombauer, Irma (née von Starkloff), birth of, 17; burial of, 331; childhood of, 17–27, 144–45; civic and cultural interests of, 42, 44–48, 59, 60, 63, 65, 68, 80, 183, 187, 289; competitive bent of, 18, 33, 48; "conversion" of, 326; cooking skills of, 56, 57, 84, 127–28; courtship and wedding of, 39–40; as culinary amateur, 2, 3, 5, 126, 127–28, 161–62, 235, 282–83; culinary and cultural influence of, 3, 5, 146, 238, 243, 252, 281–83, 331–32; daughter's relationship with, 53–55, 67, 94, 183–85, 187, 191–95, 224–25, 260, 272–73, 285, 296–97, 319, 403; death of, 331, 334, 340, 347, 379; difficult behavior of following strokes, 293–94, 318–19; drinking of, in later years, 195, 293–94; education and intellectual endowments of, 18–21, 22–23, 25–26, 29–30, 48; European sojourn of (1889–94), 23–27, 144–45; European sojourn of (1925–26), 68–72; European trip of (1936), 183; European trip of (1952), 286–88; family background of, 10–17, 24–25, 48; financial difficulties of (1930), 83–85; generosity of, 180–81, 188, 192–93, 194; "German Class" and, 183–85, 195–96; German heritage and, 20–21, 22, 24–25, 48, 62–64, 141–43, 144–45, 175, 177–78; and Mazie Hartrich, 86, 90–92, 98, 148, 154, 156, 181, 195, 199, 200, 205, 206, 222–23, 224, 295, 304, 305, 326, 379, 380–81; as hostess, 56, 128; housekeeping of, 40, 44–45; husband's breakdowns and, 41, 52, 68, 81;

Grateful acknowledgment is made to Ethan Becker for permission to quote from family papers and letters; to Simon and Schuster for permission to quote from *The Joy of Cooking* by Irma Rombauer and Marion Rombauer Becker, copyright © 1931, 1936, 1943, 1946, 1951, 1962, 1963, 1975 by Bobbs-Merrill; to the Missouri Historical Society for permission to quote from the Mary Whyte Hartrich–Irma Rombauer Correspondence, Missouri Historical Society Archives, St. Louis, Missouri; to the Lilly Library for permission to quote from the Bobbs-Merrill Archives of the Lilly Library, Indiana University, Blooming-ton, Indiana; and to Dorothy Merkel Alexander for permission to quote from a letter to me dated December 22, 1985.